Judaism

THE RELIGIOUS SITUATION OF OUR TIME

Judaism

No peace among the nations
without peace among the religions.

No peace among the religions
without dialogue between the religions.

No dialogue between the religions
without investigation of the foundations of the religions.

HANS KÜNG

Judaism

Between Yesterday and Tomorrow

CONTINUUM • NEW YORK

1996

The Continuum Publishing Company
370 Lexington Avenue, New York, NY 10017

Translated by John Bowden from the German
Die Religiöse Situation der Zeit: Das Judentum,
published 1991 by Piper Verlag, Munich

Copyright © R. Piper GmbH & Co. KG, Munich 1991

Graphics © Hans Küng and Stephan Schlensog

English Translation © John Bowden 1992

Printed in the United States of America

Library of Congress Cataloging-in-Publication Data

Küng, Hans, 1928–
    [Judentum. English]
    Judaism: between yesterday and tomorrow/Hans Küng:
[translated by John Bowden from the German].
        p.   cm. – (The Religious situation of our time)
    Translation of: Das Judentum.
    Includes bibliographical references and index.
    ISBN: 0-8264-0819-2 (pbk.)
    1. Judaism – 20th century.   2. Judaism – History.
3. Judaism – Relations – Christianity.   4. Christianity and
other religions –   Judaism.   5. Judaism – Essence, genius,
nature.   I. Title.   II. Series: Küng. Hans, 1928–   Religious
situation of our time.
BM565.K7613   1992   92–2974
296–dc20   CIP

Contents

Part Two

The Challenges of the Present

A. From the Holocaust to the State of Israel

Part Three

Possibilities for the Future

A. Judaism in the Postmodern Period

B. Conflicts in Life and the Future of the Law

Epilogue: No New World Order without a New World Ethic

For my Jewish friends throughout the world

The Purpose of this Book

There can be no analysis of the religious situation of our time without an analysis of living Judaism. What will be the future of Judaism, with a new millennium just round the corner and the whole world puzzling over it? Judaism, the oldest of the three great prophetic religions, reflects as in a burning glass all the religious problems of our time, on the threshold of the new millennium. Few though its adherents may be numerically, Judaism is still a spiritual world power. That is why it is appropriate to begin this **overall project** 'The Religious Situation of our Time', which is initially to concentrate on the three prophetic religions of Near Eastern origin, with Judaism.

My starting point is that all world religions, whether Christianity, Judaism or Islam, are living international and transcultural systems transcending the individual, which in the course of their history, reaching back over thousands of years, have gone through a variety of epoch-making paradigms. No investigation will do justice to them unless it strives to offer two things at the same time:

– **Analyses** of the spiritual forces of a history reaching back over thousands of years which are still influential today: hence a historical and systematic **diagnosis**;

– **Prospects** based on an analysis of the present which relate to the various options available for the future: hence practical and ecumenical **approaches to a solution**.

For only if we know how we have reached the present situation (**Part One: 'The Past that is Still Present'**),

can we understand where we stand (**Part Two: 'The Challenges of the Present'**),

and can we consider how the situation will develop (**Part Three: 'Possibilities for the Future'**).

Furthermore, at a time when an increasing number of spheres of human life – politics, economics, transport, environment and culture – are part of a global network, **no religion any longer lives in 'splendid** isolation'. In a world where in many places people of different religions live in the same street, work in the same office and study at the same university, what is happening in Judaism or Islam cannot be a matter of indifference to Christians. Conversely, Christians for their part will expect Jews or Muslims to formulate critically their view of the past, present and future of Christianity. In an age in which a global ecumenical consciousness has been awakened it is necessary to achieve a sense of the **ecumenical, global responsibility of all for all** – particularly in the face of the religious and ethnic antagonisms which have dramatically broken out afresh in the Gulf crisis and the Palestinian crisis.

In this connection it is exciting for Christian or Muslim readers to see how the **basic conflict between tradition and innovation** is dealt with and resolved in Judaism. Here our own problems are being dealt with representatively. It is also of crucial significance for Christian or Muslim observers to know whether, despite all the differences and conflicts, all the different trends and schools, all the battles between Orthodox, Conservative and Reform Judaism, Judaism will succeed in keeping in view the great centre, the religious substance of Judaism, and making it understandable to a new generation. Will the spiritual forces of this people, which was forced into an unparalleled identity-crisis at the climax of the modern period by assimilation and at the end of the modern period by the Holocaust, succeed in accepting the challenges of the new world era – which for Judaism are bound up with the foundation of the state of Israel – and transform them creatively into a new, postmodern global vision?

All these questions already show that here Christian theologians have no certainties, and do not merely interrogate other religions about 'their' problems 'from outside' in cold objectivity. Rather, Christian theologians are in the thick of processes of spiritual change and have come to understand that **all the great religions face similar structural problems** in the transition to 'postmodernity' (or whatever term one uses for the new age). The studies of Christianity and Islam which are to follow this book will have to bring this out with the same clarity – no religious truth without personal truthfulness! For just as Judaism, contrary to all notions of Jewish traditionalism, is not a rigid, uniform entity but a complex and dynamic unity which constantly changes, so too are Christianity and Islam. Thus to perceive a global, ecumenical responsibility involves seeing one's own problems better from the way in which they are reflected by others, and passing these experiences on further in resolving conflicts in one's own religion.

It is clear, however, that a book like this **about Judaism** is an adventure, first for the author and then for the reader. On the one hand it will provoke **Jewish readers**. How can a Christian theologian dare to involve himself like this in matters which are the internal concern of Jews? How can he dare to comment on the origin, centre and history of Judaism and intervene in the debates on such hotly disputed themes as the law and the Holocaust, the state of Israel and the Palestinian question, indeed even raise the question of the 'essence' and the spiritual 'future opportunities' of Judaism? For Jews, Judaism is its own affair. Why should Christianity bother with it, when for two thousand years it has done its best to deprive Judaism of any future?

On the other hand, however, this book will also disturb **Christians** (and perhaps some Muslims, too). How can a Christian theologian dare to go so far to meet Judaism, for example in connection with the origin of Christianity from Judaism? How can someone be so self-critical in the light of Judaism, speak so openly of the anti-Judaism of the Christian churches down the centuries and so unambiguously of the manifold Christian failures – beginning with Pius XII and the German bishops – over the mass murder perpetrated by the National Socialists? How does the future of Judaism concern a Christian? Surely for Christians the future belongs to Christianity – once and for all? Is not Judaism a religion which in principle has been 'transcended'?

The purpose of this book is to provide a counterpoint. Here **Judaism** is not seen as a past 'Old Testament' but as an **independent entity with amazing continuity, vitality and dynamism**. It is no longer permissible for any Christian theology to see Judaism in 'salvation-historical' terms as 'superseded', or to exploit Judaism as a mere 'legacy' in order heighten its own profile. No Christian church is any longer allowed simply to put itself in the place of the 'old Israel', as the 'new Israel'. No Christian has the right to ignore the reality of living Judaism and the challenge not only of the ongoing existence but also the dynamic renewal of this people and its organization of itself into an independent state.

And because our concern is a global ecumenical responsibility, it is impossible to write such a book without **sympathy** for the great religions of humankind. So this book is written out of a deep sympathy **for Judaism**; there is no incompatibility between incorruptible scholarly honesty which speaks the truth undeterred on all sides, and passionate commitment which is keen to oppose hatred and misunderstanding and support peace. At all events, no effort has been spared to analyse and describe in the light of the latest research the epoch-making changes and **the cultural and religious constellations or paradigms** arising out of them, over three thousand years of Jewish history and still valid today. No effort has been spared to survey **the transitory and the** abiding, to work out the constants and the variables. The one passion which drives this book on is a concern to understand the foundations, the development and the future opportunities of Judaism in the transition to a new world era. At the same time, it seeks to sound out the possibilities of a **growing mutual understanding,** an understanding between Jews and Jews, and, interwoven with this, between Jews and Christians and perhaps even between Jews, Christians and Muslims.

So this book sets out to be more than a book on Jewish-Christian dialogue, although it cannot leave out any of the questions which are still disputed between Christians and Jews (from the sabbath and the food laws, through questions about politics and the state, to christology and the Trinity). It seeks to describe Judaism as a **comprehensive living unity** and thus to engage its spiritual energies in the discussion with Christianity and Islam: **Judaism as a challenge** to Christianity and also to Islam.

I have described and explained the **method** used in this book in my programmatic *Global Responsibility* (1990, English translation 1991). (As early as 1987, in *Theology for the Third Millennium. An Ecumenical View*, English translation 1988/1991, I provided the hermeneutical basis for the possibility of transferring the paradigm theory to the history of religions; this was doubted by a few innocent reviewers, but here I am giving a clear demonstration of it.) I know that the **literature** on almost every chapter is enormous, and it will be easy for any specialist to point out that I should have taken note of this or that indispensable work. To this I can only reply that I have taken all conceivable care to discover, as far as it is possible for any individual, the state of academic research in the various areas, and to incorporate the most recent state of the international discussion into my own considerations. As far as possible in an **interdisciplinary survey** I wanted:

– to relate the great history of Judaism, yet at the same time to arrive at systematic explanations of the past;

– to make clear the causal connection between religion, politics and society and at the same time to further specifically theological reflection;

– to demonstrate the universal impulses of history, yet at the same time not to lose sight of the human factor, the role of important personalities;

– to allow original sources to speak for themselves where possible but not to get lost in quotations;

– to ally empathy with the relevant historical situation to a necessary sharpness of judgment.

A **technical point**: because this book is concerned with an extremely complex history and no less complicated issues, for the first time in my books of this length I have taken care to make use of additional **teaching aids**. This is not in order to exploit theology for pedagogic ends (which might offend some 'scholars' in this country, for whom scholarship seems to be bound up with complexity and pseudo-profundity), but in order to produce a text which is as clear and as transparent as possible to the reader. So I have used emphases and distinguishing marks in the text, grouped sets of questions, and introduced graphics, maps and synopses. I hope that this will make it easier to grasp the composition and conception of this long and multi-level book, the structure of which has nevertheless been planned throughout, from beginning to end.

And now, briefly, a few **personal** matters. I could not have produced this book so quickly without help, help above all from our Tübingen Institute for Ecumenical Research. Matthias Schnell (along with Michel Hofmann) was responsible for liason with libraries and for the final corrections. Eleonore Henn and Margarita Krause took great care over the preparation of the typescript, which was corrected time after time. Marianne Saur was a great help to me in criticizing not only its form but also its content. Checking the bibliographical details, designing the book, producing my schemes and translating them into graphics lay in the skilful hands of Stephan Schlensog. As always, collaboration with the editorial department of Piper Verlag, represented by Ulrich Wank, and the production department, represented by Hanns Polanetz, was a delight. The personal involvement in the whole project of the publishers, Dr Klaus Piper and Dr Ernst-Reinhard Piper, and our always warm personal relationship, have proved a constant encouragement. For all matters of content and style I have once again been able to rely on Dr Karl-Josef Kuschel, my colleague at the Institute, who is now teaching in the Catholic Theological Faculty of the University of Tübingen; he has seen the manuscript through from beginning to end. I also owe a special word of thanks to Professor Clemens Thoma, a specialist in Jewish studies at Lucerne, who read through the completed manuscript and suggested many corrections to details. I am also grateful for the help of my Old and New Testament colleagues, Professors Herbert Haag (of Tübingen and Lucerne) and Michael Theobald (of Tübingen), who gave a critical reading to the sections of the manuscript relating to the Old and New Testaments. I have also acknowledged other colleagues in particular sections. Last but not least I must also express my thanks once again to the Robert Bosch Jubilee Foundation, which has provided me with technical support, in particular with funds to further my research and immensely valuable computer systems, thus creating the practical means for the overall project of 'no world peace without peace between the religions'.

However, a book like this is not just written at a desk; above all it comes into being as a result of conversations with other people. I am of course particularly indebted to **Jewish friends and acquaintances** for my understanding of Judaism. The foundations for this were laid for me during the difficult 1930s and 1940s in Germany by natural and friendly relations with a family of Jewish neighbours in my Swiss home town of Sursee, and with Jewish fellow-pupils at the Gymnasium in Lucerne. My critical awareness of the Jewish question was sharpened, and I made a thorough study of the relationship between the church and Judaism as a result of meetings with Jews, in connection with my involvement in the Second Vatican Council between 1962 and 1965, and my first extended lecture tour through the United States in 1963. A key theological experience on my first visit to Israel, in 1967, was a question put by a young Jewish compatriot from Berne. She asked me spontaneously what we Christians found so special in this Christ who was being talked about all over Jerusalem. I tried to give her an answer in terms of the Jesus of history, and as a result of this direct encounter immediately understood how important a christology 'from below' is for Jewish-Christian dialogue. I presented this for the first time in my book *On Being a Christian* (1974), and now it also appears in this book. During my various visits to Israel – one at the invitation of the Swiss-Jewish Association (Dr Jakov Bach of Tel Aviv) – numerous conversations and meetings followed. Leaving aside a conversation with a representative of the Israeli Foreign Office and other representatives of official Israeli politics, I found meetings with Professors Ben-Chorin, Emil Fackenheim and David Flusser, Rabbi David Hartman, Mayor Teddy Kollek and Professors Yeshayahu Leibowitz, Gershom Scholem and Zwi Werblowsky, particularly important. There were also further conversations in connection with lectures at the Van Leer Institute in Jerusalem and at the University of Haifa.

Our Institute for Ecumenical Research at the University of Tübingen also held academic colloquia through Frau Evelyne Goodman-Tau (Jerusalem), in Lucerne with Dr Simon Lauer (along with Professor Thoma) and in Worms with Dr Pinchas Lapide (Frankfurt). As early as 1975, I had the opportunity to join in a radio discussion on 'The Dispute over Jesus' with Lapide, whose work towards mutual understanding between Christians and Jews in Germany cannot be valued highly enough; later we gave joint lectures on Christians and Jews in the Studium Generale at the University of Tübingen in the summer of 1989. Most recently, conversations with various rabbis from the German Länder have been particularly important to me in the context of the 'trialogue' between Jews, Christians and Muslims.

In particular, my regular visiting lectureships in the United States have made an important contribution to my understanding of living Judaism. It has always been a great honour and challenge for me when as a Christian theologian I have been able to speak in a synagogue or elsewhere to a Jewish public. In this connection I learned a great deal above all from my semester at Rice University, Texas (in conversation with Rabbi Samuel Karff), at the University of Michigan in Ann Arbor (with Rabbi Michael Brooks) and at the University of Toronto (with Rabbi Gunther Plaut and Rabbi Dow Marmour). It was a particular delight for me to be able to give one of the festal addresses on the occasion of the installation of Ismar Schorsch, the new chancellor of the Jewish Theological Seminary, New York, and later a whole series of lectures at the University of Judaism (Los Angeles and Southern California). All these occasions led to a deepening of my understanding of Judaism, and it has been a constant joy that I have had a sympathetic hearing even when I had to express criticism not only of Christians, but also of Jews.

Among the individual encounters from which I learned, I would like to mention conversations with Ambassador Arthur Burns (at the time in Bonn), Professor Hans Jonas (New York), Advocate Felicia Langer (Jerusalem and Tübingen), Consul Franz Lucas (London), Rabbi Jonathan Magonet (London), Chief Editor Adam Michnik (Warsaw), Professor Jacob Neusner (Tampa, Florida), Professor Roy Rappaport (Ann Arbor), Professor Peter Riesenberg (St Louis, Missouri), Professor Alan Segal (New York), Professor Israel Shahak (Jerusalem), Professor Fritz Stern (New York), Dr Pavel Wildstein (Warsaw) and Professor Michael Wolffsohn (Munich). Anyone who knows me personally will know that my intentions are honourable and that I am not engaged in a secret mission to the Jews, but am arguing for the conversion of all, especially of Christians. I am arguing for the conversion of all to the one true God, confessed equally by Christians, Jews and Muslims. This book is not just concerned with theoretical questions, but with eminently practical questions and the global world order of a new world society, with a view to a realistic vision of peace in the future. I am seeking to offer encouragement in this direction. Such peace is possible! It begins with us – already in our next encounter with people of Jewish or Islamic faith.

Finally, I would like to make one wish. On the whole, at the time of the celebrations of the fortieth anniversary of the end of the Second World War in Germany the air had still not been cleared, particularly over the relationship between Germans and Jews. I hope that this book will help to make it possible for the celebrations of the fiftieth anniversary in 1995 to take place in a spirit of truth, reconciliation and co-operation, directed towards the future, and that the celebrations of the fiftieth anniversary of the state of Israel in 1998 will become a real year of jubilee, that year which according to the book of Leviticus (25.8-31) is to be celebrated every fifty years for the 'liberation of all who dwell in the land...'

But am I not contradicting myself in embarking on such an ecumenical course? Not at all. I am convinced that loyalty to one's own religious faith (an internal perspective) and openness to other religious traditions (an external perspective) are not mutually exclusive for either Jews or Christians or Muslims. On the contrary, this is the only way in which it is possible to arrive at what we need: information about one another, reciprocal discussion and finally transformation on all sides. The final goal of all our efforts cannot be a uniform religion; it must be real peace among the religions. For it cannot be stressed often enough that there can be:

No peace among the nations
without peace among the religions.
No peace among the religions
without dialogue between the religions.
No dialogue between the religions
without investigation of the foundations of the religions.

Tübingen, June 1991   *Hans Küng*

Part One

THE PAST THAT IS STILL PRESENT

A. Origins

I. Abraham, the Tribal Ancestor of Three World Religions

Let us pause for a moment: are not human beings always in danger of taking themselves too seriously – with all their disputes, conflicts and wars? Would it really make any difference to the universe if the human race destroyed itself – on our insignificant star on the periphery of one of a hundred million Milky Ways? Just as the human race came into being, so it can pass away again...

1. A brief reflection on world history

Let us be quite clear. According to a number of scientists the world has existed for at least 13 billion years. There has been human life on our planet for perhaps 1,500,000 years: **early man,** a being with an upright stance (*homo erectus*), emerged from the animal kingdom by mutation and selection. So 99.9% of human history will have been primal history: a history without writing, without the name of a people or a religion, a political or a religious leader.

Secondly, let us be clear that it is possible that for 200,000 years, since the early Stone Age, there has been *homo sapiens,* as present-day human beings proudly call themselves. *Homo sapiens* was distinguished from the animal world by his awareness of himself. In the Stone Age, *homo sapiens* invented tools and weapons, learned to control fire, and seized the dens occupied by marauding beasts; at that time he was already burying his dead and offering sacrifices, and was able to produce cave paintings, reliefs and statues, motivated by magic and religion.

Thirdly, let us be clear that it is only for just on 10,000 years, from the great revolution in the late Stone Age, that alongside the hunters, fishers and gatherers there were an increasing number of **sedentary** farmers and cattle-breeders, people who established village cultures in their own settled dwelling places. These had important social consequences: a struggle for land and private property began; it became possible to wage 'just wars'; the rule of the few over the many took shape. The natural landscape now became a cultivated landscape, and villages turned into cities. The earliest city in the world that we know (along with Catal Hüyük in Asia Minor) is situated in primal biblical territory: Jericho in the Jordan Valley, whose city wall it has proved possible to date to the year 6800 BCE by radio-carbon dating.[1]

Fourthly, let us be clear that only for about 5,000 years, since the beginning of the third millennium BCE, were there **early historical high cultures and high religions**. A **first** high culture developed even before 3500 BCE in southern **Mesopotamia**, in the landscape inundated by the Euphrates and the Tigris, in the temple cities of Sumer, to which the human race is indebted not only for the inventions of the wheel, the potter's wheel, the chariot and the oldest system of calculation (for temple finances and the establishment of a divine order in the cosmic system), but above all for the invention of writing. First of all this writing was a script consisting of pictures inscribed on clay tablets, and then a cuneiform and finally a syllabic script.[2]

That brings 'prehistory' without writing to an end. It can be made to speak only indirectly on the basis of dumb stones, potsherds, tools, walls and tombs. Then written 'history' begins, which is able to speak to us for itself in a living way through its literary documents. The real **'historical' period of the human race begins**, in which an increasing number of specific peoples, religions and historical persons emerge from the primal and prehistoric darkness into the clear light of history. Now, not only information about administration and commerce, but later also myths and sagas, are recorded.

A **second** high culture developed in the **Nile valley** after 3000 BCE, influenced by Mesopotamia. Here, almost at the same time, a script was invented and agriculture proved possible only with the aid of artificial irrigation – in other words through collaboration, planning and organization: specifically through a centralized administration (with officials and a priesthood) and the formation of a state. Finally, after the high cultures on the Euphrates and the Tigris and on the Nile, around 2500 BCE **a third** early historical high culture took shape in the **Indus valley** (the Indus culture), and around 1500 a **fourth** in the **Huangho valley** in China, in the valley of the Yellow River (the Chang culture).[3]

However, these four high cultures and their religions had different fates. Whereas the Indus culture was replaced by the culture and religion of an Arian immigration, and Chinese culture and religion proved able to maintain themselves down to the twentieth century through a number of epoch-making changes and transformations, the first two cultures were completely submerged. Their impressive relics can be found in the most famous museums in the world. Yet no matter how imposing the multi-storey temple towers on the plain of the Euphrates and Tigris may have been (the later ziggurat of Babylon is also alluded to in the Hebrew Bible), as early as the seventh century BCE these Mesopotamian (Babylonian, Assyrian and Chaldaean) cultures disappeared. It is to them that we also owe the first account of a 'flood', one of doubtless several catastrophic inundations of the whole area which formed the basis for the later biblical account, as did the story of a paradise ('Eden' is a Sumerian word). Towards the end of the fourth century BCE, independent Egyptian culture and religion also succumbed – to Hellenism and finally to the Roman empire.[4]

A quite different religion was to last and have a future here. It developed in the narrow and often disputed land-bridge of Syria-Palestine, between Egypt and Mesopotamia. The Semites living there as early as the second half of the second millennium had succeeded in making the transition from syllabic script to character script. This was a transition to the Canaanite-Phoenician twenty-two-character alphabet adopted by the Greeks; the earliest instances of it are short words carved into the rocks of Mount Sinai by Semitic forced labour, employed by the Pharaoh in the copper and malachite mines there.

I am talking about the religion of **Israel**. Israel was a corridor at the interface between the great power blocs, and comparatively speaking an amazingly young people. This Israel did not follow the peoples of Egypt and Mesopotamia in seeing itself as having existed for ever and ever, and therefore did not link its history directly with a mythical history of the gods, but retained its consciousness of having become a people at a late stage.[5] It prefaced its own history with a long primal history from the creation of the world to the building of the Tower of Babel,[6] and a prehistory of patriarchs[7] described in cycles of legends.[8]

So we are talking about the religion of Israel and – after manifold transformations – **of Judaism**. This makes it easier to survey its development. As is well known, at the beginning of the new era (which is now Christian!), **Christianity** emerged from Judaism; it was to become the religion of the Roman empire and the whole of the Western world, first of Europe and then also of the two Americas. Finally, Judaism and Christianity were followed by a further religion, the latest and youngest of the world religions, Islam. With its home in Arabia, Islam, after the collapse of the Roman empire in the West and its weakening in the East, was able to embark on its incomparable victory procession to Morocco and Spain, and in the East as far as Mesopotamia, the Indus valley and the frontiers of China.

In order to approach these three religions appropriately, we begin with the question: What is common to these religions, all of which derive from the Near East? The answer can only be that they are primarily united by a name, Abraham.

2. What do we know about Abraham?

'When Abram was ninety-nine years old, Yahweh appeared to him and said: "I am **God** Almighty (El Shaddai), live always in my presence and be perfect, so that I may put my **covenant** between me and you, and I will multiply you in plenty." Then Abram fell down on his face. And God spoke with him and said: "See, this is my covenant that I make with you: You shall be the father of many nations. You will no longer be called by your name Abram; Abraham shall be your name, because I shall make you the father of many nations... I am setting up my covenant between me and you and your descendants after you as an eternal covenant, to be your God and the **God of your descendants**. And I am giving you and your descendants after you the land where you are now aliens, the whole of the **land of Canaan** as an eternal possession, and I will be God to them... You shall circumcise the flesh of your foreskin, and this shall be the sign of the covenant between me and you.'[9]

In this conversation between God and Abraham, who is almost one hundred years old – it is matched by the conversation with Abraham's wife Sarah, which is almost of equal importance![10] – the Priestly theologian, writing at the time of the Babylonian exile, has artistically worked all the promises of the patriarchs into a whole and made it the centre of his account of the patriarchs. So already in the first book of the Hebrew Bible, **the fundamental significance of Abraham** for the history, piety and theology of Israel and Judaism down to the present day is impressively brought out. The fundamental elements of Israelite faith which appear here are:

● **God** has the initiative, and human beings neither are nor will be one with him. Rather, human beings act 'before' God, and are to subject themselves 'wholly' to him. So from the beginning the religion of Abraham is not defined by a mysticism of union but by an encounter between God and human beings.

● However, an eternal **covenant** is established between the powerful

God and the human beings who are chosen, which represents a reciprocal relationship between God and humankind that is to be sealed by circumcision as the sign of the covenant.

• The two-fold promise given with the covenant to the descendants of Abraham: they will form a great people, which will be the **people of God**, and they will be given the **promised land**, the land of Canaan.

So according to the biblical texts Abram, who is programmatically renamed 'Abraham' (the later interpretation), the 'father of many nations', is clearly the primal ancestor of the people of Israel. But what is concealed behind this larger-than-life biblical figure? What do we now know about Abraham as a historical figure?[11] We have hardly any certain knowledge about him as a person; it is impossible to write a biography of Abraham. The **patriarchal narratives** in Genesis 11-35[12] are our only sources. And they are certainly not biography or history in our sense. In the case of all three patriarchs they are a series of brief, loosely-connected narratives with doublets and contradictions. More precisely, they are primarily **sagas** handed down orally for a long period before they were fixed in writing.[13] However, sagas are not fairy tales.[14] As a rule, for all their brevity, simplification and concentration on a few persons, they have a historical nucleus. So critical exegetes no longer maintain today that Abraham, Isaac and Jacob are something like depotentiated gods, purely mythical figures, fictitious ancestors of particular groups. Indeed no tribe nor clan appeals to them. And not least because of their customary Western Semitic personal names, they seem to have been historical figures, even if all attempts to date them have come to grief.

However, in the patriarchal narratives there is a glimmer of the social and cultural conditions that must have prevailed in Palestine in the roughly 500 years between 1900 and 1400 BCE. We get some information about these conditions through the story of Sinuhe, the Egyptian, who lived there among semi-nomads (in the 20th century BCE); through Egyptian execration texts which cursed rebellious rulers (19th/18th centuries); through the Mesopotamian texts from Mari on the Middle Euphrates (18th century) and from Nuzi near Kirkuk (15th/14th centuries); and finally through the letters found in Amarna on the Middle Nile from the state archive of Pharaohs Amenophis III and Amenophis IV Akenaten (14th century). This last caused a profound crisis for the Egyptian kingdom because of his novel belief in one God.[15]

However, it is also true that it is certainly not the case, as is sometimes claimed, that with Abraham, his son and his grandson we simply have a private family history extending over three generations. First of all, the religious and political implications of the promises indicated here, which depend on this story, are too serious for that. Moreover, the story is set against the horizon of world politics. For we cannot overlook the fact that the story of Abraham in the book of Genesis is linked to the **prehistory and the universal history of humankind generally**, which seems first to have been concluded with the story of the building of the tower of Babel.[16] According to the biblical tradition, which attempts to combine two traditions,[17] Abraham's family emigrated from the rich southern Mesopotamian trading city of Ur (whose ziggurat or high temple, dedicated to the moon god Sin, was excavated between 1922 and 1934) and, like so many people in the second millennium BCE from Mesopotamia and the wilderness of Syria and Arabia, left the north Mesopotamian city of Haran on the great bend of the Euphrates to enter the land of Canaan.[18]

For all the significance of the promise and gift of the land, however, Abraham's very origin was continually to be of great symbolic significance in the vicissitudes of Jewish history. From the beginning Abraham was not a native, but an immigrant, **'a stranger and sojourner'**.[19] The only property that he acquired is said to have been a burial place at Hebron,[20] and to the present day 'Abraham's tomb' is pointed out there to Jewish, Christian and Muslim pilgrims and tourists. As a semi-nomad living in the vicinity of cities and villages, Abraham certainly had some contact with the indigenous inhabitants, but his life-style will have kept him apart from them, and have prevented him and the other patriarchs from allying themselves with indigenous families through marriage. True, Abraham is described as a 'Hebrew' (*'ibri*[21]); however, according to the most recent research, that need not simply have been synonymous with 'Israelite', since the *habiru* or *hapiru* of the Mesopotamian cuneiform texts and the *'prw* of the Egyptian texts, who are probably identical with the 'Hebrews', do not so much denote a particular people as a lower social stratum and form of life. These were often aliens, itinerants, mercenaries or forced labourers, outlaws, who could nevertheless occasionally rise to the highest positions.[22]

3. The father of faith

However, a further factor is by no means insignificant for the present situation of the religions. By the sequence of generations, **by genealogy**,[23] Abraham makes his appearance **as a member of the Semitic 'family'**. Along with Abraham, his son Isaac and his grandson Jacob – possibly thus linked together only at a later stage – are regarded as the primal ancestors of Israel. Present-day critics of Islam, especially Christians, should note here that polygamy was also a matter of course for the early biblical tribal cultures. As is well known, Abraham himself had several subsidiary wives.[24] For according to the book of Genesis Abraham fathered **Isaac**,[25] the father of Esau and Jacob, by Sarah. Jacob, later called Israel, was regarded as the father of the twelve tribes. By his subsidiary Egyptian wife, the slave Hagar, Abraham fathered **Ishmael**,[26] the tribal ancestor of twelve groups which belonged to the Ishmaelite alliance. Finally, by Keturah he became the ancestor of sixteen proto-Arabian nomadic groups.[27] All this is not without significance for present-day questions: originally, Israel felt quite akin to the Semitic Aramaeans of the late second millennium and to the proto-Arabs of the first millennium in northern and north-western Arabia, who were also Semitic: at least, this is what the genealogies seek to convey (though the details in them are hardly historical).[28]

But what kind of a **God** is spoken of in these patriarchal narratives? Strikingly, these sagas are associated with particular sanctuaries, above all with Shechem, Bethel, Hebron and Beersheba. So some exegetes conjecture that they are aetiological sagas, sagas about the foundation of the sanctuaries, which set out to legitimate pre-Israelite, Canaanite sanctuaries for the cult of the Israelites by claiming that God revealed himself to the patriarchs in these places. Be this as it may, it is clear that from the beginning the God of patriarchal religion was a God who was bound neither to heaven nor to a sanctuary; he was a 'God of the father (ancestor)' to whom he had communicated his revelations: the God of Abraham, the God of Isaac, the God of Jacob, the God of the fathers. After the settlement, however, this God had taken on elements of the Canaanite God El (under different names like El Shaddai), so that the God of Genesis can be described both as God of the fathers and as El, and presents himself simultaneously as a personal and a cosmic God.[29] Thus nowadays there is agreement among the critical exegetes that neither the exalted ethic of the Bible nor strict monotheism will have prevailed as early as the time of the patriarchs. From a historical perspective, Abraham was certainly a henotheist, someone who presupposed the existence of a number of gods but who accepted only the one God, his God, as the supreme and binding authority.

But what about **circumcision**?[30] At that time it was by no means a completely new rite. It is an age-old custom (performed with a stone knife), which was originally widespread not only in Canaan, among Israel's Semitic neighbours, and in Egypt, but also in Africa, America and Australia. It was not, however, practised among the Philistines, Babylonians and Assyrians. It was not practised either for hygienic and medical reasons, for social reasons (initiation rites), or for religious reasons. Among the Israelites it was taken for granted from the time of the settlement in Canaan, so that it does not appear at all in the earliest strata of Israelite law and is mentioned only once in the book of Leviticus,[31] without particular emphasis. However, after the fall of the kingdoms of Israel and Judah and the exile among the Babylonians, who were not circumcised, circumcision (which had formerly been taken for granted) became a special religious sign of membership of the Jewish people; only now did it take on its specific significance as a branding by God which could no longer be obliterated and a sign of the covenant. This is finally formulated as a legal prescription in Gen.17.

If we follow the book of Genesis, though, what is more fundamental for Abraham is trust in God. **Faith** which is unconditional **trust** is the fundamental feature. It is said that this faith is 'reckoned to Abraham for righteousness'.[32] Nowhere in the Hebrew Bible is faith (Hebrew *aman* = 'be firm', the causative form of which is *he'emin* = 'believe, trust') understood as the acceptance of a given truth, as 'regarding as true' something which cannot be proved. Faith is unshakeable trust in a promise which cannot be realized by human beings; it is faithfulness, confidence, saying 'Amen'. Accordingly, Abraham is the primal image and model of those who believe in this sense, a man who on the basis of this faith can withstand the greatest test of all: the sacrifice of his son, which is asked of him but in the end is not willed by God.[33]

So we arrive at a **first**, pleasant **conclusion**. With good reason, the three religions which appeal to Abraham and in which human beings stand 'before' God (*coram Deo*), rely completely on God and thus believe 'in' God (*in Deum*), have been described as **religions of faith** – in contrast to the religions of mystical union in India or even the wisdom religions of China. So Abraham appears as the common **tribal ancestor of all three great religions of Semitic origin**. Consequently they are also referred to as the three **Abrahamic religions**. As I have shown in my hermeneutical-methodological groundwork for this book,[34] they can be understood as one great current of a religious system originating in the Near East, which is essentially different from systems originating in India or the Far East.

And yet, even at this point we cannot overlook the fact that already with Abraham, the tribal ancestor, for all the common features, we can also detect a **conflict** between the three Abrahamic religions. Why?

4. The dispute over Abraham's legacy

(a) How is Abraham regarded in **Judaism**? In the course of history, Jewish tradition has increasingly elevated the status of Abraham and made him the 'servant' of God,[35] a 'friend' of God,[36] whom 'no one equals in renown'.[37] In later Judaism Abraham's life is increasingly adorned with miracles and legends and virtues, and his supposed cenotaph is venerated in Hebron – nowadays in Arab-Palestinian-Muslim territory! Two apocryphal writings devoted to him came to be written, one about his election and his revelations (the 'Abraham Apocalypse'[38]) and one about his journey to paradise and his death, combined with praise of hospitality (the 'Testament of Abraham').[39] These writings may well have been handed down in Essene circles. And in the course of history the one who is described so sympathetically in the Hebrew Bible with human weaknesses, the one who during his life often slyly presented his wife as his sister,[40] the one who literally sent his subsidiary wife, Hagar the Egyptian, and her son Ishmael (the tribal ancestor of Muslims) into the wilderness on the urging of his wife Sarah,[41] the one who paid off the sons of his subsidiary wives with gifts and banished them from the house,[42] this Abraham (and here exceptions prove the rule), is increasingly celebrated as the embodiment not only of the virtues of modesty, mercy and hospitality, but also as **the** embodiment of all the virtues, which his descendants had only to imitate. Indeed, in the book of Jesus Sirach Abraham is already described as the 'father of many nations'.[43]

In rabbinic Judaism Abraham then came to be described as a saving figure, towering over all times. According to the Talmud, Abraham, who lived long before the revelation on Sinai, already observed in his life all the commandments[44] not only of the written Torah but also of the oral Torah.[45] Indeed, there is also the bold assertion that the world and all human beings were made for Abraham and his merits. It was only because one day there would be Abraham that the generations before him could exist, and the generations after him are supported by him.[46]

To be 'children of Abraham' was now in fact regarded as the exclusive privilege of the Israelites: Israel was the 'seed or the race of Abraham',[47] and the 'people of the God of Abraham'.[48] The originally universal horizon of the story of Abraham, that Abraham was to be the embodiment of the blessing on 'all the nations upon earth',[49] was often completely lost sight of behind the election of the one people. Down to the present day his name is commemorated in the liturgy, especially on New Year's Day and in the first praise of the Eighteen Benedictions, the central Jewish prayer. And yet we must not overlook the fact that individual rabbis also assumed that in a spiritual, believing, inward way they were children of Abraham – very much as in Christianity.

(b) What about Abraham in **Christianity**? In the New Testament no Old Testament figure (apart from Moses) is mentioned more frequently – more than seventy times. The significance of Abraham for salvation history is recognized just as much as is the fact that Israel is a child of Abraham.[50] In Luke's parable of the rich man and poor Lazarus it is taken completely for granted that belonging to Abraham extends right beyond death (bliss as resting in Abraham's bosom).[51] And also in the letter of James, which was written in a Jewish milieu, Abraham is called a 'friend of God'.[52]

And yet, as early as the preaching of **John the Baptist**,[53] physical descent from Abraham is no longer regarded as a guarantee of salvation. Rather, there is a call for repentance, *metanoia*; now everything depends on that. The decisive factor is not a biological link with Abraham but a spiritual one. At least according to the evangelist Mark, John the Baptist ironically repudiates any Jewish superiority quite sharply: if necessary, God can even make descendants of Abraham out of stones.[54] The same Gospel contains the polemical observation that at the eschatological meal, many people from the Gentile peoples will recline at table with Abraham, Isaac and Jacob, whereas some of the Israelites who were called first will be excluded.[55]

It was then above all the **apostle Paul** who – for all his high regard for Abraham – was to repudiate physical descent from Abraham as an exclusive condition for salvation and to stress the possibility of being a **spiritual, inward child of Abraham**,[56] just as he assumes a spiritual, inward Judaism.[57] Abraham was not justified before God by works of the law, but by his own trusting faith[58] – here there is a reference to Gen.15.6. Paul boldly interprets the story of the two wives Hagar and Sarah and their sons Ishmael and Isaac in terms of the Old and New Covenants, the earthly and the future Jerusalem, Judaism and the Christian community.[59] Here, too, it is decisive that Paul is not concerned to provide external legitimation by citing a sequence of generations or the observing of the commandments (Abraham was before the Torah!), but in an inward, spiritual way with discipleship in Abraham's unshakable faith. So for Christians Abraham is the father of all human beings, in so far as they believe like Abraham, the father of **all** believers, regardless of whether they are circumcised or not.

Moreover, the church fathers were preoccupied with the figure of Abraham in constantly new ways in their homilies and tractates, in a predominantly moralizing or allegorizing form. Some even devoted whole treatises to him. In patristic, mediaeval and finally also in Reformation writings, parallels were drawn with remarkable frequency between the sacrifice of Isaac and the crucifixion of Christ, though they were highly problematical. In the last century the Dane Kierkegaard, going far beyond mediaeval theology and Luther, even thought that Abraham, who was ready to sacrifice his son, might be stylized as the prototype of a blind Christian faith...

(c) And how is Abraham regarded in **Islam**? In the Qur'an, too, Abraham (Arabic 'Ibrahim') is the biblical figure who is mentioned most frequently after Moses; there are striking parallels not only to biblical accounts of Abraham but also to extra-biblical, rabbinic accounts. He plays a role in twenty-five surahs; one surah, the fourteenth, even bears his name. In the earlier surahs from **Mecca** Abraham appears above all as the one who fights against the idolatry of his father and his compatriots, and thus proves himself to be a spokesman of the truth and a great prophet. In the later surahs from **Medina**, Ishmael, the father of the Arabs, who is previously mentioned without any closer reference to Abraham, comes into prominence: he supports his father Abraham in an effort to make the Kaaba in Mecca a place for the pure monotheistic worship of God and to build it up as a pilgrimage centre.[60] The Qur'an also calls Abraham 'the friend of God';[61] however, what is most important for it is that Abraham 'was neither Jew nor Christian; rather... a *hanif* dedicated (to God) (in the Qur'an this is identical to a Muslim or monotheist) and not a heathen'.[62] Abraham, chosen by God, was the first to be converted to the one true God and to turn against all worship of idols.[63] He was the first to practise 'Islam', unconditional subjection to the will of God, especially when he embarked on the sacrifice of his own son (Isaac's name is not mentioned at this point;[64] traditional Islamic exegesis thinks of Ishmael).

So from an early stage, for the Muslims Abraham was a great prophet of the one God. It is understandable that in this way the claim of Judaism and Christianity that they alone were the true religion should be undermined by the Qur'an. For according to this understanding Abraham was neither Jew nor Christian, but the first Muslim: a believing monotheist, chosen by God, long before the Torah (Arabic *tawrat*) and Gospel (Arabic *injil*) – the others are certainly holy books, but unfortunately they have been falsified by Jews and Christians. Accordingly, Islam can derive its credentials as the oldest and at the same time the most authentic religion through Abraham; it is a religion which was taught by all the prophets (indeed, the same thing was

Abraham

Ancestor of all three Semitic religions
of Near Eastern origin.
Primal representative of monotheism.
Archetype of the prophetic religions:
the believer **before** God; friend of God.

	†	☽
Physical father of Isaac, whose son Jacob was called Israel; concluded an eternal covenant with God. So he is the ancestor of the **Jewish people**.	Spiritual father of all believers, whose promises have been fulfilled in Christ. So he is the ancestor of **Jews and Christians**.	Physical father of Ishmael, with whom he founded the Kaaba in Mecca as the central sanctuary of the one God. So he is the ancestor of the **Arabs**.
Model of loyal obedience to the law: the ideal Jew, justified by works, which prove his faithfulness.	Model of unshakeable faithfulness; the herald of Christ, justified by the faith which precedes works.	Model of unconditional submission (=Islam); the first Muslim; attains righteousness through belief in God, worship and a life well-pleasing to God.
Sacrifice of Isaac as the prototype for withstanding the hardest of all trials of faith.	Sacrifice of Isaac as the prototype for the surrender of the Son of God by the Father.	Departure from Ur as prototype for the migration of the prophet from Mecca (hijra).
Recipient of the promises of Israel: **people and land**.	Recipient of the promises for all peoples: **Jesus Christ** as Abraham's heir.	Recipient of the original revelation which is set down without falsification only in the **Qur'an**.

revealed to all of them), and was finally proclaimed in a new and definitive way by Muhammad, the confirming 'seal' of the prophets, after the Prophet had received it directly from the one true God through an angel without the errors and distortions of the Jews and Christians. Moreover, according to the Qur'an it is clear that the Muslims are closest to Abraham; they alone stand in the succession to Abraham as uncorrupted worshippers of God. They owe a great deal to him: their 'name' (Muslim), their faith, their liturgy in Mecca and thus also their theocentricity and their universalism.

There is a **second**, less pleasant, **conclusion**. It becomes clear even from so apparently harmless an example as Abraham that here we are dealing with extremely difficult questions, which are vigorously disputed between the religions and are also politically delicate; indeed, here the **primal identity of each of the three religions is at stake**.

But does all this mean that it is only at first glance that Abraham represents a 'common point of reference' for the three religions, and on subsequent inspection proves 'through the perspective of each particular religious tradition also to be the embodiment of what distinguishes them and divides them from one another', so that Abraham cannot unreservedly be regarded as 'an ideal starting point for present-day dialogue'?[65] If once again we look closer, while Abraham does not appear to be an ideal starting point, he is nevertheless a very real starting point for what we can nowadays call a 'trialogue' (a philological neologism) between Jews, Christians and Muslims.

5. The need for a 'trialogue' between Jews, Christians and Muslims

At a third glance it may emerge that while there is no total agreement over Abraham among the three religions, there is no total dissent either, but rather a **convergence** which makes a conversation seem meaningful. May one of the three religions lay exclusive claim to Abraham? Does not Abraham belong to all of them? Indeed, could he not be a challenge to all the religions, even today?

Even in the worst periods of hatred of the Jews in the Middle Ages or in modern times, **Christianity** could never completely forget that it derived from Judaism, which appealed to Abraham, and at the least continued to share with it the Hebrew Bible, the Psalms and many Hebrew elements of worship (from 'Hosanna' to 'Amen'). In the two major Gospels of Luke and Matthew (who himself came from Judaism), the genealogy of Jesus itself already emphatically recalls that Christ Jesus was a descendant of Abraham.[66] And the God who 'glorified his servant Jesus' was none other than the 'God of Abraham, Isaac and Jacob'.[67] Indeed, even if according to Paul Christianity insisted on justification through trusting faith, it was similarly by no means prepared to renounce good works: according to Paul, faith should be active through love.[68] Finally, with the Gospel of John,[69] the Letter of

James, which I have already mentioned, in particular puts extraordinarily sharp stress on the need for works as opposed to a 'faith' which consists only in inactive confessing.[70]

Conversely, however, in **Judaism** the rabbis, too, stress the significance of Abraham's obedience in faith.[71] And they, too, in no way exclusively associate the heritage of the promises to Abraham with physical descent. Evidently the Qur'an has a legitimate point here in the argument that it puts forward: before Abraham became the first monotheistic 'missionary', he was first of all himself a **convert** to the true faith, and that after many decades. Indeed the rabbis explain that precisely because of his very late circumcision (at the age of ninety-nine!), for the future Abraham opened up the possibility even of non-Jews going over to Judaism. So in this way he became the model not only for Jews but also for all the Gentiles (proselytes) who went over to Judaism, and thus the tribal ancestor of **all** nations. Therefore to this degree, at least, in Judaism, too, a spiritual descent from Abraham has for a time been possible. Down to the present day, the convert, when called to read from the Torah, is addressed as 'NN, son of our father Abraham'.[72] Furthermore, according to present-day Jewish theology, even Christians who want to remain Christians can be regarded along with Muslims as 'children of Abraham'. The Jerusalem scholar David Flusser points out: 'In the Jewish religion, the existence of Christianity (and Islam) can be understood as the fulfilment of God's promises to Abraham to make him the father of many peoples.'[73]

Nor can the close relations between **Islam** and Judaism be overlooked, despite all the special teaching of the Qur'an. Muslims appeal for their faith to the same Abrahamic origin, and Israelites for their part feel that from the beginning they were kin to the early Arabs. Historically, at the latest from the time of King Solomon, it was possible to point to numerous economic ties between the land of Canaan and Arabia, lasting until the time of the prophet Muhammad, when numerous Jewish communities lived in Arabia. Moreover, Islamic exegesis of the Qur'an and Islamic historiography uninhibitedly supplement what the Qur'an says about Abraham from the Hebrew Bible or the Jewish haggadah, and this in turn influences Jewish tradition and interpretation. The Hebrew Bible itself contains a whole series of allusions to the close relations between Jews and Arabs; numerous Arabic words have found their way into the books of Job and Proverbs; and even the Mishnah, much later, contains sections which relate to the conduct of Jews in Arabia. So it is not surprising that throughout their history the Jews felt some affinity to Arab culture, with the result that it was in Arab lands in particular that it proved possible for the most flourishing centres of mediaeval Judaism to develop: under the Abbasids in Iraq, under the Moorish rulers in Spain, and after the expulsion from Spain under the Ottomans in Istanbul and Saloniki.

Thus the question which needs already to be asked here, right at the beginning, is this. What unites the three religions of the Near Eastern currents of religious systems over and above all the more or less fortuitous historical relationships? What fundamentally unites Jews, Christians and Muslims? What can be regarded as **the real foundation** of a new Abrahamic ecumenism to be brought to mind and really put into practice again – despite all the independence of the three religions? What unites the three Abrahamic religions even now?

One need only face representatives of the Indian and Chinese currents of religious systems in ecumenical dialogue in the company of Jews and Muslims to be aware how much is common to Jews, Christians and Muslims, despite all their disputes. They share a broadly similar basic understanding of God, of human beings, of the world and of world history. This is a kind of **Abrahamic ecumene**, which is founded on a long history and which cannot be obliterated by all the hostility and wars. As Kurt Rudolph, the historian of religion, rightly observes, 'A tremendous inheritance is emerging in the history of the religion of our cultural complex, which governs the relationship between the three great Near Eastern religions down to the present day, even if it is often not perceived (whether consciously or unconsciously) by believers.'[74]

A **third** fundamental, and at the same time anticipatory, **conclusion** is that the three Abrahamic religions of Judaism, Christianity and Islam are bound together by the major characteristics which they have in common. These are already indicated by the name of Abraham. Despite all the differences which separate the religions, these common features are:

- **Semitic origin and language**: in structure and vocabulary, Arabic is closely related to the Hebrew of Israel and the Aramaic of Jesus and the earliest Christian community; all three Abrahamic religions derive from the Semitic language group;
- **Belief in one and the same God** of Abraham, their tribal ancestor, who according to all three traditions was the great witness to this one true and living God;
- **A view of history** which does not think in cosmic cycles but is **focussed on a goal**: a universal history of salvation progressing through time from its beginning in God's creation, directed towards an end through God's consummation;
- The **prophetic proclamation** and the revelation which is laid down once and for all in scripture and remains normative;

- The **basic ethic** of a fundamental humanity grounded in God's will: the Ten Commandments ('Decalogue') or something corresponding to them.

To put it in one sentence: Judaism, Christianity and Islam, these three Abrahamic religions, together form a **monotheistic world movement** of Near Eastern/Semitic origin and prophetic character with an ethical focus, which is fundamentally different in origin and structure from the religions of India and China – though these are not to be devalued as a result. Together they proved able to make an extremely important contribution to the ecumene of religions.[75]

The documents approved by the **Second Vatican Council** between 1962 and 1965 emphasize that for all the manifest differences, in Christianity in particular a clear recollection of the common heritage of Abraham has already come about. Here the Catholic church confesses explicitly that it would be inconceivable without Abraham and his people. And even if the text which follows is conceived and formulated all too much in terms of Christian self-understanding, it makes sufficiently clear what Jews and Christians have in common: 'Sounding the depths of the mystery which is the Church, this sacred Council remembers the spiritual ties which link the people of the new Covenant to the stock of Abraham. The Church of Christ acknowledges that in God's plan of salvation the beginning of her faith and election is to be found in the patriarchs, Moses and the prophets. She professes that all Christ's faithful, who as men of faith are sons of Abraham, are included in the same patriarch's call and that the salvation of the Church is mystically prefigured in the exodus of God's chosen people from the land of bondage.'[76]

The Council makes statements about the Muslims which reproduce even more clearly the self-understanding of the Muslims themselves. In this form they could probably also be endorsed by Muslims and Jews: 'The Church has also a high regard for the Muslims. They worship God, who is one, living and subsistent, merciful and almighty, the Creator of heaven and earth, who has also spoken to men. They strive to submit themselves without reserve to the hidden decrees of God, just as Abraham submitted himself to God's plan, to whose faith Muslims eagerly link their own.'[77]

This gives us sufficient hermeneutical and ecumenical preparation now to turn wholly to **Judaism** in its history which is always still present: Judaism – an ethnic religion, yet a world religion with a distinctive stamp, without which neither Christianity nor Islam would be conceivable.

II. Problems over Beginnings

Judaism has two manifest characterstics: it is an ethnic religion, the **religion of a people**, but at the same time it is a religion which has made world history and has itself experienced a world history – it is **a world religion**. Like other universal religions, Judaism is not a static entity, a monolithic block. Its history is full of tensions, full of deep and radical changes, at all events deeper than a Jewish or a Christian orthodoxy bent on continuity is ready to perceive. It is a history in which, as we shall see, without any pressure towards systematization, a variety of macromodels, major constellations, paradigms, can easily be established which are still present and virulent even today. Like any religion, Judaism, too, needs first to be measured by its own origins and criteria before it is compared with others. So we must go right back to the beginning in our questioning.

1. The riddle of Judaism

There is no doubt that Judaism – one of the earliest religions on our globe, which despite all the indescribable persecutions has been able to keep itself alive to the present day – is a religion with a power, warmth, serenity and humanity all of its own. What a constantly enigmatic, **unique phenomenon in the history of religions and of the world** this Judaism is – for others as well as for itself! Its nature is almost impossible to define. Unlike Islam and Christianity, it is not a multi-national power embracing hundreds of millions of people. Rather, it is a tiny people which only existed first of all in that tiny land in the centre, formed by Syria-Palestine, of the 'fertile crescent' of ancient cultivated lands extending from the Persian Gulf to the Nile valley – a strip of cultivated land, for the most part hilly and at most ninety miles wide, bordered on the west by the Mediterranean and in the east slowly giving way to the wilderness of Syria and Arabia.[1] In the centre is the deep split of the 'Syrian cleft', which stretches through the Jordan valley and the Dead Sea (the deepest region on earth, reaching well over a thousand feet below the surface of the Mediterranean) to Egypt, indeed to the lakes of central Africa, where the earliest discoveries of the human race so far have been made.

So what is this Judaism, about which Jews themselves puzzle most of all and which in its long history has been part of the Assyrian,

Babylonian, Persian, Greek, Roman and finally Christian world, and as a result was scattered all over the earth?

– A **state** and yet not a state! Why not? Because since the Babylonian exile (586 BCE) a majority, and from the second millennium after Christ until the present day by far the majority, of Jews have lived outside the 'Holy Land'. 5.7 million Jews are citizens of the United States (about 3% of the population), and until recently 1.7 million citizens of the USSR; only 3.3 million are citizens of Israel.

– A **people** and yet not a people! Why not? Because unlike any other people this people is an international entity. Countless Jews feel that politically and culturally they are Americans, English, French or German and by no means 'Israelis abroad'.

– A **race** and yet not a race. Why not? Because already from late Roman times individuals from every possible tribe and people have become Jews by marriage or conversion; some Eastern Jews are descended from the Turkish people of the Chasars and yet others from the black Falashas in Ethiopia, so that present-day Israel has become a manifestly multi-racial state with men and women of every possible colour of skin, hair and eyes.

– A **linguistic community** and yet not a linguistic community! Why not? Because Judaism knows neither a culture nor a language common to all Jews. Many Jews know neither Hebrew nor Yiddish.

– A **religious community** and yet not a religious community. Why not? Because a large number of Jews – even in Israel – do not believe in God and claim that their Jewishness has nothing to do with religion; others are indeed religious but personally reject observance of the halakhah, the Jewish religion of the law.

Quantitatively, the Jews are negligible, but in religious terms they are a great power. However one interprets the situation, it is clear that Judaism is the enigmatic **community of fate** of all those who, wherever and in whatever way, claim their descent from Jacob who was called Israel or – more precisely, in legal terms – have a Jewish mother or have been converted to Judaism. Regardless of whether or not they now have the same language, culture, race, they have the same destiny. They form a community of fate which (no matter whether it is affirmed, ignored or denied by individual members) has shown an unprecedented, incomparable, amazing power of endurance down to the present day over a history of three thousand years, through centuries of peace and centuries of persecution, indeed extermination. Is not this endurance over three thousand years in the worst of circumstances the abiding riddle of this community?

No matter how we explain it, there is no doubting that the Jews are an enigmatic community of fate, because they are a **community** with an enigmatic **experience**. And that is the case not just in the later, 'Christian' centuries, which were often so bad, but already from early times, from the beginning. So our question is: were not these early experiences, which were always handed down in faith – first orally, and after 1000 BCE also already in writing – always religious experiences? Experiences of a God of whom no images might be made, an incomprehensible and unfathomable God, in whose light or shade Israel has stood since Abraham, Isaac and Jacob? Did not the Jews, to the extent that they were religious, always continue to believe in this one God of the fathers, so that for them there was always only this one monotheistic religion and no others? And did not faith in this one God always remain the centre of Jewish **religion** – regardless of whether the majority were faithful or unfaithful? And could the Jewish **people**, scattered all over the earth, for two thousand years with no state of its own, have preserved its identity without the binding force of this faith? Have not believing Jews of all centuries shaped their life by it and survived precisely by doing so? Have not the Jews who since the modern period in Europe have become increasingly secular and worldly, or even secularist and godless, referred back to this faith when they wanted to explain to themselves or their children why the Jews are what they are? So has not a certain Jewish feeling of togetherness, a sense of solidarity and possibly also a spiritual attitude, taken shape, transcending the frontiers of countries and continents?

The Jews have survived – in the most trying of circumstances – for three thousand years: in the light of this enigmatic evidence can we completely resist the idea that this people might exist, be destined, for something special? Could this people have been preserved, chosen, by someone for something? That is precisely what its ancient religious traditions assert in amazing unanimity: they speak of an **election** of the people! Are they right? At all events, today, no matter whether we are Jews, Christians or Muslims, we cannot avoid answering the historical question – as already in the story of Abraham. Can we rely on these traditions of the origin of the people, since it is evident beyond any doubt that often they were often written down only hundreds of years after the 'events' they report? What is the present state of historical scholarship?

2. Origins shrouded in sagas

A small comparison immediately indicates the problem. There is no doubt that it would be extraordinarily difficult to reconstruct the history, say, of the **Swiss** Confederation (*Confoederatio Helvetica*, formed 'in the name of God the Almighty'!) if we depended only on the earliest Swiss **sagas**. Take the saga of the hunter and marksman William Tell, later to become the Swiss national hero, who after his bold shot at the apple in Altdorf, his arrest and subsequent flight over Lake Lucerne in a storm, is said finally to have shot the Habsburg Count Hermann Gessler, the hated oppressor of his people, thus giving the signal for a popular rebellion and leading the way to the liberation of his country from Habsburg rule. It would be extraordinarily difficult to use this to reconstruct the formation of the Confederation – despite the fact that these events are precisely located in central Switzerland. Why? Because – as I must confess to my sorrow as a Swiss citizen – the Tell story was probably originally a **saga**: a floating Nordic saga (the theme of shooting at an apple already appears in Saxo Grammaticus's *Gesta Danorum*). But the foundation of the Swiss confederacy, which is known to have taken place in the thirteenth century of our era, is guaranteed historically by a number of documents which are beyond doubt. These include the first federal letter of the primal cantons of Uri, Schwyz and Unterwalden, dated 1 August 1291 (which can still be seen in the Schwyz federal archive). But what about the Israelite 'confederation'?

The origin of the **Israelite** covenant community is even more shrouded in sagas.[2] That is not surprising when we reflect that it is to be dated as early as the thirteenth/twelfth century **before** Christ. The reign of Pharaoh Ramses II, the founder of the new residence city of Ramses in the Nile Delta (excavated forty miles west of the present Suez Canal), which lasted for sixty-six years, began in 1290 BCE. His city is mentioned in the book of Exodus (1.11), and in the view of many scholars he was the 'Pharaoh of the oppression', who conscripted to work on building projects Israelite nomads who had entered Egypt at an earlier date – forced labour was customary in Egypt. However, there are no documents relating to this 'oppression' of Israelites and their 'exodus' from Egypt.[3] The ancient Egyptian sources are silent, which is not particularly surprising: such an emigration of what was presumably a very small group would have been utterly insignificant for the scribes of Egyptian court and state history. But what about those ten public and spectacular miraculous plagues – the changing of water into blood, the frogs, flies, vermin, plague, boils, hail, locusts and darkness, culminating in the slaughter of the firstborn?[4] They are most likely to be condensed and stylized accounts of a type of natural catastrophe which was not unusual in Egypt and Palestine. Only the passover sacrifice[5] was probably originally a bloody sacrificial rite to ward off demons, practised to protect the new life of the herds at the time of the old nomadic spring festival.

Still, does not perhaps the first mention of the name 'Israel' outside the Bible occur in the famous hieroglyphic stele of Pharaoh Merneptah, the son and successor of Ramses II, who reigned from 1224 to 1204 BCE?[6] (This stele was found in 1896 in the City of the Dead, in Thebes, and can be seen in the Museum of Egypt in Cairo.) That may be, but the stele does not say a word about the defeat of a Pharaoh and a troop of pursuers who would have been caught by the returning waters of a lagoon. On the contrary, it records Merneptah's victory over the Libyans and its effects also on 'Israel', which according to the inscription lay fallow and had no seed corn... Otherwise there is nothing, nor is there anything about a man called Moses, to whose birth[7] a legend which was evidently already current in Sumer and Akkad was transferred, telling of the preservation of a boy hero who had been exposed. Such preservation is recorded for the first time in the case of King Sargon I of Akkad – in the second half of the third millennium BCE![8]

What follows from all this? Like the story of the election of Abraham, Isaac and Jacob, so too the stories of the exodus from Egypt, the making of the covenant on the mountain of God and the entry into the promised land were first of all only **handed down orally**. As the other peoples evidently had no knowledge of such events, and more extended written traditions occur in Israel itself during the late monarchy at the earliest, it is almost impossible to get historical verification for these fundamental events of early Israelite history. Given these not very favourable circumstances, a fundamental question arises:

3. How do we deal with the sources?

Indeed, the question cannot be avoided. What is the present-day reader to make of these stories? Indeed, what are present-day Jews, Christians or Muslims to make of their own age-old religious traditions, stories, sagas and legends? The alternatives are obvious:
– Are we to accept old traditions word for word, as they are written, with all the duplications, contradictions and improbabilities, in order to 'rescue' the 'fundamentals' of Jewish, Christian or Muslim faith?
– Or, now that the European Enlightenment has introduced historical

consciousness into the world – do we throw all these age-old sagas on the scrap-heap of history as unimportant myths and fairy tales?
– Or is there a third possibility of postmodern interpretation alongside fundamentalist tradition and modernist elimination?

The writer Thomas Mann spun out the Genesis stories in a brilliant way to make a four-volume Joseph novel of more than 2,000 pages or 70,000 lines (*Joseph and his Brothers*, 1926-1942). Believers in search of historical certainty will hardly want to rely on that. Nor will they want to rely on Sigmund Freud's psychoanalytical speculation (originally conceived as 'a historical novel') at the end of his life, on *Moses and Monotheism* (it was published in 1939, the year of his death). In any case, both Thomas Mann and Sigmund Freud based their works on historical research which by now is completely outdated.[9] Instead of this, with all due respect to Mann and Freud, as a twentieth-century believer who thinks in historical-critical terms, I want to attempt to make a distinction: truth and poetry require a survey with a historical basis.

As children of the Enlightenment we cannot understand either the Homeric epics or Virgil's *Aeneid*, the Song of Roland or the sagas of William Tell or the Nibelungs, or even Holy Scripture, in a literal, pre-modern way – as did the people of the Middle Ages or even the Reformers. We have to interpret even sacred texts, even the Bible itself, primarily with the aid of **historical criticism**. In so doing, where we are engaged in scholarly interpretations we have to use all the modern methods and ways of working: not only textual criticism, literary criticism, form criticism and genre criticism, but also motive criticism, tradition criticism, redaction criticism and a critical study of the influence of texts. Furthermore, we also have to use all that has been brought to light by archaeological excavations (especially stratigraphy) and surface explorations, and finally the result of sociological and structuralist investigations, which have proved illuminating in most recent times. Any monopolistic method is to be resisted.

Lay people are usually unaware that the scrupulous scholarly work achieved by **modern biblical criticism** – which in the process has stimulated and used other disciplines (classical philology, Egyptology, Assyriology and so on) – , represented by scrupulous academic work over about 300 years, belongs among the greatest intellectual achievements of the human race.[10] Has any of the great world religions outside the Jewish-Christian tradition investigated its own foundations and its own history so thoroughly and so impartially? None of them has remotely approached this. The Bible is far and away the most studied book in world literature. There is not a sentence about which countless modern academic commentaries have not been disseminated in an enormous variety of world languages. There is not a word about which countless philological and historical dictionaries and handbooks do not provide information. There is not a name which has not been subjected to more or less exhaustive investigation. There is not a theme which has not been illuminated from the most varied aspects – philological, historical, sociological, theological. The libraries which have been written about this one book, which is simply called 'the Bible' (from the Greek *biblia*, the books), are too vast for anyone to take in.[11]

The **Hebrew Bible** is also known as the Tanakh (an abbreviation based on the initial letters T = Torah = Law; N = Nebi'im = Prophets; Kh = Khetubim = Writings); Christians call it the Old Testament. It has been recognized that one of the most significant results of modern Christian biblical research is that criticism can distinguish different **sources** in the Pentateuch, which narrates history from the creation of the world to the death of Moses. The whole process of the formation of the Book of Genesis may itself have taken around five hundred years.[12]

On the basis of this source criticism, which has become increasingly sophisticated, it is impossible to overlook the fact that in contrast to the history **after** the formation of the state in the first millennium BCE, the sources for the period **before** the foundation of the Israelite state in the last two or three centuries of the second millennium BCE are extremely unhelpful and unyielding. Israel was still **a people in the making,** hardly noticed by its great neighbours.

But there can be no doubt that three 'events' came to be of basic importance for the later history of the people: first, the exodus of the people from Egypt; secondly, the making of the covenant on the mountain of God; and thirdly, the settlement. Granted, the history that lies 'behind' them is uncertain, especially as the literary traditions are by no means agreed. Originally, they were probably independent, and only at a later stage were they skilfully put together from different sources in a complicated process of literary composition, and thus edited to form more or less a unity. But of course this does not exclude a certain degree of historicity. Self-critical exegetes concede today that all too often, literary-critical hypotheses have been made the criterion for historical judgments about events that are described. As though late, or supposedly late, traditions could not refer to earlier facts! So can we still write history about the early history of Israel? And if so, how?

4. Towards an integrated history

My starting point is that any discipline needs analyses which dissect each and every thing. And yet no discipline may shirk making the syntheses that are required of it. Syntheses are not without their dangers. For biblical scholarship, too, with its various methods, is exposed to fashions. In a first stage, **historical and literary analysis** had been pushed so far that it almost did away with itself in an exaggerated form criticism; after this, it had to be corrected increasingly by **biblical archaeology**, to the point that for a while this even seemed to provide proof for the slogan 'the Bible was right'.[13] It has now become fashionable to explain the archaeological evidence with **sociological methods** and thus methodologically to spirit away the Old Testament writings (which did indeed come into being later) as evidence for the interpretation of the early history of Israel or even rule them out from the start as inadmissible. Indeed, there seem to be Old Testament scholars who no longer need the Old Testament to interpret the Old Testament... Archaeology, interpreted with comparative history and social anthropology, has taken its place.

My own conviction – and it is certainly not just mine – is that only **an integrated multi-dimensional approach** which combines literary, historical, sociological and theological methods can do justice to Israelite and Judaean history. I feel that my concern for a differentiated synthesis of this kind in the history of Israel is very much confirmed by more recent synthetic tendencies in biblical scholarship, represented for example by Norman K.Gottwald's sociological and literary intro-duction in *The Hebrew Bible* (1985). Gottwald's conclusion, directed against all isolated, absolutized methods (of course including the theological method), is: 'Historical criticism reduces events. Literary criticism reduces texts. Sociological criticism reduces societal structures and processes. Theological criticism reduces religious beliefs and prac-tices. Accordingly, the Hebrew Bible may be looked at entirely as historical, entirely as literary, entirely as social, entirely as theological, but in such a way that none of these ways of looking is able to exclude the others.'[14]

So we should not be intimidated by what in practice is the infinity of perspectives, by the impossibility of assimilating the masses of material heaped up by specialist scholarship and by the dogmas of the different methods, schools and trends. I shall venture to paint an overall picture so that as far as possible we can see the whole in the parts and the status of the parts in the whole.

For the history of Israel in particular, that means that we have to concede (and we shall be seeing much of this even more clearly) that it is impossible to provide subsequent historical verification of the great 'events of the early history of Israel' at a later date. The origins of Israel are and remain shrouded in saga in a way which, as is well known, also applies to other events of antiquity like the founding of Rome – the only difference being that Romulus and Remus, who were set adrift on the Tiber and suckled by a she-wolf, are not authorities for revelation in the same way as Moses, who inaugurates a salvation history which is binding to the present day. But does that mean that in the first epoch of Israel what was supposed to have happened triumphed completely over what actually did happen? It is not as simple as that.

5. The establishment of monotheism

At any rate we have to ask: **what** was it that produced so **strong an effect** in history that ultimately the whole tradition was shaped by it? The answer is clear from the basic statement of the texts: it was **faith in this one invisible God Yahweh who is at work in history**. This was a faith which was clearly so strong in the final redaction of the 'five books of Moses' that it could ultimately suppress all rival forms of belief in God. So the first and second commandments of the Decalogue run: 'I am the Lord, your God, who brought you out of the land of Egypt, from the house of slavery. You shall have no other gods than me. You shall not make for yourselves any image of God, any image at all.'[15]

We must therefore agree with **Yehezkel Kaufmann**, professor in the Hebrew University of Jerusalem, when in his impressive account of the religion of Israel he says that the 'basic idea of Israelite religion' is monotheism, the belief that 'God is the Most High, over all':[16] 'In short, the religious idea of the Bible, visible in the earliest strata, which even permeates the "magical" legends, is that of a supreme God who stands over every cosmic law, every destiny and every compulsion: unborn, uncreated, knowing no passion, independent of things and their powers, a God who does not fight against other deities or powers of impurity, who does not sacrifice, predict, prophesy and practise witchcraft; who does not sin and needs no atonement; a God who does not celebrate the festivals of his life. A free divine will which transcends all that is – that is the characteristic of biblical religion, and that makes it different from all the other religions on this earth.'[17]

But Yehezkel Kaufmann, who ignores the results of historical-critical research, does not answer one question. Was it like this from the beginning? Through arduous and detailed work, and by means of the historical-critical method, above all German scholars like Albrecht Alt, Martin Noth, Otto Eissfeldt and Gerhard von Rad[18] discerned and sketched out a picture of Israelite religion which has become classic. Though it already also took account of literary and sociological aspects, their historical criticism had to be supplemented not only by archaeology – as practised in particular by French, English, American and Israeli researchers – but also by more recent literary-critical and sociological methods (developed above all in America) which take the Bible seriously as a literary work and as a sociological document.[19]

One important result of the most recent research is that the picture of the **development of belief in God** in Israel has become more complex. On the basis of many indirect indications in the books of Kings and Chronicles, but also in the polemic of the prophets; on the basis of archaeological discoveries (for example the many figures of gods and goddesses to be found everywhere) and a number of place names (e.g. Bet-Anat = 'temple of Anat'), present-day scholars assume that polytheism was widespread in Israel down to the Babylonian exile. In other words (and above all the American historian Morton Smith[20] has worked this out), it was only after long controversies that strict biblical monotheism was able to establish itself. From our present perspective we have to begin from 'a chain of successive revolutions in the direction of monotheism following relatively rapidly after one another' (O.Keel).[21] The German Old Testament scholar Bernhard Lang[22] attempted to define them more closely (though an even sharper distinction needs to be made between the existence of other gods inside Israel and that of gods outside Israel):

– In the ninth century, in the early monarchical period of Israel, there was the battle against Baal, the god of Tyre, and for the one Israelite national God Yahweh: Yahweh instead of Baal. This was waged in the northern kingdom by the prophets Elijah and Elisha and – after the *coup d'état* – by the new king Jehu, and in the southern kingdom of Judah at the same time through the reforms of Kings Asa and Jehoshaphat.

– The eighth century saw the beginning of the 'Yahweh alone movement', which was at first in a minority: only this one God is to be worshipped in Israel, no matter what gods other peoples worship. This is monolatry, understood as the worship of one God without denying the existence of other gods (outside Israel); hence the sharp polemic of the prophet Hosea against the worship of other gods in Israel and prostitution in the temple sphere.

– In the seventh century this sole worship of Yahweh became established. The existence of other gods outside Israel was still not denied, but in Israel, the exclusive people of the covenant, Yahweh was to be worshipped exclusively, in exclusive worship (and not Baal or later Zeus); there was a reform programme under King Josiah with a purification and centralization of the cult and the declaration that the new cultic order was the law of the state.

– The sixth century, finally, saw the further development of the sole worship of Yahweh to the point of a strict monotheism, which now denied the existence of other gods: the conquest of Jerusalem by the Babylonians was interpreted as punishment for going astray into polytheism, and a redaction of the old writings was undertaken in a strictly monotheistic direction.

This, then, was a movement from polytheism through monolatry to monotheism, but for Israel itself at a very early stage what was important was its exclusive bond to the one 'jealous Yahweh' which excluded any alien cult, any cult of idols or stars. Should this development be branded 'blindness to history', 'fanaticism', 'intolerance', 'hatred' – terms which one can sometimes hear in more recent scholarship, particularly from Christian exegetes? Should we perhaps long for polytheism and the old Canaanite fertility cult? No. In the end, at what date one puts the origin of a strictly exclusive monotheism is ultimately a secondary question. That despite all the relics of earlier, less exclusive views, belief in the one and only God determines the **whole** of the Hebrew Bible in its definitive redaction from beginning to end is decisive not only for that time but also for today. Important though a reconstruction of the history of the literature and religion of Israel with the help of the historical-critical method may be, solving the question of **origins** is a very different matter from solving the question of **understanding**.

'Yahweh is God!' It was indeed a long way, but ultimately a clear one: from this saying by the prophet Elijah, who is swathed in legend; through the great writing prophets, Isaiah in the eighth century and Jeremiah in the seventh, for whom the gods (*elohim*) of the great powers (particularly those of the neo-Assyrian empire) are 'nothing' (*elihim*[23]), 'no-god' (*lo-elohim*[24]) and 'empty breath' (*hebel*[25]), until finally we have the clear hymnic confession of the Second Isaiah (Deutero-Isaiah). This prophet, like the prophet Ezekiel, worked in the sixth century among the exiles of the Babylonian captivity and there proclaimed the one and only God Yahweh as salvation for all peoples: 'There is no God outside me! There is no righteous and saving God beside me!'[26]

This was to be not only practical monotheism, but now also monotheism in principle; at the latest after the Babylonian exile it established itself as the basic confession of Judaism. And is it not still significant today? Believing Jews confess it to the present day in the 'Shema Israel', which is prayed morning and evening and at the time of death: 'Hear (*shema*), Israel, Yahweh is our God, Yahweh alone!'[27] Indeed that is Israel's great legacy to humankind, and for Christianity and Islam down to the present day it means three things:

- There are to be **no subsidiary deities,** as in all the religions around: their worship is not allowed either publicly or privately.
- There is to be **no rival, evil god,** as for example in Persian religion: even in the time of Persian rule, the 'adversary' or 'accuser' (Hebrew *satan*, then Greek *diabolos* = 'calumniator', hence English 'devil') failed to establish itself alongside the good principle as a second principle of equal status.[28]
- There is to be **no divine feminine consort** as elsewhere with all the main Semitic gods: there is not even a word for 'goddess' in Hebrew.

We need not concern ourselves here with hypotheses like the suggestion that a consort of Yahweh (for example the goddess Asherah) was worshipped in some Israelite circles. When God is addressed as 'Father' in post-exilic Judaism,[29] there is no sexist intent, to stress the masculinity of God and the inferiority of the woman (in fact she is created in the image of God just as the man is);[30] rather, the intention is to appeal as it were to the function of God as the head of the family to protect his kindred after the collapse of state structures.[31] In all three religions, pre-modern society certainly had a patriarchal stamp through and through, but patriarchy is by no means necessarily bound up with monotheism. However, where monotheism and patriarchy entered into an alliance, they all too often proved to be aggressive.

6. Adam and the universalism of the Hebrew Bible

Granted, fanaticism and intolerance have been and very often are associated with belief in the one God. And whereas the mystical religions of India, orientated on the oneness of all things, attempt more just to absorb other religions, relativizing them as preliminary stages and including them as aspects of the one and only truth (inclusivism), Judaism, Christianity and Islam, as prophetic religions which believe in the one God, tend almost naturally to exclude other religions from the start (exclusivism), to fight them, indeed to destroy them. Here the slogan is not community, but separation and conquest. Instead of the unity of humankind there is division. As we have just seen, this dangerously destructive tendency already has its foundations in the Hebrew Bible: the **concentration** on the one God often manifests itself not only as **confrontation** with the other religions, but at the same time also as **excommunication**, indeed – through 'holy wars' – ultimately as the **destruction** of those of other faiths.

But must that be? Must monotheism necessarily be fanaticism? It has rightly been observed that around the middle of the first millennium BCE, not only in Israel but also in Greece (the pre-Socratic philosophers), in Persia (Zarathustra), in India (Buddha) and in China (Confucius), reform movements against polytheism can be observed. These tend towards a single principle of the world, a single first and last reality, however it may be named. Thus Karl Jaspers called the period between the sixth and the fourth centuries BCE an 'axial period', an 'age of great personalities'.[32] Concentration of faith on the one God by no means necessarily excludes all-embracing breadth, but rather can be the foundation for it.

In the Hebrew Bible, strikingly it was the strictly monotheistic Priestly tradition which attached the greatest importance to the **universal horizon** of Israelite faith. We have already heard how the Abraham story, which leads into the history of Israel, was from the beginning connected to the story of the prehistory and universal history of humankind generally – told from the creation of the world and the first human beings to the story of the tower of Babel. This universal horizon becomes abundantly clear precisely from the account of these beginnings. But the beginnings could have been given quite a different form. One need only consider three questions: 1. For the Hebrew Bible, is not the first human being as a matter of course a Jew? Not at all. 2. Was not the covenant with Abraham (of which we heard above) the first covenant, excluding the rest of the human race? Not at all. 3. Does not belief in one God at any rate represent a narrowing in comparison with polytheism, which is very much more tolerant? Not at all. These answers need at least a brief explanation. So first of all the question of the first human being.

'Adam' is very often understood simply as the proper name of the first human being. But 'Adam' is identical with the Hebrew word for human being (*adam* = 'human being'): 'The name of the genus becomes the proper name, because Genesis wanted to typify the whole genus in the first human being.'[33] In fact the so-called 'creation story' in Gen.2-4 is not a fairy-tale account of a first human being in the garden of paradise. It is concerned to define the human situation; it is about the *adam* who is the prototype of all human beings. And that also means:

- The first human being is not a Jew (the history of Israel begins only after the creation stories and the stories of the patriarchs).

- Nor is the first human being a Christian (as a typological-allegorical Christian exegesis sometimes suggests);
- Nor is the first human being a Muslim (at least not unless Muslim is understood simplistically as monotheist);
- Rather, Adam is simply the human being (*adam*): **every** human being is **the image and likeness of God!**[34]

Here, right from the beginning, we can see the universal horizon of the Hebrew Bible. The mysterious Melchizedek, king of Salem and priest of God Most High[35] – later the model for the Hasmonaean priest-kings[36] and the prototype of Jesus Christ[37] – is not a Jew nor a Christian either. The concern is with the one God, beside whom there is none other, and therefore also with the human being, **any** human being: not just, say, with a single people, but with humankind as **a whole**.

This will immediately be confirmed from a wider perspective when I go into the second question. Was not the covenant with Abraham the first covenant, excluding the rest of the human race? Not at all. For before Abraham there was Noah and the covenant with him.

7. The covenant with Noah: a covenant with humankind and the human order

Because of the obvious importance of the covenant with Abraham (which is confirmed by Isaac and Jacob) and then of the covenant on Sinai (with Moses), and the significance of these covenants for the future, the **very first covenant** which according to the Hebrew Bible was made by Yahweh, the **Noachide covenant**, is often overlooked. With whom was it made? With humankind in general, indeed **with the whole creation**, with human beings and animals. After the flood Yahweh declares to Noah and his sons, the surviving representatives of the human race: 'Behold, I establish my **covenant** with you and your descendants after you, and with every living creature that is with you, the birds, the cattle, and every beast of the earth with you, as many as came out of the ark. I establish my **covenant** with you, that never again shall flesh be cut off by the waters of a flood, and never again shall there be a flood to destroy the earth.'[38]

This first covenant of God with humankind is not a bilateral undertaking (how could it be, after the almost complete destruction of the human race?), and because of this, some exegetes think, contrary to the text, that it is illegitimate to speak of a 'covenant' in the strict sense here. This is God's promise and assurance, given of his own free will, his commitment of himself and his own free offering. But by its very character it constitues a **covenant** (in an analogous but real sense): a covenant for ever with the whole of creation, 'his' covenant, which he himself 'grants', 'establishes': the creation will never perish again, and humankind along with the animals will be preserved.

So this unbelievable promise applies not just to the Jewish people but to all the human race: the uncircumcised as well as the circumcised. It is a **covenant with humankind**: there is no distinction of race or even of class or caste – indeed, not even of religion! For the sign of this covenant is not circumcision, practised by the member of a chosen people. The marvellous·symbol of this covenant with humankind, established by God himself, is the **rainbow** which spans the whole earth, which bears witness to the lordship, constancy and grace of God, towering above all.

However, we must not fail to notice that this covenant is already matched by a clear **obligation** on the **human** side – and to this degree it is indeed two-sided. For before the promise of the covenant some elementary demands are made of the new humankind which – in contrast to the later Torah – are to be binding on both Israelites and non-Israelites. These are not, as later, specific laws for a particular people, but basic demands which are to be observed by the whole of humankind. The covenant with humankind is matched with an **ethic for humankind**. One could describe these ordinances of preservation as a minimum **basic order of reverence for life**: not to murder ('since God has made human beings in his image'[39]) and not to eat the flesh of animals who are still living. In rabbinic Judaism, at a later date seven 'Noachide commandments' were derived from these moral obligations. They have been handed down in different versions: as well as the prohibition of murder there are prohibitions against theft, fornication, idolatry and blasphemy and the commandment to observe the law (to set up courts).[40] When in 1640 John Seldon, the English politician, lawyer and orientalist, published a book on the Hebrew understanding of the law of nature and of peoples, he put on the title page, in Hebrew letters, the Hebrew term for the Noachide commandments.

It is quite fundamental to the trialogue between Jews, Christians and Muslims that in the context of this Noachide covenant Jews – thus other rabbinic authorities, going against the rigorous Maimonides (who described Christians as idolaters because of the doctrine of the Trinity and their worship of images)[41] – recognize **Christians and Muslims** as 'Godfearers'! For they too have turned away from heathen gods and towards the true God. So even if their faith is allegedly mixed with error (for example, belief in the Trinity), they can **be saved**, just like the heathen Noachites, who did not know the commandments of

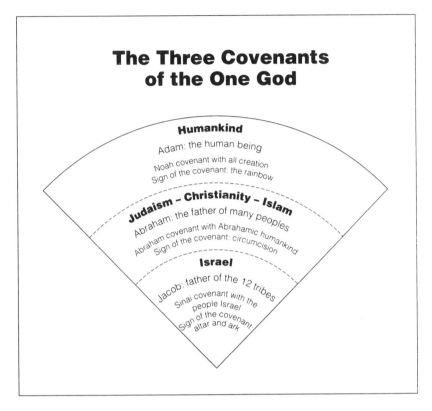

**The Three Covenants
of the One God**

Humankind
Adam: the human being
Noah covenant with all creation
Sign of the covenant: the rainbow

Judaism – Christianity – Islam
Abraham: the father of many peoples
Abraham covenant with Abrahamic humankind
Sign of the covenant: circumcision

Israel
Jacob: father of the 12 tribes
Sinai covenant with the
people Israel
Sign of the covenant:
altar and ark

Moses but were bound only by the Noachide prohibitions. In modern Judaism, for the same reason Christians are not regarded as heathen but as 'sons of Noah'.

And now to the third question: does not belief in one God represent a narrowing in comparison with polytheism, which is much more tolerant?

8. Belief in God means the fall of the gods

First of all, it has to be conceded that, on due consideration, belief in one God and belief in many gods do not go together. Down to the present day Judaism radically rejects any god alongside the one God, and even the pictorial representation of God, as *avodah zarah*, 'alien service', i.e. idolatry. In more primitive societies, belief in the one God means a radical repudiation of the divinized powers of nature in an ever-recurring cosmic dying-and-coming-into-being. But even in our often polytheistic age – for Christians and Muslims as for Jews – it means the radical repudiation of the many gods who nowadays are worshipped by men and women without any divine title: of all earthly entities with a divine function, on whom a person may feel that everyone depends, which he or she hopes for and fears more than anything else in the world. Here it makes no difference whether modern men and women – sometimes monotheists, and sometimes also polytheists – worship Mammon, sex, power or science, the nation, the church, the synagogue or the party, the leader or the pope as God. Israel's belief in one God stands over against any quasi- or pseudo-religion which absolutizes a relative. It casts down all false gods.

However, this belief in the one God need not of itself represent any spiritual narrowing. Rather, it gives **great freedom,** because it **relativizes** all the other powers and authorities in the world which so easily enslave people. By binding themselves to the one true Absolute, human beings therefore become truly free from all that is relative; it can no longer become an idol for them. So the strict, living, passionate, uncompromising belief in God, which is and remains the mark of Israel and at the same time is its gift to other peoples – and which cannot be praised enough – is to be seen against the universal human horizon of the Hebrew Bible. Today, in the transition to postmodernity, no return to the gods veiled in mythology is called for. Rather, instead of an artificial remythologizing, what is needed is a constantly new conversion to the one true God, who is the God of Jews, Christians and Muslims but who at the same time wills to be the God of all men and women.

However, this one God of all humankind – at least according to the testimony of the biblical writings – chose the people Israel in a special way from among all peoples. The **one God** and **his people** and **land:** here we move towards the centre of Israelite faith, which is of fundamental significance for the ever-renewed discovery of identity and formation of consensus in Judaism.

B. The Centre

'Centre' can be understood wrongly. For example, 'centre' does not mean a 'basic concept' or 'basic idea', in comparison with which all other concepts and ideas in Israelite religion would be just historical phenomena and developments – as it did under Hegel's influence in the nineteenth century. Nor does 'centre' mean a 'basic principle' in terms of which the whole of Israelite belief could be constructed systematically – which is what an orthodox dogmatic theologian could easily misunderstand it to mean. All attempts to derive a conceptual system or a coherent dogmatics from the Hebrew Bible have failed, and most recently come to grief on historical criticism. This criticism demonstrated that in the Hebrew Bible, already in the 'Five Books of Moses' and even more after them, there are very different traditions, periods and theologies.

But as far as I am concerned, the question will not go away. For all the variety, is there no connection between traditions and periods, persons and theologies? Is the Hebrew Bible just a conglomerate of basically different writings which have no common denominator? At least believers – Jews and also Christians – are interested in this question. Still, it needs to be answered on a historical basis, legitimated by scholarship:

– What made the different (but not completely heterogeneous) **traditions** grow together?
– What links the biblical **periods** (which are not totally different) together?
– What keeps the **theologies** (which do not simply deviate from one another) together?

So talk of a centre of Jewish faith is not focussed on the theoretical question of a systematic conception of unity. It is focussed on the practical question of what is **permanently valid** and **constantly obligatory** in Judaism, at least from a particular generation. It is neither unimportant nor even illegitimate for Jews or Christians to ask: how does Israelite religion differ from other religions? What is the special,

the typical, the specific character of Israelite religion as it has manifested itself in the Hebrew Bible, albeit in a historical process of constant reinterpretation? Or more precisely, in the various documents of Israelite faith what is
– the constant presupposition (not principle),
– normative basic conception (not dogma),
– driving force (not law)?

I. The Central Structural Elements

'Say therefore to the people of Israel, I am Yahweh, and I will bring you out from under the burdens of the Egyptians and I will deliver you from their bondage, and I will redeem you with an outstretched arm and with great acts of judgment, and I will take you for my **people**, and I will be **your God**; and you shall know that I am the Lord (Yahweh) your God, who has brought you out from under the burdens of the Egyptians.'[1]

1. Exodus: people and election

The **exodus cycle**,[2] though a skilful literary construction, is in many respects completely obscure.[3] According to the biblical tradition, only four generations lay between the time of Joseph, when the other eleven sons of Jacob had come to Egypt along with their father, and the time of Moses, when the Israelites left Egypt.[4] But a great people could hardly have grown up in this period, and there are also signs that some of the tribes or peoples which according to the book of Genesis were descended from the patriarchs were already in existence at the time of the patriarchs. Therefore present-day exegetes assume that the names of the **twelve sons of Jacob** were originally the names of **twelve tribes** from which at a later date twelve tribal ancestors of the same name were derived.[5] The consequence of this would be that the alliance of twelve tribes can hardly be derived historically from a common tribal ancestor.

Furthermore there is agreement among the experts that in no way were all the later tribes of Israel in Egypt before the settlement. This can be assumed only for particular clans or tribal groups, usually called the exodus group, the Yahweh group or the **Moses group**. These were the groups which had had particular experiences in the eastern or north-eastern part of the Sinai peninsula of a God Yahweh who was unknown in Canaan; they were the ones who brought knowledge of him to Palestine. Belief in Yahweh, which became normative for all Israel, thus rests on the early experiences of what was originally a relatively small group.

But what really took place under Ramses II and his son and successor in connection with the building of cities in the Nile delta? We do not know. The more detailed circumstances of the exodus, the exact route (one or several?) and the events by a Sea of Reeds: the nucleus of historical truth in all this can no longer be discovered. The same events were described in quite different ways, even in the different sources of the Pentateuch. And the biblical narratives of this early period have undergone successive reworking and therefore also theological inter-pretation, possibly down to the exilic or post-exilic period. It is difficult to tell from what at first was only oral tradition and from the various relatively late written sources, which do not seem very reliable for the pre-exilic period, what is history and what poetry, what is possibly just later interpretation or theological construction. However, precisely at this point, a combination of literary and archaeological methods, together with cultural sociology, might prove its worth.

To begin with, let us keep to the features which came to be influential in history, to what became the foundation of the **self-understanding of the later people of Israel**. Here one thing is completely clear. Alongside the promise to the patriarchs and the covenant with Abraham, the fundamental element is the constantly enriched and deepened **recollec-tion of a liberation** of the people from Egyptian slavery which took place at one time. Regardless of whatever may have happened here historically, at a later stage Israel understood the hour of its birth as an election, rescue and redemption of the people which was attributed to one God with the name Yahweh.

A word on this **name for God**. In the Hebrew Bible, as is well known, God's own name is denoted by four consonants, the tetragrammaton, **YHWH** (Yahweh, abbreviated to Yah).[6] However, in the last centuries before Christ Jews ceased to pronounce this name out of respect: God himself is present in the name. It was principally replaced by the word 'Adonay' (Lord), the vowels of which were attached to the name YHWH. As a result, later mediaeval theologians (and 'Jehovah's Witnesses' down to the present day) erroneously read Yahweh as Jehovah. At this point I ask Jewish readers to excuse me for keeping to the original instruction which, while prohibiting images of Yahweh, did not prohibit the pronunciation of his name. Even today this name is always paraphrased by Jews, usually with 'Adonai' ('Lord') or 'Hashem' ('the name').

But what is the meaning of that name which occurs more than 6,800 times in the Hebrew Bible? It is well known that when Moses was called at the burning bush, he was given an enigmatic answer to this question: *ehyeh asher ehyeh*.[7] Nowadays we cannot simply keep to the Greek translation of the Hebrew Bible (which is called the Septuagint, because according to legend it was produced by seventy translators): 'I am the one who is'. The verb *hayah* can indeed also mean 'be' in rare cases. But usually it means 'be there, take place, happen'. And since in Hebrew, present and future have the same form, we can translate the phrase either, 'I am there as the one who is there', or 'I am there as the one who will be there', or – as the great German Jewish translator of the Hebrew Bible, Martin Buber, rendered it: **'I will be there as the one who will be there.'**

Be this as it may, this answer does not in any way give a static and ontological definition of the being of God, of the kind that some ancient, mediaeval and modern Christian theologians have assumed: '*Sum qui sum* = 'I am who I am', hence *ipsum esse*, 'being itself'. Rather, here we have an announcement of God's declaration of his will in the form of a promise: God's dynamic being there, being present, being effective. So 'Yahweh' means: 'I will be there, present, leading the way, helping, strengthening, liberating!'

We have already heard that a fundamental and exclusive monotheism developed and established itself in Israel only slowly: from belief in the one god of a group, through the god of a people who claims sole worship, to belief in the one and only God of all peoples and the creator of heaven and earth. But one thing is certain: **belief in Yahweh** (his name is mentioned in every book of the Bible except for Koheleth [Ecclesiastes], Esther and the Song of Songs) is **the constant foundation for the people of Israel.** They believe in him, worship him and hope in him. And this Yahweh was evidently not experienced by his people as a despot and a slave owner, but as a God of liberation and redemption. If we listen to the fundamental biblical documents, it is unambiguously clear that what Israel experienced was not understood merely as a human work, but as **God's action.** Yahweh is believed in as the reason for the liberation from Egypt. So **he** is the real saviour and protector of Israel! God 'with us', 'for us'!

The confession of the one God who brought Israel out of Egypt is thus a primal confession of Israel. As we heard, it is also the introduction to the Decalogue. Very much later, the prophet Hosea put it like this: 'I am the Lord, your God from Egypt. You know no God beside me, and there is no helper but me.'[8] This liberation of the people chosen by God is remembered daily even now in Jewish morning and evening prayer, in every synagogue service, in the whole course of the Jewish calendar and especially at the feast of Pesach or Passover. It is and remains a basic datum of Jewish faith.[9]

So Israel understands itself as the **people** freed by God. Moreover 'people' (Hebrew *'am, goy*) is the term used most frequently by the Israelite tribes to describe themselves: **God's** people or – in line with the logic of this experience – God's **chosen** people. This way Jews have of describing themselves has often been misunderstood by non-Jews as an expression of Jewish superiority and arrogance. But given these beginnings there can be no question of that, no matter how individual Jews may have understood this or put it into practice. For:

1. The election of Israel is not a matter of the Israelites choosing themselves; it is **God's act** alone. And the Hebrew Bible uses a whole series of cognate verbs to describe this initiative of God's, like 'elect', 'single out', 'accept', 'embrace', 'call'... No one has a claim to election. Election is pure grace. So it is no occasion for chauvinism or exclusivism with a religious basis. The people of Israel is to be a blessing for other peoples.

2. The election of Israel does not mean the recognition of a particular quality of this people before all others, but a particular obligation. The reciprocity is only apparent: the choice by God (which is one-sided) has to be matched by the acceptance of **obligations** by Israel: Israel will not do justice to its election as people of God through pride and conceit, but only through obedient fulfilment of the regulations of the covenant. And how often has Israel failed and sinned against a call and an obligation! Only God's faithfulness preserves it from downfall. This becomes even clearer when we turn to a further guiding concept, the covenant.

2. Sinai: covenant and law

'And now, if you hear my voice and observe my **covenant**, you shall be my possession before all peoples; for the whole earth is mine. You shall become to me a kingdom of priests and a holy people. Those are the words which you are to say to the people of Israel.'[10]

What lies behind the **'Sinai' cycle**, which was not mentioned in some biblical summaries of the saving acts of God and presumably was originally handed down independently? In particular, what lies behind the narratives of the theophany of Yahweh, the Decalogue[11] and the making of the covenant?[12]

Here, too, we do not have much assured historical knowledge. Just as the route of the march to the mountain of God cannot clearly be verified, so too the **mountain of God** itself cannot be identified either. Was it really the Mount Sinai that we know, on the peninsula to the south of Israel, as the later Christian tradition in particular assumed it to be as a matter of course? Or rather was it Mount Horeb in north-east Israel, or a third location which has also been considered? And as for the **God of the mountain**, are we to conclude from the mountain of God that Yahweh was perhaps originally a mountain God of the wilderness? Was the one who revealed himself with fire and earthquake connected with a volcanic mountain? These are questions about questions, which only emphasize that we have no certain knowledge about the place of the origin of the revelation of God. Strictly speaking, we should always put 'Sinai' in quotation marks.

So what is left? What still seems most convincing to me is the interpretation that the tradition of the mountain of God was originally an autonomous tradition which was meant to illustrate the special relationship between Yahweh and Israel.[13] For there is no mistaking the fact that on this mountain of God, no matter where it is to be located, **a special relationship between Yahweh and the Yahweh group**, the primal Israel, was established. And unless we want to deny any historical nucleus to the tradition of the mountain of God in its original form, we have to begin from the fact that in the period between the exodus and the settlement, a particular, exclusive relationship came into being between the people – first of all in the form of the Moses group or the exodus group – and this God, as a result of which we call it the Yahweh group.

It is improbable that the Yahweh group itself already understood its experience of God explicitly as a '**covenant**'. However, be this as it may, we can at least say that what was later called the 'covenant' is grounded in this experience of the exodus and 'Sinai'. The reality of the covenant existed for a long time before the word 'covenant' (which occurs 287 times) was used for it. The substance – the final bond between this people and Yahweh, and thus fellowship with him – existed before the concept. Then in the time of 'Deuteronomy', in the seventh century, a time of crisis, as a result of prophetic impulses, anti-Canaanite reaction and a national freedom movement, the Hebrew word *berit* (which in the secular sphere simply means a legal relationship between two parties, regardless of whether or not they have equal rights) became the central concept of a **covenant theology**.[14] 'Covenant' now has the comprehensive meaning of God's election, God's rule and abiding communion with his people. This covenant is now the exclusive, indissoluble agreement between God and this people, which binds both sides. Through this covenant, which is the authentic sign of an incomparable, irrevocable condescension of the one God to his people, Israel clearly distinguishes itself from the polytheistic religions of its environment and their nature myths. In retrospect, the people now understood the whole of their own history in this way. After the 'covenant' with Abraham,[15] an individual, which was confirmed for his sons Isaac[16] and Jacob,[17] the covenant is now made with the **whole people**, which clearly has priority over the individual. What it signifies is that **Yahweh is the God of Israel, and Israel is his people.**

However, a special obligation in partnership is bound up with this special tie – as is already implied by the word *berit*. God's covenant **promise** is matched by the people's covenant **obligation**. Israel is to respond to God's promise of faithfulness with faithfulness, and to this extent the making of a covenant and the **giving of the law**, *berit* and **Torah,** belong together. Moreover, in the covenant-making ceremony of the book of Deuteronomy there is particularly strong stress on obedience to the regulations and obligations of the law;[18] for the covenant can be broken on the people's side. At the centre, completely bound up with the covenant event itself, are the 'Ten Words', the Decalogue, along with some expansions: apodeictic commands which express universal ethical and religious principles, a basic order which is established under the will of Yahweh. Torah, translated *nomos* in the Septuagint and the New Testament and 'law' in English, originally did not mean a corpus of law, but **instruction** generally: guidance for a truly human life which was made possible and demanded by God. And to the degree to which Christianity has literally made the 'Ten Commandments' its own and to the degree, too, that towards the end of the Mecca period (in the context of the vision of a nocturnal journey by the prophet to Jerusalem) the Qur'an offers a summary of the most important ethical obligations (with a striking number of parallels to the Decalogue – apart from those relating to the sabbath), we can speak of a **common basic ethic** of the three prophetic religions. This is a basic ethic which will need to be investigated more closely in connection with Christianity and Islam.

There was then a long **process of development** which turned the original 'instruction' into a comprehensive corpus of law. The fact that the covenant ethos originally appears at its centre as the unconditional proclamation of the will of Yahweh, as apodictic divine law, in no way means that all the legal material of the 'Book of the Covenant' in the

The Common Basic Ethic

The Jewish-Christian Decalogue	The Islamic Code of Duties
(Exodus 20.1-21)	(surah 17. 22-38)
I am the Lord your God.	In the Name of God, the merciful Lord of mercy.
You shall have no other gods besides me.	Set up no other deity alongside (the one) God.
You shall not make for yourselves any image of God. You shall not take the name of the Lord your God in vain.	Your Lord has commanded that you serve no one but Him.
Remember the sabbath day, to keep it holy.	
Honour your father and mother.	Show kindness to your parents. Give to the kinsman his due and to the needy and the wayfarer.
You shall not kill.	Do not kill your children for fear of poverty. Do not kill any man – a deed God forbids.
You shall not commit adultery.	Do not come near to adultery.
You shall not steal.	Handle the property of the orphan with integrity.
You shall not bear false witness against your neighbour.	Keep your bond. For you are accountable.
You shall not covet your neighbour's house.	Give full measure when you measure and weigh with just scales. Do not pursue things of which you have no knowledge.
You shall not covet your neighbour's wife, or his manservant or his maidservant, or his ox, or his ass, or anything that is your neighbour's.	Do not strut proudly on the earth.
(Revised Standard Version)	*(Translated by Kenneth Cragg)*

Book of Exodus,[19] far less the whole wealth of further legal definitions with the character of civil or cultic law, some of them in casuistic form, go right back to the event on the mountain. Since the basic studies by Albrecht Alt[20] and Martin Noth,[21] it has been the consensus of exegetes that, as Gerhard von Rad put it, 'Israel itself worked for a long time on the Decalogue, until in form and content it became so universal and so brief that it could be regarded as an adequate description of the whole of Yahweh's will for Israel.'[22] Granted, here too in the course of research positions have become increasingly sophisticated. Contrary to what was still assumed by Alt, the legal statements which have been designated apodeictic cannot be called genuinely Israelite or Yahwistic (they can also be found in other cultures). Nor can as it were a primal Decalogue be worked out from the various traditions of the text. However, it is quite possible that 'the Decalogue belongs to a relatively early period of Israel's life, probably within the premonarchic age'.[23] It also seems possible that individual commandments like the first three commandments in the Decalogue, or prohibitions of child sacrifice, magic and sodomy as parts of religious ceremonies, go back to Moses.

Be this as it may, in critical biblical scholarship there is nowadays agreement, to quote a statement by Georg Fohrer, 'that large portions of the apodictic rules of conduct were not brought to Palestine by the Moses host, but either, like Lev.18.7ff., derive from a non-Yahwistic nomadic environment, or only else did not come into being until after the settlement in Palestine, as an imitation of ancient forms.' So we may follow Fohrer in concluding: 'In any case, such regulations constituted the first steps along a path that led to a goal Moses can hardly have had in mind: a comprehensive system of commandments and prohibitions regulating the entire life of the nation and the individual, such as the Jewish religion of the law envisioned.'[24]

3. Canaan: land and promise

'After the death of Moses the servant of the Lord, the Lord said to Joshua the son of Nun, Moses' minister. "Moses my servant is dead; now therefore arise, go over this Jordan, you and all this people, into the **land** which I am giving to them, to the people of Israel. Every place that the sole of your foot will tread upon I have given to you, as I promised to Moses. From the wilderness and this Lebanon as far as the great river, the river Euphrates, all the land of the Hittites to the Great Sea towards the going down of the sun shall be your territory." '[25]

It is also virtually impossible to construct a clear account of what lies behind the **stories of the 'settlement'** (to use a neutral term), although the literary, archaeological and sociological research here has been particularly intensive. However, two statements may meet with widespread assent among scholars.

1. The land of Palestine, the scene of the biblical history, already had a **history of thousands of years** behind it when the Israelites began to settle there. In the late Bronze Age, 1500-1250 BCE, it may have been covered by a network of agrarian city- states each under a 'king', and all under the nominal supremacy of Egypt. It was a land not lacking in culture. Although the population was mixed, it was mostly inhabited by Semitic Canaanites, but in the coastal plain of southern Palestine there were Philistines, a 'Sea People' who had invaded from the Aegean (Crete) and gave the land its later name of Palestine. This name arose as a Graeco-Roman designation for a province which derived from the 'Philistines' (Aramaic *pelista'im*).[26]

2. At that time **Israel was not yet a political entity capable of any action**. Despite the biblical narratives in the Book of Joshua (chs 1-12), the occupation of the land by the Israelites cannot have taken place as the military action of a twelve-tribe alliance (which may not even have existed in this coherent form at that time). It must have taken place as a lengthy and complex process in the twelfth and eleventh centuries, and possibly already in the thirteen century (archaeologically the late Bronze Age, and possible the early Iron Age). But how did this 'settlement' take place? That is the historical question. There is at present more argument among scholars about this problem than about any other in the history of Israel. We shall have to go into the various models in more detail from a historical perspective.

However, no matter what decision we come to on historical questions, and no matter what religious understanding the invading Israelites may have had of themselves, for the people of Israel at a later stage it became increasingly important that the **land promised by God** also belongs to God's people. The Hebrew Bible leaves that in no doubt. So here we have something which is of theological and political significance even today. The land, or more precisely a particular 'holy' land, does not have a special saving significance either for Christianity, which understands itself as a universal people of God, tied to no ethnic or geographical frontiers, or for Islam, which despite its Arab origin and character similarly does not make any distinction in principle between the lands. However, for Judaism, which preserved its primal bond with the land of Israel (Hebrew *Eretz Israel*), even in the time of the 'dispersion' (Greek *Diaspora*), the relation to this particular land, the 'promised' land, is quite essential. To dismiss this as merely a subsequent attempt at legitimation neglects an aspect of Israel's experience of God which is attested in the biblical writings from beginning to end. Along with election, deliverance and covenant, the promise of the land is a basic element of Israelite faith. Whether or not it is convenient for others, Yahweh's chosen people and the promised land now belong together. And down to the present day the biblical promises of land[27] form the religious basis for the claims of the Jewish people to a land in Palestine.[28]

Still, it is by no means a simple matter to understand this in detail and to reconcile it with other possible rights. We must never forget that Joshua 1-12, the narratives of the settlement, form part of the Deuteronomistic history work and were written more than half a millennium after the 'events' concerned. In fact the **frontiers** of the land **changed** constantly with the changing fate of the people on its course through the centuries. So what here can be regarded as guaranteed by God? Questions for the future trialogue already become pressing.

Questions for the Future

Given the formative elements and key concepts in Jewish faith, some questions arise first of all for Judaism.

Is there not a dispute even among Jews as to whether quite specific **frontiers** for the modern state of Israel can be derived from the biblical **promises of Land?** Even in the original process of redaction, is not the promise of an Israelite empire from the Lebanon to the Euphrates[29] already a back-projection of ideal claims to territory, indeed a day-dream?

From a specifically Christian perspective the question arises: has not a concentration within Judaism on the Abraham and Sinai covenants with the chosen people often led to a neglect of that first covenant which God made with Noah and his descendants after the Flood, and which was to embrace 'everything living', including the animals: a **universal covenant** with the whole of creation, the sign of which is the rainbow,[30] a covenant which means that creation may not sink back into chaos again? So does not the Hebrew Bible presuppose a human community which underlies all national communities, to which God's universal will for salvation relates?

From a specifically Muslim perspective the question arises: according to the Hebrew Bible itself, were not **promises** also given **to Ishmael**, the father of the Arabs: that he, the son of Abraham and the Egyptian woman Hagar, should become ancestor of a great people through the twelve princes[31] of the Arab peoples between Egypt and Assyria?[32] What is the validity of these promises?

II. The Central Figure

1. Who was Moses?

I have so far spoken regularly of the Moses group, so it is impossible to avoid the question what real **historical** knowledge we have of Moses, who occupies a unique position in the salvation history of Israel. Some even see him as the founder of the Jewish religion. They put him on the same level as other founder figures, as Jesus, Muhammad, Confucius and Buddha Gautama, although, as is well known, all these figures played a very different role in the context of their religion. At all events, it has already become clear that the origins of the religion of Yahweh are extremely complex and can in no way simply be attributed to one person. And does Moses in fact have such a central position in the actual course of history? Have not perhaps numerous sagas and stories, commandments and regulations from very different sources, simply collected round his figure and crystallized there?

There is no evidence for Moses outside the Bible; he himself did not leave any literary works. However, nowadays there is no dispute over one thing: that Moses was a **historical figure** and not, say, a depotentiated moon god, as was claimed in a wild hypothesis at the beginning of this century. The name Moses is Egyptian, and Moses will have been born in Egypt, though in all probability he was not an Egyptian but a Semite. Many exegetes do not doubt his stay among the Midianites (who elsewhere are quite hostile to the Israelites), his marriage to a Midianite woman and his good relations with his father-in-law in Midian,[1] where moreover he had his decisive encounter with the God Yahweh.[2] They are as sure of this as of his connection with the Israelites,[3] whose emigration he led. However, the great question is: what precisely was Moses' **function and position**?

There is hardly a category of religious leadership[4] which has not already been applied to Moses by scholars.[5] On the basis of the sources, though, it seems impossible simply to dismiss him as a wonder-worker in the wilderness, even as a magician. On the other hand, to suppose that he founded a people seems as much of a projection back of later circumstances as to suppose that he was a theologian and representative of a monotheism which was already exclusive at that time. It also seems a rash conjecture to see Moses simply as an East Jordanian bedouin sheikh whose tomb was revered in the neighbourhood of Mount Nebo (as Martin Noth's laborious traditio-historical construction sought to demonstrate, although Deut.34.6 says that Moses' tomb is 'unknown to this day').[6] The same goes for the opposite view, that Moses was essentially already all that was attributed to him by later tradition; that he functioned at the same time as prophet, judge and mediator of the covenant, combining these functions in a specifically 'Mosaic' office.

There is no doubt that the picture of Moses[7] in the various strata of the Pentateuch has undergone a considerable development: from the messenger of Yahweh (J), leader of the people (E) and wonder-worker (JE), to God's representative radiating divine splendour (P).[8] But no matter what historians continue to dispute, all in all Moses appears as an extraordinarily complex **charismatic figure**: an inspired leader, but one who does not himself fight; a recipient of revelation who is a man with weaknesses; the founder of a cult who personally does not offer any sacrifices. Certainly Moses may not have been a prophet in the same way as the later great writing prophets of the southern kingdom and the Exile (indeed he himself did not write anything), but he was a prophet like the early charismatic prophets of the northern kingdom (Elijah, Elisha, Hosea). In short, in all probability Moses was an utterly prophetic figure who at all events **moulded the type of the three 'prophetic' religions from the start**; moreover all the Abrahamic religions recognize him as their second great leading figure.

2. The religious profile of Moses

The structural differences between the different currents of religious systems which have already been mentioned bring out Moses' profile clearly. For this Moses, who soon after the account of his call given by the Book of Exodus[9] in Midian experiences the God Yahweh in the burning bush and, veiling his face, speaks with God, is certainly **no transfigured sage in the spirit of Far Eastern harmony and humanity**, for whom the Absolute, 'heaven' and its will, are there, but only as a horizon, not as a centre. No, when confronted with God's revelation, Moses does not just want to reflect soberly on ethics and politics – like, say, the wise Confucius. Reverence for the will of heaven would not be enough for him. Moses does not look back on ideal ancestors and an earlier time. Harmony in family and state, among human beings, and between human beings and nature is not his ideal. Then what is?

Yet another differentiation: this Moses, who goes through the wilderness at the head of his 'tribes' towards a future which is completely uncertain, is also **no mystic who closes his eyes and ears in the spirit of Indian inwardness and universal unity**, who turns inward to find the Absolute; he is not like, say, the Buddha, who goes through stages of immersion in methodical meditation in order to attain enlightenment. For Moses, the Absolute, the last and first Reality, is no Nirvana, no Void, no Incomprehensible utterly dissimilar to human beings. Nor, however, is it a Brahman; it is not the all-embracing, all-permeating One, Pure, Infinite, exalted above all speech, impossible to express in thoughts and to describe in words. So yet again. What is Moses, then?

The answer can only be that Moses is a **typically prophetic figure in the spirit of a Near Eastern Semitic religion of faith and hope.** For him God is a great **personal encounter** full of power and mercy – granted, what is encountered is mysterious and hidden, but it is not completely dissimilar to human beings. God is the living, active God of anger and grace, the Lord of life and death, on whom human beings are dependent: a Thou who speaks and can be addressed. In prophetic religion people to some extent see themselves set **before** this God, to whom they owe a word, an answer, indeed responsibility, and in accordance with whose will they have to fulfil particular tasks.

Moreover, in the case of the **prophet in the strict sense**, there is a **completely personal call to a quite definite task.** The prophet is to be wholly and utterly the ambassador of God; God's word and will are to be made known to the people and the individual by a word or sign. He is no guru, who might possibly himself become God. On the contrary, he is a passionate spokesman for God, who wants to establish a bond with this one God through trusting faith. In this sense Moses becomes the instigator of the exodus, the deliverance, the wandering in the wilderness.

So what was said by Friedrich Heiler, a renowned analyst of the mystical and prophetic types, and of prophetic piety generally, applies *par excellence* to Moses, the one who proclaims the will of Yahweh and the leader of his people. Prophetic religion is 'active, challenging, desiring, ethical... In prophetic experience the emotions blaze up, the will to live asserts itself, triumphs in external defeat, and defies death and annihilation. Born of a tenacious will to life, immovable confidence, reliance and trust firm as a rock, bold adventurous hope breaks through at last... The prophet is a fighter who ever struggles upwards from doubt to assurance, from tormenting uncertainty to absolute serenity of life, from despondency to fresh courage of soul, from fear to hope, from a depressing consciousness of guilt to the blessed experience of grace and salvation.'[10]

Moses is indeed the **prototype of the prophet**: the only one in the Hebrew Bible with whom God spoke not only 'in visions' and 'dreams' but 'face to face'.[11] So in the Deuteronomic farewell speech Moses can say to his people: 'The Lord your God will raise up a prophet like me from the midst of your brothers – you shall hearken to him.'[12] Indeed, in this way Moses appears after Abraham as **the second great representative of the prophetic religions,** and is also accepted as such by Christianity and Islam. However – as already in the case of Abraham – they understand him in very different ways.

3. Moses as reflected in Judaism, Christianity and Islam

(*a*) What position does Moses have in post-biblical **Judaism**? He remains **the central figure,** approached only by Abraham, in part by Jacob and David, and then by the messiah. Innumerable legends adorn his life from birth (as a boy at Pharaoh's court) to death. In apocryphal writings not accepted into the biblical canon Moses is exalted and virtually made a hero: compare the 'Apocalypse of Moses'[13] and the 'Ascension of Moses'.[14] Presumably, once there were even more writings attributed to Moses which have not come down to us. But whereas Hellenistic Judaism idealized Moses as a genius in the face of pagan anti-Judaism, making him the teacher of Orpheus, from whom all the great sages learned, the rabbinic tradition sees Moses primarily as a teacher of the law, indeed as *the* teacher of the law. 'Moses, our rabbi' (Hebrew *Moshe Rabbenu*): of all the different possible titles for Moses, rabbinic Judaism chose just one, that of rabbi. And now not only do the laws **in the** Pentateuch form the Torah, but – and this is important – **the whole Pentateuch** is now Torah, 'the Torah of Moses'.[15]

The consequence is that everything that is to be found in the Torah from the creation through the patriarchs to future events is all now regarded as having been revealed, indeed dictated, to Moses by God. Furthermore, both the **written** Torah, from now on regarded as the 'Five Books of Moses', and the **oral** Torah with its countless regulations and applications are attributed to Moses. So Moses, the instigator of the exodus, the deliverance and the wandering in the wilderness, has increasingly become Moses, **the guardian of the tradition and of persistence.** It has become impossible to speak too highly of him, the father of wisdom and prophecy, for whose sake the world was made.

(*b*) But how is Moses now seen in **Christianity**? He is mentioned more times in the New Testament (80 times) than any other Old Testament figure. Here, too, it is taken for granted that he is the author of the Pentateuch, so here too he is seen as the prophet and lawgiver who proclaimed God's message. The commandment of Moses is the commandment of God.[16] In Luke, 'Moses and the prophets' means 'the

Torah and the prophets'. It goes without saying that they are also the Bible of the young Christian community.[17]

Indeed the picture of Moses is so powerful for the New Testament community, too, that much in the life and activity of Jesus is even seen in the light of the prophetic figure of Moses, and in some circumstances is also deliberately modelled on him. The story of Moses may already have been in the background of Matthew's infancy narrative:[18] a warning about the king, the murder of innocent children, flight into exile until the king's death... But the forty days of fasting in the wilderness and the feeding of the five thousand are also Moses typology. That means that Moses appears everywhere as **the type of Jesus Christ**, the prophet of the end-time. In the Gospel of John there is even an explicit reference to the feeding with manna in the wilderness.[19] And the ascension of Jesus, which occurs only in Luke (at the end of his Gospel and at the beginning of the Acts of the Apostles), is also like that of Moses. Indeed, according to Luke 'Moses and the Prophets' together are to be understood as virtually a prophecy of the Jesus event.[20]

However, this also brings out the dispute which from the start makes the figure of Moses in the New Testament appear ambivalent: **Moses is highly esteemed, but Jesus is esteemed even more highly**. And that applies right through the Gospels:
– in Mark, where in the story of the Transfiguration Moses joins Elijah in giving personal testimony to Jesus;
– in Matthew, where the 'Sermon on the Mount' is intended to surpass the legislation on 'Mount' Sinai;
– in Luke, where Jesus is explicitly presented as a second Moses and redeemer of his people;
– in John, according to whom the law came through Moses, but grace and truth come through Jesus Christ;
– even more in the letters of Paul and the Letter to the Hebrews, throughout which Moses represents the religion of the law. While this is not simply being done away with, it is decisively relativized by the grace of God in Jesus Christ.

(c) And in **Islam**? Here, too, Moses is the biblical figure who is mentioned most frequently alongside Abraham. It is said that Moses prophesied the coming of the Prophet Muhammad, his successor, indeed that Moses was one of the very great prophets. Why? Because like the Prophet Muhammad he **too received a book from God!** So Jews and Christians belong to the 'people of the book', to those who possess a scripture. As such, they have a part in the truth which is revealed

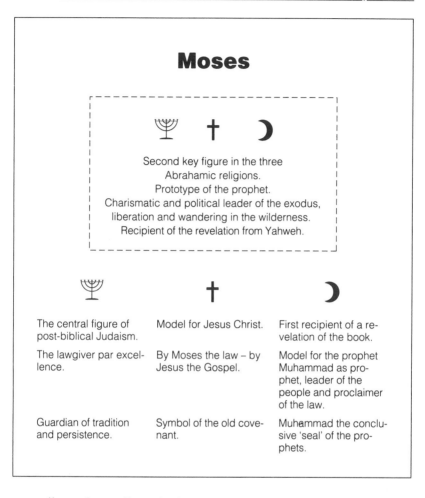

Moses

Second key figure in the three
Abrahamic religions.
Prototype of the prophet.
Charismatic and political leader of the exodus,
liberation and wandering in the wilderness.
Recipient of the revelation from Yahweh.

The central figure of post-biblical Judaism.	Model for Jesus Christ.	First recipient of a revelation of the book.
The lawgiver par excellence.	By Moses the law – by Jesus the Gospel.	Model for the prophet Muhammad as prophet, leader of the people and proclaimer of the law.
Guardian of tradition and persistence.	Symbol of the old covenant.	Muhammad the conclusive 'seal' of the prophets.

eternally and equally, which is similarly preserved in a book, the heavenly original of the Qur'an. In this way Moses as a prophet and lawgiver can be understood completely as a model for Muhammad.[21]

Some things are told of Moses in the Qur'an which can already be found in the biblical tradition or in the non-biblical tradition and in folklore. Indeed other biblical stories can be applied to Moses by the Qur'an.[22] And is there not also much in Muhammad's life which is reminiscent of Moses? The receiving of revelation (dictated and handed on by angels) and his flight (to Medina), and also his victorious leadership on the journey to the wilderness, and finally his blessed death and ascension. As is well known, this is said to have taken place in Jerusalem! Conversely, some elements from Islamic tradition have been incorporated into the Jewish Moses tradition. And yet for all the parallels, one thing is undisputed: for Muslims, Muhammad is the 'seal' of the prophets, the last and greatest of the prophets, who newly proclaims the law of Moses – unlike Jews and Christians – in an unfalsified form.

If we now look back on the previous comments, we may venture at least provisionally to define what in all the changing historical constellations is the abiding substance of the faith of Judaism (later I shall have to keep pointing this out again).

4. The abiding substance of faith and changing paradigms

What in fact, after our considerations so far, is the **centre and foundation**, what is the abiding **substance of faith** in the Jewish religion, Hebrew Bible, Israelite belief? Regardless of any criticisms, interpretations or reductions as a result of a historical, literary or sociological approach, in the light of the foundation documents of Israelite faith which have become normative and influential in history, the answer is that this central content of faith is the **God Yahweh** and the one **people Israel**. There can be no Israelite faith, no Hebrew Bible, no Jewish religion without the confession '**Yahweh is the God of Israel, and Israel is his people!**' This 'covenant formula' denotes the 'centre of the Old Testament'[23] (which in no way should be understood in static terms). The whole as it were elliptical testimony of the Hebrew Bible, the Tenak, the Old Testament, swings around the two focal points of Yahweh and Israel.[24] Of course it can be argued that the one God of Israel himself forms the centre of the Old Testament; but what is significant for the Hebrew Bible is the fact that this one God is never seen alone, but together with the people whom he has chosen. The biblical writings do not centre on the innermost 'mysteries of the Godhead', but on the history of this people with its God. To this degree a bipolar description of the centre suggests itself, as God and people (with or without the term 'covenant', which only came to be used later).[25]

If we describe the various structural elements and permanent leading ideas of Israelite-Jewish faith more closely, in the light of all that we have heard they prove to be the following:

• the **people** chosen by God, but this includes
• the **land** promised by God, since both are
• sealed by the **covenant** made with the one God, which carries with it an obligation to keep his commandments.

This special relationship of Israel to its God is in nucleus the starting point and normative centre around which crystallization takes place. And despite all the failure and obduracy of the people, reported from the beginning, it will remain the goal of the Jewish religion, a goal which is never given up. Although even as a Jew one may keep whatever one wills of this constant centre which is the motive force for everything, here are the foundations of the characteristics of the Jewish people:

• **Originality** from an early period,
• **Continuity** in its long history down the centuries,
• **Identity** despite all the difference in languages and races, cultures and religions.

So this people is the source of a legacy in world history and an incomparable obligation which later also became binding on both Christianity and Islam: the world owes to Israel belief in the one God.

However, this centre, this foundation, this substance of faith – indicated throughout our schematic description of the paradigm changes by a circle with a broken circumference – was never given abstractly and in isolation. At the beginning it is hard to indicate historically, and in any case it was constantly reinterpreted and realized in practice in ever new ways to meet the changing demands of the time. To this degree, in the chapter which follows, under the heading 'History', it has been necessary to combine a systematic-theological with a historical-chronological account: without the latter it is impossible to provide a convincing basis for the former. It will be said that this Yahweh as the one God, this Israel as the chosen people, are 'objects' of faith: that they are visible only to the eyes of faith as the revelation of God, and that is by no means a matter of course. That is true. But they are there in the biblical writings as concepts, notions, historically relevant factors, to be recognized, described and examined by historians as well – regardless of whether or not they bring the attitude of believers to them.

However, the more time goes on, the more clearly it emerges that time and again **new epoch-making constellations** of the time – of society generally, the community of faith, the proclamation and reflection of faith – reinterpret this one and the same centre and make it specific. This is what I understand by a **paradigm**, following Thomas S.Kuhn: 'an entire constellation of beliefs, values, techniques, and so on shared by the members of a given community.'[26] I have explained at some length in earlier publications how and to what degree a transference of the paradigm theory (as a 'macroparadigm') from the sphere of the natural sciences to that of religion and theology is possible and important.[27]

This history of Israel, and later of Judaism, will now become exceptionally dramatic. In it, in answer to great challenges in world history, a small people will undergo a whole series of fundamental religious changes, indeed what on a longer view is a revolutionary paradigm change.

C. History

I. The Tribal Paradigm: The Period before the State

Since the 'settlement' in Palestine the people of Israel has been a historically definable entity – whatever one has to understand initially by 'people'. From that point on, if we take note of long-term developments, we can identify **six macro-constellations** – though these are highly schematized, and we cannot consider all the complex questions of their background. Despite constant counter-trends, these macro-constellations became and remained **dominant.** Any reputable history of Israel or of the Jewish people will contain a vast amount of material relating to them: first of all the early Israelite tribal paradigm and the paradigm of the Davidic kingdom, then the post-exilic theocratic paradigm, followed by the mediaeval Jewish paradigm of the rabbis and the synagogue, finally the modern paradigm and now – who knows – perhaps the transition to a postmodern paradigm.

It will emerge that epoch-making changes are always born of a crisis which can drag on for a long time. This finally leads to a new paradigm which, according to the definition by Thomas S.Kuhn that I have already quoted, is 'an entire constellation of beliefs, values, techniques, and so on shared by the members of a given community'.[1] And yet, as we shall also see, the constants which I have just described continue in the faith and praxis of Jewish belief: there is a **continuity in all the discontinuity.** However, this does not take the form of a constant progress, as was supposed in the Enlightenment. The very history of this people will show that here history is certainly not 'eternal progress', nor does it run in accordance with the scheme of 'birth – flourishing – decline', as Oswald Spengler presupposed in his morphology of world history. Rather, constantly new paradigms are possible, each paradigm bringing with it gains **and** losses.[2] But what does that look like specifically in the history of Judaism?

1. The settlement – three attempts at reconstruction

If we follow the state of contemporary scholarship, what did the first paradigm look like, the **primal constellation** of Israel which became and remains fundamental to its whole history? A brief sketch must suffice. First we must note what is of disputed historicity and the points made in previous chapters. There is dispute as to whether all the later twelve tribes were in Egypt, then set out on the 'wandering' and were all present at the mountain of God. There is also dispute about the wandering through the wilderness, so that even the idea of all Israel as the 'wandering people of God', which is important right down to the late Christian 'Letter to the Hebrews', is uncertain; of course there is also dispute about the duration of the 'wandering' – which is supposed to have been forty years (so often a symbolic number), as a punishment until the rebellious generation had died out. And there is dispute over most features of the Israelite 'settlement'. Indeed, according to Roland de Vaux, for a long time Director of the École Biblique in Jerusalem and one of the most qualified experts, the settlement is '... the most difficult problem in the entire history of Israel'.[3]

Nowadays there is agreement among experts only on one point: the settlement will not have taken place in a kind of 'Blitzkrieg' of the kind related in the first twelve chapters of the Book of Joshua, which in any case only describe the conquest of central Palestine. We must always bear in mind that all these biblical narratives are not just history but stories.

Basically, three historical **models for reconstructing** of the settlement have been considered by scholars, all of which are more or less hypothetical.[4]

– The **conquest model** (waves of immigration). This model, based above all on **archaeology**, assumes a long-drawn-out settlement by several waves of warlike nomads coming from the wilderness. It was put forward above all by the American archaelogists W.F.Albright and G.E.Wright.[5] Nowadays it has been largely abandoned, because it has been refuted by later discoveries. Cities like Jericho and Ai had presumably long been in ruins at the time of the conquest and therefore could not have been conquered then, as Josh.6-8 reports. Many places mentioned in the Bible yield no relics whatsoever from the late Bronze Age, and many Canaanite regions show no indication of an Israelite settlement before the tenth century.

– The **immigration model** (slow infiltration). This **traditio-historical** model, outlined by A.Alt and M.Noth[6] and developed by many other scholars, assumes a successive peaceful settlement of semi-nomads on the margins of the steppes and the desert during the process of 'transhumance', the change of pasturage necessitated by the rainless summer. This hypothesis has recently been criticized above all from the sociological aspect, because a life deep in the desert would have been impossible before the domestication of the camel – on the dating of which experts differ by many centuries! So shepherds or nomads would not have been able to come from the depths of the desert.

– The **restructuring model** (revolution or evolution within Palestine). This **sociological** model, first put forward by G.E.Mendenhall in 1962,[7] further developed and 'politicized' by N.K.Gottwald as a 'revolutionary model',[8] and finally further modified to an 'evolutionary model',[9] initially commanded most assent, at least in America. Gottwald – at first far too one-sidedly indebted to a Marxist social theory – now no longer speaks of a sudden overthrow, but more of a slow series of revolutions. In his view the settlement is not to be understood in the framework of a nomadic invasion from outside, but as a **process of restructuring the population** from within during the late Bronze Age, around 1200. There is discussion as to

– whether this was a more peaceful movement on the part of the un-free farmers and tenants who withdrew from the exploitative domination of the Canaanite city-states and moved to newly-founded villages in the hill-country (Mendenhall),

– or whether this was more a political struggle and a direct revolt on the part of the peasants, organized into tribes, along with semi-nomads, mercenaries and outlaws (*apiru*), who at that time turned directly against the highly commercialized Canaanite city-states and the ruling classes there (Gottwald).

However, serious objections have also been raised against this sociological model. The Israeli archaeologist Israel Finkelstein has listed them in detail.[10] Most recent archaeological research, and important demographic and ethnographic data from the present, 'refute any theory that the Israelites were malcontents fleeing from the Canaanite polity'; rather, more recent findings would indicate 'that the new settlers in the hill-country in the Iron I period came from a pastoralist background' (352). Finkelstein concludes from this, with his own modifications,[11] that 'in the final analysis, Alt's view of Israelite settlement as a peaceful settlement in the less inhabited regions of the country came closest to the results of field studies conducted decades later.'[12]

Basically, this may be said to be the state of research at present, which is still in flux. However, must not the literary biblical evidence be taken more seriously in the whole discussion?

2. An attempt at an integrated view

Granted, it is almost impossible to dispute the fact of a restructuring of population. This is derived above all from archaeological data – and was sometimes also connected with violent clashes and the destruction of cities. But the **biblical writings** should **not** be neglected here. And the constant biblical evidence is irrefutable: that **Israel's ancestors came from the wilderness**, and were therefore nomads, not sedentary people. So central insights from both the conquest and invasion models need to be combined with the restructuring model, and sociological analysis needs to be brought into historical-critical exegesis of the traditional text. As literary analyses of the past two centuries have shown impressively, the biblical narratives indeed contain some age-old traditions, yet speak directly in quite a different way from the mute archaeological discoveries, which have to be deciphered and are usually ambiguous. They have to be incorporated constructively into an **integrated** model which is both socio-political and religious (Gottwald calls it a socio-religious model). How?

A group which immigrated from Egypt, the Moses group or the exodus Israelites, must at least have been the catalyst for this process of social restructuring, even if it did not start it. This group or groups of immigrants, who believed in the **God Yahweh**, brought with it the various traditions of an exodus from Egypt, a crossing of the Reed Sea and the making of a covenant on the mountain of God in the wilderness. It is utterly improbable that this was an exilic or a post-exilic invention. At all events, there is no question that right at the beginning of the process of the formation of a people, belief in Yahweh played an important role for the forces which at that time were in process of changing society. 'Slowly growing together, first of all in a union of El-worshippers, they became a significantly growing coalition of Yahweh-worshippers.'[13] All this means that despite the many questions which are still open, an integrated model seems to do most justice both to the newest archaeological and sociological insights and also to the biblical texts – that is, if one is not to abandon any attempt at historical reconstruction altogether.[14] Perhaps a new consensus will emerge over this question in the future.

Be this as it may, this discussion, for all its hypotheses, has demonstrated two things. The complex historical questions can hardly be given a satisfactory explanation through the Old Testament texts alone, which is what is attempted by an isolated literary criticism, with a late dating of the Yahwist and the book of Judges (though of course this is disputed).[15] So there can be **no literary reduction**; the social history of

Israel is also part of its history. However, conversely it is also the case that without the Old Testament texts – for which belief in Yahweh is central – any reconstruction of the history of Israel must come to grief. So there can be **no sociological reduction**: sweepingly and dogmatically to deny the Old Testament writings any value as sources for the pre-monarchical, indeed the pre-exilic period would amount to making the identity of Israel as a people in its specific post-exilic form come into being as it were by an utterly improbable spontaneous generation. Sociological reconstructions often require just as much 'faith' as the later re-tellings of biblical stories by traditional exegesis. No, the concerns and results of long research into the history of traditions must not be lost. The history of Israel is not just the history of Israelite society, as sociologists sometimes want to suggest.

The views of the Göttingen Old Testament scholar **Herbert Donner** point in this direction. He has accepted many of the results of sociological research in sketching out his own 'framework for the settlement of the Israelites in Palestine'. In so doing he introduces the specific concern of biblical scholarship like this: 'The conviction maintained in the Old Testament tradition that Israel came out of the wilderness cannot simply rest on invention – there is no reason for such an invention. We will hardly go far wrong if we attribute the impetus towards the formation of the consciousness of an Israelite community above all to these groups, some of which came from the south and some from the east. They brought with them Yahweh, whose home was certainly not the cultivated land of Palestine. They also brought with them the traditions of the exodus from Egypt, the crossing of the Red Sea and the making of the covenant on the mountain of God in the wilderness. They were destined to dominate and were capable of domination. In the land they encountered groups of nomads from the hill country, and in the course of the settlement the major groups of the Israelite tribes took shape, depending on the regional features. The tribes were secondary products, as the orders of clan and family are older than that of the tribe. These people felt bound, akin, to others living under similar circumstances: to those whom in a generalizing way we call Aramaeans. So we can say that **the settlement and the first beginning of the people of Israel coincide**: they are two sides of the same coin.'[16]

To make this first paradigm more precise we must note that however Canaanite society came into being (whether or not through 'retribalization'), and however it was organized (whether in an 'egalitarian' way or not), if we interpret the Old Testament writings by means of historical criticism, the difference between Canaanite and Israelite religion evidently emerged at an early stage. Belief in Yahweh, which derived from the wilderness, soon began to establish itself in the cultivated region, and the various extended families, villages, clans and tribes now came together gradually in a **community of fate** and a **narrative community**. 'United tribal Israel is the subject of the traditions.'[17] The expression 'tribal paradigm' describes this first paradigm.

3. The constant centre

Israel's history is certainly not unparalleled, but on the basis of particular religious experiences and interpretations it does have a unique, irreplaceable result. Already at this point, in this initial constellation of the formation of a people, what I have provisionally defined as the **constant centre** and **abiding foundation** of Jewish religion is confirmed: it is impossible to understand even the beginnings of Israelite society without the two factors of **Yahweh and Israel** (people and land). Here we can see not only the universal structure of 'one God, one king, one land', as in other West Semitic religions, but also that of 'one God, one people, one land'.

This belief in God is never an abstract monotheism, but always belief in a God concerned with the people; it is never an abstract social history, but always the socio-religious history of Israel as the history of a people with this God. As early as the song of Deborah in the book of Judges,[18] a 'mother in Israel'[19] – perhaps the earliest major document in the Hebrew Bible – , there is a celebration of 'Yahweh, the God of Israel',[20] to whom victory over the enemy is attributed. So **Julius Wellhausen**, one of the most significant, knowledgeable and critical scholars of the Hebrew Bible, who died in 1914, may still be right in his definition of the quintessence of Israelite religion: 'Out of necessity, in the time of Moses the people of Israel came together from kindred families and tribes and elevated itself above them. The new union was hallowed by Yahweh, who had existed beforehand, but only now took his place at the head of this people. Yahweh the God of Israel, and Israel the people of Yahweh: that is the beginning and the abiding principle of the political and religious history which follows.'[21]

If we want to define this relationship of Yahweh to his people more closely, we will do better **not** to use the concept of the '**kingship of God**', as Martin Buber did in his major treatise with this title.[22] For before the time of the monarchy Yahweh is hardly ever designated 'king' (Hebrew *melek*), and the Sinai covenant is in no way understood pointedly as a 'royal covenant', so that the term 'theocracy' could at best be used only in a very broad sense.[23] We must therefore be cautious about the statement that 'the realization of the all-embracing rule of God' was not only the 'eschaton of Israel' but also its 'proton', a primal datum of Israelite religion. It is even less possible than before to assume on the basis of the most recent state of scholarship that the self-understanding of early Israel presupposed the idea of a king.

So it is better to use the category of the **covenant** rather than that of kingship to describe the relationship of Yahweh to his people, which includes **the rule of God and the community of God**. 'Covenant' fits this communal relationship of Yahweh with his people, based on mutuality, much better than the isolated and one-sided concept of 'lordship', which is why it was widespread at the time of 'Deuteronomy' (in the seventh century BCE).[24] However, that does not mean that 'covenant' needs to be something like a mandatory general concept for a theology of the Old Testament, as happens in Walther Eichrodt's significant two-volume *Theology of the Old Testament*, in which not only the relationship between God and people but also the relationship between God and the world and God and man is forced under this concept.[25]

Thus in the period before the state the Israelite extended families, clans, villages and tribes may have been increasingly clearly associated and allied; indeed, they may have come to understand themselves as a **single people and religion**. They will not have formed an entity with a uniform organization, but a **loose federation**. And the common belief in one and the same God which was increasingly establishing itself may have furthered the people's political coherence just as, conversely, the political consolidation may have intensified faith. Such a process is not just a matter of ideas and doctrines, but of ever-new and varied experiences and recollections of the activity of the one God towards this people: stories of God's gracious election, demanding rule and abiding communion with this people – in short, everything that was later called 'covenant'.

4. The structure of the pre-state paradigm

Once again, it is **impossible to discover precisely how** this **community** took **specific form** in the period after the settlement. For a long time scholars followed Martin Noth in assuming that the twelve tribes of Israel formed a sacral amphictyony, i.e. a 'community of those dwelling around (a central sanctuary)', of the kind which existed, for example, in Greece and Italy. The ark of Yahweh – originally a mobile sanctuary

– would have been the central sanctuary of the tribes, its cultic centre. However, evidently none of the nomadic cultures had such a central sanctuary, nor is it possible to demonstrate that the ark of Yahweh was a mobile sanctuary, indeed a central sanctuary for all Israel. But it is also impossible to substantiate the opposite theory, that the confederation of the twelve tribes was not a sacral alliance but a purely political federation.

On the contrary, it is very much more probable that at a time when it was virtually impossible to separate politics and religion, **regional-political and religious factors simultaneously** played a part. And among the religious factors, belief in Yahweh, which was increasingly confessed by the tribes, played a primary role. However, it is as difficult to discover what specific historical role was played in all this by the warrior hero **Joshua** from the tribe of Ephraim, who is presented first as Moses' servant and then as his successor and finally as the one who completes his work, as it is to determine what the specific actions of individual tribes or individual heroes may have been. According to some scholars, the three Rachel tribes of Benjamin, Ephraim and Manasseh (= the house of Joseph), which settled in central Palestine, will have formed the nucleus of later 'Israel'.[26] Be this as it may, it is decisive that the Israelite tribal federation already appears in the Song of Deborah, mentioned above, as the **'people of Yahweh'**.[27] And the political and religious development led to the following constellation: 'to extended familes, protective alliances of families.. and tribes, brought together as an inter-tribal community named "Israel", "Israelites" or "tribes (or people) of Israel (or Yahweh)"'.[28]

If in these circumstances we want to describe the religious and social **structure of this tribal paradigm** of the twelfth/eleventh century (Paradigm I = P I), we must begin from the following characteristics:

- The Israelite tribes of the first period lived in a **loose federation** and increasingly grew together as a people and a religion. As in the kindred Aramaean and proto-Arabian tribes there were elders who functioned as judges, and there were leaders in the extended families and tribes – in other words, there was a **patriarchal order**. But there was still no monarchical head over all the tribes, far less a central government with an administrative apparatus.
- There were **sanctuaries of Yahweh** and thus also a **priesthood of Yahweh**. However, in this first paradigm there were as yet no religious institutions and customs of the kind that we know from later paradigms, even if in the later biblical histories they are often projected back on to this time.
- At this time there were **charismatic saviour figures** of very different

kinds, so-called judges (*shoftim*), and in times of a common threat there was a common army made up from the tribes. But there were no professional soldiers, no mercenaries and no aristocratic cavalry, nor was there what in Islam was later called a 'holy war' (Arabic *jihad*).

- In religious terms the tribes were held together by **belief in Yahweh, the God of Israel**. However, Yahweh was regarded as the Lord of families, clans and tribes, and not yet as the King of the people. This was the rule of God, but not the kingly reign of God.
- Belief in Yahweh formed the foundation for **Israel's understanding of itself as the people of Yahweh**. However, the unity of the people was a loose, dynamic tribal federation without monarchy, without the apparatus of officialdom and without professional soldiers, not a monolithic unity.

So at this early period there was a tribal, not a state society: in the twelfth and eleventh centuries the extended families, clans, villages and tribes of Israelites still lived in a pre-monarchical overall constellation which antedated the state. At that time there was the land, but no fixed frontiers; nor was there national unity, far less a focal point in a monarchy. Ideas of a coherent tribal alliance of Israel at this period, functioning as an organizational unity, are the projection of a state identity back on to a society preceding the state.

II. The Paradigm of the Kingdom: The Period of the Monarchy

'Then the men of Israel said to Gideon, "Rule over us, you and your sons and your grandsons also; for you have delivered us out of the hand of Midian." Gideon said to them, "I will not rule over you, and my son will not rule over you; the Lord will rule over you." '[1] So, there was no monarch, no monarchy, at the time of these so-called 'judges' of Israel at the end of the second millennium BCE. But things did not remain like that.

1. Crisis and paradigm shift

Epochs do not follow in succession, but conflict. Their law is not an additive linearity, but dialectic: continuity in discontinuity. When a religion – for whatever complex reasons – gets into a fundamental crisis, when the precursors of a new religious movement leave the private for the public sphere, when the opposition become representative, and when new initiatives, examples, communities become the norm; in other words, when the new not only dawns but breaks through, one can speak of a change of eras, of a shift in the entire constellation, the macro-paradigm, indeed of an epoch-making **paradigm shift**.

A social and religious **crisis** is normally the starting point for a paradigm shift, and of course the shift had always been prepared for in the preceding paradigm. This crisis can be caused from outside: a challenge posed by a new economic, political or military constellation of great powers. Or it can be a crisis which is primarily self-generated: internal economic, political and social developments. For Israel in the **transitional period from the so-called judges to a new era**, it was both these things together.

Here, first of all **long-term developments within the Israelite society** of the early Iron Age – the development of the population, the settlement, the economy, the development of crafts and military techniques, and all the changes of social structure, had a considerable effect: they represent the framework for social and religious life. These processes of development within Israel may in fact have produced the pressures which led to a monarchy.[2]

However, at the same time we must not overlook the fact that the more these very disparate extended families, clans and tribes became **sedentary**, banded together and became aware of their common destiny, the more pressure was exerted as a result of the overall social and political situation towards both a permanent internal co-ordination and a permanent common readiness for defence against external adversaries. According to the biblical evidence, the second reason in particular led to the crisis which sparked off the desire for a unitary, continuous leadership. It introduced an innovation within the nation-state which was then in its turn to become tradition: the transition **from a tribal society to a people with a state,** and as a result of this a consolidated state with a central government. Thus there was a transition from a pre-state to a state form of organization. And of course, for all the continuity of Israelite society, this was a change of extreme political, economic, social and indeed religious significance.

So was there at that time a massive **external threat** to tribal territory? Beyond doubt. It came from the Philistines (possibly Semites), who had settled on the southern part of the coast. They were a well-organized military power and attempted to extend their control all over Palestine, including the hill-country. Because of their superior technology in weaponry (iron weapons, chariots), they had to be warded off with united forces. This meant that the cumbersome Israelite levy, raised only in emergencies, had to be put under a regular command. So the requirement was not just for a temporary charismatic leader ('judges' like Othniel, Deborah, Samson, Eli and Samuel), but for a permanent elected leader. In other words, the institution which had long been a reality in the surrounding minor states had now also to be adopted in Israel: the **monarchy.**

The reason why this process leading towards an autonomous state could ultimately be completed without being impeded from abroad and with success at home – at least as far as the northern tribes were concerned, since there are doubts about the involvement of Judah – may be connected with the weakness of the major powers, not only on the Nile but also on the Tigris and Euphrates, around the end of the first millennium BCE. A **power vacuum** had come into being on the land-bridge of Syria-Palestine – that highly important region not only for military strategy but also for trade, lying between the sea and the wilderness to the west and east and the great empires to the north and south. This made possible the undisturbed establishment of an autonomous monarchy in Israel, and in the end for the first time the establishment of an indigenous empire.

How did this monarchy, which transcended the tribes, come about? Evidently not without resistance. We can detect resistance to a replacement of the sole rule of Yahweh by the rule of a king, rule by an individual man; this is already illustrated by the quotation from the book of Judges at the beginning of this section. Other anti-royal texts in Deuteronomy,[3] Judges[4] and I Samuel[5] also point in this direction. Granted, some of these texts may not come from this early period but may have been shaped in prophetic and priestly circles as a result of later hostility to the king. But we have to suppose that there will have been opposition to the king in early Israel, indeed from the beginning, in the name not only of tribal autonomy (which still managed to spark off rebellions at a later date) but also of the 'theocratic' claim of rule by Yahweh. So there was protest against the institution of a monarchy on both political and religious grounds.

And yet the monarchy began to establish itself, as is evident from other texts which are **favourable to the king**.[6] To put this in religious language: the monarchy was regarded as having been granted by Yahweh – on the insistence of the people. It was now at the service of the religion of Yahweh. **The first king** was the Benjaminite **Saul** (1012-1004). He was apparently designated by Samuel, the 'judge', seer, prophet, priest (the tradition is very obscure here), and then acclaimed by the people. The newly elected king took up residence in his home town of Gibeah (about four miles north of Jerusalem). In our day his small and primitively built fortress has been excavated; it is the first significant Israelite building known to us.

What type of monarchy was this? Was it more of a 'chiefdom', to use a term from South Pacific anthropology, than a 'kingdom'? There is no question that this fails to do it justice, for while in one way Saul continued the early tribal leadership, he also extended it to a number of tribes, as Georg Fohrer rightly stresses.[7] So Saul's kingship may not have been a tribal princedom, but already kingship over a people, though at this point it was not yet territorial, but merely national. Saul was not so much king of the land of Israel as king of the Israelites: he was thus above all the chosen king of the army, and now, in this emergency, had command over the tribal levy. Moreover he had initial successes as leader in the field (along with his son Jonathan). However, significantly we have hardly any reports of other royal functions – of a court, an internal organization, and a state structure. And anyway, Saul's reign lasted only eight years. The tone of the accounts of him may have been coloured by later historians who were well disposed towards David. That is presumably true above all of the report of Saul's sorry end, which makes David's assumption of rule seem all the more justified. For as a result of a variety of mistakes and failures the psychologically sick Saul is said to have fallen on his own sword after a catastrophic defeat at the hands of the Philistines.[8]

Might the monarchy not have remained simply an episode after this tragic suicidal end? Hardly. For the time was now ripe for the epoch-making **paradigm shift** from a pre-state constellation to a **state constellation,** and to this degree Saul's military kingship was a transitional stage.

2. The epoch-making achievements of David as king

Saul had introduced a paradigm shift, but this was really brought about, around the year 1000 BCE, by someone else: **David** (1004-965), a Judaean of simple origins from the tribal capital of Bethlehem. Initially he had been a follower of Saul, indeed his son-in-law, but was then apparently persecuted by Saul out of envy. He recognized the opportunities for a new overall model and took advantage of them. And for many Jews this has remained the great ideal down to the present day: the **kingdom of David.**

But did this David really make history? Was he indeed epoch-making?[9] There has been much discussion in our time as to whether men (and women) make history or vice versa. And as we have heard, more than ever before present-day historiography is simply social history, which is not primarily orientated on the 'individuals of world history' (Hegel), but on structural conditions and social change. Of course in the case of David, too, and his rapid rise to power, there must have been the necessary structural conditions – abroad as well as at home – for such an epoch-making change, and to this degree questions of sociology, social anthropology and historical geography always also need to be taken into account in any comprehensive historical approach. So far, so good. But precisely at this point it emerges that the description of long-term social forces must not neglect the individuals who act within the framework which these create. Concrete history is always a **dialectic of structures and persons**! And the 'factual history' of contingent individual events or agents does not just lie on the surface; it is at the centre of the historical processes of 'social history'.

So it is no coincidence that history-writing proper in Israel only began in the time of David.[10] We have better knowledge about 'David' (the name is usually interpreted as God's 'favourite') on the basis of the sources than about anyone else in Israel[11] – and this is an important difference from the previous paradigm. In fact the account of David in the books of the Old Testament can compete with later Greek historiography. Fundamental historical scepticism about the biblical sources is even less appropriate here than in connection with previous eras; and as is well known, sources for historians are not just sources composed by historians.

Indeed, in the case of David we may have an example of a man who, when the time was ripe, really did make history. In the terminology of Arnold Toynbee: there had been a great historical 'challenge', and this met with an appropriate historical response in the person of David. For what would have become of Israel without David, this man of charisma, vision and bravura, who evidently had not only religious motivations but also artistic gifts (even critical exegetes attribute the laments over Saul and Jonathan[12] and individual psalms to David)? No one knows. However, it is more than questionable:

1. Whether without this figure of extraordinary political intelligence and force the northern and southern parts of the kingdom, Israel and Judah, whose territories were so markedly different, would have succeed in forming quite an extensive Israelite 'empire', the first on Palestinian soil, though it was completely split over internal politics. David reigned 'over all Israel and Judah'[13] a good seven years after his acclamation as king of Judah – on the basis of his towering personality and with the help of departmental ministers, an official staff and a troop of mercenaries, always combat-ready, which had sworn personal obedience to him.

2. Whether the strongly fortified Canaanite city of Jerusalem, the city of the Jebusites, surrounded by three deep valleys, would ever have become the capital of this kingdom, which was united only by a personal union (it was not a unified kingdom). It was David who with his mercenaries first captured this strategically favourable city, which lay on the frontier between Judah and Israel, and made the hill of Zion with its mountain fortress his residence;[14] in that way it became his own possession and the possession of his dynasty, the 'city of David';[15]

3. Whether the new capital of Jerusalem would ever have taken on the novel sacral character which it still has to this day, had not David, in solemn procession with music and cultic dance, introduced into it the portable holy 'ark of God', the symbol of the tribal alliance and of the presence of Yahweh.[16] He did so shrewdly in order to safeguard his rule: he built the sanctuary of the ark there and will have organized and 'Yahwized' not only the military and civil administration but also the Canaanite cultic and priestly administration. Only through David did Yahweh become a kind of state deity in Jerusalem, so that Jerusalem became the cultic centre for all Israel and Judah, indeed a unique 'holy city'. Even critical historiography cannot therefore avoid noting that David's policy was already interpreted in subsequent Judaism as having been a decisive break: 'For the Deuteronomistic history, David's action

in bringing the ark to Jerusalem indicates on the one hand the continuity of the united kingdom with the past and on the other hand a complete new beginning, the new era which would end only with the destruction of the first temple in 587/86 BCE.'[17]

However, this transference of the cult to the old Canaanite city also opened the door for the influx of Canaanite ideas into the new state religion. Like former Canaanite city kings (including the priest king Melchizedek?), David, leading the cultic dance before the ark, assumed priestly functions and in so doing immediately incurred criticism. It is not easy to discover how far the fusion of Yahweh religion with Canaanite cults had already gone in the time of David.[18] Perhaps already at that time there was a kind of 'state syncretism', a royal ideology, in which the king was regarded as the 'adopted son' of God. But this is not the decisive point for future developments.

3. David's kingdom – still a paradigmatic ideal today

Quite apart from the details of the religious situation at that time, it has become clear what the paradigm shift to the **paradigm of the Davidic kingdom** (paradigm II = P II) meant for Israel, and also what has remained a dream for many Jews down to the time of David Ben-Gurion:

- an Israel with a tight state organization, united under Davidic leadership,
- Jerusalem as the religious and political centre of the kingdom ('Zion' was later a name for the whole city)
- a strong army, an administration which functioned well, and a clergy integrated into the state,
- national identity within the secure frontiers of a great empire.

As far as this last was concerned, David, who was as wise a diplomat as he was a brilliant army leader, had carried on a highly **expansionist foreign policy** at that time. What had begun as a defensive war became a campaign of conquest. Whereas the wars waged by the Israelite tribes during the settlement as described in the books of Joshua and Judges were still described as wars waged by Yahweh himself, David's wars of conquest no longer appear as wars of Yahweh or 'holy wars'. Never before and never afterwards were Israel's frontiers pushed so wide. Without any nationalistic inhibitions David, who at the time of his clash with King Saul was himself for a while a Philistine vassal and accepted other non-Israelites into the royal guard, included **non-**

Israelite areas in his Greater Israel. This is not without significance for the question of the frontiers of Israel down to the present day, and even at the time of David was to lead to considerable internal tensions and conflicts.

Just as at a much later date – if I may be allowed this comparison once again – the small Swiss Confederation (whose strength, too, lay in its control of the great international trade routes running from north to south) was able to extend southwards as far as Veltlin, and indeed Milan, at a time when the great powers were militarily and politically weak, but then had to withdraw after a heavy defeat in war, so within a few decades David succeeded in incorporating into his kingdom broad areas of Syria, with varied dependent status, without coming up against any resistance worth mentioning from the great powers of Mesopotamia and Egypt (we do not find even a mention of the name David anywhere in their records). These areas included not only the Philistine vassal states in the coastal regions, but also the kingdoms of Moab and Edom east of the Jordan, the Aramaean states (with their capital Aram-Damascus!), and finally the kingdom of the Ammonites (with its capital Rabbat-Ammon, the present-day Amman).

As we know, all these areas were lost again at a later date. At all events, the Israelite national state which comprised the territory of the twelve tribes extended only from 'Dan to Beersheba'.[19] And even within these frontiers there was a non-Israelite population, some of whom were conscripted for forced labour.[20] But possession of the areas explains why a later Deuteronomistic editor of the book of Joshua could see Yahweh's promise of land to his people as being so extensive: 'From the wilderness and this Lebanon as far as the great river, the river Euphrates, all the land of the Hittites to the Great Sea toward the going down of the sun shall be your territory.'[21] In this way the recollection of David's great empire was preserved as an ideal: it was cherished and enriched – and not just in Judaism.

Indeed, David, this most significant ruler in the history of Israel, this great politician, supreme commander and organizer, remained a model for all subsequent generations. He overcame all the opposition of the tribes, who were bent on independence (Saul's tribe of Benjamin in particular), all the revolts and intrigues, and established permanently the hegemony of the tribe of Judah and his family. It is understandable that in the course of history his image was increasingly idealized – already in the books of Chronicles as compared with the books of Samuel and Kings. In a later Deuteronomistic reworking he is even promised **everlasting rule**,[22] though this was never realized in fact. The real king increasingly becomes the ideal king, and the idea of the king becomes a royal ideology. At a later date, when for a long time no Israelite king had ruled 'over all Israel and Judah', this royal ideology was to give rise to a messialogy: the idea of **a messiah** who as the ideal Davidic king of the end-time, as David *redivivus* or as 'son of David', would restore the Davidic kingdom and fulfil the promise of an everlasting rule.

So for all Israel David remained a **prophetic figure of orientation and hope,** who centuries later, at the time of the post-exilic Second Temple as depicted in I Chronicles,[23] was even promoted to become the real founder of the Temple (of Solomon!) and of all the priestly hierarchy. Whether or not the Psalms come from him, they in fact remain the finest and most profound expression of prophetic prayer. And David remained this figure of orientation and hope to an even greater degree when this Second Temple, too, had been burned down in the Jewish War with Rome (70 CE), and Jerusalem had been completely destroyed after the last Jewish revolt against the Romans (135 CE). At that time, David's tomb in the city of David (probably in the region of Siloam), which was still well known at the time of Nehemiah[24] and of the Acts of the Apostles,[25] was destroyed and forgotten (nowadays, because of a doubtful tradition from the time of the Crusades, the many pilgrims regard a place on Mount Zion as the tomb of David). However, there is no doubt that, as C.Thoma points out, 'the biblical David, as a brilliant king and figure of charismatic piety, impressed Judaism of all times and every shade. From the second century BCE onwards David became a **primal dynastic figure** for rulers (Hasmonaeans and Herodians) and hierarchs (patriarchs and leaders in the Babylonian exile), a **model figure** for enthusiasts and revolutionaries with an eschatological orientation, and a leading **religious figure** who was concerned with the building up and consolidation of a community life in conformity with tradition'.[26]

4. David as reflected in Judaism, Christianity and Islam

These indications are enough to remind us that David, too – like Abraham and Moses – has always been perceived very selectively and brought to life very differently in each new period as the **figure of an ideal prophetic leader.** This is even more true in the case of the two other prophetic religions, Christianity and Islam. They both hold David in high esteem, but in detail they interpret him in very different ways. It is worth sketching out briefly the **different profiles of David** in the three religions.

(a) In the rabbinic writings of mediaeval **Judaism**[27] the colourful and lively figure of David – with his strengths and weaknesses an idol who is by no means without dangers – is presented in pastoral style, in three respects (quite apart from the messianic vision of the future).

– In the first place David is seen as the exemplary **man of prayer** and **prophet**, who is said to have composed or at least edited all the Psalms himself (they were probably anonymous originally, and only some were attributed to him). As 'the Psalmist' David was now regarded as an authentic prophet through whom God's word was communicated. Indeed already at that time he appears in an active role in the Israelite (rabbinic) prayer assembly; he is virtually the type of Israel, who in the Psalms speaks not only for himself but for all Israel. It follows from this that:

– David also appeared to the rabbis – since some of the Psalms praise the study of the law day and night[28] – as the one who is **faithful to the law** and who **teaches the law** in an exemplary way. He constantly studied the Torah, observed it in the minutest detail, inexorably hammered it into others and finally died peacefully on a Pentecost sabbath (he is said to have interrupted his reading of the Torah to investigate where the beautiful music that he heard was coming from).

– Finally, however, David also appears as the exemplary **sinner and penitent**, who bitterly regrets his adultery with the beautiful Bathsheba and his murder of her husband, Uriah the Hittite. He does penance and so receives forgiveness. Although David was also roundly criticized by the rabbis (for excessive self-confidence, the defective upbringing of his children, and a census of the population prompted by his own interests), he is therefore excused his adultery.

The fact that David's **great-grandmother Ruth** had been a Moabite woman,[29] i.e. a **non-Jew**, had been used as an argument by the opponents of David in individual tribes; it was still discussed in the Talmud, but then interpreted away by the rabbis. In particular David's origin from a Jewish mother – which in the rabbinic view was the essential characteristic of the true Jew – was thus by no means clear and had to be constructed. As a result, David's origin was then sometimes so exaggerated theologically that he even became virtually an archetype of God, the one for whose sake the world had been created.

The rabbis were concerned here that David should not be understood wrongly and even misused for the dangerous political adventures of messianic enthusiasts. When King Saul was persecuting him, David was for a while, at any rate, the leader of a band of outlaws in the wilderness of Judaea, before he became a Philistine vassal and later king. It is no wonder that in the late modern period, in Europe, this same David was finally rediscovered as a **political figure**, above all, of course, by Zionism. Thus regardless of the extreme changes in its history, down to the present day many Jews regard the Davidic kingdom – taken possession of 3,000 years previously – as the ideal kingdom, and it is of course the foundation for the claim of Zionism – in particular also to Jerusalem. Moreover, since the first Zionist Congress in Basel in 1897, the symbol of Zionism has been the six-pointed 'star of David' (Hebrew *magen* = 'shield' of David), which first appears in Judaism in the early Middle Ages and was then disseminated above all by the Kabbalist Isaac Luria in the fifteenth century. In 1948 it was included in Israel's state flag (so in my scheme of paradigm shifts a vertical broken line is drawn right down to the twentieth century).

(*b*) And how is David regarded in **Christianity**? David is also mentioned often, and with the utmost respect, in the writings of original Christianity: here, too, he is acknowledged as the author of the Psalms, as a model of piety and as prophet of the divine revelation. If we follow Mark's account,[30] Jesus too referred to David, and defended the rubbing of ears of corn on the sabbath with a reference to I Sam.21.2-7, where the priest Abimelech gave David and his people the shewbread which really only priests were allowed to eat.

However, the significance of David for the New Testament goes far beyond this. In particular the Gospel of Matthew, which derives from a Jewish-Christian milieu, seems to have been interested in stressing that **Jesus of Nazareth** was a direct **descendant of David**.[31] There is also some **dispute**: whereas remarkably enough the birthplace of Jesus is not mentioned by either the earliest (Mark) or the latest evangelist (John), both the major evangelists (Matthew and Luke) contain a story about Jesus' infancy (there are many differences in detail between the two and the story is embellished with legends) and insist that Bethlehem is his birthplace. Moreover, Bethlehem is explicitly called the 'city of David'.[32] Many Christian exegetes conjecture that this only happened at a later date, for theological reasons. But it is striking that the messianic expectation of the prophet Micah is taken up in both Matthew and Luke, and that it expressly relates to Bethlehem. Jesus of Nazareth is evidently to be given Davidic credentials as the Messiah of Israel. Moreover the genealogies of Jesus – which similarly occur only in Matthew[33] and Luke[34] – coincide specifically over David, but in other respects diverge widely and cannot be harmonized. This, too, brings out the theological interests of the New Testament authors.

Conversely, it means that historically it must remain an open question whether Jesus really was a descendant of David or was just given the title.

On the other hand there is **no dispute, first,** that the real home of the 'Nazarene' or 'Nazorean' was the insignificant Nazareth in the north, in Galilee, and **secondly,** that 'Son of David' as a messianic title was used of Jesus of Nazareth at a very early stage.[35] How was it understood? In good Jewish fashion it was understood in a theological, eschatological sense. That means that just as in later Jewish interpretation God already willed to be 'a Father' to King David, and as a result David became God's 'son',[36] so too it was to be possible to understand Jesus as 'son of God':[37] not of course (as in a later Greek interpretation) in terms of physical-metaphysical descent but, in the original Jewish sense, in terms of the appointment of a human being to royal power, as it were as God's representative on earth – just like David. However, 'son of David' as a title (there are about 20 instances of it in the New Testament) faded into the background with the increasing 'Hellenization of Christianity' – in favour of titles like 'Son of God' (or 'Son', 75 times) or 'Son of Man' (80 times) and even more of the Gentile-Christian, Greek title 'Christos' (around 500 times). So it is not surprising that 'son of David' also failed to be incorporated into the creeds of the Greek-speaking Hellenistic community: this title would have been incomprehensible and open to misunderstanding in the new environment. But as a type of Christ, David's story – from looking after the sheep, through the fight with Goliath (= Satan) to his laments in the Psalms – was a real treasure-trove for the church fathers and for mediaeval theologians.

In every respect David remained a popular figure, depicted countless times on frescoes, in psalteries and on church portals in royal regalia with a harp. He was a model for the Christian rulers of the Middle Ages (Charlemagne as a 'new David'); he provided legitimation for the anointing of Christian emperors and kings by the church and the pope (because of his anointing as king by the seer Samuel); and he was an appropriate church patron for mastersingers and colleges of music. Only in the Renaissance and the baroque periods did the youthful athletic figure (as in the splendid statues of David by Donatello and Michaelangelo in Florence) come wholly into the foreground.

(*c*) And what about the **Qur'an**? Like Abraham and Moses, David (Arabic 'Da'ud' or 'Dawud') is also a prominent figure in the holy book of **Islam**. The pre-Islamic Arab poets already praised David or his son Solomon (Arabic Suleiman) as the inventor of the coat of mail (chain

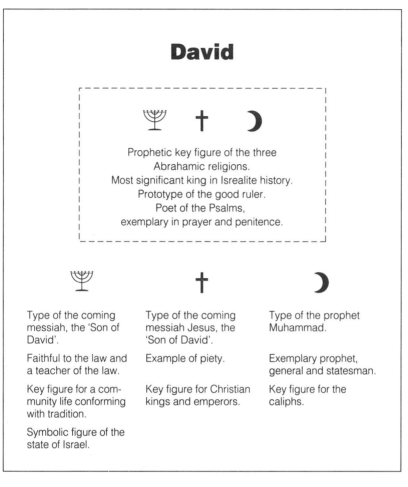

David

Prophetic key figure of the three
Abrahamic religions.
Most significant king in Isrealite history.
Prototype of the good ruler.
Poet of the Psalms,
exemplary in prayer and penitence.

Type of the coming messiah, the 'Son of David'.	Type of the coming messiah Jesus, the 'Son of David'.	Type of the prophet Muhammad.
Faithful to the law and a teacher of the law.	Example of piety.	Exemplary prophet, general and statesman.
Key figure for a community life conforming with tradition.	Key figure for Christian kings and emperors.	Key figure for the caliphs.
Symbolic figure of the state of Israel.		

mail). They also knew of David's psalms, and this of course was particularly important for the Qur'an. Here David appears as Allah's representative (Khalifa), who judges in righteousness. David is once even cited along with Jesus ('Isa'); they are both said to have cursed the unbelieving children of Israel.[38]

Despite all this, however, the various episodes from David's life are not of such significance (though here, too, we have the possibly legendary victory over the Philistine Goliath);[39] David is sometimes even confused with other biblical figures. This sheds light on the Muslim charges that Jews and Christians have falsified their own revelatory scriptures. More important than anything else is the basic fact that in the Qur'an David, like Moses before him and Jesus after him, is termed **a true prophet**, a direct recipient of the divine revelation. Why? Because he too received a **book** from God, the book of **Psalms**. So we can read in surah 17.55: 'We have exalted some prophets above others. To David we gave the Psalms.'[40] No wonder David was widely noted in the post-Qur'anic literature! For his life seems to anticipate many of the features of the biography of the Prophet – we need think only of the flight from Saul and Absalom's revolt.

5. The two faces of Solomon and the division of the kingdom

All in all, the period of the monarchy lasted only around 400 years. Whereas the accounts of Saul and David are contained in the two books of Samuel, the history of their successors is subsequently outlined in the two books of Kings. However, while it is possible to date the individual kings fairly accurately, the information about them is unfortunately very fragmentary and has been theologically filtered. So the question is: how did things go after the great David?

The one problem over which David failed completely was that of arranging for a **successor**. He had practised a skilful policy of marriages to keep himself in power: he had taken eight wives and had at least nineteen sons of various descent! But in the end this very policy was to prove negative.[41] Moreover, a variety of tragedies overshadowed David's end: the blood guilt of the oldest prince Amnon with his half-sister Tamar (the only daughter of David that we know of); the murder of Amnon on the orders of his brother Absalom; Absalom's flight and then his *coup d'état*; David's flight and the eventual killing of Absalom in the subsequent hunt and pursuit; the candidature of a further prince, Adonijah, who is then put out of harm's way; and finally, on the urging of David's court prophet Nathan and Bathsheba, whom David had once seduced, the nomination of **Solomon**,[42] Bathsheba's son, as co-regent by David immediately before his death. Last of all came Solomon's accession and with it the elimination of all the forces of the opposition, beginning with Adonijah.[43]

So from his accession on, Solomon presents an **ambiguous picture**: it is now virtually impossible to reconcile historically his ruthless actions – there are some reports of intrigues in the harem and a kind of *coup d'état* without popular assent – with his much-praised 'wisdom' and his authorship of '3,000 proverbs and 1,005 songs'.[44] Beyond question, at that time experiential wisdom was already being taken over from Egypt in the forms of sayings and songs, and then being gradually integrated into Yahwistic religion. According to a royal novella on the Egyptian pattern,[45] Solomon was granted **divine recog-**

nition (by an encounter with God) **instead of political recognition** (by a royal treaty).[46]

In I Kings the following details of Solomon's reign are given, more in a logical than a chronological order: his wisdom,[47] his buildings,[48] his trade,[49] and also his apostasy and his end.[50] At all events, the famous 'judgment of Solomon'[51] may have been a floating legend, and the literary works attributed to Solomon (Proverbs, Song of Songs, Ecclesiastes, the Wisdom of Solomon) are later pseudepigraphy. No one can avoid distinguishing the historical Solomon from the later idealistic images of Solomon.[52]

Nowadays there is agreement about that among scholars. The later proverbial **'Solomon in all his glory'** is only one side of the historical reality. It is expressed above all in the building of a splendid **temple**, though it was modest in comparison with Solomon's palace.[53] As the property of the Davidic dynasty, it became at the same time both the state sanctuary and the central sanctuary of Israel, and was given an official, hereditary royal priesthood. In comparison with the state temple, the 'ark of God' quickly lost significance; from this point on, Yahweh, who as 'king' now had a 'house', 'dwelt' in the Temple.[54] Now the king no longer merely exercised priestly functions *ad hoc*, but was 'priest for ever'. Solomon's absolutist rule was further marked by the building of fortified places and the reinforcement of a standing army; by a brilliant court and the furthering of the arts and sciences; and finally by his cultivation of international relationships, extended trade, marriage to a daughter of Pharaoh and a gigantic harem with a number of foreign wives, whose gods called for special cults in sacred Jerusalem. This probably also resulted in syncretistic worship by other subjects.

However, a high price had to be paid for all this – and that is the other, **wretched side** to the historical reality. The price was a monarchy in a city culture which now differed more and more markedly from the people, its customs and usages; the creation of a tight central government and twelve administrative districts (excluding Judah!) to supply provisions to the court; the transition to a city economy and oppressive taxes, even forced labour under the supervision of a minister of the corvée who moreover was stoned by the people after Solomon's death. Finally, the state was supported by slaves – not just prisoners of war, as under David, but now also by those who had been enslaved for debt: in other words, people who had been compelled to sell their property (which according to old Israelite ideas was the inalienable gift of God!).

Great estates and the impoverishment of the masses were the result.

Because of his enormous building activity – of which the mighty encircling walls and 'four-entry' gates of the cities of Hazor, Megiddo and Gezer unearthed by archaeologists are evidence – Solomon even had to sell a whole district of Galilee with twenty cities to the king of Tyre. And it was the harsh forced labour which was to be the chief complaint by the northern tribes against Solomon's successor and son Rehoboam. What was the fatal consequence of this conflict?

It is not surprising that the Davidic kingdom, which from the start suffered from a tension between north and south and began to crumble even under Solomon, split apart completely after Solomon's death.[55] Only about seventy years after David's accession, around 927, there was a fatal **division of the kingdom** in the central territory of David (along with successive losses of the territories which had also been conquered) into a northern kingdom and a southern kingdom, each with a different history. Here is a brief summary of what is important for our perspective.

In the **north**, the larger and stronger **kingdom of Israel** came into being; later it had a new capital, **Samaria**, newly built by King Omri and without any tradition:
– here according to some present-day historians there was a tendency more towards a charismatic than a dynastic ideal of kingship (monarchy as a free contract between the people and the man designated by Yahweh);
– here at all events kings were often overthrown with terrible blood-baths;
– here, because of the strong Canaanite element in the population, the dynasty of Omri in particular attempted to pursue a religious policy which kept the balance by tolerating alien gods and temples (images of bulls were also symbols of Yahweh);
– here, however, a strong prophetic opposition also developed, which sought to destroy all the sanctuaries of the Phoenician Baal and in Jehu's revolution attempted to exterminate the Canaanite cult.

By contrast, in the **south**, more remote and shut in on itself, the tiny **kingdom of Judah** came into being, with its capital **Jerusalem**;
– here all possible means were used to maintain the Davidic succession;
– here for a long time, until a stronger Egypt intervened once again in Palestine, there was an attempt to keep apart from the politics of the wider world;
– but here the Canaanite cult was similarly largely tolerated and the syncretism of Jerusalem also had the countryside in its grasp (despite Yahwistic reactions under kings Asa, Jehoshaphat and later above all under Hezekiah).

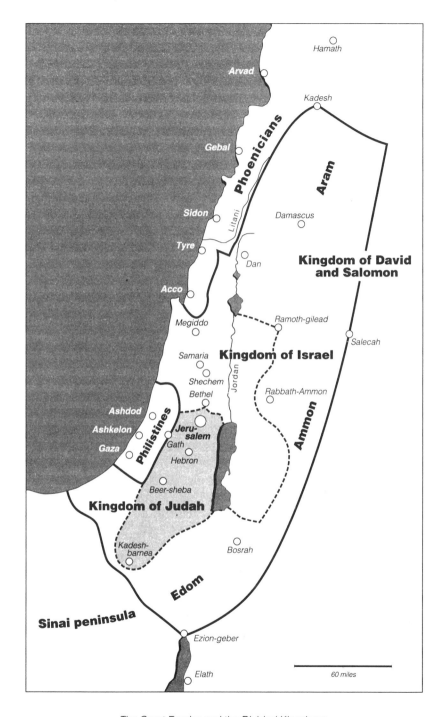

The Great Empire and the Divided Kingdoms

This period of the division of the kingdom is thus a time of increasing syncretism. But it is also the great time of classical prophecy, which marks out Israelite religion as a typically prophetic religion in a unique way.

6. The unique character of prophecy

In his well-known book *Prophecy and Religion in Ancient China*,[56] H.H.Rowley had sought to demonstrate that in ancient China, too, there were prophets like those which were known in Israel. Certainly no one doubts that in ancient China, too, there were shamans, sooth-sayers and ecstatics of very different kinds. But prophets? If we look at the evidence more closely,[57] it becomes clear that the term 'prophet' has been stretched so wide that it also covers 'reformers' and even 'statesmen'. If Confucius and the great Israelite individual prophets like Amos, Isaiah, Jeremiah and others are all brought under the same common denominator of 'prophet', all the differences are levelled out. And does not Confucius lack precisely what marks out the great Israelite prophets and at the same time distinguishes them not only from the basic Indian-mystic, but also the Chinese-wisdom type of religion?[58] Let us look more closely, first of all within the sphere of Israel.

Of course in the **sphere of ancient Israel**, too, there were soothsayers, ecstatics, seers, indeed something like 'prophets' in the broadest sense of the word. Cuneiform documents from Mari in the central Euphrates mention men who had to give a message at the behest of a god, though this message was always addressed only to the king. In Israel, too, probably already in the period before the state, ecstatics made sporadic appearances, going into raptures through dancing and instrumental music, and at that time they were even joined by King Saul. There were also organized groups of 'prophets' at certain holy places, and there were 'seers' and miracle-working 'men of God'. Nor must we forget the presumably numerous female prophets (though they are cited only by way of exception) like Aaron's sister Miriam, who led the other women in clapping hands and ring-dancing;[59] Deborah, who has already been cited;[60] the prophetess Huldah;[61] and an anonymous prophet, probably the wife of Isaiah.[62]

But who is a prophet in the strict sense? At all events, not someone who can 'predict', 'foretell' something, as popular understanding has it; such a person would be just a 'fortune teller'. No, in the original understanding of the Greek word *prophetes*, a prophet is someone who announces, proclaims something. So a prophet is an 'announcer', a 'proclaimer', a 'communicator' (as Buber put it) of God himself: a man who does not 'soothsay', but speaks the truth. The Hebrew word *nabi* indicates the decisive element; originally it means the one who 'calls', or 'is called'. That means that the prophet in the strict sense is the one who is specially 'called' by God. And this role of prophet begins in Israelite history with the institution of kingship and essentially also ends with it, in the catastrophe of the exile (post-exilic prophecy is only the postlude and echo of the earlier great prophecy).[63] So during the monarchy, with its political and social presuppositions, we find those relatively few **great individual prophets** who are distinct both from the numerous official cultic prophets of a sanctuary and from the court prophets of a king (who are so often 'false prophets'). These great individuals are not the professional representatives of a class, a guild, a sanctuary or a king; rather, snatched away from their everyday profession (as farmers or priests), they appear as **those who are specially called to give tidings of God** – that is their specific character.

In this way they represent in exemplary form what characterizes the structural type of the prophetic in the history of religion generally: according to the biblical tradition the great prophets of Israel – and this is expressed particularly in their calling – understand themselves as having been set quite personally **before God**:

just as Abraham was already called to go forth to a new land and received God's promise;

just as Moses already cast himself down before the bush which burned and yet was not consumed, the sign of God's presence;

just as, finally, David too danced and prayed before the ark of God, the sign of Yahweh's mighty presence.

These great leading figures, too, were one day directly to be called 'prophets': later, of course in retrospect, when Israelite religion had long since become the **prophetic religion** *par excellence* through its great individual prophets...

But precisely what characterized the basic attitude of the prophet? The basis of prophetic existence is neither a theological dogmatics nor a political tactic, but **trusting faith**.

Therefore – as we already saw in connection with Abraham – prophetic religions can also be called **religions of faith**. Standing before God, prostrating himself, kneeling, the prophet experiences his call as one who is aware of his inadequacy. A mysterious experience with the living God on which an outsider cannot pass judgment: a revelation in the form of a vision, audition or inspiration, as is attested by the extremely different visions accompanying the calls of Isaiah,[64] Jeremiah,[65] and Ezekiel.[66] In the face of God's superiority the prophet certainly feels himself to be small and unworthy; however, he is not enslaved, but confronted with a decision: whether to say yes or no to God's call.

Once the prophet has said the 'Yes' that is required of him, then he knows that he is quite personally chosen, moved, indeed compelled to carry out his task, renouncing all rest, satisfaction and security. In season and out of season, he has to speak to his day God's threat of disaster and, if this threat is heeded by those to whom it is addressed, God's redeeming word of salvation. Here all revolves round the present time. This prophet is not concerned with a distant future, but with the present. And in the understanding of the Hebrew Bible, only someone who truly proclaims the will of Yahweh independently of an institutional tie (of the kind which bound the professional prophets) is a true prophet. As God's spokesmen, filled with the spirit, the prophets are the inconvenient **watchers, warners, examiners, admonishers.** They are not instruments without a will of their own, but always strong-willed interpreters of the will of God. Nor are they supermen and miracle-men, but people who are seized from outside and assailed from within, made uncertain and yet sure of the grace of God. At all events, they will not be deterred from conveying God's message, even when confronted with the incalculable complexities of foreign power politics or situations of crisis within the nation. This message is conveyed through symbolic (not magical) actions and prophetic (nor predictive) sayings, reports and speeches; those who deliver it are watchful, brave and stubborn, though sometimes depressed and almost in despair. 'Thus Yahweh has spoken!' 'Thus says Yahweh!' This is publicly their constant characteristic and mark.

To clarify the situation, let us look once again at Chinese (and also Indian) religion. In the same period, between 800 and 500 BCE, not only were the Greek pre-Socratic philosophers looking for a great primal principle of the world, but **in India** pious thinkers were seeking a unity behind the superficial multiplicity of worldly phenomena and the many gods, and were developing the doctrine of the unity of all things in the Upanishads, a doctrine which has influenced almost all later religious thought in India, including Buddhism and Jainism.[67] And at the same time, **in China,** at a time of political and cultural uncertainty, the great thinkers were raising the question of the status of human beings in the universe and of social order and harmony – a humanism which culminated in the teaching of Confucius.[68]

But however many similarities there may have been in the questions and answers of the normative figures in all the three currents of religious

systems, there is no mistaking the fact that the great representatives of prophetic piety who stand in trusting faith before the God who makes personal demands (*coram Deo*) and hear and proclaim God's word are fundamentally different:
– from **those Indian mystics** who now already see themselves in God (*in Deo*), indeed who only have methodically to make themselves aware of the unity with the hidden Absolute through spiritual exercises, meditation and yoga;
– but also from **those Chinese sages** for whom it is the distant heaven **above** them (*sub divo*) which represents order, power and law and whose will they are to understand and do.

The great prophets represent a unique climax in Israel's history of faith. Elijah and Elisha, those **prophets of the word** who became legendary but were still characterized by marked ecstatic traits, were protagonists of this prophetic movement, initially intervening in the history of the people more by their actions than by their words. Their sayings are embedded in lengthy narratives (often with magical and miraculous features, even raisings of the dead):
– **Elijah**, shrouded in saga, the leader of that 'Yahweh alone party' of which we have already heard,[69] who led a passionate struggle for the uniqueness of Yahweh against any worship of Canaanite Baal and social injustice: 'I am jealous for Yahweh, the God of hosts.'[70]
– **Elisha**, who is the head of a group of prophets and stands out above all for his great miracles – of a kind which significantly are no longer reported of the later prophets.

In the eighth and seventh centuries, the line of such prophets of the word was continued by **the writing prophets** proper, who renounced political and social action and relied only on the word and on symbolic actions (which did not have a magical, mechanical effect); their words, addressed to the whole people, were collected together on the whole by pupils and then preserved in a number of books. Beginning with **Amos** and **Hosea** in the northern kingdom, through **Isaiah, Jeremiah** and **Ezekiel** in the south, down to the last prophet, the anonymous **Malachi** – how few of them there were in this long, short, period of a good two hundred years! – they admonished and warned; they threatened the downfall of the two kingdoms of Israel and Judah, and called for conversion; they were the scourge of a culture which had become worldly, and against all alien cults proclaimed a strictly monotheistic faith; they took a line which was strongly critical of society against an upper class which was increasingly enriching itself and a caste of great landowners. Scholars differ as to whether a call to repentance was already connected with the announcement of disaster among the pre-exilic prophets (the words of salvation may have often been inserted into the text by later redactors); at all events the words of judgment predominate decisively.

7. The prophet in opposition to the priests and the king

Thus the writing prophets of the eighth/seventh centuries prove to be solitary, radical great **critics of their time** in the face of the threatening judgment of God, committed to God alone. They combine recollection of the past and analysis of the present with prognosis for the future – usually in poetic form but sometimes also in powerful prose.

– They criticize the people's **conception of history**, a history which is proving no longer to be a 'history of salvation' but a history of false trust in national power and political coalitions and thus a history of failure, guilt and sin. In the face of the announcement of the punitive judgment of God, who also can act through other peoples, the whole people of Israel is challenged to a decision: total apostasy from God and downfall or a return to God and new life.

– They criticize the **worship of the priests**, which with its altars, sacrifices, songs, vows and feast-days proves not to be a 'means of salvation' but a cheating of God himself, so long as people think that they can assure themselves of God's blessing through the mechanical performance of prescribed rites and ineffective sacrifices, instead of being changed in their hearts, doing right and struggling with God in prayer.

– They criticize the **legal practice of the rulers**, the upper classes' contempt for justice, the negligence and transgressions of officials and judges, who acquit the guilty and condemn the innocent, leaving both orphans and widows in the lurch, instead of enquiring into the meaning and spirit of the law and allowing its use to be an expression of their own hearts. But they also criticize the transgressions of the merchants and the great landowners, who have done away with the freedom and equality which existed in the period before the state by buying up properties and impoverishing and enslaving those who work on the land.

So is it astonishing if social tensions increased with time, and the great communicators of the word now increasingly found themselves **opposed** to those who held power, to the **monarchy** itself and also to its **priesthood**? Certainly the prophets were not in principle against the monarchy and the priesthood; they did not foment a revolution, and both Isaiah and Jeremiah were sometimes in accord with the king. But in the light of their calling they were now the only counterbalance and corrective to the rulers and a people which was all too obedient to them.

The prophets abhorred the syncretistic religious policy and the alliance between throne and altar, and also the opportunist toing and froing in foreign politics. There were no more summons to wars of Yahweh, 'holy wars', but – in the name of Yahweh – **speeches against war**. Indeed the prophets proclaimed the expectation of **a peace among the peoples** which Yahweh would bring about: '...and they shall beat their swords into ploughshares, and their spears into pruning hooks; nation shall not lift up sword against nation, neither shall they learn war any more'.[71] No wonder that the prophets were increasingly not only ignored, attacked and ridiculed as 'fools',[72] but were also, like Jeremiah, arrested and possibly even killed. 'The fate of the prophets' has not become proverbial by chance. To relate the stories of the prophets is always also to relate a story of suffering.

The prophets were not correct in all their announcements, but in their announcement of the great judgment – as compared with the professional prophets, who toned it down – they were all too right. Moreover prophecy, which impotently staked everything simply on the word, outlived the monarchy, which along with the priesthood embodied all power. In the framework of the state paradigm of the kingdom, as non-conformists the prophets mostly represented the opposing forces which could not establish themselves at a given moment. But to the degree that their life and arguments were centred on Israelite faith – Yahweh, the God of Israel – they also remained a living force in the coming new constellation. Indeed, after their prophecy of the judgment of God on his people had been fulfilled for the kingdom of Judah as well as that of Israel, their faith was an inspiration for the very different time that was to come, as it was for the collection and editing of the holy scriptures of the Hebrew Bible which was soon to begin. Here already was the foundation for the universal extension of the religion of Yahweh to other peoples, in so far as the words of the prophets, which were often also addressed to other peoples, were directed at the individual, so that the community of the people was no longer simply identical with the community of faith. The unconditional 'Yes' to Yahweh was more important to them than membership of the people.

8. The domesticating of prophecy in Judaism, Christianity and Islam

These universalist impulses had an effect over many centuries, after the monarchy had fallen, and the prophetic message also became the heritage of other religions. So even today the **prophetic heritage** lives on in all three Abrahamic religions, albeit in different ways. **Common** to Judaism, Christianity and Islam are:

- The strict prophetic faith in one God, who tolerates no other gods, powers, rulers and figures alongside himself, and who is the God not only of one people but of all peoples; who is not a national God but the Lord of the world;
- The basic prophetic ethic: humane demands for justice, truth, loyalty, peace and love, said to be the demands of God himself;
- The prophetic criticism of the unjust and inhuman conditions under which humiliated, enslaved and exploited people have to live – no service of God without service of human beings.

To the degree that Judaism, Christianity and Islam continue and activate this prophetic heritage, they are **prophetic religions** *par excellence*. At the same time, however, we should not overlook the fact that because of developments in the subsequent period the interpretations and evaluations of the prophets turned out very differently in all three prophetic religions. The prophets are praised in retrospect, but not followed to the same degree. On the contrary: depending on particular needs, **in interpreting** these great 'outsiders' and opposition figures, who would not fit properly into any established order, attempts have been made to **domesticate them**. Let me put this in a pointed way:

- In **Judaism** the prophets were later increasingly subordinated to the teachers of the law, who regarded themselves more and more as super-prophets. Even many Jews criticize this today. Over against the 'Five Books of Moses', the Torah, the prophetic books were understood merely as interpretations which had been far surpassed by later rabbinic 'wise men', who boldly equated their own interpretations with the Torah of Moses.[73] It is no coincidence that in one tractate of the Talmud we find the saying, 'The words of the elders are more important than the words of the prophets.'[74]
- In **Christianity**, Israel's prophets were long regarded only as forerunners and announcers of Jesus of Nazareth. Even many Christians criticize this today. As though they themselves did not have critical remarks to make about society and the church. However, in comparison with Jews, Christians have been fond of referring to the prophets'

Prophets

Especially called to proclaim God.
Culminating figures of the prophetic religions.
Social, political and theological critics of society.
They watch, warn, examine and admonish.

	†	)
Alongside Moses, the great prophets are the central religious figures in Israelite history.	The prophets of Israel are significant heralds of Jesus, the Christ.	Before Muhammad the greatest prophets are Noah, Abraham, Moses, David and Jesus. They received the very message that Muhammad received later.
Israel expects the coming of the endtime prophet (Deut. 18.15).	Jesus is the promised eschatological prophet. In him the promises of the Hebrew Bible have been fulfilled; his Spirit works prophetically for the future.	Muhammad is the 'seal' which confirms and concludes all the earlier prophets.
The teachers of the Torah who emerge later replace the prophets in significance. Prophecy is suppressed.	Even in earliest Christian times the charisma of prophecy ebbed away and was absorbed into the office of bishop (who increasingly became priest, king and prophet in one person). Prophecy is domesticated.	After the death of Muhammad, those who are learned in the law are the legitimate successors of the prophet. Prophecy is institutionalized.

criticism of the Jewish religion and have clearly devalued the Torah in comparison with the prophetic books.

• Finally, in **Islam**, Adam, Abraham, Moses, David and Jesus have certainly always been highly esteemed as prophets - not only as *nabi* but as *rasul* (of Allah), as emissaries of God who gave laws and left behind a particular message and scripture. But apart from various stories about prophets (which are given only a subsidiary pedagogical and literary function), none of the major or minor prophets of Israel is thought worthy of mention in the Qur'an; none is acknowledged as a spokesman of God, as giving warning and announcing a serious-joyful message. Muhammad as the concluding 'seal of the prophets' takes the place of all of them.[75]

Of course prophetic criticism may not pass over the fact that prophecy can also be misused (the false prophets), and that the **monarchy** also **had its historical merits**, even if it was not to exist 'for ever'. Problematic though these developments may have been, without the monarchy there would have been no Yahwistic state religion, no central Temple, no national and religious ideology, no collecting and shaping of the old traditions, narratives, legal statements and poems.

But now the golden age of the monarchy was finally over, and the kingdom divided. And the ways of the two kingdoms, now separated, remained different – sometimes in fratricidal war and sometimes in a kindred fashion.

9. From the division of the kingdom to the fall of the kingdom

The fate of the two kingdoms was a sorry one. The decline of both of them – as the prophets constantly kept announcing – was to continue inexorably. The **paradigm of the kingdom** increasingly manifested a fundamental **crisis**. The history of the northern kingdom showed this as much as the history of the southern kingdom.

The **northern kingdom** was being frequently entangled in wars with Syrians, Ammonites and Moabites, when a threatening and highly-militarized great power came to loom on the Mesopotamian horizon. This was tightly organized into small provinces under direct government, and with the help of detachments of chariots and for the first time also with an extremely rapid cavalry (armed with bows and lances) had built up an unparalleled military machine. The Syrian Aramaean states along with Israel were to succumb to it. This power was the **neo-Assyrian empire**, which since the ninth century had been engaged in energetic expansion westwards; it reached the zenith of its power under Tiglath-pileser III (745-727). Power struggles within Israel made the situation worse for the northern kingdom. For when the king of Judah, Ahaz of the family of David, was on the point of being coerced by Israel and Aram-Damascus (at that time both were already Assyrian vassals) by force of arms to join an armed coalition against Assyria, he went against the advice of the prophet Isaiah in calling on the Assyrian great king himself for help. Tiglath-pileser intervened rapidly. In 733 he annexed Galilee and Gilead (and also Aram-Damascus a year later), and everywhere followed the Assyrian policy of deporting the upper classes of the cities to Mesopotamia and replacing them out of hand by alien groups. A rump state (Ephraim) was left; under a pro-Assyrian king it now became a completely dependent vassal state.

When there was another rebellion in Ephraim a decade later (in the meantime Shalmaneser V, Tiglath-pileser's son, had become king in Assyria), siege was also laid to the royal residence in Samaria and in 722 it was captured – but only after three years of resistance; Megiddo, Shechem and Hazor were destroyed. Again the upper class were carried off to northern Mespotamia and Media (according to an Assyrian source 27,280 were deported), and replaced by all kinds of alien colonists from a variety of countries. Those who were carried off were never to return.

That meant that the **end of the northern kingdom of Israel** was now definitive.[76] The northern kingdom did not experience any rebirth; the 'ten tribes of the north' had gone under and all that was left was an Assyrian province, 'Samerina'. From that point on, not only the city but also the whole area was called '**Samaria**', and was inhabited by '**Samaritans**', i.e. by **a mixed people** which was composed of the new colonizing upper class (deriving from Babylonia and Central Syria) and the indigenous population, which was leaderless. This population now worshipped both Yahweh and the new alien gods at the same time,[77] and was deeply despised by the Judaeans in the south of the country because of its syncretism.

What about the name 'Israel'? Subsequently it was claimed only by the **southern kingdom of Judah**, which still existed. Although economically and politically Judah was by far the weaker part-state, it now saw itself as the sole heir not only of the Davidic state and its ideology but also of the religious tradition of the part-state of Israel and its worship. For from the beginning people in Jerusalem had not been content with the division of the kingdom, and so were permanently interested in the re-attachment of the northern kingdom, Samaria. But was there room for a third great power between Egypt and Mesopotamia?

The request for help from Jerusalem's King Ahaz to Assyria was also to have consequences for his kingdom of Judah. The kingdom had voluntarily, though out of necessity, made itself dependent on the Assyrians, and when it too attempted to rebel, it became a vassal of the

Assyrian empire: Assyrian deities and cults could now also be found all over Judah, and even in the Temple of Jerusalem. However, as a result of the defeat and final downfall of the Assyrians in the seventh century, the kingdom of Judah was given yet another brief breathing space. The one king of Judah whom some people regard as the only king in any way comparable to David, **King Josiah** (639-609), attempted to exploit it. Josiah had come to the throne at the age of eight and later regarded the time as ripe for a fundamental reform of the cult.[78] What form did this take?

From Egypt to Mesopotamia, the seventh century BCE generally had been a time of restoration: restoration of temples, of ancient writings, of literature; thus it was a time of return to the old days in religion and politics as well.[79] King Hezekiah had already attempted a religious reform at the beginning of the century, but subsequently, towards the end of the century, one event caused a particular stir: in 621, during the renovation of Solomon's Temple, in circumstances which are not explained, a book of unknown origin was discovered which had been deposited there: this was an early form of 'Deutero-nomy' = the 'Second Law', as it was later called.[80] The book in question was a law book which must have come into being not too long beforehand under priestly and prophetic influences (presumably in the northern kingdom, and then brought to Jerusalem and revised there); it gave itself out to be the great **farewell speech of Moses,** delivered before the Israelite **settlement,** and was now also generally accepted as such.[81] However, the original book (the 'primal-Deuteronomy', and thus also the reform envisaged in it) may have been smaller than the present biblical book of Deuteronomy. At all events, at the time of King Josiah people believed that here they were hearing directly the word of Yahweh, which called for unconditional obdience. Above all the king himself – after consulting and making enquiries of the prophetess Huldah – took the message of Moses seriously: he read it out to an assembly in the Temple, and in this way solemnly made **a new covenant** between Yahweh and his people; for the king himself this covenant now also amounted to something like a constitutional obligation to a constitution.

Thus in the Hebrew Bible Josiah appears as the reforming king *par excellence*. What were the consequences of this 'Deuteronomic reform'? For a long time the **Temple,** and gradually the Temple Mount, indeed the whole city of Jerusalem – called 'Zion' in poetry – had been regarded as the seat of God and thus as a holy place. According to the Deuteronomic view, now the transcendent God made 'his name dwell'[82] in the Holy of Holies of the Temple. **Shekinah,** dwelling, means that here God's emanation is powerfully present in a way which is dangerous for any unauthorized person – a *mysterium tremendum et fascinosum*.

Only now was the **sacrificial cult concentrated** wholly on Jerusalem and its Temple; all the country priests of Yahweh were commanded to come to Jerusalem (where they became a kind of second-class clergy, who were not entitled to offer sacrifice). At the same time there was a 'purge' of pagan and syncretistic cults, their altars, implements, images and emblems: in the Temple, in the holy city, throughout Judaea and even in parts of the northern kingdom. There was a reordering of the whole of Israelite cultic life – in particular a renewal of the passover feast – which was in no way just a religious 'restoration' of the old. For the **programme of cultic unity and cultic purity** carried out here was in fact new, and pointed forward. This was a religious and political reform – probably also aimed at the new 'Davidic' unity of north and south which was constantly hoped for – under the sign of 'election' and the 'covenant' (*berit*): only now does this latter word (as we heard earlier) become a central and key concept for religious thought in Israel/Judah. We should not fail to note here that while the 'election' was understood in markedly nationalistic religious terms and as being exclusively directed against the other nations, the obligation of the covenant was now a legally codified book of law, the humane tendencies of which cannot of course be denied.

And yet the reform of this hopeful, gifted and energetic reformer king was to come to a tragic end. In the meantime, after heavy fighting, Assur was conquered in 614 and Nineveh in 612 by a coalition of Medes and Babylonians; both cities were completely destroyed (the prophet Nahum had announced this). Three years later Pharaoh Necho II marched northwards – in order to intervene in Haran in support of the remaining Assyrian armies. King Josiah dared to block the Pharaoh's march at Megiddo. There he was taken prisoner by the Egyptians in obscure circumstances – remarkably, even before the battle – and immediately executed. He was only forty. That was the end of the reform in Judah. However, the events surrounding Josiah's reform had engraved themselves deeply in the people's memory. The 'book of the law' – for the first time in the history of Israelite religion a revealed book which was *a priori* 'holy' had played a decisive role – was to have a future. But this future would come only after catastrophe.

The land was again under Egyptian control, but this in turn was soon to be replaced by another rule: that of the **neo-Babylonian empire**, which was also called the Chaldaean empire after its founder, Nabopolassar, who was of Aramaean descent. Politically, what followed Josiah was to be no more than a swansong for the kingdom. For there was no room for a buffer state steering a middle course between the two great powers in the north and south. The **end of the southern kingdom** had also come – barely 150 years after the downfall of the north. When King Jehoiakim tried to free himself from Babylonian rule, in 598/597 Babylonian troops occupied the country and laid siege to Jerusalem. Only the opening of the gates by King Jehoiachin, who had succeeded his father on the throne during the siege, prevented the destruction of the city. However, the Temple and city were plundered, the Temple treasure was taken to Babylon, and the young king, his harem and members of the upper class (nobility, priests and craftsmen) were all deported to Babylon. These were the proverbial 'top ten thousand',[83] including the later prophet Ezekiel.

A decade later, under the influence of court circles friendly to Egypt, **King Zedekiah**, who had been newly appointed by the Babylonians, once again thought that he could try to rebel against the neo-Babylonian powers – although **the prophet Jeremiah** of Jerusalem, who had been called to be a prophet as early as the thirteenth year of Josiah's reign, untiringly warned against this. The Babylonians appeared a second time before Jerusalem. This time they were commanded by the crown prince **Nebuchadnezzar II**, the son of Nabopolassar. The year was 587/86. Again the city – bereft of Egyptian help – was besieged, and finally stormed and plundered. The Temple of Solomon went up in flames, and with it probably also the old ark of the covenant, which was of no interest to the Babylonians.

This time the conquerors did the job properly. The city was levelled to the ground and the remnants of the upper class who had been left behind were deported **to Babylon**. King Zedekiah was made to watch the execution of his sons and some members of his court at the Babylonian headquarters and was then blinded; he was finally taken off to Babylon in chains,[84] and later died there.[85] However, the prophet Jeremiah, who had been suspected of high treason and arrested by King Zedekiah, was freed by the Babylonians. Unlike the Assyrians in the northern kingdom, the Babylonians did not settle any alien colonists in Judah. Jeremiah's friend, the Judaean Gedaliah, became the Babylonian high commissioner; he ruled sensibly, but three years later was murdered by a fanatic from the royal house in his residence at Mizpah. For fear of reprisals, Jeremiah was forced to emigrate to Egypt along with the inhabitants of Mizpah, and there he died – no one knows when and where.

That was the **end of the Davidic monarchy**, and with it also of the existing political state organization. Indeed (if we leave aside the interlude of the Maccabean period) it was the end of the political independence of the Jewish people as a state - for around two and a half millennia, to the middle of our century. That surely helps us to understand how the ninth day of the month Avib (July-August) remained a day of national mourning and also how many people saw in the new state of Israel under David Ben-Gurion a resurrection of the ancient kingdom of David and Solomon – Israel's golden age.

Questions for the Future

What function can David have in the future for the three prophetic religions: in youth training, in school books and instruction, in culture and politics?

What are the frontiers of the 'promised land', the 'biblical Israel'? What frontiers should the new state have under the star of David: those of the great Davidic empire, those of the original tribal territory, those of the surviving kingdom of Judah? Should Israel extend from the Lebanon to the Euphrates, from Dan to Beersheba, from Carmel to Gilead, or from Tel Aviv to Jordan?

III. The Paradigm of Theocracy: Post-Exilic Judaism

It is amazing beyond measure: the Jewish people survived even when all its state institutions were taken away. Is that simply a biological fact or more of a continuum with a psychological foundation, or is it even a historical miracle? No, the survival of the Jewish **people** is connected with the survival of the Jewish **religion**: with belief in the one **God** of this people.

1. The time of the exile and new hope

The crisis to which the collapse of the paradigm of the Davidic kingdom had led was a profound one: the Temple had been burned down; the city walls destroyed; the Davidic monarchy, which had been thought to be eternal, had been extinguished; and Judah, too, had been occupied by foreign troops and its elite executed or deported. The election of the people and the promise of the land had been bound up with Israel's fulfilment of the obligations of the covenant![1] Thus the great, inconvenient, authentic prophets and their threats had been vindicated, and no longer needed to be concerned about their credentials (there was no longer any mention of the court prophets who had conformed with the system, and it seemed more than superfluous to gather together their sayings): the kingdom of the ten tribes had gone under, and so many people of Judah had been deported to Babylon! And how hard it was 'to sing the Lord's song by the waters of Babylon, in a strange land'.[2] As a result many people also despaired of the power of Yahweh and – both in Palestine and in Babylonia! – turned to the old Canaanite or the new Babylonian gods. Alien cults, syncretistic cults, superstition and magic were widespread, along with the cult of Yahweh.

The Babylonian exile (Hebrew *golah*[3]) was to last almost fifty years (586-538), and some Israelites – especially those in Egypt – no longer had any thought of returning to Israel. The dispersion of Israel, the **Diaspora**, had begun, and remains a historical reality down to the present day. From this time on, Israel lived in and by **a tension between homeland and Diaspora**. However, time and again very important new impulses emerged from this very Diaspora. Here already it becomes evident that both homeland and foreign lands are authentic vehicles of earlier Israelite traditions.

One thing is clear: the end of the Davidic kingdom was not the end of the people of Israel. On the contrary, it proved that in the very period of the Babylonian exile this people was able to maintain an amazing **internal independence** and show a surprising spiritual fertility. In contrast to the practice of the Assyrians of an earlier period, whose custom was to disperse throughout the empire those who had been deported in order to liquidate the elite of a people both ethnically and politically, **in Babylonia** the exiles were allowed to remain together in small compact settlements. They regarded themselves as the better part of Israel, the 'holy remnant' proclaimed by the prophets. They had hardly any dealings with the indigenous Babylonian population. We must not get a wrong idea of the life of those who had been forcibly deported to Babylonia: the former king Jehoiachin and his court were able to lead a relatively pleasant life in Babylon, at that time the world capital. And even those who had been compulsorily settled in the provinces were not engaged in forced labour, but led a relatively free life as subjects – with their own houses, plantations, trade and sometimes quite a considerable income. Self-government predominated, and people lived in an order determined by families, who were governed by 'elders'.

As a result of this cohesion, the majority of the exiles kept alive the hope of return to their old homeland: the **longing for Jerusalem** which is celebrated in some psalms, despite all the lamentation.[4] The decisive idea was that Yahweh could not be worshipped properly in this foreign, unclean land, but only in Jerusalem. The Temple tax, paid annually, which was brought from Babylonia to Jerusalem, was a permanent bond of solidarity. The new cultic order of Deuteronomy and King Josiah's reform of the cult now once again had some influence. Indeed, **the beginnings of Torah piety** developed in Babylonia, with religious Torah schools (and perhaps already also synagogues and simple services of the word). Circumcision (which was not customary among the Babylonians), the sabbath commandment, regulations about purity and food, and probably also commemorative feasts now became particularly important as signs of membership of the people of Yahweh; they were characteristics which distinguished the Jews from other peoples. The status of scribes and teachers of the law, who interpreted the Torah for all everyday instances, began to emerge.

Faced with the downfall of the state, people looked for something to hold on to, and since the Temple and the Temple cult were no more, this proved to be the oral and in part also the written **traditions**. From time immemorial, on the one hand there were **stories** (Hebrew *haggadah*, narrative) to illustrate the identity of the people: 'Who are we?' And on the other hand there were **laws** (Hebrew *halakhah*, literally 'the going', 'the direction') to regulate the conduct of the people: 'How do we live?' For no other nation in the future were the written traditions to be as important for preserving their own identity, even without a state, as they were for the people of Israel. There is no doubt that already in groups of educated exiles in Babylonia, many of these remaining traditions were collected, written down and edited.

The observance of the law (which marked people out from the 'Gentiles') and the cult of Yahweh, which was now understood in exclusive terms and was centralized, may have been what held the colonies of exiles together spiritually. Indeed, it was here that the presuppositions were created for a new **paradigm shift** of a major kind which was prepared for in the exile and completed after the return. Here Babylonian influence is unmistakable – the Mesopotamian calendar, Babylonian names, a Babylonian world-view – and above all, **Aramaic** now became the vernacular of the whole region. From it Israel took over the quadratic alphabet which is still in use, in place of the Phoenician alphabet.

In the face of the epoch-making catastrophe the exiles were strengthened in their faith and encouraged to new hope by the two great prophets of the exile, Ezekiel and 'Deutero-Isaiah'.

– 'Prophet of disaster' that he was, **Ezekiel,** called in Babylonia in 593, had first of all interpreted the exile completely and utterly as a punishment for the apostasy of the people from Yahweh. But from 587/86 on he had begun increasingly clearly also to express the hope of a renewal of human beings, a restoration of the united Israelite kingdom and a rebuilding of the Temple. Read above all his great vision of the resurrection of the dead bones,[5] which even now can reduce some Jews to tears. In a new way Ezekiel addresses individuals and their personal responsibility. He expected change to come about in individuals through the forgiveness of guilt, renewal of the heart and the bestowing of the divine spirit.

– '**Deutero-Isaiah**', the 'second Isaiah', is a prophet whose name we do not know, from the last years of the exile, before the downfall of the Babylonian empire. His message has been handed down in chapters 40-55 of the book of Isaiah. He proclaims with incomparable power of conviction the liberation and homecoming of the exiles as a new exodus from Egypt: a new journey – a journey through the wilderness – to Jerusalem for the rebuilding of the Temple. Deutero-Isaiah is the first prophet to proclaim an end-time ('eschatological') message, of a completely different, new, eternal age which is to replace the present age after the execution of judgment. And this prophet is also the first to advocate not just that practical monotheism which commits Israel to

Yahweh alone, regardless of other gods, but a theoretical monotheism which in principle denies the existence of other gods in any form.[6]

But what about **Palestine**? Here, too, where the majority of the country population had been left behind to work the estates and the vineyards, a new spiritual vigour became evident. The Babylonians had divided up the land of the exiles and in so doing had gained themselves many loyal subjects. And yet the five **Lamentations** (*threni*; only the fifth is a lament of the people), composed in a skilful metrical form, are not to be regarded simply as a description of the situation in Palestine at the time of the 'Babylonian captivity'. Whether composed in Jerusalem or in the exile, but at all events under the immediate impact of the dramatic events, they are primarily about the abandonment and destruction of the Holy City; like other psalms they bewail the catastrophe as the justified penal judgment of Yahweh on a people which has incurred guilt. However, even in Palestine the situation may slowly have become normalized. According to many present-day scholars it was here that the first form of the 'Deuteronomistic' history work came into being, that history compiled by one or more redactors under the influence of the book of Deuteronomy, which was to prove so important for later times. In its final form it was to comprise the newly-composed or revised books of Joshua, Judges, Samuel and Kings, and incorporated the book of Deuteronomy (by means of the introductory chapters 1-4). In this way the authors made use of the chronology of Israelite historiography.[7]

What was the consequence? Only now was the coherent and consistent monotheistic trend in Palestine able to establish itself – represented by the great prophets Jeremiah and Ezekiel along with the author of the Priestly Writing and the Deuteronomistic historian(s). It had been learned that the one God of Israel can be worshipped all over the earth. The **basic message** was now quite exclusively that Yahweh is the one and only God, Creator and Lord of the universe, before whom all other gods are nothing, do not exist. And Israel is his chosen people. So in the midst of the exilic period, in the midst of a time of shame and often despair, the foundation for a new hope was laid. The crisis of the Babylonian exile finally produced an entire new constellation, a quite different paradigm. We shall now consider this new paradigm – first of all in the context of Persian rule.[8]

2. Post-exilic consolidation: Temple and law

He had been hailed as the righteous one,[9] the shepherd,[10] indeed as Messiah:[11] **Cyrus II** from the Persian family of the Achaemenides, who was called the Great and who for the whole of the ancient world – even for the Greeks (see Xenophon's *Education of Cyrus*) became the embodiment of the ideal ruler. After shaking off Median rule and conquering Media and Lydia (the kingdom of the proverbially rich Croesus), in 539 he had entered Babylon in triumph to become the founder of the **Persian empire, which lasted for a good 200 years.** For many Iranians, even now Cyrus is the father of the fatherland. The land-bridge of Syria-Palestine (and later Egypt) was now also in Persian hands. Under Cambyses, the son of the founder of the empire (530-522), the Persian empire, the widest that history had so far seen, extended from the Indus to the Ionian coast of Asia Minor and to the First Cataract of the Nile. Under Darius the Great (522-486), Cyrus' second successor and a brilliant organizer, the kingdom was divided into twenty provinces or satrapies with uniform taxation and currency (a network of roads and a courier service followed). Cities like Persepolis and Susa, and the famous Royal Road from Susa to Sardes in Western Asia Minor were built, and Thracia and Macedonia were also incorporated into the empire... And what about Israel, which was by no means insignificant even for the Persians in terms of military strategy?

Cyrus' accession to power represented a new opportunity for tiny Israel. Whereas the Assyrian and even the Babylonian system of rule was based on military force (plundering, destruction, occupation, deportations, contributions) and on administrative co-ordination of the occupied territories, Cyrus' system of rule, and later that of the Achaemenids, was based on an amazing tolerance: on sparing opponents and encouraging the cultural and religious characteristics of the different areas of the empire. Instead of nationalism there was now universalism. Instead of Persian as the state language there was Aramaic, which was already widespread all over the ancient East in the neo-Babylonian/Chaldaean empire ('imperial Aramaic'; biblical Aramaic is a branch of it). This political strategy of tolerance – which in view of the failure of both Assyrian and Babylonian great-power politics was extremely realistic – may not have been idealism or even modern relativism, but the result of a clear political and economic calculation on the part of a ruler of Persia who otherwise ruled in a strict and despotic way: tolerance as a way of achieving political stability among the various subject-groups and motivation to work.

And yet in both a contemporary and a present-day perspective it represents a historical achievement of the first order.

In the context of such a policy – at any rate according to the report in the Book of Ezra – Cyrus was evidently moved to issue an **edict**[12] in the very first year of his reign, 538. He allowed the rebuilding of the Temple in Jerusalem at state expense and the return of the sacred vessels of the Temple which had been confiscated by Nebuchadnezzar. Scholars dispute as to whether, as is stated in a Hebrew version of this same decree,[13] at the same time permission was given for the exiles to return.[14] But Cyrus would hardly have been celebrated as messiah had he not given permission for this homecoming.[15]

However, the return was slow in coming about:[16] it was not until twelve years after the edict of Cyrus – and against the resistance of the provincial capital and its governor – that the **building of the 'Second Temple'** was begun, in 520 BCE. This took place under the Jewish-Persian governor Zerubbabel – following the energetic admonition of the prophets Haggai[17] and Zechariah.[18] These, moreover, gratefully proclaimed Zerubbabel, who was of the line of David, as messiah – for the first time in the history of Jewish messianism the messiah was a figure of contemporary history![19] Moreover it is remarkable that to this first messianic figure the prophet Zechariah added a second: the priest Joshua.[20] So in this early post-exilic period, to begin with there was evidently a tense eschatological expectation which looked for a completely new age, with a messianic government or direct rule by God.

However, the eschatological mood soon ebbed away. For in 515 BCE the '**Second Temple**' was solemnly **consecrated**.[21] This took place under the Great King of Persia, Darius, who was subsequently to hurl himself into fateful wars against the Greek city states because of the rebellion of the Greeks of Asia Minor (the Ionian Revolt, 499), action which led to his defeat by Athens at Marathon in 490. In comparison to the Temple of Solomon, this building is thought initially to have been of more modest proportions.[22] It no longer contained an ark of the covenant, but the seven-branched 'lampstand', Hebrew **Menorah**, which was now to become one of the most important pictorial images of Jewish religious art and later the symbol of the newly created state of Israel.

The Second Temple now provided a basis on which the restored institutions could quickly gain importance. Above all the priestly-theocratic trend established itself, and many earlier traditions revived. Now, after the downfall of the monarchy, the Temple was no longer royal property and a state temple; rather, financed by the people, it was a people's temple. At the same time it is clear that precisely as a result of this the priesthood also took on a new importance. At the head of the people there was now no longer a king to whom the chief priest was subordinate, but a 'high priest', who himself was the representative of Yahweh and whose significance was to increase even more considerably in the subsequent period.

However, political and religious conditions in Jerusalem were to go on remaining tense for a long time. A good seventy years after the return, around 465 BCE, an anonymous prophet under the name of 'Malachi' ('my messenger')[23] was already again complaining about the externalization of the cult, greedy priests, faithless people and mixed marriages; moreover the Jewish tradition regards this Malachi as the last – the seal – of the prophets. The Persian Great Kings must have been concerned to have peace and order on the land-bridge of Syria-Palestine, especially as they had to secure their lines of communication because of a rebellion in Egypt (460). Be this as it may, the Persian Great King, probably under the influence of Jewish circles in Babylonia, allowed himself to be persuaded to send two officials in the service of Persia to Jerusalem as royal commissioners (with an entourage) to carry out a state-backed reorganization of the post-exilic community in Judah. These were the two reformers Nehemiah and – before, alongside or after him? – Ezra.

Although **Nehemiah** came from a family of Jewish exiles, he had risen to be cupbearer to the Great King in Susa. What was his concern when in 445 BCE he arrived in a still desolate Jerusalem – appointed by Artaxerxes I as 'governor in the land of Judah'?[24] The answer is that he had a disinterested concern (he did not acquire any property or receive any payment other than goods in kind) above all for the **external security** and **internal reorganization** of the city:
– first the rebuilding of the city walls in fifty-two days, against renewed vigorous opposition from the provincial capital of Samaria;
– then a remission of debt for impoverished citizens, which had become necessary because of the excessive usury of the Jewish landed aristocracy;
– at the same time a reordering of property-holding and a resettling of country-dwellers in the underpopulated city;
– finally, measures against the desecration of the sabbath and mixed marriages, which threatened the existence of the very small Jewish community.

These measures, however, also **led the Jewish community in practice to keep itself apart** in a way which was to have effects on world history. Nehemiah himself returned to the Persian court after twelve years;

perhaps Judah had already become an independent province under him, and that must have accelerated the already lengthy process of alienation between south and north, Judah and Samaria. The cause of the alienation was primarily political, but now also increasingly took on a religious character.

And what was **Ezra's** concern? A priest from a Zadokite family which had been carried off to Babylon, according to an earlier view he came to Jerusalem, also under Artaxerxes I, with a new caravan of returnees as early as 458 BCE. Alternatively (according to the hypothesis of A. Hoonacker,[25] accepted by many scholars), he only came later, in 398 BCE. As 'scribe of the law of the God of heaven',[26] he too was intent on **religious and cultic reform**, which was also of political interest to the Persians. He took quite fanatical and mercilessly brutal steps against mixed marriages, and in solemn assembly proclaimed 'the law' to which the people had to commit themselves through the renewal of the covenant.[27] There is a still unresolved dispute as to whether this 'law' was the whole Pentateuch, just the Priestly Writing or Deuteronomy, or, less probably, the royal Persian law.[28] Given the consequences, it may have been the main body of the Pentateuchal traditions which were now elevated to become a binding legal norm. This is confirmed by the fact that in the fourth century the Samaritans took over the Pentaeuch – which accordingly would already be a work of the Babylonian Diaspora – as the official basis of their religion.

All this already shows the pressing concern of the moment: a **concentration on the law** which had already been laid down in the exile in the spirit of Deuteronomy: attain grace by observing the law! The lawbook contained in the book of Leviticus, the 'Holiness Code',[29] might already have been given its definitive form at that time. In addition to religious and ethical instructions, it contains above all cultic regulations relating to the slaughtering of animals and the eating of their meat; to sexual intercourse and sexual transgressions; to the holiness of the Temple, of priests, sacrifices, offerings and festivals; to the sabbatical year and the year of jubilee... All in all it was a Magna Carta for the renewal of the life of the people of Israel, though 'not in the prophetical sense of reconstruction through the Spirit, but rather through organization and law', as the exegete Georg Fohrer rightly observes.[30]

Now all that also means that we must be aware of the **ambivalence** of this development:

– On the one hand, after the beginnings of the Deuteronomic reform movement there was now, as Fohrer puts it, 'a legalistic attitude and a piety of the law to which it was impossible to deny either a deep

earnestness or a readiness for obedience to the divine will'. Even an 'inward assent to the law' could be felt.[31]
– On the other hand, however, life was 'kept within the narrow bounds of the law, regulated and schematized': 'The determining factor was the correct outward act, as must be the case with a legalistic orientation. That man was righteous and devout who fulfilled the divine requirements laid down in the law.'[32] In fact, here there was already a preparation for what was later to be called 'Jewish Orthodoxy'.

Be this as it may, at any rate in the biblical 'sources' this development is seen in a completely positive light. This is the case with the '**Chronicler**', presumably a levite belonging to the cultic personnel in Jerusalem. He is the author of the Chronistic history work, which glorifies David; the work originally also included the books of Nehemiah and Ezra, as a continuation of the two books of Chronicles. He has preserved for us both Ezra's account of his actions (written for the Persian imperial government or the Jews in Babylon)[33] and the memoirs of Nehemiah[34] in a work which was probably written around 300. In it the religious history of Israel is strongly stylized. We can also see the degree to which the Jewish community (above all the Pharisees) later revered the memory of the two great reformers from the way in which they included the books of Nehemiah and Ezra among the canonical holy books. Ezra in particular, who was often compared with Moses, was regarded as the founder of **early Judaism, a Judaism governed by the cult and by the law** – and leading away from the prophetic message. It is certainly not the case (as even so understanding an interpreter as Georg Fohrer[35] thinks) that a 'new religion' was introduced after the exile. But what I would call **a new epoch-making paradigm** of Israelite religion had broken through, which we must now go on to analyse more closely.

However, the community of **Samaria**, which significantly always associated the religious separation (the 'Samaritan schism') with the name of Ezra, the zealot for the law, subsequently retained only the Pentateuch. In Samaria, people had in any case never shared in the political and religious glorification of David, Jerusalem and the Temple, and had insisted on the autonomy of the Samaritan north. From the fourth century the separation from the Jewish south must be regarded as complete. However, it is no longer possible to establish precisely when Samaria erected its own sanctuary on Mount Gerizim near Shechem.[36] Be this as it may, for us the subsequent history of Israel will be only the history of Judah: it will be Judaean and also to this extent specifically Jewish history.

3. The new, Jewish paradigm: the theocratic community

So already about ninety years after the edict of Cyrus, around the year 450, there was a definitive breakthrough of the new constellation, the **completion of the new paradigm**. Here, too, the criteria for a paradigm shift are easy to recognize:

– First had to have come the fundamental crisis of the previous paradigm, that of the Davidic kingdom: the downfall of the kingdoms of Israel and Judah and the Babylonian exile.

– The new paradigm was already prepared for in the framework of the old: by the cultic reform of King Josiah.

– It was initiated on the one hand by the prophets and Deuteronomistic writers of the exilic and post-exilic period, and on the other hand by the rebuilding of the Temple.

– It was carried through by the priesthood, which now for the first time was elevated to power in the country.

And what are the **decisive characteristics** of this new constellation? Palestine was now part of the fifth Persian satrapy, 'Trans-Euphrates', lying beyond the river. Later it was presumably a separate province independent of Samaria, in which the priesthood under its 'high priest', relatively independent of the Persian central government, had taken over the spiritual and political leadership.

● So the basic pattern was **no longer** formed by the **monarchy**, the kingdom and thus political power. For a good century political power remained with the Persians, and was then to pass over to Alexander the Great and his Greek successors, and finally to the Romans.

● The basic pattern was provided on the one hand by the **Temple and the Temple hierarchy** of the holy city of Jerusalem, which was now the exclusive religious centre, and on the other hand by the collection of the **holy scriptures**, which now became binding **law**.

● So the form of rule was **theocracy**; here, while God himself did not exercise rule over the state, he did so over the **community of those** who believed in Yahweh – by means of the priesthood (hierocracy) and the law of God (nomocracy). All in all, then, this was no longer the **paradigm** of a monarchical state, but that of a **theocratic community**.

Granted, many prayers and songs which have come down from this time in the psalter centre on **the Temple** and the law, but here, too, we should not consider reality only from a religious aspect. For in time the Temple itself also became a **factor of economic power,** and its political influence must not be underestimated. Granted, in the future Judah was politically a land ruled by a variety of governors from the different occupying powers. On the other hand, as J.A.Soggin has rightly stressed, the Temple was 'the only place in which Judah could still exercise any form of self-determination, limited though it was; in this respect, too, it was helped by the religious tolerance of the Persians. Moreover the Temple had come to have significant economic importance because of the contributions which it regularly received from the Diaspora in its own currency (the obol) and because it performed functions which we might regard as those of a bank. There is therefore nothing strange in the fact that the religious authorities came to acquire increasing importance alongside the civil government, not only in matters of cult and belief, but also in everyday life.'[37] Moreover the Jerusalem Temple treasure was often to arouse the covetousness of foreign authorities...

So the time of the Second Temple and the holy scriptures in no way just brought **restoration**, as is often claimed, but also **innovation**, with new structural elements and a new concentration: no more and no less than an entire **new post-exilic constellation**, a **specifically Jewish theocracy paradigm** (Paradigm III = P III), which succeeded the pre-state tribal paradigm and the paradigm of the Davidic kingdom.

To leave no room for doubt here, either, it should be stressed that there was still the same primal message, the same **God Yahweh and his chosen people (and land)**. This remained the constant centre and foundation, and was also the substance of faith in this third Israelite paradigm. But the whole social and political framework, the 'entire constellation of beliefs, values, techniques', the macro-paradigm, is now different. Now Yahweh no longer rules directly as in the pre-monarchical period. Now, in this post-monarchical period, Yahweh rules in a **mediated** and **institutionalized** way on the basis of the Temple and the holy scriptures. And '**Israel**' – the precise significance of the name changes with the paradigm – is now no longer a kingdom but above all **a religious community** which God chose for himself so that it can serve him through Temple worship and observance of the law. Instead of a king, the high priest as God's representative and a Temple hierarchy as intermediaries hold office, and the Torah is now the will of God made scripture. In this sense, instead of monarchy there is now **theocracy**: hierocracy and nomocracy.

This has also already made it clear that the remarkable debates of Christian exegetes about the end of the history of the people of Israel are pointless. The history of the people of Israel goes on! For all the changes, there is no mistaking the spiritual and religious identity which maintains itself and indeed now in some respects is even intensified. So here there is not a total break, which would have dissolved the substance of Israelite faith, but a paradigm shift. What changes is the entire constellation of the common beliefs, values and techniques of the Israelite community which convey this substance and at the same time shape it: 'Israel' now becomes identical with '**Judaism**', not only politically and in terms of population, but also spiritually, in a religious way. The consequences are decisive. Let us look at them more closely.

4. The rise of the Jewish religion of the book

The second half of Persian rule – a good century between Nehemiah and Alexander the Great – has been called the 'dark century'.[38] Not because nothing important or just terrible happened in this period between the middle of the fifth and the fourth centuries BCE, but because there are no direct written accounts of it. However, at this time such great works as the Song of Songs were written. Now the **process of the canonization of the Hebrew scriptures** which was grounded in Deuteronomy and then began in the exile and the post-exilic period was **brought to a conclusion**. How did this happen?

In contrast, say, to the Greeks, who were particularly interested in physics and metaphysics, the Israelites were above all interested in their history, how it was initiated and guided by the living God with living people. Indeed all the stories (*haggadah*) and instructions (*halakhah*) deal with it. Now, at the latest after the exile, these very different traditions of different ages, which I cited in the very first chapters of this book, were given their definitive fixed written form – by a variety of redactors in a strictly monotheistic spirit. Everything was to appear as a **history of the people of Israel with its God Yahweh**, progressing from beginning to end, coherent throughout, a human drama and yet meaningful in itself:

– all the old traditions, sagas and legends of the creation of the world and the fall of humankind; of the great flood and the covenant of God with humanity under Noah; of the patriarchs Abraham, Isaac and Jacob and Jacob's twelve sons; of the liberation from Egypt, the making of the covenant on the mountain of God and the entry into the promised land;

– and in addition the whole complex of legal material which had grown up in the course of centuries;

– as well as the writings of the prophets (their canonization strengthened the impression that all prophecy was concluded);

– and also all the chronicles, the Deuteronomistic history and now (probably in the fourth-third centuries) also the Chronistic history work.[39]

The Torah will have been in existence, if not already during the exile, then at least at the end of the fifth and beginning of the fourth centuries, and the 'Prophets' at the latest by the end of the third century. A third group, later called 'Writings' by the rabbis, may have been completed relatively late. As we saw, the Jews call the whole work which thus came into being 'Tanakh', after the initial letters of the three parts (Torah – Nebi'im – Khetubim); Christians call it the 'Old (not 'out-dated'!) Testament'. According to the Jewish view it consists of the following parts:[40]

- Law/instruction, 'Torah': the Pentateuch of the 'Five Books of Moses': Genesis, Exodus, Leviticus, Numbers, Deuteronomy;
- Prophets, 'Nebi'im': Joshua, Judges, and the books of Samuel and Kings; the great writing prophets Isaiah, Jeremiah, Ezekiel; and the so-called twelve 'minor' prophets;
- Writings: 'Ketubim': Psalms, Proverbs, Job, Song of Songs, Ruth, Lamentations, Koheleth, Esther, Daniel, Ezra, Nehemiah and the books of Chronicles.

These three groups of books form the 'Biblia' (originally plural: the books), the book *par excellence* which comprises the 'canonical' = 'normative' writings, which contains God's revelation: 'holy scripture', because God himself is regarded as its author. Directly or indirectly, according to the understanding of faith, in it **God's word and will** are expressed: quite directly in the Torah; more indirectly and with human collaboration through the prophets; with even greater human involvement through the other writings. All these writings are to be studied, and the most important are also to be read aloud in worship.

So now **worship through the word** more and more markedly takes its place alongside sacrificial worship; it is independent of the sacrifices and is even echoed among the Temple priesthood. And now the **synagogue** more and more markedly takes its place alongside the Temple; as we heard, its beginnings may go back to the Babylonian exile, when there was no Temple. But that means that even in Judaism the book did not stand at the beginning. Only from now on can we talk of a Jewish **religion of the book** – alongside the centralized **religion of the Temple**.

However, a religion of the book develops its own forms – with consequences for worship. From as early as the time of David onwards, incomparably personal prayers can be found in Judaism: psalms full of the deepest human emotions, an expression of despair, of trust, of anxiety, repentance and hope. But only now do we also find in Judaism alongside personal prayer **communal prayers of the people which have been fixed in writing**: hymns (psalms), confessions of sin and intercessions. These constitute the service of the word and also accompany the sacrificial cult. Indeed we may follow the leading Jewish liturgical historian Ismar Elbogen in calling the institution of fixed community prayers without exaggeration a 'radical innovation of the Second Temple period'.[41] Or, as another leading Jewish liturgical scholar, Joseph Heinemann, puts it: 'Fixed prayer, in and of itself constituting the entirety of the divine service, was a startling innovation in the ancient world, which both Christianity and Islam inherited from Judaism.'[42]

The changes for the whole of Jewish private piety, too, were far-reaching, and here the American Jewish scholar Jacob Neusner has precisely summed up the decisive feature. What does life under the law mean down to the present day? 'Life under the law means praying – morning, evening, at night and at mealtimes, both routinely and when something extraordinary happens. In order to be a Jew... one consciously lives in awareness of the presence of God and is constantly prepared to praise and thank God. The way of the Torah is the way of constant devotion to God.'[43]

To sum up: with the canonization of scripture goes something like a **canonization of the liturgy**. As the Protestant exegete James Charlesworth has worked out, there is 'the dual process of canonization of scripture and "canonization" of the liturgy'.[44] The consequence is a far more homogeneous, conformist religion, which found the prophetic talk of individuals increasingly suspicious. We might ask why.

5. The quenching of prophecy – and the consequences to the present day

Can we overlook the fact that this whole process – as far as scripture, liturgy and power structures are concerned – represented a **consolidation** and **constriction** of religion which was not without its dangers?
Referring to Georg Fohrer, I have already indicated that:
– The concentration of Judaism on the law, which was to guarantee the unity of faith and action, brought with it the threat of **legalism**.
– An excessive emphasis on the Temple, the place of God's presence, brought with it the threat of **ritualism**.
– An accretion of power to the priesthood, which claimed to provide the mediation between human beings and God, brought with it the threat of **clericalism**.

As in all religions, so too in the history of Israelite religion there was constantly consolidation and constriction. What was the difference now – after the exile? There was no longer any **prophecy** as a counterbalance to the institution. There was no charismatic protest against all kinds of fossilizations in the name of the sovereign freedom of God himself. No, prophecy too was affected by the post-exilic paradigm shift.

Certainly, there were still a few prophets after the prophets of the court and the sanctuaries had disappeared. But instead of coming forward as charismatic messengers of God, as in classical times, after the Exile they increasingly became authorized interpreters of the tradition – one might think of 'Trito-Isaiah'[45] and 'Deutero-Zechariah'[46] – scribal prophets or prophetic scribes. That is understandable. For where everything was governed by an order which had been turned into law and writings, the sayings of the prophets could be hardly more than an exploitation of earlier prophecy. Indeed, there was now a remarkable extension, but at the same time a dilution of the term 'prophet'. For **all** the authors of holy scripture, including Moses and David, were now regarded as sacred **writers**, and in this sense could quite directly be called 'prophets'. Moreover Judaism as a whole could now be called a 'prophetic' religion, in a generalized way which also perhaps made the description innocuous. In one of the Psalms we find the complaint, 'there is no prophet more...'[47] And later the rabbis were to say that after the death of the prophets Haggai, Zechariah and Malachi the Holy Spirit had departed from Israel.[48] We cannot ignore the fact that the more prophetic influence declined, the stronger legalistic piety became.

We have to pause briefly here, since we are face to face with a momentous development which also has its parallels in the two other prophetic religions. Who could ignore the fact that the ebbing away and quenching of prophecy after a heyday is also a problem in **Christianity**, where Jesus Christ is regarded as the eschatological prophet after John as his forerunner,[49] and where the male and female prophets who were at first strongly represented in the original community died out towards the end of the second century. Be this as it may, in Paul prophets were still second to the apostles in the hierarchy of charisms.[50] So what happened to the prophets, to prophetic discourse, to this important charisma?[51] According to Paul, in worship **all** should express themselves prophetically,[52] but always according to the measure of their faith in Christ.[53] According to Ephesians, the church is founded on the apostles and the prophets (of the new covenant).[54] But how did the historical development turn out? Like the scribes in Judaism after the Exile, so the bishops in the church after the first century – doubtless also faced with many false prophets and particularly in view of the Montanist crisis – began to integrate the prophetic function into their apostolic 'ministry'. The more time went on, the more they felt themselves to be successors not only of the apostles, but also of the prophets and the teachers. Hierarchical church law increasingly took the place of free prophecy. So what happened to the prophetic impulses in Christianity?

To take the question further: is not the quenching of prophecy also a problem in Islam? Certainly here the prophets before Muhammad are highly esteemed as his forerunners: alongside those who received a revelation of the book there were also many other *nabi*s (= ordinary prophet: according to tradition there were 313 of these, but according to the mystical tradition 124,900!).[55] However, after Muhammad, who once again proclaimed the message of the former prophets in its original purity and thus at the same time also brought it to a conclusion, prophetic impulses seem to have been ruled out for subsequent millennia. Muhammad is the 'seal' of any prophecy. Not least because of this 'exclusiveness' today in Islam the law, or the *shari'a*, has largely overshadowed the originally prophetic message of the Qu'ran – even in the view of some Muslims. The result is that nowadays in fact it is not so much the message of the prophet himself, as the religious law developed centuries after him that has the highest authority. What has happened to the prophetic impulses in Islam?

It is therefore clear that nowadays the quenching of prophecy is a question for all three 'prophetic' religions. Think of all the difficulties that **Christianity** had, and has, with such prophetic figures as Francis of Assisi, Martin Luther, the Wesley brothers or the Black South Africans Hendrik Witbooi of Namibia and Simon Kimbangu of Congo! Think how many problems **Judaism** had with the mediaeval Kabbalist Abraham Abulafia, then with Franz Rosenzweig or Martin Buber! Think how many difficulties modern **Islam** had with modern reformers like al-Afghani, Ahmad Khan and Mahmud Taha of the Sudan! Is prophecy to be only the charism of individuals and not a dimension of the whole people of God under the inspiration of the prophets? Are the **prophetic** religions nowadays doing justice to their own claim to be **prophetic** religions? Or is 'prophetic' religion only an academic category in the history of religions which hardly describes the specific reality of religion as it is lived out? Critical questions which point forward are justified here.

There is no doubt about it: numerous people in the prophetic religions long for the prophetic religions to be more prophetic, so that they may put more faith in their prophetic message. But the question for us now is: how did things develop in Israel after prophecy was quenched in its classical form? Who had taken the place of the prophets in Palestine?

6. Hellenistic world culture: the period of the wise men

The place of the prophets was initially taken by the wisdom teachers, whose concerns were entirely practical. However, these wise men were no longer charismatic individuals, but representatives of a school. They no longer proclaimed Yahweh's revelation and liberation, but attached importance to observing the ordinances of life, to pedagogical applications of them in the everyday world. The focus of their interest was not God and his action in history but human beings and how they were to act correctly in a great variety of spheres in life. Wisdom theology does not presuppose the recognition of the mighty acts of God in 'salvation history' (exodus and settlement play no decisive theological role here). What is important is, rather, the confidence that all of creation rests on a wise order, and that human beings are capable of correct conduct by observing this order which has been appointed by God and thus can find their place in the divine world order. In complete contrast to the prophet, in Israel the wise man is primarily an empiricist, a detached observer, one who maintains a clever balance between the extremes, though his work is focussed on the communication of existential experience.

Where are the beginnings of Israelite wisdom teaching, a kind of wisdom which can be detected throughout the whole of the ancient Near East at that time? Individual proverbial material may well go back to the time of King Solomon. In that case the term used is '**earlier wisdom**'. Throughout the monarchy there were individual wisdom teachers, and as early as the time of the prophet Jeremiah, alongside the king and the court, the priests and the prophets, there is express mention of a group of wise men.[56] During the Exile, though, both in Mesopotamia and in Egypt the exiles were exposed to an international wisdom culture; this means that the flourishing of wisdom literature after the Exile is not as surprising as all that. Nowadays it is described as '**later wisdom**': proverbs, admonitions and instructions were now reshaped or compiled and collected in books. Through the inclusion of creation and revelation, wisdom became a comprehensive theological system, wisdom theology: divine wisdom was the teacher of human beings.

However, the **crisis of wisdom** which is recorded in books like **Job** and **Koheleth** shows how little Jewish piety had really been consolidated. despite all attempts at restoration, all institutionalization and canonization. A good century after the return from Exile, above all one of the fundamental doctrines of Jewish belief in God, the doctrine of retribution, of God's righteousness which rewards and punishes, and which was advocated both by wisdom theology and by the piety of the law, had been shattered: this was the theory that there is a connection between how one does and how one fares which human beings can recognize. Do we really reap what we have sown? This is precisely what is vigorously disputed in the book of Job, and even more in a book like Koheleth, which was probably accepted into the canon only because it was attributed to Solomon. For Koheleth, a man who was more a sceptical philosopher than a theologian, the break with ancestral belief in retribution has already become a fundamental problem. Koheleth embodies the thought 'of the parting of the ways, the boundary between two times', in which 'under the impact of the spiritual crisis of early Hellenism, his critical thought could no longer make sense of traditional wisdom and... traditional piety and the cult'; but even Koheleth, with a more Socratic and conservative disposition, avoided 'breaking with the religion of the fathers and identifying God, say, with incalculable fate'.[57] In view of this crisis of wisdom, the **Book of Proverbs**, like Jesus Sirach, seeks a new trust in the divine order, in the wisdom of God the Father, in the universality and reliability of God's plan. To this degree these are books of restoration, the restoration of traditional belief in Yahweh.[58]

However, the crisis of wisdom simply reflected a more deep-seated **structural crisis of the era.** In order to understand its political dimensions we must look at northern Greece, from where the greatest danger now began to threaten for the Persian empire. For the Macedonian king **Philip II** (359-336) had been astonishingly successful in bringing together the Greek city-states, engaged in constant rivalry after the battle of Marathon, in the 'Corinthian Alliance' against the Persians; at the same time he developed a new military unit, the tightly-packed phalanx, into a feared Greek battle formation. The focal point of world history began to shift from east to west: for the first time a **major European power** appeared on the scene of world history.[59]

However, it was not Philip, but his son, who was to take up the war against the Persians finally and succesfully, in 336, after Philip's murder. **Alexander**, twenty years old, educated by the brilliant philosopher Aristotle, and known as 'the Great', changed the face of the earth, both politically and culturally, in no more than thirteen years. The first European invasion of Asia was the work of Alexander, who was a strategist on a grand scale. After the conquest of Asia Minor, in 334 he turned south, occupied the coastal cities of Phoenicia (including Tyre, the mother city of Carthage, after a seven months' siege), Palestine, and finally Egypt. There, crowned with the double crown of the Pharaohs, he had the city built which bears his name to the present day – Alexandria. What about Jerusalem? Jerusalem seems to have surrendered voluntarily on Alexander's march through the land to Egypt – in contrast to Samaria, which also tried to rebel later.

Back from Egypt, Alexander turned northwards, defeated the last Persian Great King Darius III at the battle of Gaugamela in 331, and entered Babylon without a fight. After also capturing Susa, Persepolis, and Ecbatana, and after the murder of Darius by one of his satraps, Alexander had achieved his goal. He entered into the heritage of the Achaemenids, only to press on immediately to the 'ends of the earth', the foot of the Himalayas. However, Alexander wanted more than mere military conquest. He imposed the **union of Greek and Eastern blood, ceremonial and culture.** He had ten thousand Greek officers and soldiers married to Persian women in Susa in a kind of mass wedding. So although he died in Babylon in 323 – completely unexpectedly, at the age of thirty-three, of a fever, without any heirs capable of ruling – he forcibly introduced a new age: after the Persian era came the **Hellenistic** era.

This Greek cosmopolitan '**Hellenism**' deliberately encouraged by Alexander, this mutual interpenetration of Greek and Eastern culture in the states which succeeded to Alexander's empire, and the consequent religious universalism and syncretism, represented **an enormous challenge to the Jewish religion**. Was a new paradigm shift perhaps announcing itself here? Would Judaism now also become a world religion with a universalistic orientation as a result of its encounter with the universalistic world culture of Hellenism, since its ethical monotheism already exercised a strong fascination on many non-Jews everywhere, and therefore the Jewish mission was also increasingly successful?[60]

What we note, rather, is the opposite development. Certainly there is a by no means insignificant collection of Hellenistic Jewish writings: alongside the historian Jason of Cyrene and the philosopher Aristobulus in the second century BCE there is the towering figure of the philosopher Philo of Alexandria (15/10 BCE - 40/50 CE), a contemporary of Jesus of Nazareth, who attempted to reconcile the Jewish religion with Greek philosophy by interpreting the Pentateuch in his commentaries with the help of allegorical methods of interpretation taken over from the Greek Stoa. He also attempted to discuss the creation story, the legislation of Moses and the patriarchal narratives systematically in a Hellenistic spirit. But in the end, all these efforts remained episodes. In the middle and long term the consequence of the encounter with Hellenism was, rather, a strengthening of the traditional Jewish piety of Temple and Torah.

Does all this 'no longer belong to the theme of the history of the people of Israel'?[61] No, the history of the people does not come to an end here. But it does enter into a long-drawn-out, fundamental crisis which will finally result in a further epoch-making paradigm shift.

7. The crisis of theocracy: from the revolution to the 'church state'

Beyond doubt the culture of the Hellenistic world also exerted a strong influence on Palestine, especially after the second century BCE, above all in the cities, which were becoming increasingly more numerous, and among the educated and well-to-do, particularly in Jerusalem, where the rich aristocratic priestly families lived. A marked increase in building activity and the creation of works of art, a heightening of efficiency in the economy, administration and among the military were a mark of Hellenistic culture anyway, and led to a general raising of living standards. People were concerned to show that they were enlightened. Even high priests now increasingly often had Hellenistic names. On the other hand, however, not only in the Diaspora but also in Judaea, powerful circles loyal to the law stood firm against Hellenistic influence, at least in their own religious sphere. After the first power struggles among Alexander's generals, known as the Diadochi (= successors), with their changing fortunes, this was already true for the rule of the Egyptian Ptolemies (the Thirty-First and last Egyptian dynasty) over Palestine for about a century (300-200/198 BCE).

The centre was now the rapidly growing new city of Alexandria. Here the Hellenization of Judaism was to find its most visible expression. For as the knowledge of Hebrew and Aramaic had declined in the great Jewish community of Alexandria, in succession first the Pentateuch and then the whole of the Hebrew Bible were translated into Greek. As we heard, legend attributes this work to 'seventy' translators – hence the name **Septuagint** (Greek for seventy).

However, the periods of harmony and cultural interaction were soon to be disrupted when the Seleucids, advancing from the region of Mesopotamia and Syria, displaced the Ptolemies from Palestine. After five 'Syrian wars' over the land-bridge of Syria-Palestine, the Seleucids took possession of Palestine. And after initial tolerance there were increasingly pointed attempts to advance the **Hellenization of Jerusalem** (Greek language, constitution, theatre, stadium, gymnasium...). The question was whether a reformed Judaism, adapted to the new time, could not be a significant possibility. At the time this possibility was also affirmed by some Jewish reformers.

For those who were faithful to the law, however, any reform was apostasy. At all events, opposition to this Hellenization grew among the people. There was an explosion in 169 BCE when the Seleucid king Antiochus IV Epiphanes appropriated the Temple treasure to improve the state's financial position for a campaign in Egypt. He twice had to occupy Jerusalem. Then he made the city a Hellenistic military colony, which in effect amounted to a **forcible Hellenization** of Israel. In 167 there was a ban on cultic worship in accordance with the law, circumcision and the observance of the sabbath; those loyal to the Torah were persecuted; and pagan cults were forced on the people. There was even what the book of Daniel calls the 'abomination of desolation'[62]: an altar to Zeus on the altar of burnt offering in the Temple.

The conflict between traditional Jewish and Hellenistic culture now escalated enormously, and the hour had come for **a revolution by the people of the land,** those of the old faith – inspired and led by the priest Mattathias and his five sons from the family of Hasmon: the **Hasmonaeans.**[63] The third son, Judas, called **Maccabaeus** (Aramaic *maqqabay* = the 'hammer man'), managed to defeat the Syrian Seleucid troops in three battles. In 164 BCE he entered Jerusalem and removed the pagan abomination – but without attacking the Seleucid garrison in the citadel (Akra) of Jerusalem, the sign of Syrian supremacy. On 14 December of the same year the desecrated Temple was solemnly reconsecrated, and to the present day Jews throughout the world mark this date by the feast of Hanukkah (the 'purification' of the Temple), which as the 'Feast of Lights' (with the eight-branched Hanukkah lampstand) has turned into a kind of Jewish Christmas.

What were the political consequences? Reaction among the people was split. The group of the 'pious' ("Hasidim'), from which the party of 'Pharisees' was later to come, was content with **spiritual and religious autonomy** under Syrian and Seleucid supremacy. The same was even more true of a group of radically pious Jews, called 'Essenes', who probably broke away in protest as early as this; some of them even began to emigrate into the wilderness. The Maccabaean movement took precisely the opposite view: they were now also intent on the political autonomy of Judaea – among other things by means of a dangerous defence treaty made in 161 with the rising great power of Rome! The result was a series of wearisome struggles.

The third party, the Hellenizing 'Sadducees', composed of the leading priests and aristocratic families, under pressure from both sides, eventually called on the Seleucids for help: initially, moreover, the Seleucids even defeated the Maccabees, and Judas lost his life. But his brother **Jonathan** continued the struggle, first as a guerrilla leader, then as high priest, and two years later also as '*strategos* (general) of Judaea' (150 BCE). Thus in Judaea, for the first time for more than four hundred years, spiritual and secular power were combined in one person. In 141 Jonathan's older brother and successor **Simon** – who in 142 had been recognized as high priest and independent ruler by the Seleucid rulers – also captured the Akra of Jerusalem and forced the evacuation of the Syrian occupying forces. A year later the people bestowed on him the hereditary honours of general, prince and high priest. After his murder these passed to his son **John**, with the name **Hyrcanus I** (135/4-104); he thus *de facto* became the first king (and high priest) of the Hasmonaean dynasty. Under him Judaea became politically independent and was only nominally under Seleucid supremacy. So with Simon and John the Maccabees had achieved their great aim: not only religious but political autonomy. But how was the religious renewal faring?

With such a priest-king, **theocracy** now seemed to have found **its most marked expression**. Yet in the land of Israel people were anything but content with the Hasmonaeans. The opposition became increasingly vociferous: the 'pious', the popular **'Pharisees'** (= Aramaic *perishayya*, from the Hebrew *perushim*, those 'set apart' by their piety). For these, observance of the law, interpreted in a binding way by oral tradition, was more important than any nationalism. For this group the new priest-kingship had already been all too secular, by no means religious enough, for a long time.

Faced with this pious opposition, John Hyrcanus was forced to rely completely on the Hellenistic party of the Sadducees, for whom only the Pentateuch, and not just any tradition, was binding. He was able to hold the line, but his son and successor, **Alexander Jannaeus** (103-76), who now also formally took the title of king – which according to the views of the orthodox was reserved for a son of David – had to maintain his rule with bloody terror. After his victory, Alexander ended a rebellion by the Pharisees which had gone on for several years by crucifying 800 of the rebels.[64] The wars of faith had long since become wars of conquest: not only the coastal cities and Galilee, but also large parts of Transjordan, had been seized.

The two books of Maccabees – which were not included in the Jewish canon – recount the history of the rebellion and the rule of the Maccabees from 175-135, without glossing anything over or playing it down.[65] This is a history which in our day has again become a symbol of the Jewish concern for self-assertion. As N.K.Gottwald has rightly pointed out, it is an irony of history that 'Judas, the first Maccabee, had led a majority of Jews against a small but powerful group of Jewish Hellenizers and their Seleucid backers. In a turnabout, Alexander Jannaeus, a successor of the Maccabees, now led a small but powerful group of royal supporters in a desperate battle against a majority of countrymen who saw him as an embodiment of Hellenistic corruption and oppression.'[66] Thus any exploitation of the Maccabees for contemporary political ends is questionable.

The almost eighty years of Jewish independence under the Hasmonaeans (142-63) was to remain an interlude – it lasted only as long as there was a power vacuum on the land-bridge of Palestine. That was not to be very long. The **Roman empire** had long since pushed forward its Eastern frontiers to Greece and Asia Minor, and Pompey, Caesar's rival, now chief commander in Asia, was intent on having a new order in Asia Minor.[67] Called on as an arbitrator by Hyrcanus and

Aristobulus, who were at odds over the Hasmonaean succession, Pompey in fact acceded to the request of delegates from the Jewish people: having had more than enough of any Hasmonaean royal rule, these once again called for a separation betwen religious and political rule. In other words, they wanted a **restoration of priestly rule, to be limited to the religious and cultic sphere.** They were ready to cede political rule to the new world power, Rome: 'The supporters of Hyrcanus agreed to this and handed Jerusalem over to Pompey. Aristobulus entrenched himself on the Temple Mount, which was captured after a three-month siege. Thus after almost a century of struggle, of temporary political freedom and a Jewish state, the Maccabean movement had come to grief on the selfishness of a Hasmonaean ruler who came from its ranks.'[68]

The result of this policy was that **Judaea** was now a **vassal state of Rome** – very much reduced, without the coastal cities and without access to the Mediterranean. The high priest was stripped of his power: he was denied the title of king and the right to levy taxes. Now he ruled only over the faith community in Jerusalem, and temporarily still as ethnarch by courtesy of the Romans. And what about the Hasmonaeans? Because of their dangerous political connections with the Parthians – Rome's great opponents in Asia Minor – the Romans later allowed the whole family to be exterminated. A Judaized Idumaean was to get the 'credit' for this cruel business, a district governor of Galilee who had fled to Rome, son of Antipater Hyrcanus II by the daughter of an Arabian prince, who in fact had shortly beforehand been appointed by the Roman senate as 'allied king' (*rex socius*) of Judaea – which in fact meant that he was its vassal king. This was **Herod**, later also called '**the Great**'.[69] In 37 he captured Jerusalem with Roman help and, sly, cruel and purposeful as he was, established a state which, while dependent on Rome (it was indirectly under the senate), was nevertheless relatively independent, and was no smaller than the Hasmonaean kingdom.

In Jerusalem Herod ostentatiously acted as a Judaean; he did not attack the Jewish cult and supported Diaspora Judaism: he developed Jerusalem and the Temple to give them great splendour, and secured peace and prosperity for the city and the whole country through the *Pax Romana*. However, he was deeply hated by the people, and particularly by those with a strict faith. As king he was virtually **the counterpart to the great David**. Why? A Roman and of mixed birth, he built or enlarged Hellenistic palaces, temples and cities everywhere (for example, Samaria was renamed Sebaste, Augusta, 'imperial city', in honour of Augustus), encouraged emperor worship, and built or rebuilt numerous fortresses – signs of his reign of terror (the citadels of

Jerusalem, Machaerus and Masada on the Dead Sea). Worse than that, though, he manipulated high priests at will, encouraged the separation of state and religion, violently nipped any opposition in the bud, and just on suspicion killed all potential successors in the Hasmonaean family and his own (from eight marriages in all). The victims included his second wife Mariamne, great-niece of the high priest Hyrcanus; Hyrcanus himself, at the age of eighty; and three of his own sons, the third murdered just a few days before his own death. All this forms the background to the New Testament legend of the murder of the children at Bethlehem (carried out on Herod's orders) in the Gospel of Matthew, and also provided material for the great dramatists of world literature, from Hans Sachs and Calderon through Voltaire to Friedrich Hebbel...

From the time of the Hasmonaeans, the internal political struggle in Judaea was mainly dominated by the battle between the rich Hellenized upper class of the **Sadducees**, who collaborated with the Roman forces of occupation, and those pious people who were anti-Greek, the **Pharisees**; these were interested in a life under the law, 'righteousness', and judgment. The Pharisees now gained increasing support from the people. There is no question that under Roman supremacy, with its religious toleration, the theocratic paradigm consolidated itself further and had become **a kind of church-state** – again with the **Temple** as an economic, political and religious centre.[70] Even Herod and his successors (after Herod's death in 4 BCE, the emperor Augustus divided the Herodian kingdom among his three younger sons), and also the Roman governors (procurators) with a seat in Caesarea Maris (they included the well-known Pontius Pilate, 26-36 CE), in general respected the structure of theocratic power and rule represented by the **priestly hierarchy**, which the Jews regarded as having been legitimated by God himself, the supreme Lord. Religion, the dispensation of justice, administration, and to a limited degree also politics, are here indissolubly bound up together. The central organ of government, administration and justice, responsible for all religious matters and matters of civil law, was not a Jewish king but the **Supreme Council** in Jerusalem – in Greek *synhedrion* (= 'assembly', hence Aramaic *sanhedrin*) – with the high priest at its head. The ruling classes of the country were represented in it; in addition to the Sadducaic priests and aristocrats these were above all the 'scribes' (theologian-lawyers) of both the Sadducaean-priestly and Pharisaic-popular trends. The Sanhedrin consisted of precisely seventy men under the presidency of the high priest, who, although utterly dependent on the king and the occupying forces, was still regarded as the supreme representative of the Jewish people. However, whether they were expressed openly or in secret, the expectations widespread among the people were quite different from those in the hierarchical establishment.

8. The apocalyptists – warning and interpreting the time

Under the pressure of events, on the periphery of the theocratic paradigm, among the circles of the 'Hasidim' a novel interpretation of history came into being, and a new literature of 'apocalyptic' (= 'un-veiling', 'revelation'), which took up again the earlier end-time, eschatological hope. Now above all in the form of prophecies, testaments, dreams and visions, in rich imagery and numerical speculation, it claimed to be able to 'un-veil' the divine mysteries and above all the future. What was unveiled here?[71]

The apocalyptists had already taken the place of the prophets and the wise men, warning and interpreting the time, as visionaries, seers and dreamers, in the crisis of the Maccabaen period. And it was the **book of Daniel** in which – after a number of preliminary stages in prophetic literature – the apocalyptic proclamation came to be fully elaborated. A book by the prophet Daniel? It has now been demonstrated that because of its language, its theology (the later theology of angels) and its unitary composition, the book of Daniel cannot in any way come from the seer at the Babylonian court in the sixth century BCE. Rather, its author comes from the second century, concealed behind the mask of Daniel, and writes in the time of that brutal Hellenizer Antiochus IV Epiphanes. Moreover, in the Jewish canon the book is not put among the 'Prophets', but among the 'Writings'.

The book of Daniel represents another, less political than **theological form of reaction** to political repression and the cultural struggle between Judaism and Hellenism. This now called above all for a new answer to the meaning of history: 'This extraordinarily aggressive Seleucid expansionary pressure southwards, bound up with the seductions of Hellenistic culture, which in Jerusalem led to mass if often also concealed apostasy among the well-to-do, clergy and aristocracy – even to the point of doing away with the Torah – brought about such fundamental crisis among pious circles in Judaism both externally and internally that it gave rise to that completely changed theology of history which we call apocalyptic.'[72] This changed theology of history, often bound up with the expectation of a final cosmic catastrophe and the coming of the kingdom of God, had two momentous consequences – in terms of its later historical effects.

One was that for the first time in the history of the Jewish people, belief in an **individual resurrection from the dead** came into being. That is understandable, since in the face of such a time of persecution – for the author of the book of Daniel virtually an emergency in which men, women and children were being cruelly tortured for holding firm to the law – the old problem of just retribution posed itself far more sharply than it had done generations before. New questions emerged – different ones from those in the time of the Ptolemies and Koheleth, who in his melancholy delight in this world (enjoy life while it lasts!) is far removed from the traditional theology of retribution in the wisdom literature, but equally far removed from any joyful hope for a world to come. Now, in the face of the loyalty of many martyrs to the faith – they had been faced with the crazy alternative of apostasy or death – unprecedented new questions emerge. What can be the significance of a martyr death if those who are loyal to the faith no longer receive any recompense? They do not receive it in this life, since they are already dead, nor in the life to come, since that is only a shadow existence. Where is the just God with his righteousness – in particular for those who are most righteous of all?

The answer of the apocalyptist Daniel is that this emergency will be followed by the end-time, now! Israel will be saved and – here is the new element – the dead will rise again: both the witnesses to the faith and their persecutors. The dead who have slept in the 'land of dust' will awaken. They will return to life as whole human beings (and not just, say, Platonically as 'souls'), in this this-worldly existence, but that existence will now last eternally, without end: for the wise in the form of eternal light, for the others in the form of eternal shame (this too is not elaborated on). 'The wise will shine like the splendour of the firmament and the many will be led to righteousness, like the stars for ever and ever.'[73] This passage should be noted: this text from Daniel is the earliest, indeed the **only undisputed evidence for a resurrection from the dead** in the whole of the Hebrew Bible! However, outside the Hebrew canon, in the Greek Septuagint, there are further testimonies to this hope of resurrection which emerged at so late a stage – especially in II Maccabees, which contains the oldest Jewish accounts of martyrs, accounts which became the model for the Christian acts of martyrs. Thus belief in the resurrection became a main theme of Judaism in the century and a half before Christ.

A **second development** is just as important. In view of the way in which history had gone completely astray, the traditional **messianic expectation** among the Jewish people, the coming of a 'Son of David', had lost its power of conviction – and that was as a result of history itself. Apocalyptic circles in Palestine had now become convinced that help could now come only from God's emissary sent directly from heaven: another, pre-existent bringer of salvation, kept hidden with God. So, strikingly, the Davidic messiah is completely absent from a number of apocalyptic writings. The place of the Davidic, earthly messiah is taken by the pre-existent and transcendent judge and saviour figure of the **Son of Man**: only later in Palestine was there a fusion of the Son of Man with the traditional messiah figure.[74]

This period, which was largely shaped by apocalyptic, saw the birth, barely noticed by the wider world and not listed in its chronicles, of that Jew who was to become the destiny of Judaism and Christianity: **Jesus of Nazareth**, called the 'Son of Man'. There was already vigorous controversy over him in his lifetime, and a small but rapidly growing group of Jews was firmly convinced of his resurrection to new life after a violent death.

We shall hear more of him later in this book. Here I want to recount further the history of the Jewish people, which is exciting enough, given a new shift in the times.

9. The fall of Jerusalem and the end of theocracy

Quite independently of the execution of Jesus of Nazareth around the year 30 CE – the Romans liquidated him as one of the numerous Jewish trouble-makers – the political and religious crisis of Judaism had heightened dramatically in subsequent decades. Jewish freedom fighters above all in Galilee, and urban guerrillas in Jerusalem, Zealots and Sicarii (dagger men), had already for a long time been carrying out attacks on the Roman forces of occupation. These forces were represented by rapacious, insensitive and politically incompetent procurators, who allowed themselves some very stupid incursions into the religious sphere.[75]

However, the great rebellion against Roman power only came around forty years after Jesus' death, in the years 66-70 of our era. We are well informed about the course of events, since the Jewish writer Flavius Josephus, who was himself involved in the rebellion in Galilee but later became a protégé of the Flavian emperors, described the ultimately breath-taking events in his book *On the Jewish War*. His account is detailed, but biassed throughout (against the Zealots and in favour of Rome). And yet at that time there was not just a conspiracy by a single revolutionary group or party, which then kept snowballing, as Josephus suggests to excuse the Jewish people. Rather, a general political, social and religious confrontation was in the making in the

50s and 60s.[76] The consequence was a **national popular war against the rule of Rome, a war which at the same time was a social class struggle** against the rich aristocratic establishment friendly to Rome and thus for that very reason in a most profound sense also a **religious struggle**. As a chosen people the Jews believed that they had the right to political freedom, and the renewed loyalty to the national religious institutions – zeal for Temple and law – seemed to guarantee them victory with the help of their God. Here are the most important dates on which historians are in agreement.

66 CE: Provocation by the governor Gessius Florus, riots in Caesarea and Jerusalem, seizure of the Temple Court and the Antonia citadel by Eleazar, the son of the high priest, who was himself later executed (his palace and that of the Hasmonaeans was burned down); unsuccessful intervention in Jerusalem by the Roman governor of Syria; preparations for war on both sides.

67: On the orders of the emperor Nero a slow recapture of the country under the command of the general Flavius Vespasianus and his son Titus – both later emperors and protectors of 'Flavius' Josephus. There are clashes resembling a civil war in Jerusalem; the earliest Christian community emigrates (according to certain traditions) from Jerusalem to Pella in Transjordan.

68: Nero's death and the encirclement of Jerusalem by Vespasian. As Vespasian begins to lay siege to Jerusalem in the following year, he is proclaimed emperor by the legions of the East. He hands over command to his son Titus and hastens to Rome.

70: At the beginning of the year the attack on the city of Jerusalem is launched, but there are months of vigorous Jewish resistance in house-to-house fighting. In August the Temple is burned down, and in September the citadel and the upper city are finally captured. There is an enormous blood-bath, plundering, and destruction of the city.

71: Triumphal procession of Titus in Rome. He brings with him as victor's booty the menorah, the seven-branched lampstand from the Temple. This is depicted on the triumphal arch of Titus in the Roman Forum (the original disappeared in 455 during the Vandal attack on Rome).

74: Only now was the fortress of Masada, long besieged and completely starved out, captured, after the whole 960-person Zealot garrison (apart from two women and five children) had committed suicide. Masada was long forgotten, but in our time has been identified and excavated. Against it the tremendous Roman siege ramp can still be seen.[77] Masada today is a monument of the Jewish state, and recently has become a sign of Jewish bravery to the death. For the Jews of the time it was a senseless catastrophe without parallel. For we must not forget that all in all, around a quarter of the Jewish population of Palestine – according to Josephus and Tacitus around 600,000 people – may have perished in the first Jewish-Roman war.

Some decades later, in 132-135, against all the warning signals, a second, messianically-orientated, hopeless and ultimate Jewish rebellion took place against the Romans. We do not know much about it.[78] It was led by a Simeon ben Koseba, who was hailed as messiah by Rabbi Akiba, the most influential teacher of his time, and given the title Bar Kokhba (= son of the star). However, he was then reviled by others as one who had led the people astray (as is attested in the Talmud) and given the name Bar Kosiba (= son of lies).[79] This rebellion, which was again put down methodically by the Romans, led to the final catastrophe after the capture of fifty fortresses and around a thousand fortified places. Bar Kokhba fell in battle and Rabbi Akiba suffered martyrdom, reciting the 'Shema' as he died. This second war is said to have claimed around 850,000 victims. Any one of the followers of Bar Kokhba who was not cut down was sold into slavery. The old Jerusalem was completely destroyed. And almost worse, after the end of the war a completely new, totally Hellenized, city was built. Even its name, Colonia Aelia Capitolina, was an entirely new one. Jerusalem became a Roman colony with sanctuaries of Jupiter Capitolinus, Juno and Minerva. Those who had been circumcised were prohibited from entering the city on pain of death.

This was an epoch-making break: virtually no other event had such a sustained influence on the history and self-understanding of Judaism as did the loss of Jerusalem and the Second Temple. Was this not the final end of the holy city of Israel? Throughout the following centuries the Bar Kokhba revolt was seen as a costly and senseless catastrophe – until almost two thousand years later, after the Six Day War and the recapture of Jerusalem, it was to be glorified quite directly as a heroic action. But might not what people in Israel have called the Bar-Kokhba syndrome also bring renewed danger to the Jewish people and state, instead of peace?

It is now nineteen centuries since Roman troops levelled city and Temple to the ground. And the city of Abraham, who is said to have met the priest Melchizedek and to have bound his son Isaac at God's behest there, the city of David and Solomon, the city of the Hasmonaeans and Herodians, has meanwhile become the holy city of **three world religions** in another long and eventful history. But Jerusalem, which according to Jewish popular etymology is meant to be the **'city of peace'**, has become a **city of no peace**.

There is no ignoring the fact that each of the three Abrahamic religions has a legitimate claim on Jerusalem. But at the same time none is ready to acknowledge the rights of the two others. And so today the barely thirty-five acres of the Temple Court are the most disputed piece of land on this earth, the slightest incursion into which has bloody consequences, as has been evident in our days. But many people are asking whether a Temple is an essential part of Judaism; does it not (like the monarchy) belong to certain limited constellations of a particular period? Is it part of the substance of the faith of Judaism, or just of a particular paradigm? The political positions and strategies of all three Abrahamic religions are very different, without any uniformity in this respect.

– A number of **Jews** would like to see the Temple rebuilt, and pray for that three times a day. They are already constructing a model, raising money, and training priests.

However, the vast majority of present-day Jews do not want a rebuilding of the Temple, far less the resumption of bloody animal sacrifices, which would be the consequence.

– Some **Christians**, too, want the rebuilding of the Temple, but only because for them this would be a preliminary sign of the return of Christ.

However, the majority of Christians are content with their own places of worship and do not want any rebuilding of the Temple, the result of which could quite easily be a confrontation with the Jews.

Not a few **Muslims** are ready to defend the Dome of the Rock and the mosques on the Temple Court to the last drop of blood, in order to prevent the rebuilding of the Temple.

However, the majority of Muslims do not want to wage any new war over the 'holy rock'.

This is the ambiguous and highly dangerous situation, and only one thing is certain. There will definitely be no real peace between Jews, Christians and Muslims unless a way of peaceful co-existence over Jerusalem and its Temple Mount is found. I shall be making some concrete practical suggestions about this in Part Three of this book. Here, to begin with, are a few questions to point the way.

Questions for the Future

For **Jews**, as the city of David, Jerusalem will remain the religious centre and the city of their longing, and the Temple Mount the place of the First, Second (and possibly also Third) Temple.

But: may Jews forget that the city was under Christian and Muslim rule for 1500 years and that Jerusalem is also a holy city for Christians and Muslims?

For **Christians**, as the city of Jesus Christ and the earliest community, Jerusalem will remain the mother of all churches on earth and the Temple Mount the place where Jesus prayed, worked and preached.

But: may Christians forget that for more than a millennium this city was an Israelite-Jewish city, that it also means much to Muslims, and that as Christians they are to set their hope not on the 'earthly' but on the 'heavenly' Jerusalem?

For **Muslims**, as the city of Muhammad, Jerusalem will remain the holiest city after Mecca and Medina, and the Temple Mount the place from which the prophet was transported to heaven.

But: may Muslims forget that the city of Jerusalem was for 1700 years a city first of the Jews and then of the Christians, before it became a Muslim city?

IV. The Mediaeval Paradigm: The Rabbis and the Synagogue

Could not Judaism, strongly represented all over the Roman empire by educated men, with its great leading idea of an ethical monotheism (which Christianity was to take up later), have had a great future in the Hellenistic world? But it had lost any chance of that. For what a change the wars between the Jews and Rome – which arose out of the Hellenistic crisis – had brought! At all events, this was an even sharper break than the Babylonian exile. It resulted not only in an impoverishment of the population, but also in dispossession of the land, the destruction of its stock of trees, and thus in the long term a change in climate. Whole groups of the people were now virtually wiped out:

– There was an end to the radicals of a political (revolutionary or Zealot) or apolitical (Essene or sectarian) shade, whom the war had swept away.

– There was an end to the king, to the hope for an imminent messianic liberator; an end to the holy city of Jerusalem, which now for almost two millennia ceased to be the political centre of the Jewish people.

– There was an end to the Temple, the priesthood, the Temple liturgy, the animal sacrifices, indeed to a whole system of cult and law which was bound up with the Temple, without the slightest hope that the Temple could be rebuilt in the foreseeable future and the cult could be resumed.

– In short, what had definitively collapsed was no more and no less than the theocratic paradigm which seemed so well-established. A fundamental paradigm shift was in the making.

1. Pharisees and rabbis: the new form of life

Entering the city was prohibited to all those who had been circumcised (including Jewish Christians), on pain of death; indeed initially there was even a real suppression of religion: a prohibition of circumcision, of sabbath observance, of the ordination of teachers of the law, of public teaching of the Torah and the making of proselytes. Only when the revolutionary will of the Jews in Palestine to resist had clearly been broken were the anti-Jewish decrees revised or no longer enforced. There is no question about it: the Jewish religion had become a Diaspora religion in the Jews' own land. But – and who can still be surprised at this? – that was by no means the end of it!

Who saw to the **continuity** between theocratic Israel and Israel without a Temple, between biblical and post-biblical Judaism? **The**

Pharisees! In the end of the day, of the great parties within Judaism – leaving aside the Jewish-Christian movement, which I shall be discussing later – only those representatives of that early movement of moral renewal who called themselves the 'separated ones' (the 'pious'), i.e. 'Pharisees', survived. They were mostly laity, and scattered among the people. How did that come about?

Already during the first war between the Jews and Rome, Johanan ben Zakkai, a member of the Sanhedrin and representative of the moderate Pharisees who from the start were only half-heartedly involved in the war against the power of Rome, had been smuggled out of besieged Jerusalem in a coffin and had handed himself over to the Romans. The Romans allowed him to open a house of teaching (*bet midrash*) in **Jabneh** (Greek Jamnia, on the sea near Jaffa), and after the destruction of Jerusalem this became the centre of a small gathering of scholars which trained rabbis, calculated the Jewish calendar each year, and gradually, with the assent of the Romans, also took over some of the judicial functions of the Jerusalem Sanhedrin. It was **not Masada**, soon forgotten, the place of warriors and of violent suicide, which down the centuries until the new foundation of the state of Israel remained the symbol of Jewish survival and Jewish rebirth, but rather the teaching academy in Jabneh, this place of scholars, which after the Bar-Kokhba revolt was transferred to Galilee. Instead of legitimating the war ('just' though it may have been), the rabbis now advocated the principle of non-violence.

Indeed, in their everyday life, in their families and in their villages, the Pharisees had so far already practised the same ritual purity as the priests in the Temple (not only the Temple but the whole people and the whole land was to be holy!). So they were the ones who after the destruction of the Temple provided the best basis for entering into the heritage of the priests and making a spiritual survival possible for Judaism. However, in competence and significance the new 'Great Sanhedrin', which reappeared soon after 70, consisting mostly of poor Pharisaic rabbis, was only a shadow of the old. After Johanan's retirement the leadership in Jabneh passed to Gamaliel II, the head of the ambitious house of Hillel, which had been very involved in the rebellion against Rome. He succeeded in excluding the rival school of the house of Shammai, which had its own interpretation of the law (by the excommunication of Rabbi Eliezer ben Hyrcanus) and acquiring an authority which extended beyond the region. Furthermore, after the second rebellion, Judaism was now represented to Rome, which was interested in a *modus vivendi*, by the head of the house of Hillel. As a result, the head of this house finally also managed to gain control of the former Temple tax (now an annual tax) which was to be levied from every Jew in the empire. For as *nasi* ('prince' = 'patriarch'), while he did not rule over the land, he did rule over the people (*ethnos*) in the capacity of ethnarch. This consolidated the position of the humiliated Jews *vis-à-vis* the outside world, but at the same time now made the moderate **Pharisees** (in the spirit of Hillel) the **normative Judaism**. A process of making legislation uniform and reducing the multiplicity of positions now began.

What was still left immediately after this national catastrophe to the Jews, who in Palestine now predominantly lived on agriculture, manual labour and trading in silk? There was certainly no longer any new historiography; there were no new psalms and poems; virtually no more apocalyptic visions; no wisdom literature; and no religious philosophy of the kind which had been practised by the great Alexandrian Philo, a contemporary of Jesus. Instead of this, to begin with at any rate, there was virtually only **scripture** (above all the Five Books of Moses, the Torah), the **scribes** and the **synagogue**. But now – after the fall of Jerusalem and its Temple – these were to acquire a completely **new status**.

- Scripture? The Torah scrolls now took the place of the altar, and the study of the Torah – together with prayer and good works – took the place of the Temple cult.
- The scribes? The rabbis now became the successors of the priestly caste; the status of rabbi attained by learned education increasingly replaced the hereditary status of priest and levite.
- The synagogue? The local house of assembly, prayer and community replaced the Jerusalem Temple.

All these factors allow us now to speak of a new, fourth paradigm, the **paradigm of the rabbis and the synagogue** (paradigm IV = P IV). However, here, too, people still kept holding on unshakeably to the religious centre, the central statement, the **substance of Israelite-Jewish faith**: Yahweh remains the God of Israel and Israel remains his people. Moreover the relationship of the Jewish people, now **scattered** all over the earth, to the promised **land** was never lost down all the centuries – however few Jews might have been living in it at the time. But precisely what does this paradigm of the rabbis and the synagogue mean?

(*a*) **Rabbis**: in place of the priesthood, now, in a lengthy development, the 'rabbis', the 'scribes', became the dominant power, and they now came exclusively from the Pharisaic trend. In the preceding paradigm the scribes had at best played a subordinate role. At the time of Jesus, 'rabbi' was obviously a respectful form of address for someone who knew and taught the Torah, but not yet an exclusive title for a particular group or caste, the educated and ordained teacher.[1]

But what were the rabbis now, in the second and third centuries? As they had always been, they were 'teachers of the law'. Thus from the start they were neither priests nor community leaders nor pastors nor mediators of salvation, but experts in and interpreters of the all-embracing religious law who had had a special training (and in Palestine for a long time had also been ordained). Certainly, the rabbis often worked at the same time – on the land, as manual workers or as tradespeople – when they were not paid a salary by the patriarch, the prince of the scholars, the *nasi*. But slowly they became a new social stratum which attempted to institutionalize its authority over the community (above all through the internal Jewish courts): they were increasingly a caste of scholars, often with whole scholarly dynasties, feeling themselves set apart from the common people (*am ha-aretz* = 'people of the land') who could not or would not observe the law, with all its countless regulations about purity, food and fasting. So the rabbis now replaced the priests at the top of the social ladder. However, they were not a monastic, educated elite, cut off from the people by their celibacy, as in Catholic Christianity. Rather, they were the committed experts in the law in their family and profession, who basically tried also to turn every Jew into an expert in the law. The **rabbi now became a norm and model**. And just as in the post-biblical period the Christian bishop and priest wanted to appear a 'second Christ' to his community, so now the rabbi wanted to appear as something like a Torah incarnate.

(*b*) **Synagogue**. In place of the Temple the 'synagogue', which could now be found everywhere in Judaism, took on decisive significance. The Greek word means both the assembly and the community, and the building in which the assembly takes place. As the religious centre of a local Jewish community, the synagogue represents a revolutionary development in the history of religions generally – moreover it is a model for Christian churches and Islamic mosques. In all probability it is exilic in origin – in ancient Jewish tradition it is derived from Moses. Be this as it may, the earliest certain archaeological and linguistic evidence for Israel itself is not to be found until the first century after Christ.

Beyond question the synagogue, too, grew enormously in status as a result of the fall of the central sanctuary, the Second Temple. After that there were synagogues not only from Galilee to Gaza,[2] but throughout the Roman empire, for liturgical and non-liturgical gatherings. In these synagogues communal prayers were now offered, and the Torah was systematically read and taught, commented on and discussed with narratives and interpretations. Here there now developed the typically rabbinic view that **intensive study of scripture**, regular **prayer** and good **works** could replace **Temple worship and sacrifice**: 'By three things is the world sustained: by the Torah, by the cult, and by deeds of loving-kindness.'[3] The Pharisaic tradition was to be passed on to all Jews in flesh and blood from childhood on, above all with the help of schools for children. Indeed, learning the Torah, and thus learning generally, became a lifelong process. Studying the Torah ranked above taking a part in community worship.

In both religion and politics the rabbis steered a sage **middle course**: in religion (internally) they attempted to order all spheres of life by the law ('halakhically') and at the same time to make the precise fulfilment of the law reasonably tolerable in everyday life by moderate interpretations. Here indeed they had every freedom. But politically (externally) they fell into line with the Romans. Certainly they never gave up hope of a messianic kingdom, **but they attached this messianic hope to strict obedience to the law.**

Therefore, 'When people believed that by studying the Torah and keeping the commandments they would take a critical role in the coming of the messiah, Judaism, as we have known it for nearly two millennia, was born. When, further, Jews reached the conviction that the figure of the rabbi encompassed all three – the learning, the doing, the hope – Judaism had come to full and enduring expression... So Judaism became **rabbinic**.' Thus probably the greatest expert on this revolutionary paradigm shift, the American Jewish scholar Jacob Neusner, who has worked out the significance of this epoch-making shift more perceptively than others. And in fact, 'The rabbi as model and authority, Torah as the principal and organizing symbol, study of Torah as the capital religious deed, the life of religious discipline as the prime expression of what it means to be Israel, the Jewish people', in other words everything that was to make Judaism distinctive for almost twenty centuries, would all be sought in vain in the post-exilic theocracy paradigm, even in the Maccabaean period and most of all even still in the time of Jesus: 'Judaism as we know it took shape before and after the destruction of the Temple of Jerusalem in 70 CE. By around 600 CE, it was fully worked out.'[4]

There is no doubt that with the help of the synagogue and its teachers Pharisaism now began everywhere to carry through a **comprehensive ordering of life** against any kind of resistance among the people. To this end, innovations which had long since been initiated by the assembly at Jamnia were formally sanctioned, so that they have the validity of law down to the present day in Judaism:

– The **regulation of prayers** for synagogues and individuals. Down to the present day there are two main prayers: in the morning and in the evening the 'Hear, Israel' (*Shema Yisrael*), and also in the afternoon the 'Eighteen Benedictions' (*Shemone Esre*). The Twelfth Benediction is the curse on the dissidents (*minim*) and Jewish Christians (*nosrim*); we shall discuss that later. At a later date supplementary prayers (*piyutim*) were created for synagogue services.[5]

– The definitive **establishing of the canon of the holy scriptures.** The books of the Hebrew Tanakh were fixed at twenty-four (and to the present day this is also the canon of the Protestant churches). Books that were excluded were on the one hand the seven so-called apocryphal books of Baruch, Jesus Sirach, Tobit, Judith, I and II Maccabees and the Wisdom of Solomon, which were contained in the Alexandrian Greek translation of the Bible (and are still included in the canon of the Greek Orthodox and Roman Catholic Church), and on the other the pseudepigrapha of Enoch, the Sibyllines, the Testaments of the Twelve Patriarchs, and so on (which no one took up). The standard text of the Hebrew Bible which is still accepted today was also established (only in the Middle Ages was it fixed down to its pronunciation, with the help of vowel signs).

But with the new paradigm the **cultural and spiritual centre** had also shifted: for after the destruction of Jerusalem many teachers of the law had fled, mainly **to Babylonia** with its flourishing economy[6] – there were still old connections in that direction. Jewish self-government there was headed by a powerful Jewish exilarch, allegedly of Davidic origin, who collaborated with the patriarch of Palestine (not least over the silk trade from the Far East to Syria and Europe). In that framework a lively spiritual life developed of a Judaism which, while fundamentally still Palestinian, was largely stamped by Hellenistic culture. In the third century, **rabbinic high schools** were founded, on the Palestinian model, in order to educate the people here, too, in obedience to the law as interpreted by the Pharisees. The first of these schools was that of Sura in southern Babylonia, followed by that of Nehardea/Pumbedita near Baghdad. They soon surpassed the Palestinian schools in significance.

Babylonia had gained what Palestine had lost: possibly the numerical and quantitative, but at all events the political and spiritual-cultural, primacy. The predominance of Babylonia – the remains of the synagogue of Dura Europos (destroyed in 256 CE) on the Euphrates with a wealth of biblical frescoes are the only architectural evidence to survive – is clearly evident in the process of post-biblical tradition: less in the Mishnah, which was edited in Palestine, than later in the Talmud, in which the Babylonian tradition prevailed over that of Palestine.

2. The rise of orthopraxy: Mishnah and Talmud

Of course this new paradigm was prepared for in the old paradigm, as happened in the earlier shift. As we heard, in the post-exilic period the Jewish religion had increasingly become a religion of the book. However, after the national catastrophe of 135, after the final loss of both the monarchy and of the Temple and prophecy, now even more the **Torah** – originally testimony to God's rule over Israel and the original revelation of his will – became the **sole foundation** of the relationship with God. Jewish piety was now purely and simply the **piety of the Torah**, in its Pharisaic form. There was an all-embracing 'process of rabbinization': 'the re-reading of everything in terms of the system of the rabbi'.[7] As never before, the book was exclusively given independent authority; it became a norm at the same time for membership of the elect people, for the good will of God and the welfare of human beings. The book was the source of life for a people which was increasingly scattered over the world. Wherever it was, Jewish life had to mean life under the Torah. The consequence was a comprehensive ritualizing of everyday life.

For it had already been important for the Pharisees (who were sharply opposed to the Sadducees of the Temple) that alongside the written Torah there was also an **'oral Torah'** (which had not been known at all earlier); this contained the interpretations of the written Torah (including all the different rabbinic learned opinions on the individual commandments and prohibitions). In the first phase these 'traditions of the fathers' were never set down in writing, but handed down orally, though increasingly learned off by heart by specialized 'tradents'; later, however, they were written down: first privately and then quite officially. This **process of commenting** on the Torah, which grew to an enormous extent and became increasingly complex, extends over more than half a millennium and came to its climax and conclusion in **two phases**. As we shall see, because of its interest for today we shall have to discuss it briefly.[8]

Phase 1: Mishnah.[9] As early as 200 CE, it is said, the patriarch Yehuda ha-Nasi had compiled an authoritative selection of 'oral Torah' (which at least in part went back to the Pharisees). This was the Mishnah (Hebrew 'repetition, teaching'), embracing the whole religious law of the oral tradition, the halakhah (the non-legal edifying texts of the Mishnah are unimportant). Did the patriarch Jehuda, who probably worked with a whole team, want to create in the Mishnah a collection of sources of the halakhic tradition, or a text book for instruction (or for teachers), or a legal codex proper to be used in passing judgment? Whatever the answer, he was concerned 'with handing down the tradition which for him was of course at the same time law', and at the latest fifty to a hundred years later the Mishnah had also become 'the codex of authoritative law for the whole rabbinate'.[10] Five to six generations of about 260 teachers of the law are involved here. This Mishnah (written in Hebrew) contains 63 tractates without any distinction between (religious) sacral law and (secular) civil law; they are brought together in main divisions ('Orders'), six in number, which are mostly thematic: Seeds, Set Feasts, Women, Damages, Hallowed Things (sacrifice, oaths, food regulations) and Cleannesses (only a single tractate, 'Aboth', 'The Fathers', has a non-legal, edifying content).

And now the decisive point. According to the orthodox view, this 'oral Torah' is **of equal value** to the original written, **biblical Torah**. Why? Because it was **already part of the revelation on Sinai!** This was a conception which was unknown before the fall of the Second Temple. But (as we heard) in the perspective of the rabbis Moses now became purely and simply 'our rabbi'. However, on critical investigation this oral Torah is in no way a unitary document, to some degree fallen from heaven. On the contrary, if historical criteria are applied, the work of many generations can be detected; indeed traces of editing by scribes and expositors can be recognized from as late as the period after 200.

Phase 2: Talmud.[11] In the following three centuries – it was a tremendous amount of work for many generations – the Mishnah was commented on again in its turn, in both centres of Jewish learning: in Palestine, but above all in Babylonia. This was done through the 'Gemara' (Hebrew 'expansion'), which was often composed in Aramaic dialects. Together, Gemara and Mishnah form the '**Talmud**' (Hebrew 'study', 'teaching').[12] So with all its edifying expansions the Talmud is primarily just a gigantic commentary on the Mishnah, in so far as the Mishnah's tractates are still relevant after the destruction of the Temple. It was handed down in two very different versions in both centres:
– The **Palestinian** or Jerusalem Talmud (the Talmud Yerushalmi, which was probably produced in Tiberias) comments on only thirty-nine tractates of the Mishnah. Without much order and often contradictory, it was probably completed at the beginning of the fifth century – in connection with the end of the patriarchate in 425.

– The **Babylonian** Talmud comments on only thirty-seven tractates, but is very much longer (almost 6,000 folio pages). It was only completed in the seventh/eighth centuries and established itself all over Judaism.

In terms of content, the two genres we have come across can also be distinguished in the Talmud. Here, too, there is primarily the **halakhah** (Hebrew 'the way to be taken'), the religious law with its binding regulations on religious and civil matters, inculcating the rules about the sabbath, purity and food, all precisely according to the Pharisaic interpretation. But then, in contrast to the Mishnah, in the Babylonian Talmud the **haggadah** (Hebrew 'narrative', 'proclamation') can often be found on one and the same page: narratives, legends, parables, astronomical, anatomical, medical and psychological information, ethical and theological teaching – in other words, the edifying, non-legal parts of the rabbinic tradition. So the Talmud – apart from the Mishnah which is contained in it and a few decisions by the last Babylonian redactors (= Saboraeans) – is not so much a legal codex which rules on everything as an encyclopaedic report of a discussion which notes many contradictory opinions on the law and every possible theme down the centuries. Indeed, it is 'a national library of Babylonian Judaism, the construction of which is orientated on the Mishnah'.[13]

The question is, why is this confusingly complicated and often obscure literary edifice also so important for non-Jews? Because the Babylonian Talmud – commented on and edited time and again[14] – is still the **normative** foundation for all decisions of rabbinic Judaism on the religious law, even today. And that means that it is authoritative **for the religious teaching and religious law of Jewish Orthodoxy** (and often also still of Conservative Judaism) down to the present day. So the understanding of Judaism as it developed in the fourth paradigm continues to the present. Certainly the consequence is traditionalism in teaching and practice, but for the rabbis and their successors this is not a negative factor. It was not permissible to make changes or additions even in the 'Talmudic period'. Only interpretation is allowed – with the help of rabbinic opinions, though these are countless and often contradictory, and thus on many occasions allow contrary views.

However, in order to exclude the possibility of misunderstanding on the part of non-Jews, it must be said straight away that this 'Orthodox' Judaism is **not primarily concerned with 'ortho-doxy', with 'right teaching'**; in contrast to Christianity it knows virtually nothing of dogmas, catechisms, tests of faith, Inquisition. It did not then and it does not now. For example, belief in the resurrection, over which there was once dispute, became universally established long ago; and at most, messianic speculations, calculations and movements appear primarily on the periphery. The **prime concern is rather with 'orthopraxy', with 'right living' under the Torah,** with conduct in accordance with the Torah in everyday life, though to dissidents this can seem just as dogmatic, catechizing, and indeed inquisitorial and exclusive. And yet Jewish identity becomes concrete less in the content of faith than in the practical accomplishment of faith.

Now as all the countless regulations contained in the Torah, Mishnah and Talmud (which thus go far beyond the original five books of Moses) are regarded directly or indirectly as the revealed **word of God** which stands for ever, they **must all be observed unconditionally** – down to the last precept about the sabbath, food, purity, prayer and worship. Certainly, there was no lack of attempts among the rabbis to classify the mass of 613 precepts: 248 commandments and 365 prohibitions. Not everything applies to both adults **and** those who have not yet come of age, to both men **and** women, to both Jews **and** non-Jews; at any rate, only the Noachic commandments which we have already come across apply to non-Jews. Certainly, depending on the situation, and particularly when there is danger to life, the obligation to obey individual commandments can be lifted, and the transgression of certain commandments at most carries with it only a light punishment. But all this does not mean that there is any relativizing of the individual commandments, far less is it possible to take refuge in ignorance. For in the last resort the issue is always the command of the eternal God, and that remains for ever – unalterable, unchanging, infallible.

Is this the paramountcy of tradition? Christian and Muslim readers must not judge too hastily here. For are not the parallels to developments in Christianity and Islam unmistakable? Torah **and** Mishnah, scripture **and** tradition, Qur'an **and** Sunna. In a very similar way, at a later date, in both Christianity and Islam the almost immeasurable oral tradition (*traditio*, Sunna) is given equal rights[15] alongside the original holy scripture ('New Testament', 'Qur'an'), and indeed is often in fact **set above it.** For anyone who gives the secondary element equal status in so doing demotes the primary element. And like the laws of the halakhah, so in fact the dogmas of the church tradition are already firmly established before their grounding in the Bible. The scholars could limit their biblical exegesis to 'grounding' the existing traditional doctrine in the Bible after the event, to making it conform with the system. But in the Christian tradition, too, is not a good deal carried along which seems 'grounded' in the Bible or tradition and is no longer understood today? A good deal of what was once intended for a

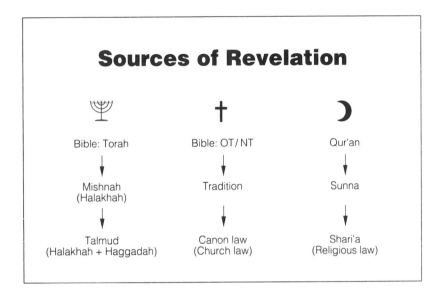

Sources of Revelation

Bible: Torah	Bible: OT/NT	Qur'an
↓	↓	↓
Mishnah (Halakhah)	Tradition	Sunna
↓	↓	↓
Talmud (Halakhah + Haggadah)	Canon law (Church law)	Shari'a (Religious law)

completely different situation is adapted by often tortuous explanations.

So we should already note here that it would be fundamentally wrong to see only the legalistic element in Judaism and its understanding of the law, and thus play off Judaism and Christianity against each other as law and freedom. Was not the Christianity of the ancient church and the Byzantine church (think of the emperor Justinian!), and even more mediaeval Roman Catholic Christianity (Pope Innocent III!) characterized by an extrardinary strong legalism? Was it not characterized by a canon law which was developed only in the Christian Middle Ages, and an increasingly elaborate science of church law which is truly no less complicated than that of Judaism or Islam? Conversely, however, it is happily also the case that not only mediaeval Christianity but also mediaeval Judaism would in principle see itself directed – precisely through the halakhah – to the study of the original 'holy scripture'. For in rabbinic Judaism the study of the Torah was understood as the way of hearing God's word and experiencing God's presence (*shekinah*). And perhaps no other religous tradition has put so much stress on the significance of the study of the sacred texts as an opening, as a way to the holy God, the author of the Torah, as has the Jewish tradition. And does one need to add that the passion for learning, for reading and writing, for books and finally for intellectual discourse and disputation that is so important for Jews and their ethos, derives in particular from the study of the Torah?

3. Judaism as a religion of the Torah: life in the Diaspora

The time of the **rabbis** – from the first to the seventh/eighth centuries – was also the time of the **church fathers**, and just as the rabbis shaped the structure of orthodox Judaism, so the church fathers shaped the structure of orthodox Christianity, that second, Greek-Hellenistic paradigm of Christianity (which followed the Jewish-Christian paradigm). But why did nothing like a Greek-Byzantine patristics develop in Judaism (in contrast to Christianity)? Why did one group create the 'introverted' Jewish Talmud in Hebrew and Aramaic, whereas the other developed a completely 'extravert' Hellenistic theology in Greek or Latin language and patterns of thought?

Culturally and in religious terms, that **no patristics** could develop in **Judaism** was not just a result of the opposition between Jewish and Greek culture generally, i.e. the fact that the Greek translation of the Bible and Greek-Jewish literature of the kind which had flourished especially in Alexandria met with virtually no response within Judaism. Nor was the political situation the sole factor, though the Greek-speaking Jews who had also rebelled against Rome in 115-117 CE in Egypt (Alexandria!), Cyrenaica, Cyprus and Syria, were largely exterminated. The deeper, real reason lies in the new rabbinic paradigm: having emerged from the Hellenistic crisis, it was so centred upon itself, so capable of defending itself, and so exclusive, that all down the centuries **within Judaism neither Hellenistic culture and philosophy nor Roman law and order could prevail against it.** The rabbinic paradigm prohibited and prevented any 'mixing' of the Jewish people with other peoples. This eventually had positive consequences for Judaism itself, but also, as we shall see, negative consequences as well.[16] It is an irony of history that whereas two centuries later the **Christian** Alexandrians Clement and Origen made history by preparing theologically for the Hellenistic paradigm of the early church and thus for the political shift, their predecessor, the **Jewish** Alexandrian Philo,[17] was no more than an episode. After the downfall of Jewish Alexandria, even his large-scale allegorical interpretation of scripture with a Platonic stamp had done its duty...

Here we find confirmation that **the rabbinic paradigm** was shaped less by theology ('learning about God') than **by jurisprudence** ('learning about the law'). And whereas representative collections of Christian literature from the first millennium (Migne's *Patrologia Graeca et Latina* or the *Corpus Christianorum*) comprise hundreds of volumes of theological writings, of which only a small part is of a legal kind, the opposite is true of Jewish writings. For the most part they centre on clarifications, developments and new applications of the law. Indeed the Mishnah itself has the form of a law book, and far more than half of the Babylonian Talmud and more than three-quarters of the Jerusalem Talmud are devoted to questions about the law; naturally, this also shaped the further commentaries and sub-commentaries of the scholars.[18] Here we have almost a 'sea of the halakhah', with many tributaries and parallel streams, persons and places, as is demonstrated by a great 'Map of the Jewish Oral Law' made by Abba Kovner in an original pictorial appendix to the supplementary volume of the Jerusalem *Encyclopaedia Judaica* of 1985. In this connection it is by no means unimportant that the first systematic Jewish theology comes only from the tenth century (we shall be returning to its author, the Gaon Saadia); by contrast, Christianity developed a science of church law only in the twelfth century, on the basis of the *Decretum Gratiani*.

It is clear that Judaism is now **no longer a national religion**, but the vast majority of the Jews live 'among the nations', in the **Diaspora**, the **'dispersion'** – literally spread over the whole world from the Hindu Kush to Gibraltar. So may 'Diaspora' simply be identified with 'exile' – as often happens in extreme Zionist circles, which in this way support their claim to the land of Israel from the Bible, and seek to persuade all Jews to 'return' to the state of Israel? Certainly that is how people may often have felt, particularly in the Jewish Middle Ages. But it cannot be denied that already before the destruction of the First Temple there were Jewish trading settlements outside the land of Israel – like the famous Jewish military colony on the island of Elephantine in Upper Egypt (of which there is evidence as early as the sixth century BCE), which was in Egyptian service. The Jewish historian Salo W.Baron estimates that in the year of the destruction of the Second Temple there must have been around two million Jews in Palestine, but four million in the Roman empire outside Palestine and a million in Babylonia and other non-Roman countries (with a great influx of converts!).[19] Not all of these were exiles! Indeed, the feeling of living in 'banishment' was clearly relativized at any time by the wishes of many Diaspora Jews who, even after the Babylonian exile, did not want to return to the land of Israel when they could have gone back. It is a fact that by far the majority of Jews even now prefer life in the Diaspora – for all their inner bond with the land of Israel. Since the destruction of the First Temple Judaism has been in a way bi-polar or, better, has existed in a **tension between homeland and the periphery**, the *Eretz Israel* (land of Israel) and the Diaspora.

But how did the situation of Judaism now take shape in the centuries after the destruction of the Second Temple? In **Palestine**, after the Roman empire had gone over to Christianity and all non-Jews had accepted the Christian faith, the Jews had become a minority, and in the Byzantine empire they were exposed to increasing restrictions, so that they felt the Islamic conquest of Palestine in 638 to be a liberation. For now, for the first time, Jews might settle in Jerusalem again, although their spiritual centre remained the learned school at Tiberias in Galilee. After the decimation of the Jews at the time of the Crusades (to which we shall return) there was renewed Jewish immigration in connection with the Arab reconquest by Sultan Saladin in 1187, and this also continued under Mamluk rule in the fourteenth/fifteenth centuries. But how were things outside Palestine?

At a very early stage Jews had penetrated the Roman empire as far as Toledo and Lyons, Cologne and Bonn. And now, at the end of antiquity and the beginning of the European Middle Ages, there were significant **centres** of Jewish life and activity in the **Diaspora** (often founded centuries earlier).
– First of all, as I have said, there were Jewish centres in **Babylonia** (despite persecutions under the Zoroastrian Sassanids and their 'magi'). With intact Jewish self-government under allegedly Davidic exilarchs, Babylonia was so to speak the Jews' second home, where there was still security and prosperity even under the Islamic caliphs of the tenth and eleventh centuries. However, with the decline and ultimate fall of the caliphate of Baghdad in the Mongol onslaught of 1258, even the Jewish communities in Babylonia sank into insignificance.
– Between the fourth and sixth centuries there were Jewish centres in the **Yemen**, in southern Arabia, the land of the fabulous Queen of Sheba. There was earlier Jewish settlement there, and even a Jewish kingdom of Himyar, but that was destroyed in 525 by Christian Ethiopia (with the aid of the emperor Justinian).
– Between the fourth and seventh centuries there were also Jewish centres in central **Arabia**[20] (above all in Medina), where Jewish tribes had already long assimilated to the Arabs in social divisions and manner of life. After initially being courted by the prophet Muhammad, they were exterminated or forced to emigrate to Syria or Mesopotamia.
– In the eighth century there were Jewish centres in the area of Russia between the Volga, the Black Sea and the Caspian Sea. Here the kingdom of the **Khazars** (a Turkish people) had converted to Jewish faith around 740 so as not to be dependent on either Byzantium or Islam, but around 950 it was forced to accept the Christian faith by the prince of Kiev.

- O   Important places in the Hellenistic Diaspora
- △   Mediaeval intellectual centres
- ◪   Sites of mediaeval massacres
- ▲   Kabbalistic Centres
- ■   Cities with important Jewish qu
- •   Other important places

Source: Encyclopaedia Britannica

*Important Historical Places in Hellenistic
and Mediaeval Judaism*

– Between the eighth and eleventh centuries there were Jewish centres especially in **Spain**. Here, after the conversion of the West Goths to Roman Catholicism, the Jews – who had already been strongly represented in the early Roman empire and then in the Aryan kingdom of the West Goths – had had to accept considerable restrictions and many compulsory baptisms. The conquest of the country by Muslim Arabs after 711, like that of Palestine as early as 638, was hailed as liberation and supported. Under the caliphate of Cordoba (755-1013) and after its destruction by fanatical Berbers, Judaism experienced a new cultural heyday in Granada and Seville (but primarily also in Christian Castile, Toledo and Aragon).

– Judaism flourished in **Central Europe** particularly in the tenth and eleventh centuries. Here Jews had settled long before the immigration of the Germanic tribes; the colonization began in the ninth century and the Jewish communities were generally protected by the kings (Merovingians, Carolingians and Ottonians) against the attacks of the church, its bishops and councils.

– Judaism flourished in the eleventh and twelfth centuries in the **Egypt** of the Ishmaelite Fatimids; the research here has been extraordinarily good because of the discovery of around 200,000 manuscripts from the Geniza (= 'hiding place' or 'store room') of the Cairo synagogues which was discovered at the end of the last century.

However, all over the world, in an amazing way, not only in prayer and worship, but also in ethos, discipline and way of life, the Jews continued to be formed and moulded by the **paradigm of the rabbis and the synagogue**, the outlines of which I have described. For every Jew all over the world, the whole course of the day (from early in the morning till late in the evening), the whole course of the year (working days, sabbath days and feast days), indeed the whole course of life (from birth and circumcision through sexual maturity, marriage and family to death and burial), was regulated by the instructions of Mishnah and Talmud. This was a quite special **life-style** with numerous binding precepts, rules of life and customs which related to every conceivable thing: hair-style and clothing, food and washing, types of prayer and times of prayer, housing and sexual life. Wherever Jews came – and in the course of urbanization they devoted themselves increasingly to crafts and trade – the Talmud came too... Gratitude for the Law, God's great gift, and delight in its fulfilment, in the human bond with God, determine rabbinic piety. There is no higher spiritual activity than the study of the Law, but this is the human answer to God's word.

Once again, there was still the same centre and foundation to Israelite-Jewish faith, the one **God**, his **people** and **land**. But as after other previous shifts, the substance of this faith was realized in a new age of the world in another totality of convictions, values and techniques; it was seen in another constellation, in a new paradigm. It is not just that the synagogue took the place of the Temple, scripture the place of the altar, the rabbi the place of the sacrificial priest. Rather, as we heard, **the national religion now became completely and utterly a religion of the Torah:**

- Of necessity Jerusalem faded into the background in favour of the Diaspora and its cultural centres;
- The home territory (Palestine) faded into the background in favour of a spiritual home in Jewish faith and life which was realized in obedience to the Torah;
- National allegiance faded into the background in favour of a ritual and moral purity which transcended all nations;
- The Bible faded into the background in favour of a tradition which was similarly normative: Mishnah and Talmud.

Amazingly enough, without a central religious or political authority the Jewish people, scattered to the four winds, succeeded in preserving the unity of its religion by:

- the **oral Torah** collected and fixed in the Talmud;
- the **common language**, Hebrew/Aramaic, which went with this, and
- the **authority of the rabbis**, which stood behind it all.

And although 'the rabbinic authority did not go unchallenged, in principle it was never overthrown until the collapse of Jewish self-government, which began in the late eighteenth century and continued in the nineteenth'.[21] Right down to the time of the European Enlightenment! We are therefore fully justified in also calling this paradigm of the rabbis and the synagogue the **Jewish-mediaeval paradigm**, the framework of which allowed a very great regional and national variety in the different communities.

However, this process of forming a new paradigm also had its shadow side: a not inconsiderable heightening of that Jewish segregation which could already be noted in pre-Christian times and which already then was the occasion for anti-Judaism, a 'pagan' anti-Judaism. We must now consider that.

4. The Jews segregate themselves: pre-Christian anti-Judaism

Externally, the Jews now lived literally without any frontiers. Internally, however, the rabbis had meanwhile extended and marked off the old regulations about purity to such a degree that in practice they became something like **internal frontiers** between the 'pure' Jewish people and an 'impure' society which at a very early stage was cosmopolitan and trans-national, and now in fact was more and more Christian. Not only the priests, as before, but as we know the whole people, was now understood as a separated 'priestly people'.

However, this did not go so far as in the mediaeval Christian church, which now formally excluded the righteous of other peoples from the kingdom of God (the Council of Florence, 1442: 'No one – not just the heathen but also the Jews, heretics and schismatics – outside the Catholic Church can have a part in eternal life, but they will go to the hell fire which is prepared for the devil and his angels, unless they allow themselves to be received into it – the Catholic Church – before death').[22] Judaism knows no dogma like 'outside Israel no salvation'. On the contrary, also according to the rabbis, any righteous non-Jew can attain eternal salvation – on the basis of his righteous works. To this degree rabbinic Judaism represents a universalism of salvation,[23] but this must be seen in conjunction with a **particularism of the people**, which alone is and remains chosen.

However, this particularism of the Jewish people has a fatal effect where it is combined with a rigorous understanding of the law (halakhah) and thus at an early stage leads to an isolationism of the Jewish people. For the momentous consequence of the very idea of the 'pure' Jewish people cannot be overlooked. As we noted, this **religious and social segregation of themselves** by Jews from non-Jews (the latter being regarded as public 'sinners'), which had its foundation in the Babylonian exile and now was carried on in a quite deliberate way, in fact amounted to a kind of **self-isolation**. Within the Jewish people itself it led to many tensions and conflicts, but long before the Christian era, among other peoples it caused a good deal of instinctive antipathy, indeed enmity and hatred – everything that comes under the fatal label **anti-Judaism**. This came about because of complicated political, social and religious-ideological circumstances; it is not, however, to be identified with modern 'antisemitism', which has a racial or economic basis, although this antisemitism does go back to the earlier anti-Judaism.[24]

It must be noted as a fact that **anti-Judaism** – a fundamental antipathy to Jews as Jews – is **centuries older than Christianity**. Already in pre-

Christian centuries (even in the tolerant Persian empire, say, of the anti-Jewish Great King Ahasuerus/Xerxes in the fifth century), there were various generally hostile reactions to Jews on the part of the 'pagan' world around, though later in the Roman empire for the most part they were respected and treated well.

But if we look back briefly, what were the **reasons** for pre-Christian pagan anti-Judaism?[25] The answer will be of some importance for our assessment of the anti-Judaism in the Christian church.

1. Jews could not and would not revere or worship **any other deities** alongside the one God. The exclusive Jewish monotheism which became established in the post-exilic period had to assert itself in the face of traditional pagan polytheism, the more recent Hellenistic ruler-cult, and finally in particular in the face of the Roman emperor-cult and the mystical idea of empire associated with it (the union of the emperor and the empire). Diaspora Judaism, which as an special ethnic and religious group in any case had a somewhat tense relationship with the indigenous population, was orientated less on Rome, the world capital, than on Jerusalem, the city of David and the Messiah. The prohibition of images also alienated the average person in antiquity. No wonder that there are anti-Jewish remarks even in classical Roman authors like Cicero, Seneca, Quintilian and Tacitus, and that Roman emperors – depending on the political opportunity – made use of the Jews as allies against the indigenous population or as scapegoats to be punished for their own failure.

2. The Jews' **aggressive description of their own salvation history** was taken as an insult by other cultivated peoples, primarily the Egyptians. In a great city of antiquity like Alexandria (with the largest Jewish community in the Diaspora) the exodus story in particular must have been counter-productive, as is evident from Flavius Josephus' apologia *contra Apionem* and the anti-Jewish authors quoted in it. According to Josephus, an anti-Jewish ideology developed above all in Egypt. Here there were increasingly violent riots, and in the year 38 CE there was a pogrom against the Jews. But as early as the third century BCE a counter-version of the origin of the Jewish nation had been related by the Egyptian priest Mantheo (or Manetho), which was later also taken over by the Romans.[26] The Jews, who were originally Egyptians, had been driven out of Egypt because they had been smitten by leprosy and other diseases. Under Moses, an apostate Egyptian priest, they had then founded a nation of their own – with Jerusalem as capital. The prohibition against eating pork was later also associated with the apparently well-founded Jewish fear of leprosy, and a variety

of other fables and historical lies (some of which were later also told of Christians) were in circulation (worshipping an ass's head, the sacrifice of children) and possibly still are.

3. As we saw, **circumcision**, old and widespread in the East, and for Israelites initially one commandment among many, became a Jewish characteristic only after the Babylonian empire. After the prohibition of circumcision by Antiochus Epiphanes and the emperor Hadrian, however, it became a test of faith and a mark of faith. To non-Jews, though, this mark of faith seemed to be more a mark of shame: physically, circumcision in itself distinguished Jewish men irrevocably from Greeks and Romans, who regarded such a bloody rite as archaic, barbaric, tasteless and superstitious.

4. However, it was above all the **commandments about purity and food** which did not just visibly distinguish the Jews from the other peoples of the Hellenistic world but also marked them off. To this degree we can note as a result something which as it were provides negative confirmation of our analysis of the rabbinic Torah paradigm: 'There can be little doubt that the reason for their strangeness in the ancient world lay in their obedience to the commandments of the law.'[27] Might a people which regarded other peoples as ritually 'unclean' and therefore rejected not only mixed marriages but also shared meals, festivals and amusements, reckon on getting much sympathy? Because of their rejection of social contacts at meals, marriages, worship and festivals, the Jews were regarded not just as aliens but as enemies and indeed as misanthropists, in particular by the Greeks – and in the Near East, too, the Greeks were the intellectual elite. In addition there was the sabbath commandment, which many people found impossible to understand (was it a fast day?). As early as the end of the fourth century BCE, Hecataeus of Abdera[28] wrote that the Jewish way of living was 'an inhuman and inhospitable form of life' – a charge which was later levelled by the notorious Antiochus Epiphanes in defence of his compulsory Hellenization, and subsequently by the Romans.

This religious, cultural and political non-conformism may have been the background to the direct **persecutions** by a state power like **Rome**. Being in any case open to syncretism, Rome had initally also been completely tolerant to the Jews in the religious sphere and had even allowed them the sabbath rest. However, wherever political resistance or even rebellion manifested itself, no matter from whom or for what reason, the Romans intervened as brutally as the Assyrians and the Seleucids before them. And it should not be forgotten that quite similar charges were raised against the Christians down to the third century because of their rejection of the emperor cult, and similar pressure was applied to them; the only difference was that at that time the Christians did not resort to violence, as did the Jews at the time of the Maccabees and the two rebellions of 68-70 and 132-135. As early as 38 CE the **first Jewish pogrom** in world history took place in the Hellenistic metropolis Alexandria; the Roman emperor Claudius found it necessary in a letter to the people of Alexandria to warn them against both the hatred of the Jews nurtured by the (indigenous) Greeks and the quest for power on the part of the Jews (orientated on the centre of the empire). Hostility against the Jews also manifested itself in the first century in Rome, on Rhodes and in Syria-Palestine. The Jewish opposition to paganism in principle (hatred of pagans), followed by terrorist actions and finally two great Jewish revolutions, further inflamed anti-Jewish resentment and ideologies in the Roman empire.

How heedlessly a Christian Byzantine emperor – Constantius II, son of Constantine the Great – could still react appeared in 351, when another Jewish revolt had broken out in Palestine in connection with a Roman defeat in the Parthian war. The bloody laws of the pagan emperor Hadrian were immediately reactivated by the Christian emperor – with catastrophic consequences for the Jews. The Jewish schools were again closed, the scholars fled, there were various legal restrictions (for example over fixing the calendar), and finally, around 425 – in circumstances which are not completely clear[29] – both the patriarchate and the Sanhedrin were abolished.

But in the new paradigm, as we have heard, Judaism was no longer attached to Sanhedrin, high priest or patriarchs, though it was attached to synagogue and Torah, Mishnah and Talmud, and thus to the rabbis, who were continually able to prevail over what was often a superstitious popular piety.

5. Judaism in the Middle Ages and the beginnings of Christian anti-Judaism

It became clear that with the paradigm of the rabbis and the synagogue the **Jewish Middle Ages**, which were to last for a long time, had begun very early. As Johann Maier, the Director of the Martin Buber Institute for Judaistics in Cologne, rightly remarks, the Jews were in existence at the end of antiquity 'as the only people – though scattered – with an unbroken unity and continuity of culture, civilization and organization', and therefore came to be 'to a particular degree the vehicles of an urban, civilizing colonization... especially as from the Diaspora of antiquity they already had a relevant tradition of trade'.[30] Neither the migration of the Germanic peoples nor the Islamic conquest resulted in a paradigm change for Judaism itself. Rather, with amazing constancy and resistance, the same rabbinic paradigm had been able to maintain itself from Roman and Byzantine rule, through Islamic rule, into the Christian high Middle Ages, the time of the Reformation and long into the modern period in Europe.[31]

These Jewish Middle Ages, which begin in the first century and last until the eighteenth, are of course fundamentally different from the Christian Middle Ages, which begin considerably later. The Christian Middle Ages were prepared for by the Roman popes of late antiquity and theologically by Augustine, but they were to dawn only after the period of popular migration, in the form of the Carolingian empire and in the eleventh century with the reform movement of Gregory VII, with papal absolutism, with scholasticism, church law, celibacy and the Crusades. What, we may already ask here, is the **difference between the Jewish and the Christian Middle Ages**? By way of clarification, this question may be answered briefly in anticipation:

• Instead of the universal church, for mediaeval Jews the Torah is the home and fortress of faith.

• Instead of Caesaro-papism (in the Christian East) and papalism (in the West), cathedocracy[32] prevails in Judaism: rule not from the chair of Peter but from the chair of the scholars.

• Whereas it is most evident that in Christianity religious faith is made precise and there is a tripartite 'creed' (with numerous dogmas, disputes over faith and heresies), in Judaism it is religious praxis that is made precise on the presupposition of strict belief in one God and thus of the 'codex' of binding law (with numerous legal regulations, disputes over the law and a variety of schools).

• Instead of the theological summas, supported by church law, in Judaism the dominant feature is an all-embracing, coherent and universal system of morality and law for behaviour in any situation.

• Instead of subjection to ideals of an elitist monasticism which sets itself apart (with celibacy and abstinence as a movement characterized by poverty), in Judaism the dominant ideal is of a pious affirmation of life and its joys, to be lived out in everyday life by all believers.

This mediaeval Jewish paradigm is anything but 'obsolete' even today. To the present day it has continued to be handed down and put into practice by one of the great groups in Judaism, **Pharisaic-Talmudic Orthodoxy**. Whether in Jerusalem, New York, London or Paris, in faithfulness to the letter attempts are still made to keep all the precepts of the law even under modern conditions. All religious adaptations to modernity and all innovations are uncompromisingly rejected. For such mediaeval-orthodox Judaism, Israel even now is not primarily a state but a spiritual home: 'Israel' is the centre of ritual and moral purity – guaranteed by observing the law, wherever one may live. We shall hear more of this; for the moment we shall primarily keep with history, but now a history which necessarily seemed quite different from what was later to be the successful history of Christianity and Islam – a **history of suffering**.

The blame for the clash between Jews and Christians (so vigorous was a dispute in Rome as early as the year 49/50 that the emperor Claudius banished both parties from the capital for a time) cannot be assigned one-sidedly. Did the young Christian 'heresy' represent a real threat to Judaism? Or conversely, in view of the time of persecution which already began with the emperor Nero, did perhaps the Christian communities note bitterly the hostile attitude of the Jewish communities? The reason why there was already a parting of the ways between Jews and Jewish Christians at a very early stage in Palestine will be discussed as a separate theme in Part Two, in connection with the present. But even without such clarification, we can understand that the Judaism which continued to exist (even after the destruction of Jerusalem) increasingly represented a challenge to Christianity, which believed that it was theologically in the right – indeed that many Christians, including the theological elite, felt the continued existence of Judaism to be a threat.

So whether perceptibly or not, the anti-Judaism of the pagan state began to turn into an **anti-Judaism** which was specifically **that of the Christian church.**[33] Here, unfortunately, we have to note a fatal difference between pagan and Christian anti-Judaism: 'Whereas pre-Christian anti-Judaism was sporadic, limited locally, unofficial and had no ideological foundation (apart from the Egyptian species and its offshoots), at least from around the time of Constantine the Christian kind was permanent, universal, officially stirred up, a matter of principle, and supported by an ideological system. It does not have its roots in historical events and conditions, but even occurs where there are no Jews.'[34] According to J.W.Parkes, the new element in the fate of Jews in Christian times was that in contrast to the pagan attitude, the Christian attitude was no longer based on contemporary Jewish conduct but 'on an interpretation of what was held to be a divinely authoritative description of Jewish character and Jewish history'.[35]

Here some **church fathers** had still learned Hebrew and the exegesis of the Bible from Jewish teachers, and as head of the catechetical school of Alexandria, the brilliant **Origen**, the first Christian theologian to work in a scientific way, lived among Jews, maintained friendly relations with them and defended them to the pagans, even if in homilies he vigorously censured them because of their rejection of the messiah Jesus. But how did it come about, one might ask, that the opposition between Jews and Christians was now to become increasingly shrill, and as early as the second century an *adversus Judaeos* literature, a literature which was explicitly hostile to the Jews (the Epistle of Barnabas, Melito of Sardes, Tertullian and Hippolytus) was to come into being?[36]

Libraries have been written about this, and after discussing the origins of the completely different lives of Jews and Christians our view will be clearer. For the moment, however, to help us to understand the fatal development which followed, I shall mention without comment some important and often overlapping **factors** which were responsible **for the anti-Judaism specific to the church**:

1. The growing alienation of the church from its Old Testament and Hebrew roots because of the Hellenization and universalization of the Christian message.

2. The exclusive claim to the Hebrew Bible by a church which no longer valued it for itself but utilized it almost exclusively for its own existence with the help of typological and allegorical exegesis.

3. The breaking off of reciprocal conversations between church and synagogue in mutual isolation, in which dialogue was usually replaced by apologetic monologue.

4. The blame for the crucifixion of Jesus which was now assigned generally to 'the Jews', indeed to all Jews, so that their expulsion and dispersion could be regarded as a legitimate divine curse on a condemned people.

So already in the second half of the second century we find in **Melito** of Sardes, a bishop in Asia Minor, that pernicious saying (prompted by an un-Jewish/anti-Jewish christology) which was to prove particularly fateful in history: 'Listen, all you families of the nations, and see! An unprecedented murder has occurred in the middle of Jerusalem... the God has been murdered; the king of Israel has been put to death by an Israelite right hand.'[37] So the charge that the Jews were 'murderers of God' was unleashed on the world. Here already the concern was no longer to convert the Jews but to fight against them.

The shift under Constantine in 312/313 – unrestricted freedom of religion and the favouring of the Catholic church by the emperor **Constantine the Great** (306-337) – did not mean any direct deterioration in the status of Judaism. Without doubt Constantine was extremely unfriendly in his choice of words about the Jews (particularly when he was addressing the church – perhaps under the influence of his Christian advisers?). However, as G.Stemberger has noted in opposition to sweeping verdicts which speak of the end of tolerance towards the Jews, it would be 'wrong to describe Constantine as an outspoken opponent of the Jews', especially as, 'the laws which Constantine enacted did not bring any real deterioration for the Jews but rather in some respects strengthened their privileges under the law'.[38]

The real shift in imperial policy came precisely a century after Constantine's death. After **Theodosius the Great** (379-395) had ended freedom of religion and in 380 had declared Christianity to be the state religion and paganism and heresy to be crimes against the state, under emperor **Theodosius II** (401-450), finally Judaism, too, by **special church-state laws** (the 'Theodosian Codex', 438), was *de facto* excluded from the sacral realm to which access was to be had only through the sacraments of the church. Because after the formation of an **imperial church** the Jews in particular now consistently also rejected the ideology of the empire with its Christian colouring (the Christian emperor and his rule as the image of the heavenly rule of God?), what had been specifically pagan anti-Judaism was formally taken over by the imperial church and powerfully strengthened by Christian motives.

The church now no longer remembered that it had once been persecuted. On the contrary, with the help of the state, that same Christian church which not too long beforehand had been a persecuted minority in the Roman empire, without rights, now made Judaism, previously at any rate a *religio licita* (''permitted religion') in the Roman empire, an entity with inferior rights. While Judaism was not to be exterminated like the heresies, it was to be separated from Christian spheres of life and socially isolated. The **first repressive measures** served this end: there was a ban on mixed marriages with proselytes (converts to Judaism); a ban on Jews holding official positions; a ban on the building or extension of synagogues; a ban on any proselytizing. This very ban on recruiting compelled Judaism, which had formerly been a missionary religion successfully on the offensive, fatefully to concentrate on itself and reproduce itself, so that it was easy to speak of it later as a distinctive 'Jewish race'! To this degree, at this period rabbinic efforts at segregation (on halakhic grounds) and the Christian practice of discrimination (on political and theological grounds) affected each other and towards the end of the Roman empire led to a complete isolation of Judaism.

So now, in the territory of the Roman empire, in practice the Jews lived outside the empire. Many Jews more than ever felt their situation to be that of a *gola*, a real exile, and once again hoped for the imminent redemptive coming of the messiah. And whereas theologians and bishops like **Augustine** still felt that they had a missionary task towards the Jews (for Augustine, contrary to the current thesis that the Jews had murdered God, despite their guilt the Jews had a hope of conversion), others like **Ambrose** of Milan prevented the rebuilding of synagogues. Indeed, bishops like **Chrysostom** in Constantinople were already preaching against the Jews in the style of later anti-Jewish agitators:[39] the synagogue was a place of opposition to the law, a sphere of evil, a bastion of the devil; the Jews were *bon viveurs* who delighted in feasting and covetous rich people who, unfit for work, were now more fit for slaughtering (!). But despite all the counter-measures, throughout the empire Judaism remained present as a living religion. Indeed at this time in Constantinople there were still Christians (*ioudaizantes* = Judaizing Christians or Jewish Christians?) who went to the synagogue on sabbaths and feast days and in other respects enjoyed Jewish ceremonies.

The situation of the Jews was even more difficult in their great Diaspora city of Alexandria: in 415 they were driven out of Alexandria by an inflamed mob. As so often, behind this action there was a bishop (priest or monk), in this case that famous/notorious patriarch **Cyril**. Subsequently, at the Council of Ephesus in 431 – before the arrival of the opposing party – this advocate of an extreme Hellenistic and thus also anti-Jewish christology (Christ has only one divine nature = monophysitism) caused the status of Mary as 'mother of God' to be defined in a consistent way: Mary was not only 'Christotokos' = 'bearer of Christ' but 'Theotokos' = 'bearer of God'. However, for the empire as a whole it was the *Corpus Iuris Civilis* of the highly orthodox emperor **Justinian** (527-565) which, in the context of the fight against the heresies, once again intensified the anti-Jewish measures of Theodosius II (a prohibition against the holding of Christian slaves, which had a ruinous economic effect, and restrictions on Jewish worship). Justinian's law book was to be normative for mediaeval legislation on the Jews in both state and church.

However, during these centuries, in the **Western empire** people were utterly absorbed by the migratory movements of the Germanic peoples. Finally even the **papacy**, which in Western Rome had assumed the rule of the Roman emperor, had to take account of them: hence – to the indignation of the Greeks, an indignation which even now they have not got over – the coronation of the 'barbarian' king Charlemagne of the Franks as Roman emperor in 800. Here a new paradigm shift was taking shape within Christianity, from the Hellenistic paradigm of the early church to the Roman Catholic paradigm of the mediaeval church. But at the time of the Carolingians the Jews, again hoping for a shift towards eschatological salvation, began a new system of dating of their own which continued the biblical chronology and, as was later asserted, was meant to begin with the year of creation (= 3761 BCE).

The papacy, which was already becoming stronger at an early date, had still practised a relatively moderate policy towards the Jews – especially Gregory the Great around 600, with a reference to the promised conversion of the Jews (conversion through gentle persuasion or the offer of material advantages, without the use of force and compulsory baptism). However, the early Christian Middle Ages in France and especially in Spain also saw the first **direct use of force** against the Jews, though these instances were to remain **isolated** until the crusades. Even Bishop Isidore of Seville (died 637), who is regarded as the last of the Western church fathers, is characterized by a dishonourable anti-Jewish polemic. He could not suspect that a good seventy years later, for more than seven centuries, Spain was to be dominated by the Muslims, and that **Islam** was to appear as a new world power and a new world religion on the European continent – as the great opponent of Christianity in particular. No wonder that the first reports of good collaboration between Muslims and Jews were to be received in the West with the utmost suspicion.

6. Moorish Spain: what binds Jews and Muslims together

Of course, even under Islamic rule there were no 'equal rights' in the modern sense: for Jews (as for Christians) there were numerous restrictions.[40] And yet precisely here Jews were extremely successful, in Babylonia as in Syria, in Egypt as in North Africa and Spain. At least in theory, on the basis of the '**Laws of Omar**' which come from the seventh/eighth century, the members of the two other 'religions of the book' (which were respected but regarded as obsolete) could not hold office in the state, could not have Muslims as slaves, could not have houses higher than those of Muslim neighbours and could not ride on horses, could not build new houses of God or practise their own religion publicly. They had to wear distinctive clothing and to pay taxes (land tax and poll tax). Here as a rule the Shi'ites proved to be stricter than the Sunnis.[41]

And yet in fact under Islam (= Ishmael, Abraham's other son!) the

Jews fared **better than under the rule of Christianity,** the Roman and Germano-Roman empire (= 'Edom', the descendants of Esau, Jacob's selfish brother). Was this simply because of the malice and hostility of the Christians? No, there was a **very real background** to this treatment and there were **very real reasons** for it.[42]

– In the Islamic empire, despite all the restrictions, there was generally a **legally binding basis** which gave the Jewish minority guaranteed rights (even of personal possessions); this was lacking in the Christian West because of the migration of peoples, and in the Byzantine empire had steadily been replaced by a legislation which was hostile to the Jews.

– From the beginning the Jews had **central spiritual authorities** which were recognized by the Islamic authorities, in the framework of a self-government which extended beyond the local community (the Babylonian exilarchs and Gaons/heads of the colleges; there were also corresponding authorities in Egypt in Spain), whereas in Christian Europe the autonomous Jewish communities had long lived alongside one another and were not represented by any supra-regional authority.

– After the loss of the Christian Syrians, the Jews could continually be of new help to the Islamic empire **in trade in the East and the Mediterranean,** whereas in the Christian sphere at a very early stage they had to surrender long-distance trade with the Islamic world to the Italian cities, which in the late Middle Ages also took the lead in the Islamic sphere.

– The Jews could use **Arabic,** which is akin to Hebrew, **as an international language for commerce and trade,** whereas they gained hardly any command of Latin which, while international, was limited to the clergy and the learned, and so were forced back on the various national idioms, which were not yet very cultivated.

– The Jews were also closer to the Muslims than to the Christians in religion, because of their **clear monotheism,** without any mysterious dogmas, and because of the **similarity of their commandments about purity and food.** They saw themselves even more separated from the Christians as a result of the doctrines of the Trinity and the Incarnation which had now been developed fully, than as a result of the original dispute over law and circumcision.

– In the Islamic sphere, at an early stage the Jews were confronted with Arab **philosophy** and only to a degree with the **theological claim of Islam.** While they had to cope with Christian theology only from the twelfth century on, here they were immediately brought face to face with the Christian claim to revelation (the exception was the court of the emperor Frederick II in Sicily in the thirteenth century).

The 'golden age' of **Moorish Spain** exemplifies the way in which, despite Muslim rule and all the restrictions, it was possible for Jews and Muslims to **live together** with some degree of **harmony**; at any rate this gives the lie to the talk of 'ancestral Jewish-Arab hostility' which is customary today. After the Jewish-Hellenistic symbiosis, this Jewish-Moorish symbiosis was the **second interaction in world history between the Jewish culture and an alien culture**. In contrast to the other European countries, here the Jews could continue to engage in agriculture to an even greater extent. However, it has to be said that here in particular the Jews were also significantly involved in the slave trade which flourished from the Near East to Eastern Europe. But in Cordoba and other centres the Jews (at least the upper classes) had adopted Arabic as their language, along with Arab clothing and customs; they played a full part in economic, political and cultural life and were clearly marked out from Jews of other countries by their aristocratic, self-conscious manner. So by far the most fruitful symbiosis between Jews and Muslims developed in Spain. It found expression in an incomparable cultural flourishing of the sciences and arts, to which Jewish philosophy and theology, linguistic science and secular poetry (the first Jewish love-poetry since the Song of Songs), natural science and medicine and a wide-ranging activity in translation (Arabic-Hebrew-Latin), made an important contribution. So in the tenth century Moorish Spain had largely replaced Babylon, where in the ninth and tenth centuries there had similarly been a fertile exchange betwen Muslims and Jews, as the spiritual centre of Judaism.

By their translation and interpretation of Platonic and Aristotelian thought, the Arab philosophers had made a decisive preparation for Jewish and Christian scholasticism. And to the present day the great symbolic figure for Spanish Judaism remains the most significant Jewish scholar of the Middle Ages: **Moses ben Maimon** (1135-1204),[43] called Maimonides in the West. He came from Cordoba and was then active above all in Morocco and Egypt. As physician, merchant, lawyer, philosopher and theologian, in his main work *Guide for the Perplexed* he tried to reconcile religious faith and reason (like the Muslim philosophers Avicenna and Averroes, and later in Christianity Albertus Magnus and Thomas Aquinas) and down to the present day has remained the great model for Jewish scholars. Maimonides' **confession of faith** of 1168, contained in his commentary on the Mishnah,[44] has stood the test of history despite all the criticism of it: it has often been given poetic form and now appears as a confession in the prayer books at the end of morning prayer. It expresses the elements of faith which Judaism shares with Christianity and Islam (belief in the existence,

What Jews believe

1. 'I believe and affirm that the Creator created and guides all creatures, and that he alone has accomplished, accomplishes and will accomplish all works.

2. I believe and affirm that the Creator is one, with a oneness which is absolutely unique, and that he alone was, is and will be our God.

3. I believe and affirm that the Creator is not a body, that there is nothing bodily about him and that none is like him.

4. I believe and affirm that the Creator is the first and will be the last.

5. I believe and affirm that the Creator alone is worthy of worship and that we should not worship anything other than him.

6. I believe and affirm that all the words of the prophets are true.

7. I believe and affirm that the prophecy of our teacher Moses is true and that he is the father of all the prophets, both of those who came before him and those who followed him.

8. I believe and affirm that the Torah which is in our possession today is the same Torah as was handed down to our teacher Moses.

9. I believe and affirm that this Torah will not be abrogated, nor shall another Torah come from God.

10. I believe and affirm that the Creator has knowledge of all the deeds and thoughts of men, for scripture says, 'He who has formed all their hearts also understands their doings.'

11. I believe and affirm that the Creator rewards those who obey his commandments and punishes those who transgress his prohibitions.

12. I believe and affirm that the messiah will come. Even should he tarry, I still long for his advent.

13. I believe and affirm that a resurrection of the dead will take place at a time which will be well pleasing to the Creator.

Praised be his name and praised be his memory for ever and ever.'

Confession of faith by Moses Maimonides

unity, incorporeality and omniscience of God and in retribution and resurrection) as clearly as what divides the three religions: over against Christianity the absolute simplicity of God and belief in a messiah who is still to come, and over against Islam and its Qur'an the eternal validity of the Torah of Moses.

Like Christian and Islamic religion, as a result of its origins Jewish religion is essentially historical, and utterly different from any nature religion. However, the question must now be raised not only from the Islamic but also from the Christian perspective: can this long, dramatic history of the Jewish people, and in particular the history of Jews with Christians, be reduced purely and simply to a history of suffering?

7. Not to be forgotten: the Jewish success story

Before we go into the sorry nadir of the mediaeval church's persecution of the Jews, we must follow Jewish historians like Salo W.Baron,[45] Bernhard Blumenkranz, Peter Riesenberg and David Biale and discuss something which is often forgotten or kept silent about – as part of the battle against hostility to the Jews and in order to achieve a possibly better way for Jews and Christians to live together in the future. For the persecution of the Jews in Christianity was not a permanent condition, but had been provoked by particular factors, not least social and economic factors. In other words, alongside the fearful history of suffering we must not overlook the **amazing history of Jewish success** – all down the centuries, already long before the formation of the state of Israel. And that is true not only for the Islamic sphere but for the Christian sphere as well.

Since in mediaeval Judaism history writing (which had flourished above all in the time of the monarchy) gave way almost completely to work on the written and oral Torah, and in any case was seriously hampered by the way in which the Jewish people were dispersed, it was only after the Enlightenment that **Jewish historiography** underwent a powerful revival. Mention should be made here of Heinrich Graetz's eleven-volume *History of the Jews from Earliest Times to the Present* (1853-1875), which is still a basic study, and in our century Simon Dubnow's classic ten-volume *World History of the Jewish People* (1925-1929). One of the newest and best works is now that of H.H.Ben-Sasson, Professor at the Hebrew University of Jerusalem, editor and co-author of the 1200-page *History of the Jewish People*,[46] which is often quoted here. Ben-Sasson has without doubt expressed the basic feeling of many Jews that 'persecution and humiliation of the Jews' were always 'acts of deliberate policy' against the Jews and that the overwhelming majority of Jews virtually 'chose the fate of unabating persecution' because they 'preferred to remain loyal to their faith and their people and their heritage'.[47]

However, other leading Jewish specialists cast doubt on such statements which at the same time both generalize persecution and make it a heroic matter.[48] Salo W.Baron of Columbia University, New York, who unlike the Diaspora-orientated Dubnow and also unlike the more recent Israel-centred historians attempts to depict the Diaspora **and Eretz Israel** as two centres of Jewish creativity, attempts throughout his multi-volume work to **correct** the interpretation of Jewish history as **a purely passive history of suffering** and with it that 'lachrymose view of Jewish history which sees the fate of the Jews in the Diaspora as a sheer sucession of misery and persecution'; instead of this, Baron everywhere attempts to emphasize areas and elements in which Jews and their environment were mutually fruitful.[49]

In his well documented work on *Jews and Christians in the Western World*, Bernard Blumenkranz of Paris[50] was able to entitle Part One, dealing with the period between 430 (the death of Augustine in the middle of the age of popular migration) and 1096 (the beginning of the Crusades) **'Good Neighbourly Relations'**. For all the fundamental differences of belief between Judaism and Christianity, despite all the theological polemic and the missionary efforts by both sides, for many centuries the difference had not simply meant opposition and conflict. Certainly there was always misuse of power on the part of those who were stronger (usually Christians, but also in Spain, by way of exception, the Jews), and majorities (of whatever kind) down to the present day usually treated minorities as – minorities, entities with lesser rights. But that should not disguise the fact that only in the eleventh century did a fundamental change make itself felt in the attitude of the Roman Catholic Church to the Jews, which then embraced the whole of Europe – a change which was reinforced by the crusades (against Muslims and Jews).

Against this wider historical horizon, Peter Riesenberg of Washington University, St Louis,[51] emphatically points out that if we do not look at the history of Judaism from the Hellenistic period to the Italian Renaissance *a priori* only through glasses darkened by the most recent events of terror, and if we see the acts of violence against Jews in the **overall context** of the fate of many national and religious minorities, xenophobia and religious intolerance, we have to say something like this. What was done to the Jews at that time – we are not yet speaking of the Holocaust – by way of humiliation, violence, banishment and finally also massacre was also, lamentably, done to some **other lesser peoples and minorities**, beginning with the Greeks, Manichaeans and Nestorians, through the crusades against Muslims, Byzantine Christians and heretics of the Western church (Albigensians and Cathari), through countless acts of terror at the time of the Reformation and the Thirty Years' War, finally down to the murder in our century of 1.5 million Armenians in Turkey... To say that is of course neither to offer a historical excuse nor to engage in a 'historicizing' which neutralizes everything and puts it on the same level; rather, it is a necessary supplementing of history.

We must not overlook the positive element in Jewish history. The Jewish **Diaspora**, the justification for the existence of which some present-day Israelis have questioned, is marked by not only economic but also cultural and spiritual achievements which are unparalleled in comparison with other minorities: by far the greater part of Jewish poetry (tens of thousands of poems in Hebrew), philosophy of religion, theology, mysticism and science comes from the Jewish Diaspora. After the decline of Jewish science in Mesopotamia, one has only to think of the significance of the rabbinic scholar Gershom ben Judah in Mainz, which rivalled the authority of the last significant Gaon (Chai, who died in 1038). He was followed by an even greater rabbi, Solomon Yizhaki, called **Rashi** (1040-1105), who for a long time was regarded as **the** commentator on Bible and Talmud.[52]

We may regard this Diaspora existence more as a way of suffering, as penitence for the sins of the fathers, as the proclamation of God's name among the nations, or simply as a place of better economic opportunities. However, the liveliness of the Jewish communities of which we have heard is beyond dispute. They existed virtually all over the then known world, from Mesopotamia to Spain, and we could say a good deal about the flourishing communities of Jews in North Africa (Kairouan?), under the Carolingians in Germany, or even in Italy as late as the fourteenth and fifteenth centuries. All in all, despite the minority status of the Jews, the strict restrictions on them, and the occasional confusions at least down to the crusades, this is a history of highly impressive achievements. So we can only endorse Riesenberg's judgment: on the whole, compared with other more powerful peoples and groupings, Judaism was the **only Diaspora minority** in the Christian world which was amazingly **successful** over a long period. Often privileged in their trading settlements, in particular throughout the German empire as 'servants of the imperial chamber', many Jews had freedom from tolls and a free market everywhere; for a long time they dominated Mediterranean trade, and when this was taken over by Italian cities, they dominated trade within Europe and with Eastern Europe. So until the Crusades a relatively large number of Jews were well-to-do and even rich (for example, between 1166 and 1185 Aaron of York was probably the richest man in England). Jews were rich above all because of their achievements not only in the economic and financial spheres but also in government, science and culture.

But what about the notorious **ghetto** for Jews? Even in the case of the separate residential quarter, the Jewish ghetto (or the *shtetl* in Eastern Europe) we do better to follow Bernhard Blumenkranz in speaking of what from the tenth/eleventh century onwards was primarily a 'Jewish quarter' chosen spontaneously and of the Jews' own accord, of the kind that existed from antiquity and was also to be found in the major Islamic cities. All this was primarily a consequence of the Jews opting for separation as described above: their chosen way of life, the demands of an orthodox Jewish life-style in terms of liturgy, diet and education. It was only later that the walls around the quarter, which were intended to protect the Jews (the first of them built in Speyer in 1084), served as barriers – as an expression of the discrimination against Jews. Only in the sixteenth century, as the result of an above-average growth in the Jewish population, were there legal restrictions on Jewish settlements which confined them to a particular part of the city. On the model of the situation in Venice, such an area was called a 'ghetto'. Because 5,000 Jewish refugees had come to Venice in the year 1515/16, it was resolved to restrict all Jews to a district at the end of the main island, called the 'ghetto nuovo', and thus to segregate them completely – albeit in the face of vigorous Jewish protests. But in the ghetto the Jews could at least feel secure and develop an intense cultural life (even today in North America not only orthodox Jews but also Chinese and other groups would like an 'ethnic neighbourhood').[53] However, sooner or later this compulsory 'ghettoization' inevitably led to terribly restricted and unhygienic living conditions, and ultimately official restrictions on marriages and children.

Be this as it may, the centuries of relative tolerance and *laisser-faire* Jewish-Christian coexistence cannot simply be brushed aside by the contemporary view of Jewish history. Of course this does not alter the Jewish history of suffering in any way. But in order to deal with the present, even in the Near East, it is extremely important to recognize what Peter Riesenberg put like this: 'Jewish history can still be Jewish history without over-emphasis on misery, persecution and special suffering. My purpose is not to deny Jewish suffering or the constructive role that memory, and even exaggeration of this suffering, has played in the past 2000 years of Jewish history. It is, rather, to make contemporary Jews more aware and indeed, proud than they have been of their long history of successful adaptation, survival and creation throughout the world. In the midst of every kind of society they have largely maintained their own identity and esprit, and have contributed to many gentile civilizations while advancing their own.'[54]

So the history of the Jews between the fall of Jerusalem and the modern age in Europe was both a history of powerlessness and a history of power. The American Jewish historian David Biale, of Berkeley, California, has put particular emphasis on this by citing the Jewish revolts in antiquity, the political theories of the rabbis and the corporate power of the Jews in the Middle Ages.[55] Israeli historians, too, warn against all meta-historical temptations and political-ideological instrumentalizations of the history and interpretation of antisemitism. The incomprehensibility of the Holocaust must not divert us into a misleadingly one-sided, retrospective 'anti-semitization' of the whole history of the relationships between Jews and non-Jews, under cover of a rational analysis of the historical course of events. So, thus warned against the constraints in Jewish history, we return to that church anti-Judaism which now of course reaches its terrifying nadir in the much-celebrated high Middle Ages of Christianity.

8. Christian persecutions of the Jews and the 'reasons' for them

What happened in the eleventh century to bring about a complete change of mood and finally a terrible **shift in the attitude of the church to Judaism**?[56] Here there is striking evidence of the interdependence of the three prophetic religions. It was the historic struggle of Christianity against Islam! Right at the beginning of the century a rumour had gone through Europe that the Jews had warned Sultan al-Hakim of Egypt that Christians would conquer his empire, including Jerusalem, unless he destroyed the Church of the Holy Sepulchre there. The Sultan did just that – in the year 1009, by beginning to persecute Christians and Jews – which was an exceptional move in Islam. What was brewing at the beginning of the century finally erupted at the end of it.

Along with the intensified fight against 'heretics' within the church in southern France (the Albigenisans), it was primarily the **Crusades** (1095-1270) which had catastrophic consequences for many Jews in Europe. The Jews were now lumped in with the Muslims. Indeed, according to more recent investigations anti-Islamism may have been a main cause of the outbreak of anti-Judaism in the high Middle Ages.[57] The first anti-Jewish riots occurred in 1096 during the First Crusade – often out of simple greed and against the will of both the authorities and the citizens. Particularly in the 'Holy Land', 'Christian' knights who had been made fanatical by preachers and were greedy for plunder thought that they had to eliminate the 'enemies of Christ' by force. In 1099 there was an indescribable blood bath of the Jews in Palestine, who here were allied with the Muslims. Only a wretched remnant of Jews remained (in Acco and Tyre). European Jews now lost their previously dominant position in long-distance trading; all that was left to them was minor retailing and money-lending. But from the time of the Second Crusade many crusaders had been guaranteed postponement of repayments or even remission of debts owed to their Jewish creditors.

Pope **Gregory VII** (1073-1085), known as the first pope to exercise absolute rule as a result of a revolution from above (and for decrees against lay investiture and the marriage of priests), who aided the breakthrough of the new mediaeval Roman Catholic paradigm, had also issued the first degrees against Jews in state office. Here the anti-Jewish theology had had an influence on legal judgments, and these in turn had an effect on theology. However, the **climax of the church's anti-Judaism** came with the pontificate of **Innocent III** (a contemporary of the very different Francis of Assisi) and the greatest council of the Middle Ages, which he was responsible for summoning: the **Fourth Lateran Synod** of 1215.[58] It was not the riots in connection with the First Crusade in 1096 but this council which fundamentally changed the situation of the Jews, both legally and theologically.[59] Because as unbelievers the Jews were 'servants of sin', it was concluded that they should now be the servants of Christian princes. So now, in Constitution 68 of the council, for the first time a special form of dress was directly prescribed for Jews, which would isolate them; they were banned from taking public office, forbidden to go out during Holy Week, and had a compulsory tax imposed on them, to be paid to the local Christian clergy. The new mendicant orders, the disciples of Dominic and sadly also of Francis, gained prominence as those who implemented the new anti-Jewish Roman policy.[60]

At the same time this anti-Judaism, too, had economic, psychological and theological roots, although virtually no new arguments against the Jews had emerged in mediaeval theology. Only in art, on the portals of Gothic cathedrals, was the self-understanding of the mediaeval church graphically portrayed in a new way: a feminine figure with eyes bound, a broken banner or tables of the law dropping from her hands, embodied the synagogue: hardened, blind, conquered, rejected Judaism. Her counterpart was the triumphant church of Christ. And even worse, from the thirteenth century 'Jewish swine' became part of the standard repertory of the pictorial calumniation of the Jews by the church.

Because of the tremendous suffering, the centuries of continuous **Jewish migratory movements** began – first of all increasingly **eastwards,** where the Jews found new fields for colonizing activity in the countries that were developing there. So countless German Jews migrated first from the cities of the Rhine and Danube to central Germany, later to Poland, and finally on to the Ukraine and Russia. The **Yiddish** (really Jewish German) spoken by the Jews in Eastern Europe, with its Middle High German basis, combined with Hebrew-Aramaic and Slavic elements, still points back towards the regions of the Rhine.

The situation in **Germany** was still comparatively tolerable. For in the 'Holy Roman Empire', after many anti-Jewish riots, in 1237 the Jews had been put under the special protection of the emperor and then of the territorial rulers as 'servants of the imperial chamber' (*servi camerae* – though this brought with it exploitation by taxation). (Since their defeat in the Jewish war against Rome, all Jews were ostensibly slaves of the Roman emperor and his legal successors!) The situation was now very much worse in the Christian states of Europe under centralized rule, where the Jews were driven out once there was no longer any economic need for them: in **France**, where at first there had been special taxation, confiscation of goods, burnings of the Talmud and forced baptisms, and particularly in **England**. After vain attempts at conversion, in the thirteenth century hundreds of Jews were hanged there, thousands imprisoned, and finally, in 1290, all were banished and their property confiscated. Here already there were 'final solutions' of the 'Jewish problem'! And all over Europe religious, social and economic resentment were now combined in a fatal form of anti-Judaism which did not need the racist basis of later 'antisemitism' to produce thousands of victims.

In **Spain,** too, the situation had become more acute with the completion of the reconquest, the end of Muslim rule which came towards the end of the fifteenth century, and the union of the two kingdoms of Castile and Aragon. The Dominican orders were entrusted with establishing the **Inquisition**; it had set itself the aim of 'converting' the Jews – by force, if necessary – under the sign of the 'church which alone brings salvation'. This was soon to have a devastating effect; in 1481 around 400 Jews were burned in Seville alone, 2,000 in the archdiocese of Cadiz, and in Spain as a whole probably more than 12,000. With the conquest of Granada (Spain's last Muslim kingdom) in 1492 and the end of the Christian reconquest, on the urging of the notorious Grand Inquisitor Torquemada, confessor to Queen Isabella of Castile, all the Jews in Spain were confronted with the alternative of baptism or emigration. Around 100,000 people emigrated, but more had themselves baptized – out of fear of the expense and hardship of emigration. However, they secretly remained Jews (= Spanish *marranos*, 'pigs', because pseudo-Christians were worse than those Jews loyal to the faith who had emigrated). Finally, in 1497, contrary to all promises, the Jews were also expelled from Portugal (and in 1501 from Provence). Ferdinand of Aragon and Isabella of Castile were given the title 'Catholic monarchs' by Pope Alexander VI (Borgia!). The Turkish empire benefited most, economically and also culturally, from the emigration of the **Spanish-Eastern** = 'Sephardic' Jews (Sepharad = Spain), as did Italy until the introduction of the Inquisition, and Holland in the north. 'Christian' Spain remained in Jewish memory as the dark and gloomy counterpart to Moorish Spain.

So the history of strife and curse between Jews and Christians moved towards its nadir. And the question arises: was there no **religious dialogue**[61] at all throughout this whole period? The answer is this:

1. On the **Christian side**, in the high Middle Ages there were **disputations**, but these were **forced** on the Jews, often initiated and carried on by Jewish converts, and arranged by the church and princely courts.[62] There was one in Paris in 1240 (at which the Talmud was then publicly burned), in Barcelona in 1263 (with the famous Rabbi Moses Nachmanides, who was later banished from the country), and above all one in Tortosa in 1413/14, between the Jewish convert Joshua Lorki (whose Christian name was Geronimo de Santa Fé) and the then leading Jewish philosopher Joseph Albo. Such disputations had little to do with dialogue in the modern sense. It was not a matter of really understanding the other side and in the last resort respecting dissent. Rather, the *a priori* concern was to provide a theological refutation of the Jews with the aim of converting them. The last of the great Jewish-Christian disputations, that in Tortosa, was not a real debate but a 'public show, indeed a public show trial'.[63] Yet even such disputations, which at any rate presupposed an exact knowledge of Jewish sources on the Christian side, came to an end after the introduction of the church Inquisition.

2. Conversely, on the **Jewish side**, too, there was an **anti-Christian polemic** parallel to the tractate *Adversus Judaeos* which was to be found in the works of almost every church father, above all the so-called *Toledot Jeshu*, a parody of the life of Jesus depicted in the

Gospels. In this work Jesus was depicted as a kind of magician who, contrary to the law, had assumed the divine name. However, more recent Christian research, too, has established 'that there is no Tannaitic (= first/second-century) "Jesus passage" and that all the Amoraean (= third- to fifth-century) mentions of Jesus are more post-Talmudic than Talmudic'. 'Only in the course of the repressive Byzantine religious policy in the fifth, sixth and seventh centuries (before the Arab conquest) did Christianity, identified with the Roman-Byzantine empire, become for Judaism an apocalyptic caricature of the fourth kingdom in Daniel and assume the character of idolatry. In this situation it was also quite possible to see the founder of Christianity in the rabbinic Ben Stada/ Ben Pandera figure, who was associated with the charge of leading people astray into idolatry.'[64] However, the Middle Ages then saw the first anti-Christian polemical literature to be taken seriously: books like *The Shame of the Saints* (1397) written in Spain by Isaac ben Moses Ephodi, or the *Abolition of the Dogmas of the Christian Religion* (1397/98), also written in Spain, by Hasdai ben Judah Crescas; or books like *Book of Refutation* (written in the thirteenth/fourteenth century in the Rhineland) or *Strengthening of Faith* by the Karaite Isaac ben Moses Halevi Troki, published in Lithuania in 1593.[65] But a third point needs to be made.

3. Much as both sides were entangled in polemic, the two polemics were not of equal importance. The Jews never had anything remotely approaching the political power of Christians. Indeed from our present perspective it is shaming for Christians, too, to see how the Christian church, of all bodies, oppressed and persecuted Jews with the force of the state in the name of the Jew Jesus, and now even more triumphantly gave itself out to be the successor, representative, heir to Israel, which had been finally rejected. What a **fatal division of roles** this was, in both theory and practice: 'the Jews' – the rejected people, to whom all the statements about judgment and the curse in the Hebrew Bible applied. And by contrast, the church – the true Israel, which could apply all the promises of the Hebrew Bible to itself. So the church was now the spiritual Israel, **the** people of God. For had not the Jewish people in fact ceased to be God's people since the crucifixion of Jesus? The punishment for this death was now finally indeed a history of suffering, unparalleled in human history. And what became of Christian love? This seemed at best to be shown to individual Jews. Not least because of such heavy theological and historical prejudices, the centuries of Judaism after the Crusades are full of enforced religious dialogues, compulsory baptisms and burnings of the Talmud; of caricatures of the 'Jewish swine' (the prohibition against eating pork), of condemnations,

expulsions, resettlements, plunderings, torture and murder. There was a convenient side-effect which was constantly desired: the debts of Christians could be wiped out by the liquidation of their Jewish creditors. As Christians must we not blush for shame even today in the face of this fearful history of blood and tears?

4. And is all this now a thing of the past? No, some **mediaeval prejudices** live on in Christianity. Granted, at that time this special economic position, forced on the Jews by the Christians themselves and sometimes certainly also exploited, which sometimes made non-Jews substantial debtors to Jews, was often a pretext for the persecution of Jews. But those ancient and sometimes mediaeval historical prejudices, repeated down to the most recent past and born of anxieties (and which unfortunately many Christians even now fail to realize are untenable), are a different matter from the complaints which were certainly sometimes justified about dubious practices in money-lending (particularly in country areas).[66] The following comments need to be made, briefly and clearly:

(a) **Are the Jews 'money-grubbers'?** There are still widespread comments about 'money-grubbing Jews' or 'Christian Jews' and about financial transactions as a characteristic of the 'synagogue'![67] But originally – in Palestine and also in Babylonia – the Jews had distinguished themselves chiefly in agriculture, cattle-breeding and market gardening, and then also in the crafts and in trade. In the Hellenistic period the Jews, along with the Greeks, were the chief agents in trade with the East, because of their lines of communication and knowledge of languages. And in the European Diaspora, too, they had continued not only in both trade and shipping, but also in agriculture; indeed in early mediaeval Europe agriculture had even been their prime occupation! It was the Christians themselves who first drove Jews out of the high offices of state, the law and the army, and then after the time of the crusades out of agriculture (in which the majority of them were employed) and the crafts. They were even explicitly prohibited from manufacturing Christian devotional materials by Pope Benedict XIII in 1415. Jewish landowners might not employ any Christian workers. The Christian order of guilds closed the crafts to the Jews. The feudal system prevented them from acquiring land and property. Foreign trade had passed into other hands. So what else could the Jews really have done if they wanted to survive? All that was left to them was minor trading and peddling.

Hypocritically, the mediaeval church itself forced Jews who could only eke out a livelihood in such a way into lending money at interest and taking pledges (and also into trade in antiques), which it forbade its own members (interest = usury!). These practices were desired by the authorities, but ostracized and hated among the populace. In any case, according to the strict rabbinic interpretation of the law, Jews had to apply the biblical prohibition against lending money at interest[68] (which had been constantly got round in earlier days) only to Jews faithful to the law. So as a result of the churches' command the Jews had a monopoly in financial transactions. Since they themselves were taxed excessively highly, they had to ask for correspondingly high interest (usually 43-100%), and in 1290 this first led to their expulsion from England. So in the late Middle Ages 'the Jew' became a hostile figure, who even in the passion plays which were widespread after the fourteenth century typically had to appear as a usurer ('son of Judas').[69] Jews had to purchase almost everything for themselves – the right to come and go, to buy and sell, to pray together, to marry, to bear a child.

(b) **Are the Jews 'condemned to dispersion'?** Who does not know the legend of the Jewish cobbler Ahasver (which in fact only emerges in the high Middle Ages)? He is said to have cursed Jesus on his way to the cross and to have been condemned to restless wandering until Christ's return! Is he not **the** symbolic figure of the Jews which some people wanted to see at the time? But not all Jews lived in the Diaspora, simply waiting for redemption in penance for their sins! In any case, the sins which according to the Jewish view made the people guilty (idolatry and hatred of one another) were not those of which Christians accused them (the rejection of Christ). Conversely, the Jewish Diaspora had begun several centuries **before** the death of Christ. As we saw, only a small proportion of the Jews were living in Palestine at the time of Jesus' birth. And a substantial number of Jews continued to live in Palestine after the conquest of Jerusalem by Titus and the Bar Kokhba rebellion. It was the Crusaders who finished them off, leaving only a tiny remnant to eke out a wretched life as dyers. So are the Jews condemned to dispersion? Here, too, it has taken the foundation of the state of Israel seriously to shake this monstrous legend.

(c) **Are the Jews 'criminal plotters'?** Who does not know of the treacherous fables which are still believed even today by some Catholics who persist in the mediaeval paradigm? These tell of the ritual murder of Christian children (the 'holy' boy William of Norwich), alleged poisoning of wells, miracles with the host and desecrations of the host (and also relate how dangerous Jewish doctors are; there was talk of a 'conspiracy' of Jewish doctors against Stalin's life as late as 1953!). And think of all the recorded anti-Jewish remarks by popes and saints! But all these sordid accusations were projections. The Hebrew Bible,

Mishnah and Talmud manifestly fear the taint of blood. And already mediaeval emperors like Frederick II and popes like Innocent II protected the Jews against such charges. But the indisputable fact is that these criminal, highly dangerous prejudices and legends have cost countless Jews their lives in constantly new persecutions and expulsions. For example, in 1475 it was alleged that Simon, an eighteen-month-old boy, had been the victim of a Jewish ritual. A cult of him came into being in Trent, the city where the council was held, and it was endorsed by Pope Sixtus V. Only in 1965, under the influence of the Second Vatican Council, was the cult abolished.

The Crusades were not even the absolute nadir of all the discrimination and persecutions. The **most serious mediaeval persecution of the Jews** took place between 1348 and 1350. In Alsace, in the Rhineland, Thuringia, Bavaria and Austria about 300 Jewish communities were exterminated and hundreds of thousands of Jews were slaughtered in religious fanaticism: a large number were forcibly converted, and only a remnant was still tolerated. Why did all this happen? It began with a fable! Originating in southern France, the charge suddenly spread throughout Europe that Jews were responsible for the plague which had broken out, taking the lives of around a third of the population: Jews had poisoned the wells. The consequences were fatal. In 1394, following the example of England a century earlier, the Jews were also banished from France – of course always with lucrative confiscations of property. This action was not to be reversed until the French Revolution.

The German empire, finally, was by no means behindhand in its actions, and in the fifteenth and sixteenth centuries one wave of expulsion of Jews followed another. Now there were major Jewish communities only in Frankfurt, Worms, Vienna and Prague. Thus the cultural decline of north European Jewry was forced upon it with incalculable results. As we have already heard, **the Jews (Ashkenasim) who came from Germany ('Ashkenasia')** emigrated eastwards. And so finally in the sixteenth and seventeenth centuries the **economic and cultural balance of Judaism shifted to Poland**: at that time Poland was a developing country where the Jews were welcome as pioneers in urban and long-distance trading; and as a middle class engaged in trade and commerce they enjoyed security, privilege, and indeed for a while even very considerable autonomy.

Before going on to recount more history, at this point, in view of the transition from the Middle Ages to the modern period in Europe, I would like to raise a question which I have hardly ever seen discussed but which is by no means unimportant for the present. Why was there no real Reformation as there was in Christianity in Judaism, which only made the transition from the Middle Ages to the modern period in the eighteenth century?

9. Why was there no Jewish reformation?

Is that perhaps a meaningless or at least a superfluous question? Even some Jews are insufficiently aware that in the face of the highly complex process of commentary and codification in rabbinic Judaism, already in the Middle Ages there was a broad **Jewish 'back to the Bible'** movement – arising from concern over Islam, which was spreading so rapidly, and as an expression of revolt against the rabbinic establishment. In the eighth century a Jewish sect had come into being in the region of Persia and Babylon whose founder was held to be a certain Anan ben David. It had rejected the Talmud and had allowed only the Hebrew Bible, the Tanakh, as the source of divine revelation. All that one needed to know to fulfil God's commandments was to be found in the Bible itself. By contrast, a post-biblical tradition, everything collected in the Mishnah and Talmud, the vast traditional material of the 'oral Torah', was useless. That is amazing. So even in Judaism there was a *sola scriptura* movement in opposition to the predominant Talmudic, rabbinic tradition: later traditions were to be measured critically by '**scripture alone**'. This was a reform movement which, like the Protestant Reformation movement, even reshaped the liturgy so that it was completely in accordance with the Bible, with the emphasis on the Psalms. This inevitably heightened opposition to the 'clerical' establishment, which here was that of the rabbis.

Even at that time, the supporters of this movement were called **Karaeans** or Karaites (Hebrew *kara'im*, from 'read' or 'call, assemble'), 'people of scripture', to distinguish them from the adherents of rabbinic Judaism (whom scholars call the 'Rabbanites').[70] Benjamin ben Moses from Nahawend in Persia (830-886) made an important contribution towards consolidating this movement. As the first Karaite systematic theologian he elevated the free and independent individual study of scripture to be a basic principle. At the same time, through a philosophical criticism of tradition inspired by Plotinus, he attempted to eliminate all the anthropomorphic features from the understanding of God in the haggadah and Jewish mysticism. Are these anti-rabbinic 'biblicists' perhaps beneath attention? Certainly not. They formed the most significant Jewish sect in the East between the ninth and the twelfth centuries; sometimes it had a majority in certain communities, and it gave official rabbinic Judaism a hard time even in Palestine, Egypt and North Africa. However, following the First Crusade in 1099, the sect was largely exterminated in Palestine: along with their Rabbanite opponents, the Karaites of Jerusalem were driven into a synagogue by the 'Crusader knights' and burnt alive.

As their spiritual and cultural contribution, in the ninth and tenth centuries the Karaites produced a significant academic literature. Famous scholars emerged in philosophy, theology, scriptural exegesis, Hebrew philology and lexicography, and compelled even official Talmudic Judaism to return to a more intensive preoccupation with the Bible itself. And despite a Rabbanite ban on marriage with the Karaites, even at a later date there were a number of Karaite communities in the Byzantine, later to become the Turkish, empire. In the twelfth century, in Byzantium alone, 500 out of 2,500 Jews were said to be Karaites; having incurred the enmity of the orthodox Rabbanites, they had to live segregated from other Jews. Between the seventeenth and the nineteenth centuries the main focus of the Karaite movement shifted to the Crimea and Lithuania. And so (apart from the Samaritans) they are the only Jewish sect to have survived more than 1200 years and still to be in existence today. It is estimated that as late as 1932 there were still around 10,000 Karaites in the Soviet Union. And after the foundation of the state of Israel in 1948, many of them came from Islamic countries to Israel, where they form a community which is recognized by the government but not very influential (in 1970 their membership was estimated at around 7,000).

But why was it that this reform movement, with all its impulses to foster and interpret the text of the Bible, **could not prevail against the rabbinic establishment?** It is no argument to say that the rabbinic establishment was too powerful – it has only to be compared with the powerful mediaeval Roman Catholic church! Rather, we might reflect on the following points:

1. In contrast to the Protestant Reformers, the founder of the Karaite movement, Anan ben David, combined an **ascetic rigorism** with his call to scripture; this was grounded in a quasi-Sadducean return to the pure Bible, and also in a reaction against the secularization of the Babylonian Jewish exilarchate. For in contrast to the Rabbanitic interpretation (along Pharisaic lines), which was often more accommodating, Karaism called for stricter regulations on sabbath rest, circumcision, ritual purity, and above all marriages with kinsfolk (following Gen.2.24, even those related by marriage were to be regarded as blood relations).

So life among those of other faiths was almost impossible; for many people emigration to Palestine was the inevitable consequence, so that in the twentieth century there was generally a marked return there by the Karaites. Consequently, as the Jewish scholars J.E.Heller and L.Nemoy point out, the Karaite founder Anan cannot be called 'a true "reformer" of Judaism; for far from making the "yoke" of the traditional law easier, he made it harder to bear'.[71]

2. Because of the individualistic maxims of their founder, 'Search boldly in the Torah and do not rely on my opinion', after his death his followers very soon **split** into different groups and parties – orientated on apocalyptic or philosophy, or believing in the Torah. There was a threat of religious anarchy, and a difference over calendar reckoning created additional problems. It was very much more difficult to survive in countless groups and parties than within the framework of a closed religious and social system.

3. A **defender of rabbinic Judaism** against the Karaites, with an encyclopaedic education, who argued in a supremely rational way, appeared in the tenth century in the person of the Gaon ('head') of the school of Sura in Babylon (which has already been mentioned). This was the Egyptian **Saadia ben Joseph** (882-942). He was the supreme scholarly authority for the Jews of his time. Not only had he translated the Hebrew Bible into Aramaic and made a skilful commentary on it, but his *Book of the Doctrine of Faith and the Grounds of Knowledge*[72] was the first systematic theological account of Jewish faith (a first formulation of ten articles of faith which Moses Maimonides then expanded to the thirteen classical articles quoted above). In so doing Saadiah deliberately took over philosophical and theological arguments from the surrounding culture. For since the ninth century the influence of classical Greek philosophy had made itself felt in both Karaite and Rabbanite Judaism, and Saadia's book was the first work of a philosophical theological character since Philo of Alexandria, who had been completely forgotten in Judaism. This same extremely famous man now wrote a series of pamphlets (the first at the early age of twenty-three) against the Karaites, whom he regarded as heretics and apostates from the mother synagogue. Followed by later great Jewish theologians like Jehuda Hallevi (who died in 1141) and Moses ben Maimon (Maimonides), he succeeded in stemming this expanding opposition movement within Judaism, so that the danger of a funda-mental reformation could be averted.

4. Thus these Karaites remained a small and increasingly conservative **minority**, which withdrew as far as possible from the world, whether this world was rabbinic, Christian or Muslim, and gave up the oppor-

tunity of further spiritual interaction with the surrounding culture. So a historical opportunity was missed. For whenever there was a concern in Judaism to reflect on the Bible, even at a later date - for example in London among the descendants of those Spanish and Portuguese Jews who had been forcibly baptized, or in nineteenth-century reformed Judaism – in other words, when quasi-Karaite arguments emerged, they could be promptly dismissed with the cry of 'Karaism' – heretical!

Questions for the Future

✝ Did the Roman Catholic Church act wisely in *a priori* rejecting all suggestions for reform by the Reformers (even a liturgy in the vernacular, the chalice for the laity and married priests) and instead of this developing the mediaeval church system into a Counter-Reformation and anti-Modernist fortress? Did not this same church have to catch up on essential points with the paradigm shift of the Reformation at the Second Vatican Council 450 years later – too late?

🕎 Did rabbinic Judaism act rightly in the long run when it rejected any radical-critical questioning which referred back to the Bible and its original message, and instead of this preferred to hold on to the mediaeval-Talmudic paradigm? Did not changed times constantly remind it of the need for reform?

☽ Was traditional Islam well advised in the long run constantly to reject reforms of the Shari'a, that mediaeval law of religion building on the Qur'an and Sunna, and to want to exclude the Ijtihad – rational independent interpretation of the law – as being dangerous? Are not some questions (for instance about the status of women and non-Muslims) which were earlier thought to be non-existent or settled returning with all the greater urgency?

V. The Modern Paradigm: Assimilation

With **Humanism**, at first a change in attitude towards the Jews seemed to be in the making. Jewish book production skills and culture flourished in northern Italy. A Hebrew linguistics developed in Germany – for a better understanding of the Hebrew Bible and post-biblical tradition. And now great attention was paid to the Jewish mysticism of the **Kabbala**. We shall investigate its understanding of God later, but here we must already ask: what does 'Kabbala' mean? In the transition from the Middle Ages to modernity, is it perhaps a new Jewish paradigm?

1. The Kabbala – not a new paradigm

'Kabbala', too, originally meant simply 'tradition'. But now the word became a synonym for a specific **secret teaching** of the Jewish tradition, which was regarded as the real content of the Torah. The leading Jewish expert on the Kabbala, Gershom Scholem, has demonstrated beyond doubt that the Kabbala is a Jewish form of **Gnosticism**, which aims at insight into, or even **knowledge of, the mysteries of the Godhead** (and in so doing found the assent at least of Martin Buber in his later years).[1] This secret doctrine had a long prehistory, hey-day and subsequent history. We need to look at it more closely.

Prehistory. There are early traces in individual enigmatic and esoteric statements in Hellenistic Jewish literature and in cosmic speculations by rabbis. According to the most recent research into the Kabbala by Moshe Idel, from the beginning of Jewish mysticism in the second century BCE there were two types of mystical experience, though from the start they cannot be clearly distinguished. In the second century CE both were represented by Rabbi Akiba. The first was the moderate form, theosophical speculation, which led the mystic through dedicated study of the Torah to the mysteries of the eternal, pre-existent Torah and thus to contemplate, indeed to influence, the Godhead itself. The second was the intensive form, which aimed at the ecstatic fulfilment of the mystic through particular techniques (magic words, the singing of divine names and hymns).[2] Only in the second half of the first millennium were there the first systematizations of the understanding of God and creation: mystical interpretations of the account of creation in the book of Genesis, a speculative doctrine of angels, and above all the developed 'chariot' (*merkaba*) mysticism, a vision of the theophany on the heavenly chariot as depicted in a great image in the vision of the prophet Ezekiel at his call. This mysticism was to be achieved through study of the Torah or through special techniques.[3] The secret doctrine also reached Europe from Palestine, especially the French and German Hasidim (the 'pious'), and was first summarized with its consequences for asceticism and penitence in the 'Book of the Pious' (*seper hasidim*).

The **Kabbalistic movement** in the strict sense developed between the twelfth and the fourteenth centuries, above all in southern France (Narbonne, Arles, Marseilles) and Spain (Gerona and Barcelona) – at the very time that ascetic Christian groups like the Cathari and the Albigensians were emerging in the same area. In Kabbalistic circles[4] the theosophical doctrine of the organism of unfolding divine potencies, powers or aeons was fully developed: one instance is the influential book entitled **Bahir** ('Book of Clarity'). Here too, finally, the main work of the 'older Kabbala' came into being, the Bible of the Jewish mystics, the quasi-canonical book **Zohar** (1240-1280). This is that *Book of Emanation* which distinguishes between the hidden aspect of the deity (*En-soph* = the Infinite) and its revealed aspect, and in so doing describes the ten attributes and powers of God and stages of the divine revelation, together with a doctrine of the migration of souls. The intensive, ecstatic type of mystical experience, now clearly distinct from the theosophical form, is represented at the same time by the Spaniard **Abraham Abulafia** from Saragossa (who died after 1291); he also used breathing techniques and introduced prophetic-messianic notes into the Kabbalistic movement, though these were only to make their full mark at a later period.

Be this as it may, philosophy and secular sciences were now rejected everywhere, and the rational scholasticism of Maimonides was increasingly forced into the background. Its place was taken by an introverted, self-contained, neo-Platonic speculative religious sensibility with an ascetic colouring, which culminated in a strict Torah piety, interpreted in mystical terms. For this piety, the Torah is the law of the world, for which all knowledge of the world is hidden in a mysterious way, and the language of which, Hebrew, was already the primal language of creation.

The Kabbalistic movement reached its **hey-day** between the fourteenth and the seventeenth centuries, to the degree that what had formerly been elitist secret knowledge of the divine mysteries was now as it were democratized by countless manuscripts, anthologies and finally printed works. Under the impact of the expulsion of the Jews from Spain in 1492 and the fearful pressure of suffering, the Kabbala had now increasingly taken on messianic traits and included eschatological speculations; it had spread from Spain into the ghettos all over the Jewish Diapora. Indeed, in the century of the Protestant Reformation there was even a popular penitential movement in expectation of the messiah, and in Central and Eastern Europe the originally esoteric Kabbala was now wholly fused with popular Ashkenasi Hasidism, which came into being in parallel to it, and also with some superstitions which were widespread among the people (demons, alphabetic magic, and the artificial man Golem...).

And yet we should note that for all the systematizing, there was never a uniform mystical system in Judaism. Whereas a mysticism pressing towards union with the deity is very much at the centre of religions of Indian origin, in the religions with a prophetic character – in Judaism, as in Christianity and Islam – this naturally remained only a powerful parallel or subordinate trend, which was either suspected, condemned and excluded by Orthodoxy, or ultimately domesticated and integrated into the traditional rabbinic system. In other words, the Kabbala, too, was **not** able to bring about a permanent change in the entire constellation, **a new paradigm**. On the contrary, the fate of the Kabbalistic movement was soon to be sealed. What was the reason?

In Palestine, where more Jews had settled once again, or more precisely in Safed in northern Galilee, where according to the Kabbala the messiah was to appear, a new Kabbala centre had meanwhile formed among exiled Jews with Moses Cordovero (1522-1570). This was to become a theological centre for Judaism generally.[5] For here the legendary 'sacred lion' **Isaac Luria** (1534-1572) now developed a new method of meditation by concentrating on the individual letters of the Torah, which for him was at the same time the sacred book of nature. The aim was to achieve union with the divine. At the same time he also presented an extremely influential speculative doctrine of God, the origin of the world, the origin of evil and the messiah. As Gershom Scholem has shown, this is a classical example of a Gnostic system of thought within orthodox Judaism. It is a great myth of exile and redemption: the 'sparks' of divine light and life are scattered throughout the world, and in their exile they long to be raised to their original place in the divine harmony of all being by human activity.

However, a century later, on this selfsame basis of Palestinian Kabbalism, in a messianic climate which had already long been inflamed, a disaster took place involving a pseudo-messiah which was to usher in the **subsequent history** of the Kabbalistic-messianic movement. In Palestine a certain **Shabbetai Zevi** (1626-1676) had himself pronounced messiah by the 'prophet' Nathan of Gaza on the basis of the Lurian Kabbala; he proclaimed the year 1666 as the year of redemption. Intense messianic expectations were concentrated on him, and these were now also shared by the majority of rabbis from Palestine and Morocco to Poland. Particularly in Poland, in 1648, there had been fearful massacres of the Jews during the revolt of Russian peasants and Cossacks against the Poles and their Jewish administrators, followed by movements of refugees. However, on his way to Constantinople to receive the Sultan's crown in Turkish waters, the 'messiah' Shabbetai was arrested and imprisoned. Indeed, faced with the choice of death or conversion, in 1666, the year of redemption, he went over to Islam to save his life. The Sultan finally exiled Shabbetai Zevi to Albania, where he died ten years later.

It is understandable that the fate of Shabbetai was a fearful disappointment for Jews all over the world, but even after the death of their messiah it did not prevent some of them, especially in Eastern Europe (they were later called Sabbatians), from continuing to believe in him and his return. The lack of realism in the Kabbalistic movement, its mystical extravagance and fixation on the other-worldly and the unearthly, were now manifest. The Kabbala was utterly in crisis again a century later because of the leader of the East European Sabbateans, **Jakob Frank** (1726-1791). He gave himself out to be the reincarnation of Shabbetai Zevi and proclaimed the 'higher' (viz., than the halakhah) or 'spiritual' 'Torah of emanation'. When Frank was excommunicated by a rabbinic court he fled to Turkey and also became a Muslim. On his return to Poland, along with his followers he underwent a second conversion, this time to Roman Catholicism. But that was not yet enough: after an eventful history – he also constructed a new Trinity ('gracious God' – 'great brother' – 'She' = the Shekinah as the Virgin Mary) – he ended up as an adherent of Russian Orthodoxy.

In truth, for many Jews the crisis of Kabbalism now finally emerged: this doctrine seemed discredited and its fate as a spiritual power sealed. Any Kabbalistic piety there still was finally came to be concentrated in **Eastern European Hasidism.**[6] This was a movement of Eastern European 'pious' ('Hasidim'), steeped in a strong sense of belonging together; it first developed in Podolia and Galicia among those frustrated by dry rabbinism and tormented by pogroms. It goes back to the wonder-working charismatic Eliezer Baal Shem Tob ('Besht' for short, 1700-1760)[7] and was handed on by the 'great *Maggid*' (Dov Baer from Mezhirech, 1703-1772) and above all by Rabbi Nachman of Bratislava (1772-1811), the organizer of the Hasidic movement. Such great 'Rebbes' or 'Zaddikim' are the leading figures. The achievement of communion with God is also the centre of Hasidism, but the Gnostic speculations about the divine mysteries are here reinterpreted in moralistic terms: in statements about human beings and their way to God, which they can find throughout everyday, secular life, even in conversations in the market place. Prayer and contemplation of the divine names are more important than study of the Torah. However, this Kabbalistic Hasidism was fought against bitterly by rabbinic Judaism (the '*Mitnaggedim*', under the leadership of Gaon Elijah ben Solomon of Vilna) because of its pantheistic ideas, and was replaced by a strict practice of the law which was often even more markedly formalistic.

Only in our century has Jewish history been treated as the history of a living people and not primarily as that of philosophical and theological ideas. And only since that has happened have people also begun to be interested in the forces which affected the life of the Jewish masses of Eastern Europe. After Simon Dubnow's pioneering research into the history of Hasidism it was above all Martin Buber who with extraordinary religious intuition and poetic skill was able to make this alien world of an alleged obscurantism comprehensible to European and American readers with his *Tales of the Hasidim*[8] (first of all the *Story of Rabbi Nachman*, 1906, and the *Legend of Baal Shem*, 1907). But as Gershom Scholem has shown,[9] Buber was not bothered about the extensive corpus of theoretical writings (tractates, Bible commentaries, sermons and lectures) and their speculations of a Kabbalistic character. Rather, he retold the legends, anecdotes and sayings of the Hasidim, making a subjective selection and combination of them and interpreting them in powerful religious and existentialist terms. In so doing he largely interpreted away the element of magic, and at the same time neglected the social character of Hasidism and its strong ties to the Torah and the commandments.

And was note taken of the Kabbala on the **Christian** side? Among the elite of Europe's theologians and philosophers, attention had first been drawn to the Kabbala at the time of Humanism; indeed only after 1480 were the sources accessible. For example, G.Pico della Mirandola had begun to occupy himself with the Kabbala, as had his admirer **Johannes Reuchlin** from Pforzheim. Trained by Jewish teachers, Reuchlin was to become the founder of Hebrew linguistics.[10] The Kabbala seemed to him to be a kind of Jewish primal wisdom (mediated by Pythagoras to the Greeks). Whereas Mirandola had only given a report, Reuchlin attempted in two works[11] to understand the Kabbala as the link in a humanistic synthesis of Judaism, Greek culture and Christianity. This was a synthesis which he was striving for in his own works. The adventure was not without its dangers.

When in a variety of pamphlets Johannes Pfefferkorn, a Jew converted to Christianity, issued a call for all Jewish books but the Bible to be confiscated and burned, since he alleged that they defamed Christianity, Reuchlin – a learned humanist and jurist – resolutely opposed him in public. In a learned opinion for the emperor Reuchlin supported the Jews' claim to possession of the Talmud by appealing to Roman law (and unfalsified canon law) over against the developed mediaeval law on the Jews (1510), and in his work *Looking-Glass* (1511) he firmly opposed Pfefferkorn.

The consequences for Reuchlin were serious, but after all that we have heard so far about the attitude of the church to the Jews they can hardly be surprising. Having now incurred marked hostility, Reuchlin got entangled in a great dispute with the Dominicans and the University of Cologne, and was arraigned in a trial which stirred up the whole learned public of the time.[12] He was acquitted in Speyer in 1514, but this did not prevent his being condemned by Pope Leo X, to whom he had dedicated his *magnum opus, On the Kabbalistic Art,* in 1520. Only by submission and entry into the secular priesthood did Reuchlin escape a worse fate: following a brief period of academic activity in Ingolstadt and Tübingen, he died two years after his condemnation. He was to be vindicated later. For, 'that Judaism belongs in the European community of law and culture was first argued by the Christian Kabbalist Reuchlin, who thus made decisive preparations for the revolution in the treatment of the Jews which broke through after the end of the eighteenth century'.[13]

Meanwhile a religious revolution had begun in Christian Germany which was to put the Reuchlin case well in the shade, a paradigm shift *par excellence*: this was Martin Luther's Reformation. Reuchlin had been the great-uncle of Melanchthon, Luther's loyal theological companion. Luther himself had served as an expert witness at Reuchlin's trial and had contributed towards his acquittal. For Luther had a very mild attitude to the Jews – at that time.

2. Luther, too, against the Jews

It was Martin Luther who, in the face of the Roman Catholic paradigm of the late mediaeval church which was now in a severe crisis, with prophetic power announced the vision of **a new, Reformation paradigm** of Christianity: back to the original gospel! And so after 1517, the year of decision, the young Reformer was convinced that in this new constellation, and with the gospel which he had rediscovered, purged of all Roman additions, a new last age had dawned for the Jews as well.[14]

Thus Luther resolutely made himself an **advocate of the Jews**. In 1523, in a series of sermons he commented on the Five Books of Moses, and at the same time composed a work with the title *That Jesus Christ was Born a Jew*.[15] In it Luther defended himself against charges made by Christians that he taught that Jesus was of the 'seed of Abraham' and thus denied Mary's perpetual virginity (before and after the birth of Jesus), and in so doing was advocating Jewish views. Here, all too understandably, Luther's starting point was now that after the introduction of the Reformation the Jews really had no reason to be converted to the true (and originally Jewish) Christianity. Indeed, in this decisively new situation Luther expected that the Jews would have a positive attitude to the Jesus Christ, born a Jew, born of the Virgin, who had been newly recognized – simply on the basis of their own biblical tradition. For basically the Jews needed only to return to the faith of their fathers, the patriarchs and prophets, to a faith in which the messiahship of Jesus was clearly predicted: 'And though we vaunt ourselves equally highly, we are nevertheless Gentiles, and the Jews are of the blood of Christ; we are kinsfolk and aliens, and they are blood-friends, cousins and brothers of our Lord.'[16]

Moreover Luther resolutely attacked slander against the Jews and any use of force against them. Instead, he called for them to be taught from the Bible and to be given a better social status. 'If we are to help them, we must exercise on them the law of Christian love, not that of the Pope, accept them in friendly fashion, attempt to win them over, and work so that they have a cause and a place to be with us and around us, to hear and see our Christian teaching and life.'[17] In 1530, at the Diet of Augsburg, Luther was still arguing for limited toleration of the Jews. For if there was already a Reformation in the **church**, why should there not soon also be a **Reformation in Judaism**?

But what was the dangerous background to this hope? It was the **apocalyptic expectation** which had again become virulent in the crisis of the late Middle Ages in Christianity:[18] the expectation of an imminent end of the world, and as a presupposition for this a mass conversion of the Jews. But this expectation proved deceptive. On the contrary, in Moravia 'some Christians' had even gone over to Judaism, had themselves circumcised and had begun to celebrate the sabbath. Luther still adopted a relatively moderate attitude in 1538 in a letter *Against* *the Sabbatarians.*[19] In good Pauline fashion he argued that in principle it was quite possible for a Christian to have himself circumcised as long as he was not convinced that this was necessary for salvation. On the other hand, according to Luther it was an unquestionable fact that the Jews had lost Temple, priesthood, liturgy, rule and land 1500 years earlier and that as a result the Mosaic law had forfeited its validity. If the Jews nevertheless wanted to practise the Mosaic law, they should found a new state of Israel! But there were now no divine promises for that, as the Jews had evidently been forsaken by God and were no longer God's people.

This attitude on the part of Luther did not bear fruit either, but rather provoked retorts from rabbis which infuriated Luther. And so in his **old age** the **Reformer** became an **advocate of the use of force** against the Jews. Three years before his death – having become depressed at the extremely ambivalent results of his Reformation and the increase in conversions to Judaism, and still in expectation of the Last Judgment – he wrote that famous, notorious, passionately anti-Jewish work, his polemical *On the Jews and their Lies* (it was no longer a missionary tract).[20] It was to have little effect at that time, but fearful consequences at the time of Hitler and Himmler.

Instead of converting the Jews, learning from them or disputing with them, Luther now wants only to talk **about** the Jews. In a long **first** part he begins by accusing them of 'arrogance', since they still claimed to be God's chosen people, appealing to their descent, circumcision, law and the promised land. In a long **second** part he then attempts by means of a mediaeval exegetical method once more to provide a proof for the messiahship of Jesus from the Hebrew Bible which is finally meant to convince even Jews. Here he no longer shrinks from repeating the usual mediaeval slander (poisoning wells, infanticide) and accusing the Jews of avarice and a lust for blood and vengeance, of blindness and hardness of heart. Furthermore, after a **third** part about polemical Jewish calumny of Mary ('a whore'), Jesus ('the child of a whore') and the Christians ('changelings'), in a **concluding** part the Reformer now also makes fatal **practical suggestions** to the state powers as to how they should proceed against the Jews.

Here readers can hardly believe their eyes: Luther, who a quarter of a century earlier had escaped the Roman Inquisition and thus the stake only because of the intervention of his own local ruler, now demands for Jews no more and no less than the burning of synagogues, the destruction of houses, the confiscation of the holy scriptures; indeed, he calls for a ban on teaching and worshipping on pain of death, an abolition of safe-conducts, confiscation of cash and jewellery, hard physical labour, and finally, if even all this is of no use, banishment from Christian lands and a return to Palestine: 'Then let us emulate the common sense of other nations such as France, Spain, Bohemia, etc., compute with them how much their usury has extorted from us, divide this amicably, but then eject them forever from the country.'[21] Luther could not suspect how his demands would one day be realized. Only four days before his death on 18 February 1546, offended by the many Jews in the neighbourhood of his home town of Eisleben, he agitated in the pulpit against the Jews and openly pleaded for their expulsion.

In all fairness, it must be mentioned here that Luther's demands also seemed too extreme to many princes of the time. Moreover in 1595 his writing against the Jews was confiscated by the emperor at the request of the Jews as being a 'shameless book of shame'. As to the historical consequences: the Reformer Martin Luther was certainly not a nationalistic and racist antisemite who declared the Jews to be socially, psychologically and even biologically inferior. No, Luther, who initially was anything but a hater of the Jews, became an anti-Jewish preacher as a result of certain basic theological convictions, above all because of a misunderstanding of apocalyptic. The most prominent example of the boorishness in his time, he reviled the Jews as liars and devils in the same nasty way as he reviled the Turks and the Pope, the eschatological antichrist. It is necessary to tackle this theology critically.

And what about the other Reformers, **Huldrych Zwingli** and **Jean Calvin**? They shared the anti-Jewish prejudices of their day, though at the same time they were no apocalyptists, but combined Reformation theology with Erasmian learning, were more restrained in talking about the Jews and did not support violent action. However, that was easy, since the Jews had long since been banished from Zurich and Geneva, as they had from most German cities. Against Luther, Calvin in particular had stressed the unity of the two Testaments in his theology and on the matter of interest had acknowledged that the Jews were right. However, all this cannot disguise the fact that even the theology of the other Reformers is not free of anti-Jewish prejudice and that even the Reformers as a whole were still often **imprisoned in mediaeval prejudices**.

This is also true of their **exegetical method**, by means of which Luther, for example, wanted to prove the dogmas of the Trinity and the Incarnation of God to the Jews from the Old Testament. As the Lutheran theologian Wilhelm Maurer notes, 'here Luther associated himself so closely with the exegetical tradition of early and mediaeval

Christianity that he could not do justice to his rabbinic opponents; here scholarly progress in theology, too, has decided against him'.[22] And as for the **political attitude** of the Reformers, for all the struggle against the mediaeval 'freedom (= power) of the church' (*libertas ecclesiae*) and for the gospel 'freedom of a Christian' (*libertas christiana*), there is not a trace in them of modern religious freedom (*libertas religiosa*), of tolerance of non-Christians in general and the acceptance of Jews in particular. No, the 'freedom' of a Christian was in no way at the same time the 'freedom' of a non-Christian! Even the time of the Reformation still saw late-mediaeval hysteria, executions of heretics (in Geneva), wars against the opposition (the Peasants' War), the burning of witches (always women!) and – 'of course' – also forced measures against Jews.

All this shows that the **Reformation** is not, as is often unthinkingly assumed, the beginning of the modern period in the strict sense. It represents a quite different entire constellation, an **epoch-making paradigm between the Middle Ages and modernity**. In many ways it points forward, but in some ways it is also clearly still rooted in the past. And this is particularly the case with the Jews: Luther's later negative attitude to the Jews can therefore rightly be described as a regression 'to a mediaeval Catholic standpoint'.[23]

We might ask, what was the situation at this time with Rome? There, despite and because of the Renaissance, which was in love with antiquity, there could be no question of a Reformation paradigm – far less a modern one. There everything so to speak pointed back to the past – and for the hierarchy of the church that meant: back to the Middle Ages.

3. The anti-Jewish popes of the Counter-Reformation

Nowadays even Catholic theology concedes that in theology, liturgy, discipline and church life the Roman Catholic Counter-Reformation sought a **restoration of the mediaeval** *status quo* – either peacefully, or if necessary with armed force. There is no question of a new paradigm! So it is understandable that its attitude towards the Jews was no more tolerant than that of the Reformation. Granted, the Renaissance popes, pragmatic and economically aware as they were, were at the same time active as protectors of the Jews and benefited from them – as did the princes and the emperor. The transitional pope Paul III Farnese (1534-1549) – a Renaissance man through and through (he had four children!), who nevertheless nominated reform cardinals, confirmed the Jesuit orders and convened the reforming Council of Trent – encouraged the settling of Jewish refugees and Marranos from Spanish territories in Rome, and promised them protection from the Inquisition.

However, 1555, the year of the religious peace of Augsburg, by which the confessional possessions in the German empire were cemented for centuries (*cuius regio, eius religio*), when the first Roman Grand Inquisitor Gian Pietro Caraffa had ascended the papal throne under the name of Paul IV (another signal), meant a new **period of repression** for the Jews, at least in the church-state. This must not be concealed.[24] Here I shall mention just the decisive persons and facts:

– **Paul IV** (1555-1559): only two months after entering office he published an anti-Jewish bull under the title *Cum nimis absurdum*, and a few days later followed the example of Venice in expelling the Jews of Rome to a bad quarter on the bank of the Tiber. 'Ghetto' now very quickly became the official name for such firmly demarcated special quarters. But the same pope had burnt in Ancona twenty-four Marranos who had fled from Portugal, under constant suspicion of being hypocrites and potential traitors. The Talmud and all its interpretations were banned.

– **Pius V** (1566-1572), Grand Inquisitor under Paul IV, who in 1570 issued the foolish bull excommunicating and deposing Elizabeth I of England, also made his mark in 1569 with an anti-Jewish bull *Hebrorum gens sola*. In practice this meant the expulsion of even long-established Jewish communities from the church-state; permission for Jewish settlements was given only in Rome and Ancona.

– **Gregory XIII** (1572-1585) was the pope who in the first year of his pontificate celebrated a *Te Deum* in gratitude for the mass-murder of Protestants on St Bartholomew's Eve in Paris, and then actively engaged in plans for the invasion of England and the murder of Queen Elizabeth I. In his anti-Jewish bull *Antiqua Judaeorum probitas* and other decrees he considerably extended the rights of the Inquisition against the Jews, again banned the possession of the Talmud and commanded compulsory sermons for Jews in Rome and throughout the church.[25] Although he attempted to protect Jews against violent attacks, in 1578 he had seven Marranos executed before the Latin Gate. Since the Jewish mission had borne hardly any fruit as far as adults were concerned, the same pope founded a boarding school for Jewish (and Muslim) children who had already become, or were to become, Christians.

Granted, later popes – above all **Sixtus V**, under whose pontificate the rise of England as a world power began, following the defeat of the Spanish Armada in 1588 – reversed the expulsion of Jews which had taken place everywhere, partly for economic reasons. But their situation in the church-state remained precarious. There was **no longer** any

theological controversy with Judaism in the **Roman Catholic sphere.**
Inquisition replaced discussion, and church power replaced the Christian spirit. However, it should be noted in passing that in the war
between Christians and Turks, Jews were at least highly prized as
prisoners and slaves. At the local centre of the Mediterranean slave
trade, on the island of Malta, under the protection of the Johannite
order(!), Jews were a favourite purchase – because they commanded
high ransoms. A flourishing 'Christian' slave trade had begun at the
expense of the Jews. This continued for a long time, until finally an end
was put to it, not by a pope, but by an heir of the French Revolution,
the emperor Napoleon.

Whereas there was now no longer any open theological discussion of
Judaism in post-Tridentine Catholicism, things were **different in the
Protestant sphere**: here, in the period between 1550 and 1650, an
increasing number of theologians and lawyers spoke out in favour of
the Jews. They were called 'philosemites',[26] and were headed by the
Dutchman Hugo Grotius, who along with the Spanish Jesuit Francisco
de Suarez initiated modern international law. A group of Protestant
theologians (among them Samuel von Pufendorf, who produced theories of constitutional law, natural law and international law) was
particularly interested in the Karaites in Eastern Europe and encouraged
publications about these Jewish 'Protestants', who rejected a post-
biblical tradition. These practitioners of natural law – and on the other
hand some Pietists under the leadership of Jakob Spener[27] – stressed
the common Old Testament roots of Jews and Christians, challenged
the general condemnation of the Jewish people, protected the Jews
against slanders like that of ritual murder, and stressed the advantages
of the Jewish people before God – though mostly with the idea at the
back of their minds that they might still finally convert the Jews to
Christianity (the Pietists even had an explicit mission programme). All
this was not completely in vain: for the first time – under the impact of
the modest, respectful and non-violent pietistic mission to the Jews –
people may have been converted from Judaism out of conviction.
However, the great mass of Jews were hardly interested in philosemitic
arguments. The walls of the ghettos had not yet fallen, even if they were
now being slowly undermined: slowly, but surely.

4. Judaism on the threshold of modernity

And yet, in the longer term the **Reformation** (and ultimately also the Counter-Reformation) had brought the Jews immense **advantages**. For the monolithic unity of faith in the West had now been burst open and the Jews were now no longer the only dissenters. Their main Catholic opponents, the mendicant orders and the Inquisition, had been put out of action in Protestant areas. At the same time sanctuaries of tolerance had opened up (Holland, for example, which around the middle of the seventeenth century possessed considerable capital and was advanced industrially), which if necessary could also become places of refuge. The **centre of economic energy** generally had shifted **from southern Europe to northern Europe** – first to Holland and then to England. To this degree the Reformation had indirectly **prepared for the modern period**, which – as the significance of the churches declined in the seventeenth century – made itself increasingly evident in politics and economics.[28] Jews were everywhere: in the founding of the modern colonial economy, in the development of a modern European economic system, and finally in the realization of the modern state, all within the framework of a revolutionary new entire constellation:[29]

(*a*) From the time of Columbus Jews were active almost everywhere (especially in the Caribbean and in Brazil) as merchants and traders in laying the foundation for the **modern colonial economy**. 1492 is a historic but also an ironic date. America was discovered in the year that the Jews were driven out of Spain. The first Jews (or Marranos) came with Christopher Columbus (who despite rumours to the contrary was not a Jew![30]) to that new world which was later to over-trump all the kingdoms of Europe.

And this is the second 'irony of history'. It was above all Sephardic Jews, expelled from Spain and Portugal, who from their base in Amsterdam made an essential contribution towards establishing the Dutch pre-eminence in world trade during the seventeenth century in the face of the Catholic Spaniards and Portuguese. In 1654 the first twenty-three Jewish refugees from Catholic Brazil, where the Inquisition had become equally active, arrived in New Amsterdam,[31] that city founded by Dutchmen which from 1664 was to be called New York (the first synagogue was founded there in 1729 and the Portuguese records have been preserved). In general it can be said that nowhere in more recent times could the Jews develop as freely as they did in North America. Here, from the beginning they were not closed off as a Jewish community, but organized themselves around individual synagogues –

as Christian immigrants organized themselves round their churches. At the end of the eighteenth century there were half a dozen communities (with between 2,000 and 3,000 members, primarily merchants) in New York, Newport, Philadelphia, Savannah, Charleston and Richmond, all in all a 'worthy orthodoxy' established according to Sephardic ritual.[32]

(b) In the development of a **European economic system** built on capital and transfer of capital, Jews soon represented a significant economic factor. Calculating soberly and rationally, and at the same time thinking in global terms, at an early stage they used their capital strength in a way which was completely market-orientated and utilized innovative new means of payment like financial facilities. They played a leading role in the creation of bonds (bills of exchange, shares) and in trading with them (the stock exchange), and they took the lead in the beginnings of modern stock-exchange speculation in the seventeenth century, first in Amsterdam and then in London. In addition, the Jews had an effective system of international information (partly based on old family links). No other closed community as a people and a faith had connections like theirs: from Baghdad to Constantinople, from Bordeaux to Hamburg, from Poland, Lithuania and the Ukraine to the other side of the ocean. The result was that Jews were often well ahead in estimating political, military and economic developments.

So the **development of modern capitalism** was not just to do with the Protestant-Calvinistic ethic, as Max Weber thought, but **also with Jewish pragmatism**. For these economic and political reasons (and also for theological, messianic reasons), Jews were admitted **to England** again in 1656 under Oliver Cromwell and the philosemite Puritans, i.e. at the time of the first immigration into North America. Here, too, a 'worthy orthodoxy' (of Sephardic and in this case also of Ashkenasy origin) established itself and still exists today.

But on the European continent there was now a mass flight back westwards, particularly from the favourite Jewish haven of **Poland**. For in 1648, in the wake of the bloody rebellions by impoverished Russian Orthodox tenants against the dominant Polish Catholic aristocracy in what at that time was still the Polish Ukraine, supported by Cossacks and Tatars from the Crimea, there were massacres – primarily of the aristocracy's Jewish agents and other officials. It was to be significant for the future physical appearance of Jews of non-European origin in Germany and America that in contrast to the Polish upper and middle classes the Jews of Poland did not adopt Western dress but kept the old Polish clothing (kaftan, fur-trimmed hats and caps); as a result these were subsequently no longer regarded as 'typically Polish' but as 'typically Jewish'. Even now, for many Jews this clothing is a distinguishing mark and a token of their confession, but for many non-Jews it is more of a curious symbol of cultural isolation.

(c) In bringing about the centralized **modern state** in Europe, the princes quite often had Jews at their side, whether as efficient sources of finance or as influential army suppliers. Indeed, in some European residences whole dynasties of 'court Jews' or 'court factors' formed, who were indispensable to the ruling aristocracy. And as the Thirty Years' War (1618-1648) had swallowed up immense sums, the need for such financial advisers and fund-raisers was in any case particularly great. This was the period in which the rise of such famous families as the Oppenheimers and the Wertheimers was to begin (the Rothschilds came later)... However, the tragedy of Joseph Süss-Oppenheimer (born in 1692), which was given literary form by Wilhelm Hauff in 1828, made into an international bestseller by Lion Feuchtwanger in 1925, and screened as a tendentious film by Veit Harlan, made in 1940 on the orders of Goebbels, is symptomatic of the popular mood. As court agent of a variety of princes, 'Jew Süss' had amassed an enormous fortune; as Financial Privy Councilor of the Duke of Württemberg, in a mercantilist-absolutist spirit he introduced numerous taxes and levies without the consent of the representatives of the people. Envied and hated for his wealth, stories about women and his luxury, immediately after the death of the Duke in 1738 he was hanged for high treason in Stuttgart at the age of forty-six.

In all this we must be clear that for Christianity the paradigm of modernity was the first constellation in world history for which the impulse did not come from within theology and the church but 'from outside': from a **society** which was rapidly becoming **worldly** and **secular**, and was thus **emancipating** itself from the rule of church and theology. Neither the Lutheran tribal lands (which in Germany had been exhausted by the war) nor the Roman Catholic bastions (Italy, Spain and Portugal), but the countries of England, France and the Netherlands, which had been less controlled by the church, were the prime forces in shaping the spirit of modernity. And here in particular the position of the Jews was comparatively good. It was increasingly to prove that the reactionary Roman church policy – anti-Protestant, anti-Jewish and anti-modern – was economically and politically counter-productive for the states which had remained Catholic, and all in all this led to a considerable loss of power for Catholicism.

(*d*) Because of all these developments there were fundamental changes in the global equilibrium: the modern **Eurocentric world-system** developed and was to prevail for around three centuries. With the shift in the economic centre, the **focal point of world history moved from the Mediterranean to the Atlantic,** which became the great sea for new world trade. After the Reformation and the Counter-Reformation and the indescribable devastations of the 'wars of religion', the age of confessionalism on the European continent finally concluded with the end of the Thirty Years War (the Peace of Westphalia in 1648). In England there followed the 'Glorious Revolution' and William III's Acts of Toleration for the Protestant Nonconformists (1688/89). Everywhere people had at last had enough of the long religious quarrel. They wanted **toleration** of the various **confessions,** and soon – after the voyages of discovery to all the continents as early as the sixteenth century – also toleration of the various **religions.**

So the modern age begins under the optimistic sign of a new **faith in human reason,** which becomes the supreme arbiter of truth in contrast to all religious authorities. And unlike the Renaissance, the modern period is not directed backwards, but forwards: belief in human reason and the nature common to all human beings (natural law) becomes belief in the better future, in progress. Now we can speak of the **modern world in the strict sense,** as it had already broken through by the **middle of the seventeenth century.**
– In **modern philosophy,** which began from the human subject: founded by Descartes, Spinoza, Leibniz and the English empiricists Locke, Hobbes and Hume, it found its first great synthesis in Kant.
– In **empirical-mathematical natural science:** after the Copernican shift, this reached its classical form through Galileo and Kepler with Newton's *Physics,* and formed the presupposition for the development of typically modern technology and industry.
– In a **secular understanding of the state and politics:** regardless of confessional or religious viewpoints, this had already been practised successfully by Cardinal Richelieu and Louis XIV in alliances with Protestants or Turks; it was now also given a theoretical foundation through the constitutional theory, grounded in natural law, of Bodin, Grotius, Hobbes, Locke and Pufendorf. The state is understood without any supernatural goal as the natural product of a contract between people and government and so can be regarded as autonomous over against the church. Human rights are grounded in natural law.
All in all this was a new and **epoch-making paradigm-shift,** which begins around the middle of the seventeenth century and is fully

developed in the eighteenth. Towards the end of the 'siècle des lumières', the philosophical-scientific and soon also the technological revolution became a political one, with the **American and French Revolutions** and their solemn proclamation of human rights; it came to full economic fruition in the nineteenth-century industrial revolution.

This modern entire constellation fundamentally changed economic society and thus in the end changed Judaism as well. Here conflicts proved unavoidable: Jewish tradition and modern innovation, the biblical-Talmudic understanding of God and the Copernican world-view stand in diametrical opposition. How were the two to be brought together?

5. The case of Spinoza and the modern understanding of God

In 1600, after cruel torture, Giordano Bruno, the late-Renaissance philosopher, was burnt by the Inquisition in Rome on the Campo dei Fiori – for pantheism and other crimes against Christian faith.[33] He was the first to draw the philosophical consequences for a modern view of the world from the Copernican shift. It was soon to prove that the new age would bring completely new challenges, for the Jewish understanding of the Bible and of God as well, and this was made evident by one of the most profound and consistent thinkers to have a modern sense of life, nature, the world and God, but who at the same time was probably the most reviled philosopher of the early modern period. This is **Baruch** (Benedict, 'the blessed') **de Spinoza** (1632-1677), son of the orthodox Jew Michael Espinosa, who had fled from Portugal, which was controlled by the Inquisition.

Like the Christian hierarchs, monks and theologians, so too the rabbis created their own dissenters. In Amsterdam in particular they had formed a no less authoritarian and patriarchal oligarchy – as so often happens, made up of a few rich related merchants and distinguished figures – who regarded the principal virtue as uncon-ditional obedience to parents (the fourth commandment!). This Jewish establishment in Amsterdam now turned against a brilliant young man from its own ranks as soon as he emerged as an independent thinker and member of a circle of free-thinkers. The consequence was that the young man, thoroughly trained in Jewish and Latin philosophy and literature, and also interested in mathematics, natural sciences and contemporary philosophy, became an outsider in his own community. In this respect he resembled another great outsider, who was possibly his neighbour in the Jewish quarter of Amsterdam, the painter Rembrandt.[34]

In the year 1656, aged twenty-four, Spinoza was **expelled** from the Amsterdam synagogue **with the great curse**, for serious false doctrines. He was expelled by those very Jews who a year earlier had pleaded for Jewish refugees to be allowed to stay in New Amsterdam (New York). Later, Spinoza was even banished from Amsterdam on Jewish urging.[35] In order to be safe from fanatics, from that time on he lived among Christians as a free philosopher – he turned down a professorial chair in Heidelberg – for the sake of an undisturbed life and intellectual freedom. He finally lived in The Hague, supported by friends; he earned his living by polishing optical glass but devoted his whole time to philosophical thought. But he did not commit suicide, as another excommunicated Jewish heretic in Amsterdam, Uriel de Costa, had done fifteen years earlier (1640). So, as the Jerusalem philospher Yirmyahu Yovel[36] emphasizes in a new book on Spinoza which has been much discussed in Israel, Spinoza was the first 'problematic Jew'. He rejected the teachings and the authority of the rabbinate and yet remained deeply indebted to his Judaism and his religion, without being converted to Christianity. His was a hopeless situation under the verdict of a 'two-fold negation, rejected by Christians as a Jew and by the Jews as a heretic'.[37]

Spinoza was able to publish only one work during his lifetime (in addition to a work on the principles of Cartesian philosophy) – and even so it had to be anonymous, and with a fictitious place of publication. This was the *Tractatus theologico-politicus* (1670).[38] He was promptly condemned. Why? Because here Spinoza proved to be not only a resolute defender of intellectually honest thought and faith, but also a resolute advocate of a modern biblical criticism. Is the Bible an inspired and therefore inerrant book of God? No, it is the often contradictory document of an authentically human faith, which can and must be interpreted by means of historical criticism. Spinoza was now the first to challenge the Mosaic authorship of the Pentateuch, and he also investigated the history of the origins of other biblical books. He thus became the **ancestor of modern biblical criticism** and no more escaped condemnation than did the Oratorian Richard Simon, the father of Catholic biblical criticism, eight years later in Paris. Simon was immediately expelled from the Oratory (1678).[39] Here once for all a debate now broke out over the Bible, which was to come to a further climax a century later within orthodox Protestantism through Lessing's publication of the 'Fragments of an Anonymous Author' (the Hamburg

Orientalist Samuel Reimarus), and even now has theology on tenterhooks.

However, it was not just biblical criticism which brought Spinoza into disrepute, but also his new **understanding of God**, which because of its cosmic dimensions was sometimes even misunderstood as atheism. Here Spinoza was basically just reacting to an extremely anthropomorphic understanding of God of the kind that had developed in late mediaeval nominalism and in the Reformation doctrine of predestination: the notion of an omnipotent God who determines and controls human beings and the world in absolute freedom (*potestas absoluta*), and so can easily be claimed by his interpreters and representatives here on earth as support for their own determinations and their own control.

So against all irrationality and arbitrariness Spinoza stresses the unity of will and reason in the infinite being of God. Following the line of classical philosophical theology from Plato and Aristotle through Thomas Aquinas to Descartes he understands this as the perfect primal ground of all reality, the necessary being (*ens necessarium*) and the one substance which is grounded in itself and through itself (*causa sui*). For Spinoza, God therefore cannot in any way be thought of as separate from the universe. For him **God is in the world** and **the world is in God**. The infinite is in the finite and the finite is in the infinite. And nature? It is a particular way in which God himself exists. And human consciousness? It is a particular way in which God himself thinks. That means that the individual self and all finite things are not simply independent substances; they are modifications of the one and only divine substance. So God is all in all.

But is that not a purely immanent and no longer a transcendent biblical God? In fact, for Spinoza God seems to be transcendent only in so far as his infinitely many attributes remain inaccessible to human beings. He is not the transcendent but rather the immanent primal cause of all things and the cause of himself (*causa sui*). And yet Spinoza's pantheism is not a simple doctrine that everything is one, a doctrine which declares any reality to be divine. Rather, Spinoza makes a subtle distinction between the one infinite substance of God as the ground of being (= *natura naturans*) and the multiplicity of individual finite forms of reality as it is extended and thought (= *natura naturata*).

However, unlike some pantheistic or pantheizing mediaeval Kabbalists, Spinoza always remained a modern Cartesian rationalist, who with the help of the geometric method even attempted to deduce **ethics as a stringent system** (of basic concepts, axioms, propositions, proofs and conclusions) in a purely logical way.[40] He had no success here, and some people now regard Spinoza's ethical tractate as 'conceptual poetry'. Spinoza's rigid predeterminism, which cannot allow anything indeterminate in the world, has also been regarded as outmoded after the rise of the new physics at the beginning of our century, though this did not prevent so brilliant a physicist of Jewish origin as Albert Einstein from retaining it. All his life Einstein refused to adopt modern quantum mechanics with its purely statistical probability and lack of sharpness (Heisenberg's 'indeterminacy principle'). And Spinoza's God in particular, whose strict necessity also applied to nature, stood behind Einstein's famous saying, 'The Old One does not play dice.'[41]

Still, apart from Spinoza's rationalism and predeterminism, it was his new understanding of God which was essentially responsible for the fact that in the German classics from Lessing to Goethe, and in German philosophical idealism from Fichte through Schelling to Hegel, '**God**' – the Godhead, the Absolute, the Absolute Spirit – was thought of **otherwise than** in the terms to which people had become used in the Middle Ages and the Reformation. Otherwise than **the Reformers**, who still took over the biblical concept of God in a completely pre-modern, pre-critical way (for not only the popes but also Luther and Melanchthon had rejected the revolutionary model of the world put forward by the Catholic canon Nicolaus Copernicus). And also otherwise than the Deists, originating in England or France, with their early-modern Enlightenment understanding of God. At a very early stage, Spinoza's picture of the world already raised the question: in a new age can God still be understood in a naive and anthropomorphic way as an omnipotent and absolutist ruler who deals with the world and human beings just as he likes, with unlimited powers? Or is he now perhaps to be understood along the lines of Enlightenment Deism, so to speak as a monarch who rules constitutionally and who, himself bound by a constitution based on the natural and moral laws, subtly removes himself from the concrete life of the world and of human beings? Spinoza rejected both these alternatives.

Spinoza's pioneering influence derived from his view that the relationship between God and the world, God and human beings, must be understood on the presuppositions of modern philosophy and an understanding of reality shaped by the natural sciences. In the face of the new picture of the world this amounted to a **worldliness of God** understood in modern terms. So rather than speaking of 'pan-theism' (everything is God) we would do better to speak of a 'pan-entheism' (everything is in God). And even the transcendent God of the Bible, who is in no way separated from the world, but is omnipresent in his actions in the world, is better understood on modern presuppositions than in terms of classical Greek or mediaeval metaphysics. So in time, as a result of the Jewish philosopher Baruch de Spinoza, the following **understanding of God for the modern paradigm** largely became established:[42]

- God is **not a supra-terrestrial being** above the clouds, in a physical heaven. Since Copernicus and Galileo this naively anthropomophic conception has been superseded. God is not a 'supreme being' dwelling 'above' the world ('the world above') in any literal or spatial sense.

- God is **not a extra-terrestrial being** beyond the stars, in a metaphysical heaven. From Spinoza's perspective the Enlightenment-Deistic conception seems *a priori* inappropriate: God is not 'outside' the world in a spiritual or metaphysical sense, an objectified, reified Being existing over against human beings in an other-worldly beyond ('the world behind'). Rather,

- God is **in** this world and this world is **in** God. **A unitary understanding of reality** holds. God is not just a (supreme) finite entity alongside the finite, as part of reality. Rather, he is the infinite **in** the finite, transcendence **in** immanence, the absolute **in** the relative. Precisely by being the Absolute, God can enter into a relationship with the world and human beings: a relationship not in the sense of weakness, dependence, relativity in the bad sense, but in the sense of strength, unlimited freedom, absolute sovereignty. So God is the Absolute who includes and creates relativity. Precisely as the One who is free, God makes relationship possible and brings it about. God is the absolute/relative, other-worldly/this-worldly, transcendent/immanent, all-embracing/all-permeating reality, the most real reality at the heart of things, in human beings, in the history of human beings, in the world.

Of course these statements, expressed in the form of theses, are still far from answering all the questions about the difference between the 'God of the philosophers and scientists' and the 'God of Abraham, Isaac and Jacob' (as the problem was posed by the mathematician and physicist, philosopher and theologian Blaise Pascal, who was a contemporary of Descartes and at the opposite pole from him). We shall have sufficient occasion later to pursue this problem, which is fundamental to all three prophetic religions. However, we may anticipate by noting that there is no way back beyond Spinoza.

Nor should it be forgotten that for all his rejection by Jews, Catholics and Protestants, Baruch de Spinoza himself remained unshakeably true to his convictions. He was profoundly convinced that he believed in a 'greater' God than did the naive believers in the Bible. Here Spinoza drew his strength from the longing for the eternal which goes beyond all that is transitory, from what he called the 'spiritual love of God'. So he also hoped that death was a way to the God-Nature which is all in one. He died in 1677 at the early age of forty-four, of consumption, outwardly withdrawn and not very emancipated, but in spirit freer and more pious than the vast majority of his contemporaries, whether Jews or Christians. He was so far ahead of his time that a century later, even the first really modern Jew barely understood him properly.

6. The first modern Jew: Moses Mendelssohn

It is significant enough that the first thinker unambiguously to speak out for unrestricted equal rights for the Jews, in 1714, was not a theologian but the English Deist, John Toland (1670-1722), who was an advocate of an undogmatic Christianity.[43] We are approaching the age of the Enlightenment and our question is: was there also **Enlightenment in the Jewish sphere?**[44]

The picture is ambiguous. Among the French representatives of the Enlightenment only Montesquieu was ready to let the Jews be Jews: i.e. to treat them 'as such' and not just 'as citizens' with equal rights. In his classical work *De l'esprit des lois* (1748), he quotes with approval the remark of a Jew against the Spanish/Portuguese Inquisition, which had just burnt an eighteen-year-old Jewish girl in Lisbon: 'You want us to be Christians, but you yourselves do not want to be Christians. But if you do not want to be Chrisitans, at least be human beings.'[45] The views of the real spokesmen of the French Enlightenment (who were mostly anti-religious) were quite different. **Voltaire**, who was not himself an atheist but a detached Deist, may have done more than anyone else before the great revolution to destroy the traditional belief in the divine right of the monarchy, the privileges of the nobility and the infallibility of the church; in so doing he also prepared indirectly for an emancipation of the Jews. On the other hand, Voltaire had always included Judaism in his indescribable hatred of Christianity and had encouraged the rise of antisemitism with his biting irony against both religions. He called the Jewish religion absurd and abominable, and its 'fables very much more stupid and absurd because they (the Jews) are the coarsest of the Asians'.[46] Diderot and Holbach spoke in similar vein, hardly proving to be spearheads of the Enlightenment on this point. The conclusion to be drawn from this is that it was the representatives of the French Enlightenment who share the responsibility for the anti-Judaism of the modern European intelligentsia! The most significant representative of the German Enlightenment, which was by no means against religion, forms a radical contrast to this. At the early age of twenty, **Gotthold Ephraim Lessing** (1729-1781) attacked anti-Jewish prejudices in his comedy *The Jews* and, as is well known, did not just dare to write the parable of the three rings (or religions). He was also bold enough for the first time in the history of the German theatre to put the figure of a noble Jew on the stage – *Nathan the Wise* (1779).[47] Here was a Jew who, moreover, in this play appears more Christian than a Christian. There is a famous remark by a Christian monk in a crucial scene with the Jew Nathan: 'You are a Christian! By God you are a Christian! There never was a better Christian!'[48] However, Nathan turns the argument upside down. 'Good for us! For what makes me a Christian to you makes you a Jew to me.' This means that formal membership of Christianity or Judaism is no longer decisive for a true life. What matters is not being a Christian or a Jew, if and to the extent that they obscure humanity. The crucial thing is being a human being, the values of qualitative humanity, which can be common to both religions. So Nathan the Wise is a Jew who is committed to humanity through and through. Is Nathan merely dramatic fiction or is he a reflection of reality?

It is no secret that a real figure lay behind this stage character, none other than **the first really modern Jew**, who lived in Berlin in Lessing's day. Coming from Dessau at the age of forty, he had received a broad general education there, had been introduced by Lessing into influential cultural circles and was bound to his exact contemporary in a lifelong friendship. This Jew was **Moses Mendelssohn** (1726-1789) – a paradigmatic figure for modern Jewish cultural, social and religious history: for many German Jews up to 1933 he was something like a modern messiah.

Attractive not so much in appearance but by virtue of his presence of mind, quick wit and urbanity, this philosopher from the school of Leibniz and Christian Wolff (**the** philosopher of the Enlightenment) at the same time made a name for himself as a literary critic, translator of the Bible and reformer. As a result, Frederick the Great, a king who was by no means well disposed towards the Jews, by a law of 1750 gave him the status of 'Jew under extraordinary protection', and the Prussian Academy of Sciences awarded him a prize for his 'treatise on evidence in the metaphysical sciences'. With Lessing's help he had begun to publish his philosophical writings - like Lessing and Herder he wrote programmatically in German and not in Latin (or Hebrew), the language of scholars. He presented his own spiritual portrait in the international bestseller *Phaedo*, in which he took up the arguments for the immortality of the soul which had been put forward by Plato and Leibniz and supplemented them with his own arguments from moral theology. So Moses Mendelssohn was a writer, philosopher, aesthete, critic and also a psychologist.[49] But was he also a Jewish thinker? He felt compelled to become one.

It is easy to understand how such a towering intellectual figure would be a provocation to the educated Christian elite in Germany. For however much the early representatives of the Enlightenment (especially in France) had borrowed arguments against Christianity from Judaism, Judaism itself had hardly emerged as an agent of Enlightenment, fully trapped in the rabbinic-Talmudic paradigm as it now was. Now all of a sudden, with Mendelssohn a paradoxical figure had emerged: **a Jew indebted to the Enlightenment**. This raised the question, could such a man still remain a Jew? Did he not have to draw the consequences of his Western-philosophical education and become a convert to Christianity? Was not an enlightened Christianity the highest level of cultural progress?

Under public pressure from the young Zurich pastor Johann Kaspar Lavater, Mendelssohn now became a **defender of his Jewish religion**, as wise as he was passionate. Four years after Lessing's *Nathan*, a little book appeared, with the title *Jerusalem, or On Religious Power and Judaism* (1783).[50] In this late work Mendelssohn described how Judaism did not prescribe any special doctrinal opinions or saving truths, but rather was identical with the rational knowledge of God himself. Judaism was essentially just **a revealed religion of the law**, by which God issued an invitation not so much to hold the content of faith to be true ('orthodoxy') as to fulfil the commandments ('orthopraxy'), an invitation to a praxis which was binding only on Jews and on no one else. Since in addition Mendelssohn regarded the political and social regulations of the Torah as time-conditioned, he did not find the remaining Jewish ceremonial law a problem either for the present-day state or for the contemporary church.

So Moses Mendelssohn represents an undogmatic, rational faith which is fully open to modernity, a faith which he attempted to combine with a loyal observance of traditional Jewish obligations and rites. He wanted to be both **modern and Jewish at the same time**, to be fully involved in the cultural and spiritual life of the world around him (German culture with its idealistic stamp was more attractive to Jews than secular French culture), and yet not to give up being a Jew – which is what some well-meaning Christians continually expected of him. What he wanted to do was not to give up Judaism, but to preserve its pure nucleus.

Thus here a new self-understanding of being a Jew had emerged: the Jew as both a human being and a citizen. For society this meant that it was possible for members of different religions – Christianity and Judaism – to participate in a common German culture. So Mendelssohn called for a revival of the Hebrew language and literature, and at the same time for an education related to the present, which was also to incorporate the content of secular education.

However, Moses Mendelssohn exercised more influence by his example and his **practical commitment** than he did by his theory of Judaism. He did so in three respects:

– by his commitment to a correct biblical Hebrew and a German translation of the Pentateuch and the Psalms, printed in Hebrew letters with a Hebrew commentary, a 'German Bible' which soon became popular (not least as a means of learning German), though it was attacked by the orthodox as a new 'Berlin religion';

– by his concern for persecuted and exiled Jewish families and his efforts to improve the legal situation of the Jews and the relationship between Jews and Christians;

– by the thoroughly humanistic style in which as a convinced Jew he argued for tolerance, humanity and good taste.

So Moses Mendelssohn provided vital help in getting the Jews out of their mediaeval ghetto and introducing them to modern culture, though he also inevitably suffered many setbacks (in 1771 Frederick II blocked his election to the Berlin Academy). And yet in word and deed and through his whole person he became the **initiator, symbol and idol of the 'Haskalah', the Jewish 'Enlightenment'**, which spread from Berlin throughout central and north-eastern Europe. However, in parallel to this a less rationalistic Jewish Enlightenment came into being, supported by the Jews of northern Italy (who since the Middle Ages and the Renaissance had already been better integrated and educated). For a long time they had been studying medicine in Padua, and were later able to found the first scientific rabbinic seminary in Europe there, the Istituto Convitto Rabbinico. By means of works in Hebrew this more moderate 'Haskalah' had an effect on the Habsburg empire as far as Bohemia, Moravia and Galicia, for in multilingual Austria-Hungary, Hebrew was well able to keep its place alongside German (now the thoroughly modern cultural language).[51]

However, even then both Jews and non-Jews were asking whether the **separation between Enlightenment theory and traditional Jewish practice of the law** as advocated by Mendelssohn could be maintained in the long run. Could Judaism be divided so simply into an ethical monotheism (with much in common with the Western philosophical tradition) on the one hand and a ceremonial Jewish tradition on the other? Did this not lead to a cultural and religious schizophrenia? And what about the constants of Israelite-Jewish faith? With his rational enlightenment Mendelssohn may not have neglected them, but he did spiritualize them completely. What still remained of Israel as God's people and God's land? Mendelssohn and the representatives of the Jewish Enlightenment (*Maskilim*) were hardly interested in a separate Jewish state. Was not Judaism as a unity of God, people and land dissolving – into the private faith of individuals?

Lessing had died in 1781, the year of Kant's *Critique of Pure Reason*, which shattered the rational proofs for the immortality of the soul and the existence of God. Shortly after that, Moses Mendelssohn was reluctantly drawn into another great public controversy, which shook him more than anything previously. This was the 'Spinoza affair' – and here one is amazed and yet not amazed. For in a work *On the Teaching of Spinoza in Letters to Herr Moses Mendelssohn*, no less a figure than Mendelssohn's friend Lessing was publicly accused of Spinozaism by F.H.Jacobi. And at that time the charge of pantheism was clearly equivalent to the charge of atheism. To refute the attacks of Jacobi and others Mendelssohn wrote *To the Friends of Lessing. An Appendix to Herr Jacobi's Correspondence about Spinoza's Teaching*. Already sick, he sent this letter off personally on 31 December; on 4 January 1786 he died. At the great funeral of this universally respected first great Jewish figure of the Enlightenment, no one suspected the turn that the Enlightenment was to take within three years: the storming of the Bastille in Paris on 14 July 1789.

7. Human rights for Jews as well

It was the enlightened Austrian monarch **Joseph II**, son of Maria Theresa, who was the first in principle to recognize equal human rights for Jews (for Bohemia and Moravia in 1781/82, for Hungary in 1783 and for Galicia in 1789), though this was in their capacity as 'citizens', not as 'Jews'. Concretely, this meant that the emperor himself had decreed the constitutional and legal emancipation of the Jews and their full incorporation into the constitutional and legal order, with the aim of making all Jews 'useful citizens of the state'. This also included the assumption of German-sounding names, which the Jews accepted only with some resistance – depending on financial resources these ranged from Schwarz and Weiss to Lilienthal and Rosenthal. However, with this very policy the brash enlightened emperor also came up against resistance among many Jewish communities and especially among their rabbis. These were communities which hitherto had lived largely in an autonomous, rabbinic way and rejected this kind of assimilation as non-Jewish. For in their view all this would inevitably lead to apostasy from the Jewish faith.

Still, despite all the prescriptions for emancipation the dialogue between church and Judaism which began with Mendelssohn in Germany was not really continued – apart from the influential liberal programmatic work by Christian Wilhelm Dohm, *On the Civic Betterment of the Jews* (1781), which was prompted by Mendelssohn. Even the verdict of the cosmopolitan Immanuel Kant on the Jews had been anything but favourable, although he was a friend of Mendelssohn's. The 'poets and thinkers' of German idealism – from Fichte via Schleiermacher to the Romantics – had the most antagonistic attitudes to Judaism. Already in the fragments written in his youth the great philosopher **G.F.W.Hegel** saw the God Yahweh only as a principle of simple unity and the people Israel as the embodiment of a split; in his lectures on the philosophy of religion he then combined a threefold Christianity and an idealized Germanhood at the expense of Judaism to form the great synthesis of 'absolute religion'.[52] And at the opposite pole to Hegel, for **Friedrich Schleiermacher,** who was to become the church father of Protestant theology in the nineteenth century, Judaism had been 'long a dead religion', the central feature of which was a view of the eternal rule of the Godhead as 'universal direct retribution' ('rewarding, punishing, chastizing').[53]

However, as is well known, the great **revolution in Germany** did not take place in politics but (unfortunately) only in **the realm of ideas,** in philosophy, poetry and music. And even the name of Mendelssohn lived on in Germany above all in the philosopher's grandson, the musician and composer Felix Mendelssohn-Bartholdy. He not only revived the work of the half-forgotten Johann Sebastian Bach by, for example, putting on a performance of his *St Matthew Passion,* but also composed an oratorio with the title *Paulus* (1836), a variety of church anthems (including *Tu es Petrus*), a symphony-cantata 'Hymn of Praise', and even a 'Reformation' symphony to celebrate the three hundredth anniversary of the Augsburg Confession in 1830. However, Felix Mendelssohn-Bartholdy had been baptized at the age of seven and had thus taken a step that his grandfather Moses had always tried to avoid, even if his children nevertheless did not: the step away from Judaism. In other words, in what was perhaps Germany's most famous Jewish family, which had produced not only philosophers and composers, but also scientists, writers and bankers, the **conflict between Judaism and the modern world** had been decided **against Judaism**. And Mendelssohn was only one of the now increasingly numerous Jewish converts to Christianity, the 'better' religion.[54] Baptism had now become what another famous German convert from Judaism, Heinrich Heine, had with sarcastic undertones called 'the entrance ticket to European culture'.

Still, the radical political consequences of the Enlightenment would first be drawn in America, and a dozen years later in France, with the **Declarations on Human Rights in the American and French Revolutions,** which also included **the Jews.** In the United States, as we have heard, from the beginning the Jewish immigrants had been so to speak free citizens, and soon after Independence they were guaranteed civil and religious equality. In Europe, however, there were prolonged controversies. 'Men are born and remain free and equal in rights'. This first sentence of the French Declaration on Human Rights in 1789 was clarified the very next month by the French National Assembly after a vigorous intervention (above all from Alsace, which had a large Jewish population), by a resolution that all Jews who took the oath as French citizens had **unconditional rights of citizenship.**

So the French Revolution had brought the formal proclamation of human rights for all men and thus also **for the Jews** – however, this was for the Jews not as a religious community (so to speak a nation within the nation) but, very much along the lines of modern individualism and liberalism, for the Jews **as individual citizens.** And even **Napoleon,** who promoted, inherited and went beyond the Revolution, was not concerned in his policy with the community of the Jews as a religion within a Christian empire: for him, religion was in any case a private matter. He was concerned to train the Jews as loyal 'French *citoyens* of Mosaic faith', within a secular state which in matters of world-view had to impose neutrality and toleration of all confessions and religions. This is how we are to understand the twelve questions which Napoleon solemnly put in 1806 to the more than one hundred delegates of French Jewry from all over the empire (including the Rhineland and Italy), and also his convening of a 'Great Sanhedrin', made up of forty-five rabbis and twenty-six lay members. But with this policy France had done more for the Jews than any other European nation – until the affair of the French Captain Dreyfus at the end of the century was to destroy illusions here as well.

And what about **Germany?** In the long run even Germany could not close itself to the lofty values of the two great revolutions – despite all the scepticism of the ruling classes about these 'Western' ideas. In any case, wherever they came to in Europe, the French armies had begun to establish the equal rights of the Jews with the help of the Napoleonic Code: they saw to the abolition of the compulsory restriction to the ghetto, of prohibitions against being engaged in certain professions and of the special taxes for Jews; at the same time there was also a new consistorial community order recognized by the state. The attempts at restoration on the part of the Ancien Régime of the Metternich era after 1815 were certainly aimed at suppressing the achievements of the Enlightenment and forgetting the emancipation of the Jews, in the name of the doctrine of the Christian state, the Romantic myth of the people, and a nationalistic patriotism which increased after the Napoleonic wars.

But in the next revolutionary wave, in 1848, in Germany too there was a proclamation of the 'basic rights of the German people' which also applied to Jews; moreover, this was made by the first German National Assembly in Frankfurt (something similar also happened the same year in Italian Piedmont). Finally, in 1869 the North German Alliance passed a law that 'all still existing restrictions on civic and state rights stemming from differences in religious confession be lifted'; for the Jews this meant a lifting of the restrictions on choice of profession and place of residence. All in all, this was an admission of Jews to full citizenship (with restrictions only for the army and senior civil service posts) and to civic society – which was then implemented all over the Wilhelmine empire. This course did not lead through the old urban middle class or through the middle class engaged in commerce, who had many links with the aristocracy, but through the **educated middle class**, on which the civil service elite kept an eye. Thus Judaism in Germany had begun to become middle-class – and the increase in the number of cultured Jews in universities and free professions showed how successful it was. As we shall see in more detail later, this German-Jewish symbiosis was, after the Jewish-Hellenistic and Jewish-Moorish interactions, the **third interaction in world history between Jewish culture and an alien culture.**[55]

However, one European state of the nineteenth century was to refuse civic and cultural equality to the Jews the longest – and after all that we have heard, its identity can hardly be surprising: the papal **church state.**[56] Right on the eve of the French Revolution, **Pius VI** had begun his pontificate with a decree on the Jews (*Editto sopra gli Ebrei*) which had resulted in new humiliations, acts of violence, compulsory baptisms and the locking up of Jewish children. And even later, under the absolutist and reactionary reign of **Pius IX**, in 1858 in Bologna the six-year-old Jewish child Edgaro Mortara was snatched from his parents by the papal police because he had been secretly baptized by a serving maid. He was carried off to Rome, and despite world-wide protests (including interventions from Napoleon III and the emperor Franz Joseph) he was inexorably given a Catholic upbringing, and indeed after a number of years was even ordained priest. It was only in 1870 that the walls of the Roman ghetto could fall, as a result of the entry of the Italian armies of liberation into the city. This was barely three months after the definition of papal primacy and infallibility, which had been made at the First Vatican Council by the same pope, as anti-liberal as he was anti-semitic, on the basis of a mediaeval/anti-Reformation/anti-modern attitude. This was a paradoxical development: as the Jews came out of the ghetto, the papacy went into a ghetto of its own making!

And in **Eastern Europe?**[57] In Russia, at the other end of Europe, it was at best members of the wafer-thin Jewish upper class, court Jews, rich merchants and some rabbis who had made acquaintance with the central European Jewish Enlightenment – as a result of business connections, journeys and education. By contrast the masses – who *a priori* had their reservations or even were opposed to the representatives of the Jewish Enlightenment with government support – remained virtually untouched by it. At this time they were for the most part still under the influence of **Hasidism**, which we have already come across, and in the face of an authoritarian cathedocracy which rejected all ecstasies, miracles and visions practised a piety of ardour and joy with a stress on feeling: joyful and loud ceremonies in their own houses of prayer, an enthusiastic or meditative form of prayer (often concentrated on the letters of the Bible), and remarkable leaders or holy men, righteous men or saints (*Zaddikim*). All in all, this was a remarkable religious world of its own, which has probably been transfigured all too poetically in our century through Martin Buber's accounts.

Only slowly, in Russia, too, a **Jewish movement** developed which **was indebted to the Enlightenment** – bitterly resisted by both the rabbis and the Hasidim. For in the Tsar's empire, where after the annexation of the Crimea, Bessarabia and above all Poland, in the nineteenth century now around two-thirds of all European Jews lived, the Jews were granted equal rights very hesitantly, if at all. How could a national assimilation of Jewish believers be at all possible there, in a land *de facto* dominated by a national religion – whether this was Russian Orthodoxy or Polish Catholicism? Moreover, the politics of the Tsars was also *de facto* aimed at a forced, purely external assimilation: Jews, too, were to be compelled to do military service and go to school. Indeed under Tsar Alexander III there were again harsh counter-measures, in which the Christian Supreme Curator of the Holy Synod had a hand. The same was the case in Poland. Here the Jews once again inevitably became the scapegoats for the general social misery. The Jewish Enlightenment was the greatest loser here. For rabbinic Ortho-doxy succeeded in allying itself with Hasidism against the Jewish Enlightenment movement, which had now been disowned by the zig-zag policy of the state: moreover in contrast to central and western Europe, no academic rabbinic seminaries were founded anywhere in Eastern Europe.

All this was also to have consequences particularly for countries to which the Jews now emigrated again in greater numbers, not least in the economic sphere. In connection with the 'unfavourable concen-tration on a few trades which had arisen in the Middle Ages', Johann Maier rightly points out: 'The problem of the unsound social structure as a disastrous legacy of the Middle Ages was not solved by the Jewish Enlightenment, but only partly modified, and it now had an effect on the surrounding world in both forms. The great Jewish majority of Eastern Europe, limited in the occupations in which its members could engage and primarily bound to tradition, represented an immense social problem. This problem also shifted to central Europe to the degree that "Eastern Jews" pressed westwards.'[58] And now, for an ever-increasing number of Jews, the West was America.

Let us recall that in 1654 the history of the Jews in the **United States** had begun with those twenty-three refugees from Brazil, and had subsequently stabilized around half a dozen Sephardic synagogues. A period of tranquil co-existence within Judaism followed, until the Ashkenasy synagogues split off at the beginning of the nineteenth century. The situation became more acute when at the beginning of the 1830s a mass **immigration of German-speaking Jews** began, so that around 1880 the Jewish population of the United States now already comprised 250,000, almost all of whom were exclusively German-speaking. For among the German immigrants there were no longer just poor traders and peddlars, but also an increasing number of well-to-do rabbis, trained at German universities, who brought from Germany ideas about the radical reform of modern worship which they could implement even better in free America, without 'church tax' and state regulation, than in the state-church system of the German states. But what effect did this confrontation with modernity have on the Jews –

their psyche, education, training, worship and community organization?

8. Identity crisis and paradigm shift: Reform Judaism

The fact can no longer be ignored that up to the Enlightenment Judaism
had been able to preserve the forms of life, law and faith which had
been shaped in the Middle Ages. But with the eighteenth/nineteenth
century the long **Jewish Middle Ages** and the 'segregation' of the Jews
from the rest of humankind, first sought by them and finally enforced
on them, had definitively **run its course**. Judaism experienced the
Enlightenment later, but therefore all the more vigorously. The Jews
were now **fully exposed to the spirit of modernity**, earlier and more
radically than, say, the Muslims because they were scattered right
across Europe and America. For as we heard, the scientific and
technological revolution of the seventeenth century and the social and
political revolution of the eighteenth century had been followed in the
nineteenth century by the industrial revolution. This had its effects on
the shape of cities: just as from the end of the eighteenth to the beginning
of the twentieth century most of the mediaeval city walls fell – as a
consequence of the tremendous growth of the cities and the increasingly
large modern agglomerations of industry – so now in succession the
walls also fell of those Jewish ghettos which had first been wanted by
and then forced on the Jews.

Now came the **exodus from the ghetto – spiritually and culturally as
well**. For in the integrated nation state a (Jewish) state within the state
was now no longer possible. Conversely, human rights for Jews
meant giving up the old Pharisaic-rabbinic autonomy and self-chosen
segregation, not only in France and England, but also in the German
states and the monarchy on the Danube. Indeed, in Germany in
particular there was a great controversy over the **reform of Judaism**.
So a religious reformation was not a presupposition for the rationalistic
Enlightenment, as in Christianity; it was the other way round: the
**rationalistic Enlightenment was a presupposition for the religious
Reformation!**

German Jewry worked deliberately and energetically to enter bourgeois society and become incorporated into it.[59] For the first time,
apostasy from the Jewish faith was no longer called for, but rather a
perfect command of the German language (instead of Yiddish), and an
adoption of the bourgeois ideal of education, of bourgeois 'respectability' and bourgeois 'morality'. As early as the 1820s isolated attempts

had begun to be made in Germany to celebrate the Jewish liturgy in the vernacular in a 'respectable' bourgeois way (without walking around and showing emotions); to allow sermons and organ accompaniments; to call Bar Mitzvah, the initiation ceremony for boys, 'confirmation'; to concentrate the observance of the law on the ethical commandments; and to attach importance to secular rather than Talmudic education. In the religious sphere there was a decided ethicizing and internalization. So, given the tremendous growth in the Jewish population, many Jews now asked whether they should not take advantage of the new possibilities of school education, training for professions and social life. **Education** and **training** became problem number one – no longer for the highly-privileged 'court Jews' of the world of princely absolutism, but in the age of democracy for any 'Jewish citizen'!

Indeed, throughout Western and Central Europe, apart from a few pockets of resistance, in Judaism, too, after a long period of stagnation a new paradigm-shift was now coming about in the face of the challenge of modernity, specifically through modern science, culture and democracy: from the mediaeval-rabbinic paradigm of the dispersed people of God to the **paradigm of modern, Enlightened-reformed Judaism** (Paradigm V = P V). So again there was a new entire constellation:

- Instead of the mediaeval segregation and autonomy of the Jewish community there was now the legal-political-social **integration of individuals and 'cultic communities' into the modern nation state**: a new ordering of the community and a partial replacement of the halakhic law with state law. 'Exile', the alien world outside, was to become home.
- Instead of the traditional rabbinic-Talmudic education there was now a **modern general education**: an education and training in public schools which was also secular, up-to-date and vocational.
- Instead of rabbis who were experts in the law and judges, there were now **rabbis** who had an academic training (in rabbinic seminaries) and explained Jewish teaching from the Bible, the Talmud, history and philosophy, thus acting as **preachers, pastors, liturgists and teachers.**
- Instead of a Hebrew liturgy which had largely become incomprehensible, formalistic and ritualistic, there was now a **reformed Jewish liturgy** in the vernacular with a sermon, which incorporated elements adapted from the surrounding culture (music, including the organ). Wearing a hat was no longer compulsory, nor were the sexes separated in choir and congregation.
- Instead of an isolating ghetto life restricted by every possible kind of

mediaeval custom there was now a **modernization of the whole Jewish life-style**, from dress to eating customs.

However, from the middle of the last century the reform stagnated in **Germany** because of the conservatism of German Jewry and its community organization, and also because of the conservatism of the German state and German society. It progressed only with the 'Science of Judaism' (from 1819), as this had been founded by Leopold Zunz and others.[60] 'Science' meant concrete and systematic research into Jewish religion, history and literature in a comprehensive source-critical way, of a kind that had not happened since the destruction of the Second Temple. A later high-point was the foundation of the Hebrew University of Jerusalem in 1925, which also included the study of Jewish poetry, Kabbala and social history. Even now, this 'Science of Judaism' exists as an international academic community, called 'Jewish Studies' or 'Judaistics'. Major contributions were made above all in the lexical sphere, as is evident not only from the *Jewish Encyclopedia* (12 vols., New York 1901-1906), but also the *Jüdische Lexikon* (5 vols., Berlin 1928-1934, new edition 1987), and now finally the imposing *Encyclopaedia Judaica* (17 vols., Jerusalem 1972). And yet even in the nineteenth century Reform Judaism could not establish itself universally – either in Germany or in the United States. Above all Jews from the lower middle classes and Jews of Eastern provenance were not involved in it.

In the **United States**, at first the development in fact took precisely the opposite direction. Here **Reform Judaism** had been substantially strengthened as early as the middle of the nineteenth century, when such significant rabbis as Leo Merzbacher, Samuel Adler, Max Lilienthal, the pragmatic organizer Isaac Mayer Wise and David Einhorn, whose concern was theoretical clarification, had immigrated from German-speaking countries. They had first of all formed 'Reform associations' and 'temples' (this name was preferred to that of synagogue). Indeed, above all on the initiative of Rabbi Isaac Mayer Wise, at a very early stage a radically reformed prayer book was published in German and Hebrew (1857). Significantly, there was no reference in it to a promised land and a restoration of the Jewish state. In 1873 there followed the foundation of the Union of American Hebrew Congregations, and two years later that of the first Jewish college, the Hebrew Union College in Cincinnati.

The culminating point of this reform movement was a **programme** which was passed in **Pittsburgh in 1885** and some years later was also accepted by the Reform rabbinate as the definitive position of Reform

Judaism. How was Judaism understood here? Judaism was explicitly defined as a 'progressive' religion, as a religion which always strove to be 'in harmony with the demands of reason' and to 'progress' in knowledge. Concretely, that meant that the modern age required the rejection of all those Mosaic laws (one might think above all of the commandments relating to food and purity), which 'are not in harmony with the views and customs of modern civilization'. It also called for the rejection of any national ambitions on the part of Judaism: 'We consider ourselves no longer a nation but a religious community, and therefore expect neither a return to Palestine nor a sacrificial worship under the administration of the sons of Aaron, nor the restoration of any of the laws concerning a Jewish state.'[61]

So this was modernization all along the line. The watchwords were no longer segregation and isolation, but adaptation, participation and assimilation. And as all this ended up in a **national and cultural adaptation**, we are fully justified in also calling the modern paradigm the **assimilation paradigm**: assimilation to the national and cultural environment of the time.

However, like any paradigm shift, this too was a far-reaching historical process in which reactions were similarly divided. For would not a rationalistic Reform Judaism of this kind inevitably end up in **conflicts**, not only with other groups but also with itself?

– Instead of the emphasis being on the 'exile', the oppression and the persecution of the people, it was now on their 'mission' among the Gentiles to disseminate the true knowledge of God – but without in fact practising this mission seriously.

– Instead of praising the Temple and its sacrificial cult, people praised the prophetic preaching of social justice – but without being particularly prominent in initiatives for social reform within society (apart from a few exceptions).

– Instead of stressing the specifically Jewish customs (for example on the sabbath, at weddings or festivals), people now stressed the humane ethos which Judaism shared with everyone else – but without wanting to give up the old rite of circumcision or really to tolerate mixed marriages.

– Instead of the emphasis being on Judaism as a community of the people, it was now on Judaism as a religious community – but without a complete abandonment of the bond with this particular people.

So it is not surprising that the reform, which seemed to be establishing itself all over America, soon found itself up against powerful opposition forces. Finally, at the end of this first main section, we must consider these opposing forces, which make the picture of Judaism seem remarkably complex. For the 'past' described here is particularly 'present' at this point. In a way unparalleled since the time of Hellenism, today great groups of Jews are living side by side, each with different theologies, forms of life and pictures of the world – in short, each dependent on different paradigms.

9. The contemporaneity of rival paradigms

Orthodox Judaism formed a **first counter-force** to Reform Judaism. For a long time, some of its representatives had looked on the process of assimilation or emancipation which began in the ninetenth century with the utmost concern; the term 'emancipation' was taken over from the Irish, fighting for their independence in Great Britain. Was all this really 'emancipation'? Did not such emancipation often simply amount to *connubium* and *conversio*, mixed marriages and apostasy from the faith? Was not the Jewish religion therefore well on the way to dissolving itself through such emancipation or assimilation?

The fact is that Reform Judaism, which towards the end of the century had spread considerably, began to pay a price for its policy of assimilation. For under the influence of rationalism, at the latest after the second half of the nineteenth century, even in the German-language Judaism of America there was now virtually no longer any sense of the values of symbol and feeling in religion: there was no sense of poetry and emotion in worship, of metaphorical and mythological modes of expression in the Bible; there was no feeling for Jewish folklore. And the price was that towards the end of the century there were increasingly clear signs of a decline in attendance at worship, in which all too little of the old Jewish religion could now be found. Even an alliance between modern Reform Judaism and liberal Christianity now no longer seemed to be ruled out.

It is not surprising that in Germany a Jewish Orthodoxy now began to organize itself (we shall be discussing it later), and that in the face of the breakthrough of reform, internal difficulties in the Orthodox synagogues and the apostasy of many Jews from the East, the **Orthodox Jews from Eastern Europe who had emigrated to the United States** also attempted to **band together**: in 1896 a first American Yeshiva, a college for rabbinic training, was founded by Rabbi Isaac Elchanan; from this in 1928 the Yeshiva College (the first general institution of higher education under Jewish direction) and in 1946 the Yeshiva University were to emerge. In 1898 there followed the founding of the Union of

Orthodox Jewish Congregations and in 1902 that of the Union of Orthodox Rabbis; this still exists today, though only some of the communities and rabbis from Eastern Europe joined it (later an English-speaking rabbinic union was also formed). But how were the Orthodox able to gain this influence even in America?

The reasons for the strengthening of Orthodoxy in America were above all **demographic**. Around 1820, only 8,000 Jews had immigrated into the United States from Eastern Europe. But in 1881/82, after terrible pogroms and anti-Jewish laws in Russia and Poland, a mass immigration began. By 1908 this had already increased the number of Jews in the United States to 1.8 million, around three-quarters of them now of Eastern European origin; for the most part this was a Jewish proletariat which, in contrast to the earlier German-Jewish merchants and traders who were distributed all over the country, as factory workers remained wholly concentrated on the great cities. They had often had no schooling, yet from the beginning they made use of every opportunity to rise socially.

The decisive point is that wherever the 'Eastern Jews', regarded as 'backward', and shaped by their mediaeval religion, fled, whether to Western Europe, Palestine or America, for the most part they persisted in their traditional patterns of life and structures (scandalizing the 'Western Jews'). They continued to cherish their previous **segregated life-style**, with at best external accommodations, say to modern means of transport, communication and payment. Just as Roman prelates, similarly imprisoned in their mediaeval paradigm, are fond of appearing in public in remarkable dress from a former age and are resolutely against birth control and in favour of a large number of children, so down to the present day Orthodox Eastern Jews, also distancing themselves socially from the seductions of modernity, go through the streets of London, Paris, Antwerp, Jerusalem and even New York in the traditional dark Sunday wear of Polish peasants.

The consequence is that in a way unparalleled since the fall of the Second Temple, depending on the religious circles, stratum of the population or nation from which a Jew comes, there were **time-lags in awareness** – with serious long-term consequences down to the present day for the internal situation within Judaism, from Eastern and Central Europe to America and Palestine. For now the consequences of the modern development were emerging increasingly clearly. Whereas in the mediaeval ghetto the identity and thus the dignity of the Jewish people remained unassailed despite all insults and hostilities (indeed their very segregation was a sign that they were God's chosen people), now that the walls of the ghetto had fallen and many Jews were seeking to join in modern secular culture, a major **identity-crisis** broke over the Jewish people. This was an identity-crisis of the kind that we can note in any paradigm shift, but it now threatened to break apart the mediaeval unity of the Jewish people and completely to undermine the age-old Jewish belief in God.

A **second counter-force** was **secularized Judaism**. Alongside Orthodoxy and Reform we need to take seriously a development which similarly began primarily and above all in **Germany**. Representatives of this movement would have nothing to do with a reform of Judaism – but for very different reasons from those of Orthodoxy. An increasing number of young Jewish intellectuals of the generation of Heinrich Heine (1797-1856) and Karl Marx (1818-1883) abandoned their Jewish belief in favour of enlightened modernity – and did so almost more radically than many of their older contemporaries from the Christian tradition.[62] Understandably, the post-revolutionary cultural trends of restoration (Metternich) and Romanticism were not very attractive to Jews because they were politically reactionary and mostly anti-Jewish. They tended more to intensify an **antipathy to religion of any kind** among Jewish intellectuals. The consequence was that conservative Christians and churches, too, regarded this development within Judaism with increasing suspicion and displeasure; they would have preferred traditional Judaism in its isolation. For shoals of these modern, secularized Jews, accustomed to reading and learning, now pressed their way into the cultural sector, the educated professions and public life, and wanted to make their mark by extraordinary achievements because they were a minority. Were they not particularly dangerous representatives of the Enlightenment – liberals, indeed Socialists and Communists? And as an upright Christian, what was one to think of Sigmund Freud and his subversive psychoanalysis?

Revolutionary, socialist and anarchistic Jews also grew up in **Eastern Europe**; they did not see themselves confronted with an ethnically homogenous society like that of Germany, to which it might have been possible to adapt by reform. The Orthodox system, rooted in rabbinic law, *a priori* excluded even the slightest reform. Indeed Jewish opponents had no option but to disown their religion completely if they were dissenters – this was a similar dilemma to that faced by many Russian Christians, who were in opposition to a Russian Orthodoxy directed by the Tsars.

For many Eastern Jews, the traditional system of law and ritual collapsed at the latest when they left their villages for the great cities of Europe or America. For it seemed increasingly less plausible that one should continue to observe such old-fashioned rules in the nine-teenth and twentieth centuries. Where was the contemporary theologi-cal justification for this age-old ritual and legal practice which to many people seemed void of meaning? Why circumcision? Why ritual slaughtering (draining the animal of blood for the sake of 'kosher' meat)? Why, finally, Hebrew in worship, not to mention the despised Yiddish? Was all this directly revealed by God and prescribed in a binding way once and for all? And conversely, why should not Jews be allowed to bury their dead in coffins? Why should they not open up corpses for the sake of medical progress and do much else that was forbidden by Jewish law?

The result was that even if people still often observed particular rites publicly, they no longer believed in them. So a completely **religionless Judaism** came into being, with **total assimilation**. And as the other side of this development, many young intellectual Jews began to join all the different forms of the new, radically secular, **quasi-religious movements of salvation** which existed at the end of the nineteenth century: socialism, anarchism or – and this was to be the determining factor for the future in Judaism – **Zionism**.

But what does 'Judaism' still mean in such circumstances? That became the **key question** in both Europe and America. Is Judaism a religion or a people or both? Does not Judaism – in contrast to Christianity and Islam – always also mean a particular **people** with a common identity, a common cultural heritage, a common origin, a common **religion**? However, conversely it could be asked: should it not also be possible to remain Jewish and yet be modern at the same time?

A **third counter-force** began to take shape – between the extreme Orthodox and secularized solutions: **Conservative Judaism**. The Jewish Theological Seminary Association was formed in 1886/87 in reaction to the Pittsburgh Manifesto of the Reform Rabbis, under the leadership of Rabbi H.Pereira Mendes. However, this Conservative Judaism gained a living religious centre only when the influential New York Jews Cyrus Adler and Jakob Schiff, both of German descent, put the Jewish Theological Seminary on a solid financial and academic footing and in 1902 called the distinguished scholar Solomon Schechter (who discovered the Geniza manuscripts in Cairo)[63] from England as presi-dent of the college; with him a newly constituted teaching body was appointed, consisting of German and Eastern European Jewish scholars. Schechter, of whom we shall be hearing more in due course, succeeded in pointing a way forward by which it was possible to endorse the modern development and yet remain faithful to the Mosaic

Torah and the rabbinic traditions and thus preserve the true Jewish spirit.

In this way the Seminary, and especially the Teachers' Institute which was associated with it in 1909 (soon, in contrast to the Reform movement, it was to give all its courses in Hebrew, and it also disseminated in America the use of the neo-Hebrew which had already become common in modern Palestine), became a bridge to Orthodoxy, which intellectually was often quite helpless. Both rabbis and teachers for some socially advanced Orthodox synagogues were trained here, since there was also a conviction that better family education (mothers should not go out to work) and the quasi-innate impulse of Jews to learn (colleges) gave the best opportunities for rising socially and for moving out of the slums into better parts of the cities (from there, in a third stage, there was a movement out into the suburbs of the great cities). Unfortunately, in this development the more religious (Orthodox) Jews came off worst, since they were the poorer ones.

Because of quotas, 1925 saw a stop to mass immigration. But in 1927 there were already 4.2 million Jews in the United States (3.6% of the total population), with 3,100 communities. However, surveys from the 1930s show that despite the imposing structures of the synagogues and the number of Jewish associations and institutions, by far the majority of children of Jewish immigrants departed from the Jewish faith. Jewish students produced a considerably higher proportion of atheists, agnostics and sceptics than their Catholic or Protestant fellow-students.[64] The Jewish school and social system which had been built up so intensively (with hospitals, and homes for orphans and old people) often had as little to do with the Jewish religion as many Jewish Youth Organizations (YMHA, YWHA Young Men/Women's Hebrew Associations) and charitable Jewish organizations (B'nai B'rith, American Jewish Committee). **Jewishness** – a popular ideology often propagated by socialists – now became more important than **Judaism**. However, this did not seem acceptable either to strict Orthodoxy or to the radical modern Reform Jews, though it was to Conservative Judaism, which cherished Jewish history, literature, language and customs.

There is no doubt that at the end of the nineteenth century and the beginning of the twentieth, the internal situation within Judaism had become drastically more acute, as a result of the now obvious **contemporaneity of divergent and rival paradigm**s, all of which had their own problems. More pressing and serious than the questions which were addressed from outside to the various Jewish trends were

the questions which Jews now put to themselves and at the same time
to others in these various schools, trends, 'sects', 'confessions' and
'denominations':

 Questions in the Face of Modernity

– To the **Orthodox**: Is it possible to take advantage of the technological
and economic possibilities of the modern world and at the same time
detach oneself spiritually, culturally and religiously from all the other
developments in society; to claim a special divine election, forbid mixed
marriages and generally feel 'in exile'? Does that not lead to the complete
isolation of a community, and thus provoke dangerous resentment and
aggression? Can Judaism remain a national religion and the nation of a
religion in an age which separates state and religion? Indeed, can religion
still play this dominant role in Judaism at all if society as a whole is generally
becoming 'secularized'?
– To the **Secular**: Is it possible simply to abandon Jewish peoplehood
and membership of the Jewish religion and live like everyone else, as a
secular citizen of German, French, British or American nationality? Will not
the non-Jewish world around sooner or later provide a reminder that one
is still a Jew, that invisible walls remain between Jews and Christians, and
in any case some doors and some areas remain closed? Is it possible to
forget the Jewish religion like this and make the Jewish people a people
like other peoples? In this religion in particular, are not anti-religious
tendencies ultimately doomed to failure?
– To the **Reformers**: Is it possible to reform Jewish liturgy, upbringing,
education and life-style and restrict Jewish observance of the law to the
purely ethical sphere without in so doing also sacrificing what is specifically
Jewish and endangering the heart of Jewish faith and community? Is it
possible simply to ignore the national element in the Jewish religion and
make Judaism a religion like other religions? In this religion in particular,
are not anti-national tendencies ultimately doomed to failure?
– To the **Conservatives**: Is it possible to keep public secular and
private Jewish life separate without succumbing to the danger of spiritual
schizophrenia – between a show of modernity and a repressed Jewishness? Must one not decide whether or not the Bible is God's revelation,
whether or not one really has to observe the Mosaic law with all its individual
commandments?

Judaism as a different religion, a different people, a different 'race'.
Tragically, these questions were soon to be matters of life and death.
But no matter which Jewish trend one belonged to, at the end of the
nineteenth century all Jews were once again confronted with a quite
different fatal development. Something that no one in 'Enlightened'

civilized Europe would have still thought possible after all the mediaeval pogroms against the Jews now happened: once again there was a radical intensification of anti-Judaism, which now took the form of an **antisemitism with a biological and racial basis.** The consequences were to be fearful: not just renewed discrimination against the Jews and expulsion of Jews, but now even a systematic extermination of the Jews.

We are compelled to look very much more closely at this disastrous development, which became a fearful fate for the whole of Jewry. And as these events concern our contemporary history, I shall report them under a new main title, 'The Challenges of the Present'.

Part Two

THE CHALLENGES OF
THE PRESENT

A. From the Holocaust to the State of Israel

Before we touch on so emotional a problem of contemporary history as the extermination of the Jews, which was attempted and almost achieved in Germany, some fundamental observations need to be made. For when confronted with such a grim past, just about every people prefers the art of forgetting to that of remembering. However, liberation does not come through forgetting and repressing, but through remembering and acknowledging.

I am not concerned here with the past in isolation, in an abstract way, nor am I concerned to cultivate a complex about the past. I am concerned with that past which will not go away, a past which still continues to determine the present and which is still virulent today among large sectors of the nations. A repressed past easily becomes a curse.

So my purpose here is not a fixation on the past, the moral condemnation of yesterday from the high horse of the generation which did not experience these events, nor a resentful criticism of the church and state of the time in the interests of contemporary politics. My concern is to make a critical and self-critical analysis of those forces and structures which governed a particular past and are still influential today. All this is with a view to a better future.

I. A Past That Will Not Go Away

Although national history or church history should obviously not be described as a single chain of omissions, failures and crimes, and the pleasant side of history should equally be noted with the greatest possible objectivity (and in a later book I shall do this for Christianity as well), so too not only the 'good past' of a people or even a religious community should be cultivated.

In principle:

• Neither a national history nor a church history may be sweepingly

'instrumentalized' in the interest of a particular party, state or church
policy as a means of creating identity. As Habermas has remarked,
history is not a 'substitute religion', capable of offering compensatory
meaning to those deprived of their roots in the process of modernization, and creating a consensus in state and church.

• Rather, both national and church history need to be examined
critically and appropriated self-critically: with a view not only to the
historical dialectic of continuity and interruption, but also to the
ethical difference between humanity and inhumanity, good and evil.

• So those who because of negative historical experiences have a critical
relationship to their own history and thus have a heightened moral
awareness and greater human sensitivity can help to avoid the
repetition of earlier mistakes. They can find a new, freer identification
with their state or their religion, which excludes the former uncritical
total identification with all its totalitarian consequences.

It is impossible to cope with the past in the sense of bidding it farewell
or neutralizing it. Whether one likes it or not, the past always remains
part of the present. However, it is possible to assimilate the past in a
critical or self-critical way. Indeed, the past which is still always present
can be utilized for the future: the causes of past tragedies can be
analysed, and theories can be derived from them. So we shall now turn
to a contemporary theme which is central to a better future for Jews
and Christians: the present-day verdict on the mass murder of six
million Jews – and there is good evidence for this figure.[1]

1. Historians in dispute

There is occasion enough for this assimilation of criticism and self-
criticism. For after forty years of late consequences it should be evident
that already in 1945 (and even more in 1946/47, after the shift in US
policy towards the Stalinist Soviet Union and a Germany which was
first occupied and then courted) a process was under way of neutralizing
and repressing guilt. So in the Federal Republic of Germany, which
was newly constituted in 1949 (and in the German Democratic Republic
with its Stalinist orientation), there was neglect of the 'mourning'[2]
which was so urgently necessary; in the West it was largely replaced by
an anti-Communism shared with the Americans (and understandable
under Stalin).

'No one was there and no one knew anything.'[3] Many people
who visited defeated Germany after the war got the impression of a

widespread lie about alleged ignorance – particularly ignorance about the·plundering, persecution and extermination of the Jews. As though this had not taken place in full public view: the massive witch-hunts against the Jews even before 1933; in 1933 the beginning of the removal of Jews from the state, business, the arts and science; in 1935 the Nuremberg race laws 'for the protection of German blood and German honour'; then in November 1938 – not three months after the Munich agreement with England and France – the organized riots and brawls, the destruction of synagogues and the pogroms, the demolition and plundering ('Arianization') of Jewish banks, businesses and department stores; and finally the arrest and deportation of tens of thousands of German Jews to the concentration camps which were notorious everywhere.[4]

However, in the Germany of the post-war decades – understandably absorbed in reconstruction and fascinated by the 'economic miracle' – people had largely bracketted off the National Socialist years from German history as an alien body. First of all they thought that they could be satisfied with moral indignation against 'a rule of violence and tyranny' supposed to have been forced on the German people from outside (by Hitler and his cronies). People spoke of what they had personally suffered: the loss of relatives, air-raids, being turned out of their homes. They forgot what the Germans had done first to others: attacks on peaceful lands in the west, north and east of Europe, the first carpet bombing, the mass executions, deportations, gassings and so on. As though they had not shared the responsibility and therefore also the guilt for this 'doom' – directly or indirectly, to a greater or lesser degree. An apologetic, euphemistic terminology began to establish itself which included the Jews among the 'victims of violence' (if possible, not mentioning them by name); there was general talk of the crime committed 'in the name of the German people' (by whom?). People showed an ambivalent attitude to the small resistance group which all too late (first on 20 July 1944) really embarked on action which, had it been successful and had Germany immediately capitulated, would have prevented the destruction of many cities (Berlin, Dresden, Heilbronn...), millions of war dead and above all the murder of further millions of Jews (were they 'traitors'?[5]).

So was it surprising that, after decades, the dispute over the responsibility for the World War and the Holocaust which had yet to be settled should have broken out with even greater vigour? As early as 1961 there was a first passionate debate among historians over Fritz Fischer's book *Grasping for World Power*,[6] and the indisputable German share of the blame for the First World War. But the real symptom of this is the so-called 'historians' dispute' over National Socialism and the Second World War which erupted in the 1980s, a good forty years after the end of the war, and which fanned into flame what had long been smouldering.

Of course this newest fundamental and highly emotional dispute over the revisionism of contemporary German historians and journalists in connection with a reassessment of the Nazi crimes[7] was also followed with great interest abroad, especially in France, Israel and America. And for some of those directly involved and some observers, carried on as it was with amazing openness, it had quite painful consequences: it opened up old wounds and split German historians into two camps.

If we now look back on the historians' debate with some detachment and try to weigh the arguments of the two sides with as little prejudice as possible, two things have to be said:

– The most recent debate was sparked off by the Berlin historian **Ernst Nolte** with **apologetic speculations**, insinuations and ambiguities: about Bolshevism as the model and pattern for the Nazi terror; about Bolshevist class murder as a presupposition for Nazi racial murder; about a 'European civil war' from '1917 (!) to 1945'; about an alleged 'declaration of war' on the Third Reich by Chaim Weizmann, the President of the Jewish Agency. These were adventurous, indeed dangerous hypotheses. Even more dangerous, however, than the talk of a preventive war by Hitler against Russia was talk of a preventive murder by Hitler of the defenceless Jews!

– In retrospect, the accusatory analysis of the philosopher **Jürgen Habermas** seems all too justified, even if he perhaps all too sweepingly lumped a number of authors together: such 'historicizing' of the Nazi past in fact ends up by relativizing everything, bringing it down to the same level and making it innocuous and trivial. It is 'a kind of damage limitation' and evidently a politically motivated 'apologetic tendency in contemporary German historiography'.[8]

Indeed, that the **Third Reich** has maintained an 'utterly negative life' down to the present day has nothing to do, as Nolte thinks, with a 'negative myth of absolute evil', but is a matter of naked historical reality.[9] Did not Nolte himself rightly in principle describe the **reasons** for this as early as 1980? Here I shall quote the **two** most important of them, following Nolte himself – in view of the significance of the question for world history and the underlying tendencies to foist off elsewhere German responsibility for a war planned over a long period,

at the outbreak of which no general mutinied and no worker went on strike, and for the Holocaust:
– First of all: 'The first, strongest and most general reason is as follows. According to a view which is hardly disputed, the Third Reich began and bore responsibility for the greatest and most costly war in human history. By his refusal to negotiate, resign or capitulate in due time, Hitler brought this war to such a catastrophic end that for Germans in particular the memory of it must be indelible. In addition there is the moral condemnation of the survivors by Hitler, so that in Germany a negative judgment is quite simply a necessity of life.'[10]
– Secondly: 'The violent acts of the Third Reich are singular. Certainly there are some precedents and parallels to the concentration camps and even to the "smashing of the workers' movement", but in motivation and execution the extermination of several million European Jews – and also many slaves, psychologically sick people and gypsies – is unprecedented, and it caused unparalleled terror in particular by the cold, inhuman, technical precision of the quasi-industrial machinery of the gas chambers.'[11]

After these statements, one wonders why later (after the political shift in the Federal Republic in 1982!) Nolte could attempt such a historical relativization of the Nazi crime, such an exoneration of the German nationalist middle class, the generals and the mass murderer Adolf Hitler. As though Nazism had been above all an answer to Bolshevism and not an originally nationalistic German delusion about race and conquest – with catastrophic conclusions for the whole world! As early as 1978, in his Notes on Hitler,[12] Sebastian Haffner made clear the global consequences of Hitler's twelve-year-old dictatorship. He may have exaggerated, but in principle he was right: 'Whether we like it or not, the world of today is the work of Hitler. Without Hitler there would be no division of Germany and Europe; without Hitler there would be no Americans and Russians in Berlin; without Hitler there would be no Israel; without Hitler there would be no end to the colonies, or at least not so rapid an end; there would be no Asian, Arab and Black African emancipation or the removal of the class system in Europe. Indeed, to put it more accurately, there would be none of this without Hitler's mistakes. For he certainly did not want any of it.'[13]

Those isolated German politicians, historians and fellow-country-men who, as veterans of the world war, forty years later presented themselves as 'defenders of the Christian West' against Bolshevism read history backwards in a very rash way. (Where had they been? In Bergen or Bordeaux? In Rotterdam or Oradour? On Corsica or Crete? Before Tobruk or Stalingrad?) They, the attackers, wanted to restyle themselves as victims. Were they all victims? Those who were invaded and the aggressors, the innocent and the criminals, the American soldiers and the SS troops (at Bitburg cemetery in 1980!)? Were they all victims? No, this kind of obliteration of guilt, at the end of which there are no perpetrators left, is a falsification of the historical account. Simply because the perpetrators finally had to pay for their atrocities, they did not become 'victims', if this word is still to have any meaning at all. No 'self-defence' can be constructed out of aggression. And no new national identity can be achieved by a 'historicizing' of National Socialism – by bridging over, levelling down or bracketting off the twelve years of Nazi rule.

After all this, we may ask whether the historians' dispute was not really superfluous. But it had its good side, since contrary to the intentions of those who embarked on them, the attempts to 'historicize' the Holocaust led to its becoming **a contemporary reality**. Instead of a 'normalization' of the history of the Third Reich there was now intensified self-critical **reflection** on the uniqueness and the indelibility of the Nazi mass murder, which evidently could not so easily be relativized historically with references to Stalin's Gulag; which could not so conveniently be redefined ideologically and rationally domesticated.[14]

But in the light of the historians' debate, how are we to assess the Holocaust today? It is necessary to avoid a false alternative.

2. How do we deal with the Holocaust?

1. There must be **no moral levelling down** of the Holocaust. Without in any way being 'obsessed' by a 'guilt complex', we must maintain (as was shown once again precisely by the German 'historians' dispute) that **the Holocaust is a singular crime**. Not because each event, each person, each age is unique; that is a truism. Rather, because the dimension of **ideological-industrial mass-murder** perpetuated here is **unprecedented, incomparable and barely imaginable** even now. 'The question occurred to us: what about the women and children? Here too, I resolved to find a clear-cut solution. I did not feel justified in exterminating the men – i.e. killing them or having them killed – and allowing avengers to grow up for our sons and grandsons in the form of children. The difficult decision had to be made to remove this people from the face of the earth.' Thus **Heinrich Himmler**, the head of the SS, on 6 October 1943. He was able to appeal to a 'Führer's order'.[15] As early as 30 January 1939, **Adolf Hitler** had threatened 'the extermi-

nation of the Jewish race in Europe' in the event of a war, and in spring 1941, in connection with the Russian campaign, he had planned and then implemented it through Heydrich's task forces. Presumably in summer 1941, at any rate at the height of his confidence in victory, he had given Himmler a secret verbal order to carry out the extermination of all European Jews in the territories under German control. Right up to his end, and even in his political testament, Hitler boasted of having exterminated the Jews in Germany and Central Europe.[16]

So I can only agree with the historian **Eberhard Jäckel** when against all moves by his fellow historians to play down the Holocaust he points out its historically unpredecented extent. The National Socialist murder of the Jews was unique 'because never before had a state resolved and announced on the authority of its duly appointed ruler that it would kill a particular group of human beings, including old people, women, children and infants, down to the last person, and put this resolve into practice with every possible state means'.[17]

No, it is historically unjustified and thus also theologically irresponsible to minimize Auschwitz, to bring it down to the level of other calvaries of world history and thus ultimately to explain the whole cruel event anthropologically and morally in terms of the ever-present weakness and sinfulness of human beings. The fact remains that to level down the Holocaust in moral terms and to harmonize it by introducing comparisons is irresponsible. After January 1942 at least two million Jews were murdered in Auschwitz-Birkenau, the largest extermination camp. No reference to the errors and crimes of other peoples (nor even a Christian cross at the entrance to the camp at Auschwitz) can and may ever divert attention from this mass murder of Jews which is unique in its inhumanity. However – while unequivocally granting all this, we must also consider another point.

2. The Holocaust must **not be made an absolute**. For all the shame and sorrow, even this gigantic crime by human beings against human beings must be looked at within the framework of German history and human history. As we have already seen, the word 'historicizing' used for this by Martin Broszat, at the time Director of the Munich Institute for Contemporary History, is inappropriate here (because it suggests archives, museums, 'relativizing', and thus plays down the event). However, we are justified in bringing out links with other genocides in our century – from the murder of the Armenians by the Turks to the Pol Pot massacres in Cambodia.[18]

In particular **Stalin's** mass murders, long ignored or relativized by many on the left, must not be passed over in silence. Constant purges of the Party, the smashing of the peasants, terrorist pressure on the intelligentsia and the proletariat, the Moscow trials (against Bucharin and his old friends) also claimed millions of victims. According to Nikita Kruschchev's account to the Twentieth Party Congress of the Soviet Communist Party in Moscow in 1956 which ushered in de-Stalinization, it is above all the historical achievement of **Alexander Solzhenitsyn** – who also kept silence for a long time on the left wing – to have been able to picture the people of the Gulag Archipelago in Communist Soviet Russia in terrifying detail.[19] Truly, all this must not be played down, because while the concentration camps and the Gulags have been done away with, the KGB and its consequences still remain. For all the immense internal problems, Mikhail Gorbachev's *glasnost* has in principle ushered in a self-critical illumination of the history of the Soviet Union – from the frustration of real democracy by Lenin's Bolsheviks in 1917 to the pact between Hitler and Stalin in 1939.[20]

Nevertheless, who would want to make a detailed comparison between the horrors of the Nazi terror and those of the Soviet terror?[21] However, once one has *a priori* ruled out all comparative harmonization, it is legitimate to introduce a counterpoint. For it seems just as historically unjustifiable and theologically irresponsible – in whatever interests – to make Auschwitz a moment or a monument detached from the human history of violence and suffering. In this way it is all too easy to foist responsibility off on some historically disastrous fate, an anti-Christ, demon or Satan. It is also all too easy in this way to forget that in other circumstances a Holocaust disposition could also come into being among the persecuted of yesterday towards the persecuted of today. So it is important to be specific and to analyse the causes, first of all seeing them in a wider European context.

3. Nationalism and racism – an explosive mixture

With welcome clarity, in recent years German historians like Eberhard Jäckel, Jürgen Kocka, Christian Meier, Hans and Wolfgang Mommsen and others[22] have again made us aware that it is wrong to regard the National Socialist dictatorship with all its criminal consequences simply as a tragic entanglement in an inescapable fate (as a consequence of a geo-political 'central position', of Germany's 'special course', and quite directly of the Versailles treaty, the world economic crisis and mass unemployment). Anyone who wants to blame everything on the one Adolf Hitler and his 'demonic' powers of seduction in order to exonerate the German people and its ruling classes in politics and diplomacy, the army, business and the academic and scientific worlds, is not just irresponsibly simplifying history, but indeed falsifying it.

However, there is no disputing the fact that the radical Nazi hatred of the Jews had a 'Christian' prehistory going back over centuries and an immediate **political and secular prehistory**. I have already given an account of this: with the utmost individual and indeed collective efforts, the Jews in Germany had succeeded in becoming citizens in the legal sense (state citizens) and also – to a large degree – in the cultural sense (educated citizens), just as at the same time other social groups (Catholics, workers, women) had to fight for social advancement and recognition.

Here the history of Jews in Germany in particular had undergone a deeply **ambivalent development**, as Shulamit Volkov, Director of the Institute for German History at the University of Tel Aviv, has brought out in a critical survey of the latest historical research. She points out that this was neither simply a step-by-step, consistent, successful process of assimilation, as depicted first in Germany and then often also among German-Jewish emigrés. Conversely, nor was it a process of ever greater obstacles on the way to legal, social and cultural integration, so that any hope of authentic emancipation was *a priori* deceptive, as is argued by the Zionist school above all in Israel.[23] Despite all the repudiation of the Jews and the hostility towards them, the history of their assimilation was often one of successful social life with their neighbours and social and cultural success. They were helped by their economic and financial connections, their great tradition of reading and learning, their family life, which generally remained intact, and their well-tried pattern of upbringing. So in fact the experiences of German Jews were extremely varied, and their development was unusually advanced, but forces were in play which tended both towards assimilation and towards dissociation and rejection. Only relatively late, in National Socialism, did the antisemitic forces gain the upper hand over the wealth of shared Jewish and German experiences, fears and hopes.[24]

Here above all the gradual rise of **nationalism** had a fateful effect, and the 'patriotism' ('love of the fatherland') which developed as early as the eighteenth century soon degenerated into a form of chauvinistic arrogance. For all their social integration, the Jews were very open to the charge of a lack of national awareness in so far as they still lived by a tradition going back over thousands of years and a sense of togetherness extending beyond national frontiers. And above all because of this nationalism – which was particularly virulent in Germany because national union came about at a late stage – in the nineteenth and twentieth centuries Jewish and German equality was often hardly more than theoretical and legal, and the symbiosis between the Jews and Germans was often only superficial: frequently it was a matter more of external acculturation than of truly integrative inculturation. It was more assimilation – which is now increasingly a term with negative connotations, even for the modern Jew who has adapted – than real community.

The Christian churches, too, often did little more than tolerate their Jewish fellow-citizens – in the hope that one day they would be completely converted. So for many people in Germany – in both business and politics, in literature, journalism and art – the Jews remained a 'disruptive element'. And whenever a step forward seemed to have been taken in the recognition of the Jews, upsurges of anti-Judaism made themselves felt in the opposite direction. All too often the Jews faced opposing forces in nationalism and the churches. This is the only explanation why after the period of the Enlightenment (which is itself already ambivalent) a great darkness should once again break in on them.

What a mysterious, uncanny development there was in eastern, western and central Europe – despite the Enlightenment! As we heard, in **Russia** (and in Poland) first of all the Jewish Enlightenment movement had had very good relations with the government. However, after the murder of Tsar Alexander II in 1881 – which rumour attributed to 'the Jews' – there were again serious riots among the mobs, who were hostile to the Jews: there were repeated waves of pogroms over subsequent years, right down to the revolutionary chaos of the period between 1917 and 1921.

What about **France**? According to Shulamit Volkov, 'Interestingly, on closer investigation it emerges that what had at first seemed to me to be unique to Germany, especially during the Kaiser's Reich, also applied to at least a further citadel of antisemitic agitation at this time, namely the France of the Third Republic.' It was above all Edouard Drumont's anti-Jewish work *La France Juive* of 1886 which attained 'more popularity and was more seriously discussed among people who mattered than anything that the German antisemites had written at this time'.[25]

Indeed in France the affair of Captain **Alfred Dreyfus** of the General Staff was to destroy any belief in the realization of the Enlightenment ideals of emancipation. Wrongfully accused of betraying his country to Germany in 1894, the Jew Dreyfus was first condemned to deportation for life and then in 1899, in manifest breach of the law, to ten years' imprisonment. This sparked off an affair which not only caused the Third Republic its greatest domestic political crisis but at the same time laid open the extent to which antisemitism was still to be found in France. For years the army, the aristocracy, the monarchists, the upper class, the right-wing press and the clergy opposed the call to reopen the trial (which came from radical Republicans, Socialists, left-wing Catholics and the liberal press). It was only in 1906 (seven years later!) that Dreyfus the Jew from Alsace secured full rehabilitation.

So along with European nationalism, and encouraged by numerous anti-Jewish clichés (which were also widespread all over Europe), an anti-Judaism had grown up in the nineteenth century which was now no longer primarily religious but had a **racial and biological** basis – very much in line with the social Darwinist spirit of the time and its principle of selection, 'the survival of the fittest'. This anti-Judaism was thus not biblical and religious but apparently scientific. History was now understood not as a struggle between classes but a struggle between races, the racial struggle of the Indo-Germanic 'Aryan' master race against the Slavs, and above all against the 'semitic' race of the Jews. This view of the world been put together by the French diplomat and writer Count **Joseph Arthur Gobineau** – and similarly also by the Anglo-German **Houston Stewart Chamberlain** (son-in-law of the anti-Jewish Richard Wagner), who had attempted to give it a 'scholarly' basis in his four-volume *Essay on the Inequality of the Human Races.*[26] The racist antisemitism of this French aristocrat (who was also a friend of Richard Wagner!) was originally directed against the Enlightenment generally, against the egalitarian ideas of 1789, against human rights, democracy, freedom and equality – and to this end needed **the** type of the 'unequal', the Jews.

Right down to the nineteenth century, the term 'semitic' had still covered the whole linguistic group of Semites, including the Arabs. But in 1879 the term **'antisemitic'** was created and popularized by a German pamphleteer called Wilhelm Marr.[27] Why? In order to give hatred of the Jews a respectable, 'scientific' name. For now at the end of the nineteenth century, in **Germany** in particular, an explosive mixture of popular enthusiasm made up of nationalism and racism was brewing. Here the state was not understood along nationalist French lines as the unity of will of a variety of different citizens but – after the patriotic wave of the Napoleonic Wars – romantically as a single 'individuality of the people (the Volk)' with a special 'spirit' and 'character' (it was often a substitute for a national religion, which did not exist). The explosive character of this mixture was largely underestimated because the attitude seemed to be no more than the well-known hostility to the Jews.

The old 'Jewish question' was by no means settled, but was now said to be 'the social question' (Otto Glogau); indeed it was made presentable as an essential component of the anti-democratic, anti-emancipatory ideology of German nationalism (Heinrich von Treitschke and the consequences). For in the meantime, in the process of assimilation, Jews had become increasingly influential in business, politics and culture, thus provoking feelings of hatred and envy among many non-Jews who had failed to make the grade. And after the First World War, in which 12,000(!) German Jews fell on the battlefield for Germany,[28] and after the collapse of the second German Reich in 1918, when a not inconsiderable number of Jewish intellectuals had begun to commit themselves to the socialist left, the terrible crop was to grow which had been sown in the second half of the nineteenth century. A specific antisemitism now became the substitute religion for the dawning National Socialist 'Third Reich'.

4. A defeat for the European Enlightenment

Nevertheless, we cannot simply derive the antisemitism of National Socialism from history, as though here we just had a recurrent cycle or an acceleration towards a final catastrophe. In the face of these widespread views, Shulamit Volkov has rightly stressed the **novelty of National Socialist antisemitism**. Now there was no longer just an antisemitism of the written word, of discussion and ideology, but an antisemitism of the spoken word, of propaganda, of outcry and action. The novelty was that only in Nazism was there large-scale **active antisemitism** which resorted to naked force, terror and ultimately extermination.[29] So at that time – quite contrary to the expectations even of the Jews, despite everything, because of what in many respects had proved a successful collaboration between Germans and Jews – there occurred that catastrophe in world history which was radically to interrupt the process of the assimiliation of Judaism, at least in Europe. It seemed to confirm the views of those Orthodox Jews who had forthrightly rejected anything modern, and compromise those forces of both liberal and conservative Judaism which had been intent on assimilation to, or at least co-existence with, the modern world. Rightly?

In retrospect, there is no doubt that racist and especially Nazi antisemitism represented an unprecedented **defeat for the European**

Enlightenment. After Gotthold Ephraim Lessing and Moses Mendelssohn; after the American and French Revolutions; after Karl Marx, Sigmund Freud, Martin Buber and Albert Einstein; after Gustav Mahler, Jakob Wassermann and Joseph Roth; after so many prominent modern Jewish philosophers, authors, artists, musicians and scientists in Germany, there was a terrifying lapse into the barbaric realms of the Middle Ages, into ancient ignorance, pernicious superstition and unheard-of cruelty towards the Jews. Beyond question this was also a repudiation of the ideals of 1789. In 1945 Thomas Mann, the representative of the German spirit at a time of Nazi barbarism, thought that the Germans were 'a people of the Romantic counter-revolution against the philosophical intellectualism and rationalism of the Enlightenment'; and the German inwardness to which the world owes German metaphysics and German music finally had a negative effect on human social life in a typical 'German dualism of the boldest speculation and political immaturity'.[30]

Indeed this cruel regression of a whole enlightened nation – bought at the price of the 'myth of the twentieth century' (the title of Rosenberg's notorious book), i.e. with legends, lies and mystifications – was an immaturity deeply rooted in the history of German life, but ultimately one which Germany had brought upon itself. And because of the tremendous possibilities of the modern world, because of modern science, technology, industry and mass mobilization, the effects were once again infinitely more terrifying than all the terror which had come upon the Jews in the Middle Ages and at the time of the Reformation.

In fact, even now we can hardly understand how in the very country in which the Jews had made the furthest cultural process, a country which many Jews loved as their home more than any country outside Palestine, a country to which they had made their most considerable cultural contributions,[31] how in this ancient cultured nation of poets, thinkers and musicians, after a persecution which was generally acknowledged and endorsed over a number of years, a monstrous mass murder of around six million Jews could ultimately be organized and carried out. Here, of all places, the crazy attempt at a '**final solution**' was made, the attempt at a total extermination of a whole people, the 'Shoah', the 'catastrophe', or the 'whole offering', the '**Holocaust**', of the Jewish people. In our day the question is still an open one and is the one that most pains the best of Germans. Where does the guilt lie? What are the consequences for the Jewish people and the German people, but also for Jewish theology, Christian faith and the Jewish-Christian dialogue? We shall have to go into all that, but first of all one thing is indispensable.

5. Naming the guilty: the elites and the masses

Adolf Hitler was neither an 'accident' in German history nor a 'decree' of 'fate'. Adolf Hitler came to power with the broad assent of the German people, and for all the hidden criticism was supported to the bitter end by the majority of the population with a loyalty which is still terrifying even today. And what would people be saying about this Hitler today if in 1941, at the height of his power, he had met with an accident or if he had even won the war against the free world (and completed the extermination of the Jews)? To the present day the phenomenon of Hitler puts a question-mark against any absolute pacifism. Peace at **any** price? Even at the price of Auschwitz?

Certainly, there was political resistance at that time against Nazi barbarism – however, that was the exception and not the rule. Certainly, we must distinguish between those who incited and those who were led astray, those who gave orders and those who obeyed – but only with the aim of clearly identifying the specific responsibility on both sides. For the Nazi dictatorship could neither have come into being nor lasted without the **failure** of 'ordinary' men and women with their own interests at heart, without the whole of everyday Fascism. But there is also another factor which in commemorative speeches is usually passed over in silence: this criminal regime would even less have been able to achieve its dominant position without the ruling **elites in German bureaucracy, industry,**[32] **the law,**[33] **medicine,**[34] **journalism**[35] and the army.[36] The majority of them had a conversative bent; they had supported the Kaiser's Reich and had been sceptical about the Weimar democracy. The same is also true of the **universities,**[37] both students and professors: the most prominent cases are Martin Heidegger, the philosopher and pliable Rector of Freiburg in 1933/34 (who was a Nazi party member until 1945),[38] and the constitutional lawyer and party member Carl Schmitt,[39] the pioneer thinker for a Führer who as the supreme judge directly made law. Like so many who had held positions of responsibility under the Nazis, even after the war neither showed any realization of failure, was at all contrite and acknowledged any guilt.

In addition – and who would deny this – all over Germany there was a widespread **anxiety about the 'East',** whether open or latent, an anxiety about the totalitarian Bolshevism which had been victorious in the Russian October Revolution and the chaotic 'soviet republic' which threatened chaos as early as 1918. On top of all this there was the traditional **'antisemitism'** (which truly extended from Spain to Poland and elsewhere). All this may at least provide the beginnings of an explanation why in Germany there **was no politically relevant protest against the suppression of the Jews**, more precisely why compassion, indignation, indeed active resistance to the Nazi anti-Jewish legislation could be found only in exceptional instances, although it has been calculated that around one million Germans were quite directly involved in the measures against the Jews. The key to an explanation for the lack of resistance might lie here: the traders, manual workers, farmers and educated classes who had come off worst in the development towards liberal capitalism were only too ready to make the Jews, supposedly rich and steadily getting richer, responsible for their own economic and social decline. The thought of scapegoats was prevalent. And the elites – now also on the pretext of opposition to Communism – carried their banners forward, while the state and the banks enriched themselves from the Jews who were expelled or exterminated.

However, in Germany probably only relatively few people had any precise knowledge about the 'final solution' of the Jewish question. **Walter Laqueur** may be right in his cautious summary: 'Millions of Germans knew by late 1942 that the Jews had disappeared. Rumours about their fate reached Germany through officers and soldiers returning from the eastern front but also through other channels. There were clear indications in the wartime speeches of the Nazi leaders that something more drastic than resettlement had happened. Knowledge about the exact manner in which they had been killed was restricted to very few. It is, in fact, quite likely that while many Germans thought that the Jews were no longer alive, they did not necessarily believe that they were dead... Very few people had an interest in the fate of the Jews. Most individuals faced a great many more important problems. It was an unpleasant topic, speculations were unprofitable, discussions of the fate of the Jews were discouraged. Consideration of this question was pushed aside, blotted out for the duration.'[40]

Even by the **churches?** On the church side the excuse is often made that the National Socialist antisemitism was the **work of godless anti-Christian criminals.** Hitler, Rosenberg, Goering, Goebbels, Himmler, Heydrich, Eichmann, along with their helpers and minions, had indeed mostly been baptized, but had long since ceased to be Christians; indeed they had resolutely refused to be Christians. They had become neo-pagans, who after the war would have 'done away with' not only the synagogues but also the churches. Had not some closed, confiscated and profaned churches and religious houses already pointed in this direction?

While this view is certainly not false, it is nevertheless only a half-truth. I shall be giving a detailed account in due course. Certainly there

Anti-Jewish Measures
The Church and the Nazis

Canon Law	Nazi Measures
Ban on marriage and sexual relations between Christians and Jews (Synod of Elvira, 306).	Law for the Protection of German Blood and German Honour (15 September 1935).
Ban on Jews and Christians eating together (Synod of Elvira, 306).	Jews are banned from using restaurant cars (Transport Minister to the Minister of the Interior, 30 December 1939).
Jews are not allowed to hold public office (Synod of Clermont, 535).	Law for the Restoration of the Civil Service (7 April 1933).
Jews are not allowed to keep Christian servants, maids or slaves (Third Synod of Orleans, 538).	Law for the Protection of German Blood and German Honour (15 September 1935).
Jews are not allowed to show themselves in the streets during Holy Week (Third Synod of Orleans, 538).	Police order authorizing local authorities to ban Jews from the streets on certain days (e.g. on Nazi festivals).
Burning of the Talmud and other Jewish Writings (Twelfth Synod of Toledo, 681).	Burning of books in Nazi Germany.
Christians are forbidden to consult Jewish doctors (Trullan Synod, 692).	Fourth Ordinance in the Reich Civil Law of 15 July 1938.
Christians are not allowed to live with Jews (Synod of Narbonne, 1050).	Order of Goering of 28 December 1938, that Jews are to be concentrated in certain houses (Bormann to Rosenberg, 17 January 1939).
Jews must pay tithes to the church like Christians (Synod of Gerona, 1078). Ban on work on Sunday (Synod of Szabolcs, 1092).	The 'Offering of Social Compensation' of 24 December 1940, in accordance with which Jews had to pay a special income tax to balance the Party contributions imposed on the Nazis.
Jews may not lay charges against Christians and cannot be witnesses against Christians (Third Lateran Council, 1179).	Proposal by the Party Chancery to ban Jews from bringing civil suits, 9 September 1942 (Bormann to the Minister of Justice. 9 September 1942).
Jews are forbidden to disinherit fellow-believers who have gone over to Christianity (Third Lateran Council, 1179).	Authorization by the Ministry of Justice to declare void wills which offend the 'healthy sensibility of the people' (31 July 1938).

Canon Law	Nazi Measures
Jews must wear a distinctive sign on their clothing (Fourth Lateran Council, 1215. The model was a decree of the caliph Omar I, 634-44, that Christians must wear blue and Jews yellow girdles).	Ordinance of 1 September 1941.
Ban on building synagogues (Council of Oxford, 1222).	Destruction of synagogues throughout the Reich on 10 November 1938 (Heydrich to Goering, 11 November 1938).
Christians are not allowed to take part in Jewish festivities (Synod of Vienna, 1267).	Ban on friendly relations with Jews, 24 October 1941 (Gestapo order).
Jews may not dispute with ordinary people about the Catholic faith (Synod of Vienna, 1267).	
Jews may live only in Jewish quarters (Synod of Breslau, 1267).	Order by Heydrich, 21 September 1939.
Christians are not allowed to sell or lease land to Jews (Synod of Ofen, 1279).	Ordinance of 3 December 1937, which provided for the compulsory purchase of Jewish land.
The conversion of a Christian to Judaism or the return of a baptized Jew to his former religion is to be treated as proven heresy (Synod of Mainz, 1310).	The conversion of Christians to Judaism exposes them to the danger of being treated as Jews (Decision of the Königsberg Court, 26 June 1942)
The sale or pledging of church objects to Jews is forbidden (Synod of Lavaur, 1368).	
Jews may not negotiate contracts between Christians, especially as marriage brokers (Council of Basel, 1434).	Law of 6 July 1938 on the dissolution of Jewish estate agencies and marriage bureaus with non-Jewish clients.
Jews may not acquire any academic degrees (Council of Basel, 1434).	Law against the over-filling of German schools and colleges (25 April 1933).

(Source: R. Hilberg, *Die Vernichtung der europäischen Juden.*
Die Gesamtgeschichte des Holocaust, Berlin 1982, 15f.)

was the Protestant 'Confessing Church' and some silent resistance from part of the Catholic clergy. But there was never any convincing resistance against the persecution of the Jews on a broad front by the official churches either. Why not? The basic answer can already be given here – in the light of the story which I told in the first part of this book. It is connected with the deeply-rooted religious, Christian anti-Judaism which even for a Catholic like Joseph Goebbels was the basis of his commitment to National Socialism – along with the Führer cult.[41] Bitter though this recognition may be, it cannot be passed over in silence. The racist antisemitism which reached its climax of terrorism in the Holocaust would not have been possible **without the prehistory of the religious anti-Judaism of the Christian church extending over almost two thousand years.**[42] And is not the case of the Austrian Catholic Adolf Hitler the most abysmal example of this? Even now many people do not recognize the religious roots of his antisemitism.

6. The fatal antisemitism of a Catholic: Adolf Hitler

Despite all the necessary historical structural analyses of National Socialist antisemitism, we cannot leave out of account the decisive and quite personal role played by Adolf Hitler and his henchmen.[43] If historiography can never attain mathematical exactitude, far less can the description of economic and social developments and patterns. Only a combination of structural history, political historiography and biographical interpretation can come anywhere near to doing justice to reality.

To see Hitler's way to power, to total rule, to war and to the murder of the Jews, one might read the summary analyses of, say, the Stuttgart historian Eberhard Jäckel. His concerns were **Hitler's** 'world-view'[44] and **Hitler's** 'rule'.[45] Or one might read the great synthesis of Germany between 1933 and 1945 by the Münster historian Hans-Ulrich Thamer, entitled *Seduction and Violence*.[46] On the Nazi policy of the extermination of the Jews Jäckel notes that 'the removal of the Jews was Hitler's earliest aim'.[47] And Thamer comments: 'There is no mistaking the fact that with Hitler's entry into politics, antisemitism played the central role in his political thought and agitation, and antisemitism remained his policy.'[48] One might reflect that as early as September 1919 (when he was still in the army), Hitler had written: 'Purely on grounds of feeling, antisemitism will find its ultimate expression in the form of progroms [sic]. However, the antisemitism of reason must lead to a systematic legal fight against and removal of the privileges of the Jew, which he possesses in contrast to the other aliens who live among us (legislation on aliens). But his ultimate aim must immovably be the complete removal of the Jews.'[49]

What does that mean? It means that even before Hitler became a nationalist whose ideal was a Greater Germany, he was radically **antisemitic**. And just as others saw history simply as class struggle, Hitler saw it as **racial struggle** (I have already drawn attention to the fatal line of tradition). For Hitler, the one race above all which had to be conquered in this battle was 'international world Jewry', public enemy number one! For Adolf Hitler, from the beginning the **conquest of 'living space'** and the **extermination of the Jews**, the two central points in the programme of the National Socialist movement, belonged together. The World War and the Holocaust have their foundations here.

Already as a schoolchild, Hitler, who at the age of six became a choirboy and served at mass, and had 'excellent opportunity to intoxicate myself with the solemn splendour of the brilliant church festivals',[50] must have been made irreligious by a primitive authoritarian religious instruction. The pupils had been influenced above all by the anti-Jewish statements of the Gospel of John ('children of light' = Christians; 'children of darkness' = Jews) and later, too, Hitler's hatred of the Jews is unthinkable without the antisemitic climate of Austria and Vienna, its church and Christian Socialist party. It is well known that from as early as the Enlightenment, Austria's Catholic church had fuelled the **traditional anti-Judaism of the Austrian population** and indeed had deliberately used it as a political instrument both against the monarchy and against democracy. This anti-Judaism was first turned against the enlightened Emperor Joseph II, who was highly respected by the Jewish population because of his Patent of Tolerance; then against Emperor Franz Joseph I, because of his personal connections with Jews; and finally also against the middle-class liberals, who were regarded as 'infected with Judaism' and as being responsible for the downfall of the Danube monarchy. So it is no coincidence that after 1918 it was Karl Lueger, the extremely popular Mayor of Vienna, the antisemitic founder and leader of the Christian Socialist party, who became Hitler's first model as a great charismatic leader of the masses. The Austrian historian Friedrich Heer has said all that is necessary in this connection in his monumental study of the belief of Adolf Hitler (1968) – far too little noted in Catholic circles.[51]

How had things been at that time? Towards the end of the nineteenth century **Vienna**, the melting pot for countless peoples and popular elements, had had increasing social problems. Old prejudices had revived: Jews, the proportion of whom in the population of the imperial city which had nurtured them had grown from around 6,200 in 1857 to well above 200,000 in 1923, were becoming increasingly dominant in finance and trade, in medicine and the law, and finally in journalism and the university. However, after Austria's defeat at Königgrätz in 1866 and even more after the stock exchange crash of 1873, they had once again been produced as scapegoats for the deterioration in the economic and social condition of the masses. All the immense problems of modern urbanization, industrialization and early capitalism were loaded on 'the Jews'. 'The Jews' were supposed to be lurking behind everything: behind enlightenment, liberalism and libertinism, and also behind Socialism and Marxism. How convenient it was for the churches and bourgeois parties, and also parts of the Social Democratic movement, suddenly to have a common opponent in their fight for the favour of the masses. 'The Jews' were regarded not only as the authors of the economic crisis but also as conspirators against the church, the clergy and the religious order. And what about the Catholic Adolf Hitler? From his youth up he deeply imbibed this antisemitic air of Vienna and Austria.

At the same time, however, it has to be said clearly that **Hitler's personal antisemitism** was essentially **more than the religious anti-Judaism** of the church, which had never been intent on physical extermination but only on segregation or conversion. It was also essentially **more than the socially rooted antisemitism** of those in debt financially, which was directed against Jewish moneylenders and not, say, against Jewish doctors. No, Hitler's antisemitism was **biological and racist**, and thus **total** – he was quite simply against 'the Jews'. The confused works of an ex-monk, a certain Georg Lanz von Liebenfels,[52] already had an important influence on the young Hitler; so too did Hitler's 'friend Bernhard', Bernhard Stempfle, that ex-member of a Catholic order who was involved in the editing of *Mein Kampf* and was still close to Hitler in Munich when he was shot by the SS by mistake in the Röhm Putsch of 1934 (Hitler was furious: 'These swine have also killed my good Father Stempfle!'[53]).

Certainly, once he had become party leader, Hitler despised the German bishops as weaklings, although as a man of power he would marvel at the organization, dogmatic stability and liturgical splendour of the two-thousand-year-old Roman church (and in particular the discipline of the Jesuits). And though he punctiliously paid his church tax to the Catholic church to the bitter end, for the period after the war he was planning vengeance on numerous silent, rebellious Catholic pastors and chaplains. But Hitler hated the Jews more than anything else in the world.

And truly when, in the face of total defeat, he committed suicide on

30 April 1945, he would really have almost have offered a '**holocaust**', a '**whole offering**', to his ideological and pathological will for destruction. Almost six million people died, simply because they were Jews, and in addition there were also 500,000 non-Jewish captives. 'Holocaust' (a term introduced by Elie Wiesel, the American Jewish author and survivor of Auschwitz) is a word which is not without its problems, since originally in the religious sense it denotes a 'whole offering' or 'burnt offering'. However, the Jews who were exterminated in no way wanted to be sacrificial 'offerings', 'victims', but to live. And those who exterminated them did not really mean to offer a 'sacrifice' (for whom would that have been?); they were intent on total extermination. That is why many Jews nowadays prefer to use the term '**Shoah**' for this mass extermination: it comes from Isaiah 47.11 and means 'disaster', '**catastrophe**'. But have people really reflected enough here that in Isaiah the word *shoah* is not applied to Israel but to Babylon? Until an adequate word has been found, we will do best to keep to the most widespread term, 'Holocaust'.

Of course concentration on the 'Führer' **does not yet answer** the **question who was guilty** of the Holocaust. Too many people – and certainly not just the more than ten million party members – took refuge in lies after the war. However, the schematic allied campaign of denazification, which was extended to the whole population, itself led people astray into believing that what they had written on the questionnaires relieved them of their burdens, and that this settled the matter. So the chief culprits became the incriminated, the incriminated became the fellow-travellers, and the fellow-travellers became the exonerated. Moreover, the prime concern now was to find something to eat and somewhere to live; to rebuild the devastated cities, reorganize economic life and build up a new democratic state! Let bygones be bygones!?

So it is not surprising that the questions about responsibility, initially suppressed and then kept down for so long, should only break out again decades later. It is striking that the time of the historians' dispute was also the time of the case of the Gestapo butcher Barbie in Lyons and the 'case' of the former General Secretary of the United Nations, **Kurt Waldheim**, in Vienna. Elected as Austrian Federal President at the urging of the Christian Socialists, of all people, Waldheim, who was increasingly convicted of being a collaborator in Hitler's war machine, proved to be an almost ideal figure for many of his compatriots to identify with, dealing with the past by lying or repressing his own share of the guilt.[54]

It is worth reflecting that the criticism of Waldheim's conduct made not only by Jewish organizations but also by countless people in Austria, did not so much lead to self-examination as to a clearly detectable **upsurge of antisemitism in Austria**. No less a figure than the suffragan bishop of Vienna, Bishop Krätzl, therefore felt compelled to comment on such tendencies in March 1988: 'We cannot make antisemitism disappear with silence and patient waiting. Until recently I still believed that it was an exaggeration to suppose that there was still all too much antisemitism in Austria. But since I preached at the National Festival in Mariazell about how un-Christian antisemitism really is, I have been taught otherwise. I was vigorously criticized for what I said, in person immediately after the mass, and later in letters and by telephone. We Christians, I was told, should have nothing whatsoever to do with the Jews. We must put all the blame for antisemitism squarely on the Jews. Talking about antisemitism only provokes it again. Someone even sank so low as to claim that the atrocities of Auschwitz which have been mentioned over and over again were simply a historical falsehood. So it again seems necessary to investigate the roots of antisemitism and to ask: was it really still there, or has it been inflamed again?'[55]

To describe the church situation in particular, four areas especially need further illumination, including historical illumination: the responsibility of the German Protestants, of the Vatican, of the German Catholic bishops, and of Polish Catholicism.

II. The Repression of Guilt

'In the night of 10 November 1938 the District President of the East Prussian district of Schlossberg, Wichard von Bredow, received a teletype from the Gauleitung, informing him that at this time all the synagogues in Germany were being burned. The police and the fire brigade were not to intervene. Bredow put on his army uniform and said farewell to his wife, the mother of their five children, with the words: "I am going to the synagogue in Schierwindt and as a Christian and a German mean to prevent one of the greatest crimes within my jurisdiction." He knew that he was risking his life or could be put in a concentration camp by the Gestapo. "I cannot do otherwise." When the SA, SS and Party members arrived to set fire to the synagogue, the District President was already standing in front of it. He drew his pistol: the way into the synagogue would be over his dead body. Thereupon the arsonists withdrew. The synagogue was the only one in the region to remain intact. No one dared to move against the District President.'[1]

Without doubt many other heroic actions of this kind could be reported from the years of terror between 1933 and 1945.[2] But they remained exceptions. This one synagogue was not destroyed, but at least 267 synagogues and chapels were destroyed in the night of 10 November 1938, cynically called 'Reichskristallnacht', either by the fanatical antisemitic propaganda minister Joseph Goebbels himself or by Berlin street talk – as though only the window-panes had been broken (and this damage alone amounted to millions of Reichmarks).

1. What would have happened if . . . ?

Without doubt many Germans, whether Protestants, Catholics, Socialists or humanists of all kinds, attempted in individual cases to help their Jewish fellow-citizens, and it is important that such actions should be collected and documented in detail. But that would leave out one thing: such uncounted details would distract attention from the essentials and shift the emphasis. Here are some facts about 'Reichskristallnacht'.[3] 8,000 Jewish businesses were destroyed in a night; countless homes were devastated and plundered; more than 100 German Jews were murdered; many were maltreated, assaulted and stripped of their human dignity. 10,000 of the most well-to-do Jews were arrested in order to get at their possessions, compel them to emigrate or to send them to concentration camps. By 1938, of the 520,000 German Jews,

130,000 had already left their homes. This emigration was now to be accelerated – but not without prior confiscations and plundering (at that time the total income of the Jews in Germany was estimated at 8.5 billion Reichsmarks).

It should not be forgotten that the totalitarian, deeply antidemocratic and antisemitic character of Adolf Hitler's personal, confessional document *Mein Kampf* and of the Nazi Party programme ('No Jew can be a member of the people') was generally known from the beginning – not just in 1938 but already in 1933. Could not much have been prevented had there been some other brave district presidents, mayors, civil servants, soldiers, businessmen and university professors, who like the district president mentioned at the beginning of this chapter had said – regardless of the consequences – 'I cannot do otherwise...' Indeed, what would have happened had even the active Christians, pastors, bishops and the pope shown more Christian courage?[4] To be specific:

First, we might imagine: what would have happened if the **German episcopate** had warned against the manifestly antisemitic programme of the Nazis – instead of capitulating to National Socialism after Hitler's government declaration of 23 March 1933, to the dismay of many Catholics?[5] What if they had protested publicly in the face of the acts of terror and violence against all those with free and open minds, which immediately began?

Secondly, we might imagine: what would have happened if the **Vatican,** instead of being the first foreign power to give Hitler respectability with a concordat as early as 20 July 1933, had warned Germany and the world again of a man whose devastating intentions had quite unambiguously been presented in *Mein Kampf* and in the twenty-four points of his party's programme? A man who had begun to implement his programme as early as the beginning of 1933 with a boycott on Jewish businesses, doctors and lawyers, and other discriminatory measures against Jewish citizens?

Thirdly, we might imagine: what would have happened, as Pastor Martin Niemöller, one of the few churchmen to resist, asked after the war, if instead of keeping silent or even joining in, the 14,000 Protestant pastors in Germany had dared from the beginning to form an active front against the Nazi regime and to call for political resistance?

But I can already hear the objections of political and church apologists: all this is just illusory speculation.

2. Is it all just illusory speculation?

No, there were quite realistic possibilities. And the verdicts of historians today show what failed to be done: 'The churches were the only institutions which could either escape or even resist the totalitarian ideological claims of National Socialism, but they issued no call to political resistance. The attempt to co-ordinate them failed, but their predominantly conservative and nationalistic basic attitude continued to ensure their loyalty to the state.'[6]

But again I can hear the objections of the apologists. Anyone who wants to talk about this must have been there: how can a historian born in 1943 allow himself to pass judgment on this time! But is that not in fact to deny legitimation to any form of history-writing? Does one have to have taken part in the Napoleonic Wars to be able to arrive at an informed and fair judgment on them? Might not the opposite be the case, that those who were not only 'there' at the time, but were actively involved, with all their obligations and interests, are the last people capable of giving a reasonably well-informed, fair verdict on this time? When I asked the Protestant theologian Helmut Gollwitzer, a member of the Confessing Church, why after forty years people could perhaps speak more openly about that time and about the failure of even the churches, his answer was significant: because those who bore responsibility at that time are now slowly disappearing from the scene.

No, the criticism of historians born after the event – in the Catholic sphere one prominent figure is Georg Denzler, who as a result is often attacked by his Catholic colleagues – is in no way just an external one, thought up at a later date. In view of the fact that in order to protect itself the German Catholic Episcopal Conference is still attempting to disguise its own failure with the help of biased historians and by collecting instances of 'resistance' among Catholics (of which there were isolated cases), I shall cite here a verdict on the attitude of the German episcopate during the Nazi period given by someone who is above suspicion, from the year 1946. A letter dated 23 February 1946 from the Catholic Lord Mayor of Cologne, who was dismissed by the Nazis and then became the first Chancellor of the Federal Republic of Germany, **Konrad Adenauer**, to Pastor Dr Bernhard Custodis of Bonn, reads as follows:

'In my view the German people and also the bishops and clergy bear a good deal of blame for what went on in the concentration camps. It is correct that later perhaps there was not a lot that could be done. The guilt lies earlier. The German people, and also to a great extent the bishops and clergy, succumbed to the National Socialist agitation. They allowed themselves to be co-ordinated... without resisting, indeed sometimes with enthusiasm. That is where their guilt lies. Moreover people also knew – even if they did not know the whole extent of what went on in the camps – that personal freedom, every principle of law, was being trampled under foot; that the Gestapo, our SS and also some of our troops in Poland and Germany were committing unspeakable atrocities on the civil population. The pogroms against the Jews in 1933 and 1938 took place in full public view. The murder of hostages in France was announced to us officially. So it cannot really be claimed that the public knew nothing, that the National Socialist government and the army leaders in principle constantly offended against natural law, against the Hague Convention and against the simplest demands of humanity.' Adenauer's letter ends: 'I believe that if all the bishops had together made public statements from the pulpit on a particular day, they could have prevented a great deal. That did not happen, and there is no excuse for it. It would have been no bad thing if the bishops had all been put in prison or in concentration camp as a result. Quite the contrary. But none of that happened and therefore it is best to keep quiet.'[7]

'Best to keep quiet'? This is what the other great Catholic from Cologne, the writer and Nobel prizewinner Heinrich Böll, just could not understand. No, even Konrad Adenauer, that prominent Chancellor, is not free of responsibility for the repression of guilt in state and church after the war. Certainly from the beginning he was opposed to Hitler's Reich, which in his view was taking the line of the expansionist Prussian German Reich (the line from Frederick II to Bismarck to Wilhelm II to Hitler) and was completely given the cold shoulder by the Nazis. And after the war he in particular did fundamental work in collaboration with Israel's first prime minister, David Ben-Gurion, towards reconciling Germans and Jews, not least by showing political wisdom – unlike the unteachable Pius XII – in leading the way towards the recognition of Israel by the Federal Republic in the face of all Arab opposition, and even insisting on financial reparations in the face of all his opponents within Germany. However, his policy of restoration and the far-reaching integration of even the major Nazis (think of the Globke case!) after 1945 – there was no 'zero hour'! – did a good deal to encourage the churches' impenitence. And had truth been respected then, in the 1940s and 1950s, as is happening now in the 1990s with the publication of the Stasi records, far from leading to a 'spiritual civil war', it might have led to insight.

So, given the infinite amount which failed to be done, then and in subsequent decades, and which is still poisoning the present, only one thing can help towards celebrating the fiftieth anniversary of the end of Nazi rule and the Second World War in 1995 with a better conscience: to demonstrate once again by means of some irrefutable facts **what actually happened** as compared with **what could have happened**. Only if we remind ourselves in unqualified openness of what happened and what failed to be done, will it be possible to arrive at a liberating confession of guilt. The remarks which follow should not be understood as a subsequent condemnation by those who were born after the event, but as a help towards assimilating the past which is orientated on the future. So:

3. Protestants who did not protest: German Christians

German Protestantism had been affected in quite a different way from Catholicism by the crisis of the modern-bourgeois paradigm in 1918. For with the downfall of the thousand-year-old German empire, the four-hundred-year old Protestant system of state churches which had been preserved down to modern times had also collapsed. In the absence of the princes, the organization of the Protestant church had for the first time to rely upon itself: economically, politically, spiritually and in religious terms.[8] Previously Protestants had identified in every respect with the German nation and its war: 'God with us!' What now? After such a catastrophic defeat, sealed by the Versailles treaty, could one continue to make that claim? Still, by arrangement with the Weimar Republic, which was also very unpopular with the church governments, and with the help of the German Evangelical Church Federation and its organs, the Protestant provincial churches, which were now autonomous, had been able to find a new national unity. Once again they represented a powerful presence, with a highly respectable theology and numerous groups, organizations and associations.

However, because of their strong German nationalist tradition, from the beginning the Protestant churches in Germany were much better disposed to National Socialism than the Catholic Church. And in 1933, the year of the 'new salvation', from the start there was now a concern to take an active part in shaping the future which was a contrast to the time of the new order in 1918. Whereas Catholicism, as we shall see, capitulated to Hitler principally because of the 'Reich concordat' and then largely assented with enthusiasm, right from the beginning a large proportion of Protestants openly endorsed the National Socialist movement – not least because at the same time it represented a 'no' to Marxism, liberalism and atheism. The promised 'Reich Church' was to many Protestants what their 'Reich Concordat' was to the Catholics. And whereas Catholic theologians played down the relationship between Nazism and Catholicism by comparing it to the relationship between the natural and the supernatural order (what Nazism achieved on the 'natural' level, Catholicism achieved on the 'supernatural' level!), for Protestants Martin Luther was a great landmark in whom Christianity and Germanhood, Protestantism and National Socialism, were allegedly combined from the start. It was thought that the people – the Volk –, peoplehood and the people's movement were now part of the 'divinely willed ordinance of creation'. Why should one protest against the abolition of basic democratic rights as early as 28 February 1933, or against the enabling law of 23 March 1933, or against the establishment of the first concentration camps? Certainly, from the first day onwards the new regime proved to be a regime of terror, but the terror first of all struck those who were unpopular in any case: Communists, Social Democrats, Jews... Why should one not follow Adolf Hitler, the man of 'providence', in being against Marxism, Judaism and atheism, and for the rebirth of the German nation and the social renewal of the German people?

The National Socialists exploited the situation skilfully. In the Faith Movement of the '**German Christians**', to which initially one-fifth of the Protestant pastors and even more laity belonged, already from the end of the 1920s the Party had at its disposal an organization of sympathizers within the Protestant church. And this was almost pre-destined to be a synthesis of the church and National Socialism. To put it bluntly, the movement was aiming at a church which had been co-ordinated in accordance with the Führer principle, a church which was completely subordinate to the state. *A priori*, Luther's doctrine of two kingdoms, understood as a *laisser-faire* juxtaposition of state and church, therefore seemed to offer the best theological basis and to concede to the state a sphere of interest in which the church would not interfere, provided that the state respected its autonomy. But at best the church felt itself responsible for the Jewish Christians – the rest of the Jews were the state's responsibility.[9]

The guidelines of the Faith Movement of 'German Christians' dated 26 May 1932(!) called for an 'affirmative faith in Christ, fitting our race', of a kind that corresponded to the German spirit of Luther and heroic piety: 'We see in race, nationality and nation, orders of life given and entrusted to us by God, to care for the preservation of which is for us God's law. For these reasons, racial miscegenation has to be opposed. On the strength of its experience, the German Foreign Mission has been admonishing the German nation for a long time: "Keep your race pure." [10] So what was excluded *a priori* by the constitution of the Catholic church became possible in Protestantism: the rapid foundation of a 'Reich Church' under a 'Reich bishop', the former military chaplain Ludwig Müller, who was Hitler's choice.

This development inevitably had fateful consequences, particularly for the **Jewish question**, for the state very soon required the church to follow it in this respect. As early as 6 September 1933, the General Synod of the Old Prussian Union, albeit against massive opposition, had to resolve to apply the state's Aryan paragraph in the church as well: 'No one who is not of Aryan descent, or who is married to a person of non-Aryan descent, may be called as a minister or official of the church's administration. Clergy and officials of Aryan descent who enter into marriage with a person of non-Aryan descent are to be dismissed.' [11] However, now an opposition movement within the church also took shape very quickly.

4. Opposition within the church and the confession of guilt

A few days after the General Synod, a 'Pastors' Emergency League' was founded on the initiative of Pastor Martin Niemöller. Around 6000 pastors joined it that very same year, 1933, and committed themselves in a declaration to 'exercise their office as servants of the Word only in allegiance to Holy Scripture and the confessions of the Reformation as the true interpretation of Holy Scripture'. [12] And yet there was a proviso: since some pastors wanted to acknowledge the Aryan ruling in the state sphere, article 4 of the declaration went too far for them: 'Under such an obligation I bear witness that the application of the Aryan paragraph within the sphere of the church of Christ is a violation of the state of confession.' [13] And what about the Protestant faculties? In their judgments on the issue, the Erlangen faculty (with Paul Althaus! [14]) endorsed and the Marburg faculty (with Rudolf Bultmann! [15]) opposed the introduction of an Aryan paragraph into the church.

However, when subsequently the 'German Christians' increasingly clearly attached themselves to the National Socialist ideology, indeed to the folkish religion of Alfred Rosenberg (rejecting the 'Jewish' Old Testament and the 'rabbi' Paul in favour of the Aryan hero Jesus), they increasingly lost their basis in the church, so that they dissolved into smaller groups. In the end the Reich Bishop no longer felt able to provide effective leadership in the church. With a 'muzzling decree' the regime now banned all statements on church politics from the pulpits – one could go on telling this story endlessly, but that is not our task here. In any case, the complicated 'preliminary history and time of illusions, 1918-1934', and above all the dramatic developments in the 'year of disillusionment, 1934', with the Synod of Barmen, have been abundantly documented in the two volumes of *The Churches and the Third Reich*, written by my Tübingen colleague Klaus Scholder, who died all too prematurely. They have now become standard works.

For us it is important to see that at any rate in contrast to the Catholic sphere, in Protestantism, along with all the assent, there was also public opposition to the Nazi policy. Granted, there was **no active political resistance** against the totalitarian regime, but there was **organized resistance within the church**. For when a crisis similarly developed in the Pastors' Emergency League, in the face of all the attempts by the state at co-ordination and persecution, the **Confessing Church** was founded, on the inspiration of the Swiss Reformed professor of theology **Karl Barth**, who was teaching in Bonn at the time.[16] He and other like-minded friends from 'dialectical theology' wanted to establish 'Christ's claim to rule' over all areas, including the state.

Moreover this endeavour was given visible expression in the **Confessing Synod of Barmen** in May 1934, where a clear confession was made of Jesus Christ as the sole 'Lord' of the church.[17] This had to be understood as a clear repudiation of the 'Führer principle' as understood by National Socialism. However, at that time the Confessing Church did not want to make any statement on the Jewish question, not least because its high dogmatic christology was hardly capable of coping with the Jew Jesus. But already at that early stage Karl Barth was dismissed from his professorial chair, and in future taught in Basel.[18] Only in May 1936 did the provisional church government of the Confessing Church compose a memorandum which also attacked the racial policy and the tyranny of the regime.[19] **Martin Niemöller** was put in a concentration camp in 1937; **Dietrich Bonhoeffer**, a champion against the persecution and extermination of the Jews, was banned from speaking and writing, joined a political resistance group in 1940, at the height of German power, and was executed after the attempt on Hitler's life on 20 June 1944.[20] But this Confessing Church, which based itself solely on the gospel, managed to hold out until the end of the war – despite all the increasing tension between the church and the government. It was a support in the most difficult of times not only for many pastors, but also for countless faithful. To the dismay of their rulers, in the 1940 census 95% of Germans still acknowledged allegiance to their churches, whether Protestant or Catholic.

It must also be acknowledged that after the war it was similarly the

Protestant church in Germany which showed the greatest awareness of its complicity in the endless suffering under the Nazi terror. In the 'Stuttgart Confession of Guilt' of 19 October 1945,[21] the council of the Evangelical Church stated – though without mentioning the Jews, and to the indignation of many Protestants who were still blind to what had happened: 'Through us infinite suffering has been brought upon many peoples and lands... we accuse ourselves of not having confessed more boldly, not having prayed more faithfully, not having believed more joyfully and not having loved more ardently'. The 'Darmstadt Statement' of the Confessing Church on 8 August 1947 spoke out even more clearly – though again without mentioning the Jews. Martin Niemöller and Gustav Heinemann, later to become Federal President, contributed to it, but others, like Martin Dibelius, the prominent bishop of Berlin, felt that it had gone too far because the roots of disaster were not seen first in the person of Hitler: 'We went wrong when we began to dream the dream of a special German mission, as though the German character could cure the world. As a result we prepared the way for the unrestricted use of political power and set our nation on God's throne. – It was disastrous that we began to ground our state internally on a strong government alone, and externally only on the development of military power.'[22]

The numerous obstacles which got in the way of the 'Statement on the Jewish Question' made by the Evangelical Church in Germany in April 1950 show how difficult this church found it to cope at all with the Jewish question after 1945; how little people were bothered about the Christians who were persecuted because of their descent, especially the Jewish Christians; how little people had come to terms with the anti-Jewish traditions in the church; and how interested they were in a mission to the Jews rather than a public declaration of guilt.[23]

Not least because of the manner of their **criticism of denazification,** the majority of bishops and church governments encouraged the repression of how disastrously close they themselves were to National Socialism. Still trapped in their leanings towards German nationalism, some of them, while verbally acknowledging the aims of the denazification measures of the military government, still encouraged the minimalization of the National Socialist misdeeds (especially in 1948, when at last there was an opportunity to condemn the main culprits). They kept imputing base motives to their champions. Did they not contribute in this way to the failure of the measures?[24]

Not least the **World Council of Churches** shows how difficult the Protestant churches also still found it to cope with their relationship to Judaism on a world level. The First General Assembly of the World

Council of Churches in Amsterdam (in which the Catholic Church under Pius XII had refused to participate) had accepted a final report on 'The Christian Attitude to the Jews' and had commended it to the individual churches. By contrast, the Second General Assembly in Evanston in 1954 rejected a passage on the main theme 'Christ our Hope' which referred to Israel, and since then, remarkably, this theme has failed to appear on the agenda of any WCC General Assembly. Certainly there have been statememts on antisemitism and the Near East conflict which have touched on theological questions. But it is again striking that the 1968 General Assembly in Uppsala ventured to approve a statement 'On the Situation in the Middle East' without even mentioning the state of Israel. Diplomatic considerations? Theological constraints? Or a lack of Christian courage?

But enough of the attitude of the Protestant churches to Judaism during the war and in the post-war period. What about the Catholic church?

5. A pope who kept silent: Pius XII

It is probably a consequence of the papal claim to 'infallibility' that even where there are no formally 'infallible' statements, there is the greatest difficulty in acknowledging errors. It is precisely the same as with other authoritarian regimes. Could not the acknowledgment of even a single error shatter the whole claim to infallibility, since though officially it concerns 'only' questions of dogma and morality, it indirectly bathes all the statements of the pope in the same aura? We come to **Pius XII**. It is impossible here to make an overall assessment of the pontificate of this 'Pastor Angelicus', whom, with all the world, I admired at the beginning of my studies in Rome between 1948 and 1955. However, I came increasingly to see his policies as being open to criticism – because of his dictatorial 'internal politics' and his highly diplomatic 'Jewish policy', with which we are concerned here. It is a cruel irony that the very Pius XII, the last unchallenged representative of the pre-conciliar mediaeval, Counter-Reformation, anti-modernist paradigm, who immediately after the Second World War moved very energetically to define an 'infallible' dogma about Mary (in 1950), had been extremely hesitant to issue a public condemnation of National Socialism and antisemitism while at the same time banning worker priests and dismissing the most important theologians of his time.

Why? To cut a long story short, because as a result of his career, Eugenio Pacelli: 1. was surrounded by expressly Germanophile and exclusively German colleagues (he was known as 'the pope of the Germans'); 2. thought above all in legal and diplomatic terms, rather than in terms of theology and the gospel; 3. had a fixation on the Curia and the institution rather than relating to pastoral work and people; 4. since the shock of the 'soviet republic' in Munich in 1918 had been obsessed with a phobia about physical contact and a fear of Communism and had a deeply authoritarian and anti-democratic attitude ('Führer Catholicism'). 5. He was thus predisposed to a pragmatic and anti-Communist alliance with totalitarian Nazism. What was important for Pacelli, the professional diplomat, was the 'freedom of the church', understood as the widest possible state recognition of the institution of the church and the new canon law, the new *Codex Iuris Canonici*, in the development of which he had been involved and which he promulgated in 1917, in the midst of the war, without the assent of the world episcopate. 'Human rights' and 'democracy' were fundamentally alien to this pope. And as for the Jews: even while he was a cardinal, he no longer regarded Jerusalem and its people as the city and the people of God. No, for him as a Roman, Rome – not the Romans, but Rome and always Rome – was the new Zion and the Roman people was the people who lived in the Roman faith. In this mediaeval, anti-Jewish sense Pacelli was **Roman Catholic**.[25]

To put this positively: Cardinal Secretary of State Pacelli, unexpectedly elected pope on 2 March 1939, was first and last a '**man of the church**', as I was told in my years of study in Rome by his private secretary and closest confidant, Fr Robert Leiber SJ. That meant that Pius XII was 'no saint' (thus, not without a critical undertone, the same Fr Leiber), despite all descriptions of him by others and by himself. However, in this connection the decisive question is: was Eugenio Pacelli also the prophetic figure who was so desperately needed at this time?

Pacelli was a monarch of the church who impressed the whole world. As pope he had primarily the interests of the institutional church and the Vatican in view and was therefore involved in a **conflict of conscience** where National Socialism and Judaism were concerned. The Jewish scholar Pinchas Lapide may well have been right in his well-intentioned study on *Rome and the Jews* (1967): Catholics (at that time the Catholic press said 'the pope') may have preserved 'hundreds of thousands' of Jews in all from certain death (I do not want to go into the highly uncertain figure here). But what is that compared with the murder of six million Jews?

It is an indisputable fact of world history that Eugenio Pacelli, the
Cardinal Secretary of State, who as early as August 1931(!) had forced
the German Catholic Chancellor Brüning into a coalition with the
National Socialists and who broke with Brüning when the latter
refused, conferred unprecedented political status on Hitler before the
world public (here too he 'only' had the interest of the church and the
Curia at heart). As early as 20 July 1933 he was the first to conclude
an international treaty with the new regime on the model of the Lateran
Treaty with Mussolini (1929), the unfortunate '**Reich Concordat**'.[26]
This was only a few months after the brown-shirted 'Führer' had come
to power (similar treaties followed later with the dictators Franco in
Spain and Salazar in Portugal). What Pacelli took into account was
that this treaty brought Hitler both recognition by other countries and
the integration of the Catholic part of the population into the Nazi
system. For Article 32 (the 'de-politicizing clause') banned Catholic
clergy from any political activity. This was already a provision in the
Mussolini concordat (though as is evident from the cases of Prelate
Seipel, the Austrian Chancellor and the Slovakian state president Tiso,
this also had its problematical aspects). However, what was probably
even more important was that the neutralization of the Catholic
associations in accordance with Article 31 (the 'clause for the protection
of associations'), which was pressed for by the German hishops from
as early as 1928, was aimed at the complete abolition of the lay
associations and thus also of the Catholic Centre Party.[27] In this way
crucial preparations were made for a totalitarian one-party rule.

It was a fatal misreading of the brown-shirted terrorist regime
that while the **Catholic Church** was not co-ordinated, in fact it was
condemned to **political neutrality**. How is that to be explained? I have
already indicated the degree to which the traditionalist Roman lawyer
and diplomat Pacelli had a fixation on the church as an institution (the
protection of Catholic corporations, schools, associations, pastoral
letters, freedom of religious practice). And secondly, there was an
affinity between his **authoritarian understanding of the church** (i.e. an
anti-Protestant, anti-liberal, anti-socialist and anti-modern understanding) and an **authoritarian**, i.e. Fascist, **understanding of the state**.
(This was even stated openly by Prelate Kaas, who was the go-between
in the concordat.) For were not 'unity', 'order', 'discipline' and the
'Führer principle' to hold on the natural level of the state, as they did
on the supernatural level of the church?

This at any rate was at first the view even of 'progressive' German
Catholic theologians, like the dogmatic theologian Michael Schmaus
from Münster, the church historian Joseph Lortz from Braunsberg,

and Karl Adam from Tübingen. As early as 1933, Adam, the famous dogmatic theologian – after enthusiastic praise of the 'people's Chancellor' Hitler ('he came from the Catholic south but we did not know him') – pointed out that 'nationalism and Catholicism' were not 'intrinsically opposed', but belonged together 'like nature and supernature'. 'The German demand for purity of blood' was 'in line with the Old Testament revelation of God', and it was the 'right and duty of the state to protect the purity of the blood of its people by appropriate regulations'.[28] That even in 1943 (after the Wannsee conference and the measures which followed) Adam used the dogma of the 'immaculate conception' of Mary to show that Jesus Christ was no 'descendant of a Jew', because his 'mother Mary had no physical and moral connection with those ugly dispositions and powers which we condemn in those who are full-blooded Jews',[29] shows the bankruptcy of such dogmatics.

Once again: it is to the credit of Pinchas Lapide (the numerous Roman Catholic apologists do not count here) that he defended Pius XII against sweeping attacks. It is in fact wrong to assert that Pius XII 'did nothing for the Jews', was racist or antisemitic, or kept silent either out of cowardice or to protect the financial interests of the Vatican. Rather, what is true is that particularly towards the end of the war Pacelli made efforts to rescue **individual Jews** or groups of Jews, above all in Italy and Rome, and twice – in his 1942 Christmas address and in the secret consistory of cardinals on 2 June 1943 – lamented briefly, abstractly and in general terms, the fate of the 'unfortunate people' who were being persecuted because of their race. That is beyond question. But the basic question remains: was that enough at this moment in history? Was it enough for someone who claimed to be the 'representative of Christ on earth'?

Almost certainly not. For what is all that compared with what this same **pope did not do**? This too is a fact – and the personal background of this pope makes some things more understandable here.

1. In all his statements the pope used bewilderingly general phrases. He spoke of 'unfortunate people'; moulded by the traditional anti-Jewish Roman theology, **he evidently never uttered the word 'Jews'.** At the same time the Roman Jesuit journal which appeared under the direct supervision of his Secretary of State was publishing anti-Jewish articles.

2. Pacelli evidently saw no need to say even a word of explicit condemnation of the **German attack on Poland** which broke all international law and which precipitated a whole people (a Catholic people at that!) into disaster. Not even a protest note, public or private,

went to Berlin. Rather, in the face of this crime he always asserted his 'neutrality' and at best expressed his sympathy with the suffering of the Polish people, without providing effective help for these Catholics whose representatives had asked him for a word or a gesture of support.[30]

3. Because of the distortions of attitude brought about by his professional training, the pope, who thought in terms of church politics and church law, enormously **overestimated** the influence of **diplomacy and concordats**. For him, the old Roman saying *Quod non est in actis non est in mundo* ('What is not in the records is not in the world') had almost the opposite sense: *Quod est in actis est in mundo* ('what is in the records is in the world').

4. Infinitely more important for this resolute anti-Zionist than the vexatious Jewish question were **two political aims**: the fight against **Soviet Communism**, which was feared more than anything else: a fight and which was being won by the Germans, and – of course here also – the preservation of **the institutional church**, which had to be rescued from the war. The interests of a particular minority and fundamentally also of world peace had to take a back seat behind that.

5. Pacelli, having been made pope, did not publish the **encyclical against racism and antisemitism** which was already being worked on under his predecessor Pius XI (who in 1937 had issued the encyclical *Mit brennender Sorge* against National Socialism)[31] – in any case in 1938 it was too late.[32] Nor did he support the Dutch bishops who had intervened openly for the Jews, so that the Nazi butchers had a free hand there.

6. Although the public protest of just one German bishop (Clemens August Graf von Galen in Münster in 1941) against Hitler's monstrous 'euthanasia programme', while far too late (1941), made a considerable impact on the public (the episcopal conference, which had already been informed since autumn 1940, could not rouse itself to issue a protest), and the Lutheran bishops of Denmark were also successful in their public intervention on behalf of the Jews, Pacelli, as secretary of state and pope – although otherwise making statements on every possible topic in thousands of addresses – **avoided any public protest against antisemitism** or even taking the obvious step of cancelling the concordat, which from the start had constantly been abused by the Nazis (or the concordat with Fascist Italy).

We cannot conceal the fact that even **before the Second World War** there was:

– **no protest** against the Nazi acts of violence in 1933 immediately

before and after the concordat;
– no protest against the Nuremberg race laws of 1935;
– no protest against the invasion of Ethiopia in 1936 by Mussolini, whom Pacelli publicly praised for having restored that imperial Rome which had been destined by divine providence to be capital of the world and the central seat of religion;
– no protest against the persecution of the Jews in the encyclical *Mit brennender Sorge* of 1937, in which the word 'race' is mentioned only once and the word 'Jew' is not mentioned at all, although the charge against the Jews that they murdered Christ is repeated;
– no protest against the pogrom of the so-called 'Kristallnacht' on 9/10 November 1938;
– no joint protest with the leaders of the other Christian churches against Hitler's unbridled urge for conquest, after his annexation of Bohemia and Moravia, as was suggested by Dr Lang, the Archbishop of Canterbury, on 20 May 1939;
– no protest against the invasion of Albania by Fascist Italy on Good Friday 1939;
– no protest against the outbreak of the Second World War caused by the National Socialist criminals on 1 September 1939.

The world waited in vain. Pius XII, whose appeals for peace kept resounding, always stressed his 'neutrality', expressed his compassion for some victims, but otherwise, **even during the war,** preferred **to keep silent.** Not only did he keep silent over the notorious German war crimes all over Europe and the ethnically and politically motivated mass-murder of at least ten thousand Orthodox Serbs by the radical right-wing Catholic Utasha regime in Croatia between 1941 and 1945;[33] he **even** kept silent **over the extermination of the Jews,** the greatest mass murder of all times, about which after 1942 he was probably better informed (through Nuncio Bernardini in Berne and Italian military chaplains in Russia) than any other statesmen of the West. And Pacelli (with his fixation on his two goals) would not change his mind even when during the course of the war he was increasingly asked to take a public stand, not only by Bishop Konrad von Preysing of Berlin, the only German bishop with any political stature, but also by Jewish organizations, even by President Roosevelt and other Western statesmen, and finally also by Chief Rabbi Herzog of Palestine. This continued to be his attitude during and after the short non-violent occupation of Rome by the Germans (between October 1943 and 1944) – although at that time the 'final solution' was coming to a climax with the deportation of the Jews of Hungary to the gas chambers of Auschwitz.[34]

Certainly, Pius XII, who was personally by no means a coward, had a not unjustified anxiety about retributory measures by the Nazis, primarily against the Catholic church and – after the occupation of Rome by German troops – also against the Vatican. Moreover, even when the Jews of Rome were deported in October 1943, the then German ambassador to the Vatican, **Ernst von Weizsäcker**, reported to Berlin that 'although from what I hear the pope has been assailed from various sides, he has not allowed himself to be drawn into any demonstrative statement against the deportation of the Jews', although 'the event took place as it were under the pope's windows'.[35] Indeed, 'even on this delicate question' the Pope had 'done everything possible not to put any strain on the relationship between the German government and the German posts in Rome'. While an official communiqué on the Pope's charitable actions was published in the *Osservatore Romano* on 25/26 October, as usual in this paper it was 'very tortuous and unclear': the Pope 'extends his paternal care to all men without distinction of nationality, religion and race'. On this the ambassador commented: 'Objections to this publication are all the more out of place since only very few people will understand its wording... as a special reference to the Jewish question.'[36]

It is paradoxical enough that although Pope Pacelli did not show the slightest inhibitions after the war, in 1949, about excommunicating all Communist members throughout the world at a stroke (because of the Curia's short-sighted interest in Italian elections), he refrained not only from any excommunication of such prominent 'Catholics' and mass murderers as Hitler, Himmler, Goebbels and Bormann (Goering, Eichmann and other leading Nazis were nominally Protestants), but even from any public condemnation of them – not to mention of antisemitic Catholic prelates and state presidents like Tiso of occupied Slovakia, the similarly antisemitic Ustasha leader Ante Pavelic and the French Marshal Pétain. He never received Alcide de Gasperi, the great anti-Fascist leader of the Italian Democrazia Cristiana, and the first prime minister of Italy after the war.[37] During the Fascist period de Gasperi was employed as an auxiliary librarian in the Vatican: to Pacelli, who wanted to keep the monarchy in Italy and later even suggested an electoral pact with the neo-Fascists to him, de Gasperi seemed too unclerical and too devout.

6. Vatican diplomacy and John XXIII

No, there is no getting round the comment by the American Catholic priest John F.Morley, made in connection with the eleven-volume collection of documents, *Vatican Diplomacy and the Jews during the Holocaust, 1939-1949*, which had been published in the meantime.[38] In the first years of the war the Vatican was predominantly concerned with the **baptized** Jews. Having fallen victim to a diplomacy which had almost become an end in itself, it largely ignored the suffering of the great mass of the Jewish people. Of the papal diplomats of this ilk Morley in fact says: 'While highly active in defence of Church rights, their involvement in the Jewish problem was tangential at best and minimal at worst.' He then draws the conclusion: 'It must be concluded that Vatican diplomacy failed the Jews during the Holocaust by not doing all that it was possible for it to do on their behalf. It also failed itself because in neglecting the needs of the Jews, and pursuing a goal of reserve rather than humanitarian concern, it betrayed the ideals that it had set for itself. The nuncios, the secretary of state, and, most of all, the Pope share the responsibility for this dual failure.'[39] That applies above all to Pius XII himself, who never showed any personal sympathy for the Jews, but regarded them as the people who murdered God, and who as a triumphalistic representative of the Roman ideology regarded Christ as a Roman and thought that Jerusalem had been replaced by Rome. So from the beginning – like his predecessor and the whole of the Roman Curia – he had **opposed the foundation of a Jewish state in Palestine.**

There is no longer any doubt: whereas even his shrewd German confidante Sr Pasqualina Lehnert[40] and others like Cardinal Eugenio Tisserant kept pressing him to take a clear stand against the National Socialist regime, the pope himself remained silent publicly – despite increasing information about the Holocaust. This was more than a political failure; it was a moral failure. It was a still incomprehensible **refusal on the part of a Christian who formally claimed to be 'Christ's representative'** *par excellence* **to make a moral protest free of any political opportunism.** However, it is even more incomprehensible that this selfsame pope **repressed his error after the war** and compensated for it by authoritarian measures against dissenters within Catholicism, especially in France. Following the new anti-Modernist encyclical *Humani generis* of 1950, three French Jesuit provincials were dismissed, along with the famous Jesuit theologians P.Teilhard de Chardin, H.de Lubac and H.Bouillard (and three other professors); then, following the ban on worker priests, such important Dominican theologians as

M.-D.Chenu, Y.Congar and H.-M.Féret suffered the same fate . . . And it is most incomprehensible of all (or only too comprehensible, given the terrible history which had gone before) that after the Holocaust, Pius, who had made a pact with Hitler and other dictators, **refused diplomatic recognition** to the young democratic **state of Israel** through all the years up to his death in 1958.[41]

That was the pontificate of Pius XII.

Doubtless he had the best of intentions, and he published a pioneering encyclical for Catholic biblical exegesis (*Divino afflante Spiritu*, 1943), but on almost all decisive points (liturgical reform, ecumenism, anti-Communism, freedom of religion, the Jewish question, the 'modern world') he had to be corrected by his successor and his Council.

He spoke more in public than any pope before him, but kept silent about the greatest crime of his time;

He was tirelessly active for his church, yet remained passive in the face of the greatest catastrophe of his pontificate;

He paternalistically trained Catholics in childlike obedience to himself, but also to Hitler, Mussolini, Franco and Salazar, simply in order to rescue 'the church', its 'law', its apparatus and its institutions.

He made pacts with the real enemies of Christianity, but carried on a merciless church struggle against all 'deviants' and 'innovators' in his own church.

So for all its outward splendour, this pontificate was truly 'a **Christian tragedy**'.

Twenty-five years later, people were still protesting against the play with this sub-title, Rolf Hochhuth's *The Representative* of 1963 – as did the Archbishop of Munich, the General Secretary of the German Episcopal Conference, the Minister of Science and their tame press organs in 1988, on the occasion of a new production in Munich. However, this shows not only that they were not studying history without prejudice, but also that they had learned absolutely nothing in the meantime. They would have done better to adopt John XXIII's comment. According to Hannah Arendt, when asked what one could do about Hochhuth's play, he remarked, 'Do? What can one do about the truth?'

So the basic problems of *The Representative* (which are not all the views of its author, Hochhuth) will continue to remain on the agenda – to the scandal of uninformed bishops and inflamed Catholics – until one day the Vatican concedes its guilt, recognizes the state of Israel and at the same time makes **all** the relevant documents available to unprejudiced historical research. Nothing needs to be added to Joachim Kaiser's comment on the occasion of the new production of *The*

Representative in the Prince Regent Theatre in Munich: 'Has so little changed? Must not critical and liberal spirits recognize with some irony that now, too, the spokesmen of the Catholic establishment whom Hochhuth accused in his controversial play *The Representative* of joining Pope Pius XII at that time in behaving too **tactically**, too much on the basis of well-considered **political** considerations, are **tactically** and **politically** evading the play, whereas a Karl Jaspers or a Golo Mann took it seriously... Even believing Christians would do well to show that they had been affected in some way by the urgency of Hochhuth's moral commitment. Instead of this, they put pressure on Munich's subsidized theatre over this play for twenty-five years.'[42]

Truly, it is also a public scandal for all informed Catholics that the very institution which bears the main blame for Roman Catholic anti-Judaism all down the centuries, from the thirteenth century on, could not act here with more sensitivity, simply in a Christian way. Unfortunately, the scandal has in no way been done away with even by **John Paul II**, despite his spectacular but not exactly 'historical' visit to a synagogue on 13 April 1986. There has been no unequivocal confession of guilt and no diplomatic recognition of the state of Israel by the Vatican, even under the Polish pope.[43] This only confirms the deep-seated resentment and the intrinsic contradictoriness of the Roman Curia and its policy towards the Jewish state. As the famous Jewish Italian historian Arnaldo Momigliano, professor at the universities of Pisa and Chicago, remarked in one of the last books published before he died, at that time a combination of clericalism and pro-Nazism made the extermination of the Jews acceptable to the Italians.[44] And even now in the Roman Curia, which at that time was largely Fascist and is still authoritarian, a barely disguised suspicion of the Jews remain. Many Catholics found it painful that even after the first Iraqi missile attack on Tel Aviv, Pope John Paul II, while lamenting the extension of the war and the victims, strictly avoided mentioning Israel by name. The Jewish community in Rome was reminded of Pius XII's silence, protested, and again appealed to the pope finally to recognize the state of Israel. And in the meantime countless Catholics throughout the world were asking whether someone who constantly preaches conversion to the whole world must not first be converted if he is to become really credible.

That the situation for the Roman papacy does not look even more pitiful is something for which the church is indebted to **John XXIII**, the first Roman pope also to take a different line over relations with the Jews. As Apostolic Delegate in Turkey, already during the Second World War he had rescued thousands of Jews, especially children, from

Romania and Bulgaria (by means of blank baptismal certificates). In 1958, the very year in which he became pope, he abolished the prayer against 'the faithless Jews' (*'Oremus pro perfidis Judaeis'*) in the intercessions in the Good Friday liturgy and substituted for it inter- cessions for the Jews; this was rightly understood as a signal for a new attitude towards this people.[45]

In 1960, for the first time this pope received a group of more than 100 American Jews, and to their surprise welcomed them with the words of the biblical Joseph in Egypt, 'Son io, Giuseppe il fratello vestro! – I am Joseph your brother.' Thus, as an expression of a new beginning, instead of using his official name he used his own name, Giuseppe, clothed in a biblical quotation. Quite spontaneously (without all the now customary, calculated media hype), one day this pope had his car stop at the synagogue in Rome to bless the Jews who happened to be pouring out of it. No wonder that on the night before John XXIII's death, the Chief Rabbi of Rome himself went with countless Jewish believers to the Piazza S.Petro to join the Catholics in watching and praying! John XXIII died, all too early, on 3 June 1963, after a brief but epoch-making pontificate of barely five years, after the first session of the **Second Vatican Council,** which he had convened to everyone's complete surprise, and which met for the first time in autumn 1962.

In this spirit, in 1965 the Council finally – in the face of vehement opposition from the traditionally anti-Jewish Roman Curia and the bishops from the Near East – made the epoch-making declaration on the 'Relationship of the Church to the Non-Christian Religions'. This was on 28 October 1965, the seventh anniversary of the date of Pope John's election. In section 4 of this declaration (*Nostra Aetate*), for the first time in a council clarity was achieved on the question which, as we have heard, has brought infinite suffering to Jews all down the centuries: the question of a 'collective guilt' of the Jewish people then or even now for the death of Jesus. The Council declared unmistakably: 'Even though the Jewish authorities and those who followed their lead pressed for the death of Christ, neither all Jews indiscriminately at that time, nor Jews today, can be charged with the crimes committed during his passion.' At the same time, in this document the church at last reflects on the statements by the apostle Paul in Romans 9-11 which have so often been betrayed in the history of the church: one may not conclude from the fact that the church is the new people of God that the Jews are 'rejected or accursed by God'.[46]

However, even at that time – Pope John was already dead – many Jews and Christians did not understand that after the dismaying mass murders and a long history of Christian anti-Judaism, the Catholic church as a whole had only been able to struggle through to vague formulas of 'lament': once again a *condemnare* ('condemn') was deleted from the draft statement. And on his visit to the United Nations, even Pope John Paul II, while solemnly uttering the word 'Auschwitz', long avoided speaking a clear word of condemnation on specifically Catholic or even Roman antisemitism. And what about the German Catholic bishops? What role did they play?

7. An episcopate which capitulated: the German bishops

Already in the nineteenth century the German episcopate had consider-able reservations about the modern state, which the church had opposed in the Kulturkampf, as it did later about the young Weimar democracy after the First World War. The bishops found themselves in a dilemma: theologically they were now in principle against liberalism and social-ism, but in practice they wanted to exploit the democratic system as far as possible for their own ends. And what about their attitude to National Socialism – the sole theme of this short chapter?[47] National Socialism was rejected for its racial programme, but its anti-liberalism and anti-Bolshevism was noted with some sympathy ('better Brown than Red'). So because of its own anti-Judaism, the church also had an ambiguous attitude to racial antisemitism.

Against this historical background it was not so surprising that the leader of political Catholicism, prelate Ludwig Kaas, a friend of Pacelli's, with his Centre Party **voted for Hitler's 'Enabling Law'** and thus provided the decisive majority for the coming 'Führer'. Even Catholic historians now concede this to be **'the cardinal error of German Catholicism'**.[48] Or, as the Protestant historian Klaus Scholder puts it, this was 'the capitulation of Catholicism' – primarily, as is now accepted as a quite unambiguous historical fact, for the sake of the Reich concordat which Hitler held in prospect.[49] Before that, as Scholder also notes, 'German Catholicism, in both the church and politics, with what must be generally seen as an admirable steadfastness and solidarity', had rejected 'National Socialism, until for the higher reasons of its concordat policy, Rome thought it necessary to withdraw on this front'.[50] However, precisely this dangerous conformist solidarity made the church incapable of acting politically. Taken by surprise by the Vatican shift, in the end all the German bishops went along with it. Now they too were concerned solely for the Reich concordat, heedless of the fate of those 'outside', the 'others' (Communists, Socialists, Slavs, Jews), and of democracy generally. In religious, cultural, educational terms this concordat was supposed to guarantee the self-preservation of the church: 'The pressure from Hitler, Kaas's policy, and the desires and illusions of Rome had put the German bishops in a situation in which in fact they had no alternative but to capitulate.'[51]

Capitulate? In fact, from now on there could no longer be any question of political resistance to the system. Not only was resistance virtually impossible to justify on the basis of the official Catholic doctrine of the state as developed by Leo XIII, but in addition, as we saw, by the concordat (with its clauses relating to depoliticization and the protection of the associations), the Catholic Church had volunteered **to keep out of politics**. So protests and admonitions in sermons remained isolated, and petitions were mostly useless. No, there would be no need to discuss all this again if the truth were conceded officially, with plainness and clarity. As it is, however, in view of the regrettable self-righteousness of the German episcopate, it is necessary to state clearly what official statements are all too ready to kept quiet about or to cover up.

1. It is bad that because of the situation brought about by Hitler, Kaas and the Vatican, a few days after Hitler's government declaration on 23 March 1933 the German episcopate **capitulated** to the National Socialists who had come to power, despite their well-known nationalist and racist programme, and despite all their acts of terror against anyone who thought otherwise – to the clear dismay of many clergy and laity, many of whom even later persisted in a tacit and silent opposition to the regime.

2. It is worse that the German episcopate, whose sole concern was the 'independence' of the church, did **not** venture to make **a single public statement on behalf of the Jews** throughout the whole period of National Socialism (and hardly dared to say anything on behalf of quite a few Catholic priests and lay people who had been arrested). Full of loyalty to the criminal Nazi regime even after 'Kristallnacht' and the attack on Poland, after 1940 most of the German bishops prayed for a German victory with increasing frequency.[52]

3. It is even worse that the German bishops, who in their pastoral letter immediately after the war, in August 1945, were painfully concerned above all about their confessional schools, and even then described the Jews in Nazi fashion as 'non-Aryans', have **even now still avoided making a clear confession of the guilt of the episcopate in particular.**

4. It is worst of all that in the almost fifty years since the end of the war the hierarchy has done everything possible to **restyle as 'resistance'**

the silence, toleration and co-operation of the church authorities during Nazi rule. They have praised the pope and themselves, with apologetic, with beatifications, surveys and co-operative historians. As though the few real heroes of the resistance and a few others had stood for the hierarchy of the church and had not usually been left in the lurch by them (as also had the conscientious objectors)! One might think of the Provost of Berlin, **Bernhard Lichtenberg**, who prayed publicly for the Jews and died on the way to Dachau; of the Jesuit Fr **Alfred Delp**, who was executed; and of Pastor Dr **Max Joseph Metzger**, the inspiration of the peace movement and the ecumenical movement, who was beheaded. If only at least, at a late stage, the bishops had approved the pastoral letter drafted to be read out from all pulpits on the Second Sunday in Advent, 1941, which took the Nazi regime sharply to task; or even the very watered-down draft pastoral letter of March 1942. But there were no written petitions to state authorities, and in accordance with the wishes of the pope there was not a single clear public statement against a regime which after the Jews would doubtless also have liquidated the churches.

Granted, the German Catholic bishops were no Nazis. And in many respects – generally to a greater extent than the majority of their Protestant brothers-in-office – the pastoral clergy showed a non-conformist attitude of opposition. As a result there was something like a 'natural' testimony on the part of some Catholics, who showed an everyday power of resistance and had the courage to make specific interventions.[53] But now, from the beginning, the bishops and clergy had allowed themselves to be forced back into the 'religious' sphere, and despite some discussions they always refrained from any public protest. Even in 1941, an advisory committee of the episcopal conference referred to the scope of a public declaration in the following dramatic words: 'One day it will be of tremendous historical significance if in the hour of decision for the church of Germany the German bishops have publicly abused divine and natural law and thus pre-empted the decision for millions of souls. On the other hand, if the bishops keep silent, the way will be blocked not just temporarily but for decades and longer... Moreover, the question of success or failure may not be significant. The only decisive question is what our duty is at the present moment. What does conscience require? What does God, what do believers, expect of their bishops?'[54] But there was no kind of public declaration, although the Protestant leaders had approached the episcopate to make a joint protest.

And as far as the **Jews** were concerned: it is well known that even

Bishop Graf Galen of Münster, the only bishop who – as we heard – finally had the courage to make a late public protest against the murder of the mentally ill (and later the closure and appropriation of Catholic institutions), with his German nationalist bent and in faithfulness to the Roman line, never risked a word on behalf of the Jews.[55] This although as early as 1937 his cousin Konrad von Preyssing, the Bishop of Berlin, had argued for a clear strategy of confrontation with the Nazi regime,[56] and Johann Baptista Sproll, the Bishop of Rottenburg, who was disposed towards opposition, also took a lone stand in daring public confrontation (particularly by publicly abstaining in the vote on the annexation of Austria in April 1938). As a result he was exiled.[57] No, the German bishops did not use the word 'Jews' publicly any more than did their pope, and that was still the case in their first pastoral letter after the war!

On this question, then, there was failure all along the line, and this fact cannot be obscured by subsequent beatifications (in Germany under Pope John Paul II). Even many Catholics understood these as self-obfuscation by a church institution which has never convincingly acknowledged its failure. Respect for uncompromising figures like the Jesuit father **Rupert Mayer** (who was spared, because he had been a officer in the First World War) and the Jewish Carmelite **Edith Stein**! But even many Carmelites, men and women, had a question about the beatifications. Was the distinguished philosopher Edith Stein gassed because she was a member of a Catholic order? Was it not rather because she was a Jew – the woman who as early as 1933 had asked the pope (in vain) for an encyclical against racial hatred and antisemitism? In the Carmel, at any rate, as a Jew she was completely isolated and misunderstood. Where was the protest of the church hierarchy and her superiors in the order when Edith Stein was being dragged away? We did not hear anything about that from the pope at the time of the beatification celebrations in Cologne in 1987.[58]

So as a Christian one could only sympathize with the protests of many Jews when in 1989 a convent of the Carmelite order was to be built on the site of the former **concentration camp of Auschwitz**, of all places, with a giant cross as a visible symbol. Granted, the motives of the sisters there may have been honourable. But the statements by the primate of Poland, Cardinal Glemp, and the telling silence of the Polish pope, again raised questions about the antisemitism (and the honesty) of the Catholic hierarchy. Only after world-wide Jewish and Christian protests was the action abandoned. But the cross was still standing in September 1990, when I visited Auschwitz. Cannot people really understand that Auschwitz is now a place which Jews all over the world regard as a **Jewish mass grave**, not to be taken over by Christians?

This, too, is a story which we cannot pursue further here. Once again I would draw attention to the publications of the critical Catholic historian **Georg Denzler**, who has boldly opposed all public repression of guilt, all glorification and creation of legends (about general 'ignorance' and 'church resistance'). Here one can read all that is worth knowing about what is on the whole the pitiful attitude of the German episcopal conference.[59] One can also read all that is necessary about the scandalous treatment of those Catholic priests who had to suffer in concentration camps and who right up to their deaths were refused access to their files. Why? Because in this way the attitude of particular episcopal authorities to the Fascist brown-shirts at that time would have come to light. There were the eleven priests from the diocese of Freiburg imprisoned in a concentration camp who after the war complained bitterly but vainly against 'Brown Conrad' (as their Archbishop Gröber was called in the Nazi period); they had their equivalents in almost every diocese. But it was only in 1991 – as a result of the television programme 'Persil Coupons and False Passes' by Ernst Klee, distinguished author of a number of publications on the subject – that a wider public became aware of 'how the churches (and particularly the Vatican) helped the Nazis after the war'.

The Catholic hierarchy of Germany, well-equipped with the 'Reich concordat' (which was unfortunately declared to be 'valid' by the Supreme Court), and with billions of marks in church taxes, was the most highly bureaucratized and richest church in the world. In the post-war period it could arrogantly and impatiently ride roughshod over its own people and their needs, At the same time, standing on the right wing of the world episcopate, it could mercilessly suppress dissenters, men and women, among youth organizations, student communities, teachers of religion, pastors and theologians, and force them into exile or muzzle them. Truly, 1945 was even less a striking new beginning for the church than it was for the state.

Indeed, it was only in 1980, thirty-five years after the end of the Nazi regime, and fifteen years after the end of the Second Vatican Council, that the **Catholic episcopal conference** took a stand on the Jewish question – and that only because it was forced to. Even then, it avoided anything which could have been regarded as an unambiguous confession of its **own** historical **complicity**. So to end this section – precisely because, disappointingly, there was nothing of this kind in the declaration of the German episcopate 'On the Relationship of the

Church to Judaism' of 28 April 1980 – [60] I shall quote the clear confession of guilt which was expressed as early as 1975, under the influence of theologians and lay people, in the **Declaration of the Joint Synod of Catholic Dioceses of the Federal Republic of Germany**: 'We are the country whose most recent political history is darkened by the attempt systematically to exterminate the Jewish people. In this time of National Socialism, despite exemplary conduct by individuals and groups, as a whole we were a church community which went on living too much with our backs turned on the fate of this persecuted Jewish people. We allowed our gaze to be fixed too firmly on the threat to our own institutions and kept quiet about the crimes perpetrated on the Jews and Judaism. Here many people incurred guilt out of sheer anxiety about their lives. It weighs particularly heavily on us that Christians even collaborated in this persecution. The practical honesty of our concern for renewal depends also upon our confessing this guilt and being ready to learn a painful lesson from this history of the guilt of our country and also our church. Here our German church in particular must be alive to all tendencies to abolish human rights and to misuse political power. It must give special help to all those who today are being persecuted for racist or other ideological motives. And above all it must take on special responsibilities for the burdens of relations between the whole church and the Jewish people and its religion.'[61]

8. A repressive church: the church of Poland

As early as 1965, within the framework of the Second Vatican Council, there was a 'historic' correspondence between the Polish bishops, who gave and asked for forgiveness, and the German bishops. At that time I was personally able to note in the Council how lamely and with what confusion the German bishops reacted to this noble (if also not unselfish) offer of reconciliation. They did not want to give up their jurisdiction over the eastern territories which were now Polish. But finally, in 1989, they were completely overtaken by political developments. 'Life punishes the one who comes too late,' as Mikhail Gorbachev remarked!? But even in November 1990 – yes, 1990! – no agreement was reached in joint discussions between ten German and fifteen Polish bishops on the question of guilt, expulsion (which manifestly did not take place at the wish of the Poles, but on Allied orders) and on pastoral care for German minorities in Poland.[62]

But here a counterpoint is appropriate. When it comes to antisemitism and the Holocaust, the question of the responsibility of the German hierarchy must not conceal that of the complicity of another hierarchy, the Catholic hierarchy in **Poland**. For in the Nazi period, amazingly, it made no **official statement protesting against the annihilation of the Polish Jews.**

Granted, it is more than understandable that even now the Poles still regard themselves as the second greatest victims of Nazi rule after the Jews (six million Polish people also died). And as a member of a small nation I cannot disguise my sympathy for the infinitely brave Polish nation, constantly caught between great powers. I first made its acquaintance in 1940, at the age of twelve, in the persons of Poles interned in Switzerland. Terrible things were done to the Polish people which have left their mark even today. Not only was the Polish nation invaded and terrorized by Hitler's armies, but in an agreement between Hitler and Stalin, for the fourth time in its history (after the three partitions in the late eighteenth century) it was dismembered and finally, in the third act of the tragedy, incorporated into the sphere of rule of Stalin and his successors with the co-operation of the Western powers. 2,800 Polish clergy are said to have been imprisoned in Dachau, and the Polish religious **Maximilian Kolbe**, who went to certain death in Auschwitz in place of the father of a family, is a shining example of Christian self-sacrifice.[63] There is no doubt about it: Poland is a nation which only now has been liberated and which deserves our heartfelt admiration. Here the name of the workers' leader Lech Walensa (for a long time abandoned by the Roman curia) may stand for others. And yet here one is amazed, for was it not also Lech Walensa, Nobel prizewinner and now state president, who, while not antisemitic himself, confirmed antisemitic phobias through statements he made during the election? Evidently there is a group of 'real Poles' in the Solidarity movement who are characterized by 'intolerance of those of other views, repression of criticism and primitive chauvinism'(B.Borusewicz), to whom the church hierarchy stands close.[64]

So it is impossible to suppress certain questions. Does the German rule of force excuse the attitude of the Catholic church of Poland to the Jews during and after the war? Of the six million dead Poles, were not half Jews, around a fifth of the Polish population? Why did not a single Polish bishop raise his voice over the genocide which was being perpetrated by Germans on Jews on Polish soil? And was there not also much indifference, indeed secret joy, among the Polish people at what the Nazis were doing? Even Polish historians sometimes obscure essential facts here. **'Blood which has been shed unites us'** runs the dramatic title of the book by the Catholic historian Vladislav

Bartoszewski on 'Jews and Poles at the time of the "Final Solution"'
(of great merit because of the fate of many Jews).[65] So are both entirely
victims? But is such a general statement true? Jews resolutely reject
such a posthumous offering and assertion of a 'common recollection'.
That may seem astonishing at first sight, but it is easily understood.
Why?

Anti-Judaism with a religious basis, indeed racist **antisemitism**, was
deeply rooted and widespread **even in pre-war Poland**. One example
may be enough. 'There will be the Jewish problem as long as the Jews
remain. It is a fact that the Jews are fighting against the Catholic
Church, persisting in freethinking, and are the vanguard of godlessness,
Bolshevism and subversion. It is a fact that the Jewish influence on
morality is pernicious and that their publishing houses disseminate
pornography. It is a fact that the Jews deceive, levy interest, and are
pimps. It is a fact that the religious and ethical influence of the Jewish
young people on Polish young people is a negative one.' Is that the
authentic voice of the Catholic and Nazi propaganda minister Joseph
Goebbels? No, this passage can be found in a pastoral letter of 1936,
written by the Catholic primate of Poland, Cardinal Hlond.[66]

On this, the Director of the Salomon Ludwig Steinheim Institute for
German-Jewish History, Professor Julius H.Schoeps, remarks: 'The
practice of antisemitism in pre-war Poland matched that in Germany
before the pogrom of 9 November 1938 – perhaps with the sole
difference that no formal anti-Jewish laws were needed for it. In Poland,
too, there was massive discrimination against Jews in professional and
business life. Physical maltreatment of Jewish pupils and students at
Polish schools and universities was an everyday occurrence at the end
of the 1930s. The professional associations of doctors, architects and
engineers expelled their Jewish members "with reference to Aryan
regulations" which were unmistakably orientated on the paragraph in
the Nuremberg Laws of 1935 and indicate that Polish society, too, had
been infected by the bacillus of antisemitism.'[67]

In 1939 there were around 3.5 million Jews in Poland; after the
United States, Poland was the second largest Jewish diaspora in the
world, with 30 Jewish daily newspapers and 400 Jewish cemeteries.
Almost a third of the population of Warsaw and around 16% of the
population of Poland were Jewish. The Nazis killed three million of
them, more than half of all the Jews exterminated by the Nazis. Take
the shattering book of photographs by the two young non-Jewish Poles
Malgorzata Nierzabitowska and Tomasz Tomaszewski on *The Last
Jews in Poland*, and look at the pictures.[68] As I heard from Dr Pawel

Wildstein, President of the Jewish Co-ordination Committee in Poland, only between 8,000 and 10,000 Jews are still living in Poland, old and frail and not distinctive in the clothes they wear. And this is not just because of the Nazis! Are we to keep quiet about all this – despite all our admiration for the freedom-loving Polish people? I do not think that we should. Here, very briefly, are the **historical facts**.

– The German occupation did not tone down the traditional Polish anti-Judaism but intensified it; the Germans also had Polish collaborators in the Holocaust.

– Conversely, many Polish Jews enthusiastically welcomed the invasion by Soviet troops in 1940 because Poland was not a home for them, and so became stooges of the Soviet forces of occupation.

– A Polish 'Auxiliary Council' for Jews ('Zegota') was set up only in 1942, when a large proportion of the inhabitants of the Jewish ghettos had already been sent to the death camps.

– Support for the Jews from the Polish resistance movement in the Warsaw Ghetto uprising of 1943 was extremely hesitant and half-hearted.

– After the war, anti-Judaism in Poland was as strong as ever. Indeed, when some Jews (including not a few Communists) wanted to return to their old homeland there were serious anti-Jewish riots, real pogroms: in Krakow on 11 August 1945 and in Kielce on 4 July 1946 (with between sixty and seventy dead). The church authorities did not make any public statement on them.[69] In 1945 alone there is evidence that 353 Jews were killed by mobs, resulting in a mass flight of around 80,000 Polish Jews to the West.[70]

– There was another mass exodus in 1968 after a campaign of antisemitism organized by the state, again without any protest from the church; in 1970 the last rabbi finally left Poland.

So they are contributory reasons for the fact that today barely 10,000 Jews are left in Poland. 'Blood which has been shed unites us'? On his Polish 'pilgrimages', **Karol Wojtyla**, ordained priest in 1946, the year of the pogrom, later Archbishop of Krakow and now Roman Pontifex, who censured Auschwitz (thirty miles west of Krakow) dramatically, but in very general terms, at the United Nations in New York in 1979, never took account of all these painful questions. Why does he maintain silence on them, when like Pius XII he gives addresses on almost every question, past and present?

It is all the more welcome that in North America and Britain at least, attempts are being made by organizations on both sides to **improve Jewish-Polish relations** and to clarify existing historical and relevant contemporary questions. Here I would refer simply to the Polish-Jewish congresses at Columbia University in New York in 1983, and in England at Oxford in 1984, arranged by the Oxford Institute of Polish-Jewish Studies. Since 1986 the Institute has published annually a *Journal of Polish-Jewish Studies* (edited by A.Polonsky).

In Poland itself, where this question of Polish antisemitism was tabu throughout the whole post-war period, it was the 1985 film *Shoah* by the French Jew Claude Lanzmann which set discussion going over possible Polish complicity in the Holocaust. No wonder that the Polish government lodged a protest with the French Foreign Minister over some passages in the film – but without banning it.[71] No wonder, either, that the film led to vigorous protests among the population, since it does not paint a very flattering picture of the country and its people at this time.

And yet the **discussion** was fruitful even in Poland. In Poland, too, many people wanted to know the truth. Moreover, in the Catholic weekly *Tygodnik Powszechny* of 11 January 1987, the distinguished Polish literary scholar **Jan Blonski** with some courage said of the usual Polish self-justifications: 'We should stop putting the blame on political, social and economic conditions and first say, "Yes, we are guilty."' In connection with the pogroms after the war, Blonski continues: 'We could not even welcome the survivors and receive them honourably, even if they were embittered, confused and perhaps also a burden on us. In short, instead of calculating and excusing ourselves, we should first examine ourselves, consider our sin and our weakness. This moral conversion, in particular, is absolutely necessary in our relationship to the Polish-Jewish past.'[72]

But although Blonski carefully distinguished 'between participation and complicity', the paper received hundreds of mostly critical and polemical communications, so that its chief editor **Jerzy Turowicz** finally felt obliged to make the following statement: 'We must note with shame that even if some authors deny it, these very letters prove that antisemitism is still widespread in Poland, although virtually no Jews are now left in our country.'[73] This leading Catholic of Poland boldly and honestly stated that unlike the Poles, their Jewish fellow countrymen and women were condemned to death from the start. And although the Polish citizens, with three million dead, had to mourn as many victims as their Jewish compatriots, 95% per cent of the Jewish minority in Poland had been exterminated as compared with only 10% of the Polish population as a whole. He argued that the traditional thought-pattern – as long as we Poles were victims we are completely innocent – had to be given up.

There is an amazing phenomenon in Catholic Poland similar to that in Catholic Austria: an **antisemitism without Jews**! Although practically no Jews are still left in Poland, on a visit in 1990 I myself noted that antisemitism is still so virulent that even the then Masowiecki government could be sweepingly dismissed as 'infected with Jewishness' – without being defended in any way by the hierarchy. Conversely, I had to note that the overwhelming proportion of Jewish victims (including Polish Jews) is not sufficiently stressed either in Auschwitz or in the City Museum in Warsaw.[74] So the insensitivity of the primate of Poland, Cardinal Joseph Glemp (long supported by the silent Polish pope), over the Carmelite House in Auschwitz, and then the anti-Jewish statements by Lech Walensa, are not so surprising. At any rate the latter asked the Jews for forgiveness when he was in Jerusalem in May 1991.

However, finally, at last, consciences are being examined even in the Polish hierarchy. Not only has the Polish episcopate formed a sub-commission for dialogue with Judaism, but eventually on 20 January 1991 – provoked and put under pressure by the negative reaction of the world public – for the first time it made a formal condemnation of antisemitism and expressed its 'honest regret for all tendencies towards antisemitism which have taken place on Polish soil whenever and by whomever': 'We do this in the deep conviction that any manifestation of antisemitism is irreconcilable with the spirit of the gospel.'[75] However, the use of the obscure formulation 'whenever and by whomever', coupled with a protest against mention of a 'Polish antisemitism' as a particularly dangerous form of antisemitism, makes it clear that the past has not been sufficiently assimilated even in the church of Poland.

These and similar events compel me to draw the basic conclusion (and truly, not just for Poland) that relations between Jews and Christians are evidently still far from being purged – historically, emotionally and theologically. A new constructive relationship between Jews and Christians is possible only if Christians, whatever their position, openly confess their guilt in the Holocaust without any disguise or apologetic. There is a need not to foster a guilt-complex but to arrive at authentic repentance, deeper understanding and closer collaboration with Jewish fellow-citizens. And such critical self-examination is also called for in other Christian lands where Jews have lived.

Murdered Jews

in Nazi-Occupied Europe
1 September 1939 – 8 May 1945

Poland **3,000,000**
Soviet Union **1,000,000**
Czechoslovakia **217,000**
Hungary **200,000**
Bessarabia **200,000**
Germany **160,000**
Lithuania **135,000**
Bukowina **124,632**
Holland **106,000**
Northern Transylvania **105,000**
France **83,000**
Latvia **80,000**
Greece **65,000**
Austria **65,000**
Yugoslavia **60,000**
Carpathian Ukraine **60,000**
Rumania **40,000**
Belgium **24,387**
Italy **8,000**
Memel **8,000**
Macedonia **7,122**
Thrace **4,221**
Rhodes **1,700**
Estonia **1,000**
Danzig **1,000**
Norway **728**
Luxembourg **700**
Libya **562**
Crete **260**
Albania **200**
Cos **120**
Denmark **77**
Finland **11**

Numbers: M. Gilbert, *Endlösung*, Reinbek 1982

9. No nation is innocent: Switzerland, the USA?

Hardly a nation has any occasion for self-righteousness over the Jewish question. When a conference was arranged by thirty-two states on 6 July 1938 in Evian by Lake Geneva on the initiative of President Franklin D.Roosevelt to seek a solution to the refugee problem, it was evident how little inclination there was to accept German or Jewish refugees. That is too little known. During the war those very countries with a large amount of space, like the states of North and South America and Australia, tended to restrict the admission of Jewish refugees rather than open their frontiers. It is symptomatic of this that in May 1939 the ship St Louis, with a full load of German Jews, had to return to Europe because no state was prepared to accept it. Great Britain closed the doors in Palestine to those persecuted by the Nazis. One asks, what could have been done for the Jews in all the occupied European countries from Poland to France – following, say, the example of Denmark, its king and its Lutheran episcopate, where in an unprecedented action almost all the Jewish population (around 7,000 people) was smuggled to Sweden by the Danish underground? Indeed, how much antisemitism was there also in other European countries?

Even in neutral Switzerland, where during the Second World War around 300,000 refugees were accepted for longer or shorter periods, people were highly restrictive over the policy of asylum for fear of Hitler's wrath and the constant threat of a German invasion. There was a widespread view that no more Jews could be admitted into the country. 'The boat is full', was the excuse of many Swiss at the time, and it made them politically blind to the need, as can be read in the depressing report under this title by Alfred A.Häsler on *Switzerland and the Refugees, 1933-1945*.[76] Great figures from German literature, art and culture had been accepted.[77] At the end of the war, on 8 May 1945, Switzerland was still sheltering more than 115,000 refugees. But in the time between August 1942 and 1945 alone, 9,751 refugees had been turned away, and countless had been deterred from the start.[78]

So there is no occasion for Swiss self-satisfaction and self-righteousness – which is still widespread. Only on the fiftieth anniversary of so-called 'Kristallnacht', in November 1988, did a church body in Switzerland finally make a clear confession of guilt – this honour goes to the Evangelical Church Alliance. The confession recalled that only two days after that Nazi pogrom, Switzerland officially signed an agreement with Germany which in fact made it impossible for Jews to travel legally out of Germany. Even today, the statement said, it fills the church with 'great shame' that thousands of those wanting to travel, with a 'J stamp' in their passports, were turned away on the frontiers of Switzerland, 'and at a time when people could be aware that they were sending these people back to certain death'.[79]

It might be mentioned just briefly that even the **International Committee of the Red Cross** in October 1942 did not enlighten the world about the Holocaust – despite what was beyond doubt its immense service in mitigating the distress of war, caring for prisoners and providing humanitarian help of all kinds. Confronted with a great power which sought to obliterate a whole race, the Committee thought that it could do virtually nothing, and felt obliged to be unpartisan and neutral. But in reality here, too, there was no great interest in rescuing the European Jews. Many leading members of the International Committee of the Red Cross, above all C.J.Burckhardt, were terrified of making a public protest, primarily for Swiss reasons of state – and this although at the latest since autumn 1942 people in Geneva had precise knowledge of the content of the Wannsee Conference. They largely took refuge behind fragmentary information. Thousands of Jews could probably have been saved had the Red Cross intervened energetically at the right time – as had originally been planned.[80]

And what about **France**? More than 75,000 Jews were carried off from France and murdered, and, as Serge Klarsfeld has pointed out, countless French people – from members of the Vichy Goverment and senior civil servants to simple gendarmes – collaborated in the 'final solution'.[81] What lies hidden in the black years of 1940-1945, between occupation and liberation, behind the Vichy regime and 'collaboration'? 'Red and white stripes in the French memory' is something that Alfred Grosser writes about in an extended chapter.[82] No, despite the ideals of 1789, France too was anything but friendly to the Jews (even a poet of the status of Paul Claudel saw France under Pétain as freed from the yoke of the anti-Catholic party – professors, lawyers, freemasons and Jews!). Only when Bishop Théas and Cardinals Saliège and Gerlier protested in pastoral letters against the inhuman treatment of the Jews (albeit in antipathy to the republic on the side of Marshal Petain) did Vichy in 1943 rejected the stripping of citizenship from all Jews naturalized since 1927.

And **North America**? What was done in the **United States** which, like the Vatican, had received the first news about the 'final solution' from Switzerland? David S.Wyman entitled his investigations into 'America and the Holocaust' *The Abandonment of the Jews* (1984).[83] To the horror of many people, Wyman succeeded in copiously documenting the fact that in the United States (as in Canada) in the 1930s and 1940s, first political opportunism, secondly general hostility to immigration, and thirdly traditional antisemitism had largely paralysed not only the media (even the *New York Times*), the churches, the parties and the trade unions, but also Congress, the State Department and above all President Franklin D.Roosevelt, who in any case was under considerable suspicion of 'friendliness towards the Jews' (Roosevelt's 'New Deal' programme was mockingly referred to as the 'Jew Deal').

The Catholic theologian Ronald Modras has recently pointed out that probably the most influential radio preacher in the United States in the 1930s was the Catholic priest **Charles Coughlin**, who with his Sunday afternoon addresses is said sometimes to have reached more than 30 million hearers. In addition he edited a weekly newspaper with a circulation of around 185,000. With the tacit toleration of the episcopate and the Vatican, Coughlin, avowedly antisemitic, served up Nazi stories about Jewish influence in the Soviet Union, and in 1938 managed to justify even 'Kristallnacht' to his hearers as a defensive action on the part of the Nazis against Jewish-inspired Communism. Coughlin found widespread support, since according to more recent research, right up until 1943 half of all Americans held more or less clearly antisemitic views.[84]

Given this general mood, it is not so surprising that reports about the Holocaust tended to be either ignored or suppressed in the USA – until even from here all help came too late.

But was there any alternative at that time? Certainly. As Wyman remarks: 'If nothing else, a few forceful statements by the President would have brought the extermination news out of obscurity and into the headlines. But he had little to say about the problem and gave no priority at all to rescue.'[85] Here the author has in mind rescue measures which would have been completely compatible with the Allied war plans. At any rate, with Allied help it proved possible to evacuate hundreds of thousands of non-Jewish refugees from Europe without any problem. However, at the same time there was no possibility of transport or accommodation for the majority of European Jews. Despite relevant information, even in the Jewish auxiliary organizations of America, only at a very late stage, indeed perhaps too late, were people willing to recognize the extent of the National Socialist extermination measures. This is demonstrated by Yehuda Bauer in the case of the American Jewish Joint Distribution Committee.[86] But the 'American apathy', to quote the title of a study by Chaim Genizi, affected not only Jewish but also non-Jewish Christian refugees, who made up about thirty per cent of the total number – and that despite the amazing work of some small and financially weak Christian auxiliary organizations.[87]

A historiography which is not just political history might be able to demonstrate on all sides that just as there is **no innocent religion**, so too there is **no innocent nation**. However, the aim of my historical analysis is not accusation but an assimilation of guilt. The question is: what positive conclusions for the present are to be drawn from this sorry historical evidence about a past which will not easily go away? Indeed, historical questions everywhere prove to have considerable political relevance, and contemporary political questions prove to be historically determined. But it has also become clear that both historical and contemporary political questions all too often have a religious and theological background and foundation. What basic religious and theological attitude is called for here?

10. Drawing a line under the Holocaust: is that a strategy?

If true reconciliation and true peace are to be achieved, conversion and penitence are called for from both sides – despite the fundamental difference between perpetrators and victims. As a Jewish citizen of Israel and professor at a German college, **Michael Wolffsohn** has a right to address both sides clearly when in an acute analysis he makes the following statements in connection with the Holocaust.
– Theoretically and academically, individual and collective guilt can be neatly divided, but hardly in politics and in practice. Everyone, whether old or young, high or low, guilty or innocent, is entangled in a national web of guilt which cannot completely be unravelled;
– Germany's National Socialist past 'has already for a long time ceased to be pure history'. 'It has become a political instrument', an 'instrument of anti-Germanism', which non-Germans can use when they need to, whether or not they are Jews.
– The 'political mechanics' of anti-Germanism threaten to end up in the same way as those of anti-Judaism (for Wolffsohn, both are a kind of 'political biologism' which simply shackles human beings to their birth): 'Just as the Jews around two thousand years ago were branded murderers of Christ, so too the Holocaust, the murder of the Jews, will hang round the Germans' necks for centuries. In neither instance were the people of the time collectively guilty; in neither case do subsequent generations bear any blame at all, either individually or collectively. However, in both cases the sign of Cain remains an instrument and argument which is used against their ancestors, themselves and their successors. Afterwards the political reaction of the world is like that of Pavlov's dog: the conditioned reflex associated with the Jews is

"murderers of Christ"; that associated with Germany is – and will long continue to be – Auschwitz.'[88]

But, I ask myself, does this really have to be the long-term relationship between Germans and Jews? And would it be a good thing if, in order to unburden themselves, the Germans increasingly turned from the past and the Jews – perhaps to create their own identity – increasingly fixed themselves on the past, the Holocaust?

(a) How often one hears in Germany the slogan, '**Forget, at last forget!**' At last a line must be drawn under the whole history. A steadily increasing majority of German men and women in fact suffer from the fact that although they personally are not responsible for the crimes of their ancestors, internationally they are branded for this at every opportunity, in what is often a very self-righteous way. My question is: would not sometimes much-praised comprehension or compassion be more appropriate here? Martin Buber, far too little valued and not taken seriously enough in Israel, showed this comprehension and compassion when in 1953 he received the Peace Prize of the German Book Trade in the Paulskirche in Frankfurt. On this occasion he said: 'When I think of the German people of the days of Auschwitz and Treblinka, first of all I see the very many people who knew that the atrocity was happening and did not object: but my heart, which knows about human weakness, refuses to condemn my neighbour becuse he did not have it in him to become a martyr.'[89]

However, there is one thing that Germans must not expect: a forgetting of guilt. That would be historical irresponsibility. In 1984 the German Chancellor spoke innocently in Jerusalem (against the background of an arms deal with Saudi Arabia) of the 'dispensation of late birth' because at the time of the atrocities he was not yet of age or even in office. He did so to exclude himself, as the political representative of the nation, from the general responsibility of his people and to avoid a clear public confession of guilt in the name of the nation. But in so doing he was encouraging that mentality of repression which is so politically dangerous. German politics cannot be detached from history in this way, nor can relations between Germans, Jews and Israelis. Granted, awareness of guilt is not 'obsession with guilt'. And if a voluntary confession of guilt is **rejected**, the accusation becomes all the sharper. For those who do not themselves remember are remembered. Here a 'Christian' Democrat in particular has more occasion than other democrats to remember the web of guilt in which the generations are entangled. This has nothing to do with either a mythological 'original sin' or an ideological 'collective guilt'. No, instead of wanting to emerge 'from the shadow of one's own history', as F.J.Strauss put it, it is important both theologically and politically to stand in the history of one's own people in the present too, as did the German Federal President Richard von Weizsäcker (also a Christian Democrat), in a speech delivered forty years after 1945.

The **1991 Gulf War** shows vividly what the forgetting of history can lead to. Numerous Germans are hurt that the reputation of reunited Germany was seriously damaged in the eyes of the world and especially in Israel by unscrupulous firms and businesses tolerated by the governments. For the sake of their profits, they heedlessly contravened laws or passed them by in order to build a bomb-proof bunker for the warmonger Saddam Hussein, to adapt Soviet missiles to fly longer distances, and to produce poison gas. Cynical and blind to history, they were aware that these fearful weapons could also be used against Israel. And this after the millionfold murder of Jews! No, there can be progress here only if in the future arms production and exports are changed.

Questions for the Future

† The Holocaust is a past which also has an influence on Germany's present. So in future, should not German politicians, journalists, businessmen, scholars or church people accept that drawing a line under it cannot be a strategy? That what is needed is **reconciliation, not by forgetting**, hushing up, suppressing and 'normalizing'? In the meantime, how is reconciliation to be translated into political action on the basis of critical **recollection** (by the state, businesses, the academic world and the churches)?

(*b*) But a question can be asked in return. Does that not perpetuate guilt? Many Jews think that the guilt of the Germans must time and again be notched anew into the growing tree of history and immortalized. So their slogan is, '**No forgiving, ever!**' Your guilt lasts for ever... However, a steadily increasing majority of Jewish and also Israeli men and women (more than 60% of Israeli citizens have now been born after the war) know of the infinite sorrow of the Holocaust only from recollections. And even in Jerusalem, some younger people do not want to live with a constant fixation on the past. So one can understand the intensive efforts all over the world, particularly on the part of the older generation, to keep alive the memory of the Holocaust. As long as crimes can still be uncovered and guilt can still be atoned for, courts will be active. In any case, antisemitism has not died out, and Jews cannot feel sufficiently safe even in the state of Israel to rule out the possibility of a new Holocaust – as was shown by the 1973 Yom Kippur War and the missiles of the Iraqi dictator Saddam Hussein in 1991. One Jewish trauma which remains from the Nazi period is the determination that never again will Jews be led unresisting like lambs to the slaughter.

However, there is also something that Jews should not aim at: the perpetuation of guilt. To nurture and foster guilt-feelings is not a long-term policy, as was recognized at a very early stage by Israel's first prime minister, David Ben-Gurion. In April 1987, at the site of the former concentration camp of Bergen-Belsen, an Israeli prime minister could still proclaim, 'I have brought no forgiving with me – and no forgetting.' One may certainly agree with the political representative of that country in the reason he gave, 'The living are not allowed to forget'. However – and here too I shall allow myself to speak with some Swiss boldness – I would just as resolutely contradict him, in the name of the Hebrew Bible, when he claims, 'Only the dead have the right to forgive.' I ask myself, 'Is that really what is written?' And how could one really imagine a true reconciliation if not only any forgetting must be ruled out (rightly), but also any forgiving? (I know that this is a delicate point, and we must return to it.) No, instead of diplomatically covering up an abyss of guilt for considerations of foreign and domestic policy, the political and theological imperative is to forgive guilt.

Again, it is the **Gulf War** which shows in a terrifying way the consequences of not discussing the question of the forgiveness of guilt seriously. Heavy strains were put on the relationship between the Germans and the Israelis not only by the criminal activities of German firms but also by the **anti-Germanism** which could flare up in Israeli 'popular anger' and in the Israeli media and which – after almost half a century of German-Israeli collaboration – was unfortunately complete confirmation of Wolffsohn's thesis to the degree that it completely distorted and concealed the situation in present-day Germany. The all-too-justified complaints against the business deals of German firms (above all in connection with the production of poison gas) threatened to rub off on 'the Germans' generally. By contrast, there were hardly any complaints about the involvement of other states in the arming of the Iraqi dictator: about France, which had delivered 880 Exocet missiles and 113 Mirage fighter-bombers to Iraq; about the USSR, which had delivered 2,000 Scuds, 1,000 T-72 tanks and 64 MIGs; about South Africa, which had supplied Iraq with 200 pieces of heavy artillery; about the sea and land mines which were delivered by

Russia, Taiwan and Italy; or about the radar installations which came from Brazil, England and France.[90]

One cannot fail to be struck by the fact that Germany does not figure in this list of arms deliveries. And yet there was massive and often hate-filled protest against that country. And there were insinuations of a German collective guilt, so that German politicians – unlike Adenauer, who embodied atonement with personal dignity and political steadfast-ness – felt compelled to make penitential pilgrimages to Jerusalem in hordes, there to listen to public accusations and tirades, even in the Israeli parliament. The Israeli president would not shake hands with any German, not even the woman president of the German Parliament. As a Swiss citizen I ask myself: did not more come through here in Israel than legitimate protest against unscrupulous German profiteers? If this happens, does not the political argument of the Holocaust become threadbare or even boomerang – as far as the Palestinian question is concerned? Is not all this connected with an inability to discuss the question of guilt in the spirit of reconciliation? As a friend of German-Israeli understanding I ask myself whether such a fixation on the Holocaust, such a reactivation of the Holocaust, does any service to the understanding between Germans and Israelis. Michael Wolffsohn, who as a committed advocate of objectivity in German-Jewish relations often has to defend himself against his German-Jewish fellow believers, remarks: 'Anyone who uses Auschwitz for political ends is spiritually desecrating graves.'[91] No, no crime should be excused, no enlightenment prevented, no punishment suppressed. Self-critical questions are in place, but they must be self-critical questions to both sides, in Germany and in Israel. And these questions are connected with the problem of reconciliation and forgiveness. So this question, too, is unavoidable for the future.

Questions for the Future

In Israel, the Holocaust can be used at any time as an argument and an instrument in domestic and foreign policy. But in future should not Jewish politicians, journalists, businessmen, scholars or theo-logians accept that a historical policy fixated on the Holocaust cannot be a strategy? That what is needed is **reconciliation, not by perpetuating**, intimidating or buying, **but by forgiving**? But how is such forgiving, which is not to be understood as playing down or erasing the past, to be directed fruitfully towards a new relationship to the past in the light of new possibilities for the future?

But these questions will not be discussed in greater theological depth until a later stage. In any case, they cannot be discussed adequately in the abstract, as they have countless political presuppositions and implications. And the main presupposition is the question of the **state of Israel**. It cannot be bracketted off as merely a political question, as in some church documents. Complex religious and theological problems are involved here. So it is now time for us to turn directly to the Jewish state. In this second part, first of all I shall relate the history of its formation and its self-assertion in the present; then, in Part Three, I shall investigate the question of the future of this state, including the religious and theological dimension.

III. The Return to Israel

'By the waters of Babylon,
there we sat down and wept,
when we thought of Zion.'

So the Jews were already praying in the Psalms.[1] Weeping, for Zion, the mountain which already at that time was a synonym for Jerusalem? Since the destruction of the First Temple and the exile in Babylon there has indeed been a Jewish Diaspora, but in Jewish tradition there is also the experience of exile from the 'land of Israel' (*Eretz Israel*), the longing for liberation and homesickness for **Zion**: homesickness for Jerusalem, the city of God. However, only since the nineteenth century has the longing for return among the Jewish people been combined with the idea of a nation: in Zionism, which has built the state of Israel.

Today – almost half a century after the Holocaust and the foundation of the state – the state of Israel is still at the centre of passionate controversy: political controversy between Israelis and Arabs and religious controversy between Jews, Christians and Muslims. As the Gulf War has again shown, the now already almost fifty-year-old dispute over the state of Israel is the main reason for the tensions between the Western world and the Arab world. So the state of Israel is still a political **and** theological challenge of the first order. This has to be recognized if peace is to be served in this unpeaceful part of our world. For there will only be real peace if not only a diplomatic solution is sought, but a deeper political, ethical and religious understanding is striven for. The Near Eastern region cannot go on being virtually a symbol of political fanaticism, nationalistic passions and religious blockages. The following remarks by a Christian theologian are meant to be understood in this sense – remote from any involvement in party politics. I hope that they may contribute towards understanding and peace.

1. Zionism instead of assimilation: Leon Pinsker

Zion is an old word, but **Zionism**[2] is a modern one, used only since the end of the last century. It was coined by Nathan Birnbaum in his journal *Self-Emancipation*, which later appeared with the sub-title *An Organ of the Zionists*. From the beginning, Zionism was not understood in practical philanthropic terms, but specifically in party-political terms;

it aimed at the institutionalization of a national political Zionist party for the liberation of the Jewish people and for their organization into a state.

So the state of Israel is in no way the result of the Holocaust, as non-Jews have often assumed. There would have been a state of Israel even without Hitler. As we have heard, for centuries Jews have been expecting the restoration of the kingdom of Israel. After the failure of the pseudo-messianic movement of Shabbetai Zevi in the seventeenth century, however, the basic attitude was a very passive one: everything was made dependent on the scrupulously exact fulfilment of the commandments of the Torah, and thus the establishment of the kingdom was expected by the powerful intervention of God 'from above', to some degree through the coming of the messiah. One can call this the **eschatological-messianic** Zion-expectation, and to the present day it is shared by certain Orthodox Jewish groups even in Israel, who therefore reject a secular state of Israel.

In contrast to this purely religious expectation about Zion, **Zionism** is a **political and social** movement which seeks to achieve the establishment of a Jewish state (whether in Palestine or elsewhere) 'from below', i.e. by human activity and action. Here of course the ideological and emotional colouring provided by the old messianism is also present. This is especially true for the two Eastern European forerunners of Zionism, the Rabbi **Yehudah Alkalai** and the scholar **Zevi Hirsch Kalischer**, whose ideas began to have an effect after the 1860s.

Accordingly, political Zionism is not just a reaction to racist antisemitism. Rather, it is to be seen in connection with the Jewish Enlightenment (Haskalah) in the eighteenth century, and also with Romantic ideas about the 'people' and the rise of **nationalism** among the European peoples in the nineteenth century. This nationalism found expression in Judaism primarily in the renewal and modernization of **Hebrew** (= 'Ivrit') as a literary and national language: it owes its revival as a vernacular generally in schools and families above all to **Eliezer Ben Yehuda**. Having emigrated to Palestine in 1881, he created many new words and produced the first neo-Hebrew dictionary; he also founded a Hebrew newspaper and, along with others, the Hebrew Language Committee. To this degree, political and social Zionism is a **typically modern movement** which **increasingly secularized and politicized the religious promise**. Mention should be made here above all of the third great forerunner of Zionism, the Socialist rabbi **Moses Hess**, who in Paris also inspired Karl Marx, the baptized Jew from Trier. Hess was influenced in his views by the greatest Jewish historian of the nineteenth century, Heinrich Graetz.

It was only after the 1860s, however, that the ideas of these three significant Zionists began to have an effect, even if there was no exodus of Jews from Europe to Israel worth mentioning until the 1870s. Only after the persecution of Jews in Romania, the pogroms in Russia following the murder of Tsar Alexander II (1881) and the growing antisemitism in Germany and Austria, after 1882, was there more large-scale emigration also to Israel and the organization of a movement. This movement at first called itself Hibbat Zion, 'love of Zion', but later was incorporated into the Zionist movement. So with the immigration of largely Orthodox 'Friends of Zion', the year 1882 marked the beginning of the first *aliyah* or immigration into Israel.[3]

It was a Russian Jew and enlightened doctor by the name of **Leon Pinsker** (1821-1891) who gave the first passionate and at the same time acutely analytical expression to the political Zion-movements.[4] After the pogrom of 1881 he had begun to doubt the viability of the assimilation which he had at first fully affirmed. In a pamphlet on *Auto-emancipation*,[5] written in German, he finally offered an eloquent account of the intellectual foundations of political and social Zionism. Pinsker's **diagnosis** was that the central problem was not the distress of the Jewish individual but the homelessness of the Jewish people. 'The essence of the problem, as we see it, lies in the fact that, in the midst of the nations among whom the Jews reside, they form a distinctive element which cannot be assimilated, which cannot be readily digested by any nation.'[6] So antisemitism is not a phenomenon limited by time and space, but everywhere quite understandably an inherited social and pathological phenomenon which in the face of a 'spiritual nation' must be diagnosed as Judaeophobia. Everywhere Jewry is only a minority: it is not a nation, merely individuals; Jews are at best guests, never hosts: never with equal rights, eternally despised.

And the **remedy**? According to Pinsker, this cannot come about through civil and political equality but only through 'self-liberation', through a **new homeland**: not necessarily the 'holy' land, but the Jews' 'own' land – at first Pinsker thought more of America than of Palestine – to which they would contribute their most holy things, namely the idea of God and the Bible. At all events, this would be a land where Jews were no longer aliens but their own masters. 'The proper, the only remedy, would be the creation of a Jewish nationality, of a people living upon its own soil, the auto-emancipation of the Jews: their emenacipation as a nation among nations by the acquisition of a home of their own.'[7]

So the Zionists, too, understood the difference between Jews and non-Jews primarily in **ethnic** terms; for them Judaism was not primarily a religious community but the **community of a people**. However, Zionism naturally drew the opposite consequences to antisemitism: the construction of their own secular Jewish state was indispensable for the Jewish people. This programme now also had to be realized in practice. And so at that time, under Pinsker's leadership, the Odessa committee of the Organization for the Colonization of Palestine succeeded in bringing about 25,000 Jews to the Holy Land. This had to be done in the face of a ban imposed by the government of the Osman empire, which in the nineteenth century still ruled all the territory from Asia Minor to the Balkans and from Egypt to Mesopotamia, of course also including Palestine. However, Pinsker had no success whatsoever among German Jews during his lifetime. Only decades after his death, in 1934, were his bones moved to Jerusalem and there solemnly interred on Mount Scopus. Meanwhile, the decisive impulse towards a Jewish state had come from someone else, who was able to speak to the German Jews as well.

2. A state for the Jews: Theodor Herzl

It is indisputably the achievement of the Jewish lawyer and Viennese journalist Dr **Theodor Herzl** (1860-1904)[8] that Zionism was able to organize itself as a political force. A man who in his every action radiated the aura of a prophetic figure, without knowing Pinsker's writing and work Herzl now put forward the demand for a state for the Jews in his lucidly argued, programmatic and pragmatic pamphlet of 1896, *The Jewish State*.[9] This was a visionary work in which (here the English version of the title is misleading) Herzl was concerned not just with a 'Jewish state' but a 'state of Jews' (as the German title has it). For what was decisive for this pioneer thinker was not the Jewish religion but the **Jewish people**. With his slogan 'We are a people – **one** people!'[10] he addressed both Eastern and Western Jews. For Herzl, at first a return to *Eretz Israel*, the 'land of Israel', was not a necessity – for religious reasons. What was decisive for him was the growing 'misery of the Jews',[11] which could not be overcome by any assimilation. So the only meaningful solution was the organization by the Jewish people of itself in the form of a state, wherever that might be.

To understand this we have to realize that Herzl himself was an enlightened, assimilated Jew, with the detachment from Jewish tradition, culture and religion which went with that. He was a Viennese intellectual who, for example, did not think much of reviving Hebrew for Jews. For him the question of the Jews was neither religious nor social, but **national**. At an early stage he once even wondered whether he should not lead all the Jews of Vienna to St Stephen's Cathedral for baptism, so as once and for all to do away with any basis for antisemitism.

The subsequent change in Herzl's life had to do with two factors. First there was the trial of Dreyfus in Paris and the outcry of the Paris mob, 'Death to the Jew', at the public degradation of the Jewish Captain Dreyfus. Herzl was very personally involved, since he reported this as Paris correspondent of a liberal Vienna newspaper. This trial opened his eyes to the antisemitism which was evidently ineradicable, despite all the enlightenment. If even a country like France, which had in fact been the first European country to proclaim human rights specifically for the Jews as well, had experienced such a terrible lapse into hatred of the Jews, what might happen elsewhere! The second factor was the growing antisemitism in Vienna. Though Emperor Franz Joseph I repudiated it three times, in 1897 it led to the election of Karl Lueger, the Christian Socialist and opportunistically antisemitic tribune of the people, as Lord Mayor of Vienna. It was Lueger who was later to become the idol of the young Adolf Hitler.

Like Pinsker, Herzl too was now convinced that a total assimilation of the Jews could not be achieved, because none of the host countries really wanted it. And that despite all the great achievements of Jews not only in business and banking, but also in literature, art and culture! Rather, the more Jews emancipated themselves, the more threatening and hated they seemed to be. So those who still felt aliens rather than members of their particular European 'host-people', who felt Jews, should now go to the new land of the Jews, whether this were in Palestine, in Argentina or somewhere else. The decisive thing was that the '**people without a land**' at last needed a '**land without people**'.

Herzl envisaged a well-organized exodus from the slavery of 'Egypt': first the poor, those without rights and the persecuted; then the skilled workers; then the middle class with possessions; and finally the rich. In this way everyone could move in groups to the land allotted them in a new state – led by their rabbis – after achieving rights under a Jewish charter. Herzl rejected a gradual illegal infiltration. The power behind the state, the *persona* recognized as the legal representative of the wandering people, would be the 'Society of Jews'. Distinct from this was the 'Jewish Company', as the acquiring body and the representative of the community which held the land by law. There could be help from a development bank, and all this would be organized and looked after by a supervisory committee. Religious feelings and the longing for a homeland would help. But one thing was also clear to the enlightened Herzl: this state of Jews was not to be a hierocratic state of God, but a modern state with freedom and social justice (and a seven-hour working day!), committed to tolerance on all sides.

Theodor Herzl was not just an inspiring speaker, a brilliant pamphleteer, a passionate dramatist and a visionary Romantic, whose 1902 Zionist novel of the future, *Old New Land*, stirred the imagination of many Jews as much as his programmatic work *The Jewish State*. He was also a gifted organizer and diplomat who quickly made his mark on the international scene. Thus he succeeded in bringing together the Zionist movements, giving them an organizational and programmatic basis, and preserving their unity despite enormous difficulties. In 1897 – three years after the Dreyfus trial – the First **International Zionist Congress** took place in Basel, led by Herzl. It approved a first basic programme for the Zionist movement, the 'Basel programme'. At the centre of this programme stood the 'creation of a home for the Jewish people, publicly secured by law'. It was to be (and here Herzl had to fall into line) 'in Palestine'.

On this basis, as President of the World Zionist Organization (WZO), Herzl now fought for his ideas, always caught up in battles to lay down demarcation lines to the right and the left (his central organ was the Viennese journal *Die Welt*). For Herzl was opposed both to a depoliticizing of Zionism by the culture Zionism of an Achad ha-Am, who put forward the idea of a cultural spiritual centre and neglected the political dimension, and to a religious loading by nationalistically religious Orthodox Jews. Finally, he was also opposed to a one-sided politicization which sought to express itself in the establishment of a socialist political party. So from the start, Herzl's movement was under considerable pressure; he personally suffered as a result of the marked tensions and pamphlet campaigns. He was even indignantly accused by Russian Jews of betraying the land of Israel because he argued in favour of Jewish charter rights in British Uganda: a substitute solution in the face of new pogroms. And over the question of Palestine itself, despite negotiations with Kaiser Wilhelm II and the Turkish sultan, along with Baron Edmond de Rothschild (who in 1882 had founded the Zikhron Ya'akov settlement) and other Jewish personalities, he could not achieve any concrete results with the pope and the British government.

All the conflicts, abuse and disappointments sapped Herzl's strength and were a contributory cause to his exhaustion and sudden death at the age of forty-four, on 3 July 1904, before he could reap the fruits of his restless work. But, as tends to happen, after Herzl's death and an enormous funeral in Vienna, it became clear to all that this selfless man was the real father of the Jewish state. Moreover, very soon after the foundation of the state of Israel, in August 1949, in accordance with his wishes his bones were brought from Vienna to Jerusalem, where they were interred in a memorial on Mount Herzl.

The year of Herzl's death in fact marked the second *aliyah* – after the pogroms in Russia and Poland. The first Hebrew high school (in Jaffa) and academy of art (in Jerusalem) were founded in 1906; the first kibbutz (Degania south of Lake Kinneret) and the first modern Jewish city (Tel Aviv) were founded in 1909, as was the first Jewish self-defence movement, Ha-Shomer ('The Watcher'); it had manifestly become necessary.

3. Towards the foundation of a state: Chaim Weizmann

It was only because Herzl had made the weak Zionist movement a strong international organization that it was recognized by the British government, which as early as 1914 declared war on the Osman empire and was thus to be directly confronted with the Palestine question. The most important figure in the Zionist movement at the time of the First World War was Dr **Chaim Weizmann** (1874-1952), born in Pinsk and educated in Berlin and Freiburg, Switzerland.[13] Enthused by Herzl's ideas at an early stage, he advocated, however, a 'synthetic Zionism' which would combine the aims of political Zionism with Jewish culture. From 1903 Professor of Biochemistry in Manchester, between 1916 and 1919 he was head of the munitions laboratories of the British Admiralty. He was the one who was now to make the decisive contacts with the British statesman James Arthur Balfour. As early as 1916 the British government had made a secret agreement (the Sykes-Picot agreement) with the French over the partition of the Holy Land, which excluded the territory west of the Jordan from Arab territory. When British troops advanced towards Palestine in 1916/1917, the British government was of course highly interested in Jewish support against the Turks.

This was the historical opportunity for which the Zionists had waited so long, and which they now thought to exploit. In 1917 Weizmann received from Lord Balfour, now British Foreign Minister, the official declaration (in a letter to Lord Rothschild) that 'Her Majesty's Government' viewed with favour the establishment of a '**national home**' for the Jewish people in Palestine and would use its best endeavours to facilitate the achievement of this object.[14] 'A national home'! That had been the demand of the First International Zionist Congress. At last it had been confirmed in a politically relevant document – and by England, the world power at the time. Had the Zionists achieved their goal?

This so-called **Balfour Declaration** seems clear, and yet it contains an addition which should not be suppressed. For the Declaration states at the same time: 'it being clearly understood that nothing shall be done which may prejudice the civil and religious rights of existing non-Jewish communities in Palestine, or the rights and political status enjoyed by Jews in any other country'.[15] It was on this precise point that the conflict was to focus: the 'civil and religious rights of existing non-Jewish communities in Palestine'. For not a few of the leading Zionist thought from the beginning only of their own rights, those of the Jewish immigrants, and not the rights of others, of an Arab population which had been settled for more than a millennium.

A few weeks after the Balfour Declaration, at Hanukkah 1917, General Allenby – the bridge between Jordan and the West Bank still recalls his name even now – entered Jerusalem at the head of the British troops: the four-hundred-year-old Osman Islamic rule was ended. The president of the Zionist Commission now formed at the wish of the British government, as a link between the British government and the Jewish population, was to be none other than Chaim Weizmann. As early as 1918 he founded the Hebrew University of Jerusalem; it was dedicated in 1925 on Mount Scopus. From 1920 to 1931, and again from 1935-1946, he served as President of the World Zionist Organization. But how did the story unfold?

As early as 1919, the World Zionist Organization – using the Balfour Declaration as its Magna Carta – had presented a map at the Paris Peace Conference. On it the 'home' of the Jews comprised all Palestine, including Transjordan – i.e. far more than the territories of a 'Greater Israel' which have been occupied since 1967. As the old Zionist and historian Simha Flapan (Secretary of the Mapai Party between 1954 and 1981 and head of the Department for Arab Affairs) has only recently emphasized,[16] this remained the aim of the key Zionist leaders, propagated more secretly than openly. They differed only over methods – whether these should be more diplomatic and evolutionary or implemented by military force. In 1937, for example, the Twentieth Zionist Congress confirmed, with the support of all parties, that the Jews had an unalienable right to settle in all parts of Palestine – on both sides of the Jordan.

In order to justify such rights and settle people of different nations, languages, cultures and socio-economic backgrounds from all over the world in this one country, the Zionists, the majority of whom were secularized, had to appeal to religion and the Bible. They had to appeal to the religious traditions binding on all Jews: to the memory of the state sovereignty which had been lost two thousand years previously; to the frontiers of the empire of David and Solomon in the heyday of the old Israel. And here already it becomes clear that **different paradigms** were to be thought valid and disputed in the coming Jewish state: not only elements of the modern Enlightenment paradigm (P V: a parliamentary democracy), but also those of the paradigm of the Davidic empire (P II: the union of the kingdom of Judah and the northern kingdom, with Jerusalem as capital and the frontiers extended as widely as possible). Small religious parties and the Chief Rabbi's office would ensure that an independent religious jurisdiction was introduced (P III), and that the mediaeval rabbinic paradigm (P IV) would be brought to bear in determining who was a Jew and deciding some questions of private and family law.

However, there was still some way to go to achieve the goal of the foundation of a state. Still, after the First World War a **third** *aliyah* took place, made up above all of Polish immigrants, the majority of whom founded agricultural settlements. Within the Zionist organization, which had meanwhile become a mass movement, there were increasingly vigorous discussions about the aims and methods of Zionism: about strategy and tactics, about economic policy, about the foundation of a Jewish Agency for Palestine (as desired by the League of Nations), but above all about what attitude to have to England, the power with the mandate. For in 1920, by a resolution of the League of Nations, Palestine became an **official British mandate**: the land east of the Jordan (Transjordan) was detached to form a separate territory, and in 1921 the British put it under the Hashemite Emir Abdallah in Amman, who after independence in 1946 was to become King of Jordan (Abdallah's younger brother Faisal was similarly installed as king of Iraq in 1921; the monarchy fell in 1958). In 1922 the League of Nations called on Great Britain 'in recognition of the historical links between the Jewish people and Palestine to facilitate Jewish immigration and settlement in the country'. However, despite all Jewish demands, Great Britain continued to prohibit this in Transjordan.

So in 1924 there began the **fourth** *aliyah*. This was again made up of Poles, the majority of whom settled in the cities on the Mediterranean coast. However, the different ideological wings of Zionism (in addition to the religious Orthodox there were also numerous Jewish Socialists and Communists) would still not be reconciled. Finally, in 1929, a **Jewish Agency** was founded in Zurich – made up of Zionists and non-Zionists. Chaim Weizmann had advocated a conciliatory policy towards Israel at this time: instead of exhausting themselves in military clashes, the Jews should devote all their energies to building up economic positions in Palestine which would become trumps for later political claims. And no one can dispute that the Jewish resettlement of Palestine led to a quite remarkable economic boom in a country which under Osman rule had been largely under-farmed, impoverished, desolated and deforested. Here, contrary to all the widespread caricatures, the Jews showed what they could achieve in the agriculture with which they had persevered for so long.

However, it had long since become evident that the position put forward in the Balfour Declaration was essentially a **contradictory** one. It made a decisive contribution towards Palestine becoming one of the most contested lands on earth. For experts on the situation and leading Zionists knew one thing which was underestimated by many who took a stand in the spirit of European nationalism and colonialism. Palestine was not the **'land without people'** into which the 'people without land' could simply move. In Palestine, Herzl's all-too-understandable great vision did not seem to work.

4. Not a land without people: the problem of the Palestinians

The reason is simple: in the relatively small land of Palestine there was already a **considerable indigenous population,** six out of every seven of whom were **Arabs.**[17] However, if they were not simply ignored by the settlers, they were looked on with indifference or at best condescension, and their status and rights were increasingly abused – as though the settlers alone had the right to all Palestine.

The consequence was that, although to begin with the Palestinian Arabs had hardly any political organization, they began increasingly to defend themselves against the waves of Jewish immigrants. There were anti-Jewish 'revolts' as early as 1920 and 1929, by no means just by Arab extremists, but by inhabitants of Palestine who had been settled there for centuries. For the number of Zionist settlers was increasing rapidly – here Herzl's vision was being fulfilled. Settlers grew almost tenfold, from 60,000 in 1919 to around 600,000 in the 1940s.[18] The chief motivation for immigration was not so much the Zionist vision as simply anxiety about antisemitism - first particularly in the Ukraine and Poland, where there was the largest Jewish community outside the United States and where in addition to numerous legal restrictions the Jews had to endure real pogroms; then of course in Nazi Germany; and finally throughout Europe. But how was this problem in Palestine to be deal with?

Within the Zionist movement **two main parties** formed over the Arab question; they became engaged in vigorous conflict, and were embodied in two personalities.

– On the one side was **David Ben-Gurion** (1886-1973),[19] born in Poland. As early as 1906 he was moved by Herzl's ideas to emigrate to Palestine, where he first worked on the land. He soon became a leader of the Jewish workers' movement, was expelled by the Turks, and then advanced in the USA to become the organizer of the Jewish Legion. He returned to Palestine in 1918, and in 1920 became co-founder and General Secretary of the Jewish trade union Histadrut; in 1930 he also founded the Workers' Party (Mapai). Ben-Gurion and the Zionist socialists (supported by the liberals) were primarily interested in building up a socialist society in Palestine. Through immigration and settlement a viable Jewish economic structure was to be built up as far as possible without conflict, but rather in co-operation with the Arab workers. In this way, step by step, a Jewish state was to be established. Ben-Gurion's view was that in the more distant future this should also embrace Transjordan.

– On the other side there was **Vladimir Jabotinsky** (1880-1940),[20] a journalist born in Odessa, a multilingual and powerful orator and already at an early stage a leading Zionist activist in pre-Revolutionary Russia. During the First World War he became the founder of the Jewish Legion which fought with the Allies against the Turks for the liberation of Palestine. The direct aim of Vladimir Jabotinsky and his Revisionist Party was a Jewish state within the biblical frontiers on both sides of the Jordan, which could not be achieved without armed force. There was need for battle-trained young Jews from Palestine and all over the world. A sovereign state backed up by military power was the presupposition for a mass Jewish immigration. So a trial of strength with the British and the Arabs was inevitable.

As a result, as early as 1920 the right-wing Zionist Jabotinsky organized the Haganah, that Jewish underground army which drew its recruits from the Jewish Legion and the defence organizations of the Jewish settlements in Palestine. In Jerusalem at Easter 1920 it ventured on a first public confrontation with excited Arab masses. Jabotinsky and the leaders of the Haganah were arrested by the British, but set free again. In 1925, now in open dispute with the moderate Weizmann, Jabotinsky founded his own aggressive New Zionist Organization, with Fascist and terrorist features. This worked for 'a Jewish state on both sides of the Jordan' and for 'social justice without class struggles' (a 'Revisionist Zionism' as opposed to the Socialists). Jabotinsky thought that the Arabs of Palestine could eventually settle in other Arab countries, but not the Jews.

However, not only he, but also Ben-Gurion, whose whole policy had from the start had been aimed at the greatest possible territorial expansion of the Jewish 'home', counted on so-called 'transfers' of the 'Arab population'. In the age of nationalism, imperialism and colonialism (not to mention the resettlements by Stalin and Hitler), these were largely accepted as political means. Indeed England and France had arbitrarily divided up the whole of the Near and Middle East – breaking the British pledge to the Arabs! – by sometimes arbitrary frontiers and 'zones of influence', in which a people without power and a lobby, like the Muslim Kurds (and the Christian Armenians earlier) had no chance.

But immediately after the founding of the Jewish Agency in Palestine there was again considerable unrest among the Arabs and a massacre of Jews in Hebron. So, long ago, there began that endless cycle of violence and counter-violence which reached a first climax between 1936 and 1939, and which even now has Israel and the world on edge. After 1937, Jabotinsky was commander of the terrorist underground movement Irgun Tzvai Leumi (Etzel) which in 1931 broke away from the Hagana, the military arm of the radical right-wing Revisionist Party. Irgun wanted deliberately to sow hatred and hostility by planned provocations and arbitrary bombings, and to attempt to fight the Arabs with the terrorist methods and practices which thirty years later were to be the model for Al-Fatah, the Palestinian terrorist organization under the leadership of Yassir Arafat.[21]

Already at that time the Arab resistance was largely underestimated by the Zionists, who on the whole constantly pursued a policy of economic, political and later above all military *faits accomplis*. Of course the Arabs in Palestine were not yet organized into a state or quasi-state. Since the sixteenth century they had been under Osman rule; since the First World War they had been under British rule; and, as we have heard, the present-day frontiers were laid down only after the First World War by England and France. At first these Palestinian Arabs could hardly conceive of an independent state. And yet the Palestinian Arabs, too, had their own identity, which distinguished them from Syrian, Egyptian or Mesopotamian Arabs – not to mention Palestinian Jews. And particularly the Zionist immigrants, who since the 1880s had become increasingly numerous, provoked a growing

Palestinian nationalism, indeed a modern Palestinian nation.[22] When the Palestinian people, to whom the Jews long attempted to deny the character of a people, nationality, and often even a name and an existence, would gain the right to national self-determination was only a matter of time.[23]

The general strike in May 1936 and the subsequent three-year revolt (with almost 3,000 Arab, 1,200 Jewish and 700 British victims) manifested a strong national consciousness on the part of the Palestinians. However, here it became quite evident that the Palestinians, with a good deal of passion but without much sense of reality or readiness for co-operation, were putting themselves on the wrong side. Because no one in the West took it seriously, from 1936 to 1943 the Palestinian nationalist movement even collaborated under the Mufti of Jerusalem, Amin el-Husseini, with Hitler's Germany, just as half a century later, out of frustration, Yassir Arafat was to collaborate with Iraq's dictator Saddam Hussein.

And what about the **British government**? Having promised Palestine to the Arabs and the Jews during the First World War, in the face of these fronts it increasingly manoeuvred itself into a **hopeless policy**. How could it both further the new Jewish home and defend the rights of the old indigenous Arab population at the same time? That could not work out in the long run. But what was to be done about the armed conflicts between Jews and Arabs which had kept increasing since the late 1930s? What was to be done about the illegal immigration of so many European Jews which had resulted in a **fifth** *aliyah* after the Nazi seizure of power in 1933? What was to be done about the fact that the Hagana was now fighting simultaneously against both the Arabs **and** the British?

As early as 1937, the report of the British Peel Commission recommended the division of west Palestine into a Jewish and an Arab state. This was firmly rejected by the Arabs, but was accepted by Ben-Gurion, the leader of the Workers' Party, the strongest force within Zionism, for wise tactical considerations (as a cloak for the gradual conquest of the whole of Palestine) . However, one thing seemed clear to the British. There was no question of setting up a Jewish state against the will of the Arabs (this was still stated in a White Paper of 1939). On the contrary, the Jewish immigration was now to be limited to 75,000 annually, with a total halt after five years.

But the **Second World War** (1939-1945) also brought the collapse of this policy. For now once again the British were glad of any support from the Jews, who moreover were volunteering in Palestine for the

British Army. So the British did away with the restrictions on acquiring land in Palestine and transferred control over Jewish immigration to the Jewish Agency.

Nevertheless, terrorism continued against the British, above all from Irgun Tzvai Leumi, which was now under the leadership of **Menachem Begin** (born 1913) – Jabotinsky, more controversial than any of the other Zionists, had died suddenly of a heart attack in America in 1940.[24] Begin was a young Polish lawyer who emigrated to Palestine in 1942; it was his declared intent to bomb the British out of Palestine. The Polish Jews, increasingly oppressed since the regaining of independence by their homeland, manifestly seemed more ready than others to take violent action. Above all Begin's Irgun (along with Lehi – the 'Stern Gang') bears responsibility for terrorist attacks in the Arab markets of Jerusalem and Haifa; for the murder of the British Commissioner for the Near East, Lord Moyne, in 1944; for the partial destruction of the King David Hotel in Jerusalem, used by the British government, in 1946, with the death of ninety-one victims; and in 1948 for the murder (by Lehi), greeted with indignation all over the world, of the United Nations mediator Count Folke Bernadotte after he had put forward a new plan for partition. These terrorist attacks were always officially condemned by the Jewish Agency (whose residence had been bombed by the Arabs in 1948) and Haganah, but in fact they were tolerated. When about 200,000 survivors of the Holocaust were secretly brought to Palestine ('illegal immigration', *'aliyah beth'*) with the support of Haganah and all the Jewish underground movements, the increasing conflicts between the Jewish and Arab population forced a decision.

Nahum Goldmann (1895-1982), a leading Zionist who fled from Germany in 1933, was a real contrast to Begin, and also to Ben-Gurion. He was with the League of Nations in Geneva from 1936 to 1940 as the representative of the Jewish Agency, and later worked in America towards the foundation of the state of Israel as a 'statesman without a state'.[25] However, in contrast to Ben-Gurion and other leading Zionists, Goldmann, who is also one of the founders of the great *Encyclopaedia Judaica*, was from the start, and particularly as President of the Jewish World Congress (1949-1977), decisively in favour of co-operation between Jews and Arabs. As an untiring sponsor of Jewish-Arab understanding, this man, who was highly respected inside and outside the Jewish world, of necessity came into conflict with those right-wing and left-wing Israeli politicians who were working openly or clandestinely for a homogenous Jewish state to extend over all or at least the greater part of Palestine. Even a Chaim Weizmann was unwilling to grant the Palestinians any national rights or aims, which he quite naturally claimed for the Jews. We cannot overlook the fact that from the beginning a shadow fell on the foundation of the state of Israel – in complete contrast to the intentions of Herzl and many other Zionists. How differently so much would have turned out had people listened more to Nahum Goldmann (or Martin Buber).

5. The state of Israel: David Ben-Gurion

One thing was certain: the dream which many Zionists had of a home had only been half-fulfilled in Palestine. Certainly a land had been found, even the land of the Jews, but peace and quiet for the Jewish people had not been achieved even now. On the contrary, the 'Jewish problem' had been transferred from Europe to Palestine. And this problem was to become even more acute when Zionism, which in the period between the wars had established communal autonomy, far-reaching self-government and indeed a parliament, Israel's Knesset (= assembly, its name and the number of its delegates, 120, being taken over from the 'great assembly' of Ezra and Nehemiah), finally achieved its goal, the foundation of a state. The World War and the Holocaust had not laid the foundation for it, but they did help to speed it on.

As early as May 1942, **David Ben-Gurion**, the rival of the liberal Weizmann, had got the better of the more conciliatory elements at a Zionist conference in New York with the help of militant American Zionists: his 'Biltmore Programme' (named after the Biltmore Hotel, where it was presented) in fact aimed at a state embracing **the whole of Palestine**; there was no mention either of any involvement of the Arabs in shaping it or of any frontiers. The aim was not a Jewish state in Palestine, but Palestine as a Jewish state.

However, when a new constellation of powers took shape after the end of the Second World War and the **United Nations** now assumed responsibility, things turned out differently. The British mandate was to end on 14 May 1948. Nahum Goldmann had previously argued for partitioning and the creation of a viable Jewish state in an appropriate part of Palestine, and Chaim Weizmann presented a draft plan for partition which underwent further major changes. A solid UN majority (USA and the USSR) finally resolved on 29 November 1947 to **partition Palestine** into a Jewish and an Arab state – with clearly defined borders, an economic union of the two states, and the internationalization of Jerusalem under UN administration. The Jews, who at this point in time owned 10% of the land in Palestine, were to be given 55%, around 15,000 square kilometres, and the Arab population, which at 1.3

million was almost twice as numerous, 11,000. The Arabs – the main powers in the Arab League (at that time the Palestinians still had no political representation or organization) – rejected this partitioning. This was to prove a serious historical mistake, since in this way **the Arabs** missed the opportunity of **founding their own Palestinian state,** which they now want so badly.

However, with their rejection the Arabs in fact played into the hands of Ben-Gurion, head not only of the Workers' Party, but from 1935 also of the Jewish Agency and the Zionist executive in Palestine. He had always been secretly striving for a Jewish state which would comprise the whole of Palestine. Moreover, with greater political wisdom than the Arabs, despite his reservations, Ben-Gurion agreed to the partition plan and resolutely moved towards the foundation of a state. On 15 May 1948 **the state of Israel was proclaimed** by the National Jewish Council. That in contrast to the representatives of the Jewish Agency in Washington David Ben-Gurion, who went on to become Israel's first Prime Minister and Minister of Defence (1948-1953 and 1955-1963), omitted in the Declaration of Independence to mention the frontiers laid down by the United Nations was a cause of concern for some people at the time.

Now very recently – since the publication in 1982 by the Israeli state archive of Ben-Gurion's war diaries, and thousands of documents relating to the foundation of the state which had previously been kept secret – we have obtained precise information about the motives and intentions of Ben-Gurion and leading Zionists. And thanks to the labours of the Israeli historian and journalist **Simha Flapan** (1911-1987), whom I have already mentioned, the enormous material was closely investigated with the support of American foundations and a large team of scholars at Harvard University. Flapan, who after his early years in Poland was active on behalf of Socialist Zionism, lived for more than forty years on an Israeli *kibbutz* and for almost thirty years served as General Secretary of the left-wing Mapam Party, the only party within Zionism to recognize the right of the Arab Palestinians to self-determination. It worked with other small groups for peaceful collaboration between Jews and Arabs. Flapan is above all suspicion of hostility to Israel. And if here, as a European Christian theologian, basing myself on these researches, for the sake of historical truth I have to speak of the ambiguous role of significant Jewish personalities in the 'birth of Israel', I do not want for a moment to forget the monstrous history of Christian and European guilt which forms the background to this birth. Nor do I want to allow any shadow of doubt to arise over the justification for this state of Israel to exist and over its right to live within secure and recognized frontiers. I shall return to this in detail in Part Three. Yet none of this tells against the need for demythologization where myths threaten to suppress or conceal the truth.

This is the very point at which Simha Flapan began, and in a first book published just before his death he was able to present his conclusions on the foundation of the state. In the introduction he acknowledges how, like most Israelis, he had 'always been under the influence of certain myths that had been accepted as historical truth'.[26] The first of seven myths on which he claims that the whole 'mythology of the state of Israel' is built up runs: 'Zionist acceptance of the United Nations Partition Resolution of November 29, 1947, was a far-reaching compromise by which the Jewish community abandoned the concept of a Jewish state in the whole of Palestine and recognized the right of the Palestinians to their own state. Israel accepted this sacrifice because it anticipated the implementation of the resolution in peace and cooperation with the Palestinians.'[27]

But as the researches of Flapan and his team have demonstrated, this was 'actually only a tactical move in an overall strategy aimed first at thwarting the creation of an Palestinian Arab state through a secret agreement with Abdallah of Transjordan, whose annexation of the territory allocated for a Palestinian state was to be the first step in his dream of a Greater Syria. Second, it sought to increase the territory assigned by the UN to the Jewish state.'[28]

So was the war between Jews and Arabs really inevitable? This is often said to have been the case. But before Israel's Declaration of Independence many Palestinian leaders and groups had made considerable efforts towards a modus vivendi. It was Ben-Gurion's resistance to a Palestinian state which had first driven the Palestinians into the arms of the Mufti of Jerusalem, who was a fanatical opponent of the state of Israel and therefore was not afraid even to make contact with the Jews' deadly enemy, Adolf Hitler. The Arabs accepted an American proposal for mediation presented at the last minute: this provided for a three-months ceasefire on condition that Israel temporarily postponed its declaration of independence. However, the provisional Israeli government under Ben-Gurion rejected it by a narrow majority (6: 4). So did Israel, as is often claimed, keep holding out its hand for a peace treaty but, since no Arab leader had recognized the right of Israel to exist, found no one with whom peace discussions could be carried on? 'On the contrary,' Flapan explains at length, 'from the end of World War II to 1952, Israel turned down successive proposals made by Arab states and by neutral mediators that might have brought about an accommodation.'[29] So Ben-Gurion had deliberately reckoned on an ongoing conflict with the Arab world; he knew that the USA and the Western world were on his side – not least the Federal Republic of Germany, which had been newly founded in 1949.

After the foundation of the state, **political reconciliation with Germany** was Ben-Gurion's greatest achievement as a statesman. Ben-Gurion really sought an understanding with Adenauer's Germany – and that so few years after the Holocaust! Adenauer and Ben-Gurion were both politicians with extraordinary skills; they were very aware of their power and responsibility, but also extremely pragmatic and matter-of-fact. Ben-Gurion was convinced that the payment of reparations would help Israel economically and Germany morally, and when in 1952 Menachem Begin, then still in opposition, openly branded all Germans (even Adenauer) Nazis and murderers, and threatened civil war, Ben-Gurion called the ideology of such opponents to reparations Fascist, and threatened them with military intervention. So he succeeded in agreeing reparations with the Federal Republic of Germany (the Luxembourg Agreement, the treaty with Israel) which granted Israel more than 3.45 billion Deutschemark up to 1965 (above all for the settlement and reinstatement of Jewish refugees in Israel). In 1965 diplomatic relations were also established, under Chancellor Ludwig Erhard.

Finally, after the withdrawal of the British troops, Ben-Gurion was able to safeguard the existence of the state of Israel in the first two decisive wars with the Arabs and took decisive steps towards both the technological-economic and scientific-cultural development of the state of Israel and the incorporation of the enormous masses of immigrants from all over the world. However, he was not able to create peace for his state. On the contrary, because the whole policy of this 'armed prophet' was *a priori* aimed at the maximum possible territorial expansion of the state of Israel and thus *ipso facto* against a state of Palestine, and there had been no move towards reconciliation on the Arab side, he laid the foundation for an arms race, for constantly new wars, for a high level of state debt and an economic (some Israelis even say a moral) decline. From 1948 on, all Arab efforts were addressed towards reversing the foundation of the state of Israel and settling the situation in Palestine in their favour by force. The consequence was that from the day of its founding onwards, the young state was in fact on a war footing with its Arab neighbours.

6. Five wars – and no peace

Five bloody wars of different characters were to be fought between Arabs and Israelis within the next twenty-five years.[30] To anticipate the result: the small state of Israel fighting for independence became the military power of Greater Israel, occupying wide areas of Arab territory; and the indigenous Palestinian people of around 5 million became an oppressed and refugee people (in the West all too often sweepingly described as 'extremists' and 'terrorists').

1. The **War of Independence** which broke out on the day the state was founded was fought from 15 May 1948 to 24 February 1949. Egypt, Iraq, Syria and Lebanon were caught up in it. It ended in Israeli victory because of the lack of unity in the Arab camp and the poor quality of its armies. The partition of Jerusalem was confirmed; Israel's territory was now considerably greater than that promised by the UN partition plan: part of the territory west of the Jordan was granted to the Jordanians (the 'West Bank'). The dark side of the victory was that because of war, anxiety and intimidation (the attack, massacre and shooting of the women and children of the peaceful Palestinian village of Dir Yassin planned in cold blood by Irgun and Lehi acted as a signal throughout Palestine), there was a mass flight which spread rapidly, along with the expulsion of around 850,000 Arabs from their ancestral lands into the adjoining Arab states (this was not planned, but it was tolerated by the state of Israel). 360 Arab villages and 14 cities within the state of Israel were razed to the ground, thus making it impossible for the Arab refugees to return; hence the great refugee camps and the rise of the Palestinian liberation movements.

In the following years there were mass immigrations of Jews, mostly from Africa and Asia, so that the Jewish population (which in 1947 was still around 600,000) more than doubled. A remarkable agricultural cultivation of the land began. For unlike the Arabs, the Israelis were able to exploit the scientific, technological and industrial capacity offered by the modern paradigm to the full.

2. The **Sinai campaign** lasted from 29 October to 8 November 1956. After Arab terrorist attacks and the closure of the vital Strait of Tiran, Israel launched a preventive war against Gamal Abd-el Nasser's Egypt – precisely timed to coincide with the disastrous Franco-British military intervention (the Suez crisis). The Gaza strip and the Sinai peninsula were occupied. Forced to a cease-fire by the USSR and the USA, in December 1956 Israel withdrew from Sinai and then also from the

Gaza strip in return for the guarantee of free navigation in the Gulf of Akaba.

3. The **Six Day War** lasted from 5-11 June 1967. Israel again pre-empted the massive advance of Egyptian, Syrian and Jordanian troops by a preventive war and the destruction of the Egyptian air force on the ground. In a war on three fronts the 25-mile long Gaza strip controlled by Egypt was occupied, along with Sinai, the Syrian Golan heights, the West Bank of the Jordan (about 70 miles long by 30 miles wide), and above all Arab Jerusalem.

There were several indirect consequences. For the first time – out of anxiety about a new Holocaust and then in proud joy at the victory – even the non-Zionist Jews throughout the world, and above all in the United States, identified themselves with the state of Israel. Along with this went massive economic and financial support, which led to an intensified economic boom and, even more importantly, to a renewal of the awareness of being not only an international religious community but really a people. However, **Israel now lost the historical opportunity to achieve real peace** from a position of strength (as was desired by many Israeli intellectuals and politicians) in exchange for the occupied territories and to collaborate in the establishment of a peaceful independent Arab state of Palestine. Israel became an **occupying power**, and from now on became mainly responsible for the absence of peace in the Near East.

4. The **Yom Kippur War**, from 6-25 October 1973, began with a surprise attack by Egypt and Syria, supported by the Soviet Union. Egypt on the Suez Canal and Syria on the Golan Heights launched a massive and initially successful offensive which could only be stopped with heavy Israeli losses. After more than two weeks of bitter fighting there was a ceasefire and then later – in 1974, under pressure from the USA – an agreement over troop withdrawal with Egypt and Syria. But again there was no peace.

On the contrary, the Jewish settlements in the occupied territories, principally called for by the religious parties, have since then been a constant object of dispute. It was above all the tensions over the controversial Jewish settlements in the occupied territories which in 1976/77 led to the resignation of the Labour Government and new elections. For the first time in the history of Israel the Labour Party (Mapai) was now in opposition. The Herut Party, founded in 1948 in the spirit of the right-wing extremist Jabotinsky, or rather the right-wing conservative Likud bloc, came to power, all under the former

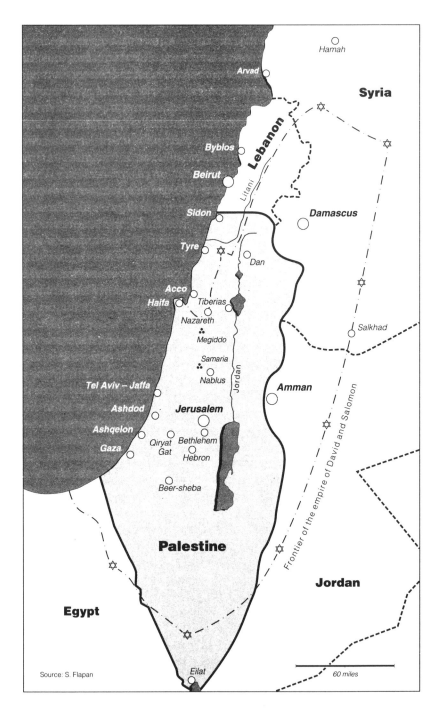

Zionist Plan of Palestine, 1919

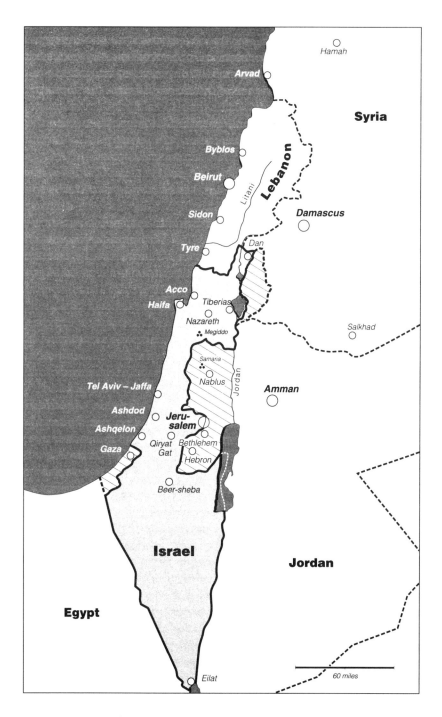

The State of Israel Today with the Occupied Territories

terrorist and notorious Irgun head **Menachem Begin,** who was now prime minister and called for direct negotiations. It should not be forgotten that he was the first prime minister of Israel to have been affected directly by the Holocaust.

Then the Egyptian president **Anwar el-Sadat** took a bold initiative. In November 1977 he visited Jerusalem for three days – in the hope that all occupied territories would be given back for the sake of peace with the Arabs. However, Begin refused this. Only after American intervention was there **an agreement** (three decades after the foundation of the state) – on 17 September 1978 – between Egypt, the United States and Israel. This **Camp David Agreement** came about through the mediation of the American President Jimmy Carter. Finally, on 26 March 1979, under pressure from Washington, Israel concluded a peace treaty with Israel which led to Israel's withdrawal from Sinai.

However, because the main issue, the **Palestinian question**, was not included in the solution, all the other states now sabotaged not only Israel but also Egypt. So there was still no peace. The military situation in the Near East remained unstable; Israel fulfilled hardly any of the pledges relating to Palestinian autonomy contained in the treaty; the terrorist actions, now carried on by the Palestinians, continued; and after a Palestinian attack on a bus in Tel Aviv which claimed 45 victims, the Israeli forces occupied the whole of Southern Lebanon (15 March to 13 June 1978).

5. The **invasion of Lebanon** which followed on 6 July 1982 was disguised as 'Operation Peace for Galilee'. It was quite clearly an **aggressive war,** pursued right up to the Lebanese capital Beirut, and directed above all against the 'terrorist' PLO. In it Christian militia, under the cover of the Israeli military, could commit massacres in the Palestinian Sabra and Shatila camps which shocked the world. The aim was the final liquidation of the Palestinians and the establishment of a Christian rump state of Lebanon. Prime Minister Begin, forced to justify his aggressive policy by the first mass peace demonstration in Israel, appealed – rightly, as historical investigations have meanwhile shown – to the example of the first prime minister of Israel, who through a secret policy had striven for what Begin was doing openly: 'He cited Ben-Gurion's plan to divide Lebanon by setting up a Christian state north of the Litani river, his relentless efforts to prevent the creation of a Palestinian state; and, during the 1948 war, his wholesale destruction of Arab villages and townships within the borders of Israel and the expulsion of their inhabitants from the country – all in the interest of establishing a homogeneous Jewish state.'[31]

Through Israel's intervention, the chaos in a country already torn into a variety of Muslim and Christian factions was even more complete. The PLO had to withdraw, but it was unbeaten. The Israeli troops, themselves in a hopeless situation, had to withdraw again: a lost war. Menachem Begin was now replaced by Yitzhak Shamir. However, in Lebanon Syria had the best cards, and the fanatical Christian general, Michel Aoun, dropped by the Americans and the French, finally had to capitulate in autumn 1990. Since then Syria has controlled the whole of Lebanon. The conflict of Israel with the Palestinian Arabs and also the conflict with Syria and Jordan continue to rumble on. Indeed the Palestinian Liberation Organization, already thought to be dead, is now becoming even more of a popular movement.

Because of the latest research, my account of the foundation of the state and its consequences turned out more critical than I originally assumed and had written in an earlier draft; I note this with regret. And what will the future be? At the time of writing (after the Gulf War in June 1991) no one knows. We shall have to return to this tragic conflict in Part Three, and then survey the possibilities for a solution.

In a broader perspective, despite the development of the state of Israel in a way which is also disappointing to many Jews, it has to be noted that for Judaism, unlike Christianity, faith, people and land now belong together. Being a Jew is not adequately defined in either religious or ethnic terms. Certainly, as we also saw, Judaism has survived the almost two-thousand-year-period remarkably well without a temple and state, as a 'republic of scholars': despite all the catastrophes, it has an intense community life. But even if both ultra-orthodox and left-wing political, secular Jews still see the **state of Israel** as a problem: **it has fundamentally changed the situation of world Jewry.** The government of Israel has in fact taken over the central task of the Zionist World Organization: for the Zionist movement, on the other hand, the only Zionists are those who have a serious intention, or at least the ideal, of immigrating into the new state. Indeed, in Israel there are Zionists who believe that if all six million Jews in the USA, who are now disobeying the word of God, returned to their senses tomorrow and came to the promised land, the day of redemption would arrive. In the face of such Zionist exaggerations on the one hand and some Christian understatements on the other, critical questions of principle arise (and I shall go into them directly in Part Three).

Questions for the Future

🕎 Since the Holocaust it has been widely recognized that a Jewish state is an unavoidable necessity in **Judaism**. However, cannot Jewishness still be lived out as meaningfully as before, both in the land of Israel itself and in the Diaspora? The majority of Jews throughout the world do not want to return to Israel. From a religious perspective, is an independent state which is not absolutely necessary for **Judaism**, as was proved in history from 70 to 1948, really an end in itself? It may be a state of the Jewish people, but is it also a state of the Jewish religion?

✝ Should not **Christians** have understood more clearly than before that the people of the Jews, wherever it may be scattered over the world, now has its ethnic roots in the land of Israel? Even completely secularized Jews still feel different from other fellow-citizens. So is not the state of Israel a means and a sign of the ongoing existence of the covenant of God with his people?

But, some people will object from the Christian side, is it still possible from the perspective of Christian theology to go on talking of the continued existence of the covenant? Can one conceal the fact that for Christians, Jesus Christ has brought a **new covenant** which made the earlier covenant the **old covenant**? Indeed, at this point, on the dividing line between old and new, does there not stand the figure of the Jew Jesus of Nazareth, who for Christians – and only for Christians – is the Christ? Beyond dispute there is a gigantic rock in the way of Jewish-Christian understanding: for Jews a stone of stumbling, but for Christians the foundation stone.

Even in politics, we cannot avoid the theological controversy over Jesus of Nazareth which has continued down to the present day. This has happened all too often in inter-religious dialogue, out of anxiety or for convenience, on both the Jewish and the Christian sides. But I am convinced that the conditions for an open and fair dialogue are more favourable today than they have been for decades.

B. The Dispute between Jews and Christians

I. Jesus in Jewish-Christian Dialogue Today

Let us not fool ourselves: this is the most difficult question between Jews and Christians because it is fraught with quite insuperable prejudices and misunderstandings. And once again the 1980 Declaration of the German Catholic bishops on the relationship of 'the church' to Judaism, which is fundamentally positive, shows how difficult it is to formulate in a way which is not open to misunderstanding.[1] Right at the beginning of this document we read: 'Today Jewish authors, too, are discovering the "Jewishness" of Jesus', and 'anyone who encounters Jesus Christ, encounters Judaism'.[2] But should not the statements here in fact have been put the other way round? For in reality the Christian churches had begun to discover the ' "Jewishness" of Jesus' which for so long they had not wanted to perceive and take seriously (even long before the time of National Socialism), because they were interested in only one thing: 'Whoever encounters Jesus Christ, encounters Christianity.' The substantive questions are complicated and cannot all be discussed here.[3] Here the important thing is quite briefly to indicate the current state of research, in dialogue above all with Jewish authors.

1. Jesus as a Jew and Jewish scholarship

In the year 1900, **Adolf von Harnack**, the great historian and synthesist of liberal theology, had published his lectures *What is Christianity?*[4] The next year saw a response to him from a twenty-seven-year-old rabbi who shortly beforehand had gained a doctorate with the philosopher Wilhelm Dilthey in Berlin and was to become a leading figure in Judaism between the two world wars. The man was **Leo Baeck** (1873-1956): 'Most of those who describe the life of Jesus omit to point out that in each of his traits Jesus is an authentic Jewish character through and through, that a man like him could only grow up on Jewish ground, only there and nowhere else. Jesus is an authentically Jewish personality: all that he strives for and does, endures and feels, says and keeps silent about, has the stamp of a Jewish nature, is in the mould of Jewish idealism, the best that there was and is in Judaism, and was to be found only in Judaism at that time. He was a Jew among Jews: a man like him could not have emerged from any other people, and a man like him could not have been active in any other people.'[5] Could we dispute that?

After writing his *The Essence of Judaism* (1905) and other publications Leo Baeck was, amazingly, able to publish his picture of Jesus as late as 1938 in *The Gospel as a Document of the History of Jewish Faith*. The next year he was put under house arrest by the Gestapo in the College for the Science of Judaism in Berlin, where he had taught for a quarter of a century, and in 1943 was deported to Theresienstadt concentration camp, where he barely survived. He was not in fact the first Jewish scholar to have occupied himself with the figure of Jesus of Nazareth. With the paradigm shift to the modern world, it had become possible for Jews to adopt a freer attitude to their own Jewish tradition. And in this liberal atmosphere, in the nineteenth century a modern Jewish theology also came into being which applied historical criticism not only to the Hebrew Bible, the Mishnah and Talmud, but also to the New Testament.[6]

I need only mention in passing that all Jewish scholars take it for granted that Jesus of Nazareth is not a myth but a historical figure who can be dated and located: he is a quite concrete figure of Jewish history at the beginning of the 'common era' (the Christian reckoning of time), who can be investigated by **the means and methods of modern history.** In French Judaism, which had become emancipated earlier than elsewhere, it had been the philosopher of history **Joseph Salvador** who as early as 1838 had inaugurated modern Jewish research into Jesus with a two-volume scientific monograph *Jesus Christ and His Doctrine* – a historical investigation, as was shown by the subtitle: 'The History of the Birth of the Church, its Organization and its Progress during the First Century'.[7]

And what about the German-speaking world? Here the first Jew to concern himself in depth with the figure of Jesus was the Reform rabbi and philosopher of religion **Samuel Hirsch,** in his book *The System of the Religious Views of the Jews and its Relationship to Paganism, Christianity and Absolute Philosophy* (1842).[8] He was followed by **Abraham Geiger,** with his *Judaism and its History* (1864), for whom the study of the Jewish history of the time was an essential presupposition for any understanding of Jesus.[9] Then finally the great Jewish historian **Heinrich Graetz**, whom we have already encountered, also set standards in connection with Jesus and the 'origin of Christianity' in the third volume of his eleven-volume *History of the Jews* under the headings 'Sinai and Golgotha'.[10] What was new in this development? It was that all the Jewish scholars were prepared to see the **Jesus of history as a thoroughly positive figure**, but also one whom they now reclaimed completely for Judaism – as opposed to the Christian churches? Why? Because the Jesus of history, it was held, did not teach anything that a Jew of his time could not also have said, whether he regarded himself as the messiah (thus Salvador and Geiger) or not (thus Hirsch and Graetz).

This trend was to continue in the twentieth century. In 1922 – still before the period of National Socialism – what is probably the most famous Jewish book on Jesus appeared, written by **Joseph Klausner**: *Jesus of Nazareth. His Time, His Life, and His Teachings*. It was the first book on Jesus to be written in Hebrew (in Jerusalem) and was then translated into numerous other languages.[11] For Klausner, Jesus is 'more Jewish' than the Jews and is dangerous to 'national Judaism' precisely because of his '**exaggerated** Judaism'.[12] Mention should also be made of the important works by **Claude G. Montefiore**, the leading representative of English Reform Judaism and the universalist President of the liberal World Union for Progressive Judaism. As early as 1909 he had investigated the synoptic sources of the story of Jesus.[13] **Max Nordau**, the loyal collaborator with Theodor Herzl, the founder of the Zionist movement, may have caught the mood of many Jewish scholars of the time with the impressive formula: 'Jesus is the soul of our soul, as he is the flesh of our flesh. So who can exclude him from the Jewish people?'[14]

Then came the Holocaust – and did it bring Jewish research into Jesus to a standstill? The pleasant surprise is that, while the Holocaust interrupted research into Jesus, it did not stop it. And since the foundation of the state of Israel, the new Jewish self-awareness has produced as many publications about Jesus of Nazareth in a few decades as formerly appeared over centuries. Thus the Jewish theologian **Pinchas Lapide** can write: 'The 187 Hebrew books, researches, poems, plays, monographs, dissertations and articles which have been written about Jesus in the last twenty-seven years, since the foundation of the state of Israel, justify the press reports of a "Jesus wave" in the present-day literature of the Jewish state.'[15] And in a dialogue the same scholar told me that the common denominator of all the twenty-nine books on Jesus that he had investigated, was a sympathy and a love for Jesus of Nazareth of a kind 'which had been impossible for eighteen centuries'.[16]

However, the word 'love' may perhaps be an exaggeration: 'sympathy' is more apt, with all the connotations of respect, attention and understanding that it carries. In this context the declaration of the German episcopal conference mentioned above rightly begins by quoting the great Jewish thinker **Martin Buber**, who in his work *Two Types of Faith* described Jesus as his 'great brother',[17] whose message had been primally Jewish. Buber's pupil **Shalom Ben-Chorin** took a similar view, and clarified Buber's remark as follows: 'For me Jesus is the eternal brother; not just a human brother but my Jewish brother. I can feel his brotherly hand grasping me, for me to follow him... His faith, his unconditional faith, his simple trust in God the Father, his readiness to humble himself completely under the will of God, that is the attitude which is lived out for us in Jesus and which can bind us Jews and Christians together.'[18]

But here too we need to treat a quotation from the bishops' declaration cautiously. For what is contained in the sentences the omission of which is indicated by the three points? The points conceal Ben-Chorin's decisive reservation, and to omit this reservation from a quotation in a church document is bordering on intellectual dishonesty: 'It is not the hand of the messiah, this hand signed with the marks of the wounds; it is definitely not a divine hand, but a human hand in whose lines the deepest suffering is engraved... The faith of Jesus unites us, but faith in Jesus divides us.'[19] In other words, for Ben-Chorin, as for Buber and many other Jewish interpreters of Jesus, Jesus is a model Jew – but only a Jew; a model man – but only a man. And whatever objections Christians may have here, the important thing is that these Jewish interpreters of Jesus have overcome the reservations that many Jews still have about the New Testament, which in many respects seems to them to have been written explicitly against 'the Jews'.

2. How would the dialogue over Jesus have to begin?

One thing must be clear in the Jewish-Christian dialogue from the start. It is not only the **Jewish researchers into Jesus** from the last century, but also those of our own century, who **firmly reject the Christ of later church dogmatics**: Jesus of Nazareth, the carpenter's son – the second person of the divine Trinity? Believing Jews say that that is unacceptable – precisely because Jesus of Nazareth was a Jew. In its declaration, the

German episcopal conference confirms these difficulties in a surprising way. There we read that 'the Son of God who is consubstantial with God' seems to 'many' (it would have been better to say 'all') Jews 'something radically un-Jewish', 'something which absolutely contradicts the strict monotheism which is expressed daily for pious Jews particularly in the "Shema Israel", and may even seem blasphemy.'[20]

Truly, what would Jesus the Jew have said to all this, that Jewish Jesus whose saying has been handed down, 'Why do you call me good? No one is good but God alone'?[21] What would the Jew Jesus have made of such dogmatic formulations of Greek Hellenistic Christianity as his being 'of the same substance as God'? Jewish scholars, at any rate, are all of the opinion that it would have been impossible for Jesus as a Jew to have said anything like this of himself. And is not this perhaps also important for Christians, since for the foundation of their belief in Christ they appeal to the Jew Jesus of Nazareth? But the bishops' declaration evidently did not want to go into that more closely. On the contrary, as if they were anxious about the consequences, they ended any further discussion with a remark which brings little comfort to either side. 'The Christian must have an understanding' for this 'deepest difference of belief' between Jews and Christians, 'even if he himself does not see any contradiction to monotheism in the doctrine that Jesus has the dignity of Son of God'.[22]

An urgent question arises: in this way, is not the **dialogue** about Jesus, who for Christians is the Christ, broken off before it has really begun? At any rate, we are not shown any way out of the cul-de-sac at this decisive point. But cannot this way really be found? Years before this declaration, in a conversation with the Jewish scholar Pinchas Lapide, who is also a pupil of Martin Buber, I had suggested that the Jewish-Christian dialogue should begin not **'from above'**, as it were from heaven, from the high christology of the councils, in which unfortunately no Jewish Christians could any longer take part, as they did in the so-called 'Apostolic Council' in Jerusalem, but **'from below'**. We should 'look at Jesus and his history from the earth, from the perspective of the people of the time, and ask, "What did men and women really see in him, and how did his disciples understand him?"'[23] Did the Jewish disciples of Jesus begin with an already manifest messiah or even a heavenly Son of God? Did they not rather begin with a Jewish man? This perspective 'from below' would enable us 'to go a long stretch of the way in company with the Jews, because they too could ask themselves, "Who was he really?"'[24]

At that time the pointed response of my Jewish dialogue partner was: 'By doing theology from below we can go together for thirty-three

years, the whole span of the earthly life of Jesus, and that is certainly a
good deal. What really separate us are the last forty-eight hours, from
the afternoon of the first Good Friday. They are barely two days, but
of course they are the decisive days, on which virtually the whole of
christology rests.'[25] That will now, of course, have to be discussed in
much more detail and in a more complex way. At any rate, in my 1974
book *On Being a Christian*, which formed the basis for our dialogue
in 1976, I attempted to sum up the consensus of Christian historical-
critical scholarship in the matter of the 'Jesus of history' and to analyse
it systematically. Here, I would like to to combine this consensus (which
is still valid, even though some corrections are needed)[26] with the
findings of present-day Jewish interpreters of Jesus – the aim being not
just to show a helpless sympathy for Jewish dialogue-partners who
unfortunately cannot understand such a high christology, with its
sophisticated concepts, but also a growing authentic understanding.

In the meantime, **Werner Vogler**, the Protestant theologian from
Leipzig, has produced a knowledgeable and fair survey under the title
Jewish Interpretations of Jesus in Christian Perspective (1988).[27] In its
criticism, it too recognizes the method 'from below', and its survey of
the positions of individual Jewish authors is very helpful. At the same
time, more recent works by Christian theologians and Judaists who are
engaged in discussion with their Jewish professional colleagues can be
of help here. By way of anticipation, it may be said that research into
Jesus must in future be put on even more of a sound footing! For **Jewish
interpreters of Jesus** can again make visible in a concrete way the links
between Jesus and the Jewish fellow-believers of his time. **Christian
interpreters of Jesus**, for their part, could help to bring out more clearly
the original profile of Jesus. In this way it might prove that this Jesus
is a stranger to both sides, to Jews and to non-Jews, and that the
encounter with him is a challenge to both sides.

However, here the Christian theologian will always remain aware
that the Jewish interpreter of Jesus approaches this figure from quite a
different history and with quite different feelings. Christians must not
forget for a moment all the monstrous things which have been done to
Jews over the course of time 'in the name of Jesus Christ', and
consequently what it means for a Jew to approach this figure without
antipathy and resentment, not to mention to investigate him with
'sympathy'. I cannot get out of my head something that **Samuel
Sandmel**, the Reform rabbi and professor at Hebrew Union College,
Cincinnati, and one of the greatest Jewish experts on the New Testament, who died all too early, confided to me as recently as 1968 at a
congress on the Gospels at Pittsburgh Theological Seminary. His father

still used to spit whenever the name Jesus was mentioned. So it is a minor miracle that the son should later have been publicly concerned with *A Jewish Understanding of the New Testament*.[28]

But what can we know of Jesus of Nazareth, since even according to Jewish scholars, the New Testament writings are the only source of authentic information about him?

3. What can we know of Jesus?

These **New Testament writings** are in fact by no means disinterested documentary reports, far less neutral scientific historiography. Rather, they are **committed testimonies of faith,** which already evoke faith in this Jesus. They are not interested in a real chronology, topology, even psychology of the life of Jesus. Indeed, they do not seek to offer a 'life of Jesus' in the modern sense: only two of the four Gospels contain stories about the childhood of Jesus, and none of the four contains anything further about the period before Jesus was thirty. As is well known, they begin with his preaching at that age.

But does this means that they are ruled out as historical sources for what the earthly, historical, Jewish Jesus himself said, did and suffered? Contrary to the assertions in the first half of the century of Karl Barth, Rudolf Bultmann and Paul Tillich, and on the Jewish side Samuel Sandmel and other Jewish scholars, often wrongly appealing to Albert Schweitzer's *The Quest of the Historical Jesus*[29] and based on prior dogmatic judgments, it has proved quite possible, meaningful and indeed necessary to enquire behind the testimonies of faith to the Jesus of history. For while these testimonies may not be simply reports, they do contain reports, and **have their foundation in reports of the real Jesus.** In other words, the stories of Jesus themselves prompt questions about his real history.

In the face of a still all too widespread historical scepticism it should be said that in the long and often stormy history of modern exegesis, historically the Jesus tradition has proved to be relatively reliable. And only a historical-critical method applied as comprehensively as possible can find the right way between the superficial credulity of the uncritical reader and the radical scepticism of the hyper-critical reader. It is **not** a question of constructing a **biography** with a continuous development, **but** of discovering what really happened with Jesus, discovering **the characteristic features and outlines of his preaching, conduct and fate.**

Those dogmatic theologians of Christian or Jewish provenance who are sceptical about the sources have in fact always begun from this point. So much so, that even Rudolf Bultmann could write an extremely concentrated and substantial book on Jesus (1926).[30] And Samuel Sandmel, too, wanted at least to maintain that 'certain bare facts' were 'historically not to be doubted'. 'Jesus, who emerged into public notice in Galilee when Herod Antipas was its Tetrach, was a real person, the leader of a movement. He had followers, called disciples. The claim was made, either by or for him, that he was the long-awaited Jewish Messiah. He journeyed from Galilee to Jerusalem, possibly in 29 or 30, and there he was executed, crucified by the Romans as a political rebel. After his death, his disciples believed that he was resurrected, and had gone to heaven, but would return to earth at the appointed time for the final divine judgment of mankind.'[31]

However, most Jewish researchers into Jesus now think that they can say considerably more about the characteristic features and outlines of Jesus' preaching, conduct and fate, and most of this accords with what is said by the leading Christian exegetes. There seems to be a broad **Jewish-Christian consensus** on the following historical findings:[32]
– that Jesus came from Nazareth in Galilee;
– that he was born the son of the carpenter Joseph and Miriam;
– that he grew up with several brothers and sisters:
– that he had himself baptized by John, the ascetic preacher of repentance (however that baptism is to be understood);
– that only then did he see himself called to public activity, and that the Jesus movement emerged (more or less directly) from the baptist movement;
– that as an itinerant preacher he announced the proximity of the eschatological kingdom of God and summoned his people to repentance;
– that in so doing he also performed numerous healing miracles, particularly on those who were psychologically ill;
– that he broke with his own family, his mother, brothers and sisters, and gathered a group of disciples around himself;
– that he found a hearing above all among the 'poor' of all kinds, the outcast, the outlaws, the sick and especially women;
– that already in Galilee he found himself embroiled in a deepening conflict with the Jewish authorities;
– that as a result he found less and less response from the people;
– that he then had an apparent failure with his preaching in Jerusalem, and finally met with a violent death.

Most Christian exegetes prove to have rather more reservations about miraculous phenomena (e.g. the historicity of the heavenly voice at the baptism or the nature miracles[33]) and about a messianic consciousness on the part of Jesus.[34] Be this as it may, the exegete James H.Charlesworth thinks that he can assert from the American perspective for the 1980s that 'not since Reimarus have so many scholars published so many remarkable books about the historical Jesus'.[35] Among more than thirty scholarly works, on the Christian side he singles out F.F.Bruce[36] and E.P.Sanders,[37] and on the Jewish side G.Cornfeld,[38] D.Flusser[39] and G.Vermes.[40]

4. Is Christianity a Jewish religion or a religion on its own?

A welcome shift is unmistakable **in exegesis**, though its exaggerations are also open to criticism. Whereas formerly exegesis worked in black and white, and it was impossible to do enough to make Jesus of Nazareth shine out at the expense of the Pharisees, now the opposite tendency can be noted, even among individual Christian exegetes. Jesus and Judaism are painted to such a degree as grey on grey that it is now very difficult to recognize Jesus' own distinctive profile, and even impossible to understand why a religion different from Judaism came into being, one which from the beginning took his name and not that of anyone else.

Questions flood in. Can we foist the whole of Jesus' controversy over the law on to the earliest community (was it so inventive?) and make Jesus himself a harmless liberal (and unoriginal) Pharisee, who would then of course not have anything decisive to say today to either Christians or Jews? Can we simply whisk away Jesus' dispute with the scribes over the sabbath, regulations about purity and food, and with the help of exegetical vivisection and parallels demonstrate that the Sermon on the Mount and its antitheses is essentially material common to all Judaism? No, such a hermeneutic delivers us over to subjective whim, and moreover leads to quite contradictory results. In this way the opposition between Jews and Christians is reduced to one long, two-thousand-year-old misunderstanding, and Jewish-Christian dialogue to shadow-boxing. Neither Jews nor Christians are helped by illusions. But some Christian exegetes – particularly German exegetes – seem to be afraid of criticizing a deliberate exegetical levelling-out[41] because they could so easily be accused of antisemitism.[42] The Holocaust is exploited not only as a political but sometimes also as a theological argument.[43]

In the following account I shall take pains to oppose any exaggerated contrasts between Jesus and Pharisaism, but without ignoring or trivializing the conflicts which according to the biblical sources as a whole led to Jesus' arrest and death.[44] For we have to explain both the continuity and the discontinuity. On the one hand Christianity is wholly rooted in Judaism (as David Flusser put it, 'Christianity is a Jewish religion').[45] But on the other hand, Christianity is a different religion from Judaism: Christianity is a distinctive religion which appeals to Christ and in this sense is Christian.[46]

Here we should remember that the Jesus movement could have been a reform movement in Judaism – and yet it became a separate world religion. Why? As we shall see, the apostle Paul is not the sole explanation. Without Jesus the Christ, by whom Saul saw himself 'sent', there would be no Paul. Against the *'terribles simplificateurs'* of our days, Joseph Klausner rightly maintains: '*Ex nihilo nihil fit* (nothing comes out of nothing): had not Jesus' teaching contained a kernel of opposition to Judaism, Paul could never **in the name of Jesus** have set aside the ceremonial laws, and broken through the barriers of national Judaism. There can be no doubt that in Jesus Paul found justifying support. In detailing the life of Jesus we have already come across various opposing points of view between the teaching of Jesus and that of the Pharisees (the latter representing traditional and also Scriptural Judaism.'[47]

The situation in **Christian dogmatics** is different from that in exegesis. There the dominant feature is still a doctrine of the Trinity and a christology which are remote from their Jewish roots, and build entirely on the Hellenistic councils of the early church. This is a dogmatics of the kind for which **Karl Barth** most recently once again laid the foundations in the Prolegomena to his *Church Dogmatics*, and which was then developed in what is beyond doubt a magnificent way in his Doctrine of Reconciliation. But on the basis of a dogmatics which begins with the 'triune God' and 'God the Son',[48] a dialogue with Jews is hardly possible.[49]

It is therefore most welcome that even in systematic theology an increasing number of authors are beginning to meet the requirements of Jewish-Christian dialogue by starting from Jesus of Nazareth, the man and the Jew. **Jürgen Moltmann**, the Protestant theologian from Tübingen, stands out for his programmatic attempt 'on the basis of a common messianic hope... to develop a christology in Christian-Jewish dialogue'.[50] In so doing he begins from the messianic hope and expectation of the Son of Man in ancient Israel, and from this develops a 'Spirit-christology which apprehends Jesus as the messianic prophet of the poor'.[51] Here, however, right from the beginning he sees himself already confronted with the Jewish objections to Jesus' messianic consciousness (e.g. those of Buber, Ben-Chorin, Scholem – and here

Moltmann could also have quoted Christian exegetes).[52] To cope with them, Moltmann sharply criticizes the christology of the Hellenistic councils, which speaks of a human and a divine nature in Jesus. In its place, in good New Testament fashion he wants 'to start from Jesus' special relationship to God, whom he called Abba, dear Father'.[53] However, here Moltmann *a priori* presupposes a 'trinitarian concept of God'.[54] In an earlier book he had developed an extraordinarily massive doctrine of the Trinity in the steps of Karl Barth and Karl Rahner, with constant polemic against monotheism, and his latest christology, too, culminates in 'divine self-relations in which Jesus discovers and finds himself...'[55] But are such divine self-relations a subject for dialogue with Jews?

Without giving in to the 'subjectivity' of a purely 'anthropological christology' (Schleiermacher, K.Rahner), which Moltmann rightly criticizes, one can at least ask whether it is not necessary to choose a less speculative starting point and to take a more consistent course. Those who want to go 'forward' (Moltmann's claim) must know whether they are coming 'from above' (from the 'heaven' of the Trinity) or 'from below' (from the 'earth' of Jesus of Nazareth). In my view it is possible to do justice to the problematical situation of Christian-Jewish (and Christian-Islamic) dialogue only if one presupposes neither a trinitarian concept of God nor *a priori* a messianic consciousness and a spiritual birth of Jesus. Jesus must be seen as **a Jew** in his contemporary Jewish context (with historical detachment) and at the same time in his significance for the present (with historical relevance).

Moreover another Protestant systematic theologian, **Friedrich-Wilhelm Marquardt**, has a different starting point for his christology, which bears the provocative title *The Christian Confession of Jesus, the Jew*:[56] without trinitarian presuppositions, he starts with the Jesus of the New Testament as he is understood today by Christian and Jewish scholars. Here, however, Marquardt does not go more closely into the conflicts between Jesus and the religious groupings of his time – the whole dispute over the law and the temple – which were a threat to Jesus' life.

A pendant to these systematic outlines from the American side is **Paul van Buren**'s now three-volume *Theology of the Jewish-Christian Reality*, which moves from 'discerning the way' through 'a Christian theology of the people Israel' to a 'christology in context'.[57] From the reality of the Holocaust (and the state of Israel), van Buren derives a special obligation for Christian theology and the church not to weaken the Jewish people, to refrain from a mission to the Jews and to engage in dialogue and co-operation: the church and theology should learn from their historical mistakes. However, at the same time van Buren warns against any Jewish-Christian tendencies to syncretism, against Christians simply taking over Jewish customs and traditions for themselves. It is not a question of creating a 'Judaism for Gentiles'. There is now one way for Jews and one way for Christians. Christians are to respect and recognize the independent way of the Jews, for behind it stands the reality of the one God of Israel, who is also the God of the church. This God called Israel to follow the Torah, and the same God called the church (which should not name itself Israel) to follow Jesus Christ. So there are two ways, but one and the same covenant and not two covenants, the old and the new. According to the New Testament itself, Jesus Christ is to be seen in the framework of the eternal covenant between God and the Jewish people.

We shall come back to the substantive questions raised here, but first of all there is an important fundamental question. How, specifically, are we to regard Jesus? In what sphere, what field of force, what camp, does he stand? Unmistakably, there are considerable **differences** between individual Jewish authors, and also among their Christian partners, when attempts are made to assign Jesus and his programme to a quite specific **religious party** in the Judaism of the time. Who was he? Was he a man of the Sadducean establishment or a political revolutionary? Was he a monastic ascetic or a pious Pharisee? Of course, in this book on Judaism I must make an effort to be as brief as possible, to limit myself to the relationship of Jesus to his Jewish contemporaries, and with a few exceptions dispense with scriptural references and bibliographies (I provided a wealth of them in *On Being a Christian*).[58] Anyone who has even a slight acquaintance with the New Testament will in any case recognize statements from this special Bible of the Christians in many sentences.

II. Who was Jesus?

'It is precisely the teachings of Jesus – and not Christology, in both its broader and its more restricted senses – that are the area in which Jews and Christians can most easily meet, help one another, and learn from one another.' These are the words of David Flusser, Professor of New Testament Studies at the Hebrew University of Jerusalem, in his article 'Christianity' in the representative theological dictionary *Contemporary Jewish Religious Thought*. And Flusser refers to the trends expressly focussed on Jesus in church history, which are orientated less on a church dogmatics than on the Jesus of the Synoptic Gospels: many peacable Christians and martyrs in the period before Constantine, but also the evangelical movements in the Middle Ages and the time of the Reformation (the Bohemian Brethren, Mennonites, Quakers and also Erasmus), then the stress on the ethics of Jesus by the Enlightenment, and after the Second World War by many Catholic theologians, who argued for a return to Jesus' message of social love.[1] However, that brings us to the very controversial question: Who was Jesus really? What was the Jesus of history?

1. A political revolutionary?

There is agreement among Jewish and Christian scholars that Jesus was **not a man of the Jewish establishment**. He was not a Sadducee; he was neither a priest nor a theologian. He was a 'layman'. He did not see his place among the ruling class and nowhere showed himself to be a conformist, an apologist for the *status quo* or a defender of law and order. One can only agree with the Jewish scholar Joseph Klausner when he says: 'Jesus and his disciples, who came not from the ruling and wealthy classes, but from the common people, were but slightly affected by the Sadducees... The Galilean carpenter and son of a carpenter and the simple fishermen who accompanied him... were as remote from Sadducaeanism as the highly-connected priests were from the simple-minded common people. The bare fact that the Sadducees denied the resurrection of the dead and did not develop the messianic idea must have alienated Jesus and his disciples.'[2]

However, the important question is: was Jesus therefore **a political revolutionary?** That is how he was seen by Robert Eisler,[3] Joel Carmichael,[4] S.G.F.Brandon[5] and (at least for the last stage of Jesus' life, with strongly messianic overtones) Pinchas Lapide[6] – and that is just a first group of largely Jewish interpreters.

Now beyond question the Gospels show us a clear-sighted, resolute, unbending Jesus who was also militant and combative when he had to be; in any case he was fearless. He had come to cast fire on the earth. One had not to fear those who could only kill the body and no more than that. A time of the sword, a time of great distress and danger, was imminent. Or does this text,[7] in which Jesus calls on his disciples to buy a sword for this emergency, represent a shift towards militancy? It is significant that his disciples could only point to two swords, which were hardly enough for bringing about a revolution, so that Jesus eventually broke off: 'Enough of that!'

No, Jesus is no **preacher of violence**. The question of the use of violence is later answered in the negative, in full accord with the Sermon on the Mount.[8] When he is arrested, Jesus says, 'Put your sword back into its place: for all who take the sword will perish by the sword.'[9] When he was arrested, Jesus himself was unarmed, defenceless, powerless. And so the disciples, who were doubtless arrested with him as political conspirators, were left unmolested.

But what about the **cleansing of the Temple**,[10] which is sometimes interpreted as an occupation of the Temple? Jesus certainly had the courage for symbolic provocation. He was by no means as meek and mild as the 'Nazarenes' of the nineteenth century loved to paint him. But according to the sources, there can be no question of his having occupied the Temple; indeed, had he attempted to do so, the Roman cohorts from the Antonia citadel would also have intervened immediately, and the passion story would have taken another course. No, the sources describe how the traders and money-changers were driven out: this is a symbolic intervention, an individual **prophetic provocation**, which amounts to a partisan demonstration: against the marketing and the profit derived from it by the hierarchy and the profiteers, and for the holiness of the place as a place of prayer. This action in the Temple was possibly connected with a threat about the destruction of the Temple and its rebuilding in the eschatological age. Jesus issued a bold challenge not only to the clerical hierarchy but also to those circles among the population who had a financial interest in the pilgrimage business and in the further development of the Temple. The Temple evidently played an important, if not exclusive, role in the later condemnation of Jesus.[11]

However, to make the point once again: there can be **no question of a Zionist messianic revolution**:

– Did Jesus call for a refusal to pay taxes? Hardly! 'Render to Caesar what is Caesar's!'[12] was his answer, and that is no call to boycott taxes. But conversely that means, 'Do not give to Caesar what is God's! Just as the currency belongs to the emperor, so people themselves belong to God.'

– Did Jesus proclaim a national war of liberation? No: as is well known, he accepted invitations to meals with the worst of collaborators, and he presented the Samaritans, an enemy hated almost more than the Gentiles, as a model.

– Did Jesus propagate the class struggle? How? He did not divide people into friends and foes, as did so many militants of his time.

– Did Jesus abolish the law for the sake of revolution? No, he wanted to help, to heal, to save; he wanted no happiness forced on people in accordance with the will of individuals. First the kingdom of God, and then everything else will be given to you!

So Jesus' message of the kingdom of God did not culminate in an appeal to bring in the better future by force. Those who take the sword will perish by the sword. His message aims at a renunciation of violence. Do not resist the evil one; do good to those who hate us; bless those who curse us; pray for those who persecute us. In this sense Jesus was a 'revolutionary' whose demands were fundamentally more radical than those of the political revolutionaries and transcended the alternatives of established order and socio-political revolution. Thus, rightly understood, Jesus was **more revolutionary than the revolutionaries**:

• Love your enemies instead of annihilating them!
• Forgive unconditionally instead of striking back!
• Be ready to suffer instead of using force!
• Bless the peacemakers rather than singing songs of hatred and revenge.

Subsequently, was it not also a result of Jesus' message and attitude that those **Jews who followed Jesus** did not make common cause with the Zealot revolutionaries in the great Jewish rebellion but fled from Jerusalem – to Pella on the other side of the Jordan? Is it a coincidence that the Christians were subsequently even persecuted fanatically in the second great revolt under Bar Kokhba? Is it a coincidence that, significantly, the Romans did not take any steps against the Christians until Nero's persecution? Hardly. For like Jesus himself, his disciples manifestly did not aim at any political and social revolution, but at a non-violent revolution, a revolution of the innermost and most hidden kind, from the centre of a person, from the human 'heart' – with a view to fellowship. The concern was to overcome the evil which lies not only in the system, in the structures, but also in human beings themselves.

So I can only agree with Werner Vogler in his very pertinent assessments of *Jewish Interpretations of Jesus in a Christian Perspective* (1988) when he raises serious methodological and hermeneutical objections to a political and messianic interpretation in the style of Eisler and Carmichael and concludes: 'On the basis of their own way of working, both authors have succeeded in sketching a picture of Jesus which shows that they are extraordinarily imaginative, but does not enrich research into Jesus. Even though the socio-critical features of their picture of Jesus represent a kind of corrective to the (Christian) research into Jesus in the past which has failed to take note of the elements of social criticism in the message and conduct of Jesus, neither Eisler nor Carmichael has produced scientific proof for their interpretation of Jesus as a social revolutionary. Similarly, should it be the case "that Jesus was transformed by the evangelists from a militant political messiah into a pacificist redeemer, as some Christian theologians are also ready to concede" (G.Baumbach), both Eisler and Carmichael still fail to produce convincing proof for their understanding of Jesus as a Jewish freedom-fighter.'[13] But does that mean that Jesus was the advocate of a piety which turned its back on the world?

2. An ascetic monk?

It has been known since the middle of this century that there were monks at that time, in the **monastery of Qumran** by the Dead Sea. And from the time of the historian Flavius Josephus it has been known that there were 'pious' Jews (Aramaic *hasdiyya*, Hebrew *hasidim*) living in the villages (and in isolated instances even in the cities), separated from the world, now called 'Essenes'. It was above all the historian Heinrich Graetz who wanted to understand Jesus as an Essene: David Flusser and A.Winkel (in his dissertation) argue that Jesus' background was both Essene and Pharisaic. In the hey-day of Qumran scholarship there was a constant concern to find connections between Qumran and John the Baptist (which are possible) and even between Qumran and Jesus, but this has proved to be an increasingly more improbable hypothesis. Neither the Qumran community nor the Essene movement are so much as mentioned in the New Testament writings, just as, conversely, there is no mention of the name of Jesus in the Qumran writings. Today, both Jewish and Christian exegetes will agree with Hans-Joachim Schoeps, the Jewish historian of religion, when he categorically states: 'The attempt has often been made to depict Jesus as a secret supporter or member of the Essene community. But there is no basis for such conjectures, far less certain proof.'[14]

It was above all Albert Schweitzer who pointed out to the good middle-class liberals that the Gospels do **not** present Jesus as **a figure who conforms to society**.[15] During his public activity Jesus leads an insecure itinerant life remote from his family, with the result that they want to get him back on the grounds that he is 'crazy'. Jesus was also evidently unmarried, and this has constantly seduced the imagination of novelists, film directors and musical composers to wild speculations. He was *A Marginal Jew* – thus the title of the most recent book on Jesus (by John P.Meier, New York 1991).

And despite everything, Jesus **was not a highly spiritual member of a religious order or an ascetic monk**. What distinguished him?

– Jesus did not live in seclusion from the world: his activity was quite public, in the villages and cities, in human society. He even made contact with the socially disreputable, with those who were 'unclean' according to the law and written off by Qumran, and as a result incurred scandal. For him purity of heart was more important than any regulations about cleanness.

– Jesus did not preach any division of humanity: it was not his concern to classify people as sons of light and sons of darkness, good and evil – *a priori* and from the beginning. Everyone has to repent, and everyone can repent: forgiveness is offered to all.

– Jesus did not live an ascetic life; he was not a zealot for the law, like members of the Essene and Qumran orders. He did not stipulate abstinence for the sake of abstinence, or any special ascetic disciplines. Rather, he joined in, ate and drank with his followers, and accepted invitations to dinners. Compared with the Baptist, he evidently incurred the charge of being a glutton and a winebibber. He made an unforgettable impression on his disciples, not by baptism, but by the supper he had with them under the threat of his arrest. For him marriage was not something that made people unclean but the will of the Creator. Renunciation of marriage was voluntary, and he did not impose a law of celibacy on anyone. It was not even necessary to renounce material possessions to be a disciple.

– Jesus did not lay down any religious rule: he stood upside down the hierarchical system which was customary even in the religious orders: the lowliest were to be the highest and the highest the servants of all. Subordination had to be mutual, for the common good. And for that there was no need of a novitiate, an entrance oath, a vow. Jesus did not call for any regular pious practices, any long prayers, any ritual meals and baths, any distinctive clothes. What marked him out was a lack of regulations, a matter-of-factness, a spontaneity and a freedom which for Qumran would have been criminal. For Jesus, incessant praying

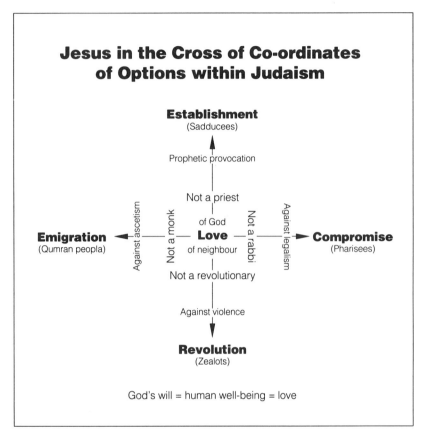

**Jesus in the Cross of Co-ordinates
of Options within Judaism**

Establishment
(Sadducees)

Prophetic provocation

Not a priest

of God

Emigration   Love   Compromise
(Qumran peopla)   of neighbour   (Pharisees)

Against ascetism   Not a monk   Not a rabbi   Against legalism

Not a revolutionary

Against violence

Revolution
(Zealots)

God's will = human well-being = love

did not mean an hour of prayer or an interminable liturgy of prayer, but a constant attitude of prayer on the part of those who expect everything from God all the time.

But what is left? If Jesus was not part of the establishment, and on the other hand did not want to adopt either the political radicalism of a violent revolution or the apolitical radicalism of the pious who opted out of society, must not then the fourth possible option within the Judaism of the time apply to him: the option of moral compromise, the harmonization of the demands of the law with everyday demands? That had been the concept of the Pharisaism of the day. So the question is: was Jesus a pious Pharisee?

3. A pious Pharisee?

I have already indicated that the picture of the **Pharisees**[16] in the Gospels is partly a caricature: indeed, they were the only representatives of official Judaism left after the fall of the Temple and the whole city of Jerusalem. They were now the main opponents of the young Christian communities. Nowadays, even in many church documents one can find a call for rethinking on the Pharisees: the Pharisees were resolutely concerned to bring the Torah up to date, as the word of God which imposes obligations in the present. As the 1980 declaration of the German episcopal conference puts it: 'They were men who had a serious concern for God's cause. One of the tasks of present-day exegesis, catechesis and homiletic is to speak about the Pharisees in the right way.'[17]

The name Pharisees, which, as we have heard, means 'those who are set apart', would also have fitted the Essenes and the Qumran monks, who made themselves independent as a kind of 'radical wing' of this movement. The Pharisees wanted two things: they wanted to **take God's commandments with** unconditional **seriousness** and to observe them with scrupulous precision. Indeed, beginning from the conviction that Israel was 'a kingdom of priests and a holy people',[18] they wanted of their own accord to observe strictly the rules about purity which according to the law were binding only on priests (and particularly also the rules about tithes). At the same time, though, as men who were close to the people in quite a different way from the priests in the Temple, they wanted to make the **law tolerable in everyday life by skilfully adapting it** to the present. They wanted to relieve people's consciences, give them security: they wanted to define precisely how far one could go without sinning. In other words, the Pharisees wanted to offer ways out where it seemed all too difficult to observe the law. For example, the law says that one may not work on the sabbath, and thirty-nine kinds of work prohibited on the sabbath are not to be done. But are there exceptions? Yes. Where life is in danger one may break the sabbath. Or, on the sabbath one may not carry anything outside the house. Outside? Outside, if one understands the courtyards of several houses to be common to them. Or, on the sabbath one may not do any hard labour. And in an emergency? Yes, if an ox falls into a pit, then one may get it out – in complete contrast to the rule in Qumran.

And what about Jesus? Did he not have a good deal in common with the Pharisees in particular? The relationship between Jesus and the Pharisees has to be discussed very carefully.[19] All too often, at the expense of Judaism, Christian interpreters of Jesus have tendentiously

overlooked or neglected **what Jesus has in common with the Pharisees.**
Like the Pharisees, Jesus lived among the people; he worked, discussed,
and taught in synagogues as they did. Jesus had contacts with the
Pharisees, and according to Luke also ate and drank with them. Indeed,
if one follows Jewish and Christian authors, some rabbinic parallels
and analogies could be indicated for every verse of the Sermon on the
Mount.

No wonder, then, that most Jewish interpreters of Jesus see him as
having been close to the Pharisees.[20] Indeed, like Abraham Geiger and
Paul Winter, some go even further and assert that Jesus was nothing
but a Pharisee, an instance of the 'love Pharisee' who is mentioned in
the Talmud, where he is listed as the one good type of Pharisee out of
seven. Is this a convincing solution? No, it is not as simple as that. We
need a counterpoint.

In fact, for Jesus the authority of Moses was not in question, any more
than it was for the Pharisees. There should never have been any dispute
about this: Jesus, too, did not want to do away with the Torah, to
abolish it, but to 'fulfil' it.[21] But what 'fulfil' means emerges from the
passages in the Sermon on the Mount which follow this saying. Today
there is a wide consensus that for Jesus, to 'fulfil' means **to deepen,
concentrate and radicalize the law of God** in the light of its innermost
dimension, namely God's basic purpose. It is Jesus' conviction that
nothing which contradicts this basic purpose may be read out of the
law or into it. The law is the will of God, which aims at human well-
being. Of course this applies particularly to the halakhic part of the
Torah, which with its words, commands and legal maxims might make
up barely a fifth of the Pentateuch. In concrete, 'fulfil' means:

- to deepen the law by resolutely taking seriously the will of God in
  the law;
- to concentrate the law by combining love of God with love of
  neighbour: love as the nucleus and criterion of the law;
- to radicalize the law by extending love of neighbour beyond the other
  members of one's people to enemies; by insisting on unbounded
  forgiveness, a renunciation of power and rights without anything in
  return, and service without superordination and subordination.

So will Jesus really have been nothing but a so-called 'love Pharisee'?
Such a claim leaves completely out of account the **contrasts between
Jesus and the Pharisees** which I have mentioned. According to the
primary sources, from the very beginning the Pharisees form the
problematical background to Jesus' preaching of the kingdom of God,

and moreover are taken seriously by most Jewish interpreters. There is no lack of material about conflict. As for the rabbinic parallels and analogies to the Sermon on the Mount (and the preaching of Jesus generally), Pinchas Lapide may be right in saying that the Sermon on the Mount is as different from the Jewish parallels as a building is from the stones of the quarry of which it was built.[22] That is the only explanation of the tremendous weight of its message, which has constantly put Christians themselves to shame, and which could even inspire people from a completely different cultural circle, like Mahatma Gandhi. It makes a difference whether there is evidence for three dozen sentences in three dozen different rabbis or whether they appear in only one, and in a pointed form at that. It is not the individual statements made by Jesus which are not interchangeable, but his message as a whole. And the question is not whether love of God and love of neighbour can also already be found in the Hebrew Bible (indisputably they can), but what role they have in the preaching of the rabbi from Nazareth and what status they are given.

Certainly the great achievements of the Pharisees in popular piety cannot be denied. But at the same time the nature of Pharisaic piety must not be played down and trivialized – by compiling particular Pharisaic texts and neglecting critical texts from the Gospels – as sometimes happens today, out of well-meaning compensation for an erstwhile pernicious anti-Pharisaism. We cannot overlook the fact that among contemporaries at any time, positive and negative judgments about the Pharisees are in balance. The Regensburg exegete Franz Mussner[23] points out 'that the Rabbinic tradition also in part exercised a criticism of the Pharisees'.[24] And, as I have already mentioned, in the Talmud[25] 'seven types of Pharisees are distinguished: the "shoulder" Pharisee (who carries his good deeds on his shoulder); the "wait yet Pharisee", the Pharisee "with the blue mark" (who banged his head on the wall in order to avoid looking at a woman); the "pestle Pharisee" (who is only apparently humble); the "bookkeeper Pharisee" (who keeps score of his virtues); the "fear Pharisee" (who obeys God only out of fear); the "love Pharisee" (who obeys God out of love). And **only the latter is the true Pharisee.**' Moreover there are allusions to most of these other Pharisees in the Gospels. Jesus even singles out for sharp criticism the 'shoulder' Pharisees, 'who carry their good deeds (*misvata*) on their shoulders)': 'They bind heavy burdens, hard to bear, and lay them on men's shoulders; but they themselves do not move them with their finger.'[26]

Truly, nothing is to be said against the Pharisees 'in themselves' and their authentic virtues. The Pharisee who is cited by Jesus in the famous parable as an example[27] is not a hypocrite. He is a quite honourable, pious man, who speaks the unadorned truth. Had he not done all that he was convinced that the law required of him? The morals of the Pharisees were generally quite exemplary, and accordingly they were respected by those who did not go as far as they did. So what is to be said against them?

The answer can only be that **Jesus differed** not just in details of everyday life but **in his whole basic religious attitude.** We find no pride in his own achievements, his own righteousness, no contempt for the ordinary people (the *am-ha-aretz*) who knew nothing of the law. There is no exclusion of the unclean and sinners, no strict doctrine of retribution. What then? Trust only in God's grace and mercy: 'God, be merciful to me, a sinner!'[28]

No, on the basis of the sources there is no getting round the conclusion that Jesus just was not a typical Pharisee with 'delight in the commandments' and casuistic exegesis. It is important not only to compare individual statements out of context but to read the texts in context. Do that, and it is clear that all the Gospels are in complete agreement in attesting that the 613 commandments and prohibitions of the law, which were so important for the Pharisees, were not what Jesus wanted to inculcate. Nowhere does he require his disciples to study the Torah. Nowhere does he seek to follow the Pharisees in building a 'hedge round the law' with rules for behaviour, a protection to guarantee that the commandments are observed. Nowhere does he seek to extend the ideals of the cleanness and holiness of the priests in Temple service to the laity and their everyday practice.

In short, the basic attitude, the overall tendency, is different: compared with all the Pharisees, Jesus is astoundingly liberal. Must it not have undermined the whole moral system for someone to show such solidarity with the unclean and the sinners, indeed to eat with them? What does it mean for the lost and dissolute son to fare better with his father than the well-bred son who stays at home, and for the crooked tax-collector to fare better with God than the pious Pharisee, who really is not like other people, like liars and adulterers?

4. Not the usual scholastic disputes, but confrontation and conflict

Most Jewish and Christian interpreters of Jesus nowadays agree that Jesus, 'the greatest observer and critic of Pharisaic spirituality',[29] **was not concerned with observing the Torah for its own sake, but with actual people.** So his freer attitude to the law and his dealings with those who were ignorant of the law, or who broke it, had serious consequences. This is the unambiguous overall picture: Jesus specifically caused offence, scandal, not only by criticizing the Temple but by his different interpretation of the law, indeed his whole basic attitude – and interpreters should not allow Jesus any less coherence and consistency than they allow themselves. According to the sources, Jesus' interpretation related above all to the **regulations about purity, fasting and the sabbath.**[30]

Different Jewish authors have interpreted differently the fact that Jesus caused specific offence by his own interpretation of the law and his attitude. The scandal arose:[31]

– because Jesus wanted to penetrate what Martin Buber called the 'primal purpose of God', the 'primal unconditioned nature of the law' which is incomprehensible to human beings;

– because Jesus repudiated individual regulations for carrying out commandments of the Torah, because he called for a freedom from the letter of the law and an uncompromising commitment on the part of individuals to the dual commandment to love God and love one's neighbour, thus attacking the main principle of Pharisaic thought (Claude Montefiore);

– because Jesus set over against the casuistic trivialization practised by certain schools of Pharisees the primal purpose of the law, and in this way 'totally' fulfilled the law by internalizing it so that love was the decisive motive (Shalom Ben-Chorin);

– because Jesus stressed the moral aspect of life in contrast to the purely formal aspect of the practice of the law. Indeed, by so radicalizing the commandment to love – the commandment to love one's enemy, with its un-Pharisaic concern for the 'sinners' – Jesus broke through barriers, with the result that, as David Flusser has indicated, the basic religious approach could be combined with the social aspect.

While as a Christian ecumenist I object to the Christian isolation of Jesus from his Jewish roots, conversely Jewish ecumenists will also object to the Jewish levelling down of the message of Jesus, so long repudiated in Judaism. From a historical perspective, is it really enough to call Jesus a great Pharisee who, like other great Pharisees, had his 'special teaching', and to bring his conflict, which ended in his death, down to the level of ordinary exegetical disputes within Pharisaic schools? Did Jesus of Nazareth die because of scholastic disputes?

Here, above all, Jewish scholars like **Hans-Joachim Schoeps**, with his historical-critical training, clearly put the emphasis elsewhere. They agree with Christian interpretations that while Jesus affirmed the Torah and also observed the ceremonial laws,

1. 'He distinguishes between the will of God and the law of the *Thora le Moshe mi Sinai* which expresses it. This means that literal observance of the law is not identical with doing the divine will. He claims the right to decide when the law expresses God's will and when it does not';

2. 'In accordance with this distinction... he sees different levels in the law, from ethical laws (which are essential) to ritual and ceremonial laws (which are less so), but does not in principle dispute the binding character of the latter';

3. 'He distinguishes between the authority of the word of scripture and the authority of rabbinic precepts. So he opposes the rabbinic principle of tradition by regarding it as a new institution from his own present, and reserving the right to his own interpretation of scripture and of the behaviour in each particular situation which is grounded in it';

4. He sought 'to fulfil the law', and therefore was 'not moving towards a new halakhah of his own'.[32]

Along with other Jewish authors, Joseph Klausner, too, is of the opinion that Jesus' concentration on the religious and ethical dimension and his bracketing off of national life is un-Jewish, indeed is dangerous for Judaism because it dissolves it. However, let us leave that to one side. At all events, it was Jesus of Nazareth and not one of the other 'liberal' rabbis who was drawn into a conflict which ended in his death. If we follow the sources, these conflicts continually raised the question: by what right, with what authority do you speak and do that? This question of authority cannot be passed over, and we must now pay specific attention to it.

5. In whose name?

As a question already asked before Easter, it permeates the Gospels which were written after Easter, and even now has not been put to rest. What do you think of him? Who is he? **One of the prophets?** Or more? Today even conservative Christian theologians concede that Jesus himself put the kingdom of God at the centre of his preaching and not his own role, person, dignity.

That is also true of the **title messiah**. According to the Synoptic Gospels – unlike, of course, the late Gospel of John with its theological reflectiveness (it already speaks of the 'Son of God') – Jesus himself never used the designation messiah or any other honorific title of

himself, except perhaps the ambiguous title 'Son of Man'. On this
nowadays Christian and Jewish interpreters largely agree. The earliest
evangelist Mark still treats the messiahship of Jesus as a secret which
is hidden from the wider public until it is confessed under the cross and
proclaimed after Easter. Why? Only in the light of the Easter experience
could one clearly see the Jesus tradition in a messianic light and thus
introduce the messianic confession into the account of the history of
Jesus. And before that? Jesus' proclamation and praxis had hardly
matched the messianic expectations of his contemporaries which were
contradictory and mostly theo-political – most of the rabbis, too,
expected a triumphant messiah.

Now precisely because Jesus cannot be understood adequately under
any of the current titles, precisely because the issue is **not one of saying
yes or a no to a particular dignity**, a particular office or even a particular
dogma, rite and law, the question which the first disciples already put
becomes acute. Who may this man who cannot be grasped with any
title really have been?

The great question about his person remains. Was he the messiah?
The avoidance of all titles makes the riddle more profound. This is a
riddle which is posed in a special way precisely because of Jesus' violent
death. Can **the death of Jesus be detached from the question of his
message and person?** Here had appeared a man who regardless of the
hierarchy and its experts, in word and deed had in practice set himself
above the cultic tabus, customary fasts, and particularly the sabbath
commandment, which at the time was largely regarded as the 'chief
commandment'. Indeed, without backing up his opinion with scriptural
quotations, as was customary with heads of Pharisaic schools, Jesus
challenged the then normative Jewish traditions of interpreting the
Torah ('the traditions of the elders'): in prohibiting divorce, prohibiting
retribution, in the command to love one's enemy. While he did not do
away with even the 'least commandments',[33] in case after case he
relativized them. And though the fact is also disputed by some Jewish
interpreters, according to the Gospels, in sovereign freedom from the
prevailing teaching and practice which was the teaching and practice
of the ruling class this Jesus claimed an authority of a kind which made
the scribes ask, 'How can this man speak like this? He blasphemes
God.'[34] But – did he blaspheme God?

The evidence is unanimous that Jesus acted on the basis of an unusual
experience of God, bond with God, and immediacy to God, when in
confrontation with the rulers he proclaimed God's rule and will and
did not simply accept the conditions of human domination:
– when he was open to **all groups;**

– when he was unwilling to deliver **wives** over to the whim of their husbands in marriage;
– when he defended **children** against adults, **the poor** against the rich, the **small** against the great – when he even stood up for those with **other religious beliefs**, those who had been **compromised politically**, the **moral failures**, those who had been sexually exploited, those who had been forced to the periphery of society. Perhaps he even – as the height of arrogance – promised them forgiveness, something that was permitted only to the high priest in a cultic context.

However, the amazing thing is that nowhere does Jesus give any grounds for his claim. Indeed, in the discussion on authority he expressly refuses to give any grounds for it. He claims this authority, he acts on the basis of it, without appealing to a higher authority with the prophetic 'Thus says the Lord!' And whereas it was the practice in rabbinic schools for a rabbi to contrast his view with that of another rabbi, using the antithesis 'It has been said' – 'But I say', in the antitheses of the Sermon on the Mount Jesus' word is set over against that of the Torah: not only no murder but no anger; not only no adultery but also no evil desires; not only no perjury, but no swearing at all; not divorce on certain conditions but no divorce at all. The community was to have problems with such radical words of Jesus and sometimes toned them down: it certainly did not invent them itself.

According to all the sources, Jesus had an underived, highly personal authority. How should one describe it? He differed from the typical 'rabbi' (though that was how he was addressed) and from the charismatic 'itinerant preacher' (although without doubt he performed healings). He has been described as the eschatological 'prophet', though as far as possible this particular title is avoided in any direct description of him in the Gospels (and even in the very old sayings source Q, which was used by Matthew and Luke). Whatever title he is given, here we do not just have the words of an expert and a specialist, as in the case of the priests and teachers of the law. Rather, we have one who without any derivation or justification authoritatively preaches the will of God in word and deed, whose aim is human well-being; who identifies himself with God's cause, which is the human cause; who is utterly taken up with this cause; who in this way becomes the highly **personal advocate of God and human beings** without any claim to titles and dignities. As a result, could not questions arise like, 'Is more than Jonah (and the prophets) here?';[35] 'Is more than Solomon (and all the wisdom teachers) here?'.[36] According to the sources, this is where the reason for the trial of Jesus must quite clearly be sought.

6. Who is to blame for Jesus' death?

Much **remains uncertain** about the **trial of Jesus** before the Jewish authorities. This may have been held before a committee (composed principally of Sadducees) rather than a plenary session of the Sanhedrin. Strikingly, the Pharisees are not mentioned in the reports of the trial. Rather than pronouncing a formal death sentence, the body may simply have resolved to hand Jesus over to Pilate. Indeed, rather than a regular trial, perhaps there was merely an interrogation to define the precise points of the charge – to be sent on to the Roman prefect. It is somewhat improbable that the direct, formal question whether Jesus was messiah or son of God was the accusation: that can be attributed to the later community. 'Many' charges are mentioned, but these are not brought, apart from a saying against the Temple (a point which often fails to be noted). The charges have to be inferred from the Gospels as a whole. And as the Gospels have plenty of conflicts to report, this cannot simply be said to be a retrospective projection of the conflict between the earliest church and the synagogue; it will be a reflection of the historical conflict which had already broken out between the historical Jesus and the Jewish establishment.

If we examine the Gospels, the **charges** which point to some completely coherent basic attitude can be summed up as follows:

- The Jew Jesus was a radical **critic of the** traditional religious practice of many **pious Jews.**
- Jesus' protest and prophecy against the **Temple** and thus against its guardians and those who benefited from it seemed arrogant.
- Jesus' understanding of the **law,** focussed wholly on human beings, was provocative.
- Jesus' **solidarity** with ordinary people who were ignorant of the law, and his dealings with notorious law-breakers and outcasts, were scandalous.
- Jesus' **criticism of the ruling groups,** to whom he was more than a nuisance because of his numerous followers among the people, was sweeping.

But no matter what the details of the court proceedings may have been, all the evangelists agree that Jesus was handed over **by the Jewish authorities to the Roman governor Pontius Pilate and crucified in accordance with Roman practice.** And according to all the reports, before Pilate, upon whose term as governor of Judaea (26-36 CE) there are very negative verdicts in contemporary sources, the term 'king of the Jews' – which was never used later by the community as a messianic title – was a major factor. In accordance with Roman custom the inscription on the cross records the particular grounds for condemnation (*causa damnationis*). 'King of the Jews' could only be understood in political terms by the Romans: the claim to a royal title was an infringement of Roman majesty (*crimen laesae maiestatis*). Although Jesus, this preacher of non-violence, had never made such a political claim, it was natural for outsiders to put him in this category.

So who killed Jesus? Was it just the Roman law, the *Lex Julia Maiestatis*, as Jews sometimes assert? Was it the Romans, while Jewish women and men mourned Jesus on his way to the cross? Such a division of roles may well be an illegitimate oversimplification of the actual history.

– Beyond doubt we must object to the ongoing exoneration of the **Roman authorities** which is evident in the Gospels. But similarly, there can be no suggestion that the sole initiative and the sole guilt lay with the Romans. In the legal sense the Roman procurator was responsible for what happened on Golgothá: at that time he alone had the *ius gladii*, the right to carry out executions, and crucifixion is a Roman form of execution.[37] But regardless of how Roman cohorts may have been involved in the arrest, they are not mentioned in the early Gospel of Mark,[38] but only by John.[39]

– According to all the reports, Jesus was first taken into custody by the **Jewish authorities** of the time. Furthermore, Roman proceedings against Jesus would hardly have been instituted without a denunciation and the assent of at least the high priest in office. According to all the sources, Jewish authorities were involved in the 'case' of Jesus of Nazareth – at least key members of the Sanhedrin around the high priest – before the Roman proceedings. The argument of Jewish exegetes, that according to Jewish law a trial on a capital charge could not have taken place at night, and that a death sentence could have been pronounced only on the day after the trial, only applies to rabbinic law as codified in the Mishnah around the end of the second century CE. There are no such regulations in the Torah, which is what the Sadducean establishment went by.

What was the issue? If we follow the sources, in the case of Jesus it was not political agitation but primarily religious provocation. This may have been the reason why the Jewish authorities were brought in from the start, because basically a religious charge lay behind the political one. And according to the Gospels, this religious charge can only have had to do with Jesus' critical attitude to the law and the Temple, and to their representatives. As a purely political agitator, Jesus would presumably have been forgotten like others, apart from his name. But as a **religious figure**, like other prophetic figures he also left an abiding and unique impression on people's memories by his message and his conduct. From the standpoint of the prevailing interpretation of the law and the Temple religion, the Jewish hierarchy would not have had to take action against a messianic pretender or false messiah, but they would against a false teacher, a lying prophet, someone who led the people astray and blasphemed God. The most recent analysis of the legal textual material by A.Strobel (1980)[40] indicates that it was not prejudice and malice which led to Jesus' condemnation, as J.Blinzler still thought in his well-known book *The Trial of Jesus*.[41] Rather, 'the role and position of Caiaphas derived from his unconditional commitment and fidelity to the law. So tragically he also had to carry out the law in the case of Jesus.'[42]

So at that time, the cruel death of Jesus could only mean that the law had triumphed. As one who hung on the tree of shame, Jesus was evidently someone who had blasphemed God, and this is also attested by contemporary Jewish writings. The sentence to death by crucifixion, which only the Roman procurator could in fact impose, could also have been a Jewish punishment, and – as Y.Yadin has clearly demonstrated by means of the Temple scroll discovered at Qumran[43] – on the basis of Deut.21.22f. was understood as a punishment for blasphemy and at the same time a sign that the crucified person was accursed by God.[44] Moreover, Josephus reports one more case: a prophet Jesus, son of Ananias, prophesied the downfall of the Temple and was therefore handed over by the Jewish authorities to the Romans, who scourged him. In another instance Josephus similarly attests that the high priest and leaders were present at a trial before the Roman procurator.[45]

In other words, the proceedings against Jesus were concerned with 'reframing the Jewish charge, which amounted to a religious misdemeanour, as a political charge of high treason'.[46] That means:

- The political charge that Jesus was seeking political power, calling on people to refuse to pay taxes to the occupying forces and inciting unrest, and thus understood himself as a political messiah-king of the Jews, was a false charge.
- But Jesus, the religious trouble-maker, was presented as a political revolutionary, i.e as a militant opponent of Roman power. For Pilate this was a plausible charge, especially as political unrest and troublemakers were hardly unusual in the circumstances of the time. That means that Jesus was condemned as a political revolutionary, though this was precisely what he was not.

So who is **to blame for Jesus' death**? The correct historical answer can only be that the Jewish and Roman authorities were **each** entangled in this case **in their own way**. For today, however, there is another decisive factor:

- Even at that time the Jews as a people did not reject Jesus; there should never have been any talk of the collective guilt of the Jewish people of the time (why not also of the Roman people?).
- To impute collective guilt to the later Jewish people is even more absurd: accusations that the present Jewish nation is guilty of the death of Jesus were and are abstruse, and have brought an infinite amount of sorrow upon this people.

Here, in the face of a monstrous history of guilt on the part of Christians, the Second Vatican Council has at last cleared up the charge that 'the Jews' are murderers of Christ, indeed murderers of God': 'Even though the Jewish authorities and those who followed their lead pressed for the death of Christ, neither all Jews indiscriminately at that time, nor Jews today, can be charged with the crime committed during his passion.'[47]

So after all that we have heard, is that 'bringing home' of Jesus to Judaism of which Jewish authors speak possible today? No and yes. Perhaps not home to the halakhah, which, having been relativized by Jesus, faded into the background and moreover was no longer regarded as unconditionally necessary for salvation by those who later believed in Jesus as the Christ. But certainly home to the Jewish people, the permanently chosen people who had long rejected, indeed for long had to reject, the rabbi from Nazareth. Today, however, even to many Jews, Jesus of Nazareth appears as the primal figure of the Jewish people, persecuted in the world and condemned to unspeakable sorrow. And if he returned today, as in Dostoievsky's story of the Grand Inquisitor, whom would he have to fear the most? Who would more readily accept him — the synagogue or the church?

However, the question is: why are his message, his way of life and his destiny still so alive? Why is he still so alive as a person?

III. Belief in Jesus as the Messiah?

Was everything finished after Jesus' death? Evidently not. It is an undisputed fact that the movement which arose from Jesus only really began after his death; only now did it really make history. Why was that? The reason was the conviction and belief of the Jewish followers of Jesus that he had risen from the dead.[1]

1. Resurrection from the dead – un-Jewish?

This was the one adamant conviction of the first Christian community which, like the apostle Paul, appealed to spiritual experiences: this crucified Jesus did not fall into nothingness. From transitory, corruptible, impermanent reality, he entered into the true, eternal life of God. Was this a 'super-natural' intervention of a *deus ex machina*? Rather, it was a 'natural' dying and being taken up into the real, true reality, at all events into a final state without any suffering. In the same way, in Luke's Gospel, Jesus' dying cry, 'My God, my God, why have you forsaken me?' (Mark 15.34), is already given a positive twist by means of a saying from the Psalms, 'Father, into your hands I commend my spirit' ((Ps.31.6; Luke 23.46); in John it then becomes 'It is fulfilled!' (19.30).

Granted, this message is not without difficulties. Legends are formed or there are legendary elaborations; there are developments conditioned by situations ('appearances'), extensions (the 'ascension') and shifts of accent (the 'empty tomb'). And yet, the fundamental aim was a simple one, and in the early period it was conveyed in brief formulae, which have been preserved in the New Testament letters and the Acts of the Apostles: 'God, who raised him/Jesus from the dead',[2] or 'God raised him from the dead'[3] (from Sheol, the shadowy realm of the dead). Only later is this faith developed in narrative form by means of the story of the empty tomb. But despite all discrepancies, indeed contradictions over time and place, the persons involved and the sequence of events, the various earliest Christian witnesses – Peter, Paul and James, the letters, the Gospels and Acts – agree that **the crucified Jesus lives for ever with God, as an obligation and a hope for us.**[4] The Jewish Christians and Gentile Christians from the New Testament communities are borne up, indeed fascinated, by the certainty that the one who was killed did not remain dead, but is alive, and that anyone who stands by him and follows him will live in the same way. The new, eternal life of the one is a challenge and a real hope for all.

However, from the beginning there was no historical proof that with the death of Jesus everything was not over, that he himself did not remain dead but had entered into God's eternal life. Throughout the New Testament there are no 'eye-witnesses' of the resurrection, nor is there any direct description of it. From the beginning, resurrection was always a **conviction of faith** – though there were reasons for it. But is a raising from the dead by God himself – and only in this sense can there be any talk of a 'rising again' – *a priori* an un-Jewish thought, a miracle, without analogy in the Jewish experience of faith? What is the meaning of the 'Easter' event? Do Judaism and Christianity part company here?

Not at all. 'Belief in the resurrection from the dead (*teḥiyyat ha-metim*) is an explicit dogma of classical Judaism, reaffirmed and elaborated by Moses Maimonides, treated by Hasdai Crescas as a "true belief" (rather than as a fundamental principle of Judaism), retracted to a more debatable level of a deduction by Joseph Albo, and all but lost as a central teaching ever since the close of the medieval discourse. Nevertheless, despite its fall from the dogmatic eminence in which it, among other beliefs, was regarded as a *sine qua non* of rabbinic eschatological teaching, resurrection continues to be affirmed in the traditional liturgy. Introduced as the second blessing of the Eighteen Benedictions (the *Shemoneh Esreh*), recited during the *Amidah* (lit. standing prayer), it asserts that God keeps faith with those who lie in the dust and will according to his mercy, raise the dead, restore them bodily and grant them eternal life.' That is how Arthur A.Cohen (1928-1986), Buber's biographer and professor at the University of Chicago, describes the eventful history of belief in the resurrection in Judaism.[5]

So 'resurrection' by God is thoroughly Jewish. Not only is the **content** of the confession of faith in Jesus' resurrection Jewish – 'You are blessed, Yahweh, you bring the dead to life' (thus the wording of the second blessing, which is also that of the funeral liturgy) – but also the **form**: 'God, who raised him from the dead' resembles the Jewish expressions of faith which are often used: 'God, who made heaven and earth', or, 'God who led you up out of Egypt.'

But the question remains: why was belief in the resurrection connected with Jesus in particular? Why could people associate any kind of hope with such a hopeless end? Why could people proclaim the one who had been judged by God to be God's messiah? Why could the gallows of shame be declared to be the sign of hope; why could the manifest bankruptcy of the movement be made the starting point for a phenomenal revival?

Here we simply have to note that according to the evidence the first disciples of Jesus gave the God of Israel and Jesus himself as the reason for their faith, newly awakened at Easter. In so doing they referred to their **experiences** of God and the exalted Lord. Certainly, our knowledge of spiritual experiences, ecstasies, visions, extensions of consciousness and 'mystical' experiences are still too limited for us to be able to explain what kind of reality ultimately underlies such stories. But certainly we cannot either simply dismiss these experiences as hallucinations[6] or explain them within the supernaturalist scheme as a divine intervention from above or from outside. Probably they will have been inner visions, not some external reality. But the 'subjective', psychological activity of the disciples and the 'objective' activity of God are in no way exclusive, since God also acts through the human psyche. At all events, visions or auditions are not neutral, objective knowledge, but a believing trust which by no means excludes doubt. These are **experiences of faith**, with which the best comparison is the **experiences** of the prophets of Israel **at their calling**. The apostles, too, now begin to feel themselves called, to proclaim the message and to commit their lives to it.

Now it has constantly been pointed out that in antiquity there is also evidence of other resurrections. Time and again, there is mention above all of the story of an appearance of Apollonius of Tyana after his death, as reported by Philostratos.[7] But note the difference from the resurrection of Jesus. Did the story of this resurrection of Apollonius ever convince anyone to change their whole life, convince them that God had spoken and acted decisively through this one person? We do not know how far Jesus himself, who indeed had expected a dramatic eschatological shift during his lifetime, had prepared his disciples for such a dramatic event. Be this as it may, the prophecies of his death and resurrection in the form in which they are reported in the Gospels are certainly later compositions.

The one thing that is certain is that the disciples, who had expected the kingdom of God imminently, now first of all saw this expectation as having been fulfilled – in the light of the resurrection of Jesus to new life. This was understood as the beginning of the eschatological redemption. At that time that, too, was a 'good Jewish' idea: not only the Jewish followers of Jesus, but also many Jews, expected the resurrection of the dead, since, as we heard, belief in the general resurrection of the dead (or at least of the righteous) had emerged for the first time in the book of Daniel and in the apocalyptic literature.

However, for the young Christian community, what many Jews expected for all human beings in the future had been already anticipated in this one event: the **resurrection of Jesus** was the **beginning of the general resurrection of the dead**, the beginning of a new time. All this had a good basis in the contemporary Jewish world of faith.

Moreover, Pinchas Lapide is one of the few present-day Jewish theologians who has had the courage to put stress once again on 'resurrection' as an authentically 'Jewish experience of faith'.[8] He has rightly emphasized that 'the resurrection belongs in the category of truly real and influential events': 'Something must have happened that we can call a historical event, since its consequences were historical – although we are completely incapable of understanding the precise nature of the experience.' However, it is not completely clear whether here Lapide is thinking of a 'fact of history' or just of 'faith with a subjective foundation'. I would be more precise: the faith of the disciples is a historical event (which can be grasped by historical means), but God's raising of Jesus to eternal life is not a historical event that can be envisaged and imagined, nor even a biological event, though it is nevertheless a real event. What does that mean? Critical examination of the sources can help here, since it can bring out the decisive element of belief in the resurrection which underlies all the legendary developments. He is alive: but what does 'alive' mean here?

At this point scholarship shows very clearly that the earliest New Testament witnesses do **not** understand the resurrection of Jesus as a **resuscitation to earthly life**, as Pinchas Lapide assumes, analogous to the three Old Testament resuscitations by prophets. Rather, against the apocalyptic-Jewish horizon of expectation, this is clearly the **exaltation** of this man from Nazareth, who has been executed and buried, **by God to God**, to the God whom he himself had called 'Abba', 'Father'. So what is meant is never – as, say, in the Greek world – just an immortality of the 'soul' but a new life of the whole person in God, since in Judaism the human being is always seen as a physical-psychological unity. It is only later, of course, that texts above all in Luke and John give a legendary account of what is virtually physical contact between the risen Jesus with his disciples. So what does resurrection mean – for our day?

- Resurrection does **not mean any return to life in our space and time.** Death is not reversed (there is no resuscitation of a corpse), but definitively overcome. Here is an entry into a quite different, incorruptible, eternal, 'heavenly' life.
- Resurrection does **not mean a continuation of this life in space and**

time. Talk of 'after' death is already misleading: there is no 'before' and 'after' in eternity. Rather, eternity means a new life in God's invisible, incomprehensible sphere (= 'heaven'), which transcends the dimensions of space and time.

• **Positively, resurrection means** that Jesus did not die and become nothing, but in death and from death died into that incomprehensible and comprehensive last and first reality, was taken up by that most real of realities to which we give the name God. Where human beings achieve their eschaton, the ultimate in their lives, what do they expect to find? Not nothingness, but that All which is God. Believers know that death is a transition to God, is an entry into God's hiddenness, into that sphere which transcends all conceptions, which no human eye has ever seen, beyond our grasp, understanding, reflection and imagination!

So from the Christian side, should the resurrection be understood triumphalistically as a victory over Judaism? Without doubt that has often been the case, and A.Roy and Alice L.Eckardt, who as Christian theologians have laudably committed themselves to the revision of dangerous Christian positions in the light of the Holocaust, think that belief in the resurrection of Jesus is the root of all Christian anti-Judaism. With belief in the resurrection, 'Christianity has legitimized historically-theologically its supersessionism and triumphalism over Judaism and the Jewish people'.[9]

Granted, as the two theologians also know, the resurrection of Jesus is part of the indispensable basic substance of Christian faith. However, as we also saw, it must not be misunderstood in a fundamentalistic way. Paul already reminds the Christian triumphalists in Corinth that the risen Christ is the crucified Jesus, and that no human being has any reason to boast. If the resurrection is understood in accordance with scripture, it may certainly not be understood as a message against the Jews, but only as a message also for the Jews. It is not an un-Jewish truth, aimed at smashing Judaism, but a Jewish truth aimed at giving hope. It is not supersession but preservation: not only because the risen Lord is manifested by the resurrection as being identical with the Jew Jesus of Nazareth, but also because the risen Lord is an invitation to a great decision which is open to all: to any human being.

Everyone, whether Jew, Christian, or non-believer, is here faced with the last great alternative. Do we die into nothingness or into the ultimate reality? Belief in a resurrection is trust that we **die into God**, instead of assuming that life is ultimately meaningless. So death and resurrection are very closely connected. The resurrection comes about with death, in death, from death. In the case of Jesus, this is brought out most clearly in early pre-Pauline hymns, in which Jesus' exaltation seems to take place even from the cross ('to death on the cross. Therefore God has highly exalted him and given him the name which is above every name...'[10]). This is the case particularly in the Gospel of John, where Jesus' 'exaltation' means at the same time both his exaltation on the cross and his 'glorification', and both mean a return to the Father. But belief in a resurrection is basically a radical belief – not in any special religious element, but in God himself, who is the subject of the action. Therefore a second process of reflection is necessary, which similarly need not seem un-Jewish to a Jew.

2. Radicalization of belief in the God of Israel

Dying into God is anything but a matter of course. It is not a natural development, not a desideratum of human nature, to be fulfilled unconditionally. Death and resurrection must be distinguished, not necessarily in time but in substance. This is also stressed by the old detail, 'rose again on the third day', which is presumably not so much historical as symbolic: 'three', not as a calendar date but as the saving date for a day of salvation. **Death** is a **human affair**, but **new life** can only be God's affair. Human beings are taken up, called, brought home, in other words finally accepted and rescued, by God himself into God's incomprehensible, all-embracing ultimate reality. This happens in death, or better, from death, as a separate event, grounded in God's action and faithfulness. As at the first creation, this is a hidden, unimaginable, new creative act of the one who calls into being that which is not. And therefore it is a real event, as real as God himself is utterly real for those who believe – and not a supernatural 'intervention', contrary to the laws of nature.

Whether understood in Jewish or Christian terms, belief in the resurrection is not an addition to belief in God but a radicalization of belief in God. It is a belief in the God who does not stop half-way but continues consistently right to the end. It is a faith in which, without strictly rational proofs, but in completely **reasonable trust**, human beings rely on the fact that the God of the beginning is also the God of the end; that just as he is the creator of the world and of human beings, so too he is their perfecter.

So belief in the resurrection is not to be understood just as an existentialist internalization or social change, but as a radicalization of belief in the creator God. Resurrection means the real **overcoming of**

death by the creator God to whom believers entrust all things, including the last things, and even the overcoming of death. It is the end that is a new beginning. Isn't this consistent? Those who begin their creed with belief in 'God the almighty creator' may also confidently end it with belief in 'eternal life'. Because God is the Alpha, he is also the Omega. That means that the almighty creator who calls into being from nothingness may also call from death to life.[11]

Only from this position is it now also possible to answer the question of the **messiahship of Jesus.** I have already described how, as far as we know, Jesus never claimed this title and in various ways avoided messianic homage from the people.[12] And yet now, in the light of the resurrection, the title 'messiah' becomes profoundly significant and authentically credible when it is applied to him. As a Christian theologian, I cannot emphasize sufficiently that it was Jewish followers of Jesus who, on the basis of their tradition of faith, drew the consequences of belief in the resurrection. It was the Jewish horizon of apocalyptic which already contained categories (e.g. 'Son of Man', 'messiah', 'judge') and notions (e.g. the exaltation of Enoch) for expressing the 'unveiling' (= *apokalypsis*) now, already, of the one who had been exalted to God and the hope for his return in the future.

Where is the risen Christ now? For the first Christians, Psalm 110.1 gave the answer to this extremely urgent question: 'Sit at my right hand...' The one who had been exalted to the right hand of God could now be regarded as the one who had been **justified by God.** Although an obvious failure among human beings, he had been justified by God. God had identified his own self with this godforsaken one. Accordingly, for these Jewish followers, resurrection meant that God took the side of the one who had given his life for God's cause and the human cause. God acknowledged him, and not the hierarchy of Jerusalem which had put him on trial, or the Roman military power which had executed him. God said 'yes' to his proclamation, his conduct, his fate.

Now that means something like a 'revaluation of all values', a revaluation above all of suffering. In content, the Christian expectation of the messiah **reversed the polarity of the** traditional Jewish title of messiah and the traditional **expectation of the messiah.** As we saw, the title messiah, used for the plenipotentiary and bringer of salvation expected in the end-time, could mean a good deal. Understood in the broadest political and nationalistic Jewish sense, and later often fused with the apocalyptic title Son of man, 'messiah of God' denoted the mighty warrior hero of the end-time and the royal liberator of the people. But as a result of the fate of Jesus, the title messiah was now given a completely new interpretation. Now it denoted a non-violent, defenceless, misunderstood, persecuted, betrayed and finally even suffering and dying messiah. To normal Jewish understanding this must have sounded as scandalous as the corresponding title put on the cross at the passion, 'King of the Jews'. In this completely transformed sense, even after the New Testament the title messiah, in Greek Christ, remained the most frequent honorific name for Jesus of Nazareth. There is no doubt about it; here we have come to the decisive theological turning point in the dialogue between Christians and Jews.

3. A decision of faith

Although there may be a historical dispute over the question of the preaching, actions and self-understanding of Jesus, the profile of Jesus' Jewishness and the belief of the earliest Jewish-Christian community, this question remains in the sphere of historical research, which deals in categories of more or less, more probable or less probable. However, at this point another dimension comes into play: the dimension of God himself, which is real, but not under historical control. At this point Christians must contribute their own reasonable trust, their decision of faith, which they cannot force on anyone else. Here there is no more or less, more probable or less probable, but only a yes or no. This, in fact, is a decision of faith, to which there is no compulsion, but a manifold invitation: a decision that God himself, the God of creation and the exodus, the God of the prophets and the wise men of Israel, has spoken, acted and revealed himself, not just through the prophets and wise men, but finally and ultimately also through the crucified Jesus of Nazareth.

However – and again Jews and Christians basically agree here – the resurrection of the one is still not the consummation of the whole. Christians should not contradict Jews, whose view has always been that even after the Christ-event the world has not been wholly changed: its distress is too great. **Even for Christians, the eschatological redemption and consummation has still to take place**: there has been a delay in the 'parousia'. For Jews and Christians, God's kingdom will first come comprehensively and in an all-determining way. So the 'Our Father' can include Jesus's petition: Thy kingdom 'come'.

On the other hand, however, it was already the conviction of the Jews who followed Jesus that everything must not be expected from this coming kingdom: in Jesus himself, his liberating words and healing actions, the power of the coming kingdom has now already dawned, and signs have been set for the coming redemption of the world; the beginning of redemption, an 'initial redemption', has already taken place. Though Jesus and his first followers may even have been 'deceived', this fact of a 'present eschatology' also opens up a perspective on the future whose consummation Jews and Christians together await. For Christians, however, Jesus is the one who has come, someone who does not just proclaim the kingdom of God but in his words and deeds is at the same time its guarantee. For Christians he is the messiah, the Christ – the decisive reason why the Jews who followed Jesus at that time could already be called 'Christians' in Greek.

As the great Jewish theologian Franz Rosenzweig once said, whether Jesus was the messiah will become evident for Jews when the messiah comes. This saying has been quoted often in Jewish-Christian dialogue. Christians can understand the remark like this: when the messiah comes, then, as Christians are convinced, he will be none other than Jesus of Nazareth, the crucified and risen one. The one who has already been raised by God to life and justified is the hope of ultimate redemption for all.

4. What Jews and Christians continue to have in common

And yet, before we have to speak not only of the tense relationship between Christians and Jews – starting from the decision of faith that I have mentioned – but also of the fatal history of their alienation,[13] we need to be reminded of what Jews and Christians continue to have in common. And fortunately, today there is no church document, whether Catholic, Protestant or ecumenical, which on the relationship between Jews and Christians does not start from these common factors. These common factors are also important for ecumenical dialogue in the future.

There is no dispute over the **Jewish basis of Christianity**.

1. Jesus' mother (Miriam) was a Jew, and so Jesus grew up quite naturally as a Jew in a Jewish family, in Nazareth in Galilee, and initially did not make any public appearance.

2. The name given to him was a good Jewish name (Hebrew *Yeshua*, a late form of *Yehoshua* = 'Yahweh is help'), as were the holy scriptures which he knew and read, the worship which he attended, the feasts which he celebrated and the prayers which he spoke. All these were Jewish through and through.

3. He worked among Jews, for Jews: his message was addressed to the whole Jewish people; the disciples, male and female, whom he

gathered around him, and all his followers, were Jews from the Jewish community.

4. The earliest community, which after Jesus' arrest and execution had initially scattered, but then reassembled in belief in him as having been raised to God, consisted of Aramaic-speaking Jews who understood themselves as a group within Judaism.

And to the extent that Jesus and those who followed him were Jews, despite a cruel history full of conflicts, **features common** to Jews and Christians **have persisted right down to the present day:**

- belief in the one **God,** or more precisely in the one God of Abraham, Isaac and Jacob, in whom men and women may trust as creator, sustainer and perfecter of the world and history;
- the collection of sacred **scriptures** (the Tanakh or the 'Old' Testament) which is the source of a common faith and of numerous common values and thought-structures;
- **worship,** in which many elements (the Psalms), many basic actions (prayers, readings) and elements with a religious content have been handed down;
- the **ethos** of justice and of love of God and neighbour, as shown above all by the Ten Commandments;
- belief in God's ongoing history with his people and its **consummation** in full communion with God.

But in addition there was far too little awareness of what the Jews who followed Jesus and the rest of the Jews **similarly at first had in common,** and would **give up only later** – in an extremely complex history. First of all, the Jewish followers of Jesus also accepted:

– the performance of circumcision;[14]
– the hallowing of the sabbath;[15]
– the observance of Jewish festivals;[16]
– obedience to the legal demands for cleanness;[17]
– and up until the destruction of the Temple also participation in Temple worship,[18] at which the 'Shema Israel' ('Hear, O Israel') and the confession of the one and only God resounded, and the 'Shemoneh Esreh', the Eighteen Benedictions, and other prayers were spoken.

These Jews who followed Jesus as their messiah were not confined to Jerusalem and Palestine but later carried on their mission everywhere. So they were also to be found in Greece and Asia Minor, in Syria and Egypt. It is therefore not surprising, as James H.Charlesworth has recently once again reminded us:[19]

– that young Christianity everywhere took over not only the Jewish

tradition of spontaneous personal prayers but also fixed **liturgical prayers**;
– that in the writings of the New Testament, not only the Psalms but in particular **hymns** were taken over from Judaism, adapted or even reformulated under the influence of Jewish tradition;
– that even in the fourth century, we can see the influence not only of Jewish **exegesis** (e.g. on Origen and Jerome) but also of Jewish **liturgy**. Indeed, Chrysostom attests that in individual cases, Christians still took part in synagogue worship in Constantinople.

In fact, any Christians who take part in synagogue services or even in the great Jewish festivals today, will be delighted to find that they are familiar with all that they encounter there, from scripture readings, beginning with the Psalms, to the hymns. What is there that one cannot join in whole-heartedly? Despite all the differences, is a new fellowship so out of the question for the future?

IV. The History of an Alienation

As we saw, what Judaism and Christianity have in common is particularly clear in the liturgy; at all events, some prayers are common or at least mutually so acceptable that nowadays ecumenical worship is possible and is even practised now and again. This is a good sign for authentic ecumenical progress. However, from the perspective of Judaism there is still no simple mutuality. Christians can take part in a Jewish service, but Jews cannot just take part in a specifically Christian service, no matter how many Jewish elements it may contain. Why not? Because up to the present day Jews note a **fundamental difference** in the Christian liturgy. It is the name of that Jew who now stands at the centre of specifically Christian liturgy. It is better not to even to mention this name at all in Jewish liturgy, far less praise it, on the basis of a very old and very important tradition.

1. What distinguishes Christians and Jews from the beginning

It would indeed be wrong to overlook the **differences** between the Jews who followed Jesus (whom we call Jewish Christians) and the rest of the Jews, which **became evident at a very early stage**. The Harvard exegete Helmut Koester has summed them up as follows:[1]
– enthusiastic awareness of possessing the Spirit: the outpouring of that Spirit of God which leads to speaking in tongues, prophesying and healing miracles (the key story here is the Pentecost event at the beginning of the Acts of the Apostles);
– provisional structures, against a background of the imminent expectation of the apocalyptic end: the group of Twelve, who were understood not as apostles or community leaders but as representatives of the twelve tribes of the Israel of the end-time (only with Luke, who wrote his Gospel and Acts after the fall of the Second Temple, do the Twelve become the 'twelve apostles', who form a kind of Jerusalem senior presbytery for the whole church):
– eschatological baptism: taken over from John the Baptist, but now administered 'in the name of Jesus', as a means of entrusting oneself completely to him, the Christ, and thus receiving the Spirit;
– the shared eschatological meal: just as Jesus himself had already celebrated such a meal with his followers, so now it was celebrated as the 'Lord's Supper', in memory and in expectation of the returning 'Lord', Aramaic '*Maran*', hence the prayer '*Maran atha*' ('Lord, come

soon').

Thus it is evident that right from the beginning, the **name of Jesus of Nazareth** stood at the very **centre of the dispute** between Jews and Christians. He had been firmly repudiated by official Judaism as a false messiah, but accepted by a young Jewish community as the true messiah. We heard why: because after the shock of his execution, Jewish men and women had different kinds of spiritual experiences (visions, auditions) against the background of the Jewish resurrection hope. They regarded these experiences, not as an interpretation which they themselves had produced, but as a revelation given by God. The very one who had been put to shame and humiliated was exalted by God himself and now ruled over the world in the place of honour 'at the right hand of God'. So he is now the bearer of the hope of the coming kingdom of God: the pioneer and bringer of salvation, who will soon be adorned with every possible Jewish honorific title.

Consequently it would be frivolous and of no service to Jewish-Christian understanding if nowadays one were simply to conceal and bracket off something what was the cause of dispute down all the centuries. Despite all the common features of faith in the one God and the one salvation history, the holy scriptures, worship, ethics and the coming consummation, right from the beginning **a basic theological difference** made itself felt: all faith and hope were concentrated on this Jesus. And that had consequences for the centre of Jewish faith:

- Here the people (who in any case were soon scattered) and the land (which in any case was soon lost) stood less and less at the **centre** as an expression of the covenant. The centre was this **Jesus** as the guarantor of the covenant, who was expected as the 'messiah' or 'Lord' ('Son of Man', 'Son of David' or whatever title), and who himself increasingly clearly stood at the centre of faith as the representative of the one God: 'Jesus is the Lord', runs one of the oldest confessions of early Christianity.

- So despite all the unchanged faith in the one God, there was a **new definition of the centre of faith**: the name of Jesus became symbolic of the kingdom of God whose coming Jesus had proclaimed. So belief in God took a specifically christological form, indeed was personified. There was no second God alongside the one God, no bitheism instead of monotheism. But the one God of Israel was seen anew through this his last prophet, emissary, messiah and Christ, who was himself understood afresh: as God's Image, Word and Son.

The question is: is this new Jesus movement perhaps just a paradigm shift within Judaism, just another time-conditioned constellation of convictions, values, procedures? We need to get a clearer view of the difference which developed at that time. The circumstances are considerably more complicated than was assumed for a long time.

2. The Hellenistic Jewish Christians

For decades it had been assumed, in the wake of Rudolf Bultmann and the history-of-religions school, that earliest Christian history (up to the 'Apostolic Council', around 49) was to be explained in terms of a **three-communities scheme**. Many Jewish scholars also took this view. The original Aramaic-speaking community of Jews with a Christian orientation, or 'Jewish Christians', in Jerusalem, whose faith and praxis had still largely remained within the framework of Judaism (fidelity to the Temple and the Torah), had been succeeded outside Jerusalem and Palestine by a Greek-speaking community made up of 'Gentile Christians'. These had fused Christianity with Hellenistic syncretism, and had made it the basis of a 'wholly new religion' before Paul founded further Gentile-Christian communities. The original community still appears in this scheme as a purely 'eschatological sect within Judaism'.[2]

However, since the 1960s and 1970s, this picture has been decisively corrected by leading exegetes.[3] Close **connections** can already be demonstrated **between 'Judaism and Hellenism'** (to quote the title of Martin Hengel's classic book[4]) in Palestine, with effects extending to the followers of Jesus and the earliest community. So we have to ask: what happened in Jerusalem and what happened in Antioch?[5]

There is a phenomenon which has been known for a long time but has not been sufficiently analysed historically: after Jesus' death, in Jerusalem the community of disciples of Jesus may by no means have consisted solely of Aramaic-speaking Jews; it may also have included a not inconsiderable number of **Greek-speaking Hellenistic Jews.** At any rate, the conflict over the daily provision for widows reported in Acts 6.1[6] seems to reflect already in the earliest community itself a sharp division between 'Hellenists' on the one hand and 'Hebrews' on the other. It is further underlined by the fact that, to all appearances, both Jewish-Christian groups had their own synagogues and their own house communities, in which scripture was read in worship either in Hebrew or in Greek. Socially and culturally, the Jewish Christians who spoke Greek as their mother tongue came from the urban milieu of Hellenistic Diaspora Judaism and, because they were more educated and probably had more active intellects, may have been led by the circle around Stephen, who are similarly mentioned in Acts ('the Seven', all of whom have purely Greek names). They were probably relatively independent of the group of apostles representing the Hebrews ('the Twelve', who represented the twelve tribes of Israel). At the same time that means that the 'Seven' will hardly have been simply welfare officers subordinate to the 'Twelve', as Luke's Acts of the Apostles reported a generation later. Rather, they will have to be seen as the 'leaders of an independent group in the community', which was already carrying on an active mission in Jerusalem at that time.[7]

The decisive point here is that soon after Jesus' death, in the earliest community – probably in the years 32-34, and at any rate before the apostle Paul – a **conflict with the synagogue establishment** must have broken out, not primarily because of the Aramaic-speaking Jewish Christians, who largely continued to be faithful to the Law and the Temple, but because of these more active Hellenistic Jewish Christians, who came from the Diaspora and therefore may have been more open to criticism of the Law and the Temple. At all events, Acts reports a conflict over alleged blasphemy against the Temple and the Law in the name of Jesus,[8] which comes to a climax with the arrest[9] and stoning of Stephen[10] and the expulsion from Jerusalem of the Hellenistic Jewish Christians (but not the Aramaic Christians: the 'apostles' remained!)[11] As we know, the Hellenistic Jewish Christians continued their missionary activity in Judaea and Samaria, but also in Phoenicia, Cyprus and Antioch. **Antioch**, 180 miles north-east of Jerusalem on the river Orontes, had a special significance, since after Rome and Alexandria it was the third most important city in the Roman empire, capital of the then Roman dual province of Syria and Cilicia.[12] So our starting point must be that the division caused by linguistic barriers on the one hand and 'liturgical independence'[13] on the other was the institutional presupposition for the ' "Hellenists" to be able to develop into a group with a special profile – on the basis of the special presuppositions of the cultural tradition of Diaspora Judaism'.[14]

Thus initially the Antiochene community, which may have been founded by those who were expelled from Jerusalem in the middle of the 30s, by no means consisted solely of Hellenistic Gentile Christians, whose syncretistic bent will have turned the kerygma of the earliest community into a completely new, mystical-cultic religion. Initially Antioch is to be seen, rather, as a community of **Greek-speaking Jewish Christians** who had **not broken free of the Law but were critical of it.** They were the ones who, given the high proportion of Jews in the population of this city (between 20,000 and 40,000), attempted first of all to carry on the mission 'only to the Jews',[15] and then, when they were rejected by the Jews, increasingly went on 'to preach the gospel

The Jesus Movement

Believed in
Jesus Christ

Jews
(='Jewish Christians')

Aramaic-speaking, from Palestine:
'Hebrews' with the 'Twelve'; **faithful to** the Temple and **the Law**

Greek-speaking, from the Diaspora:
'Hellenists' with the 'Seven'; **critical of** the Temple and **the Law**

**The apocalyptic paradigm
of primitive Christianity**

· **Saul/Paul**
apostle of the Gentiles

Non-Jews
(='Gentile Christians'): Greek / Latin-speaking; **free of the Law**

World religion:

**The Hellenistic paradigm
of the early church**

of the Lord Jesus to the Greeks also'.[16] Thus a Gentile Christianity without the law only gradually took its place in Antioch alongside a Hellenistic Jewish Christianity which was critical of the law and which continued to have an independent existence. Not until after the year 48 will the former have replaced the latter.[17]

3. How did a break between Christians and Jews come about?

In my sketch of the **theocratic paradigm** (P III) of post-exilic Judaism, I described at length the degree to which Palestinian Judaism at that time was fixed **on law and Temple**: ' "Zeal for the Law and sanctuary" was a regular feature of Jewish piety in Palestine between Herod and AD 70... Within Palestinian Judaism there was no freedom for open criticism of the Torah and the sanctuary which related to Moses himself.'[18] This easily explains why any **criticism of Torah and Temple** within Judaism inevitably came up against more or less vigorous resistance from the leading authorities, especially if it appealed to an itinerant Galilean prophet who had just been executed as a religious agitator.

We have heard that Jesus himself certainly did not have an antinomian attitude, but in individual cases was quite critical of the Law and the Temple. The whole movement of his followers could appeal to him after his death – but in quite different ways. For whereas the Aramaic-speaking Jewish-Christian community, like Jesus himself, was evidently still concerned to be loyal to Torah and Temple, it is understandable that, as Martin Hengel puts it, 'it was the "Hellenists" who, under the unique, dynamic and creative impulse of the Spirit, developed further the eschatologically motivated trend of the message of Jesus, which was critical of the Torah. The words of Jesus, newly interpreted through the experience of the Spirit and the certainty of the dawn of the end-time, provided the strength to break through the strong traditional link between Torah and cult. As a result, the holy scriptures were no longer interpreted primarily from the perspective of the law and its 613 commands and prohibitions, but as a prophetic promise focussed on Jesus.'[19]

In other words, the theocratic paradigm was in fact gradually undermined by the Hellenistic Jewish Christians in the spirit of the Kyrios Jesus who had been exalted to God. And it may have been here that the **main source of the conflict** with official Judaism lay. Had such Jewish Christians only spiritualized the Temple and the Law, the great dispute might possibly not have come about. Perhaps even the proclamation of Jesus as messiah would still have been tolerated. But the consequence that **Torah and prophets** were to be interpreted specifically in terms of Jesus and with a view to Jesus, and that salvation was in him alone, was quite unacceptable. The Jewish Torah and Temple establishment reacted to such a monstrous claim with harsh and, if necessary, violent **counter-measures**.

So it came about that, conversely, the christological and pneumatological interpretation of the Torah almost automatically took on an increasingly **anti-Jewish bias**: to the degree that people found in the Hebrew Bible 'prophecies' not only of the messiah, but also of his opponents. That can already be seen in the early New Testament writings: the concentration of the young Christian community on the exalted Jesus Christ, ruling as Kyrios and present in the Spirit, resulted in increasing polemic against a synagogue which repudiated him. So there was heightened polemic not only against particular Jewish authorities but against whole groups, 'the Pharisees and scribes', indeed finally and sweepingly against 'the Jews' generally. So we cannot avoid the painful question: do not the roots of hostility to the Jews, anti-Judaism, perhaps even antisemitism, already lie in the New Testament itself?

4. Anti-Judaism in the New Testament

A racist antisemitism cannot be found in the New Testament, any more than it can be found elsewhere in antiquity. As we heard, it is a product of the nineteenth century. However, there can hardly be any dispute that already in the New Testament there is an anti-Judaism which was to have devastating consequences in later times. The decisive question, of course, is **how we are to assess this anti-Judaism in the New Testament**.

– For centuries Christian theologians had no difficulty in convincing the world that the young church was in the right and was wrongly persecuted by the synagogue.

– Today, in understandable reaction to modern antisemitism, the opposite tendency prevails in both Jewish and Christian publications: the young Christian community is put in the wrong from the start, and the hostile reaction of the Jewish establishment is played down.

– If we attempt to assess the positions of both sides with as little prejudice as possible, we cannot help noticing that the **process of alienation was mutual**. Further evidence will be given for this in what follows. Already at an early stage there was a complete separation, and the increasing repudiation of 'the Jews' in the New Testament writings went hand in hand with the no less radical repudiation of 'the Nazarenes' by the synagogue. In other words, traditional Judaism repudiated the small but rapidly growing Christian community as an apocalyptic-messianic sect which had been overtaken by the course of events. Conversely, the young church increasingly attacked the synagogue as a religion of the Temple and the Law which had been made obsolete by Jesus. It is difficult here to reconstruct precisely and in detail who was echoing whom, what was action and what was reaction.

As the Catholic theologian Rosemary Ruether writes in her study of the roots of antisemitism: 'Thus, Church and Synagogue, like the two brothers of Rebekah's womb, were born with the younger holding on to the heel of the elder – and claiming to be the rightful heir. The Church, elaborating its theology between the second and fifth centuries, and Judaism, codifying its oral Torah into the Talmud the same period, stand as parallel but mutually exclusive answers to the same question of how Hebrew national faith finds its way into a postnational future.'[20]

Thus two rival, indeed irreconcilable, interpretations of scripture came into being. And it must be conceded on the Christian side, without any ifs and buts, that the **christological exegesis** of the Hebrew Bible brought an **anti-Jewish exegesis in its train.** Anyone who reads the New Testament writings will be able to note without having it pointed out to them that:

– under the pressure of the need to legitimate itself, the young Christian community increasingly presented the official Judaism which rejected it as a fallen, apostate Israel;

– priests and scribes are increasingly slandered as being not only uncomprehending but 'blind leaders', indeed as a 'generation of vipers', 'whitewashed sepulchres' and so on:[21]

– the Jewish people as a whole begins to be regarded as a 'wicked and faithless generation';[22]

– in particular the Pharisees, the dominant group after the fall of the Second Temple, are dismissed in the Gospel written by the Jewish Christian Matthew as 'hypocrites', as representatives of a pure legalism and formalism;[23]

– the Romans are exonerated as far as possible from responsibility for the death of Jesus, at the expense of the Jews;[24]

– the term 'the Jews' in the New Testament increasingly takes on negative connotations, instead of being used purely descriptively, and the word 'Jewish' is constantly avoided as a designation of young Christianity as such;

– finally, with a reference to the alleged fate of earlier prophets, 'the

Jews' are said to have a deadly intent and to have brought their fate upon themselves. Worst of all is the statement. 'Then all the people cried out (before Pilate), "His blood be on us and on our children."'[25] This was to have the most pernicious results, but it is hardly historical.

5. The excommunication of the Christians

Such anti-Judaism cannot be excused. But it must be seen in its historical context – which does not mean diluting it or playing it down. And yet it is not unimportant to remind ourselves that at that time Christianity was anything but a powerful state church which could have taken action against Jews, as was to happen later. Rather, in comparison with the powerful Jewish majority, young Christianity was a small, helpless group, which had to fight for its right to exist. This sometimes happened in the face of violent attempts at repression by an establishment which had already been unsettled by a relatively small opposition group. Three historical cases provide food for thought and may not be suppressed either.

1. **The case of Stephen.** Certainly, Stephen's speech in Acts[26] is a Lucan composition and cannot be used uncritically for the historical reconstruction of the views of Stephen and his supporters. What Stephen says about Israel's apostasy and the killing of the prophets is primarily to be attributed to the redactor, Luke. But a historical nucleus may have been preserved here: any criticism of Moses, any assertion that the Temple and the Law were provisional, coupled with a reference to Jesus, could easily have been denounced as blasphemy. Granted, it is equally uncertain whether Stephen was involved in a formal trial before the Sanhedrin at which he will have had the occasion to give an extended mission sermon. However, it is certain that the case of Stephen ended badly, in a kind of Jewish 'lynch law', which came to a climax with the stoning of the delinquent.[27]

2. **The case of Saul.** Whatever may be said about the theological position of the controversial apostle Paul, the case of the Hellenistic Diaspora Jew Saul from Tarsus, trained by the Pharisees, shows more clearly than that of Stephen that the Jewish establishment did not handle certain Jewish Christians with kid gloves. 'But Saul laid waste the church, and entering house after house, he dragged off men and women and committed them to prison.' So runs the account in Acts[28] about this Diaspora Jew who gained a religious profile as the persecutor,

presumably above all of those Hellenistic Jewish Christians (in Damascus or Jerusalem) who continued Jesus' criticism of the law. The authenticity of this report is confirmed by the fact that Paul himself acknowledges, in his correspondence with Philippi, that he was 'circumcised on the eighth day, of the people of Israel, a Hebrew born of Hebrews; as to the law a Pharisee, as to zeal a persecutor of the church, as to righteousness under the law blameless'.[29]

So Paul – this Pharisee of strict observance, 'zealous for the traditions of my fathers' –[30] had seen his Pharisaic zeal for God and God's law challenged by questioning of the law. Fanatic that he was, he had resolved on an active fight 'beyond measure', indeed 'in an attempt to destroy' the church, as we read in Galatians.[31] The scandal which the assertion of a messiah crucified under the curse of the law represented to any Jews had merely confirmed him in his boundless zeal for persecution.[32] So Jews did persecute Christians.

But Paul is also the archetypal example of a great mid-life change, from persecuting Christians to proclaiming Christ – however difficult that may be to explain in retrospect, either historically or psychologically. At all events, Paul himself does not attribute this radical change to human teaching, to a new self-understanding, a heroic effort or a conversion which he himself achieved. Rather, he attributes it to an experience of the living Christ, a 'revelation' (a 'seeing') of the crucified one who had been raised from the dead. This is an experience which he does not elaborate on, however it may be interpreted.[33] He understood it less as an individual conversion than as a call to be an apostle, the accredited missionary to the Gentiles.[34] And if we do not doubt that there is an authentic nucleus to the accounts of the calls of Hebrew prophets like Isaiah, Jeremiah and Ezekiel, *a priori* we should not doubt that there is also an authentic nucleus to the story of the calling of Saul, the Pharisee.

At all events, it is now the former persecutor of Christians who himself has to endure discrimination, persecution, imprisonment and chastisement from the Jewish establishment during his missionary journeys. Acts is full of this, and here, too, Paul himself confirms the authenticity of such reports – above all when he has to defend himself, and especially in the second correspondence with Corinth: 'With far greater labours, far more imprisonments, with countless beatings, and often near death. Five times have I received at the hands of the Jews the forty lashes less one. Three times I have been beaten with rods; once I was stoned. Three times I have been shipwrecked; a night and a day I have been adrift at sea; on frequent journeys, in danger from rivers, danger from robbers, danger from my own people, danger from

Gentiles, danger in the city, danger in the wilderness, danger at sea, danger from false brethren.'[35] But despite all this, all his life, as a Jew he held firmly to the promises of God to his people. We shall be hearing more of this.

3. **The case of the Johannine community**. There is no doubt that the Fourth Gospel, written around 100, contains the sharpest anti-Jewish passages. 'The Jews' not only become a hostile collective stereotype (there is no longer any terminological distinction even of groups within Judaism) but are identified programmatically with all that is evil and dark in the world. By comparison, the Christian community appears as the new, internalized, spiritual community of the new age. Instead of the Torah it is Jesus who is now 'the way, the truth and the life'; only through him does one come to the Father.[36] And Jesus is not condemned to death by the Romans as a political agitator but by the Jewish authorities, for the religious crime of blasphemy.

The religious, political and social background of this New Testament text must also be noted. If we follow the latest research, originally the Johannine community may similarly have consisted of Jewish Christians. But these must have come into conflict with the Jewish establishment at the latest at the moment when – under whatever influence – they arrived at their very high christology (Jesus the heavenly Son of God already existing before Abraham) and their equally high understanding of the eucharist ('I am the bread of life').[37] This must have seemed blasphemy to the Jewish establishment. At any rate, the Gospel of John clearly reflects this charge – in contrast to the Synoptic Gospels, in which Jesus was in conflict with the law (the sabbath)! 'This was why the Jews sought all the more to kill him, because he not only broke the sabbath but also called God his Father, making himself equal with God.'[38]

For this group, too, the consequences were serious; for the Jewish synagogue evidently excluded John's Jewish-Christian community formally from the Jewish company of faith, presumably on the charge of blasphemy: 'We stone you for no good work but for blasphemy because you, being a man, make yourself God.'[39] What appears here as a charge levelled against Jesus reflects the repudiation of the community itself.[40]

But we must also see the Gospel of John against the whole contemporary background; it was written when the formal 'excommunication' of Christians was already in force. Indeed, we heard how after the catastrophe of 70, Pharisaism re-established itself as Jewish orthodoxy in the city of Jabneh (near Jaffa) and aimed at a fundamental new ordering and reconstitution of Judaism. The theocratic paradigm no longer had any basis. The temple hierarchy had lost its function; the Sadducean upper class had been liquidated or dispersed; the Zealots were entangled in a hopeless fight to the death with the Romans (Masada!). Only the Pharisees were left as a coherent group, and they now attempted to establish themselves in the new **Temple-less rabbinic paradigm** (P IV) as a kind of 'normative Judaism', and to 'eliminate' other Jewish groups and trends.

From Jabneh and its teaching academy (first under the leadership of Rabbi Johanan ben Zakkai and then under Rabbi Gamaliel II), the Pharisaic rabbinate had evidently begun to take strict precautions so that no one deviated from the prescribed line. Only in this context can we understand a fateful text, the notorious '**cursing of heretics**' which was composed at the so-called 'council' in Jabneh, probably on the instructions of Gamaliel, two to three decades after the destruction of the Temple, around the years 90 to 100. At that time it was inserted as a twelfth benediction into the Eighteen Benedictions – the Jewish prayer, which is said three times a day and is part of the liturgy. Probably already at that time the Jewish Christians were mentioned alongside the heretics. In an early version it runs as follows: 'For the apostates let there be no hope. And let the arrogant government be speedily uprooted in our days. Let the Nazarenes (*nosrim*) and the heretics (*minim*) be destroyed in a moment. And let them be blotted out of the Book of Life and not be inscribed together with the righteous. Blessed art thou, O Lord, who humblest the arrogant.'[41]

So the curses are not directed exclusively against the Jewish Christians but, as P.Schäfer shows, 'both against a hostile authority and against different groups of heretics'.[42] It would certainly be an exaggeration to follow I.Elbogen in seeing them as a 'means of completely separating the two religions'.[43] In fact such a curse – spoken at the beginning of every service – must have led to the exclusion of Jewish Christians from the synagogue.

Here it should be noted that at the time this exclusion from the synagogue was more than a purely 'religious measure'. To be branded as a heretic and to be excluded from the community of faith had above all social and economic consequences, which changed the whole life of those involved: 'Old ties were totally cut off, all personal and social converse was forbidden, and all help ruled out.'[44] So it is understandable that this must have led to the prevalence of an **atmosphere of anxiety** in the Johannine community: the parents of the man born blind cannot concede that Jesus was the miraculous healer 'because they were afraid of the Jews';[45] many 'of the leading men of Israel' did not dare to confess their belief in Jesus openly 'so as not to be excluded from the synagogue';[46] Nicodemus the Pharisee found it better to go to Jesus by night; and even Joseph of Arimathea remained only a 'secret disciple of Jesus' – 'for fear of the Jews'.[47]

If we take all this together, there can hardly be any disputing the fact that the **excommunication of Christians** by Jews **preceded the persecution of Jews** by Christians. The New Testament reflects both the Jewish persecutions and the anti-Jewish polemic.[48] And unfortunately it has to be added that this **polemic** became increasingly **worse**, again **on both sides**. Later Jewish works, still hawked around today, claim that Jesus was the bastard offspring of a Roman soldier, Joseph Pandera, and the young girl Miriam, and that he was stoned for using the divine name in magic. The slanderous *Toledot Jeshu* (Generations, History of Jesus), based on legends and false history, were to grow in size right down to the Middle Ages. For their part, Christians increasingly resorted to the sweeping charges that in any case Jews were 'murderers of Christ', indeed 'murderers of God', which in turn is a grotesque misrepresentation of the New Testament. That had the worst consequences of all. But we have heard enough of these horrors in connection with the long history leading from anti-Judaism to antisemitism. Here we are interested in the question: what were the real differences now, where the church of Jews was evidently becoming more and more a church of Gentiles?

V. A First Christian Paradigm Shift:
From Jewish Christianity to Gentile Christianity

We can now answer the question from which we started: the new Jesus movement was not just a paradigm shift within Judaism, but the more time went on, the more it became another rival religion. This process is understandable only if we take into account the fact that at a very early stage **the young Christianity also already had a first paradigm shift of its own**: the **transition from Jewish Christianity** (which was partly Aramaic-speaking and partly Greek-speaking) **to an exclusively Greek-** (or later Latin-)**speaking Gentile Christianity.**

1. The controversial Paul

And here we must now consider above all that man whose personal change, from persecutor to disciple, was finally to lead to a decisive change in the history of early Christianity, indeed of the ancient world: the **apostle Paul**.[1] But precisely at this point we have arrived at what is perhaps the most delicate point of Jewish-Christian dialogue.[2] For the fact is, that some Jews repudiate the Jew Paul from Tarsus even more decisively than the Jew Jesus of Nazareth. As we heard, quite a number of Jews, above all the well-informed, have approached the prophetic figure of Jesus of Nazareth with sympathy. But Paul? 'Just about everything has been said about Paul from the Jewish side over 1,900 years,' remarks Pinchas Lapide: 'that he quotes the Torah eighty times only to do away with it; that he frequently contradicts himself in his letters; that he invented an un-Jewish disease, original sin, in order to cure it with an anti-Jewish means – with a human sacrifice as an atoning death. That further he became everyman to everyone in order to save some, as he says in I Corinthians (9.22); that he was thus prepared to abandon his principles for the sake of propaganda; that he falsified the faith of Jesus so that it became faith in Jesus; that he transformed the creation optimism of Genesis, according to which human beings are good, into a Hellenistic pessimism according to which human beings are too sinful and too weak by nature to prove themselves worthy of redemption without the grace of God.'[3]

An unfortunately not untypical recent example of a polemical and tendentious account which is academically untenable is **Hyam Maccoby**'s book on Paul, *The Mythmaker*, with the sub-title 'Paul and the Invention of Christianity'.[4] By contrast, a study which Christian readers, too, will find an impressive piece of scholarship is the latest book on Paul by **Alan Segal**, the Jewish historian of religion from Columbia University, *Paul the Convert*. This seeks to bring out two things: 'The apostolate and the apostasy of Saul, the Pharisee'.[5] In contrast to numerous texts from the Mishnah and the Talmud which cannot with any degree of certainty be attributed to the Judaism of the time of Jesus, the writings of Paul are (apart from those of Josephus) the 'only personal writings which have been left behind by a Pharisee of the first century'. They in particular should 'be used as a main source for the study of Judaism in the first century', contrary to the practice of Jewish research hitherto, which rules out Paul because of prejudice.[6] As Segal brings out in extensive historical and psychological analyses, here we must take 'the authenticity of Paul's conversion experience' seriously.[7] It was this one **conversion of the Pharisee Saul from Pharisaism to belief in Jesus Christ** (whose living presence he experienced in a vision) which was to prove to be very much more than just a paradigm shift within Judaism.

Two things must be presupposed here:

1. Already long before Paul's personal conversion to belief in Christ, right from their Easter experiences of the Risen One, Jewish disciples of Jesus had begun to understand the one God anew in the light of the crucified man who had been exalted to God; in this way their belief in God took on an increasingly messianic and christological orientation and content.

2. The Jew Paul who was converted to belief in Christ understood the messiah of Israel as messiah of the whole world of Jews and Gentiles. But the thought never occurred to him of replacing the Jewish faith in one God with a Christian faith in two Gods. Rather, he too saw the Jesus who had been exalted by God's Spirit as constantly subordinate to the one God and Father: as messiah, Christ, image, son of the one God. His christocentricity was grounded in and culminated in theocentricity: 'from God through Jesus Christ' – 'through Jesus Christ to God'.[8] In the end 'God himself (*ho theos*) will be all in all'.[9]

In other words, Paul is not responsible for the fundamental shift from the faith of Jesus to the community's faith in Christ. Rather, the 'responsibility' lies with the Easter experience of the risen Jesus, since as a result of this a particular group of Jews could no longer believe in the God of Israel without the messiah Jesus who had come. However, Paul **is** responsible for the fact that despite the universal monotheism of Judaism, which at the time was also engaged in an intensive mission, it was **not Judaism but Christianity which became a universal religion of humanity.**

So that is the significance of the apostle Paul for world history. The one who everywhere preached first to Jews, but was mostly rejected by them, resolutely made a way for non-Jews to gain access to Jewish belief in God and thus initiated the first paradigm shift in Christianity – from Jewish Christianity to Hellenistic Gentile Christianity. To what extent? To the extent that in the face of the leading circles of Jerusalem Christians he carried through the decision that **Gentiles** too could have **access to the universal God of Israel without** previously having to adopt **circumcision** and the Jewish laws of purity which alienated them – the halakhic regulations about food and the sabbath, the 'works of the law'.[10] In other words, a Gentile could become a Christian without becoming a Jew first. The consequences of this fundamental decision proved immense for the whole of the Western world (and not just the Western world):

– Only through Paul did the Christian mission to the Gentiles (which was already being carried on before and alongside Paul) become a resounding success, in contrast to the Jewish Hellenistic mission.

– Only through Paul did the community of Palestinian and Hellenistic Jews become a community of Jews and Gentiles.

– Only through Paul did the small Jewish 'sect' finally develop into a 'world religion' in which East and West were more closely bound together even than they had been by Alexander the Great.

– So, without Paul there would have been no Catholic Church, no Greek and Latin patristic theology, no Christian-Hellenistic culture, no Constantinian shift.

The role of the apostle Paul in world history is nowadays also stressed by Jewish theologians like Pinchas Lapide: 'For me, Paul is above all a hero of faith, whose tragic failure – like that of his lord and redeemer – was crowned only after his death with the greatest missionary success in world history. Three times repudiated, by Judaism, by Gnosticism and the Gentile cults and by his own mother church in Jerusalem, this cosmopolitan fought his way through to a global ecumenism by virtue of which he representatively peformed for Israel the prophetic task of being "a light for the nations" (Isa.49.6). Franz Rosenzweig rightly observed that it was not Jerusalem but Christianity which brought the Hebrew Bible to the remotest islands, very much in line with the prophecies of Isaiah.'[11]

But the question remains: did not Paul misunderstand Jesus, and in that respect did he not become the real founder of Christianity?

2. The sympathetic transformation

It has already become abundantly clear that in fact decisive changes came about in early Christianity as a result of Paul and his restless spiritual, theological and missionary church-political activity. But closer consideration confirms Paul's own conviction: this did not happen in contradiction to Jesus but **in connection with Jesus**, of whom Paul, on the basis of his contacts with eye-witnesses in Jerusalem and elsewhere, had doubtless heard more than is suggested by his few letters, which are mostly fragmentary occasional writings.[12] For the conflict with the law which decisively led to Jesus' death also became the conflict between the Pharisee Saul, who was so blamelessly faithful to the law, and Jesus' community. The teaching of the law put forward by Paul, who had been converted from Pharisaic persecutor to apostle of Christ, specifically presents itself as a continuation of the proclamation and conduct of Jesus himself.

However, it was a radical continuation. For what stands between the proclamation of Jesus the Jew and the proclamation of Paul the Jew? The answer is: **Jesus' execution**, which – as Saul the zealot for the Law had already heard, and Paul the critic of the Law was convinced – had been caused by a questioning of the law and not, say, by political rebellion (Paul takes the political instigator hypothesis *ad absurdum*). And for Paul, this execution had acquired meaning through the visionary experience of the crucified Jesus as one who had been raised to life. Paul knew even better than the later church how presumptuous it was for Jews to believe in a crucified messiah, and for Gentiles to believe in a crucified hero or Son of God. The belief was possible only because the crucified one had proved to be alive.

So when Paul sees all that the historical Jesus brought, lived out and maintained to the end concentrated in his death on the cross; when he uses the term **'the word of the cross'**[13] for the Christian message; when he sees this as the focus and culmination of the 'gospel' which was a life-and-death commitment for him, he does not just mean the 'cross' and nothing but the cross. Rather, he means the word **from the** cross, i.e. the proclamation that God has justified the crucified Jesus, raised him through his Spirit, and exalted him to himself. So the 'word of the cross' always also means belief in the **resurrection** of the crucified Jesus.

It is from the risen, crucified Jesus that the theology of Paul derives that deep passion and critical sharpness which sets it apart from others. From this centre – even in Paul it is not the whole – he sees God and man, approaches all situations and problems; he reprimands the confused conservative Jewish Christian moralists in the district of

Galatia in Asia Minor, who regarded circumcision, Jewish ritual, the sabbath and the calendar as decisive for salvation,[14] just as he reprimands the progressive pneumatic enthusiasts in the great Hellenistic port of Corinth, who misunderstood their newly-won spiritual freedom and misused it in a 'fleshly' way.[15] From this centre the apostle Paul could also give a theological explanation of what Jesus had in fact done and often said only implicitly. So he becomes the **first 'Christian theologian'**. To this end Paul used his rabbinic training, especially in exegesis, and the often very free application of biblical texts (Paul was possibly a pupil of the famous Gamaliel I in Jerusalem) as arbitrarily as he did some concepts and notions from his Hellenistic environment (Tarsus, the birthplace of the Roman citizen Paul, was a centre of Hellenistic education). So to those Jews and Christians who came to the letters of Paul from the Jesus tradition, which at that time was still oral, the message of Jesus must at first have appeared in a somewhat alien light: fused to quite different perspectives, categories and conceptions, translated into quite a different entire constellation.

Nevertheless, if we look more closely, we recognize that in Paul, who always modestly yet proudly described himself as an authorized 'messenger', indeed 'apostle' of Jesus Christ to the Gentiles, very much more of the preaching of Jesus is preserved than is indicated by individual 'words of the Lord' which he happens to include in his letters. Indeed the **'substance' of the preaching of Jesus** has been quite **sympathetically transformed** into the preaching of Paul.
– Paul too still had a quite intense **expectation of the coming kingdom of God**. However, whereas Jesus had looked into the future, Paul now at the same time looks back, to the kingdom of God which had already dawned through the death and resurrection of Jesus: now already the name of Jesus Christ stands for God's kingdom.
– Paul, too, begins from the *de facto* **sinfulness** of human beings (not a sexually-transmitted original sin!), particularly the sinfulness of people who, while they are righteous, pious, and faithful to the law, are nevertheless lost. But he develops this insight theologically: by using biblical, rabbinic and Hellenistic material and contrasting Adam and Christ as types of the old and the new.
– Paul, too, sees human beings as in a **crisis**; he summons to **faith** and calls for **repentance**. However, for him the message of the kingdom of God is concentrated on the word of Christ's cross which, by causing a scandal, provokes a crisis for both the Jewish and the Greek ways of 'boasting' before God. He criticizes on the one hand the legalistic obedience to the Law among Jewish Christians (as, say, in Galatians)

and on the other hand the arrogant wisdom speculation of the Gentile Christians (say in I Corinthians).

– Paul, too, claims **God** for his activity. But he does so in the light of the cross and resurrection of Jesus, where for him the activity of God, who is a God of the living and not of the dead, has made the definitive break-through. Even before Paul and then through Paul, after the death and resurrection of Jesus, Jesus' implicit and *de facto* christology has become the explicit christology of the community.

– In a quite practical way, Paul too went beyond the limits of the law in turning to the poor, the lost, the oppressed, the outsiders, the lawless, the lawbreakers, and advocated a **universalism** in word and deed. However, in the light of the cross and resurrection, in Paul, Jesus' fundamental universalism towards Israel and *de facto* or virtual universalism towards the Gentile world has now become a direct universalism with respect to **Israel and the Gentile world** which virtually requires the proclamation of the good news among the Gentiles.

– Paul, too, presents the forgiveness of sins as pure grace: the acquittal, **justification of the sinner** not on the basis of the works of the Law (Jesus' parable of the Pharisee in the Temple) but on the basis of an unconditional trust (faith) in the gracious and merciful God. However, his message of the justification of the sinner without the works of the law (without circumcision and other ritual accomplishments) presupposes Jesus' death on the cross. Here the messiah is executed as a criminal under a curse in the name of the law, before the guardians of law and order, but then appears as the risen one, justified before the law by the God who makes alive. The result was that the negative side of the law was now became evident to Paul.

– Paul, too, proclaimed the **love of God and neighbour** as the *de facto* fulfilment of the law and lived it out in the most radical way, in unconditional obedience to God and selfless commitment to his fellow human beings, even his enemies. But Paul recognized specifically in the death of Jesus the deepest revelation of this love on the part of God and Jesus himself, which may be the basis of human love for God and neighbour.

By now it should have become clear that Paul, who despite his high emotions, powerful rhetoric and some extremely polemical statements, was never a man of hatred but of love, a real 'messenger of good tidings', did not invent a new religion. He did not construct a new system or create a new 'substance of faith'. As a Jew – albeit in a completely new paradigmatic constellation – he built on that foundation which in his own words has been laid once and for all: Jesus

Christ.[16] Jesus Christ is also the origin, content and criterion of Paul's preaching. So in the light of a fundamentally different situation after Jesus' death and resurrection, he did not advocate a different cause but the same cause: the **cause of Jesus**, which is none other than **God's cause** and the **human cause** – but which now, sealed by the death and resurrection of Jesus, can be understood in brief summary as the **cause of Jesus Christ**.[17] This Jesus Christ whose living presence Paul experienced was for him the origin and criterion of the new freedom, the immovable centre and norm of what is Christian.

Ultimately, Paul's preaching is a **radically intensified understanding of God** – in the light of Jesus Christ. So since then Jews and Christians have been struggling, each in a different way – and Ernst Käsemann, the well-known Protestant exegete of Paul, has recently enlarged on this in a response to Pinchas Lapide. In fact, if we look at the history of Israel from the wandering in the wilderness through the history of the prophets and the Qumran sect down to the present, we see how the people of Israel was always faced with the need to separate itself from false worship. The writings of the Hebrew Bible are full of this: God is not only unrecognized among the heathen, he is also unrecognized even by his own people. And this people constantly experienced dramatic and tragic tensions and divisions, constantly struggled with apostates and rebels for the true God and for right, perfect worship. So in the case of Jesus, too, the last and deepest question is: 'Where and when and how is the God hidden in heaven rightly known and appropriately worshipped on earth? The Jew Paul also starts from this question asked by Israel and answers it by adopting a christological orientation to belief in God... Today perhaps, we honour the rabbi of Nazareth on both sides, whether as a teacher, a prophet, or a brother. For Paul, the crucified Christ alone is the image of the divine will, the countenance of the God who seeks out the godless, who scandalizes the pious and the moral, those who are faithful to the law and those who always need norms, and blesses the fallen, lost world as his creation. The whole theology of the apostle is to be understood and can be understood from there.'[18]

So Paul did no more and no less than consistently draw out those lines which had already been charted in the preaching, conduct and death of Jesus. In so doing he attempted to make the message understandable beyond Israel, for the whole of the then known world. Now perhaps Jews, too, will be able to understand how, with the few of his letters which are still left, that Paul who, as a disciple of his master, having committed his life in such a tremendous way, suffered the violent death of a witness to the faith in Rome under the emperor Nero (probably in 66), has constantly given new impetus to Christianity all down the centuries in a way that no one else has done but Jesus – impetus to rediscover the true Christ and to follow him. Since then it has become clear that what is distinctive about **Christianity, its 'essence'** as opposed to Judaism, the old world religions and modern humanism, is this **Christ Jesus himself.** Precisely as the one who was crucified, he differs both from the many risen, exalted and living gods and divinized founders of religions, Caesars, genies, lords and heroes of world history.

That may have been sufficient explanation of why in Christianity, after Jesus had been repudiated by the majority of the people of Israel, we do not have just **another paradigm within Judaism,** but in the end really a **different religion, although of course it has indispensable Jewish roots.** The consequences emerged clearly in a closer examination of the consequences of that first paradigm shift within Christianity, from Jewish Christianity to Gentile Christianity.

3. A universal religion of humanity

The consequence of this paradigm shift which was first prepared for by the Hellenistic Jewish Christians and then had its foundations laid by Paul was a radically new understanding of the Bible, the law and the people, the presupposition for which is Christianity as a universal religion of humanity. Let us sum up the changes briefly.

First of all, the **understanding of the Bible** changed. Jewish groups which repudiated Jesus naturally maintained their traditional exegesis of the biblical writings and at first continued to await the coming of the messiah, until the messianic hope was permanently to be shattered after the last revolt against the Romans under Bar Kokhba, who was proclaimed as the messiah.

But those Jews who followed Jesus, the Aramaic- or Greek-speaking **Jewish Christians,** now began to read the holy scriptures differently, as it were retrospectively. The Jesus event could not just be a matter of blind chance or divine whim. On the contrary, only now in retrospect did people learn to understand many of the 'promises' of the prophets 'rightly' – including the figure of the 'suffering servant' whom Deutero-Isaiah had depicted so impressively. So it was now possible to transfer to Jesus the interpretations and honorific titles which had already been coined in the Jewish holy scriptures: 'Messiah', 'Lord', 'Son of David', 'Son of Man', 'Son of God'. For example, Nathan's prophecy of the eternal rule of a descendant of David, which at that time, in Qumran and elsewhere, was given an eschatological reference to the messianic age, was now related to Jesus, who according to all the sources was of Davidic descent: 'I will be his father, and he shall be my son.'[19] So Jesus was now understood in good Jewish fashion as 'God's Son'.

However, in a non-Jewish context some of these typically Jewish honorific titles (in particular 'Son of David' or 'Son of Man') proved difficult for Hellenistic **Gentile Christians** to understand. So they do not appear in the early or classical Christian confessions of faith which were formulated in Greek or Latin. But precisely the opposite happened with the title 'Son of God'. In the Hebrew scriptures it was used only on isolated occasions for Israel's king and the whole people, but it became extraordinarily popular among the Hellenistic Gentile Christians – because it was also used for the emperor and other heroes. So popular was 'Son of God', that it now increasingly came to be understood in Graeco-Hellenistic terms as denoting a nature, and became increasingly remote from its Jewish origin. At this specific point a theological micro-paradigm shift took place within the macro-paradigm shift in the church, one which was to have serious consequences. In Jewish eyes, at any rate, as reflected in the Gospel of John, the Christians seemed increasingly to have set Jesus of Nazareth on the same level as God and thus to have endangered belief in the one and only God.

Secondly, though, the **understanding of the law** also changed. We shall be hearing more about this. After the shift from the theocratic paradigm to a new rabbinic paradigm in the second century CE, increasing weight was attached in Judaism to the scrupulous observance and codification of the halakhah (the legal parts of the Torah) and the commandments (*mizvot*) in everyday life. In synagogues and Torah schools Pharisaic circles put increasing emphasis on the strict observance not only of the Torah but also of its expansions in the Mishnah and Talmud, the traditions of the fathers, the 'oral' Torah, i.e. the whole Law, the whole halakhah.

However, for those Jews who followed Jesus, the **Jewish Christians,** all the ceremonial and ritual commandments were less important than the ethical commandments. In the spirit of Jesus, the Hellenistic Jewish Christians from the Diaspora in particular had begun to concentrate their teaching on the central ethical statements of the Torah. Their ideal was not so much righteousness in the sense of the law as active love, the chief commandment set above all the rest, made concrete and radicalized in the spirit of the Sermon on the Mount.

Finally, the **Gentile Christians** no longer felt themselves bound by the Jewish ritual law. In practice that meant that they felt under no pressure to be circumcised or to observe the ritual halakhah. They did not have to become Jews before they could become Christians. No longer circumcision, which for Jews was a sign of identity but which was abhorrent to Greeks and Romans, but rather faith and baptism were regarded as the decisive sign of Christian identity and the covenant with God. It was no longer observance of the law but faith in and discipleship of Christ that was the decisive factor.

Thirdly, the **understanding of the people of God** changed. Certainly, Jews accepted that there was also a possibility of salvation outside Judaism; righteous Gentiles, too, could attain eternal salvation on the basis of their just works (we have already considered the Jewish universalism of salvation in Part One). But at the same time Jews maintained that belonging to the people of God was identical with belonging to the people of Israel (the particularism of the Jewish people). The Jewish people comes before the individual Jew. Above all after the loss of any constitutional independence (in 70 CE), there was even more stress by Jews on the inner, spiritual unity of their own, chosen people.[20] One was born into this chosen people through one's mother, or joined it through authentic conversion.

The **Jewish Christians** felt that they still belonged fully to the people of Israel, although the Greek-speaking Hellenistic Jewish Christians had a more remote relationship to the Temple and the law than did the Aramaic-speaking Jewish Christians.

However, the **Gentile Christians,** who were now becoming increasingly numerous, did not belong to the chosen people from the start and did not have to join it by circumcision in order to become Christians. So almost automatically, they also reinterpreted the understanding of the people of God. Belief in Jesus Christ, rather than descent, was now decisive for membership. With this belief went what was originally the Jewish initiation rite of baptism, now performed in the name of Jesus Christ. The repudiation of belief in Christ by the majority of Jews everywhere strengthened even further the idea of a 'new covenant' and a 'new people of God', consisting of the 'true children of Abraham'. And after the evacuation of the community of Christians from Jerusalem at the time of the Jewish-Roman war and the destruction of the Temple, even shared Temple worship was no longer possible and there was virtually no way in which Jews and Christians could avoid living completely separate lives.[21] Finally, in the subsequent period, intellectual discussion was unfortunately reduced more and more to a constant battle over proof-texts for or against the fulfilment of the biblical promises in Jesus – until even this ultimately became superfluous and tedious.

This far-reaching process of inheritance, which above all involved filling the term 'people of God' with new content, more than anything else helps us to understand why relations between Jews and Christians over the course of the next 1500 years of shared history had been so poisoned from earliest times. But have things always to be like that? It is a sign of hope that today it is emphasisized even from the Jewish side that neither of the two religions, Christianity or Judaism, can be completely understood without the other. They belong together like 'Rebecca's children'. In a book with this title the Jewish scholar **Alan Segal** made the following programmatic statement: 'The prophecy about Jacob and Esau, Rebecca's twin children, in Genesis 25.23 was used by both Judaism and in Christianity to further their competing claims to divine favour (e.g. Midrash Rabba *ad loc.*, Romans 9.6-13). Both Judaism and Christianity consider themselves to be the heirs to the promises given to Abraham and Isaac and they are indeed fraternal twins emerging from the nation-state of second commonwealth of Israel. As brothers often do, they picked different, even opposing ways to preserve this family's heritage. These differences became so important that for two millennia few people have been able to appreciate their underlying commonalities and, hence, the reasons for their differences. Though they are twins, it is difficult to judge which religion is the older and which the younger, for this birthright is one issue separating them. Both now claim to be Jacob, the younger child who received the birthright. Rabbinic Judaism maintains that it has preserved the traditions of Israel, Jacob's new name after he wrestled with God. Christianity maintains that it is the new Israel, preserving the intentions of Israel's prophets. Because of the two religions' overwhelming similarities and in spite of their great areas of difference, both statements are true. Furthermore, neither religion can be fully understood in isolation from the other. The witness of each is needed to show the truth of the other.'[22]

Now part of that, of course, is the need to take seriously the specific features of each religion. And just as the specific feature of Christianity is the confession of Jesus Christ as 'Son of God', so the specific feature of Judaism is the belief that Israel and only Israel is the 'people of God'. As we saw right at the beginning of this book, three key terms – God's people (land), God's son (messiah) and God's word (book) – express simultaneously both the unity and the difference between the three prophetic religions of Semitic origin: Judaism, Christianity and Islam. The unity is grounded in faith in one and the same God, and the difference is grounded in faith in a central saving event which is different in each case, and which teaches believers in each case to see this faith in God in a new light. The centuries-old dispute between the prophetic religions which are in such intimate enmity with one another – a dispute which is so often linked with contempt and oppression – constantly came to a head over these various key statements about the right understanding of God. Perhaps it is because of their monotheism that the three religions have been continually characterized by exclusiveness, aggression and intolerance.

As far as Christianity is concerned, the high christological statements about Son of God, Incarnation and Trinity have constantly burdened the dialogue with Jews. And if as a Christian theologian one seriously wants to make contact with Jewish dialogue partners, it is impossible to avoid the Jewish questions over these doctrinal statements in particular. So to end this major section I want briefly to face this task – in full awareness of the difficulties. But I believe that I owe it to readers honestly to indicate how the difficult dogmas of Christianity can be 'introduced' into the dialogue in such a way as to preserve the identity of Christian faith while showing the utmost possible ecumenical openness.

VI. Christian Self-Criticism in the Light of Judaism

According to David Flusser, the teachings of Jesus, not christology, are the area in which Jews and Christians could meet most easily and learn from one another. And without ignoring the many trends in Christianity which are orientated on the Jesus of the Gospels, he adds: 'For many Christians, however, such a clarification does not directly touch their main Christian experience and interest, even though it may prove helpful and strengthen their own belief. Knowledge of the "historical", Jewish Jesus is but a necessary frame for the core of their belief, namely, the metahistorical drama of Christianity.'[1] By this last phrase Flusser means the Christ who is pre-existent with God, his incarnation and his atoning death on the cross, his resurrection, his return to his Father and his coming again.

Indeed, above all the pre-existence and incarnation of Christ, and then the Trinity, are regarded as the 'central dogmas of Christianity'. And we cannot avoid these questions of Christian dogmatics, since Gotthold Ephraim Lessing already distinguished between the 'religion of Jesus' and the 'Christian religion', Martin Buber also distinguished between 'the faith of Jesus' and 'faith in Jesus', and numerous Jews define dialogue by the slogan, 'The faith of Jesus unites us, faith in Jesus divides us'.

1. Christian self-criticism

However, it will only be possible credibly to follow an ecumenical path to peace with the other prophetic religions if that path involves resolute Christian self-criticism – on the basis of the New Testament. Welcome signs of this self-criticism can be seen, in the sphere of the churches as well.

Let us recall the 1980 statement by the German Catholic bishops that 'certain statements of Christian faith like those about the "Son of God who is of the same nature as God" appear to Jews to be radically un-Jewish' because they seem to be 'in utter conflict with strict monotheism'. The Guidelines on Religious Relations with the Jews, issued in 1974 in connection with the Vatican Council Declaration *Nostra Aetate* no.4 of 1974,[2] were particularly understanding over issues related to incarnation: 'They (the Catholics) will likewise strive to understand the difficulties which arise for the Jewish soul – rightly imbued with an extremely high, pure notion of the divine transcendence

– when faced with the mystery of the incarnate Word.' And the most recent Protestant document, the 1990 European 'Declaration on the Encounter between Lutheran Christians and Jews',[3] also stresses that the relationship between Christians and Jews is rooted 'in the testimony of the one God and his faithfulness to his covenant, as this has been handed down in books of the holy scripture of the Old Testament, which we have in common'.[4] Granted, the document does not go into the question of trinitarian faith, but in principle it does make the demand: 'The indispensable presupposition for our encounter is the readiness of Christians to listen to the testimony of Jews, to learn from their experience of faith and life, and through this to perceive new sides of the biblical tradition.'[5]

To this degree one can only emphatically endorse all the efforts which are aimed at something like a 'Christian theology of Judaism'. By this **Clemens Thoma,** one of the best Christian experts on the Jewish tradition, understands 'radically serious consideration and interpretation by Christians of the function of Judaism for the Christian churches as their origin, contradiction and companion'.[6] For the Christian churches this means 'a theology which is critical of the churches because and in so far as it reminds the Christian churches of the Jewish legacy which is inherent in Christianity and the Christian element which is alive in Judaism, and indicates that failure to note these facts is partly responsible for the superficiality, the confusion and the mistakes of yesterday and today'.[7]

Now it is no secret that neither Jews nor Muslims have been enlightened by the **distinctions** in God used by Christians in the doctrine of the Trinity (**three** persons, but **one** nature). Why, they ask, is the faith in one God, represented by Abraham and resolutely maintained by both Moses and Jesus, not being abandoned when it is assumed that from eternity along with the one Godhead, the one divine nature, there is a second person, indeed even that there are three persons in God?

Simply to attribute 'blindness' or even 'hardness of heart' to the Jews in these questions, as has happened for centuries, is to overlook our own Christian problems.[8] For at the latest since the Enlightenment and the beginning of historical-critical exegesis, which was followed by a historical-critical historiography of dogma, critical Christians have also had their questions here. With Jews and Muslims they share the view that the terms deriving from Syriac, Greek and Latin with which the Christian doctrine of God was thought through in history are nowadays often more misleading than illuminating. The Christian doctrine of God which has found expression in the classical doctrine of the Trinity has become terribly complicated. It is a confusing conceptual game involving three hypostases, persons or prosopa, two processions and four relations. And how many hundreds of pages have Christian theologians since Augustine needed to explain in high dialectic all that for Paul and John was still so simple!

Jews still keep asking questions which Christian theologians are not very keen to entertain, far less to answer. What do all these dialectical theological concepts have to do with the one God? Why, and for what reason, is there a distinction between nature and person in the absolutely one and only God? For the New Testament, too, is not God absolutely simple, not composed in this way or that – the one and only? So what is the use of a real difference in God between Father, Son and Spirit, which is nevertheless not meant to do away with the real unity of God? And on the other hand, what is the use of a logical difference between God as 'Father' and God's 'nature', which is nevertheless meant to have a substantial foundation? Is that the message of the New Testament? Why seek to add anything to the unity and uniqueness which can only water down or do away with the concept of unity and uniqueness?

Of course in this connection Jewish dialogue partners will want to know why such a complex development of dogma had to come about in Christianity anyway. However, this volume on Judaism is **not** the place to unfold and relate **the history of Christian dogmas,** to relate how statements about metaphysical Sonship, incarnation and Trinity came about in the post-biblical period. I shall be describing this development of Christian doctrine in the context of the Hellenistic paradigm of the early church in the study on Christianity which is to follow this book, and there I shall evaluate it critically. Here, on the basis of my earlier remarks[9] and the material that we have again worked through in our Institute,[10] I simply want to sketch out briefly how those 'central Christian dogmas' can at least be made sufficiently understandable in the light of the New Testament, the **original Christian message**, not to seem *a priori* to be quite absurd, or even blasphemous, to Jews. Everything depends on avoiding false positions in dialogue with our brothers and sisters of other religions.

And here, from the Christian side, it would in fact be absurd to require something 'radically un-Jewish' of Jews, something absolutely contradictory to 'strict monotheism', because the Jews are the guardians of belief in the one God. Have not Christians, too, inherited belief in the one and only God from their Jewish masters? Thus an 'understanding' of the 'Jewish soul', attention to the 'testimony of the Jews', only gets anywhere when it leads to reflection by Christians on their Jewish origins. To this degree we can again follow Clemens Thoma in defining the 'Christian theology of Judaism' in another way: 'It is an attempt by Christian theology to demonstrate and describe the consequences which follow for Christianity from the fact that Jesus Christ, his first disciples and the evangelists were Jews and lived in a Jewish environment.'[11]

So in a series of brief preliminary reflections on the possibility of a better Jewish-Christian understanding at the centre of theology I want to attempt to consider afresh and self-critically the questions of divine sonship, incarnation and Trinity in the light of their originally **Jewish roots**. First of all we turn to the question:

2. What does it mean to say that God has a Son?

It is often far too little known, even to Jews, at any rate to Muslims, and sometimes also to Christians, that the word 'Father' is also used for God in **Judaism**, in the Hebrew Bible,[12] and that in the Hebrew Bible, too, the term 'son' of God is used for human beings: for example, for the people of Israel,[13] for the Israelites as 'children of God',[14] or as 'sons of the living God',[15] but above all for the king of Israel as 'son' of God.[16]

Our question now is: did the Jew **Jesus of Nazareth** ever call himself Son of God? Here, first of all, we must remember that, like Judaism generally, Jesus of Nazareth himself was evidently not preoccupied with formulae and dogmas. One need only read the Synoptic Gospels to note that Jesus neither engaged in profound speculations like Greek philosophers or mystics nor in learned halakhic casuistry like the rabbis. In generally understandable, approachable sayings, brief stories, parables from unadorned everyday life which were open to anyone, he put at the centre of his preaching not his own person, role, or dignity but **God**: may **God's** kingdom come, **God's** name be hallowed, **God's** will be done. God's will, which is to be fulfilled by human beings in the service of their fellows. There are no secret revelations, no profound allegories with a number of unknown features. Jesus does not require the true faith, an orthodox confession, or observance of the halakhah from anyone. He does not expect theoretical reflection, but the response of a practical decision: discipleship, orthopraxy in the radical sense of committed love.

For Jews, such a way of proclaiming God was certainly not *a priori* unacceptable; at all events, it was not 'radically un-Jewish'. But how is one to help Jews to see to some extent how this person who proclaimed the kingdom of God is also to be called the Son of God – even God, according to some? In these circumstances, is it not surprising that Jesus, too, did not use the terminology of later theology and proclaim as a great 'mystery': 'God is one, of one nature but in three persons, and I am the second, divine person, who has assumed a second, human nature'?

But that raises, conversely, the constructive question: how, according to the New Testament itself, is Jesus' relationship to God to be seen? That is the **original** christological question (and in nucleus it is also the question of the Trinity).

According to the sources, there is no doubt about three things.

– Jesus spoke, prayed, fought and suffered on the basis of an ultimately inexplicable experience of God, presence of God, certainty of God, indeed unity with God as his Father.

– However, as present-day historical-critical exegesis of both Jewish and Christian provenance agrees, he did not use the title 'Son of God' of himself.

– And yet (this is where the Jewish-Christian dispute begins) **in fact his claim went beyond that of a prophet,** to the degree that in the face of the prevalent teaching and praxis, i.e. the teaching and praxis of the ruling authorities, he claimed God's authority for himself. Here, in him – and this could be assessed both positively and negatively – in fact there was 'more than Moses', more than the prophets. In fact he put in question as absolutes not only the Temple but also the Law, hallowed traditions and ordinances, and also the dividing lines betwen clean and unclean, righteous and unrighteous. Nor did he proclaim all this for one day in the future, but – against an eschatological background – for here and now.

But how do we explain that despite Jesus' shameful death, a Jesus movement came into being, that Jesus was believed in as Son of God? Only **after** his death, when on the basis of the Easter experiences people could believe that he had been taken up into God's eternal life, had been 'exalted' by God through God to God, his 'Father', **did the believing community begin to use the title 'Son' or 'Son of God' for him.** Why? This might also be something that a present-day Jew could pursue.

– First of all, for Jews who followed Jesus there was a firm basis and an inner logic to the fact that the one who had unabashedly called God his 'Father' was subsequently also explicitly called 'Son' by his believing followers. The proclamation of this God was now indissolubly bound up with his person. This 'Father' could no longer be had without the

'Son'. It was not the king of Israel, but he, the messiah, who was God's Son.

– Secondly, a Jew could easily think of exaltation to God in terms of the enthronement of the Israelite king. According to Jewish tradition, at the moment of his accession the king was instituted 'son of God', as was now the crucified Jesus through his resurrection and exaltation. In Psalm 2 such an enthronement ritual has been handed down in the statement, 'You are my son, today I have begotten you.'[17] Here 'begetting' is a synonym for exaltation. There is still no trace in the New Testament of a physical-sexual (or even a metaphysical) begetting like that of the Hellenistic sons of God!

So it can be said in the introduction to the letter to the Romans, in one of the earliest creeds (which is probably already pre-Pauline), that Jesus Christ was 'designated Son of God in power by his resurrection from the dead'. And in Acts this enthronement Psalm 2 can be taken up and applied to Jesus: 'He (God) said to me (according to Ps.2.7, to the king, to the anointed, but according to Acts 13.33 to Jesus), "You are my son, today I have begotten you".' And why can all this happen? Because here in the New Testament, in good Jewish fashion, the thought is still that Jesus is 'begotten' as king, 'begotten' as anointed (= messiah, Christ), begotten as representative and Son, 'today'. In Acts this clearly does not mean Christmas but Easter; not the feast of the 'incarnation' but the feast of the resurrection and exaltation of Jesus. In the same sense, Ps.110.1 is also applied by the priest-king in the New Testament[18] to the Jesus exalted to God to show that he is 'Son' of God: 'The Lord said to my Lord, "Sit at my right hand."' No sentence from the Hebrew Bible has been more quoted than this statement about what Martin Hengel has called a 'throne-fellowship' between the one who has been exalted to God and God himself.

So what was originally meant in Judaism, and thus also in the New Testament, by this being Son of God? Beyond question the statement is not about any origin, but has the sense that it has in the **Hebrew Bible, the Old Testament**, of appointment to a position of judgment and power. It is not about the kind of physical sonship of God that Jews still assume and rightly reject today, but about an **election and authorization** of Jesus by God, wholly in keeping with the Hebrew Bible. Jewish belief in one God would hardly have had any fundamental objections to such an understanding of the Son of God; this view could have been held by the earliest Jewish Christian community. So it seems that today, too, there can hardly be any fundamental objections to this on the part of Jewish monotheism.

And yet that is not the whole story. In the **Gentile-Christian–Hellenistic paradigm** the original dispute between Jews and Christians over the Jew Jesus of Nazareth was later to lead to a dogmatic exaltation of Jesus as Son of God which gave him complete equality with God himself. Indeed it led to his being formally worshipped by Christians. This later dogmatization of christology in Hellenistic categories (in 325, at the Council of Nicaea, Jesus Christ was defined as being 'of one substance with the Father'), and even more in the doctrine of the Trinity, the concepts of which were developed at the end of the fourth century (the neo-Nicene confession of 'one God in three persons'), seemed to Jews (as to Muslims three and a half centuries later) to be a clear infringement of the first commandment: 'No God but the one true God'. Would the Aramaic-speaking community of Jewish Christians in Jerusalem ever have understood such a doctrine?

There is also the fact that, **from as early as the first century, the Jewish Christians** who had moved eastwards were largely no longer in existence as a **corrective** to Western Hellenistic speculation and Roman organization in the church. When, after the total destruction of Jerusalem in 135 CE and their expulsion from Palestine, the Jewish people had declined and become an insignificant group, at least in the West, and when on the other hand in the third century the long-persecuted Gentile Christian church grew increasingly strong, so that at the beginning of the fourth century, with the Constantinian shift it could rise to become the powerful imperial church, it was all too easy for this church to see itself as being now the only legitimate people of God and the heir to the promises of Israel. But in order to indicate a way towards understanding over this difficult christological question, here, very briefly, I must take up a question which will be discussed in more detail in the second volume, on Christianity, in the light of the history of dogma.

3. What is incarnation?

In **Judaism**, too, **God's word** is seen as mediator between God and human beings. And the very first modern Jewish systematic theologian, Kaufmann Kohler, drew attention to the fact that the creation of the world by God's creative word means: 'The word appears... as the first created messenger, which worked and works as mediator between the world spirit and the visible world order. Even more significantly than in the realm of the visible creation, the word of God has become the mediator of the spiritual-moral world order in the revelation of God to the people of earlier times as to Israel: as the one who conveys the teaching, the **word** (Hebrew *ma-amar*, Aramaic *Memra* and Greek *Logos*) was therefore mentioned for a long time in the older haggadah alongside the Shekinah as the medium or middle being of God's revelation.'[19]

But above all the proclamation of Christ as the Word incarnate has repressed this notion in Jewish theology. According to Kohler, it 'gradually transpired that in Hellenistic circles, under the influence of Platonic and Stoic philosophy, after Philo of Alexandria a personality was attributed to this saying of God or Logos as "the first created Son of God", which exalted him to a kind of divine governor. From there it was only a small step to his further exaltation to a seat alongside God, and this was a step which the church took with the Word made flesh in Christ.'[20]

So for **Judaism**, too, the infinite God can be very close to human beings, and human beings to the infinite God. The one who is highly exalted can incline towards, descend to human beings, and be with them, accompany them. As the book of Isaiah says, 'I dwell in the high and holy place, and also walk with him who is of a contrite and humble spirit'.[21] So Israel's God is the God of **Israel**, the gracious and merciful one who constantly remains near to the people even in its darkest hours: 'For what great nation is there that has a God so near to it as the Lord our God is to us, whenever we call upon him?'[22]

However, no matter how near God and human beings can be to each other, they always remain **different**, so that down to the present day Jews hold it blasphemy to claim that God has become man at any time in human history. For many Jews that cannot be the case, simply because the Christian assertion of an incarnation of God has brought forth 'bad fruits' for the people of God. But as Clemens Thoma rightly points out, for Jews a doctrine 'cannot be true and real if it is directed in a hostile or dismissive way against God's people the Jews and the Sinai revelation to which this people bears witness'.[23] However, the real objection is: with the incarnation – as already with the worship of the golden calf by the Israelites in the wilderness, there is a *shittup*, a blasphemous 'confusion', 'mixture', 'combination' of that which is created and human with God. And in fact these questions must also occur to Christians: is not also something similar happening in the worship of the man Jesus as God?

But Christians have never asserted such a 'mixture', far less is there any question of there being a 'rival to God'. Still, as I have suggested, with the expansion of Christianity into the world of Hellenistic thought and the first paradigm shift in Christianity from the apocalyptic-Jewish-Christian to the Hellenistic-Gentile-Christian entire constellation, as Son of God Jesus had increasingly been **put on the same level of being as the Father,** and this inevitably led to growing theological difficulties. For the more attempts were made to define this relationship between Father and Son with Hellenistic categories of nature in an unimaginably complex history of dogma, the more problems there were in holding together belief in one God and the divine Sonship, and of expressing at the same time both the distinction of the Son of God from God and his unity with God.

So the more time went on, the more the relationship between Father, Son and Spirit became a *mysterium logicum* in which – as we should note carefully – the contradiction between unity and multiplicity seemed to be overcome **only verbally,** by means of constantly new terminological distinctions (last of all nature and person). God: one divine nature, three divine persons? Jesus Christ: one divine person – two natures, one divine and one human!? In view of such theological distinctions it was hardly surprising that in the subsequent period it became increasingly impossible to preach the message of this God (of Israel) and this (Jewish) Jesus as his anointed, messiah, Christ, credibly to the Jews and later to the Muslims. So later there were hardly ever any conversions to the faith from Judaism (and from Islam). The name of Jesus was often desperately kept quiet by the Jews in the Christian empire.

Was not a total dead end reached here in dialogue with the Jews? Not necessarily. For if we return from dogmatics to the New Testament, the decisive question here is not, 'What is the relationship between the three persons in one divine nature in God?', or, 'How do the two natures come together in one person in Christ?' Such questions arise only more or less of necessity if one attempts to think in the Hellenistic categories of nature. In the language of the New Testament the question is, rather, 'How is the unity of God and Jesus, of Father and Son (and moreover of the Spirit) to be thought of and to be confessed? And that in such a way that the unity and uniqueness of God are preserved to the same degree as the identity of the person of Jesus Christ?'

Now the New Testament speaks of a 'sending'[24] of the Son of God or a 'becoming flesh' of the word of God[25] – i.e. not of God, the Father himself, but of his word. How is that to be understood? Does this of itself already break down all the bridges to Judaism, as Kaufmann Kohler thought, along with many other Jewish theologians? In his major study of pre-existence christology, Karl-Joseph Kuschel has been able to demonstrate convincingly that the **Pauline statements** about the **sending** of the Son of God do not presuppose any pre-existence of Christ as a heavenly being, understood in mythological terms, but can be understood in good Jewish fashion in the context of the prophetic tradition: 'The metaphor of sending (borrowed from the prophetic tradition) expresses the conviction that the person and work of Jesus do not originate within history, but are completely the result of God's initiative.'[26] Referring to Catholic exegetes, he has demonstrated that 'of pre-existence and equality of being with God we cannot discover any trace in Paul's letters. On the contrary, for quality of being is incompatible with the thought that the Son of God is the image of his Father.'[27]

The same can be said of the **Gospel of John.** In this Gospel, at any rate, there cannot yet be any question of a 'metahistorical drama of Christ', the objection often put forward by the Jewish side.[28] Precisely in this late, fourth Gospel, we still have statements like: 'And this is eternal life, that they may know the only true God, and Jesus Christ whom you have sent.'[29] Or, 'I am ascending to my Father and your Father, to my God and your God.'[30] Here there is a clear distinction between God and Jesus Christ. No, this Gospel too does not contain any speculative metaphysical christology – torn from its Jewish roots – but rather a christology of sending and revelation associated with the world of Jewish Christianity. However, its statement about pre-existence, understood in an unmythological way, takes on heightened significance: 'John does not investigate the metaphysical nature and being of the pre-existent Christ; he is not concerned about the insight that before the incarnation there were two pre-existent divine persons who were bound together in the one divine nature. This way of conceiving of things is alien to John. So too is the conception of a "begetting within the Godhead". "I and the Father are one." This statement has nothing to do with any dogmatic-speculative statements about the relationship of the natures within the Godhead.'[31] So what was John's positive concern? 'What stands in the foreground is the confession that the man Jesus of Nazareth is the Logos of God in person. And he is the Logos as a mortal man; but he is the Logos only for those who are prepared to believe, trusting God's word in his word, God's actions in his praxis, God's history in his career, and God's compassion in his cross.'[32]

So what about the '**incarnation**' of the Son of God? Certainly the category of 'incarnation' is alien to Jewish thinking, and derives from the Hellenistic world. And yet this word, too, can be understood rightly in the light of the Jewish context. For in the case of the incarnation it would be quite wrong for Christians to fix themselves on the 'mathematical' or 'mystical' point of the conception or the birth of Jesus.[33] The Greek conceptual model of incarnation must to some degree be earthed in the context of the story of Jesus the Jew. If that is done, as I have indicated, incarnation is rightly understood only in terms of **the whole life and death and new life of Jesus.** For in all his talking and preaching, in all his behaviour, his fate and indeed his whole person, the man Jesus did not act as God's rival but proclaimed, manifested, revealed, the one word and will of God. So we can also say that in this man God's word and will took human form. Indeed, even in a Jewish context the statement could be ventured that the one in whom, according to the testimonies, word and action, teaching and life, being and action, completely coincided, is God's 'Word', 'Will', 'Son' in human form. Here we have a unity of Jesus with God. But even according to the christological councils, this is not a 'mixture' and a 'combination' but – according to the New Testament – a unity of knowledge, of will, of action, in short of the revelation of God through Jesus.

4. The Trinity – an unsurmountable obstacle?

If the **Jewish tradition** has always held unshakeably to a basic truth of Jewish faith, then it is the 'Shema Israel', 'Hear, O Israel, Yahweh is our God, Yahweh alone!',[34] which has been constantly reinterpreted and explained anew down the centuries, in a way which has been summarized by another Jewish systematic theologian, **Louis Jacobs.**[35] This confession of the unity and uniqueness of God meant the strict repudiation not only of any dualism but also of any trinitarianism. Granted, in the Middle Ages Jewish critics accused the Kabbalists of tendencies towards trinitarianism, but the latter always emphatically rejected such charges. Jewish martyrs would give up their lives rather than accept trinitarian faith.

In later centuries, the Jews felt extraordinarily reinforced by the strict monotheism of **Islam,** which meanwhile had become a world power that threatened Christianity. The triumph of Islam over faith in Christ also seemed to the Jews a triumph of the one God of Abraham over the threefold God of the Christians. In the mediaeval debates in Spain in particular, of which we have heard, the Trinity played a major role on both sides; however, on the Christian side the arguments often made use of problematical analogies which could easily be repudiated instead of directly referring to the New Testament.

Conversely, informed Jews also knew, and of course still know, that the classical **Christian tradition** has always held firm to the **unity of God**, at least in principle. The general Christian understanding is that talk of Father, Son and Spirit may in no way be made into a doctrine of two (or three) gods (like e.g. Brahman, Shiva and Vishnu in India, or Osiris, Isis and Horus in Egypt). No, for Jesus as for Christians of all ages, God has always remained the one and only God. Completely in keeping with the Hebrew Bible, for Christians, outside God there is no other God from all eternity. Also according to the New Testament, despite all the theological speculations which blossomed again, there is no third faith between monotheism and polytheism. Nor, according to the New Testament, is there any simple identity between God and Jesus, as came about in heterodox trends in the first centuries (monarchianism and modalism). The Son is not God the Father; conversely, God the Father is not the Son. 'Son' is not simply a name (mode) of God.

The transcendent God in immanence? No, that is not blasphemy; that is anything but an un-Jewish idea. Judaism, too, knows of an approach and a condescension of God, which does not do away with God's divine being but confirms it. The presence, the existence, the active power of God who was, is, and will be is expressed in all that is meant in rabbinic Judaism by **'Shekinah'** (from 'dwell'): God's dwelling, but at the same time also God's 'glory' (*kabod*) and splendour (*hod*) among men and women of this earth. And the rabbis already made it clear that God's special presence is not just bestowed in the sanctuary, in the tent of meeting and the Temple; God can also take up his abode in the community of the people – even when they go into exile. 'Im-manu-el', 'God is with us'!

And why should not God's presence, Shekinah, for once take its abode in an individual human being instead of a temple, so that in him God's hidden 'glory' can shine out for those who rely on him in trust? No kind of separation, splitting, division in the one and unique God can be meant here. But the reference can be to the Shekinah, the indwelling and revelation of the one and only God in this one man, even if that can only be experienced in faith. God's wisdom (Logos), veiled in the 'flesh', manifest only to believers: 'And the Word became flesh and dwelt among us, and we beheld his glory, the glory of the only-begotten of the Father, full of grace and truth.'[36] So runs the Johannine prologue. And the Pauline tradition states: 'In him dwells the whole fullness of the Godhead bodily.'[37]

So only against a Jewish horizon can we properly understand the common confession of twenty centuries of Christianity and all the churches. In Christianity the ground and centre of faith is not simply a holy book or law. The ground and centre of faith is **God himself**, as in Judaism and Islam ('theocentricity'). However, as the first Jewish Christians already experienced, God has finally revealed himself as he manifests himself in the historical **person of Jesus Christ** (i.e. 'theocentricity' expressed specifically in 'christocentricity'). And what is called for is commitment to this person – not to a book or a law – as the definitive criterion of the Christian understanding of God and humankind.

I know that here we Christians are asking too much of our Jewish (and Muslim) partners in dialogue, and I wish with all my heart that the dialogue could go on at this point – not to prove who is right, but in order to deepen our faith in God. For one thing must be conceded to our Jewish partners in dialogue from the start, as a common basis. According to the New Testament, too, the **principle of unity** is not a divine 'nature' common to a number of entities, as has been imagined since the neo-Nicene theology of the fourth century, but **the one God** (*ho theos*: **the** God = the Father), from whom are all things and to whom are all things. So according to the New Testament, the issue is not one of metaphysical and ontological statements about God in himself and his innermost nature; about a static inner nature of a triune God which rests on itself and is manifest to us. Rather, the issue is one of soteriological and christological statements about the manner and mode of the **revelation of God** through Jesus Christ in this world; about his dynamic and universal activity in history; about his relationship to human beings and about the relationship of human beings to him. But, someone may ask, on these New Testament presuppositions, how would belief in Father, Son and Spirit need to be understood and expressed for the dialogue with Judaism and Islam – a test case for any Christian theology – against the Jewish background? Let me attempt to give a brief summary of what will be clarified in the volume on Christianity:

- According to the New Testament, to believe in God the Father means to believe in the one God. This belief in God is something that Judaism, Christianity and Islam have in common.
- To believe in the Holy Spirit means to believe in God's effective power in human beings and the world: this belief in God's spirit can also be common to Jews, Christians and Muslims.
- To believe in the Son of God means to believe in the revelation of the one God in the man Jesus of Nazareth. This decisive difference needs

to be discussed further, in particular among the three prophetic religions.

5. Does God need the sacrifice of his own Son?

All too naturally, Christians, and especially Christian theologians, see the execution of Jesus as a sacrificial death and the supreme proof of the love of God. 'For God so loved the world that he gave his only Son, that whoever believes in him should not perish but have eternal life.' People are fond of quoting this sentence from the Gospel of John,[38] but unthinkingly.

Completely in line with the **Jewish tradition**, Pinchas Lapide also makes a highly critical comment on this: 'That God needs a human sacrifice to reconcile his own creation with himself, that he, the ruler of the world, cannot justify anyone without a blood sacrifice, is as incomprehensible to Jews as it is contrary to the Bible.'[39] Human sacrifices are an abomination to God. And Lapide then asks the question: 'What kind of God is it who can say yes to the sadistic death-pangs of his child, indeed even bring about this bestial punishment, simply to assume the purely pagan torture of crucifixion: as vicarious atonement, which is what Paul claims;... as a sacrifice to assuage the wrath of God according to Roman custom, which is how Augustine puts it; as a ransom from the devil in a kind of exchange between God and Satan, which is what Origen thinks; or as feudal satisfaction and payment of debt, which is what Anselm of Canterbury seeks to prove in his doctrine of satisfaction?'[40]

What can be said to this in the light of the **Christian tradition**? Here indeed some traditional conceptions, a number of which already have a basis in the New Testament, need to be **corrected**. To put it in simple terms: the death of Jesus was caused by human beings; it may not be explained in post-Easter exuberance as God's counsel and will for salvation, so that it is virtually made the act of God. What God allowed, he did not explicitly will or initiate in a calculated way. The God of the New Testament is none other than the God of the 'Old Testament', to whom human sacrifices are an abomination. As if God had rejected the sacrifice of Isaac in the Old Testament, only to carry it out cruelly in the New Testament in the person of his Son!

But to avoid the impression that this problem has arisen in Christian theology only as a result of Jewish objections, let me quote what I wrote on this question a number of years ago on the basis of New Testament exegesis: 'Can there be any doubt about the fact that the concept of expiatory sacrifice in particular – in popular exposition at least – often creates really painful misunderstanding, linked as it is with pagan sacrifice? Is God so cruel, even sadistic, that his anger can be appeased only by the blood of his Son? Does an innocent person have to serve as scapegoat, whipping-boy and substitute for the real sinners?'[41] In answering this question I made it clear that:

1. According to the New Testament the first Jewish followers of Jesus were faced with the tremendously difficult question **how** – in the light of belief in his new life with God – Jesus's painful, contradictory, **shameful death could be understood**. As a disaster – but in that case, where was God? As a saving event – but in that case why this death? What we see in the New Testament are the first attempts to explain this death and above all its abiding significance and positive effect for human beings, for us. In the Synoptic Gospels the idea of an atoning death at best plays a marginal role.

2. There is **no exclusive normative model for interpreting the death of Jesus** either in the New Testament or in patristics. Instead, there are a variety of interpretations, at many levels and overlapping one another: the legal interpretation (Jesus' death as a judgment on the sinner) and the cultic meaning (as representative, sacrifice, sanctification); the financial (as payment of a ransom) and finally even the military interpretation (as a battle with the evil powers).

3. So **Jesus himself** was seen in very **different images** and yet, as far as his fate was concerned, ultimately in the same dialectic: as the teacher – and yet rejected; as the prophet – and yet misunderstood; as the witness – and yet betrayed; as the judge – and yet judged; as the high priest – and yet himself sacrificed; as the king – and yet crowned with thorns; as the victor – and yet crucified.

4. Accordingly, the **result** of the event of the cross is also **described in different ways**: as example, redemption, liberation, forgiveness of sins, purification, sanctification, reconciliation and justification.

One may well ask whether it is really surprising that **not all of these** concepts and images, each of which is meant in different ways to bring out the saving significance of Jesus' death, **are still equally comprehensible today**. Some thought-models from that time have become alien to us. Some can be directly misleading.[42]

Now there is no mistaking the fact that in the New Testament **Jesus' death** is understood as a **human act**. Jews and Gentiles together are made responsible for it. And yet, similarly, the fact cannot be overlooked that the death of Jesus on the cross also has to do with God himself:

God at least allowed his 'only Son' to be executed, even if he did not directly will this or even initiate it.

But how is it then possible that in the New Testament, individual passages also say that the crucifixion of Jesus is directly an **act of God**, not only allowed but also willed and initiated by him, indeed that it is an event which blots out sin? The Leipzig exegete Werner Vogler has made a critical investigation of this second set of statements in the New Testament and comes to the conclusion that the crucifixion of Jesus is 'solely a human act. But Easter shows that God carried through his unalterable will for salvation even in the suffering and death of Jesus.'[43] The early Christian community will have thought something like this: 'If Easter was more than a subsequent correction of the execution of the Son of God which God did not prevent, then the death of Jesus could not have been a catastrophe, but must have been in accordance with the saving will of God. In that case Jesus' crucifixion was not an arbitrary human act against God; rather, this event, which first of all seemed so enigmatic, was in accordance with the will of God.'[44] But Vogler also knows that the misunderstandings of the relevant New Testament passages are 'already very old' and therefore that the church will have to 'say farewell to part of its history of spirituality (for example, in a number of hymns)'. There is need for a 'thorough clean-out'.[45]

The 'thorough clean-out' that is in fact necessary would have to involve in particular the doctrine of satisfaction put forward by Anselm of Canterbury. Here we really do have a questionable 'metahistorical drama of Christ'. This 'feudal' doctrine of redemption can only be understood against the background of a jurisprudence which flourished in the early Middle Ages, where it seemed helpful to provide a rational demonstration of the need for the incarnation and above all for redemption through the death of Jesus on the cross by means of a large-scale and apparently seamless proof. But judged by the New Testament, this doctrine of satisfaction, which Thomas Aquinas already claimed not to find logically compelling, can no longer be ours, any more than the other doctrine of an ontological transformation of this world into Good Friday night or Easter day. Redemption through Jesus Christ, understood in keeping with scripture and our time, means really making possible the transformation of our selves in trusting faith and in love practised in discipleship.

That must be enough in this book to indicate the direction in which a dialogue between Christians, Jews (and indeed Muslims) about all the difficult questions of the doctrine of God, Christ and redemption would have to take. And however difficult this may be for Jewish and

Muslim partners to understand and to accept, in order to avoid discussions on false premises it must be said quite unambiguously from the Christian side that the **criterion for being a Christian** does not lie in the church's theories of Trinity, incarnation and satisfaction developed centuries later (otherwise the early Christians would not be Christians), but in belief in the one and only God, practical discipleship of Jesus Christ, trusting in the power of God's Holy Spirit. And this Spirit, which I am convinced is also at work in the dialogue with Jewish (and Muslim) brothers and sisters, works **where** it wills and will lead us where **it** wills.

However, the question now is whether Christian self-criticism in the light of Judaism does not have a reverse side which needs to be illuminated equally clearly. If Jesus the Jew forces a revision of christology, does not this same Jew Jesus with his message also represent a challenge to some traditional Jewish views which could be taken up by Jews? Here are just a few suggestions in that direction, in which theology and politics cannot be separated completely.

VII. Jewish Self-Criticism in the Light of the Sermon on the Mount?

I am well aware of the risk of holding up the New Testament **Sermon on the Mount** as a mirror to Jews in particular, even if the Sermon on the Mount is not at all a threatening message, but quite certainly good news. Both Christians and non-Christians have attested this: Jacobins at the French Revolution and socialists in the spirit of the Russian Revolution (K.Kautsky); moralists of all kinds, including such great figures as Leo Tolstoy, Albert Schweitzer and Mahatma Gandhi. And at the same time it must be added how often in the course of a long history the Sermon on the Mount has been betrayed by Christians themselves – not least where Jews were concerned...

However, despite a monstrous history of misuse, this message has in no way been refuted. On the contrary, the cause itself proved all the more urgent, the cause of the Jew of Nazareth, as it was taken up by the Jews who were his first disciples. We need not go into the problems of textual criticism and literary criticism here. Nowadays it is a commonplace of exegesis that Jesus of Nazareth did not really sit on a 'mountain' literally to 'preach', as the evangelist Matthew would have us believe. The parallel passage in the Gospel of Luke already speaks of a 'Sermon on the Plain' rather than a 'Sermon on the Mount'. No, these texts collected and edited by the two evangelists Matthew and Luke are short sayings and groups of sayings, principally from the sayings-source Q, in which the preaching of Jesus of Nazareth is given a particular profile, a profile which is not watered down by the fact that nowadays we can indicate numerous parallels between individual sentences in the Sermon on the Mount and the Hebrew Bible or rabbinic literature. Indeed they actually make the uniqueness of Jesus' message clear. In it these statements are not isolated, but concentrated and compact, as it were personified. At the same time his teaching is matched by his life, conduct, his whole fate.

The question raised for me in this context is this. If the Sermon on the Mount has always been applied self-critically to one's own community of faith, must it not be permissible also to apply this message, which is so characteristic of Jesus the Jew, to his own people – without any Christian self-righteousness and arrogance? And if the Christian faith-community must always allow itself to be measured critically against the demand to be ready to forgive and to renounce rights and power which is expressed in the Sermon on the Mount, would it be inappropriate to keep quiet about this to the Jewish people or any other people? Here I am presupposing that it is well known that the Sermon on the Mount is not just a purely private message for personal and family relationships but also a message with political implications. Certainly it does not make superfluous a social order and a state constitution, state power and legal order, the police and the army, but it does radically relativize them by its aim at converting 'hearts'.

1. Readiness for forgiveness?

The forgiveness of sins between human beings is not 'natural', is not something that can be taken for granted. Already in connection with the Holocaust I have argued against the perpetuation of guilt and for a forgiveness (not a forgetting) of guilt, since only in this way can reconciliation come about between Israelis and Germans, Jews and Christians. But whenever I have spoken either in private or in public **against forgetting** and at the same time **for forgiving** the excessive amount of guilt, two arguments in particular have been produced against me from the Jewish side:
– Those who believe in God will say that forgiveness is not our concern but **God's**: only God can forgive guilt, and this guilt in particular.
– Those who do not believe in God will object that the living cannot forgive the guilt, **but only the victims themselves**. And as the victims are no longer among the living, the guilty ones have to live with the guilt.

So in neither case can there be forgiveness between individuals, between peoples; rather, they must endure an eternal guilt. In this way the German guilt towards the Jews can never end – either in this generation or in the next. This was the very reason used, for example, by Prime Minister Begin in calling for the unconditional support of the Israeli state by the Germans. What is the answer to this?
– That only the **dead** could forgive guilt does not sound convincing, in particular to those who might have to pay the debts for the 'second', 'third' and umpteenth generations. The survivors of the Holocaust and their descendants readily accept the confessions of guilt and the material reparations, as representatives of the victims. Why should they not also be able to forgive, as their representatives, in the same way as, for example, children can forgive injuries to their dead parents – for the sake of peace between families?
– That only **God** can forgive guilt is contrary to the Jewish tradition. Certainly the Hebrew Bible hardly calls for forgiveness of one person

by another. But there are at least isolated instances of it in the Talmud.[1] Indeed, in the book of Jesus Sirach from the second century BCE, which has been handed down only in a Greek translation and therefore is non-canonical, we read: 'Remember the end of your life, and cease from enmity... remember the covenant of the Most High, and forgive guilt.'[2]

However, caution is needed. How often have Christians, too, failed to forgive one another's guilt and that of yet others? And how often in the course of the centuries have there been calls for vengeance rather than forgiveness between 'Christian nations', which necessarily led to a hardening of peoples' hearts, to constantly new hatred and ultimately to new wars? That is evident from that irreconcilable 'ancestral enmity' between France and Germany which was dominated by ideas of mutual 'revenge' – and resulted in three great wars and many times the six million Jewish dead![3]

My question is, in this situation could not the message of Jesus in particular be a challenge to Jews and Christians? For Jesus asserts, not just somewhere, incidentally, but quite centrally, that there can be no reconciliation with God without reconciliation with one's brother. Divine forgiveness is bound up with forgiveness between human beings. So in the Lord's Prayer, after the petitions for the coming of the kingdom of God and the doing of God's will, there is the petition, 'Forgive us our trespasses as we forgive those who trespass against us.'[4] Human beings cannot receive God's great forgiveness and then refuse lesser forgiveness to fellow human beings: they must pass on the forgiveness. That is the meaning of the parable of the generous king who forgives his minister an enormous amount of debt: Jesus condemns the action of the minister extraordinarly sharply, because having been forgiven this great debt he now has his own debtor thrown into prison for a small sum.[5]

So even now, that seems to be the provocative element in this message. Jesus pleads for an unbounded readiness to forgive: not seven times but seventy-seven times – in other words, time and again, endlessly,[6] and to everyone without exception. Moreover, as he hung on the cross in his last hour he is said to have spoken a word of forgiveness: 'Father, forgive them, for they know not what they do.'[7] And characteristically of Jesus, in this connection we also have a ban on judging.[8] The other is not subject to my judgment; in the end, all are subject to the judgment of God. So for Jesus the dominant thought is not that God alone can forgive, but that God alone should judge. Human beings should forgive one another.

Some Jews will object that such an ethic is impracticable and exaggerated. Is that really so? The important thing here is to avoid misunderstanding. Jesus' demand for forgiveness must not be interpreted legalistically. He is **not** instituting **a new law** on the principle that one should forgive seventy-seven times but not seventy-eight. So Jesus' demand cannot just be turned into a constitutional law; it does not put human courts out of business. **However**, Jesus' demand is a **moral appeal** to human generosity and warm-heartedness, to individual men and women – in some circumstances even to the representatives of the state – in a quite specific situation as it were to get round the law: to forgive and to keep on forgiving.

Europe, sorely tried with suffering, had the good fortune that from the midst of catastrophe statesmen emerged of the stature of Charles de Gaulle, Konrad Adenauer, Maurice Schumann, Jean Monnet, Alcide de Gasperi and others. They wanted not merely to organize Europe technocratically, in Brussels style, but also to inspire and change it on the basis of political, ethical and religious stimuli. In this way they were able to make a **new beginning** and usher in a **real understanding** which buried old enmities and today makes a new war between European nations, especially between the French and the Germans, quite unthinkable. And by a moving ceremony of reconciliation in the cathedral at Reims, where the French kings had been crowned, de Gaulle and Adenauer showed how much the mutual forgiveness had a religious basis.

There is no doubt that this was a Christian action, but that does not mean that it was un-Jewish. When a rabbi and former Knesset delegate like Meir Kahane proclaimed 'retaliation' as a 'primal Jewish concept' it made him not only a hero to some extremists in the Jewish state but also at the same time the victim of an assassination attempt. And what about the 'eye for an eye, tooth for a tooth', which is much quoted here and is unfortunately practised all too often even in 'Christian' politics? Experts know that this statement in the Bible was not originally meant in the sense of maximum retribution but was aimed at limiting the damage: no more than one eye, no more than one tooth.

No, what is expressed in the Psalms, indeed what Christians have learned from the Jews, is fully in accord with deep Jewish piety: 'Out of the depths I cry to you, O Lord. If you, O Lord, should mark iniquities, Lord, who could stand? But there is forgiveness with you.'[9] Who indeed could stand – the Germans or the Swiss, the Americans or the Israelis?

'But there is forgiveness with you.' So our guilt should not be 'marked', but 'forgiven'. And Jesus' demand is that this forgiveness, this mercy, granted by God to human beings, should also be handed on by them. 'Should not you have had mercy on your fellow servant, as I had mercy on you?', is the answer of the king to the unmerciful minister.[10] However, one cannot require forgiveness – not even after billions of Deutschemarks in reparations. One can only ask for forgiveness! Forgiveness is a gift, is grace. Hence my question: could it not be worth while to reflect in particular about forgiveness between Germans and Israelis, Christians and Jews, in a historical, political and theological perspective, talking together in a free, open and sympathetic dialogue – without any forgetting, sparing, repressing, excusing and justifying: as a viable basis for constructive collaboration?

Here is a reflection, not just on the immediate present but also on the future. It will soon be half a century since the Holocaust, and at this very moment in the United States, in addition to the many smaller Holocaust memorials (there is a brand new one, built in 1990 at the cost of three million dollars at Miami Beach, a bronze 'arm of the six million', more than seventy feet high), three new **Holocaust museums** are being built in central locations on public land which has been donated in Washington, New York and Los Angeles, none of them costing less than 100 million dollars. One can understand how the Holocaust generation, which is slowly dying out, wants to keep the memory of the Holocaust alive. Indeed to many American Jews today the Holocaust is more important for finding their identity than belief in the God of Abraham, Isaac and Jacob. And there is no doubt that the fight for the Holocaust not to be forgotten is more than legitimate.

And yet, even some American Jews are asking, 'Why Holocaust museums in America, now? Is this an excuse for our own omissions? Is it a long-term political action?' And why are some Jews against commemorating the five million dead from the other peoples (Slavs, gypsies and so on) in addition to the six million Jews? Why did the Israeli ambassador and other Jews, of all people, protest at a memorial day on 24 April 1990 for the almost two million (Christian) Armenians who were brutally and mercilessly murdered by the Turks in 1915? Does not a monopolizing of suffering all too easily obscure the suffering inflicted on others? What would people say if the around 600,000 Muslims of New York wanted to call for a museum on public land for the Palestinians driven out of Palestine, the Israeli occupation policy and the more than 1,000 victims of the Intifada?

It is not for me to pass judgment, but I venture to say quite frankly that the remembrance of the Holocaust which is necessary would be more appropriate, more worthy of its victims, and more effective in fighting against antisemitism if instead of the stately artistic memorials to unimaginable atrocities, **temples of peace** and reconciliation were built – for shared recollection, prayer and dialogue – in which reminders of the deadly past were combined with the prospects of a living new beginning. Quite literally a 'Temple of Understanding' (the name of a world-wide organization of Jews, Christians, Muslims and other religions, aimed at religious understanding), like the famous ecumenical chapel in Houston, Texas, which was founded by the Christian Dominique de Menil and decorated by the Jewish painter Mark Rothko with monumental mystical fields of colour in black and gray.

There are examples of concrete and active reconciliation. A particulary moving one is provided by Rabbi **Albert H.Friedlander**, the Dean of Leo Baeck College in London, who was born in Germany. Exactly fifty years after he left Germany, in 1988, instead of spending a lengthy study leave in Jerusalem, to the unease of his London congregation he chose to spend his study leave in Germany, as a prominent visiting professor, speaker and dialogue partner. He had not forgotten anything (not even the Swiss frontier police, who in 1940 seized his wife's uncle, fleeing from the Nazis, and after entertaining him well sent him back over the border to meet his end in Auschwitz). So why did he want to go back to Germany? Not to forget, but in order to seek reconciliation, after the dark night to see in the slow grey of dawn a 'white line on the horizon', a 'thread of gold'. This can 'also happen between people, in the sphere of reconciliation'.[11] 'I wanted to go to Germany to find the beginning of an inner journey towards reconciliation. Reconciliation itself lies in the future, because I cannot determine the inner course of the Germans and Germany.'[12]

But now there are also already countless Jews in the world who at present are living out and practising active reconciliation not only between Jews and Christians but also between Jews and Germans. I shall mention just one as a representative, **Franz Lucas**, the Consul General in London, son of the famous German rabbi Dr Leopold Lucas who was murdered in Theresienstadt. He founded a prize for reconciliation between peoples, at the University of Tübingen, worth 50,000 DM, to be given annually to scholars in the humanities.[13] In such an atittude of concrete reconciliation, let us also consider another difficult point which we cannot avoid here.

2. Renunciation of rights and power?

We have already heard of the problems surrounding the foundation of the state of Israel and the dispute of two peoples over the same land. To renounce rights and power comes hard, nor is it 'natural'. And when I have suggested to Jews that particular political positions (say in Jerusalem) or territories (above all West Jordan) might be given up, I have often received the answer, 'All that is our right; we cannot give that up; and now at last we also have the power to assert this right. Land for peace? On the contrary, we shall go on extending our power as we have done so far. For the whole land belongs to us. And there will be peace only if our claims are respected, not otherwise.'

But caution is also needed here. How often have Christians contravened the rights of others? How often have they oppressed and exploited others? And how long even in recent decades have 'Christian' nations, have Germany (with six million dead Poles on its conscience) and Poland (over the centuries more than seven million Germans were expelled from their homes in what is now Poland),[14] asserted rights over precisely the same territories (Silesia, eastern Brandenberg, Pomerania, south-east Prussia)? 'Renunciation politicians' was a term of scorn used to describe all those in Germany who would not fall in with a plan for a particular policy of expulsion.

Here, too, the message of the Jew Jesus of Nazareth represents a **challenge for Jews and Christians** equally; for Jesus not only called for the negative renunciation, of evil in thought, word and deed, that can be found throughout the Hebrew Bible. In addition Jesus called for positive renunciation, renunciation of rights and power: moreover, not only when one is compelled to this by others, but also – in given situations – voluntarily. This is what seems to be provocative about this message even now: Jesus calls for a **voluntary renunciation without anything in return**. Specifically, this can mean:

– Renunciation of rights in favour of others: going two miles with someone who has forced you to go one mile with him;[15]

– Renunciation of power at one's own expense: giving your cloak to someone who has taken your shirt;[16]

– Renunciation of counter-violence: offering your left cheek to someone who has struck you on the right.[17]

Some Jews will object at this point, even more than over a readiness to forgive, that such an ethic of renunciation is unrealistic and asks too much of people. It was Jews who in the Nazi period had to pay dearly for renunciation of any resistance. But here too, more than before, there is a need to emphasize that Jesus' demands must **not** be misunderstood as

absolute laws to be followed literally; they are and remain ethical appeals. Jesus does not put forward the view that one cannot retaliate over a blow on the left cheek, but one can over a punch on the jaw. The Sermon on the Mount does not contain legal clauses which regulate precisely what is allowed and what is forbidden. Nor does renunciation of counter-violence *a priori* mean renunciation of all resistance: Jesus himself, always fearless, when struck on one cheek did not offer the other, but rebelled; so renunciation should not be confused with weakness.

Jesus' demands are not concerned with moral, even ascetic, achievements which would make sense in themselves. Rather, here his concern is to give **provocative instances** and issue a **drastic summons** to radical fulfilment of the will of God – in every case in favour of one's fellow human being. So any renunciation is only the negative side of a new and positive practice of peace.

From the '**German question**' in particular, one can illustrate how this basic atittude can also work out in politics. For decades relations between the Federal Republic and the Eastern states were blocked above all because of the shift of Polish territory westwards enforced by Stalin and the unwillingness of Germany to recognize the new frontiers. As we heard, already at the end of the Second Vatican Council in 1965 the Polish bishops had declared to their German brothers-in-office, 'We offer forgiveness and we ask for forgiveness.' However, on the German side the rigid fronts only began to move when the Evangelical Church in Germany published a memorandum in which it referred to the need for reconciliation between Germans and Poles as well. But this reconciliation could not be brought about without the renunciation of particular territories.

This 'Memorandum' in the spirit of a renunciation of rights and power brought about a new spiritual climate in Poland which now also facilitated a specific policy at government level. For without this change of mind-set and the support of the churches, given that about 12 million Germans had been driven out,[18] it would have been impossible for the 1970/1971 Brandt-Scheel government to conclude the German-Soviet and German-Polish treaties, which in principle settled 'the German question' externally (the Oder-Neisse line), so that after the reunion in 1989 the Kohl/Genscher government could also definitively confirm this *status quo*.

In other words, in this particular historical situation there was no attempt at retaliation, nor were existing rights insisted on or power exploited. Rather, albeit after long to-ing and fro-ing, rights and the exercise of power were largely renounced. Will it be possible to proceed in the same way over the 'Palestinian question', which has similarly caused constant unrest in the world since the Second World War, without giving up rights (perhaps on both sides)? As it is, in recent years we have hardly heard any word from Israeli politicians of the ruling Likud block more often than 'retaliation' – 'retaliatory measures', 'retaliatory strikes', which can refer to anything from closing schools or destroying houses to air attacks; this will have to be discussed later. In the Gulf War it was only the influence of the USA which prevented an immediate attack by the politicians and military, always ready for retaliation, and later prevented retaliatory strikes after the fortunately few Scud missile attacks on Tel Aviv. Most of the retaliatory measures carried out as planned have gone far beyond the *ius talionis* allowed by the Hebrew Bible, the 'eye for an eye', which, as we heard, only allowed appropriate 'retribution', and not an over-reaction.

Here is just one illustration, which was the subject of a controversy in Germany. On the occasion of the award of the Heinrich Heine Prize of the city of Düsseldorf to the editor of *Die Zeit*, **Marion Countess Dönhoff**, the Countess dared to refer to a 'double standard': the over-reaction of Israel to the death of its soldiers, and its indifference to the shooting of Palestinians which went on every week. 'Recently,' she said, 'a two-year-old girl and a fifteen-year-old boy were shot on the same day. There was no outcry or even moral indignation among the friends of Israel. Yet when an Israeli soldier was murdered the same week, in retaliation 114 houses in a village were razed to the ground, 800 people were deported and the farmers' wells were blown up with dynamite.'[19] The President of the Central Council of Jews in Germany, **Heinz Galinski**, thereupon called for the speaker to give public expression to the 'astonishment' of the Central Council 'at such a lack of sensitivity'. To this reprimand the Countess replied: 'I do not know who is lacking in sensitivity, those who make war with automatic weapons on stone-throwing children or those who write about it. In the end sensitivity is not shown by shrouding crimes against humanity in silence. It is not difficult to imagine the fatal situation in which the Israelis find themselves, but as long as they rely exclusively on weapons and reject negotiations which could lead to a guarantee by the great powers, the spiral of violence will constantly grow.'

In addition we must ask: will the spirals of violence stop and the troublesome Palestinian question be solved unless here, in this particular historical situation too, people are prepared to renounce some rights and the exercise of power for the sake of peace and humanity? Here, too, is not an **alternative policy** required, for the sake of a peaceful solution? Could not politicians be found in Israel of the stature of Vaclav Havel, the new State President of Czechoslovakia, who without in any way excusing the Nazi crimes in his country during the war nevertheless apologized on behalf of his country for the expulsion of three million Germans after the war, and precisely in so doing fought very effectively against the spirit of vengeance, against hatred and anxiety on both sides?

However, it is now time once again to turn directly to problems within Judaism itself. Now that we have surveyed the paradigms of the past and faced the challenges of the present, the question arises: where does Judaism stand today on the threshold of the third millennium? That is the main question with which this book is concerned. To put it more precisely, how can the present identity-crisis of modernity be overcome? What basic religious options should Judaism follow? And in decisive questions cannot a reflection on the Jewish origin of Christianity be a help not only for Christians but also for Jews? This chapter is meant to open up the way for us beyond modernity, into the postmodernity to which the future belongs.

C. The Overcoming of Modernity

One thing was already clear at the beginning of the twentieth century: the reactions of Jews to the invasion of their world by modernity had proved very different. And for this reason alone there never was a uniform 'world Jewry' or even a 'conspiracy of world Jewry', as many people down to Adolf Hitler supposed, blinded in their hatred of the Jews and their delusions about them. Nothing would be more wrong than to understand Judaism, then as today, as a monolithic block, and to overlook its plurality: the plurality of trends, groups, parties, which often engage in bitter clashes. To put it in a more comprehensive and more appropriate way: we must not overlook the **plurality of rival paradigms** even within present-day Judaism. At the end of Part One I established that, as can be demonstrated for Christianity and Islam, traditional paradigms are still alive in present-day Judaism, having been more or less transformed. Indeed, as we saw, in the United States already at the beginning of the twentieth century three Jewish 'confessions' had come into being, each with its own observance of the law, organization, places of education, individual synagogues, and each going its autonomous way: 'Orthodox – Conservative – Reform'.[1] How did these three trends develop, and how do they see the future?

I. Ways out of the Identity Crisis

In the period after the Second World War and the founding of the state of Israel, several factors were of decisive influence for Jews all over the world, and especially in the United States. These stabilized the situation of Judaism, above all in America. Whereas today 3.3 million Jews are living in the state of Israel, 5.7 million are living in the United States. So, having considered the various *aliyahs* (immigrations) and the founding of the state of Israel, we must now turn our attention particularly to America, which has not only by far the largest but also by far the most active Diaspora community in all Jewish history.

1. Crisis and renewal

First, increasing **social prosperity and political influence** already during and even more after the Second World War brought American Jewry together into what was socially a far more homogeneous, middle-class society than before, despite all the divergent individual groupings. The distinction between Jews from Germany and Jews from Eastern Europe became largely insignificant. Already as a consequence of President Roosevelt's 'New Deal', socialism had retreated and been absorbed into the Democrat party, and for the American Jewish consciousness after the Second World War at first the catastrophe of the Shoah largely faded into the background.

Secondly, there was manifestly **a religious renewal in the 1950s and 1960s.** For many Jews who now no longer lived in a Jewish quarter but often in isolation, in Christian surroundings, as a result of their migration to the suburbs, this renewal was caused not least by a heightened need for a religious and social 'home' in which to bring up children. 'Jewishness' now retreated in favour of 'Judaism': in other words, Jews now primarily defined themselves by their religion, and not just by a secular culture and a quasi-national feeling. Throughout the cities of America synagogues were now rebuilt, and there was much more active participation in community life and the systematic development of a religious school system with corresponding religious instruction; indeed, there was even a heightened interest in Jewish literature and theology. Alongside Protestantism and Catholicism, Judaism had become the third largest religious community. A famous book by Will Herberg was called *Protestant – Catholic – Jew*. Herberg had been born in New York in 1906,[2] and his career from the Young Communist League through editorship of Communist Party publications in the 1930s to becoming a Jewish writer and theologian in the 1940s and 1950s is typical.[3]

Thirdly, the **Israeli Six Day War in 1967** had decisive political and psychological consequences. In a flash it became clear just how much the state of Israel was on the edge of an abyss and there was the possibility of a new Holocaust. Sobriety set in among Jews who had previously been often euphoric, and a renewed feeling of being left on their own (both by the American government and public and by Christian churches and associations) took hold. As a result, Jews who previously had been anti-Zionist now also **identified** themselves **with the state of Israel**. This led to unprecedented fund-raising; indeed the sense of Jewish identity was deepened, and involvement in the shared Jewish destiny became more intense. So Judaism as a whole, if not necessarily the state of Israel (which at that time had passed up the opportunity for a peace treaty), emerged from the crisis strengthened.

Fourthly, at the beginning of the 1990s Judaism had definitively found its place in American society: 'America is ours; we belong to it' is the much-quoted statement of a minority which was formerly so often scorned and oppressed, but today is more prosperous and influential than ever before. It also has access to financial circles which were previously closed to it. With great self-confidence Judaism now manifests and emphasizes its distinctiveness in the cultural sector: in literature, theatre, films, television, art and music. It pursues its political aims with great emphasis at all levels – local, regional, national and international – by means of numerous organizations and publications, and does not hesitate to persuade and lobby in public where vital interests of the state of Israel are concerned.

So in the last decades of the second millennium an optimistic Jewish self-assessment could be the basic mood, the mood shown, for example, by Charles E.Silberman in his success story of the American Jews, *A Certain People*.[4] Nor may the new edition (1979) of the book on the American Jew by A.J.Feldman first published in 1937 have appeared completely by chance. It ends with the following description: '**The American Jew!** He is the Jew in America who, regardless of the geographic origins of his fathers, takes his place in the American community and occupies it with dignity and worth and self-respect, living honorably and usefully as a Jew and as an American. A human being keenly patriotic, splendidly advancing, finely contributing, nobly aggressive, culturally creative, socially-minded and progressive; a composite personality, made up of the best of the centuries of creative endeavor and spiritual groping of world Jewry, striking his roots into the congenial and blessed soil of America – that is **the American Jew!**'[5] However, since the 1980s this optimism has been disturbed by two things, which make some American Jews fear for the continuity and identity of Judaism in America.

2. Anxieties over continuity and identity

In numerous Jewish publications and in many forums in the 1980s, two complexes of questions were discussed time and again. They cast gloom on the future of American Judaism which had been so successful.

(*a*) Anxiety over **continuity**. What is meant here is not primarily the fact that with the growing integration of Jews into American society its proportional share in American addictions – alcohol, drugs, AIDS – has also risen (though investigations have also been set up into this). What is meant here is, rather, the general social and demographic development. For a growing **assimilation** of many Jews to the non-Jewish environment prompts fears, as also does a reduced Jewish **birthrate** and an increasing number of single households, along with a marked increase in the number of **mixed marriages**, estimated at being between a quarter and a third. In American Judaism these are called out-marriages, whether the non-Jewish partner converts to Judaism (intermarriage) or not (mixed marriage).

I need not go into the dispute within Judaism over the interpretation of the demographic data and the corresponding prognoses for the future.[6] But many Jews have been alarmed by the fact that the Jewish proportion of the total population of the USA in 1937 was still 3.7%, whereas in 1985/86 – despite immigration from the Soviet Union, Israel and Iran – it amounted to only 2.5%. However, in addition to the so to speak external, demographic threat to Judaism, there is also an internal threat which strikes at the very essence of Judaism.

(*b*) Anxiety over **identity**. Since the 1980s, the material prosperity of Jews has increasingly been coupled with a striking religious intolerance between the different Jewish denominations which has led to major polarizations and splits. Here each denomination blames the other. Who is at fault?
– **Orthodox** Judaism, in the USA as in Israel? It in fact refuses to recognize the legitimacy of the non-Orthodox system, thus questioning the validity of all marriages, divorces and conversions by Conservative or Reform rabbis.
– **Conservative** Judaism? To the utmost scandal of the Orthodox, against all Jewish tradition it in fact introduced the ordination of women rabbis in 1983.
– **Reform** Judaism? As well as ordaining women, it has even recognized Jewish descent through the father. Even children of non-Jewish mothers

but Jewish fathers are therefore to be regarded as Jews. This is still firmly rejected by both Orthodox and Conservatives.

And who is right? In the view of all concerned these questions are concerned with no more and no less than the identity of Judaism. Who is a Jew? Which synagogue is authentically Jewish? At the same time there is a fear that these conflicts could lead to an irreparable **split** in Judaism. How serious the situation is is shown by the fact that in 1986 the leaders of the different denominations gathered for a conference in Princeton under the title 'Will There Be One Jewish People by the Year 2000?' Indeed, what will the future be?

There is no doubt about it: these Jewish disputes have numerous effects on communal life within Judaism, and especially also in the state of Israel. They also have an effect on relations between Judaism and the other religions, and Christianity in particular. Finally, they contribute to the fact that a not inconsiderable part of American Jewry does not engage in any religious activity at all. We must discuss this basic option of not believing, or at least not practising, before we consider the various basic religious options.

3. Being a Jew without religion

Just as there are many people in Christianity who do not feel that they belong to any church (the unchurched Christians), so too in Judaism there are many people who do not belong to any synagogue. There are many reasons for this non-affiliation.

– First of all they can be **secular** – or more precisely, selfish and financial (why make financial sacrifices for the benefit of the synagogue?).

– Secondly, they can be completely **religious**: people cannot identify with the religious, political and financial concerns of the synagogues (the churches and their representatives). So non-practising Jews (Christians) are by no means to be counted irreligious, atheists or agnostics – even in religious statistics!

– Thirdly, they can also really be **anti-religious**: because people are basically against religion (as opium, repression, resentment, regression) or because they cannot cope with the catastrophe of the Holocaust, at least in religious terms.

There is certainly no doubt that many typically modern Jews are totally alienated from religion simply for biographical reasons. In the eyes of the Jews, to become an atheist, agnostic or crypto-agnostic in the last century was not half as bad as continuing to believe in God and becoming Christian – after such famous models as Felix Mendelssohn-

Bartholdy, Heinrich Heine or Benjamin Disraeli. That explains why before the Second World War the synagogues of all three trends (Orthodox – Conservative – Reform) formed a minority among American Jews: only between a quarter and a third of Jews belonged to them.

As I have indicated, this changed after the Second World War. And yet even in 1947 the proportion of those attending synagogue was clearly lower than that of those attending Protestant and Catholic churches. Moreover today there are still many Jews (the numbers cannot be quantified accurately) who affirm their Jewishness but reject Judaism – Jewish religion, Jewish faith. They are the successors of those **secular Jews** who already in the last century (and how many there were between Marx and Freud!) moved in the direction of **radical assimilation.** I described how these Jews emerged from the ghetto both outwardly and inwardly and adapted themselves completely to modernity: they gave up observing the Jewish ritual law, which from their perspective seemed quite meaningless, along with all external distinguishing features. They represent the **modern paradigm without religion.**

And yet such un-religious Jews are by no means *a priori* 'nihilists' who do not believe in anything or do not want to commit themselves to anything. Many of them are '**humanists**' or '**moralists**' or '**socialists**' in pursuit of thoroughly ethical aims; they apply ethical standards and in practice devote all their energies to a great variety of humanitarian, moral or social enterprises – whether specifically Jewish or generally humanist. And there is no question that in Judaism in particular (especially in America), a large number of Jews want to be humane, moral or social in this sense without being able to be religious.

However, there are now also numerous Jews who want to be humane, moral and social precisely **because** they are religious. Indeed, **because** they are religious, they think that they can explain why they should be **unconditionally** humane, moral and social. And in connection with such Jewish religious feeling, here, by way of example, I shall outline a Jewish theology which more than any other in America after the Second World War clearly brought theological anthropology and ethics into play even for unbelievers. It is connected with the name of Abraham Joshua Heschel.

4. The religious Jew: Abraham Heschel

Abraham Joshua Heschel was unusually creative precisely because –
like so many other Jewish theologians with whom we shall become
acquainted – he was the **inhabitant of two worlds**: he was born in
Warsaw in 1907[7] and died in New York in 1972. So as a Polish Jew he
already bore within himself from his origins the living piety of an
emotionally coloured Hasidism. But at the same time he was one of the
numerous Jewish theologians who – after a traditional training in
Talmud and Kabbala – was given a solid academic formation for the
whole of his life at the Berlin College for the Science of Judaism.
Moreover, the first works which Heschel had published were written
in German: his dissertation was a phenomenological study of prophecy
(1936)[8] and a biography of the great mediaeval systematic theologian
Maimonides (1935).[9] Both of these were to be indicative of his own
work. In 1937, on the instigation of Martin Buber, he became Buber's
successor at the free Jewish house of learning in Frankfurt.

And yet this theologian would never have become what he was later
to be had he not a year later – having first been deported by the Nazis
to Warsaw – emigrated to North America via London. From 1940
Heschel taught at Hebrew Union College in Cincinnati (Ohio), the
leading training centre in Reform Judaism, and from 1945 until
his death, at the Jewish Theological Seminary in New York, the
headquarters of Conservative Judaism, where his field was Jewish
ethics and mysticism. A brilliant stylist, he wrote his main works in
English, but he also published in Hebrew, Yiddish and Polish. And if
on the one hand he worked intensively on the classical sources of
Judaism and continued to study Talmud, Kabbala and Hasidism, on
the other hand, more than anyone else in America he was concerned
for a contemporary theology which attempted to apply the questions
of modern men and women to the classical insights.

Abraham Heschel sought a way between the **fundamentalists**, who
asserted that all the ultimate questions had been solved, and the
positivists, who asserted that all ultimate questions were meaningless.
Sufficiently familiar with the spirituality of Western Europe, Heschel
saw himself faced above all with the fact that in the modern world
many Jews were **largely alienated from religious reality**. For Heschel,
this process of alienation was not just the result of people's intellectual
difficulties, nor even the fault of religious traditionalism, however much
Heschel might criticize that. Rather, it was connected with the failure
of modern men and women generally to accept that dimension of reality
of which religion is a part and which human reason is capable of

understanding only to a limited degree: grasping that dimension in which the encounter between God and man can take place.

Confronted with this situation, as early as 1951 Heschel had published a first systematic work on the philosophy of religion in which he attempted to demonstrate, with a concentration on the problem of God and the problem of living, that 'man is not alone'. This was a philosophy of religion culminating in a description of the truly pious person.[10]

Five years later Heschel made another new beginning, with the central systematic work from which all his other numerous publications can be understood: a **philosophy of Judaism** with the title *God in Search of Man*.[11] This is:

– a **philosophy**, because unlike theology (as Heschel understood it) it does not begin with the descriptive and the normative, with dogmas and solutions, but with questions and problems, with religion's own explanation and exploration of itself, in order to arrive at a new critical estimation, concentrated less on the content and articles of faith than on the achievement and the act of faith, the depth and basic levels of which need to be investigated. This is what Heschel calls a 'depth theology'.

– a philosophy of **Judaism**, in which Judaism is not the object of critical examination but the subject, the source of ideas: like the insights of Plato or Kant in philosophy. So, for Heschel, Judaism is not just a feeling or an experience but above all a reality, a drama in history with events, teachings and duties which have to be understood.

The statement with which Heschel describes the situation of modern Jews and of modern human beings generally is characteristic: 'The Bible is an answer to the supreme question: what does God demand of us? Yet the question has gone out of the world. God is portrayed as a mass of vagueness behind a veil of enigmas. His voice has become alien to our minds, to our hearts, to our souls. We have learned to listen to every "I" except the "I" of God. The man of our time may proudly declare: nothing animal is alien to me but everything divine is. This is the status of the Bible in modern life: it is a sublime answer, but we do not know the question any more. Unless we recover the question, there is no hope of understanding the Bible.'[12] But how are modern men and women to rediscover God?

Even if this tends to be concealed by Heschel's style of thought, which circles around individual themes rather than progressing from argument to argument, it becomes clear that Abraham Heschel fundamentally recognizes '**three ways**' in the search for God, '**three starting points of contemplation about God**', to which the three parts of his work (God – Revelation – Answer) correspond:[13]

– The first is the way 'of sensing the presence of God in the world, in things'.
– The second is the way of 'sensing His presence in the Bible'.
– The third is the way of 'sensing his presence in sacred deeds (= the commandments)'.

On the first: since the religious dimension already given with human existence and the existence of the world is being suppressed and buried in European modernity, men and women must be freed from a basically unnatural scepticism. They must again get a 'sense of mystery'. Indeed, they must once again learn **radical astonishment** at what is apparently a matter of course: that there is something and not nothing; that a person's own being already contains a mystery; that even a desacralized nature still radiates power, beauty and sublimity and yet is not the ultimate. With amazement, human beings can learn again to be true to themselves and open to the reality of God: **the experience of God in the world**. Heschel does not want to offer proofs with a series of arguments; he simply wants to point out what is there. He wants to show what men and women could really see for themselves. He wants to illuminate the human situation and interpret creation and nature in all their transitoriness so as to make it possible to experience the reality of God anew.

This first way of experiencing God in the world, in things, **secondly** opens up the way to the **experience of God in the biblical revelation**. This is a revelation with which those who have learned to wonder anew are constantly confronted. For Heschel, God is the constant 'ontological premise', the ground of our being, the presupposition of reality. But at the very point when human beings have wonderingly become aware of this presupposition, they are also capable of understanding the message and challenge of the Bible anew. We may experience God's presence in nature, but we do not hear a 'voice'. However, in the Bible we perceive God in a quite concrete way; we hear his word. There is a direct encounter between God and human beings here, an answer to human wonderment.

But if men and women heed the biblical revelation, they can become aware that they do not need constantly to seek God, to some degree by their own efforts. Rather, here they have to do with a **God** who has already long **been in search of them**. 'God seeks man.' That describes the decisive shift of perspective which this theologian constantly wants to achieve anew, chapter by chapter. It is a shift in perspective as it were from below upwards, from immanence to transcendence, from human beings to God. 'It is not right for us to be waiting for God, as if he had never entered history. In his quest for God, the man who lives after the age of Sinai must learn to understand the realness of God's search for man. He must not forget the prophet's world, God's waiting for man.'[14]

'...must not forget the prophet's world.' It is in fact the **prophets** through whom Heschel makes it clear how God's revelation specifically takes place among human beings. And more than any other Jewish theologian, Heschel shows here the degree to which Judaism has remained a prophetic religion. For Heschel, in the Bible revelation as such is not described by empirical concepts; it is announced by evocative and indicative words. The experience of the prophets cannot be reconstituted, either historically or psychologically. The one certain thing is that the prophet does not so much stand on the level of an encounter between I and Thou as in a relationship of prophetic 'sympathy' with God. This does not mean any emotion or ecstasy, but complete openness and responsiveness to God's word itself. The prophet does not just encounter God; he also learns something from him and about him. He experiences God, not just as a Thou but as a reality with superior power which therefore enables him. Nor does he just experience God and write down the words afterwards; he hears, remembers and communicates the very word and demand which has come to him, and through him to others. Sympathy is the opposite to projection; it is complete openness and receptivity to God.

And in fact that is the decisive point: it is not a question of psychological or historical verification of the event of revelation (Heschel is not interested in historical-critical questions), or of dogmatic fixation and sterile credulity in the letter, which buttresses itself on the 'objective revelational character of the Bible'.[15] For Heschel, revelation is not a monologue, nor dictation. Revelation takes place in the living relationship of tension between God and man on the basis of the covenant: 'It is incorrect to maintain that all words in the Bible originated in the spririt of God. The blasphemous tirades of Pharaoh, the rebellious utterances of Korah, the subterfuge of Ephron, the words of the soldiers in the camp of Midian, emanated from the spirit of man. What the prophet says to God when addressed by him is not considered less holy than what God says to the prophet in addressing him. Thus the Bible is more than the word of God: it is the word of God **and** man, a record of both revelation and response; the drama of covenant between God and man. The canonization and preservation of the Bible are the work of Israel.'[16]

As to the **third** way, the circle is closed with the human 'answer', the

fulfilling of the commandments, the doing of the works of the law. For this is the way to a God who is not a philosophical abstraction or a psychological projection but a living dynamic reality who shows a passionate concern for his creatures. In this way Heschel represents a Judaism which is essentially more than that 'religon of reason' propagated by the neo-Kantian Hermann Cohen; nor is it just reduced to a personal divine relationship between the I and the great Thou, which Martin Buber ultimately understood all too individualistically. Heschel's Judaism is also a Judaism to be practised together, indeed a Judaism of the community of believers. Judaism can be practised in the context of the state of Israel, about which Heschel's comments were relatively restrained. But it can also be practised in the context of the Jewish Diaspora, which brings out its special social commitment. For it is no coincidence that as a Jew Heschel was later a committed supporter of civil rights for the Blacks, an opponent of the Vietnam war and a supporter of the Soviet Jews.

And he sought to do all this in the spirit of authentic Judaism itself. But what is this '**spirit of Judaism**'? What makes a Jew a Jew? At the end of his great outline *God in Search of Man*, Heschel once again explicitly takes up this question, and answers it in quite a different way from A.J.Feldman, who – as we have just heard – described the ideal progressive American Jew. For Heschel, the 'Spirit of Judaism' is not the spirit of conformity to American secular society, but above all the **spirit of protest**, embodied in the great prophets, against a confusion of the true God with the many earthly, false 'idols' of this society. However, this is a protest which must also be made on matters of religion and belief in the law: 'Even the laws of the Torah are not absolutes. Nothing is deified: neither power nor wisdom, neither heroes nor institutions. To ascribe divine qualities to all of these, to anything, sublime and lofty as it may be, is to distort both the idea it represents and the concept of the divine which we bestow upon it.'[17] That is what makes the identity of the Jew as a Jew: 'To be a Jew is to renounce allegiance to false gods; to be sensitive to God's infinite stake in every finite situation; to bear witness to this presence in the hours of His concealment; to remember that the world is unredeemed. We are born to be an answer to this question. Our way is either a pilgrimage or a flight. We are chosen to remain free of infatuation with worldly triumphs, to retain independence of hysteria and deceptive glories; never to succumb to splendour, even at the price of remaining strangers to fashion.'[18]

All in all, this is an imposing Jewish theology, which attempts simultaneously to be in keeping with the time and with scripture. But the wide-ranging conversation which the 'American Buber' carries on with modern and religious men and women in such an understanding way also raises questions. It does so in three respects:

5. Questions

In the **first** approach to God – through the reality of the world – Heschel's theology rightly begins with the situation of modern men and women, with modern science, anthropology and philosophy. But does not this Jewish theologian lapse all too quickly into a confrontational pattern of question and answer? Can anthropology and theology be divided so simply into a world of questions and answers, as if there were no answers in 'secular' anthropology and no self-critical questions in Jewish theology? Indeed, it is legitimate to doubt whether Heschel ever took modern anthropology seriously in intellectual terms and did not make it a function of his theological anthropology, which was established *a priori*. Heschel avoids any struggle over the question of the rights of philosophical anthropology and the elements of truth in it, any **critical discussion with the modern criticism of religion.** He suppresses any radical questioning of his own 'ontological premises'. Statements like 'man is meaningless without God'[19] betray a tendency towards a suspicious generalization, perhaps even a bad theological habit, that of speaking out theologically for contemporaries who have become sceptical before they are allowed to express their own self-understanding.[20]

As for the **second** approach to God – through the biblical revelation – Heschel rightly dissociates himself critically from a dogmatic fundamentalism and a sterile belief in the letter. But can one thus ignore the **questions of historical biblical criticism** with impunity, as though there had been no historical-critical investigation of the Bible (Spinoza, Reimarus, Lessing, Wellhausen) for almost three hundred years? For all Heschel's efforts to bring out the living reality of God in his revelation, in close contact with scripture and with a sense of the existential human needs and hopes, in the long run does not the absence of historical criticism take its revenge when he accepts uncritically the whole tradition not only of the Torah but also of the halakhah? 'The prophets' inspirations and the sages' interpretations are equally important... The savants are heirs to the prophets.'[21] Do not sentences like this sovereignly cover up the precise problem within Judaism – the domination of tradition over scripture, against which one must be able to protest once again in the spirit of the 'prophets'? If the biblical scholars, the rabbis, have become prophets, who may then protest prophetically against such 'prophets'? Does that not amount to surrendering the prophetic heritage completely to the rabbis and thus depriving the prophetic heritage of the very thing which has always marked it out: the right in the name of the living God to resist all traditions, the right to protest against a confusion between the reality of God and the traditions and interpretations, systems and hierarchies fabricated by human beings.

As for the **third** approach – doing the works of the law – Heschel rightly makes an effort to free Judaism from the prejudices, restraints and caricatures associated with a 'religion of legalism'. But for all his efforts to bring out the polarity between 'law and inwardness, love and fear, understanding and obedience, joy and discipline',[22] does not the fact that here, too, Heschel blurs the question of a theologically responsible **criticism of observance of the law** take its revenge? For all his awareness of the fact that 'the modern Jew cannot accept the way of static obedience as a short cut to the mystery of the divine will,'[23] does Heschel really take those modern Jews who are alienated from observing the law seriously when in the last resort he does accept all the commandments and gives them a spiritual sense? Do not statements like 'to say that the *mizvot* (commandments) have meaning is less accurate than saying that they lead to wells of emergent meaning and to experiences which are full of hidden brilliance'[24] suggest that Heschel does not want to make a critical interpretation of the laws, but only to transcend them spiritually? But can laws which seem meaningless to the modern Jew really lead to spiritual 'wells'? Can one want to exclude human reason like this in such questions? Is it any help to modern Jews with their questions, their criticisms, when in respect of all the commandments which so prompt their critical questions, one replies: 'We should, therefore, not evaluate the *mizvot* (commandments) by the amount of rational meaning which we may discover at their basis. Religion is not within but beyond the limits of mere reason; its task is not to compete with reason, to be a source of speculative ideas, but to aid us where reason is of little aid.'[25] May we play off reason and religon against each other like this without bidding farewell to the spirituality of modernity?

Question after question. And after this reconnaissance which Abraham Joshua Heschel's great systematic work has provided for us, we have now penetrated deeply into the problems of modern Jewish philosophy, which we may feel free to call theology. We can now ask the basic question: what do the different basic **religious** options look like for a Jew today – given that there is no creed which is binding on all Jews, nor any universal teaching authority?

II. Basic Religious Options for the Future?

The dispute over the past is also a dispute over the future. And there is no mistaking the fact that while each of the three Jewish denominations claims to be representing the original Judaism, in each case it has proved impossible to avoid adaptations (superficial, moderate or radical) to the constantly changing situation of the time. Here only indirect mention can be made of the small Jewish groups on the periphery (Jewish humanism, Jewish science, Black Judaism). How are the three main trends in Judaism developing, the trends which I already discussed as historical phenomena at the end of Part One? The problem which must now concern us further is this: what are the spiritual and religious options in the future for Orthodoxy, Conservative Judaism and Reform Judaism? By way of anticipation it can be said that all three groups, which first formed above all in Germany and then developed further in America, are changing. A renewed convergence cannot be ruled out in the future, despite all the polarizations and the individual groups which are incapable of change.

1. Classical Orthodoxy: Samson R.Hirsch

Only in 1795 was the word 'Orthodoxy', which in the nineteenth century became a customary term to mark a distinction from Reform Judaism, used for the first time with reference to Judaism: as a synonym for '**fidelity to the Law**', '**fidelity to the Torah**'. Down to the present day all those Jews count themselves part of Jewish Orthodoxy who still feel obligated to the 'written Torah' as the inspired word of God and the 'oral Torah' as its interpretation: indeed, these represent the two main sources of the halakhah, the Jewish law, by which the Orthodox have to lead their everyday life.[1]

Our historical analysis of the macro-paradigms has shown that here the issue is the handing on of the **paradigm of the rabbis and the synagogue**, which is put forward and defended resolutely by radically traditionalist Orthodoxy, particularly in the face of the incursion of the modern world. From all that we have heard, its profile is clear. When the external walls were falling in Europe and religious commitment was clearly on the wane, those who continued in the strict observance of the Torah strengthened the inner walls around the Jewish soul with countless internalized legal regulations and interpretations for every day of the year, and the sabbath in particular. Here, down to the present day, belonging to the people and belonging to the religion go together. But religion is tradition, and the synagogue (like the Roman church earlier), is a stronghold with mostly closed doors and windows, though never so exclusive an institution of salvation that (to put it in Christian terms) there is 'no salvation outside it'.

And what about the modernity outside the walls? Initially it was fundamentally ignored by the Orthodox, and the frequent failure of the modern West in moral matters provided confirmation here. Like Roman Catholics before Vatican II and even some afterwards, and also like many Muslims in the various countries of the globe, down to the present day these Jews perpetuate the **mediaeval paradigm** of religion, heedless of Reformation and Enlightenment, with only purely external adaptations (transportation, communication and financial facilities). It is enriched with elements from the post-exilic theocracy paradigm and given an anti-modernist focus. As Roman Catholics did for a long time, they also advise their children to choose 'safe' professions so as not to endanger their faith: business, law, medicine, but in no way the arts or social sciences, least of all history, Jewish history.

So is not a renewal of Judaism necessary? Yes and no. Already in the nineteenth century a man like **Samson Raphael Hirsch** (1803-1888), still the acknowledged supreme head of German neo-Orthodoxy, passionately argued, against all schismatic tendencies, that a **renewal** of Judaism was very **necessary**.[2] However, he did not call for a renewal in a progressive direction, as demanded by the reformers, through scientific criticism, changes in belief and the abandonment of many traditional laws. Rather, he called for a **conservative** renewal, through reflection on the eternal, unchanging, infallible biblical and Talmudic revelation which is God's seamless truth. The literal sense of its laws, as immutable as those of nature, had first of all to be understood, and then their real religious significance would emerge in the symbolic content which would be disclosed in each case – here impulses from the Kabbala are taken up.

And what about biblical criticism? Hirsch brushes its arguments aside. If the statement 'And God spoke to Moses and said', with which all the laws of the Torah are now introduced, is true, then this Torah is to be accepted without any ifs and buts; it is in fact to be translated into action at any time and in any situation. Or, as much of Orthodoxy now puts the alternative in a pointed way: either one accepts everything that is written – or it is best to give up being a Jew. This is an attitude towards Torah and halakhah which is not dissimilar to that of

Protestant fundamentalists towards the infallible word of the Bible or that of Catholic traditionalists towards the infallible word of the pope.

Today Orthodox Jews live dispersed throughout Europe in relatively small numbers, and then in some American cities (where the really practising Orthodox make up hardly more than 5% of the Jewish population), but above all in Israel – though even there they represent only a small minority in the country as a whole. However, it is important that with 330,000 members, in **Jerusalem** they form around a third of the Jewish population, and by tipping the scales have considerable political influence in the formation of governments. But in their day-dreams of an ideal form of state and government, some Orthodox have for a long time been anti-Zionist and against a secular state of Israel. Today, though, the great majority of Orthodox adherents are also Zionists out of religious conviction. This is just one sign that change and renewal are possible even within the framework of Orthodoxy.

Like the other denominations, orthodoxy too is **not a monolithic block** today. Rather, it is something like an alliance of independent synagogues, each with its own interpretation of the halakhah, and all attempting to surmount their crises in their own way. For during the course of the twentieth century, Eastern European Orthodoxy had already lost most of its members to the United States in the second generation.[3] Indeed, already at the beginning of the twentieth century the older Orthodoxy of the first immigrants had largely disappeared: many children of the immigrants had become Christians by marriage or conversion, and others – particularly those from Western Europe – were later absorbed by Conservative Judaism.

In addition, even many Jews who preserve links with the Orthodox synagogue and in particular give it generous material support (especially its well-developed school system), give themselves the clear conscience they need by financial contributions. Thus a good deal of the powerful backing collected for Israeli interests since the Six Day War has landed in the coffers of Orthodoxy – in both America and Israel. Even for some secular Jews, the rule of thumb seems to be: if you give money for Jewish causes, then give it to the 'right (= Orthodox) Jews... In this way, even most recently the different groups of Hasidic Jews (e.g. the Lubavich Hasidim) who immigrated from Eastern Europe have been able to develop quite a successful missionary activity with modern means, though their subjective emotionalism has caused them to be mistrusted by the other Jewish denominations.

However, a distinction needs to be made between such traditionally Orthodox Jews and those Orthodox Jews who not only have no fear of modernity but seek a symbiosis between Orthodoxy and the modern world. They fully affirm secular education and contemporary culture. These enlightened Orthodox – as they sometimes call themselves – seek a genuine synthesis of the best of both worlds. This is what the first President of the Yeshiva University, Bernard Revel, used to call for, convinced that Judaism could only be deepened and enriched in this way. And this modern, enlightened Orthodoxy already has a significant modern tradition in its turn.[4]

2. Enlightened Orthodoxy: Joseph D. Soloveitchik

Orthodoxy lives on today, above all in America. It is astounding that after a long period in which it seemed doomed to decline, in the 1970s and 1980s it not only increased in numbers but also came more strongly to the foreground among the American public. What was the reason for this? Was it simply that after the Second World War a considerable number of survivors of the Holocaust had emigrated there, and that after their fearful experiences they wanted beyond question to retain their Jewish way of life? Or was it that almost all over the world the revolutionary 1960s and 1970s were followed in the 1980s by something like a conservative backlash? Or that many Jews felt permissive Western civilization to be amoral and repellent, and that in face of the tremendously accelerated social change (which included a change in values) observance of the law promised to give them the detachment, moral steadfastness and security of world-view that they needed?

Without doubt all these factors played their part, but they are hardly a sufficient explanation. We also have this modern, **enlightened Orthodoxy** which did not want to shut itself off in a sectarian way, but to show itself open to a new, different time. To the degree that such Orthodoxy combines classical halakhic Judaism (for example, ritual bathing) with American culture (for example sport), to some younger Jews in America it represents a real option, indeed it offers a new life-style.

In this way, then, a literature was disseminated from the Orthodox Yeshiva University in New York, of all places, which in no way simply centred on esoteric problems of the exegesis of the Torah, but also addressed the everyday needs and hopes of non-Orthodox Jews. The undisputed leader of this enlightened Orthodoxy is Rabbi **Joseph D.Soloveitchik** (born 1903), Professor at the Yeshiva University, who comes from a famous rabbinic dynasty. He has been able to combine the two worlds of the Talmud and modern philosophy in his person (as Heschel combined his Eastern European origin and his philosophical doctorate in Berlin[5]). His theology is a 'theology of the halakhah', since what primarily determine a Jewish life-style and morality are not the narratives of the haggadah but primarily the legal regulations of the halakhah. This is the ideal of 'halakhic man', his world-view, life and creative capacity.

Rabbi Soloveitchik presents this **ideal of 'halakhic man'** (*ish ha-halakha* = 'man of the halakhah') eloquently and yet in a concentrated way, with numerous references to everyday life, to modern philosophy and the Jewish tradition. Like a mathematician who begins from an ideal world which is given *a priori*, 'halakhic man orients himself to the world by means of fixed statutes and firm principles'. 'An entire corpus of precepts and laws guides him along the path leading to existence.'[6] Here halakhic man, unlike the *homo religiosus*, is not primarily concerned with the reality of transcendence, but with empirical reality here and now. It is the ideal of halakhic man 'to subject reality to the yoke of the halakhah'.[7] Certainly he, too, has 'fear of death',[8] but although he believes in an eternal life, 'he strives for the redemption of the world, not via a higher world but via the world itself, via the adaptation of empirical reality to the ideal patterns of Halakhah'.[9] To this degree he is concerned 'to bring transcendence down into this valley of the shadow of death – i.e. into our world – and to transform it into a land of the living'.[10]

So what function does the **halakhah** have for this Jewish philosopher of religion? It is the 'crystallization of the fleeting individual experience into fixed principles and universal norms': 'Halakhah is the objectifying instrument of our religious consciousness'.[11] So Soloveitchik does not think of interpreting or constructing the halakhah, say, historically and genetically: he is sharply polemical against any kind of 'sociological and psychological genetics'.[12] Rather, he seeks to reconstruct the halakhah phenomenologically and existentially: 'If the commensurability of traditional beliefs with modern religious experience is to be investigated, the method of retrospective exploration, the regressive movement from objective religious symbols to subjective flux – must be applied.' For, 'If an objective compass be lacking, the final port of landing is uncertain.'[13] And for Soloveitchik this objective compass is not mediaeval Jewish philosophy (whose concepts in any case came from Greek and Arabic philosophy), as it is for most Jewish philosophers, but the halakhah, which is to be illuminated typologically from an overall context with the help of modern philosophy.

What does this overall systematic context look like? Soloveitchik, trained not least in Hegel's dialectic, sees human beings first of all as individuals, as completely contradictory beings (indeed, the biblical creation story already tells of this), stretched between unlimited possibilities and limited capacities, between a simultaneous affirmation and denial of the self, between freedom and necessity, anxiety and hope, fear of God and love of God. However, this Orthodox rabbi does not want to make any room for a Christian pessimism of the Fall; rather, he wants to encourage a realistic human self-estimation. This contradictory human situation, in which even the experience of alienation can be a source of creativity, can be coped with by human beings if they gain spiritual control of themselves and the temporal currents which oppress them. But this does not happen (as it does in Christianity) through any divine act of redemption or redeemer, but through the Torah given by God on Sinai, which is the expression of God's will.

In other words, through a life in accord with the halakhah which gives human beings firm guidance at all levels of life in the specific everyday world, a person may bring the contradictory tendencies of his existence into the necessary equilibrium. Soloveitchik does not think that the halakhah is holy in itself (any more than Mount Sinai shows traces of the descent of God); rather, it becomes holy through human devotion to it, just as Mount Moriah was hallowed by the ascent of Abraham in his readiness to sacrifice to God. Through observation of the law the Jew becomes a man of the halakhah and is taken into covenant community with God. In this way he is able to achieve his goal, nearness to God – though in lifelong tension between activity and passivity, commitment and taking back, responsibility and resignation.

Thus for this modern Orthodox theologian there is 'only a single source from which the philosophical world-view of Judaism could proceed: the objective order – the halakhah'.[14] And so Soloveitchik's second key essay on the halakhic mind[15] ends with the statement: 'Out of the sources of Halakhah, a new world view awaits formulation.'

Even as an outsider, one can understand how many Orthodox Jews can recognize themselves in this halakhah theology of Soloveitchik, who is also a great orator, since it is so close to life and presented so evocatively. Indeed, even non-Jews can share many of the anthropological and ethical conceptions about 'halakhic man' developed here. And yet here, too, questions arise, though they are difficult to formulate, since Soloveitchik has yet to publish his synthesis of anthropology and theology in book form. However, they are questions which Jews and Christians can share in putting.

3. Questions on revelation and the Law

Soloveitchik does not speak of the word of the Bible and the Talmud as the infallible word of God in so sheerly fundamentalist a way as Hirsch. But his view of the halakhah is also static. Hence the question: is the halakhah really such an 'objective ordinance' as the principle of Pythagoras, which holds independently of any psychological and sociological development? Does the theologian need to bother as little about the **history** of his 'discipline' as the mathematician and physicist does about that of his? If according to Soloveitchik the Hegelian view that all philosophy is in a constant state of becoming has become a truism, then given the long and complex history of the tradition which I have sketched out, is it convincing to leave the historical development of the halakhah itself out of account in favour of a phenomenological-existentialist approach which over large areas simply confirms the Orthodox-mediaeval interpretation?

Furthermore, did not the first great mediaeval systematic theologians criticized by Soloveitchik, Gaon Saadia (tenth century) and Bachya (eleventh century), who distinguished between rational and traditional commandments, and Maimonides (twelfth century), who laboured over a rational synthesis, get further in their awareness and solution of the problem, even if they were not yet reflecting on the historical development? Should we for example, as Soloveitchik requires in contrast to Saadia, ignore all historical reasons, say for the blowing of the shophar (a relic from nomadic times as a warning or to mark the beginning of a festival), in favour of a symbolic explanation (a call to penitence and conversion)? Can a symbolic-typological explanation remove all the real difficulties of the halakhah (for example over the rules for the sabbath, purity, or food), which deter the majority of Jews from the Orthodox way of the halakhah?

The church fathers and their successors in the twentieth century also thought that they could cope with the real difficulties in the Bible with symbolic-typological exegesis. But is it still really a convincing approach today, instead of employing resolutely historical-theological criticism, to elevate certain commandments or doctrines to some extent into a sphere of higher anthropological reason, just as some Catholic dogmatic theologians attempt to make incomprehensible traditional dogmas 'understandable' by means of theological or typological reinterpretation? Are there not also regulations in the halakhah (for example those limiting the rights of women), the rationality of which is no longer at all clear today, and which no one would proscribe nowadays if they were not already 'God's commandment'? But in that case, does not theonomy, which is supposed to fulfil human autonomy, become a heteronomy which violates human reason? It should be possible nowadays to have discussions about these and similar questions between Jewish and Christian theologians – but unfortunately Rabbi Soloveitchik rejects this.

However, the Orthodox themselves point out to us that there is a **broad spectrum of basic theological positions** in 'theory' and 'practice' even within Orthodoxy, depending on the choice of sources and methods of interpretation. Further information about them is given, for example, by the Orthodox President of the Bar Ilan University in Israel, Rabbi Emanuel Rackman.[16] Specifically, there are two main complexes.

First, revelation and faith. Here **all** Orthodox recognize the **Torah** as God's revelation to humankind, **but**:
– For some, God dictated this revelation to Moses at the time, word for word, so even today it is to be accepted in faith, word for word – down to the age of the world, which according to the Bible is around 5,000 years.
– For others, the manner of revelation is not clear, but at all events it needs interpretation, so that the age of the earth, the origin of the human race and other things must be discovered more from the natural sciences.
– For the third group, especially scientists, it is important to hold on to the traditional view of faith in personal life, but in research and life to go by scientific methods and results; contradictions between the two are covered up or suppressed.

The same holds for the **further sources** of revelation:
– For some, the biblical books outside the Pentateuch were also composed by the holy Spirit word for word; for others, the different authorship, period of composition and literary genre of the individual biblical writings are to be taken with the utmost seriousness.
– For some, the doctrine of inviolability applies not only to the Torah but to all holy scriptures, including all statements of the Mishnah and the Talmud; for others, with an appeal to the Mishnah, Talmud and mediaeval Jewish philosophy, only the five books of Moses are inviolable.

Secondly, the Law and fulfilment of the Law. All Orthodox regard the legal parts of the Torah, which are in fact the primary basis of the halakhah, as the expression of the will of God. **But**:

– Some regard these laws as eternal and absolutely unchangeable.
– Others, with the help of the oral Torah, also assume that there are non-eternal and changeable laws: laws (say about blood vengeance or about the nomination of the king) which are not absolute commands but only recommendations.

Not only questions of theology but also **questions of politics** are involved here. Orthodoxy in America fosters its self-awareness not least by the fact that it is the only form of Judaism recognized in the state of Israel. However, this is precisely the point at which the questions of the other Jews begin. Is it right that it should be taken for granted that rabbis (most recently even women rabbis within the Reform movement and Conservative Judaism) of all three Jewish trends in America can perform valid marriages, divorces and conversions, while in the state of Israel only Orthodox are allowed to do this – because of the dominant position which they had already attained in the Osman empire? All official efforts, personal connections and even financial support from American Jewry have so far been to no avail here. Neither the Conservative nor the Reform rabbis and congregations have been able to secure official recognition in Israel. Certainly they are there in the land, but they do not have any legal status comparable to the Orthodox.

The consequence is intolerable polarization, indeed in fact a **split in Judaism** for which Orthodoxy, as the most intolerant and most aggressive of all the Jewish trends, bears a good deal of the responsibility. In practice, extraordinary difficulties arise here which have already been reported: some hyper-Orthodox Jews (in this respect similar to hyper-Orthodox Christians or Muslims) are obsessed with an almost mediaeval fanaticism and in their appeals to the Torah are fighting not so much against unbelievers and Gentiles as against their own fellow-believers who have deviated from tradition. Strict separation from public sinners and refusal of any collaboration are enjoined, so that resentment is now being aroused against such a kind of Judaism even among Jews, just as in antiquity it was aroused among Gentiles. Indeed, the Orthodox even justify acts of violence against those who in their view break the sabbath (for example by sport or by driving automobiles), or who violate good morals (for example by advertising)... But the very fact that in some circumstances counter-violence can be used against the hyper-Orthodox and their institutions (as happened in a spectacular case in Israel), has led to some reflection.[17] Even the hyper-Orthodox could not tolerate a civil war.

Cannot, must not, a way of tolerance be found here in time? Even in the private life of most Orthodox there has long since ceased to be any abhorrence of what earlier generations would still have regarded as sin: secular education, modern social life, modern music. For a long time the defensiveness and encapsulation in some Orthodox synagogues, at any rate in America, is no longer as total as it used to be. And have not enlightened Orthodox shown that with reference to the Torah and without betraying the halakhah one can practise tolerance, show understanding towards other Jewish groups and work together – at any rate in the social sphere and perhaps also in the religious sphere – not only as individuals but also as organizations? Might it not be possible to reach agreement here that any kind of compulsion in religious matters must cease, even in the state of Israel? Should not a dialogue be possible among all Jews, because so many people are affected? Cannot a common solution be found to the painful problems which, for example, Jewish family law throws up, and in particular cannot the position of women be improved?

Orthodox voices, too, are calling for an understanding here and are attempting to point a way into the future, not least by taking seriously the historical, psychological and philosophical aspects of the interpretation of the halakhah. And even if they do not like Reform Judaism, informed Orthodox at least concede that in some things this has pointed the way to the future. That the question of the law is utterly central to this way into the future is plausible, and the consequences of this will have to occupy us further. But first of all let us turn to the positions which run counter to Orthodoxy.

4. Rationalistic Reform Judaism: Abraham Geiger

I also sketched out briefly in Part One the history of Reform Judaism: the history of those Jews who wanted to understand Judaism not as a legalistic, ritualistic religion, but as a **prophetic-ethical** religion, and who with a universalistic religious and political orientation had brought about something like a fundamental renewal (analogous to that in Protestantism in the sixteenth century). In both theory and practice this Reform Judaism thinks in evolutionary, historical terms.

The counterpart to Samson Raphael Hirsch is **Abraham Geiger** (1810-74),[18] a fellow-student and at first a friend, the most significant representative of German Reform Judaism and many-sided co-founder of the Science of Judaism. Geiger was firmly convinced that a religious reform, a renewal of Jewish theology and Judaism generally, could be achieved only through science and historical criticism. In his view the true nature of Judaism developed in the religion of the prophets, who as we know did not inculcate the observation of a ritual but belief in the one holy God. This has to be preserved in practice by righteousness, mercy and a love of fellow human beings which cannot be limited by any bounds (even national bounds).

Peoplehood, belonging to a people, is no longer decisive for this trend, as it was in former times. What is now decisive – and here there is a contrast with those who are fully secularized, is the religious tie, the religious confession and an enlightened religious praxis (Maimonides already gives medical or hygienic reasons for some ritual precepts). So this Reform movement **no longer** understands Judaism primarily as a nation separated from others, as the **community of a people**, but – in loyalty to former host nations – as a **religious community** living among all nations: a community of **faith**. The distinctive Jewish feature which has developed here is the ethical monotheism of the prophetic tradition.

From there, it is not much of a step to the possibility of describing such a religion, without any cultural or national elements, as a universal **religion of reason** – not, of course, to be confused with a philosophy of religion. And what could there be about it that was contrary to reason – if it is concerned above all with devotion to the one idea of God and the resultant messianic ethic? Granted, both these elements go beyond pure philosophy, but they are not irrational. So even a philosopher like **Hermann Cohen** (1842-1918) could advocate such a Jewish religion of reason with conviction. The founder of the Marburg school of neo-Kantianism, the son of a cantor who claimed never to have turned away from Judaism, towards the end of his life, as a lecturer, he devoted himself completely to rational Judaism understood in this way. His posthumously published book is also his testament: *The Religion of Reason from the Sources of Judaism*.[19] Here we have science and ethics again writ large, along with nurture and education – all very much in line with classical Reform Judaism.

So whereas Orthodoxy was essentially concerned with the preservation of the mediaeval *status quo*, in Reform Judaism we have an amazing **religious and cultural reformation**, a reform of the Jewish law, Jewish upbringing, language, liturgy, synagogue architecture and lifestyle generally. And as we saw, this is not a presupposition of the Enlightenment, as in Christianity, but its consequence (now that it had come about in Europe and North America). In the awareness that despite secularization the modern world has remained moulded by the Judaeo-Christian tradition, down to art and music, such Jews strive for their own **living synthesis between the modern world and Judaism**. They live in the modern paradigm, but preserve belief in the one God and the prophetic ethos as the 'substance' of Judaism. It is the great merit of this Reform Judaism that it gives greater expression in Jewish liturgy and upbringing to the **universal** dimensions of the divine covenant and the religion of humanity – at least initially, though, without any reference to the Holy Land.

But objections come to mind: can Jewish religion simply be derived from dedication to the idea of God and ethics? Is not life deeper than logic and are not certain depths of the human soul better reached through ritual? Are there not basic human needs for experiences, emotions, feelings, traditions? Even Jews orientated on reform would feel deficiencies here. And like Orthodox Judaism, so too this Reform Judaism which originally had an Enlightenment, rationalistic stamp, directed against tradition and against nationalism, has already changed decisively since the 1920s. A postmodern development is setting in, especially in the United States. However, progress cannot be made without conflicts.

5. Tradition and reform in conflict: Louis Jacobs

There were several causes of change: first the antipathy of the now largely 'Americanized' Reformers to the modern rationalism of German origin in the context of the paradigm shift after the First World War, which put a stop to German immigration; secondly the antisemitism which increasingly threatenened in both Europe and America; and thirdly Eastern Judaism, which was now numerically by far the most prominent in America.[20] The German-speaking Jews in America – doctors, lawyers, businessmen – constantly had everyday dealings with such Jews as their clientele. For the new generation of Jews from the East, social betterment usually went with a move from Orthodoxy to Conservative or Reform Judaism; as early as 1930, half the Reform synagogues consisted of former 'Orthodox'. It was important to take their problems seriously – Zionism, Yiddish/Hebrew, the traditional Jewish heritage.

The seizure of power by the National Socialists in 1933 with its catastrophic consequences for the European Jews also had an effect on American Jews. A violent brake was put on the optimistic development of the Reform movement. With increasing inwardness people now sought a new foundation for their own religious feeling: in 1937 the Reform rabbis approved new 'Guiding Principles of Reform Judaism' in Columbus, Ohio. In line with the Pittsburgh Declaration of 1885 the principle of progress in religion was still recognized: 'Revelation is a continuous process, not limited to any particular group or time.' However, in other respects there were quite new accents in this 'Columbus Platform'.[21]

1. On the **Torah**, it was still maintained that 'certain laws had now lost their binding force – with the disappearance of the conditions which had given rise to them'. However, at the same time it was now proclaimed: 'As a treasury of abiding spiritual ideals the Torah remains the living source of the life of Israel.' The food laws and commandments for priestly purity and clothing were still regarded as being time-conditioned, but now there was an interest in a positive formulation of religious obligations with the help of the 'commandments' (*mizvot*).

2. On Israel as **people** and **land** it was still maintained that Israel, now living scattered throughout the world, is held together by the bond of a comman history and above all by the legacy of a common faith. But at the same time it was now proclaimed: 'In the rehabilitation of Palestine, the land hallowed by memories and hopes, we behold the promise of renewed life for many of our brethren. We affirm the obligation of all Jewry to aid in its upbuilding as a Jewish homeland by endeavoring to make it not only a haven and refuge for the oppressed but also a center of Jewish culture and spiritual life.'

3. On **liturgy**, it was resolved soon afterwards to reintroduce traditional symbols, customs and music (a purely Jewish choir, and a cantor). Thus came about the introduction of the Friday evening service (with the ceremony of lighting candles), which proved much more popular than the Saturday morning service. In 1940 a *Union Prayer Book* appeared, revised in this direction (this also once again contained the Kiddush, the prayer over the cup of wine on the sabbath). Moreover, **Hebrew studies** were now also encouraged by Reform Judaism, and Hebrew Union College (in Cincinnati, later also in New York), which was responsible in Reform Judaism for training rabbis and teachers, opened a branch settlement in the state of Israel. In the United States today there are about 1.3 million members of Reform Judaism.

But as with Orthodoxy, so too with the **Reform version of Jewish religion, questions arise.** In many cases (like culture Protestantism before it), did it not prove to conform all too closely to a quite specific ideology of the bourgeois middle class? Is the most important thing for a religion in fact always to live in harmony with science, psychotherapy and liberal politics? Is the battle against antisemitism enough in itself to create identity? Can it replace the Jewish faith? Can commitment to the state of Israel be compared with the prophetic commitment to justice? Did not the prophets in particular always also criticize contemporary Israel? Moreover, is not a liberal religion all too much a religion without barbs, without contradiction, without resistance to the spirit of the time? Can this be the truly Jewish religion? Is not the truly Jewish religion the legal, halakhic religion? But how does Reform Judaism relate to this legal, halakhic tradition in particular?

The problem of tradition and reform has become the fate of some Jews, as of some Christians and Muslims. A spectacular case, which also attracted attention in America, was that of the distinguished halakhic scholar, Rabbi **Louis Jacobs** (born in Manchester in 1920). He worked successfully as a rabbi in London and as tutor at Jews' College there (later he was also visiting professor at Harvard Divinity School), but finally his career as lecturer and rabbi was blocked by a twice-repeated veto by the Chief Rabbi of the United Hebrew Congregations of the British Commonwealth in London.[22]

An increasing polarization had developed in **English Jewry** after the Second World War: between the Orthodox wing, consisting of originally Spanish and Portuguese congregations which had been reinforced by refugees from Central Europe, Hungary and Poland, and the liberal wing, which was showing its strength by the founding of new synagogues and of Leo Baeck College in London. The two wings had still been able to celebrate the 300th anniversary of the resettlement of the Jews in Great Britain with pomp and circumstance. But only six years later, a dispute erupted which was crystallized in the person of Rabbi Jacobs, on the point of his being elected Principal of Jews' College, London, in succession to the strictly Orthodox Isidore Epstein.[23] What was the charge? He was said to have denied the divine origin of parts of the Torah and to want to leave to human reason the selection of what was divine and what was not. So vigorous was the dispute that the local synagogue leaders, who supported Rabbi Jacobs and allowed him to preach even without a licence, were dismissed by the governing body of the central London synagogues. Thereupon Jacobs' followers made him director of a specially founded Society for the Study of Jewish Theology, and in 1964 even founded a synagogue specially for him.

Now even Jacobs' most vehement opponents could not dispute that this 'heretic' was a very well trained rabbi, responsible for some acute analysis, and a deeply committed scholar who could listen to both legal and ethical, mystical and philosophical voices and integrate them. Continuing to **practise as an Orthodox**, he had published a number of studies on the Kabbala and on Hasidism, and also a book on Jewish prayer and introductions to the feasts of Yom Kippur (the feast of reconciliation) and Rosh Hashanah (the Jewish New Year Festival), along with studies on Talmudic logic and methodology and finally translations of important works from Hebrew into English. But what was it that made his opponents so implacable? It was above all the fact that this rabbi had introduced the most important results of modern **historical criticism** into English Jewry, that he challenged the divine inspiration of the Pentateuch and attempted to take seriously a historical development in the composition of the books of the Bible and the Talmud, which was now *a priori* excluded by so enlightened an Orthodox as Rabbi Soloveitchik.

But what was Rabbi Jacobs' positive concern? He already states it in the foreword to his analysis of Moses Maimonides' classic confession of faith: 'This book is an attempt to discuss what a modern Jew can believe'.[24] In other words, without wanting to make Jewish faith 'attractive' on the cheap, this rabbi, who describes his position as that of a 'modernism within traditional Judaism',[25] also sees himself confronted in his own way with the fact that many intelligent Jewish women and men are also seeking to deepen their faith. They have understood that Judaism is more than a voluntary way of life; it is an authentic religion. But how can an 'intelligent' person believe all the articles of the classical Jewish confession of faith if present-day facts about the universe (e.g. evolution, and the age of the world and the human race) contradict the statements of the old confession of faith? Is one perhaps to call for a sacrifice of the intellect, which was how the conflicts between reason and revelation used to be resolved?

This was indeed no incidental matter. For nowhere, Jacobs thought, was the conflict so serious as in the eighth article of Maimonides' confession of faith: the Torah is of divine origin. Simply to abandon this principle would be to abandon Judaism as a religion. Simply to maintain this principle, as required by the great mediaeval sage from Cordobà, meant attaching Judaism once and for all to fundamentalism and obscurantism. So what was to be done? A new interpretation was needed. Jacobs already presents it here and was soon afterwards to develop it independently of Maimonides' thirteen articles.

A decade later, Jacobs had the courage to publish his **own systematic account of the main themes of Jewish theology** on a secure historical basis – *A Jewish Theology*[26]. This was a work of a kind really attempted before him only by the famous Jewish systematic theologian **Kaufmann Kohler**, who was born in Fürth in 1843 and died in New York in 1926. Like Jacobs, Kohler, too, came from Orthodoxy (the neo-Orthodoxy of S.R.Hirsch), but he was not given a rabbinate in Germany because of his critical attitude to the Bible. So he emigrated to the USA, became a Reform rabbi in Detroit and New York, and finally in 1903 became

president of Hebrew Union College in Cincinnati, the central educational institution of Reform Judaism. In this capacity he wrote an
Outline of a Systematic Theology on a Jewish Basis, which was
published in German in 1910 and in English in 1918.[27] Since Kohler's
work was now out of date in many respects and, while many Jewish
theologians had written on many themes, none of them had ventured
a new historical-critical systematic account, Jacobs' work was to fulfil
this function for 'modern Jews'. Beginning with the doctrine of God
and creation, moving through themes of anthropology and ethics to
the questions of the people of God, the state of Israel, the messianic
hope and life after death, Jacobs discussed all the theological themes
in context on the basis of a historical understanding of the biblical,
rabbinic and modern tradition.

It goes without saying that in Jacobs' systematic theology, too, the
really problematical point was the theme of **revelation**, i.e. Torah and
halakhah. Against the static understanding of revelation in Orthodoxy,
which regarded the whole Torah (the Pentateuch, the other biblical
writings and the oral Torah of the rabbinic wise men) as God's literal
and eternally valid revelation (which was therefore to be observed
literally), Jacobs followed the whole of modern biblical scholarship in
recognizing that the Torah too – and even already the Pentateuch –
had undergone a long history. However, this history had not been a
'progressive revelation' of ideas or true propositions, as still seems to
have been assumed by the 'Columbus Platform' of 1937. Rather, it had
been a history of **encounters with God**, of which **human beings** had
then given a **record** in the biblical writings, in their own words. Thus
for example the Genesis narrative as a whole deals with the covenant,
with God who finds Israel, and with Israel which finds God and brings
him to humankind. And what is true of the Genesis narrative is also
true of the rest of the Bible: 'It is all the record of a people's tremendous
attempt – the believer declares a successful attempt – to meet God. The
various propositions are, then not themselves revelation, but are the
by-product of revelation.'[28] Moreover, the present-day believer need
no longer accept the words of the Bible as the direct words of the
prophet, even of God himself, yet can still discover God's word and
will in them: 'Revelation can thus be seen as the disclosure of God
Himself.'[29]

But such an understanding of revelation also has consequences. For
what does it mean for praxis, or more precisely for the **commandments**
(*mizvot*) which are to guide praxis? According to Jacobs, such a view
of revelation makes it possible to **distinguish** between the different
commandments in the Bible. Given the problems of the present, in

today's state of knowledge three categories of commands can be distinguished:
– **significant**: food laws, the sabbath, Yom Kippur and other festivals, and also prayer shawls and phylacteries;
– **insignificant**: the prohibitions against shaving or wearing material woven of wool and cotton:
– **detrimental**: restrictions on the rights of women and particularly also children who are the issue of adulterous or incestuous unions, and who are prohibited from marrying.

It may also have become evident from the case of Rabbi Louis Jacobs to what degree the historical fronts have shifted again in the course of historical developments. Jacobs, who comes from Orthodoxy and still describes his views as being quite orthodox (in his sense), in fact represents a Reform Judaism – by being, as we heard, 'a modern in traditional Judaism'. His position raises questions for both Orthodoxy and Reform Judaism, but these are also questions for Conservative Judaism, to which he is similarly close. To that we now turn.

6. Conservatism as a middle way: Zacharias Frankel

In contrast to the Orthodox, who completely reject modernity, and the reformers, who conform all too closely to modernity, in America since the beginning of the 1920s there has also been the **middle way of Conservative Judaism**.[30] I also gave an account of that in Part One. Here 'development' and 'progress' are affirmed in principle; indeed efforts were made towards a spiritual **co-existence with the modern world**, but there was no desire to fall victim to the temptations of modernity. So the accent lay in fact on preservation, on history, on tradition.

Thus alongside Hirsch on the right and Geiger on the left, mention must in fact also be made of a third 'precursor', the German rabbinic scholar **Zacharias Frankel** (1801-1875).[31] Many Conservatives in America, too, appeal to the 'positive-historical Judaism' of Frankel's Breslau school. At that time he had been the recognized leader of the middle party which attempted to combine tradition and historical scholarship in the face of the immobility of Orthodoxy and the tendencies of Reform Judaism to disintegrate. How? Frankel's answer was that there are already sufficient possibilities for progress within the teachings of Judaism. Openness to modernity must be possible without betraying the tradition. Historical-critical interpretation is acceptable as long as it does not do away with scripture altogether by means of a 'higher biblical criticism'.That means no fundamentalism, but also no neglect of the law, which now represents the form of the Jewish spirit. Whatever may need to be said historically about the sabbath or the food laws, in practice they should simply be observed. In the end the law has a meaning in itself.

But even this mediating Conservativism along the lines of Zacharias Frankel and above all **Solomon Schechter**, whom we have likewise already encountered, which was able to combine in an exemplary way both objective science and deep piety, tradition and innovation, and regarded not just the Bible but also the experience of the whole people of Israel (the 'Catholic Israel' in Palestine and in the Diaspora) as the source of Jewish authority,[32] changed considerably under the pressure of developments.[33] The centre of Conservative Judaism, the Jewish Theological Seminary of America in New York, now came under the leadership above all of Jews from Eastern Europe (from 1940 to 1972 Louis Finkelstein was its President and Chancellor). The teachers working here were certainly open to progress in theory, but in practice they mostly kept to tradition.

Understandably, this conservative attitude leads to tensions between rabbinic scholars in the academic world and Jewish laity in real life. For many laity, who in their secular everyday life have quite different concerns from their rabbis, do not, indeed cannot, follow all the strict interpretations of the Law called for here. No wonder that in these circumstances disputes kept breaking out between the Jewish lay organization (the United Synagogue of America, founded in 1913) and the Rabbinical Assembly, founded in 1919. But that also had positive effects: the Conservative movement was the first Jewish denomination to introduce an initiation ceremony for girls (*bat mitzvah*) alongside that for boys (*bar mitzvah*). After intensive discussion, driving an automobile to synagogue on the sabbath was also allowed – when it was observed that otherwise hardly anyone in the suburbs would come to worship. However, there were those who asked themselves whether changes would always be introduced only when there was a threat of decline in membership and loss of income.

Thus evidently a conservative middle way, too, is not easy to find. Now of course the Conservatives would not have been Conservatives had they not been concerned **to preserve the past**. And in fact:
– The **strength** of Jewish conservatism lies in the fact that through intensive historical research it has given Jews of all trends quite new insights into their history. This concern for accurate texts, semitic philology and Jewish cultural history made an important contribution

towards answering the question: what do the Bible, the Talmud, Saadia and Maimonides really say?
– Here, however, also lies the **weakness** of Conservative Judaism. It is all too concerned with the past. It neglects terribly the urgent questions of what one has to believe and do today in completely changed social circumstances.

So here, too, **critical questions** cannot be suppressed. Is not Judaism more than history? May the concern for the past be at the expense of the present and the future? The concern for tradition at the expense of the Bible? The concern for history and law at the expense of theology and religion? What is then left of belief in the one God who casts down gods old and new? What about the protest of the prophets, whom no arguments from tradition could frighten?

So it is not so surprising that a new movement emerged from Conservative Judaism itself, which was now concerned quite specifically with the relevance of Judaism for today and tomorrow, and therefore called for a **reconstruction** of Judaism directed towards the future instead of **a restoration** with a historical orientation.

7. Reconstruction of Judaism: Mordecai M. Kaplan

Within the Conservative movement it was Rabbi **Mordecai M.Kaplan** (1881-1983) who, alienated from Orthodoxy at a very early stage, decisively inclined towards change, progress, the present and the future.[34]. For thirty-five years Director of the Conservative Teachers Institute (right next door to the Conservative Jewish Theological Seminary), he became the first significant Jewish theologian to have grown up wholly in America. His experience was like that of Rabbi Jacobs: many students from Orthodox families entered the Seminary and the Teachers Institute because they wanted to remain Jewish, indeed to make an intensive study of Hebrew language and history, literature, culture and national hope. But unfortunately they could no longer make much of belief in the biblical God, the God of Abraham, Isaac and Jacob.

However, for Kaplan this was just one of the symptoms of the general **crisis of American Judaism** in modern times, a crisis which in his view had not come about with either the rationalism of the eighteenth century or the liberalism of the nineteenth century: the evaporation of Jewishness had been caused by the non-Jewish environment and the indifference to the Jewish heritage, the spiritual stagnation and psychological frustration, of so many who came from Jewish families and did not know where they belonged spiritually. The question was: in such an identity crisis could, say, the rationalistic stress on the universal features of faith and ethics (belief in one God, the brotherhood of all human beings, righteousness as a great ethical ideal) help, as it did in Reform Judaism? Or the simple affirmation in faith of the unique supernatural origin of Jewish religion, as was customary in neo-Orthodoxy? According to Kaplan, neither rationality nor revelation could help unless one reflected on the decisive factor: **Judaism is not just a religion** but more than a religion. More than religion?

Kaplan had been called to the new Teachers Institute by Solomon Schechter, after Schechter had heard a lecture by the young rabbi. In the middle of his own crisis over Orthodoxy, Kaplan had put forward the thesis 'that the future of Judaism demanded that all Jewish teaching and practical activity be based on the proposition that the Jewish religion existed for the Jewish people and not the Jewish people for the Jewish religion'.[35] Solomon Schechter, the representative of the authority of the people of Israel, liked this particular thesis.

So as early as 1918, when Kaplan saw that Jewish literature and preaching alone were hardly reaching people, he had founded the first Jewish Centre or neighbourhood centre: a synagogue which at the same time served as a social, cultural, recreational and sports centre. And in 1934 – in the midst of the economic crisis (a devaluation of the dollar by 59.06%), which had resulted in a terrifying rise of antisemitism in the USA as well – Kaplan had published his almost 600-page programmatic work on 'the reconstruction of American Jewish life' under the title *Judaism as a Civilization*.[36] His main thesis was that 'Judaism as otherness is thus something far more comprehensive than Jewish religion. It includes the nexus of history, literature, language, social organization, folk sanctions, standards of conduct, social and spiritual ideals, aesthetic values, which in their totality form a civilization.'[37]

That was the decisive element, and a good American solution: according to Kaplan, Jews had to learn to accept not only their physiological heritage but also their **social heritage**: this nexus of characteristic customs, ideas, standards and codes of behaviour. All this is what is meant by civilization: 'the accumulation of knowledge, skills, tools, arts, literatures, laws, religions and philosophies, which stands between man and external nature.'[38] In other words, Judaism was to be understood primarily in social, cultural and evolutionary terms as a religious culture in which religion represents an important factor, but only one among many.

So it was consistent that Kaplan should stress the organic connection between **people** and **land** and decisively choose the Zionist option. It was also consistent that for Kaplan, in extreme cases even an atheist or an agnostic can be a good Jew, because it is not religion alone that decides who is a Jew. As for the 'reconstruction of Judaism', Kaplan is interested more in pragmatic and utilitarian questions than questions of metaphysics and theology. Does assimilation stem from the essence of Judaism? Will it enrich Jewish life? Is it intrinsically interesting? A good American pragmatism – with Jewish colouring.

And what about **religion**? What role will religion go on to play in the future? The answer of this exponent of left-wing conservatism is that while religion is not to be underestimated, it is not to be overestimated either. For just as one cannot identify Jewish civilization with religion, so one cannot separate civilization from religion either. As Kaplan put it: 'Of all civilizations, Judaism can least afford to omit religion ... Take religion out and Judaism becomes an empty shell.'[39] And yet: it is not the Torah, the Law, now become alien to many modern Jews, that is to decide how Jews are have to live today, but here again religious civilization. At this point Kaplan agrees very closely with Conservatism. The foundation of Judaism is the Jewish people and its tradition. And the Jewish religion? It is the expression of an awareness of this people. So the stronger the Jewish awareness of being a people, the stronger the Jewish culture, the stronger the solidarity and ultimately the stronger the religion.

In other words, like Jacobs, Kaplan claims the freedom **not to take over all the statements of faith and the practices of the Law into the new time.** The authorities of the past have a right to join in the dialogue, but no right of veto. For Kaplan does not believe in a supernatural divine revelation, a divine election of the people or a divine authority of the Law. And the Bible? For him it is a human book.[40] And yet Kaplan – of course condemned by Orthodoxy as a liberal and a naturalist – never left any doubt that he regarded himself as someone who believed in God. But he wants to follow a course between supernatural traditionalism and an irreligiosity which only seemingly has a foundation (Freud). So he does not want to understand God anthropomorphically, but as the non-human, transcendent power of life in the universe that brings salvation – we are reminded of Spinoza. Utterly positive in his motivation, Kaplan wants to preserve the traditional Jewish practices as far as they can still be lived out in modern life, and simply to replace the antiquated reasons for them with new ones. Jews must be able to observe the sabbath and the festivals, the food laws and the blessings, with a good conscience.

So the aim of this theology **is not a restoration** but a **'reconstruction'** of Judaism in the light of the present time and the present state of knowledge. To be specific: Kaplan, too, can for example celebrate Passover with the great Jewish tradition, even if he no longer understands this feast in the light of the alleged exodus from Egypt and the entry into the promised land, but in the light of the Holocaust and the building of the state of Israel. Indeed, Kaplan can accept and practise Jewish rites and ceremonies with conviction, as a bond with the Jewish people all over the world: sabbath, food laws and blessings. However, all these are not commandments revealed by God but helpful folkways which can help, enrich and delight.

It was completely in this sense that in 1935 Kaplan founded the Reconstructionist journal and the Reconstructionist movement, which for many people in the USA has become something like a **fourth Jewish denomination**, with its own Rabbinical College and its own organization: for the advance of Judaism as a distinctive religious civilization, the building up of the land of Israel and the furtherance of universal freedom, justice and peace.[41] In the preface to a new edition of his *magnum opus* issued in 1957, after almost a quarter of a century Kaplan once again brings out his basic intentions clearly: far from explaining Judaism only as a socio-psychological and not a theological problem, and far from encouraging religious indifference and ritual laxity (which are the charges of his opponents, he has 'the following needs: 1. to reaffirm Jewish peoplehood; 2. to revitalize Jewish religion; 3. to form a network of organic communities; 4. to strengthen the State of Israel; 5. to further Jewish cultural creativity; and 6. to cooperate with the general community in all endeavours in behalf of freedom, justice and peace. May God grant that our People heed the call.'[42]

But this imposing systematic reconstruction, too, raises **critical questions** for Jews and Christians. It is doubtless an illusion that a single Jewish religious model could become established in which all Jews would subject themselves to the same code of law and the same doctrine of faith. But does that mean that the Jewish faith has no 'substance' at all which would be common to all the denominations? Should the religion solely consist of everything that encourages a creative social interaction between Jews? But in that case is it a matter of complete indifference what a Jew believes? Is it enough to know that religion is good for human beings, for their spiritual health and for the cohesion of all Jews? But is what one ultimately holds to a matter of indifference?

Or, to put the questions theologically: can one abandon the Torah as the expression of the will of God (this is also, for example, Louis Jacobs' question to Kaplan's reconstruction[43]) and reduce the covenant with God to human solidarity? Can one so simply replace God's law with Jewish society, the people, and God's commandments with popular customs? Is the common denominator which guarantees the 'continuity of the Jewish people' in its different historical stages simply the 'continuous life of the Jewish people'[44]? Is there not a circular argument here, if the **norm** of Judaism is meant to be precisely what is **in fact current** social practice? Especially in Germany in the 1930s, did it not emerge what problematical entities 'the people' and 'the voice of the people' are? Do not some in Jewry also complain that so many Jews hardly know anything about the principles and constants of Judaism, and sometimes even claim that there are no such things, or that such questions about the essence of Judaism are 'typically Christian'? Is there not a need for a basic consensus over essentials even in Judaism? And precisely if there is no general creed and no central authority in Judaism, does not the question of what the centre of Jewish faith might be prove all the more urgent?

To make the point once again: the dispute over the past in this present is a dispute over the future. I have sketched out the origin and transformation of all three Jewish denominations, and also seriously considered the option of being a Jew without a religion. I have indicated the intrinsic problems of all the options within Judaism. And what is the result as far as the future is concerned? Many Jews will also agree when I say that none of the six options that I have described – classical and enlightened Orthodoxy, rationalistic and corrected Reform Judaism, Conservative or Reconstructed Judaism, is wholly satisfying. One cannot describe any of the different great theologians from Hirsch and Soloveitchik, through Geiger and Jacobs, Frankel and Schechter, to Kaplan and Heschel, as the Jewish position of the future. So one must choose – if yes, what? However, here we come up against a very much more basic question, a question about essence.

8. Has Judaism lost its 'essence'?

Towards the end of his very informative and concise history of American Judaism, Professor **Nathan Glazer**, the Harvard Professor of Education, has made the following basic comments on contemporary problems within Judaism. They could also do with being noted more in many Jewish-Christian discussions: 'There is much in Jewish religion that is not law and observance. Yet its essence, as developed over a period of two thousand years, was a complete pattern of life, in which a daily round of prayers and observances, punctuated by the more intense observances of the Sabbath and the festivals, reminded all Jews that they were a holy people. This pattern of life was Judaism.'⁴⁵

And how are things today? Today – according to Glazer – this pattern of life is still maintained by only a small minority: 'Since only a minority observe it, it has changed its character. The observances are no longer the outward form of the Jew but the ideological platform of only one of several trends in Jewish life. Judasim, which was the religion of all the Jewish people, has become Orthodoxy, which is the position of only some of them. This creates a more serious break in the continuity of Jewish history than the murder of six million Jews. Jewish history has known, and Judaism has been prepared for, massacre; Jewish history has not known, nor is Judaism prepared for, the abandonment of the law.'⁴⁶ Does not the abandonment of the law in our days in fact surrender the 'essence' of Judaism?

The most recent prognosis for the future by **Yeshayahu Leibowitz**, professor of chemistry, rabbinic scholar and one of the most important spiritual presences in today's state of Israel, is also extremely pessimistic. Granted, for Leibowitz, 'the Jewish people is... one of the strongest and most constant phenomena in the whole of human history'.⁴⁷ But in his view 'modern Orthodoxy... has found no answer to the contemporary problems of Judaism and the Jewish people, indeed it really has no understanding of these problems. – If I were to sum up my words on this theme I would have to say that the future of the Jewish people really is not clear to me, either in Israel or in the Diaspora. Possibly there really is no solution to the internal crisis which began in the nineteenth century.'⁴⁸

Time and again I am struck by the way how in Israel, the land of the prophets, so much more than in Islam, and even more than in Christianity, there are people who dare to address the conscience of their people regardless. For Leibowitz the radical question is 'whether the Jewish people still exists at all from the halakhic standpoint. "Neturei-Karta" people (a small group of extremely anti-Zionist ultra-Orthodox Jews who reject the state of Israel) say that they alone are Jews. If we say that the "free", i.e. people who do not observe the *mizvot* (commandments of the law) are also Jews, that has far-reaching consequences for the halakhah. It characterizes the impotence and helplessness of a religious Judaism which ignores the fact that the very Jewish people for which it seeks to lay down laws and ordinances is not the Jewish people of whom the halakhah speaks.'⁴⁹

But however correct Nathan Glazer and Yeshayahu Leibowitz may be in their analyses of the actual state of Judaism, another view must be possible of the basic problem with which they are concerned. My question is: is the 'essence' of Judaism really lost (as Glazer thinks)? Is the Jewish people really caught up in an unstoppable 'process of inner upheaval, collapse and disintegration' (which is Leibowitz's view)?[50] Certainly on two points I would agree *a priori* with these two highly respected Jewish scholars.

– Beyond doubt the **strict observance of the law** which was widespread among Jews down to modern times is now practised in full only by a tiny minority (though they are often very visible and audible); even modern Orthodoxy could not avoid certain conformist moves.

– Beyond doubt **modern Reform Judaism** has sometimes suffered from such a loss of profile that the substance and constants of Jewish faith have seemed to be ignored, trivialized, denied in favour of humanitarian, moral, social and above all political concerns.

Nevertheless – and this is my question: is what is in crisis really, as Glazer thinks, the true essence of the Jewish religion and the Jewish people as it has persisted over a period of 2,000 years? My answer is that there can be no disputing the fact that a **twofold crisis** is still working itself out in Judaism. But this relates to two epoch-making constellations, not to the real substance of Jewish faith. It is:

• a crisis for the paradigm of the rabbis and the synagogue (P IV), the halakhic religion of the Torah, with all the consequences for the future of this Judaism;

• a crisis also for the modern paradigm of assimilation (P V), with all the consequences for the ongoing existence of Judaism as a religion;

• however, all this does not directly affect the unchanging 'essence' of the Jewish religion, but only a particular historical form.

The paradigm analysis made earlier was able to demonstrate that the paradigm of the rabbis and the synagogue only developed fully after the fall of the Second Temple, whereas the modern paradigm of emancipation did not emerge until the Enlightenment, and then became profoundly questionable as a result of the First and Second World Wars. There is no doubt that **both** paradigms are at present in crisis. But so that we can be clear for the future, to end this second part, entitled 'Challenges of the Present', and as a transition to Part Three, let us bring the two present extreme positions together in a conversation, which of course must necessarily become a heated dispute. Here we have a fundamentalist (on the right of the Orthodox wing) and a secularist (as it were left of Reform Judaism).

9. A dispute

An honest theological dispute is better than an uneasy peace, especially when there are such manifest contrasts. One extreme position as it were mirrors the other, and when they are set against each other in sharp profile, they seem to cancel each other out. One can easily imagine a dispute between representatives of the two positions, even if in reality they hardly engage in dialogue, but rather tend usually to ignore each other or attack each other as opponents. But let us listen.

The fundamentalist: You progressive 'moderns' are really no longer Jews. You've abandoned all religious substance for sheer conformity to the modern world. You represent a Judaism which has lost its religious centre: a belief in God and the election of the people Israel — a belief which is thousands of years old.

The secularist: And what about you conceited pious? You're really no longer real human beings! You've completely isolated yourselves from the world and the human race for sheer fixation on your belief and your laws. You represent a Judaism which has become blind to reality and self-righteous, and so you've lost the sympathy of other human beings.

The fundamentalist: Can't you see that you have a modern substitute religion instead of the one true religion? At best you believe in Israel, whatever you understand by that, rather than in God! And if you have a common conviction at all, it's your fixation on the Holocaust, as though one could reduce the long history of God with his people to that. Of course you would never go to the Temple, even if it were to be rebuilt for you; the secular Holocaust memorial, Yad Vashem, is enough for you. There you celebrate the day which is more important to you than any other: not Yom Kippur, reconciliation with God, but the day of the Shoah, the human catastrophe. And you really don't need a religious service for that.

The secularist: You can only talk like that because spiritually you don't live in our time, but in the Middle Ages, and you've constructed a substitute world for yourselves. You only **seem** to believe in God; at heart you believe in the Law, which you've made your God. And if any common conviction unites you, it's your blatant legalism — scorning all historical progress. That is why you pray bobbing up and down at the Wailing Wall and at the same time keep the women away from it. That is why you celebrate Yom Kippur so ardently, the day on which you supposedly receive forgiveness for your numerous sins.

The fundamentalist: I can see your basic problem clearly. You don't think much of the written Torah, God's word, and you've long since abandoned the oral Torah. That's your prime fault. And yet you think that you're a good Jew simply because you identify yourself with Jewish 'history' and the Jewish state. Can't you see how you're reducing the thousands of years of the history of Israel and Judah to modern times, making them the universal criterion? You're slaves to a modernity remote from God instead of serving the Creator of heaven and earth and the Lord of history by observing the commandments given by God.

The secularist: No, the basic problem is the other way round. You've neglected the Bible often enough, you've fallen victim completely to tradition, and you think someone is a good Jew simply if he can quote the Mishnah and Talmud on any occasion. So you reduce our history to the Middle Ages, which for you will obviously never end. You've remained prisoners of your past instead of facing the new challenges of the present and the possibilities of the future.

That, then, is how the extreme positions are staked out – have I exaggerated? Will there ever be any reconciliation in this dispute? Perhaps the two sides have not sufficiently realized that the modern world, which itself was the occasion for the great dispute, is itself in a profound crisis, and that the world has entered into a postmodern constellation. This may require new decisions from the Jews as well, and indeed perhaps make it possible for them to find a way out of the modern dilemma. We must turn to the rise of postmodernism and its consequences for Judaism before we can discuss the fundamental problems of the future Judaism in detail: existential conflicts and the future of the law; Jews, Muslims and the future of the state of Israel; and the Holocaust and the future of talk of God.

Part Three

POSSIBILITIES FOR THE FUTURE

A. Judaism in the Postmodern Period

The modern world, which began in the middle of the seventeenth century, reached its height in the nineteenth century, and then was fatally shaken in the First World War, was a **Eurocentric** world. In the modern period, the worlds of Asia, the two Americas and Africa were dominated by the European nation states. This modern world was also increasingly a **secularized** world. In the developing Western industrialized societies religion was increasingly banned from the public sphere – some of this was its own fault – and shifted into the private and subjective sphere. Even in the human psyche, religious feelings were often repressed just as much as sexuality, and in the social sphere religion quite often had to suffer repression and even oppression – sometimes for understandable reasons. Everywhere we have only been able to consider the macro-history, but it can be filled out and enriched at will. It is certain that while the whole world of European science, technology, industrialization and unfortunately also militarization developed, at the same time it was also increasingly threatened. For Jews, this European modernity represented the invitation to assimilation, then the failure of this assimilation, at least in Europe, and finally the cruel catastrophe of the **Holocaust**. As we saw, the Holocaust is the **nadir and the end-point of modernity**. This period now seems finally to have come to an end, even for Judaism. But what will follow? What is coming in the **postmodern** period? What are the essential trends of development?

I. The Advent of Postmodernity

If Judaism, too, is said definitively to have entered the postmodern phase, first of all we must answer the question: precisely what does 'postmodern' mean? In what sense is the word used here? At this point I cannot enter into the wide-ranging discussion of postmodernity in which I engaged in *Global Responsibility*[1] and which I plan to take further in the volume on Christianity. Here, in relation to Judaism, a brief summary will be enough. We shall then turn to the problems which are orientated on the future.

1. What does postmodern mean?

Our age still has no name or nickname (like 'baroque' or 'rococo'). But we need at least a **provisional name** to characterize our age as it has taken shape since the First and Second World Wars. So I have chosen the term 'postmodern'. For me it is not a fashionable slogan to describe a cultural situation of radical plurality, but a **'search term'** (a heuristic term) to define what distinguishes our age from modernity. As we saw, this modern world began around the middle of the seventeenth century, found itself in deep crisis with the First World War and came to a definitive end with the Second World War and the Holocaust. So for me 'postmodern' is a term to denote an age, a term to describe the experiences of the crisis of modernity (hence post-**modern**) and the quest for new syntheses in theory and practice (hence **post**-modern). For in the most varied spheres of life the experience of crisis has long since replaced the search for the new, or the new has long since become reality. If we attempt to survey and weigh up the wider context:

– Geopolitically we have a **post-Eurocentric** constellation: gone is rule of the world by five rival European nation states (England, France, Austria, Prussia/Germany, Russia). Today we are confronted with a **polycentric constellation of different regions of the world**: in the lead North America, Soviet Russia, the European Community, Japan, and later probably also China and India.

– In foreign relations we have to reckon with **a post-colonialist** and **post-imperialist** world society. Concretely (in the ideal case) this means **truly united nations** which co-operate on an international scale.

– In economic policy a **post-capitalist, post-socialist** economy is developing. With some justification we can call it an **eco-social market economy**.

– In social policy a **post-industrial** society is increasingly coming into being. In the developed countries it will increasingly be a society **characterized by competition and communication**.

– In society, in the relationship between the sexes a **post-patriarchal system** is in the making. More of a **partnership between men and women** is clearly developing in family, business life and in the public domain.

– Culturally, we are moving in the direction of a **post-ideological**

culture, which in future will be a **culture with a more pluralist, wholistic orientation.**
– In religion, a **post-confessional and inter-religious world** is becoming evident. That means that slowly and laboriously a **multi-confessional, ecumenical world community** is developing.

But a fundamental **change in values** (not necessarily a loss of values) is bound up with the paradigm shift from modernity to postmodernity, which promises a reinforcement of the ethical-religious world-view:
– from a **science** with no ethics to an ethically responsible science:
– from a technocracy which dominates human beings to a **technology** which serves their humanity;
– from an **industry** which destroys the environment to an industry whch furthers true human interests and needs, in harmony with nature;
– from a **democracy** in the sphere of formal law to a democracy which is actually practised, in which freedom and justice are reconciled.

Now if the new postmodern constellation means a **multi-religious world society,** then with the dying out of the modern ideologies of progress the **Jewish religion,** too, might **again have a new opportunity.** If the Holocaust was the nadir and end of modernity, the rise of the **state of Israel** is the **starting point and the beginning** of postmodernity. Just as Jewish religion and postmodern theology continue to have a negative stamp as a result of the catastrophe, the Shoah, so too they have a positive stamp as a result of the rebirth of a Jewish state. This change in the overall constellation since the First and Second World Wars is of the utmost significance not only for the state of Israel, which came into being after the Holocaust, but also for Jews in America and throughout the world. Globalization and plurality are not exclusive. Despite all the constraints and reactionary movements, we might be slowly moving towards a post-confessional and inter-religious humanity, whose ideal might slowly prove to be a multiform ecumenical world community, despite all the old antagonisms and new tensions.

For Judaism, such a multi-religious world society will not be without its advantages. Just as from the sixteenth century onwards, Judaism as a minority profited from the rise of rival Christian churches which balanced one another out, so too as the smallest of the world religions it could profit from an ecumenical understanding between the competing great religions in the one world society – if there should be an end to fanaticism, exclusivism and triumphalism in favour of the peaceful co-existence of various religions with equal rights. The Gulf War has shown that this world society can less than ever afford to wage wars for the sake of religions – 'in the name of Allah', or 'with God's help' – or allow political, social and economic conflicts to escalate as a result of religion.

2. Future opportunities for religion

For religion, postmodernity means that those who want to be religious today need no longer be against science (Galileo!), technology, industry and democracy (1789!), as most churches have been in the modern period. But conversely, for the criticism of religion postmodernity means that those who from Feuerbach and Marx to Nietzsche and Freud have prophesied the end of religion with a reference to modern achievements have been discredited. From a global perspective, **religion is alive** – no matter how problematical and open to criticism its forms may be. A basic religious attitude on the one hand and a scientific world-view and political commitment on the other are no longer exclusive.

So what does the postmodern constellation mean for religion?

A revitalization of repressed religion, a renovation of lost religion and a liberating transformation of traditionalist religion are all within the realms of possibility.

– Religion need no longer be ignored, privatized, repressed or even persecuted, as in the modern paradigm;

– But religion may not be absolutized and grow too big for its own good, be objectified and institutionalized, as in the mediaeval paradigm.

– Rather, in the postmodern paradigm, religion could again be taken seriously, for all the secularity: as the deepest dimension of human existence and society, always seen along with the no less important economic, psychological, legal, social, political and aesthetic dimensions.

Indeed, it could even become a characteristic of postmodernity that religion is no longer used to oppress people, as in the modern period (the '*Ancien Régime*'), but can commit itself in a new, human way for **human liberation** – where it does not again take on a reactionary and fundamentalist or even an ethnocentric and military garb:

– for psychological and psychotherapeutic liberation: towards the identity and psychological maturity of the individual (the 'upright stance');

– for political and social liberation: towards a non-violent changing of inhuman social conditions (from South Africa to South America, from Eastern Europe to the Philippines).

However, there is still also the old repressive and regressive form of religion, for which the name fundamentalism has become established in all religions – a term originally used only for a biblicistic Protestantism. But like all the other religions, Judaism too will be measured by whether it contributes to the humanization of men and women, the furtherance of freedom, respect for human rights and the rise of democracy. For like Christianity (and Islam), Judaism too is constantly faced in quite concrete terms with a choice.

- Religions can be authoritarian, tyrannical and reactionary, as Christianity all too often was. But in some circumstances Judaism, too, can produce anxiety, intolerance, injustice, frustration and social segregation; it can legitimate immorality and social abuse and inspire wars.
- Religions can also be liberating, orientated on the future and positive towards men and women, and this has been the case with both Christianity and Judaism: they can disseminate trust in life, broadmindedness, tolerance, solidarity, creativity and social commitment; they can further spiritual renewal, social reforms and world peace.

In this new polycentric, transcultural and multi-religious world-constellation it goes without saying that the more a religion is at one with itself and does not squander itself in fights between competing trends, the more easily and more effectively it can make a common contribution to these aims. In recent decades the Second Vatican Council and the World Council of Churches have brought Catholic, Protestant and Orthodox Christians and churches considerably closer together, despite all the difficulties and differences which remain. But what about Judaism? One great transitional Jewish figure, who was born at the height of the modern period and died in Jerusalem in a completely different world and time, may illuminate and facilitate our entry into these problems. He is Martin Buber.

3. Liberating transformation of religion: Martin Buber

Martin Buber[2] is one of those people who seem, in retrospect, to have lived three lives at the same time: each of his great achievements could have more than filled an average lifetime.

– First, we have already heard that right at the beginning of the century Martin Buber, who was born in Vienna in 1878 and grew up as a child in Lemberg with his grandfather Salomon Buber, a rabbinic scholar of considerable stature, had gained an immortal reputation for his work on the **Hasidic thought** of Eastern Europe. This could not fail to have an influence on the development of his 'dialogical principle'.

– Secondly, we have already heard that Buber, who had studied at the universities of Vienna, Leipzig, Zurich and finally Berlin (with Wilhelm Dilthey and Georg Simmel), and who from 1925 was lecturer and from 1930 to 1933 professor of Jewish religion and ethics in the University of Frankfurt, had from the 1920s worked with Franz Rosenzweig to produce for the first time a German translation of the Bible congenial to the flow of Hebrew language,[3] and had written significant biblical studies – *The Kingship of God* (1932), *The Prophetic Faith* (1940), *Moses* (1945).[4] The Hebrew Bible was and remained the source of Buber's power and his ultimate criterion.

– Thirdly, however, it has to be mentioned that Buber, who had joined the Zionist movement as early as 1898 and had already spoken out at the Third Zionist Congress (in 1899) for less propaganda and more education in Palestine, became an increasingly firm supporter of a **cultural Zionism**, and so became an increasingly vigorous opponent of a purely political Zionism. He was restlessly active in writing and teaching, as an editor of journals (*Die Welt*, later *Der Jude*), as the founder of a publishing house (Jüdischer Verlag, Berlin), as the inspiration of the Jewish Youth Movement (Bar Kokhba) and then as co-founder in Berlin of a Jewish National Committee for Jews in Eastern Europe at the outbreak of the First World War. But as a Zionist in a mould of his own, at a very early stage he also gave support to the Arabs, though without finding much of a response.

Martin Buber is further evidence of what a decisive change in epochs the First World War was for the thinkers of his time. 'This is the decisive change which came about in a series of intellects at the time of the First World War. It made itself felt in many senses and spheres, but the fundamental agreement which derives from the resultant change in the human situation is unmistakable.'[5] What does Buber mean by this 'decisive change'?

In the middle of the war, in 1916, Buber had sketched out his famous philosophical work *I and Thou*. He drafted it in 1919 and it was published in 1923 – at the very time when Karl Barth had sketched out, written and rewritten his *Commentary on Romans*, that commentary which was to revolutionize Protestant theology and which is synonymous with the beginning of postmodernity for German Protestant theology. Interestingly, however, like Barth, the biblically orientated

Buber did not simply begin with the Bible, but with a philosophical reflection, in which he concentrated completely on anthropology. Moreover, Buber later criticized Barth's theology, because while in the theological anthropology of his *Church Dogmatics* Barth had taken over important insights from idealistic believers like Jacobi who did not belong to the church; unbelieving sensualists like Feuerbach; and some believing Jews, on the other hand he had not been able to 'concede that such a view of humanity could have grown up on other ground than that of christology'.[6]

Who is man, and how can he find himself in this world? That is Buber's basic question, and in answering it he very soon became clear that the age of idealistic philosophy, which in its construction of reality had started from the human subject, and which with Descartes, Kant, Hegel and English empiricism had essentially shaped European modernity, was over. An attitude to this world is not simply adopted in the human consciousness – at any rate not in the way that the existential philosophy which was soon to develop at this time would think, i.e. in human existence set against the background of a general co-humanity, what Heidegger termed an anonymous 'they'. No, man *a priori* stands in not only an I-It relationship but an I-Thou relationship – and here Buber uses the insights of F.H.Jacobi, Ludwig Feuerbach, Eugen Rosenstock and Ferdinand Ebner.[7] And the starting point of philosophy is not to be seen 'in the sphere of subjectivity' but in the sphere 'between beings': for Buber and some other thinkers, precisely this was the 'decisive change which took place at the time of the First World War'.[8]

So we could describe Buber's philosophical approach like this: at the beginning we do not have *cogito*, 'I think', but *relatio*, 'relationship'. He does not want to begin either with human beings or simply with the world, but between them: with the **relationship between man and the world**. According to Buber, all real life is **encounter**. However – and this is the important thing for him – encounter can take place in basically two ways: as an encounter of I and It and as an encounter of I and Thou.

What is this I-It relationship? For Buber, **I-It** characterizes the sphere of 'experience', of objects (which may be trees or human beings), without which of course human beings cannot live, but which in the last resort must remain alien to them. Modernity has led to this world being increasingly opened up and controlled by human beings, but very often at the cost of their power to relate to it.

Over against this stands the **I-Thou** relationship. The key term 'I-Thou' denotes the **'world of relation'**,[9] the three spheres of which are life with nature, life with human beings, and life with spiritual entities. Here it is decisive that only through the relationship to a Thou does man become an I. In contrast to the I-It relationship, the I-Thou relationship is characterized by mutuality, openness, directness and presence. And it is immediately clear that in terms of the analysis of this basic structure, the step from anthropology to a theology is only a small one.

Indeed, Buber focusses his reflection on the dialogical principle, written in a language which is as highly abstract as it is highly expressive, in a theological point. The ultimate conviction behind his book is that any I-Thou relationship points to an eternal Thou: 'The extended lines of relations meet in the eternal Thou... that by its nature cannot become ·It.'[10] This eternal Thou is recognized not through theoretical statements or metaphysical speculations but through the personal relationship to the One whom human beings can find everywhere, in persons, animals, nature or works of art.

Hence we can understand that, for Buber, in personal encounters with the eternal Thou revelation takes place not there and then, on Sinai, but here and now – always when we are open to receive it. The Bible, too, is not a dead book, but a living account of dialogical encounters between human beings and God; and even the laws are not a direct revelation of God but a human answer to God's revelation. We can see that this is no view of Jewish religion which is simply assimilated to modernity, but **a view of Jewish religion that has undergone a liberating transformation.** As we shall see later, however, it has considerable and highly controversial consequences for religious praxis.

But all this can only hint at why Buber is enthusiastically revered by many Jews (he was honoured with a great torchlight procession by the students of the Hebrew University of Jerusalem on his eighty-fifth birthday, two years before his death), and also regarded as a remarkably fertile and inspiring thinker by countless Christians, both theologians and non-theologians. I think that it is a correct definition of his position to see him as one of the intellectual precursors, indeed one of the **founder figures,** of the world epoch which began with the First World War, and which – for want of a more precise word – I am now calling postmodernity. Moreover, it is in keeping with this picture that in his reflections on the phenomenon of Napoleon, Buber (in contrast to Heidegger, who because of the decisionism in his existential philosophy was prone to Nazism and the Führer principle) already described the type of the leader who does not know 'the dimension of the Thou', and wrote: 'the lord of the age, this demonic Thou, to which no one can become Thou... towering in times of destiny, fraught with destiny. Towards him everything flames but his fire is cold. To him a thousand several relations lead, but from him none...'[11]

However, the key term for the future was to remain the comprehensive concept which Buber similarly developed as early as the eve of the First World War and also presented publicly in the fateful year 1933 (when he had been nominated Director of the Centre for Jewish Adult Education and Director of the Jewish House of Learning in Frankfurt) immediately after Hitler's 'seizure of power': '**Hebrew humanism**'.[12] As early as at the Sixteenth Zionist Congress in Zurich in 1939, Buber had explained what he still 'thought was missing in the educational system of Jewish Palestine' after three decades of experience in the nationalist Jewish movement. What he 'would have liked', was a 'Hebrew humanism in its truest meaning'.[13] The activation of the people and the renewal of the Hebrew language were not enough. At the same time there was a need for a spiritual movement: the 'knowledge and demand' in history and literature for 'discernment between true and false words', and 'the derivation of order and judgment', in the light of tradition, from the great foundation document of the Bible.[14] This was a provocative programme for purely nationalistic Zionists which it was better to ignore.

However, for Buber a purely formal 'renaissance' of the Jewish people was 'inflated nonsense'; a 'Hebrew man' was something very different from a 'man speaking Hebrew'. For Buber it was certain that 'the future of the community which is beginning again on our old native soil depends on the **rebirth of normative primal powers**'.[15] By this rebirth he did not mean, say, the Romantic programme of a mediaeval restoration, nor by a return to the Bible did he mean 'a recurrence or continuation of something long past', but 'its renewal in a genuinely contemporary manifestation'.[16] So a 'Hebrew man' is not simply a 'biblical man', but rather a '**man worthy of the Bible**', who 'wants to do and hear what the mouth of the Unconditioned commands him'.[17] And to this degree – and not say, in the sense of a literal belief in Bible and Law – Buber can also speak of a '**biblical humanism**'.[18] So this is and remains Buber's programme for a Judaism which is not only national but has undergone a spiritual renewal, a programme which is not utterly mediaeval and orthodox, nor simply liberal and modern, but – one might reasonably say – innovatory and postmodern. It is, moreover, a quite specific programme, as I can explain by making just three points.

1. On the basis of his personal paradigm shift from the subjective-monological to the dialogical principle, at a very early stage Buber strove for a position **beyond individualism and collectivism**. Already in the early 1940s, when many Western intellectuals believed in Fascism and National Socialism or in Marxism-Leninism-Stalinism, Buber wrote that despite all attempts to revive individualism, its time was past and collectivism was 'at the height of its development'. Buber's answer was: 'Here there is no other way out than the revolt of the person for the sake of the liberation of relationships. I see rising on the horizon, with the slowness of all processes in true human history, a great dissatisfaction which is unlike any that has gone before. Human beings will no longer revolt against a particular dominant tendency for the sake of other tendencies, as they have done so far, but revolt against the false realization of a great struggle, the struggle for community for the sake of an authentic realization.'[19] At the latest in 1989, there was general awareness of the end to collectivism expected by Buber.

2. In contrast to, say, Abraham Heschel, Martin Buber grappled with the **modern criticism of religion** and concerned himself at length not only with Kant and Hegel, Heidegger and Scheler, but also with Feuerbach, Marx and Nietzsche. He knows the phenomenon of the modern 'darkness of God', but also the possibility of the new relationship to an eternal Thou. More than anyone else he gave expression to the tremendous **misuse** – but also the **indispensability** – of the **word God**, which has now again been put to shame in the Gulf War – and not just by one side:

'Yes, it is the most heavy-laden of all human words. None has become so soiled, so mutilated. Just for this reason I may not abandon it. Generations of men have laid the burden of their anxious lives upon this word and weighed it to the ground; it lies in the dust and bears their whole burden. The races of man with their religious factions have torn the word to pieces; they have killed for it and died for it, and it bears their finger-marks and their blood. Where might I find a word like it to describe the highest! If I took the purest, most sparkling concept from the inner treasure-chamber of the philosophers, I could only capture thereby an unbinding product of thought. I could not capture the presence of Him whom the generations of men have honoured and degraded with their awesome living and dying. We must esteem those who interdict it because they rebel against the injustice and wrong which are so readily referred to "God" for authorization. But we may not give it up. How understandable it is that some suggest we should remain silent about the "last things" for a time in order that the misused words may be redeemed! But they are not to be redeemed thus. We cannot cleanse the word "God" and we cannot make it whole; but, defiled and mutilated as it is, we can raise it from the ground and set it over an hour **of great care.**'[20]

No, even in postmodernity there is **no alternative to the word God.** And for us that can only mean that simply to speak of God as before, in religion and politics, is mediaeval. No longer to speak of God at all was typically 'modern'. Nowadays it is vitally important for theologians and philosophers to learn to talk cautiously about God anew: liberating, transformed talk of God, which takes up the impulses from Spinoza to Buber.

3. Against militants in his own ranks, at a very early stage Martin Buber argued for a **peaceful co-existence of Jews and Arabs** – at that time even in the hope of a shared state. That was in vain, because nowadays no one thinks any longer of a shared state. But precisely for this reason we must recall that already in 1921, at the Zionist Congress, Buber proposed a resolution that the Jewish people should proclaim its 'wish to live in peace and brotherhood with the Arab people and to develop the common homeland into a republic in which both peoples will have the possibility of free development'.[21] Later, we shall have to consider how this can be possible in present-day circumstances (after the Gulf War).

Should we, can we, also pose questions in respect of Buber? The objection by Buber's colleague at the Hebrew University of Jerusalem, Yeshayahu Leibowitz, who, as he himself has said, has called Buber 'with sharp words a Jewish theologian for non-Jews',[22] must be answered from the Jewish side; to me this seems to be unjust even in relation to Buber's very personal I-Thou philosophy. Be this as it may, nowadays even some Jews are asking whether it would not have been a good thing to listen more to thinkers like Martin Buber (instead of to generals like Ariel Sharon) on questions of the humane co-existence of Jews with Jews, and Jews with Arabs. We shall have to discuss the question of the state of Israel at length later. And if Leibowitz goes on to accuse Buber of having views that bear 'no relationship to historical Judaism – which is a Judaism of the Torah and the *mizvot*',[23] we shall have occasion later to pay more attention to Buber's view of the Torah and *mizvot* when we turn to the question of the Law. But however one may react to his specific views, Martin Buber, the doyen of German Jewry, is beyond dispute a great figure, and he will also have important things to say in the future for both Jews and Christians.

II. Judaism in Postmodernity

In going on to investigate the possibilities of Judaism in a postmodern age I do not want to slip into the garb of a seer or futurologist but to continue a matter-of-fact analysis. And here first of all it must be noted that many Jews, too, complain that since the beginning of European modernity there has ceased to be any agreement among them as to what authentic Judaism is. A further exacerbating factor is that Judaism no longer has any representative universal organ which could be an arbiter on disputed questions.

Has Judaism lost its 'essence'? That is the radical question which arises at the end of modernity. To anticipate my answer: no. Unless all the signs are deceptive, Judaism is in process of bringing its 'essence' to light afresh in postmodernity. But given the epoch-making change, the basic options that we have analysed – Orthodox? Conservative? Reform? – must be reflected on again, in particular with respect to human beings, the state and God. After all that we have seen, it might be important to avoid the historical mistakes of modernity and find a way between total repudiation and total fusion.

1. Between total repudiation and total fusion

In principle, not just Judaism but also Christianity and Islam face such a task. For Judaism cannot, any more than Christianity and Islam, **repudiate all social integration and cultural assimilation** in the postmodern era, as it is constantly asked to do by the antimodernists, fundamentalists or traditionalists rooted in their own Middle Ages.

It had not in fact been a fundamental mistake in the modern period for Jews in the nineteenth and twentieth centuries, first in Germany, France and England, and then in America, to adopt the external and internal values of modern culture and to conform to their surroundings in clothing, language and education, to adapt Jewish customs and religious rituals to modern aesthetic demands and to become involved in all the spheres of modern science, art, literature and journalism. To this degree the social integration of Jews in pre-Nazi Germany cannot be said to have been unsuccessful or a failure.

Similarly, it was not a fundamental mistake for large numbers of Jews, above all in Germany and then later in America (especially those living in the great cities) to adapt to modern living conditions. (In some respects they did so even earlier than their non-Jewish fellow citizens.[1])

On the contrary, it is a paradox of world history that already at the end of the nineteenth century those many tens of thousands of Jews who immigrated to Breslau and Berlin from the Polish province of Posen decided earlier than everyone else to limit fertility in marriage and have a smaller number of children – whereas at the end of the twentieth century a Catholic pope from the Polish provincial city of Krakow, with no understanding of the conditions of modern life, thinks that he can oppose birth control and the responsible use of contraceptives which has become necessary all over the world. And whereas already in the last century Jews were striving for a better, if possible an academic, education for their daughters, in mediaeval fashion the same pope is still refusing Catholic women public and legal equality in the church liturgy and theology...

Thus it is evident that to be trapped in an earlier paradigm can make a religion and its representatives lose credibility. Religious traditionalism is not a helpful slogan either for Judaism or for Christianity and Islam. It forgets the changed times.

However, the other extreme position cannot escape criticism either. Judaism in postmodernity cannot any more than Christianity and Islam give way to that **total assimilation and complete fusion with secular society** required, often even now, of all three religions by modern ideologists of unity who want to obtain freedom, unity and equality by abolishing or levelling out all special features.

But was it not disastrous that like so many Christians, so too so many Jews in the nineteenth and twentieth centuries, first of all in Germany and then also in America, all too readily abandoned many characteristics of their own way of life and many ties to the great religious tradition? Thus family tradition and family ethos, too, were largely sacrificed to the modern 'competitive society'. Was it not disastrous in good middle-class fashion to sell one's soul to economic and cultural sucess, money and power, and to be obligated now to a patriotic, even nationalistic, world-view rather than a religious one? Could possessions, education and nation – the three indispensable characteristics of the bourgeois world – replace religion? Was this not tantamount to losing all religious substance, so that when the Nazi state denied them nationality ('Germanhood'), many Jews in Germany at that time could literally have their 'last possession' taken from them? And however important the Holocaust and the state of Israel are and will remain for postmodern Judaism, can a fixation on the Holocaust also provide a Jewish identity for the descendants of the descendants of the survivors? Can concentration on the state of Israel replace the substance of the Jewish faith?

Here it becomes evident that like total Germanization, so too the total Americanization of the Jews can hardly be the right way into the future. It is not just religious traditionalism but also irreligious modernism which attaches importance only to economic, cultural and national success, and it cannot provide a viable programme for the future: either for Judaism, or for Christianity and Islam. Such modernism, we must note, leads to a forgetfulness of the 'special element', the 'substance', the 'essence' of Judaism (as also of Christianity and Islam).

And the detrimental consequence seems to be the loss of the necessary basic religious consensus which formerly held all Jews together; it may not have been affirmed by absolutely all of them, but it was by the great majority. Without doubt the halakhah, understood literally, no longer provides such a basic consensus. But, the question now arises, is perhaps a new basic consensus taking shape in the face of new challenges?

2. A new basic consensus?

The American Jewish scholar **Ben Halpern** thinks that certain laws, rituals, linguistic and literary traditions, and also the myths of the exodus, the exile and redemption, are no longer universal values which would hold all Jews together. And yet Judaism has not fallen apart. From this he concludes that nowadays the 'Jewish consensus' is based less on a **community of faith** than a **community of fate**: 'Only because they (the Jews) are constantly involved in the consequences of each others' acts need each care what the other wants.'[2] And so the Jews remain what they always were: a special people which is not like all the rest. Here Judaism no longer functions as the vehicle of a divine providence, but as the vehicle of the different yet common Jewish experiences. Still, I ask myself, from where does the community of fate touch the Jews in such different regions, nations and situations?

Halpern's American colleague Jacob Neusner does not simply contradict his analysis, but he does see a deeper common factor among Jews, in the fact that 'the fundamental mythic structure' of Judaism 'in important ways is unbroken'.[3] Even very secular Jews would not only recognize the sociological factors of their group life but even think them very important and thoroughly worth preserving and handing on to their children: 'And the vast majority of Jews, secular and religious, still continue to respond to this-worldly events, through **the pattern** of the classical Judaic myth.'[4] This is shown, for example, in the understanding of the Holocaust and the foundation of the state of Israel as the fulfilment of the prophetic proclamation, as death and resurrection, as a return to Zion; in other words, in the interpretation of them with the symbols of creation, revelation and redemption.

'The pattern of the classical Judaic myth'? Since the ambiguous term 'myth' (despite or because of the very different attempts to define it in religious studies) has been constantly understood to denote that which is not real, not true, I would prefer to speak more clearly of patterns or structures of **Jewish faith** – which are maintained, and also constantly buried. Neusner could presumably agree with this. For as he himself objects: 'What seems to be a continuity of myth – an abiding effort to interpret events in the light of ancient archetypes of suffering and atonement, disaster and salvation' – could in reality be just 'sentimentality': 'Where does mythical being end and bourgeois nostalgia begin?'[5]

Indeed distinctions are needed here; a clarification of what is abiding is indispensable. Certainly an 'archaic piety' is not 'the only true piety'; certainly 'modernity' does not exclude the 'possibility of true religiosity'; certainly there is the 'self-understanding of modern people, aware of the abyss between themselves and the classical formulation of their ancient religious traditions, yet nonetheless sure of the authenticity and reality of their religious experience'. If we take all this seriously, then for Judaism, according to Neusner, there is no escaping the observation, 'Then religiosity endures'.[6] Only, I would already want to understand this Jewish religious feeling as **postmodern** religious feeling – beyond total repudiation and total fusion, after the Holocaust and the foundation of the state of Israel. However, this is a postmodern religious feeling which can in no way dispense with certain 'classical' constants of faith if it wants to go on remaining **Jewish** religious feeling.

3. The indispensable constants of Judaism

The thorough analysis in Part One of this book already made it quite clear that neither the paradigm of the rabbis and the synagogue nor the modern paradigm of assimilation can simply be identified with the essence of Judaism. The centre of the original Jewish religion as attested by the Hebrew Bible is indubitable even after all historical criticism, and it persists through all the changes of epoch and paradigm shifts: the **one God** and the one **people Israel**. The whole as it were elliptical testimony of the Hebrew Bible and finally also that of the Mishnah and the Talmud, of mediaeval Judaism, swings round these two focal points.

Judaism on the Way to Postmodernity?

The Jewish dilemma in the modern world

Fundamentalist Orthodoxy ◄———	———► **Radical Secularism**
Judaism in **religious isolation**: religious substance unrelated to the world.	Judaism **devoid of religion**: related to the world without religious substance.
Mediaeval substitute world: legalism, fixed on the Torah as **law**.	Modern substitute religion: Israelism, fixated on history as **Holocaust**.
Symbolic sanctuary: the Wailing Wall. Holiest day: Yom Kippur.	Symbolic sanctuary: Yad Vashem. Holiest Day: Shoah Day.
Jewish identity through **Mishnah and Talmud**.	Jewish identity through Jewish **history and state**.
Curtailment of Israelite-Jewish history to the mediaeval paradigm.	Curtailment of Israelite-Jewish history to the modern paradigm.
Consequence: a **mediaeval ghetto**: Israel isolated in a world shaped by Christianity.	Consequence: a **modern vacuum**: Israel diffused in the modern world.

Postmodern Judaism?

Judaism after **religious emancipation**: religious substance related to the world.

The original Jewish religion: Yahweh the God of Israel and Israel his people.

Its constant point of reference: **liberation from Egypt** and **revelation on Sinai**.

Jewish identity through renewed **belief in the one God** of Israel and his **election**. An uncurtailed Jewish-prophetic historical consciousness, but in the postmodern paradigm.

Consequence: **postmodern emancipation**: communication with the present-day world of nations and religions.

The central structural elements and leading ideas of Israelite faith are therefore the **people** chosen by **God**, and with them the **land** promised by God.

This special relationship of Israel to its God, attested throughout all the sources, is later expressed by the word *berit*, '**covenant**': the special covenant of this people, made with the one God, which consequently carries with it the obligation to obey God's **commandments**, the *mizvot*. The covenant is the fundamental element from which the obligation, the commandments, follow. But note: in this relationship between Israel and its God is grounded from the beginning the **originality** of the Jewish people, and then its **continuity** in the long history down the millennia; finally, in it too is grounded the **identity** of the Jewish people, despite all the differences of nations, languages and cultures.

So the question of the 'essence' of Judaism has been raised again under the conditions of the shift in epochs from modernity to postmodernity. Should not the **goal** be the **true emancipation** of Judaism, rather than total assimilation and fusion? The emancipation of a Judaism which under quite different political conditions in the world remains mindful of the reality of that covenant of God with this people which has left a deep impression on the thousands of years of Jewish history, through all the paradigm shifts, even where it has been ignored or denied? In the modern paradigm of assimilation the resigned saying was going the rounds among Jews, 'If you forget that you are a Jew, others will remind you of the fact.' In the postmodern paradigm of emancipation it could be replaced by a modest expression of self-awareness: 'If you do not forget that you are a Jew, you may also remind the others of the fact.'

And what would be the **way to** this goal of **postmodern emancipation**? In terms of modern options, for postmodernity a way would have to be sought between a rigorously traditionalistic Orthodoxy and a liberal Judaism which was all too uprooted and void of content. And as we have heard, many denominations within Judaism have attempted to find this way, which is not simply the 'conservative' one. In this transition, unless all appearances are deceptive, those **constants** of Jewish faith which had been buried, suppressed or forgotten under the pressure of the modern process of Enlightenment and secularization will emerge more clearly – despite and partly because of the vigorous controversies between the different groups within Judaism. This will happen in all the three Jewish trends that I have mentioned:

- Where in modernity people saw above all the demands of the new secular time (*vox temporis*), now in postmodernity they are recognizing anew the central significance of the biblical **belief in God** (*vox Dei*):

- Where in modernity there was all too one-sided a stress on the universal human significance of the Jewish belief in God ('universality'), now in postmodernity there is again a recognition of its roots in the Jewish **people** ('particularity').
- Where in modernity there was primarily a stress on the dimension of Jewish belief in God in human history ('Diaspora') in postmodernity there is again a relationship to the Jewish **land** ('homeland').

A new identity, a renewed self-awareness, and a true emancipation of Judaism can be attained only if these indispensable constants are again raised to the level of general awareness – while taking the countless variables into account. However, to want to strive for any uniformity would of course be a sheer illusion.

4. The future without a model of unity

As a result of the dialectic of the Enlightenment, modernity, which was originally able to establish a single concept of freedom, equality and brotherhood by appealing to universal reason and universal human nature, has found itself in a random late-modern preferential pluralism which endangers Judaism along with Christianity and Islam. This preferential pluralism, for which there is no universal truth, no universally binding ethic; for which there are no universal human rights to be respected, should be firmly rejected: here above all by a heightened awareness of abiding religious constants.

But for that very reason a unitary conception should certainly not be established – certainly not a modern one, far less a mediaeval one. As we saw, the postmodern constellation is determined by a social **pluralism** – from a religious perspective in two respects.
– There is an externalistic pluralism: in the face of a now polycentric, transcultural and multireligious postmodern world horizon;
– There is an internalistic pluralism: in the face of the mutiplicity of trends, schools and parties within Judaism since modernity.

(*a*) For Judaism, **externalistic pluralism** means God's people and land – these, after all, are the abiding constants of the essence of Judaism. But this **centre of Jewish faith** needs to be reflected on anew against the horizon of the Hebrew Bible (already described in Part One of this book), which while being in no way exclusive, is a **universal horizon**:
– that God is the creator of heaven and earth and thus of all human beings, all races and nations;
– that the first human being is not the first Jew, but is 'man', like 'Adam';

– that the first covenant after the Flood was concluded with Noah and thus with the whole human race;
– that even the first covenant with the patriarchs in no way already meant conflict with other peoples, and that in Abraham all the nations of the earth were to be blessed;
– that the Joseph story (the longest narrative in the book of Genesis, chs 37-50) takes it for granted that the Egyptians, too, know the one true God;
– that Israel's prophets (in particular Amos, Jonah and Deutero- Isaiah) are also concerned about other people;
– that even more, Jewish wisdom literature (Proverbs, Job, Koheleth), like the wisdom of the ancient Near East generally, presupposed a universal concept of God: the God of the wise men is the creator of the world and the guarantor of their order, and as such is accessible to all people of all religions;
– that even Job, the prototype of patience, like Adam and Noah was not an Israelite.

(b) For Judaism, **internalistic pluralism** means that a way has to be found which is characterized by an understanding of all the different trends or parties within Judaism. This must be an undestanding above all of what are at present the three main trends. Certainly many Jews would agree with Rabbi Dov Marmour of Toronto when he demarcates them like this, referring back to the experiences of British Jewry:
– Openness on the one hand 'for stress on the tradition, as brought out by Orthodoxy, but without its fundamentalist standpoint and legalistic extremism'.
– Openness on the other hand 'to the influences of the non-Jewish world, but without branching off into a kind of unitarianism, which is expressed in many Jewish-liberal circles'.
– Therefore a middle way, but not that of mediocrity: this middle position is 'passionately concerned with Jewish education, and now fully recognizes the force of Zionism and Israel in these endeavours, and yet it refuses to shut out the world from Jewish consciousness. It pays attention to the yearning for religious experience but without the extremism of Chasidism.'[7]

So this is a middle way in tension between assimilation and resistance, universalism and particularism, Diaspora and homeland. To many Jews it seems that this would have to be the foundation of a postmodern Judaism. For three thousand years – through all the epochs and paradigms – the decisive and central elements of Jewish faith have been the covenant, God's relation to his people, which has a relation to a particular land. However, this faith has no individualistic or nationalistic constraints, but is lived out in the community of the Jewish people in shared responsibility for the survival and well-being of humankind generally.

Even a **Judaism in the postmodern paradigm** will therefore embrace different currents, confessions and denominations, but they might not be exclusivist towards one another; they could converge and communicate. To sum up:

- A postmodern Judaism would be neither a secularistic and assimilated Judaism (P V) nor a fundamentalist and reactionary Judaism (P IV), but a Judaism which had achieved real religious **emancipation** (P VI).
- So it would not be void of religious content nor isolated; rather, the abiding religious 'substance' of Judaism would constantly be related to the changing world. Its religious **centre** ('essence') would be the same as that of the **original Jewish religion**: Yahweh the God of Israel, and Israel his people; the fundamental point of reference in history would remain the liberation from Egypt and the revelation of the Torah at Sinai; in a word, the covenant.

Now a number of equally basic **questions** arise from these very basic statements – statements which may perhaps at first seem general and abstract to some readers. For us, these questions mark the transition to some sets of problems which are extremely concrete and practical for Judaism; they will take up most of this third part, which is devoted to the future of Judaism, and they will also prove relevant for Christianity.

Questions for a Postmodern Judaism

 What could be a realistic postmodern aim for the different denominations in Judaism?

- In the face of all the secularization of modern life: an anchorage in the **Jewish *people*** – but without legalistic narrowness?

- In the face of all the loss of history and roots in modern life: a tie to the **Jewish *land*** – but without nationalistic aggression?

- In the face of all the modern agnosticisms: in Judaism, too, belief in the living **reality of God** – but without traditionalistic rigidity?

So with a view to a better future we shall have to turn to **three sets of problems**:

1. How is it possible to have an anchorage in the Jewish people without legalism? Is not the observance of the commandments, **all** the commandments, an indispensable part of being a Jew? Problems of understanding the Torah arise, in particular the question of the relationship between existential conflicts and the **future understanding of the law**.

2. How is it possible to be tied to the Jewish land without nationalism? Is it not necessary to fight passionately for this one land? Problems of the promise of the land must be discussed, specifically the question of the relations between Jews, Muslims and the **future of the state of Israel**.

3. How is it possible to believe in the living reality of God without any traditionalism? Is not the faith of Israel utterly hereditary, a tradition of fathers and mothers? Problems for the understanding of God must be discussed here, in particular the question of the **Holocaust and the future of talk of God**.

B. Conflicts in Life and the Future of the Law

There has been constant talk in this book of the problems of the law. This is the place to reflect on them in a quite fundamental way. For the Jewish version of Gretchen's famous question about religion goes like this: 'Now tell me, where do you stand on the law?' The problem is not the Torah (the 'instruction') in itself, nor the haggadic part of the Torah and the Talmud (the narratives), but its **halakhic** part: the laws, which result in many conflicts, sometimes even for non-Jews. As we saw,[1] this question does not arise for Reform Judaism or even Conservative Judaism, where the law is a problem particularly for the laity, and the rabbi is no longer really regarded as an interpreter and judge, in the way it does for Orthodoxy. What then? Is there a way out of the dilemma here? A way into the future?

I. The Ambivalence of the Law

But first of all the basic question: is not the law completely and utterly good? **Christians** most of all may find it hard to imagine that Jews could be happy with the law, with the halakhah, i.e. with the scrupulous observance of all the commandments in their everyday world.[2] In any case does not law mean a lack of freedom, subjection, alien control? And what about Christ? Did he not bring freedom from the law, independence, the gospel? However, it is not as simple as that! First of all from the perspective of Judaism itself.

1. The law as liberation: David Hartman

At all events, Christians must note that both Orthodox and Conservative **Jews** do not find observing the commandments oppressive; for them it is a great human possibility, an **opportunity** given anew time and again. A recent sympathetic advocate of this view is the Orthodox Israeli rabbi **David Hartman**, Director of the Shalom Hartmann Institute for Advanced Jewish Studies in Jerusalem. He stands in the tradition of Joseph Soloveitchik and Yeshayahu Leibowitz and at the same time offers a corrective. His book *A Living Covenant. The Innovative Spirit in Traditional Judaism*,[3] which I am taking as an example here, is a committed plea for a picture of God and human beings which is open to the world and ready for dialogue, and which also shows an understanding of non-believing and non-practising Jews.

According to rabbinic, 'halakhic' understanding, the community accepts the commandments of God not because it has to be forced to, but 'because it loves God and because it appreciates the significance of the way of life charted out by the *mitzvot*'.[4] For the rabbis, the God of Sinai is not comparable with an authoritarian dictator but with a 'teacher who encourages his pupils to think for themselves and assume intellectual responsibility for the way Torah is to be understood and practised'.[5] In other words, God has certainly decreed the commandments which may not be transgressed, but at the same time he has left it to human intellectual freedom to interpret and apply them. So for all their binding character, a good deal of freedom is left to human creativity. And rabbinic thought in particular cannot therefore do enough to stress human autonomy and initiative. The relationship between God and human beings is characterized by a fascinating tension between self-assertion and subjection, anxiety and repudiation, strangeness and familiarity.

Christian theologians cannot fail to respect such a Jewish theology, which so impressively emphasizes both tradition **and** innovation, both continuity **and** renewal, both clear criteria in thought and action **and** modern flexibility in converse and application. After all, it is grounded in a view that Christians cannot dispute in any way: that the covenant of God with the Jewish people continues, and thus also further enables the fulfilment of the commandments. According to Hartmann, indeed, the central significance of the new Israel lies in the reality of 'the fullest actualization of the world of the commandments'.[6]

The covenant is also fundamental for Rabbi Hartman. For him, **'living covenant'** is the centre of Jewish faith. It is from this centre that the world of the *mizvot* and the halakhah must also be ordered. This is also the deepest reason why in the end Hartman critically dissociates himself from Soloveitchik's ideal of 'halakhic man' which is so splendid in its strictness. In the case of a conflict between divine commandment and human reason, whereas Soloveitchik argued for unconditional obedience and a surrender of reason, Hartman – taking up the mediaeval tradition of Maimonides – argues for a **balance with reason**. Passionate love for God does not call for the subjection of human rationality and the sacrifice of the ethical sense. This is what he says: 'Maimonides declares that if a philosophical view collides with the literal significance of the Bible, we have to ask whether the philosophical assertion is really proved. If not, then we are to accept what the Bible literally says. But if it is proved, then we are obliged to reinterpret the Bible symbolically. That means that Maimonides allows the Torah to put some widespread philosophical views in question, but he could not imagine the Torah requiring us to sacrifice our human powers of reason. So similarly I too concede that the Torah puts some currently accepted patterns of behaviour in question, but I cannot imagine that it requires us to sacrifice our capacity to judge what is good and fair. The covenant is an invitation to a community, to act and take responsiblity for the state of this human world. This invitation to full responsibility in history would become ridiculous if the rational or moral forces of the community were denied specifically in the act of commitment required by the covenant.'[7] There is no question that this seeks to be a covenant theology positive towards human beings, which affirms life and is open to the world.

So what is unconvincing, when here there is such clear commitment to love of God and human beings, to freedom, creativity, readiness to learn, moral obligations, prayer and community? Could not Christians in particular agree here to celebrate what they have in common with their Jewish brothers and sisters? So what separates Jews from Christians in this respect? On the contrary, is it not old-fashioned to follow Paul or Luther in setting the law **against** the gospel, when one evidently becomes **free** for God and human beings precisely **through the law**? So is the law a true liberation?

And yet I ask myself: does such a theology of the law really remove the difficulties which not only Christians, but also countless Jews, have with the law? Does such a theology in the tradition of the rabbis really answer the most urgent questions of modern Jews who live in Israel, America or Europe, in the midst of modern culture, and who with the best will in the world cannot take over Jewish tradition without cutting out substantial parts of it? We must also hear other Jewish voices.

2. The law as a burden: difficulties with life as it is lived

Why are many modern Jews unable to accept an answer like Harman's? Because it seems to them too theoretical, too abstract, too theological. In their ordinary everyday life, with the best will in the world they cannot feel this 'fullest actualization of the world of the commandments' to be liberation. They feel it as a burden, indeed as a **contradiction to modern human autonomy**.

It seems to me that the problems which so many Jews feel so strongly today, particularly in Jerusalem, but also in any other Orthodox and Conservative milieu, need to be taken with the utmost seriousness. And remarkably enough, the questions at issue are still the same old questions as in the time of Jesus of Nazareth, though they have been slightly changed in the modern context:

– For many, the **regulations about purity** are a burden: in Israel the rules for kosher food apply in all public institutions, even in the army and in prisons.

– For quite a few the **regulations about fasting** are also a burden: according to the ancient law, harvesting and consumption are forbidden every seventh year, so tremendous economic and financial difficulties arise in attempts to observe this seventh year without damage to people's own economy.

– For most, perhaps, the commandments about the **sabbath** are a burden. The hallowing of the sabbath, the strict observance of which is a general obligation, is in fact still something like the chief commandment, and thus for many Jews it is the main problem posed by the law. For from a biblical perspective the sabbath is now the sign of the covenant between God and Israel. It is the only ritual commandment in the Decalogue; in the Bible violation of the sabbath was treated as a capital offence, a crime which merited the death penalty. Accordingly, the Orthodox interpretation is opposed to even the slightest violation of the sabbath commandment: no electric switches may be used because making fire is forbidden, no umbrellas may be opened because pitching tents is forbidden.

However, the **reality of everyday life** looks different from the written law. And even in the state of Israel, while the great majority respect the sabbath as a rest day on which no work is done, only a small minority practises the halakhah to its full extent. So mention must be made of the apparently trivial questions which Jews themselves put to the traditionally Orthodox in Israel:

– 'Why may I not drive an automobile on the sabbath, even to the synagogue? Why is it regarded as forbidden work if on the day of rest

I switch on the light, light the gas fire or open the door of my refrigerator?'
– 'Why may I not eat when and what I want without radical rigorists looking at my plate? Why should I accept from cradle to grave a religious decree reminiscent of the Middle Ages?'
– 'Why may I not regard women as equals? Why should I follow Jewish men in thanking the creator every day "that you have not made me a woman"?'

In order to understand the urgency of the problem, as Christians too, without any self-righteousness (for there were and are quite similar problems in legalistic Roman Catholicism), we must allow such Jewish voices to be heard. The journalist **Henri Zoller** moved from Berlin to Jerusalem as early as 1948, and paradoxically had a conflict of conscience over his Judaism only in the Jewish state, under the pressure of these religious compulsions. He has spoken for many Jewish contemporaries in making his criticisms.[8]

However, these difficulties are also widely mentioned in relevant **academic works**, for example the problem of travelling on the sabbath and the use of electricity. Here the Conservatives prove to be more understanding about present-day difficulties than some Orthodox rabbis.[9] But will present-day Jews be content with being allowed to switch on the light, to telephone, to use the refrigerator, the radio and the television on the sabbath, but not to cook and bake, to use an electric razor, washing- machine or iron?[10]

There is no doubt that the criticism of mounting religious and political pressure in the direction of **a return to the mediaeval Jewish paradigm** is widespread today among Israelis. To quote Zoller again: 'For religious practice is normatively determined by an increasingly aggressive Orthodoxy. Religious compulsion threatens individual civil rights. By contrast we open Jews – after our long march from the ghetto to the golf course – do not want to return to a reactionary society in which "the rabbinic authorities claim the same privileges as the Catholic Church possessed in the Middle Ages".' And precisely because in reaction to assimilation and antisemitism Zoller nevertheless believes in 'a new Judaism, what Max Brod has called 'a renewal of Judaism from its innermost soul', he also wants to believe in the freedom of conscience which allows all citizens to practise their faith in the way they think right: 'On the other hand I find it hard to accept that decrees from biblical times should determine the life of Israel in 1986, as though the synagogues had been made first of all, and then the world around them.'[11]

'Back to a reactionary society in which the rabbinic authorities claim the same privileges as the Catholic Church possessed in the Middle Ages?' Here it becomes clear that the problem of law and legalism is not just a problem within Judaism, but at the same time a Christian, or more precisely a Roman Catholic, problem.

3. Prisoners of their own doctrine of infallibility?

Let us have no illusions: any religion, whether Jewish, Christian or Islamic, which is primarily orientated on laws to bring about a relationship between God and human beings, poses similar problems for its faithful. Regardless of whether these laws are principally **doctrinal statements** or '**dogmas**' (about God, Christ, the church, Mary, the pope) as in Roman Catholicism, or **ritual laws** or *mizvot* (relating to the sabbath, food laws and purity laws), as in rabbinic Judaism, new generations constantly find themselves facing the question: what are we to do in all the conflicts of life about earlier laws, dogmas or commandments which the majority of our own believers no longer feel to be in keeping with the time?

For **a positivistic interpretation of the law**, which takes any law literally – characteristic of the Vatican or the Chief Rabbi's Office in Jerusalem (not to mention the authorities in Tehran) – the answer is relatively simple: 'The law comes from God and no human being may change it.' How a law came into being, how it changed, what meaning it still has today, how this meaning could perhaps be better preserved – all these are irrelevant questions. Just as dogmatic positivism regards 'Denzinger' (that selection of conciliar and papal doctrinal statements as expressions of 'the' Catholic tradition, which is extremely problematical because it is so one-sided)[12] as the beginning and end of all theology, so the rabbinic positivism of the commandments regards the existing halakhah as the beginning and end of law and righteousness. Anything not included here is regarded as 'un-Catholic' or as 'un-Jewish' (also 'un-Islamic'). No account whatsoever is taken of the origin of a doctrine or a commandment in a completely different situation, of its complex history and finally of the situation in which it applies today and the better future which is to be ushered in. 'Take it or leave it', and anyone who does not want the food set in front of them will have to go hungry. As if there were not a mass of other 'eating places' in the present situation, which is not that of the Jewish or Catholic (or also Islamic) Middle Ages!

However, an objection might be made: did not the great **halakhists,**

those post-Talmudic teachers of the law in Judaism – whose generosity
and humanity are praised – use considerable acuity to preserve the post-
biblical halakhah in its multiplicity and flexibility from fossilization, in
a constant effort to make it practicable again? And similarly, did not
the great **scholastics**, those post-patristic dogmatic theologians of
Christianity – whose use of Greek and Arab philosophy and whose
systematic power is still a source of admiration today – create powerful
works to make post-biblical dogmas and doctrines comprehensible and
credible for a time which had changed yet again?

Certainly we cannot blame a Moses Maimonides any more than a
Thomas Aquinas because they did not know and apply the historical-
critical method at the height of the development of the mediaeval
paradigm. Both the halakhists and the scholastics took for granted the
infallibility (or inerrance) **of holy scripture** (as still did the Protestant
Reformers). But in the rabbinic or scholastic interpretation the infallibility of scripture also meant in principle the infallibility of the Talmudic
rabbis or the councils of bishops and the popes. They claim to be the
only and definitive arbiters in matters of faith and morals.

But it is precisely this *de facto* or explicit claim to infallibility, this
impossibility of changing (of reforming) the laws of faith, which is
causing us such great difficulties today, whether we are Jews or
Christians (or indeed Muslims).[13] Here we are children of the Enlightenment. For it was the Enlightenment, which had emerged from the crisis
of the Christian mediaeval and Reformation paradigms, that put the
decisive critical question, the question of the **historicity** of all reality.
Was it really always like that? How did the giant dogmatic structures
of the scholastics and the legal edifices of the halakhists come into
being, and how did they develop? And even more fundamentally, how
did the holy scripture to which they refer itself develop: the written
revelation (the Torah, the New Testament) and then the oral material
(the Talmud, the church tradition) which was put on the same level?

We can no longer close our eyes to the fact that modern scholarship
has finally been able to convince most Jewish teachers of the law and
Christian dogmatic theologians that even scripture, the Pentateuch and
the Gospels, has a **history**. That means that it, too, is composed of
various sources, was **edited by human beings** and was **not directly
communicated by God**, even dictated literally. In other words, the
Torah and the Gospels are qualified **human words**, though they seek
in a human way to bear **witness to God's revelation** and thus are
indirectly God's word. But infallibility may not be attributed to them
any more than to the rabbinic or church tradition, all the individual

dogmas and *mizvot*, which follow them. Only God is infallible; he alone cannot err, deceive or be deceived. Happily, nowadays even relatively traditional Jewish and Christian scholars no longer deny that at least part of the Pentateuch is a post-Mosaic book and that a variety of sources (however these may be explained in detail) have been used in it – particularly in connection with the legal material. But that takes the ground from under the view that all the laws and ordinances are eternally binding and cannot be changed. What then?

4. Expedients: reinterpret or simply ignore?

So what is to be done with all the disputed dogmas or commandments? For not a few Jewish halakhists, as for Christian scholastics, the expedient was **reinterpretation**. Indeed, down to most recent times, halakhists and scholastics of every hue have been well able to retain the literal wording of dogmas or *mizvot* to maintain formal Orthodoxy but to reinterpret their content sufficiently to achieve the desired result in the end. This highly formal dialectic of lawyers and theologians commands our admiration, but any violent treatment of the text provokes conflict.

That is because the preservation of old formulae, coupled with dissociation from their content, evacuates them of their original meaning and turns them into their opposites.[14] That gives the impression of intellectual dishonesty. Here are some examples. Since the Council of Florence in 1442, in Roman Catholicism there has been the 'infallible' doctrinal statement 'outside the church there is no salvation': this is a clear demarcation against and repudiation of those who do not acknowledge the Roman Catholic Church before their deaths – whether they be Jews, heathen, heretics or schismatics.[15] But since the Second Vatican Council this same church has held that those of other faiths or even non-believers with a good conscience can by God's grace attain eternal salvation.[16] There is a clear contradiction between Florence and Vatican II, as one can see, but down to the present day this has not led the official *magisterium* of the Catholic Church to give up the old formulae.

The same is true of the commandment of the law in rabbinic Judaism. It is certainly forbidden to carry anything out of an enclosed private area into a public area on the sabbath or to carry any object more than four ells (say two metres) wide[17] in a public area. But at the same time use is made of the expedient of a Sabbath-Eruv (= 'connection', 'mixing'):[18] by a legal construct a number of houses, villages or even a whole city are declared an enclosed area in which people then cheerfully go about their business (similarly, two days are 'connected', in order to make it permissible to cook and switch on the light on the sabbath)...

But such reinterpretations are not always needed: there are striking cases in both the Jewish and the Christian spheres in which, while the law is preserved in theory, in practice it just is not observed. The expedient lies in tacitly **ignoring** it. This is amazingly the case in both Judaism and Christianity over the precarious question of **contraception**. Contraception is officially forbidden in both Orthodox Judaism and Roman Catholicism, whereas it is morally permissible both in Reform Judaism and in Anglican and Protestant Christianity. However, as in Roman Catholicism, so too in Orthodox Judaism, by far the majority of believers reject the official doctrine in their private lives. In North America not only the Orthodox Jewish families but also the Orthodox rabbis have strikingly few children – and not just because they practise more 'continence' than others! Nor is it any secret that in Catholicism Paul VI's encyclical *Humanae Vitae* (1968) could not establish itself (nowadays more than 90% of North American Catholics under thirty reject the official teaching).

Now the conflicts over contraception and family planning run their course in the most personal of all human spheres, into which even the disciplinary authority of the Chief Rabbis of Jerusalem and the Popes of Rome do not reach. But there are other instances which the law can seize on: in both Christianity and Judaism, for example, the problems of marriage and divorce. Down to the present day, Orthodox Judaism does not recognize civil regulations in marriage, and here orthodox Catholicism, too, has blocked solutions for centuries. Thus for example in Italy, the pope (Paul VI) had to be compelled by a popular referendum to accept state legislation on divorce. But in the state of Israel, where civil marriage is still not allowed, Judaism faces a very different problem, which seems quite intractable.

5. An intractable conflict? The case of a *mamser*

The only case in Jewish law (contrary to a statement by the prophet Ezekiel) in which children have to do penance for the sins of their parents is the case of a **mamser** (plural *mamserim*), which nowadays is being discussed more than ever. Etymologically the term *mamser* is derived from 'disgrace', and it is now usually translated 'bastard'.[19] What is a *mamser*? Not just any illegitimate child, but all Jewish children begotten in incest or adultery. They are mentioned only twice in the Bible.[20] In Catholic church law today such children are no longer discriminated against. However, in rabbinic law they are punished from the start. They and their descendants (!) are never allowed to get married – allegedly to ensure the purity of the family and of marriage. According to Deut.23.2, no *mamser* down to even the tenth generation may enter the assembly of the Eternal One (i.e. there is no temporal limitation), i.e. enter into marriage with a Jew, male or female. Marriage is allowed only with another *mamser* (or a female proselyte), and the children of a *mamser* are and remain *mamserim* and may only marry among themselves. Until when? Until the messiah comes and frees the *mamserim* from their impurity.

There is no doubt about it: here children do penance in a terrifying way for the sins for their parents, down to the present day. According to newspaper reports, in Jerusalem, as in some other places, the Chief Rabbinate keeps a register of hundreds of *mamserim*, to all of whom marriage with Jews is prohibited. And as there is no civil marriage in Israel, it is extremely difficult for the *mamserim* to enter into a legal marriage at all. However, some people in Israel see a danger that this marriage legislation will lead to a schism and that because of the constant extension of the 'disgrace' there will be a caste of 'dishonourables' who cannot marry. This is probably why in the USA even Orthodox rabbis refuse to make very precise enquiries in suspicious cases, and prefer to advise people to move somewhere else.

One can understand that many Jews feel such a law to be unjust, even immoral, and are urgently calling for a change in the law. After the catastrophe of the Holocaust the expedients recommended and practised earlier (e.g. mixed marriage with a non-Jew) are increasingly felt to be problematical, since today Judaism can less than ever afford to lose people.[21] Often a famous passage of the Mishnah is referred to in connection with a change in the law. Rabbi Nathan 'interpreted' the saying in the Psalm, 'It is time for the Lord to act, for they have violated the law', as: 'Violate the law because (*mishum*) it is time for the Lord to act.'[22] However, others object, should **God's** command be discriminating and unethical? That would be a monstrosity.

Very different attempts at interpretation have been proposed by halakhists in the course of the centuries. And most recently contemporary attempts at a solution by Orthodox rabbis have been investigated once again. The London rabbi Louis Jacobs, whom we have already encountered, puts one forward in his book *A Tree of Life*. Here he investigates the 'diversity, flexibility and creativity in Jewish law' with much learning, and devotes an appendix to the problem of the *mamser*.[23]

But the conflict between law and ethics seems hopeless – unless there is a change: 'But where the Halakhah, as it is presently practised, results in the kind of injustice that reasonable persons would see as detrimental to Judaism itself, a frank avowal is called for that there must be changes in the law.'[24] Thus Jacobs. Or is this merely a private problem?

Not at all. A case that was still being passionately discussed in the state of Israel in the 1980s was that of the **Langer** family. Those involved were two children from an Israeli marriage in which the mother of the children had married for the second time because she thought her first husband dead; he was supposed to have been killed by the Nazis. But this assumption proved false, since he returned. As the first marriage had not been legally dissolved, and the second was therefore to be regarded as invalid and adulterous, the children of the woman's second marriage, a brother and sister, overnight became *mamserim*: not allowed to marry until the tenth generation. When they reported to the Rabbinate for marriage, they were promptly rejected. In the public outcry over this decision, however, even Orthodox Jews asked the Rabbinate to make use of its interpretative authority in order to find a legal way out. The Ashkenasy Chief Rabbi Shlomo Goren finally annulled the first marriage for some technical reasons, declared the second marriage valid, and personally married the Langer children.

And yet the sharp protest against this by extreme traditionalists in Israel and America was maintained. Even the authority of the Chief Rabbinate was disputed, because evidently it had sacrificed one of the strictest and clearest regulations of the halakhah in an unsound compromise. For the decisive factor here was not the good intention of the mother, nor even the civil rights of the children, but only the clear will of God – and it was felt that this must be clear to any believing Jew. Here the utterly fundamental question arises which Jews and Christians (and Muslims) must put to themselves. What does God's law really require? For whom is God's law, for whom are God's commandments: for God or for human beings?

II. For God's Sake?

Since Talmudic times, the number of commandments in the Torah has been put at 613 – 365 of them prohibitions. As late as 1987, one of the best-known Israeli scholars confirmed the traditional rabbinic view.

1. For whom are the commandments there? Yeshayahu Leibowitz

Yeshayahu Leibowitz, Professor of Biochemistry at the University of Jerusalem, was born in Riga. As early as 1924 he had gained a doctorate at the University of Berlin and ten years later a medical doctorate at the University of Basel. From 1934 in Jerusalem, even after his retirement in 1970, in addition to scientific publications he has kept producing publications on religious and topical political issues.[1] He has again made clear as plainly as could be desired that the **commandments are not there for the sake of human beings but for God's sake.** The commandments (*mizvot*), for the Jews the 'way of life', are in no way a means to an end but an end in themselves: 'Indeed, most of the *mizvot* have no sense unless we regard them in this manner, as an expression of selfless divine service. Most of the *mizvot* have no instrumental or utilitarian value and cannot be be construed as helping a person fulfil his earthly or spiritual needs.'[2]

Indeed, Leibowitz goes so far as to say: 'If *mizvot* are service to God and not service to man, they do not have to be intended or directed to man's needs. Every reason given for the *mizvot* that bases itself on human needs – be they intellectual, ethical, social or national – voids the *mizvot* of all religious meaning.'[3] So anyone who uses the commandments in this way 'does not serve God but uses the Torah of God for human benefit and as a means to satisfy human needs'.[4]

And the **sabbath:** is it not there specifically for **human** rest? Let the secretary of the labour union take care of the workers' need for rest; this has nothing to do with God's commandment: 'The divine Presence did not descend upon Mount Sinai to fulfil that function.'[5] Indeed, according to Leibowitz the sabbath would be completely meaningless if it had a social or national significance: 'If the Sabbath does not have the meaning of holiness – and holiness is a concept utterly devoid of humanistic and anthropocentric meaning – then it has no meaning at all.'[6]

Of course even Leibowitz knows that most Jews do not follow such a rigorous understanding of the commandments. And they will hardly be convinced by the argument that 'there is no freedom from the chains of nature except through accepting the yoke of the Torah and *mizvot*, a yoke not imposed by nature'.[7] But for Leibowitz this is now, conversely, the occasion to remark, as he did in a long conversation with Michael Shashar, that the Jewish religion is today in a crisis which is 'perhaps its last crisis'. This crisis began 'a hundred years before the foundation of the state of Israel'.[8] What is specifically meant here is that today Judaism is confronted with the 'great meta-halakhic problem' which came about when a majority of the Jewish people no longer regarded itself as the 'people of the Torah'.[9] So for the most part Judaism lives in a post-halakhic situation.

Here Leibowitz's analysis of the situation within Judaism is inexorable and sharp: 'Halakhah as we know it does not accept any reality of a Jewish people which is not the people of the Torah. But precisely that has been the reality of our people since the beginning of the nineteenth century. Therefore it is not possible to discuss or – and I hardly need to stress this – decide any general problem concerning the state in the light of the halakhah. No political problem, no problem of the economic system and no problem of war and peace can be discussed or decided on the basis of the halakhah, since the starting point of the halakhah is the Jewish people as the people of the Torah, about whose constitutional and social forms of behaviour the halakhah gives instructions. Instead, there is a Jewish people which is not the people of the Torah, among whom the halakhic thought-world is a squaring of the circle. The question how the state of Israel is to act in accordance with a Torah whose authority it does not recognize, for example over the question of the occupied territories, is incomprehensible and senseless. With what can we compare this situation? With a non-kosher slaughterer who comes to the rabbi to ask him for a kosher knife for slaughtering pigs.'[10]

And indeed, no one can seriously doubt that this is largely the situation of contemporary Judaism: many Jews either lead a completely secular life, content themselves with a compromise between assimilation and ethnic affirmation, or in other ways show a positive concern for Jewish identity, for example by choosing from the multi-volume *Jewish Catalog* some Jewish laws and customs which can be observed and which suit them. Surely it is evident that the strict view of the commandments is in conflict with the modern understanding of freedom, however difficult such 'autonomous' decisions may be to make and personal responsibility is to bear.

But is it a matter here of 'all or nothing', as Leibowitz thinks? Must one either call for a return of the Jewish people under the 'yoke of the Torah and the halakhah' or present this Jewish people with a pessimistic prognosis for the future? Must one so identify Judaism with Torah and halakhah? Is there no biblical and theological middle way on which law and freedom could be reconciled on the basis of a genuinely Jewish heritage? This is precisely the problem which not only many Israelis but also many American Jews carry around with them.

2. A test case – the position of women: Judith Plaskow

For countless Jewish women and men today a decisive test-case for the question of a future understanding of the law is the status and role of women as currently regulated in the halakhah. It begins, say, with a wife being unable to ask for a divorce. Only the husband can do that. In some circumstances this law can have intolerable consequences. Thus a married woman remains tied to her husband even when he has disappeared or left her. In Hebrew such a woman is called *agunah*. And women's groups and lawyers estimate the number of these *agunoth* in Israel at between 8,000 and 10,000.

In Israeli public life, too, women are hopelessly under-represented. At present only 7 of the 120 members of the Knesset are women, and not a single woman holds the post of minister or deputy minister, although women have to do military service. There are numerous complaints from women, not least about their treatment before exclusively male rabbinic courts, where they are at a disadvantage: Orthodox rabbis sometimes make women in distress wait ten or twenty years for assent to divorce from the husband. Divorce laws which are two thousand years old still prevail, and nowadays they are more like fetters for women.[11] Thus there is patriarchy instead of dignity and rights.

However, it would be quite wrong to see the 'women's problem' as an exclusively Jewish problem. After all, all world religions have considerable problems over equal rights for women. In Christianity, alongside the Eastern Orthodox churches, which at any rate accept married priests (but not bishops), it is again the Roman Catholic Church which, contrary to the original composition of the Christian communities, keeps women in an inferior status. This is indicated by the prohibition against their serving mass or being ordained to the offices of deacon and priest, and also by the negative attitude to contraception and divorce.

Granted, in recent years in the Catholic Church, too, despite all the official blockages, progress has been made at the parish level over the emancipation of women. But this is also true of Judaism: in contrast to a century ago, even in Orthodox Jewish families women have a full education and training. Nevertheless, they are still some way from having completely equal rights. Although the very first page of the Bible[12] says that human beings are created in the image of God, male and female, the Orthodox male Jew in his morning prayer every day thanks God that he has not been created a woman. This is a passage which cannot be reinterpreted by any apologetics and which is omitted or at least changed in Conservative and Reformed Jewish prayer books. As in Christianity, so too in Judaism an increasing number of restrictions on the active involvement of women in public worship can be noted. A woman may now no longer read from the Torah, nor do women count for the quorum (*minyan*) needed for public worship to be held (according to Orthodox understanding at least ten men are necessary). Down to the present day, strict physical segregation of men and women is still observed in Orthodox synagogues.

The consequences were not just individual spontaneous protest actions by Jewish women before the Wailing Wall. More important, and in the long run more fruitful, is the fact that Jewish women theologians have themselves begun to work critically on the patriarchal legacy of Judaism and sketch out their own **Jewish feminist theology**. Their chief representative is the American **Judith Plaskow**, professor at Manhattan College in New York, who in her most recent programmatic book, *Standing again at Sinai*, has outlined a vision of Judaism from a 'feminist perspective'. This may certainly seem scandalous to some conservative Jews, but it cannot in any way be ignored.[13] Taking up Christian feminist hermeneutics,[14] Judith Plaskow sees through the utterly **patriarchal character of Jewish theology and history**: 'The central Jewish categories of Torah, Israel and God are all constructed from male perspectives. Torah is revelation as men perceived it, the story of Israel told from their standpoint, the law unfolded according to their needs. Israel is the male collectivity, the children of Jacob who had a daughter, but whose sons became the twelve tribes.'[15]

What is the alternative? The project of Jewish feminist theology must begin with memory, for Jewish existence is rooted in Jewish memory: 'Both the patriarchal character of Judaism and resources for transforming the tradition are grounded in the Jewish past. Feminists cannot hope to understand women's marginalization within Judaism without understanding where we have come from.'[16] Jewish women should learn to understand that they too were present when God made the covenant with his people on Mount Sinai! Jewish women may not allow themselves to be robbed of this central basic experience of Judaism, as already seems to have happened in the exodus narrative. For there we read: 'Be ready for the third day; Do not go near a woman.'[17] That sounds (and was understood) as though Moses had addressed the community of the people as merely a community of males. Does that mean that women were invisible at the most important moment of Jewish history?[18] Indeed – thus goes the question of radical Jewish feminists – in that case did women 'ever have a covenant in the first place? Are women Jews?' Here Judith Plaskow sees an injustice in the Torah: 'Of course we were at Sinai: how is it then that the text could imply that we were not there?'[19]

In the light of this self-awareness we can understand why Plaskow asks for this **to be taken into account in dealing with the halakhah**: 'The assumption that halakhah is sacred in all its details because it was given by God to Moses on Sinai is challenged by a feminist **"hermeneutics of suspicion"** that regards the law as a human creation and examines it critically in light of the social order it presupposes and creates. Halakhah may represent a response to profound religious experience, but the law itself is not divine; it is formulated by men in a patriarchal culture. Halakhah is thoroughly androcentric. It envisions and supports a patriarchal order. Those whom the law benefits may see it as God-given, but the outsider, the other, knows it differently... Any halakhah that is part of a feminist Judaism would have to look very different from halakhah as it has been. It would be different not only in its specifics but in its fundamentals.'[20]

So that is what this Jewish feminist theology is aiming at: a **new community** which does not need to exclude women from public worship or study of the Torah and reduce them to a place in a family under patriarchal domination: 'The central issue in the feminist redefinition of Israel is the place of difference in community. Judaism can absorb many women rabbis, teachers, and communal leaders; it can ignore or change certain laws and make adjustments around the edges; it can live with the ensuing contradictions and tensions without fundamentally altering its self-understanding. But when women, with our own history and spirituality and attitudes and experiences, demand equality in a community that will allow itself to be changed by our differences, when we ask that our memories become part of Jewish memory and our presence change the present, then we make a demand that is radical and transforming. Then we begin the arduous experiment of trying to create a Jewish community in which difference is neither hierarchalized nor tolerated but truly honoured. Then we begin to struggle for the only equality that is genuine.'[21]

Here the problem of law and freedom is once again addressed in a radical way. Judith Plaskow, who in contrast to other feminists does not reject the Torah, but would like to work with it, hopes for collaboration 'with liberal Jews'.[22] So are there possibilities of the reconciliation of law and freedom from the Jewish heritage? Let us listen to a third voice alongside Leibowitz and Plaskow.

3. Are law and freedom compatible? Eugene B.Borowitz

The New York rabbi **Eugene B.Borowitz**, since 1962 Professor of Education and Jewish Religious Thought at Hebrew Union College/ Jewish Institute of Religions in New York, is one of the leading spokesmen of American Reform Judaism, but is distinguished for his understanding of the Orthodox and Conservative positions as well. More clearly than others he has given a historical and systematic analysis of the options for present-day Jews in his *Choices in Modern Jewish Thought*.[23] This 'partisan guide' is of welcome objectivity and fairness, but at the end it speaks out clearly and at the same time self-critically for human freedom and autonomy in the face of the law. For Borowitz knows that the 'crux of liberal Jewish thought is the personal autonomy' which is now the 'basic axiom of modernity'.[24] But how does Borowitz himself now attempt to mediate between human self-determination and the Jewish law?

Borowitz is no more anxious than Plaskow to go back to the nineteenth-century liberalism which insisted uncritically on human autonomy and science. In the same major work on central Jewish concepts in which Leibowitz wrote on commandments, Borowitz discusses the term 'freedom'.[25] Here he argues that human autonomy cannot simply be derived from the human reason which allegedly directs the self, as in Kant and Hermann Cohen. Rather, in the face of the threat of modern individualism, autonomy must be understood in terms of personal relationship with God and thus of the covenant of God with his people: hence the Jew is a self 'with the personal right to determine what God now demands of the people of Israel and of any particular member of it'.[26]

So it is not surprising that Eugene Borowitz explicitly describes his position as **postmodern,** in so far as he does not share the optimism over progress characteristic of modernity; in so far as he puts only limited trust in science and technology; and to this degree does not want to give up his own Jewish tradition but to change it radically. He too goes on to speak of the cases I have mentioned in which the Jewish law conflicts with contemporary ethics. And in so doing he cites a particuarly significant case which is passionately discussed in the state of Israel and once again has more to do with the **sabbath commandment**. A Jew wanted to help a non-Jew who had been badly injured in a road accident; he went to the home of an Orthodox Jew and was not allowed to use the telephone to call an ambulance. Why? Because it was the sabbath! Certainly the sabbath commandment may be broken when it is a matter of life and death – but on one condition: the victim must be a Jew and not a Gentile.

In other words, like Leibowitz and Plaskow, Borowitz too begins from the presupposition that 'the vast majority of modern Jews understand themselves to be essentially self-legislating (and this regardless of party label or institutional adherence)'. He is also convinced that today we have 'an unprecedented, full-scale abandonment of the "halakhic" system', which is 'unlikely to be reversed'.[27] However, in contrast to Leibowitz and like Plaskow, Borowitz immediately adds: 'The fundamental relationship in which the Jew stands is the covenant.'[28]

That might indeed also be the perspective from which other Jewish theologians, male and female, might solve the problems connected with the law:

– A premodern affirmation of obedience to the Torah without the affirmation of a personal autonomy (as in Orthodoxy) can hardly be capable of overcoming the severe identity-crisis within Judaism. There can no longer be a return to blind submission to the law. Blind obedience to a religious or state law has caused too much disaster in the course of history for one ever to be able to rule out the decision, and in some circumstances also the resistance, of the conscience. However, at the same time it is the case that:

– A modern affirmation of human autonomy without affirmation of the Jewish legacy might similarly not be a contribution to the resolution of the identity-crisis. For in the last resort human autonomy must remain unfounded unless it is rooted in belief in a God who has created human beings in his own image and has made a covenant with them. So:

– Personal autonomy and human obligation to God's covenant with his people must be thought of together. While no modern, subjectivist understanding of human freedom can be derived from the great Jewish covenant tradition, a postmodern-personal understanding of human freedom possibly can.

But what does this mean for specific decisions? That one must make decisions depending on the situation? Borowitz's view is that, 'Often this personalist approach to Jewish duty will lead to acknowledging the lasting value of classic Jewish teaching and thus to simple obedience. But it may also require modification and abandonment of an old practice or the creation of a new form adequate to the continuing reality of an ancient relationship.'[29] In other words, the credentials and criterion of being a Jew cannot continue to consist in the most literal observation of the law; they must be provided by the living answer to God's will which is also determined by the situation. Present-day commitment to God's covenant with his people cannot be a simple repetition of classical Jewish faith.

Personal decision, and in some circumstances personal dissent – this, then, is also the central objection which Borowitz makes even to Louis Jacobs, with whom otherwise he fully agrees. After the modern emancipation, 'the postmodern affirmation of the covenant must therefore include the right of conscientious dissent from what the Jewish tradition formerly required or strictly urged'.[30] But here we are now at the decisive shift towards a possible understanding of the law in the future and must once again remember what I have already hinted at in the chapter on the postmodern paradigm.

4. The covenant remains fundamental

Indeed, in dialogue within Judaism and also in dialogue between Jews and Christians, much will depend on whether a consensus can be achieved over the statement '**The fundamental relationship in which the Jew stands is the covenant.**'

Historical analysis, at any rate, provides a decisive verification of this statement. For we already saw in the historical section that the **covenant** – the basic reality of the relationship with God, not the word *berit* – was significant from the very time of the formation of the people; it played a role in the kingdom of David and Solomon, in the formation of the state; it was of central importance in the divided monarchies; it survived the shock of the conquest of the two kingdoms and the exile; it became the key word which shaped the restoration and the rebuilding, and even after the Roman conquest of Jerusalem and the destruction of the Second Temple it remained at the centre of religious awareness for the Jews scattered over the world. It was the bond with God, with the Lord himself, which remained through all the distress of the dispersion the election and consequent obligation of the people to the Torah. The conclusion must be that no matter whether the paradigm was the tribal paradigm of the period before the state (P I), the paradigm of the kingdom in the monarchical period (P II), the constellation which was that of post-exilic Jewish theocracy (P III) or of the orthodoxy of the rabbis and the synagogue in the Jewish Middle Ages (P IV), the centre of Jewish faith remained the same: 'Yahweh is the God of Israel, and Israel is his people.'[31]

In the face of the modern paradigm (P V) which had come into being outside official Judaism and Christanity and which ushered in a world of science and technology, of industry and democracy, it seemed increasingly difficult to preserve the 'substance' of both Christianity and Judaism. However, not least the Holocaust (the nadir of godless modernity) and then the foundation of the state of Israel (for Judaism, the beginning of a new era) have led to reflection on the covenant of God with his people. So the question now is: how will this 'essence' of Judaism now take shape in **the postmodern** paradigm (P VI)?

On the basis of the development over three thousand years which I have depicted above, and the five epoch-making paradigm shifts in Judaism, the answer can now be given quite clearly: compared with the covenant **the 'halakhic system' is not primary but secondary.** All down the centuries decisive, identity-forming power has accrued, not to the halakhah but to the covenant. Conversely, that means that if nowadays the halakhic system is 'completely abandoned' by many Jews as never before, and it is hardly possible to reverse this development towards a meta- or post-halakhic situation, then it is not necessarily the case here that something essentially Jewish has been lost. At best, what has been lost is a particular historical form. For our historical analysis has also shown that the halakhic system first established itself in this form in the post-exilic period (P III) and then developed fully in the epoch of the rabbis and the synagogue (P IV), when the synagogue had taken the place of the Temple and scripture the place of the altar, when the tradition of Mishnah and Talmud was given the same status as the Torah itself – all of which is now clearly in crisis in the modern period (P V). Even the hyper-Orthodox should not underestimate the explosiveness of these questions, which can easily backfire on Jewish belief. Is it not worth discussing such explosive questions again within Judaism at a time which is not just post-halakhic but also postmodern – without polemic, suspicions or exclusions?

5. What understanding of the law will there be in the future? A
question for Jews and Christians

It is not just in our day that there have been witnesses within Judaism
to a constructive theological solution to the problems of the law. As
early as the 1920s, the two most significant Jewish thinkers of the
period between the wars, **Martin Buber** and **Franz Rosenzweig**, the
philosopher of religion, educationalist and translator of the Bible
(1886-1929),[32] agreed against all politically liberal and modern secular
Zionists with at best a cultural orientation, that the **foundation of
Jewish existence** is the **covenant** of the people with God. The living
personal relationship with God had to stand at the centre. So this centre
was not just the universally human idea of an 'ethical monotheism', as
it was for Jewish liberals before the First World War, nor, as for the
mediaeval Orthodox, was it primarily the halakhah, the law of the
Jewish religion. No, the **Law** was just a **consequence** of the covenant;
it was not an end but **a means**. As we have already heard from Buber,
it is not God himself who has made all these individual rules, but human
beings, who were seized by belief in God and whom human freedom
might not enslave.

Rosenzweig, who for a while, like many of his friends and relations,
even pondered conversion to Christianity but definitively decided for
Jewishness after a long Yom Kippur service in 1913, was co-founder
in Frankfurt in 1919 of the 'Free Jewish House of Learning', and in
1921 published his magnum opus *The Star of Redemption*.[33] He saw
the observance of the traditional Jewish law as binding beyond all
ethics. For him, loyalty to the law as the hallowed form of life of the
one people of Israel was important. However, he made an important
concession to modern men and women and their autonomy: as far as
human beings are capable of this! He did not want a division between
Jews and non-Jews, but a distinction.[34]

Buber differed.[35] He was not concerned to make the law from the
past generally binding on Jewish men and women today. For him God's
revelation is not legislation. No law made by human beings should
stand between the human I and the eternal Thou of God: the eternal
Thou alone commands or prohibits. Some or other precepts of the law
may be included, but in principle, not the traditional law but the will
of God is to be the supreme norm that lays a quite personal obligation
on me. To this extent the law does not hold universally for Jews, as
Rosenzweig would have it, but personally.

Buber's early lectures, which were collected and published in his

Speeches on Judaism, were given in the Bar Kokhba Association in Prague. In the audience was Franz Kafka, who in his novel *The Trial* had a chaplain tell Kafka's main character an enigmatic parable under the title 'Before the law'. But regardless of how this debate is carried on within Judaism, here too Christians may be challenged to take up a position. This will be not to play the Jewish dialogue partners off against one another, nor even to administer a panacea, as those who know better, but because from the origins of their faith, Christians are profoundly concerned with the problems of the law. After all, the first Christians were Jews who still felt themselves bound by the Mosaic law. After all, the Jew Jesus of Nazareth had in no way come to dissolve and abolish the law. After all, Jesus himself had made the will of God the ground and norm of fulfilling the law.

So it may help Jewish-Christian understanding if we compare the two basic positions represented by Buber and Rosenzweig with the original Christian options. If we do that, an amazing double parallel appears:

– **Rosenzweig**'s positive attitude to the Jewish law seems largely to correspond to the attitude of those **Jews** who followed Jesus, but in principle, albeit with their own particular focus and possibly even criticism (particularly the Hellenistic Jews), wanted to go on living in accordance with the Jewish law and observed the sabbath along with the other commandments.

– **Buber**'s negative attitude to the Jewish law, however, seems to come very close to the attitude of the **Gentiles** who followed Jesus, who repudiated any observance of the traditional law over and above the ethical commandments and primarily wanted to hold to what God wanted them to do, to God's will.

In all this it is important to note that **both** the Jews and the Gentiles who followed Jesus could at that time appeal to Jesus of Nazareth and his attitude to the law in support of their views in different situations. 'He was under the law', Jewish Christians could say. But in his letter to Galatia, the Jewish Christian Paul had added, in favour of the Gentile Christians, 'to redeem those under the law'.[36] Before we pursue this thought further, it might be appropriate to note what Jews and Christians possibly have in common. For should not a basic consensus be possible between them on ethics and the law – after all, they both appeal to God's covenant with Noah and with Abraham and his descendants, though in different ways.

Questions to Jews and Christians

Jews and Christians agree that the human being, as God's unique covenant partner, created in the image of God, is not allowed any anarchic autonomy or individualistic libertinism. **God's ethical commandments**, the Decalogue with all its implications, are **still an obligation on men and women today**. However, there is a question:

✝ Cannot Christians also recognize that in addition to having a universal human ethic, Jews want to be rooted in the community of their people, in the **Jewish tradition**, which one day will perhaps again lead to a basically common Jewish life-style? A common Jewish way of life on festivals and working days, with specific forms, rites and customs in the family, in worship and in everyday living?

However, precisely because human beings are God's covenant partner, they cannot be expected to show pious servility and blind obedience to the law: **God's ethical commandments** are **not simply identical with the halakhic system**, which was developed in the course of a long history and in many respects has survived. Hence the question:

🕎 Cannot Jews, too, be obligated to a legal system only in so far as they can make laws their own in personal responsibility? Should not every Jew understand that others see the obligation deriving from the Torah in a different way and that Christians, while respecting the special way of the Jewish people, will constantly also already be drawn to the **universal horizon** of the Hebrew Bible?

Precisely because as a Christian used to suffering in this cause I can well understand the traditional problems over the law within Judaism, in view of all the disputes I ask myself, 'What would that other Jew of 2,000 years ago, the master of Nazareth, have said to all this?' If a 'conscientious dissent' is to be possible today in Judaism, could it not be helpful in this question to pay attention to the great dissenter of that time, whose original voice is perhaps still heard too little in Judaism – in Judaism and Christianity?

III. For the Sake of Human Beings

1. What is the supreme norm?

In the long section on the question 'How are we to see Jesus today?',[1] I said all that needs to be said on the attitude of Jesus to Pharisaism, and especially to the law. Here, basically, we need only recall that the great dissenter from Nazareth did not come forward at that time to reject the law of God in principle but to 'fulfil' it. To this degree, Jews who followed him at that time and yet wanted to go on observing the Jewish law at least in principle did full justice to their master. Jesus himself had lived in complete obedience to the law as a Jew among Jews: he was not an antinomian. And yet, in the view of most present-day exegetes the conservative saying in Matthew[2] that heaven and earth will pass away before a jot or tittle will perish from the ceremonial law is not an authentic saying of Jesus but a construction of Jewish Christianity, which held firmly to the law – and was directed against the Jewish-Hellenistic community and its criticism of the ceremonial law, or even against the Gentile-Christian community which rejected the ceremonial law. It is already worth noting the Matthaean addition, which is in any case to be taken seriously as a principle for interpreting the Sermon on the Mount, that the righteousness of the disciples of Jesus will have[3] far to exceed that of the scribes and Pharisees.[4] This alone once again makes it clear that Jesus was certainly no antinomian; far less was he a Pharisee who piously observed the law. What did he want?

This, too, should be remembered. Jesus wanted to achieve a single great concentration, above all in practice: the supreme norm was to be love, and it is precisely this which is reported of the earliest community itself in the Acts of the Apostles – albeit transformed into an idealistic picture. Indeed Jesus himself had explicitly praised that teacher of the law who had asked him about the supreme commandment, and had replied 'understandingly' with love of God and love of neighbour, 'which are far more than all burnt offerings and all sacrifices'. Jesus' reaction was: 'You are not far from the kingdom of God.'[5]

There is no mistaking the fact that, even as reflected by the Jewish-Christian Gospel of Matthew, Jesus has retained his own original profile, and in the six so-called antitheses (or 'supertheses') in defence of marriage and family, in the cause of truthfulness, non-violence and love of enemy, took a very resolute stand against interpretations of the law which are attested for that time: the understanding of adultery and

ongoing forgiveness in rabbinic Judaism, and of hatred of the enemy in Qumranic Judaism. In the face of the coming kingdom a fundamental change in human beings is expected, one that will embrace not only outward appearances, which can be controlled, but also that which is within, and **cannot be controlled** – the human heart:
– reconciliation instead of anger and murder;
– self-control instead of adultery;
– fidelity instead of divorce;
– the renunciation of violence instead of vengeance and retribution;
– love of enemy instead of hatred of enemy.[6]

No, the master from Nazareth did not have anything in principle against either the law or teachers of the law. And yet here that small difference had emerged which, though at first sight it might seem unimportant, was capable of breaking the law apart in a decisively new situation: breaking it apart in order to show something 'greater', the other, the 'better righteousness'! The rabbi of Nazareth did not reject the keeping of the commandments. But by subsuming them all with great boldness under the chief commandment of love of God and neighbour,[7] he decisively **relativized** the individual commandments in a way different from that in the Torah – **in favour of human beings.**

And it was precisely that to which the **Gentiles** who later followed Jesus could refer. Living in a completely different, Hellenistic world outside Palestine, they were now to draw radical consequences – as Paul had done in his consideration of the one who had been crucified because of the law. For it was also a fact that Jesus did not bind his followers to the old rabbinic order of the law, nor had he given them a new halakhah of his own, to regulate all spheres of life down to the smallest detail. Instead of this, he issued a summons to obedience to God and love of neighbour with simple, liberating appeals and parables, while at the same time being provocative in his healings of individuals. This was a summons to obedience towards God's will which, while indeed meant to embrace the whole of life, was concerned completely with human well-being, that of the neighbour.

Nowhere does this become more clear than in the command which, as we saw, had become the central feature of Jewish piety, the **sabbath commandment.** According to the Jewish understanding, too, people can be helped on the sabbath if their lives are in acute danger; at least, Rabbi Simeon ben Menasya had justified this in 180 CE with what is possibly an older statement, 'The sabbath is subject to you, and you are not subject to the sabbath.'[8] But Jesus is even more basic. He does not call for literal observance of the sabbath Torah but for an all-embracing love of neighbour, behind which even the all-holy sabbath commandment has to retreat. For the **sabbath is there for human beings,** and human beings are not there for the sabbath, not only in matters of life or death or in case of attack, surprise or war, not only where Jews are involved, but **everywhere** and **always.**[9] Thus the sabbath commandment is deliberately given 'a new direction' which is a constant: 'Human beings may not be delivered over to the sabbath and made its slave.'[10] Thus not doing good is identified with doing evil.[11] Or, as Jesus himself quite explicitly says in the Gospel of Matthew: 'Therefore it is permissible to do good on the sabbath.'[12]

The sabbath, and indeed all the less important **commandments,** are **there for the sake of human beings.** Love embraces them all, and this should happen without any great words (Jesus himself hardly used the word love) but in a quite practical way – love should be shown to the first person who needs me, even if he happens to be a non-Jewish Samaritan (or an Arab).[13] And what are all the implications of this for today? What – one might add hypothetically – would the rabbi of those days say to an Orthodox rabbi today?

2. The rabbi – then and now

The rabbi of those days would presumably say to the present-day rabbi: 'You do well to speak of the living covenant as the foundation of the law. But in the end of the day, what significance do you attach to the law, indeed to legalism? Are the Torah and the halakhah, the written and the oral law, both equally revealed? And are both therefore unchangeable, infallible and irreformable, inerrant and incapable of improvement? Is everything in scripture and tradition to be fulfilled by human beings down to the last word – with reference to God and the revelation on Sinai? Are these commandments really dictated directly by God or are they divine law attested and formulated by human beings? And surely not all the liturgical, ethical, dietary regulations have the same status? Even the rabbis distinguished between chief commandments and subsidiary commandments. So is there not a scale of values, a "hierarchy of truths", a concentration on essentials, a mean in the law? Surely everything is not equally the will of God? Were things originally like **this** in God's plan with humankind?' That is roughly how the rabbi of those days would talk to the present-day rabbi.

And the present-day rabbi would presumably reply to the rabbi of those days: 'Nowadays, at least those among us who are not hyper-Orthodox often relativize the individual commandments: for example, the sabbath commandment in order to save a human life; or fasting on Yom Kippur, if human health is in danger. And after all, the Talmud explicitly states that certain commandments of the Torah may be ignored – in the interest of the "dignity of creatures". In our legal tradition, each individual commandment should simply be a way of confirming the covenant, hallowing God's name and bearing witness to God. And even now there are situations in life where only the understanding of the love of God in us and our obligation to the other can decide how a particular commandment is to be fulfilled.'

I could imagine that the rabbi of those days might similarly reply to the present-day rabbi, 'You are not far from the kingdom of God.'[14] But at the same time he would encourage him to go further. For what is love? Does it not mean the capacity also for the sake of human beings to **relativize** and to **transcend the law of God,** which is after all **there for human beings**? Does it not mean that infectious freedom which the rabbi of those days already proclaimed and practised over and above the prevalent legalistic interpretations of the law? Does it not mean a basic attitude which must be dangerous for any religious system or any religious apparatus, just as Jesus of Nazareth was ultimately a disruptive influence on all those who wanted to twist God's arm with the law and gain control?

No, even today's rabbi should not overlook the fact that Jesus of Nazareth at that time did not simply want to pour new wine into old wineskins. Had he done that, he would have hardly caused offence. If, very much in the prophetic tradition, he had simply recalled people to true observance of the law – like the prophets who acknowledged the authority of Moses; if, like the rabbis of his time, he had simply called for honest worship, a cultivation of delight in the commandments, an analysis of individual cases and in given instances the preference of one commandment to another, would that conflict have arisen?

Hardly. For Jesus of Nazareth had realized to the full the love which the Torah itself already requires for the 'alien':[15] to the point of boundless forgiveness, service regardless of rank, renunciation of rights, power and force without anything in return. In this disposition, which elevates the ten commandments to love of the 'neighbour' in the positive sense, if need be, and to the scandal of the Jewish establishment, Jesus set himself above the dominant teaching, the teaching of the rulers, the tradition, the oral tradition of the fathers, the 'halakhah'.

That was how people put the question then, and that is how they put it now. Isn't this rabbi really too liberal, too humane? In this way doesn't he make human beings the criterion of God's commandments, when he proclaims that the sabbath is made for man and not man for the sabbath? And in his whole behaviour doesn't he call for a love of fellow human beings, a love of neighbour and a love of enemy which no longer takes any notice of the natural laws between aliens and non-aliens, Jews and Samaritans/Arabs? In this way, in the long run doesn't he ultimately relativize the significance of people and descent, indeed of law and morality? Especially when he so often acts provocatively by taking the side of those who break the law against those who are faithful to it, and is even said in specific instances to have promised them forgiveness instead of punishment? So is it a coincidence that the conflict with the guardians of the law and the Temple came to a fatal climax, that this one Jew and no other rabbi suffered this fate and made history; that he not only gathered together a school but proclaimed a gospel, gathered a community, indeed by his proclamation, his behaviour and his fate sparked off a movement in world history and thus fundamentally changed the course of the world and the position of Judaism?

This raises a **basic question** for religious self-understanding which today must be **addressed to all representatives of a religious legalism.** It is truly a crucial question not only for the Jewish Orthodox but also for Islamic fundamentalists, and even more so for traditionalistic Roman Catholics and Protestant pietists who claim to be liberated from the Jewish law, only to set up a new church law. In confrontation with the executed Jew, Jesus of Nazareth, the decisive question is: is God's will expressed in the exact observance of the law – whether this be halakhah, canon law or *shari'a* – or **in that doing of the will of God aimed at love which is above any law**? This complex of problems once again comes to a head in the case of the Jew Paul. As we have heard, it is particularly over Paul that Christianity and Judaism seem to have parted company radically at a very early stage. Is there not here, too, indeed precisely here, a need for critical and self-critical rethinking?

3. Paul against the law?

To any one who has ever been confronted with Jewish Orthodoxy, it is evident that the complex of problems associated with Paul and the law are not just a Jewish problem of that time, but also a Jewish problem of today. As over so much else, there is a dispute today among Pauline scholars over how far it is possible to assume that Paul personally was in personal conflict with the law; he had indeed described himself as 'blameless in the righteousness which is according to the law'.[16] But beyond doubt his letters reflect structures of the

Pharisaic observance of the law which are particularly illuminating for present-day Jews. That is understood better by some Jewish interpreters than by some Christian exegetes.

Shalom Ben-Chorin, for example, thinks that his own particular affinity to the figure of Paul has grown 'out of his suffering under the law'. Only those who have made an attempt 'to put their lives under the law of Israel, to observe and practise the customs and precepts of the rabbinic tradition', Ben-Chorin says, can understand Paul rightly. And he adds: 'I have attempted to take upon myself the law in its Orthodox interpretation without finding in it the satisfaction, that peace, which Paul calls justification before God.'[17] What he is referring to here are experiences of zeal for the law and falling short of the law: 'Nowadays in Jerusalem we know this type of fanatical Yeshiva pupil from the Diaspora, though of course he no longer comes from Tarsus, but from New York or London. In demonstrations against those who are peacefully driving their automobiles on the Sabbath he is very often to be found among the zealots for the law who throw stones at cars and drivers – those Talmudic students from abroad. Presumably they would not react in this way to a formal desecration of the Sabbath in New York or London, but in Jerusalem they want to legitimate themselves as one-hundred-and-fifty-per-cent Jews. This is precisely how we must imagine the young Saul from Tarsus, who emphasizes that he surpassed many in Judaism in his conduct, that he was zealous for the law and that he delighted in the stoning of heretics (how similar it all is, how topical!). – However, we must now understand what it is to experience the iron discipline of the law, the halakhah, the *mizvot*, day after day, without experiencing any real proximity of God from it, without getting rid of the burdensome feeling of trangression, *averah*, sin... Does not the multiplicity of human commandments and precepts ensnare people?'[18]

After all this, the question becomes all the more pressing: was not Paul justified in definitively abolishing the Jewish law, introducing its end? For centuries this was something which was regarded as settled in Christian exegesis. And particularly if one reads Paul through the spectacles of German exegesis, especially the exegesis inspired by Luther and impressively given systematic form by Bultmann in his *Theology of the New Testament*, then the conviction is hardened that:

– With the death and resurrection of Jesus Christ, for Paul the Jewish law is finished once and for all. Now the gospel prevails instead of the law.

– For Christians, the Jewish law is insignificant, and all that matters is belief in Jesus Christ; instead of the law, faith is now what counts.

– Together with the Jewish law, in the end Judaism itself is now also superseded: the new people of God, the church, is now taking the place of the old people of God.
– What about an example? **Hans Hübner,** for whom Israel has 'perverted' the Torah,[19] is one skilful interpreter of this Lutheran exegesis; he is particularly interested in 'Paul's own theology' and like Luther before him interprets the more balanced letter to the Romans (Paul's letter of introduction to the Roman community)[20] in terms of the polemical and antinomian Galatians (which was provoked by rival Judaizing missionaries in Galatia).[21] If we follow him, then in Galatians Paul has made it quite unambiguously clear:
– that 'the one who believes in Christ **may not stand** "under the law"';
– that 'for the Christian, existence under the law and consequently existence as a Jew are by definition excluded!';
– that 'in principle, being a Christian may be defined as not being allowed to be a Jew'.[22]

One asks oneself whether such statements do not nurture the suspicion that the Lutheran exegesis of Paul is openly or cryptically anti-Jewish. Are not Paul's pro-Jewish statements here either suppressed, reinterpreted or conjured away? And with reference to the Jewish Christians one asks onself: would Paul really no longer have been a religious opponent of the possibility of a Jewish Christianity which observes the Jewish law, including circumcision, kosher food and the sabbath commandment? Even Hans Hübner must concede in the same breath that in Galatians Paul did not 'require of Jewish Christians a negation of their Jewishness', but rejects this as a 'kind of contradiction' in Paul. But can we be content with such exegesis, which thinks that it can censure Paul at those points where he does not fit into the totally antagonistic Lutheran scheme of 'law and gospel'? Given the extremely confused state of scholarship, there is no way of avoiding as clear an investigation as possible into this controversy over the validity of the law. And indeed today, more than any other, it not only polarizes Jewish and Christian exegetes of Paul but also brings about a polarization among Christian exegetes of Paul, regardless of the artificial national fronts which have recently been erected.[23]

4. Is the law abolished?

First of all the **preliminary question**. Precisely what are the **difficulties** which make clarity on this matter so hard to achieve? They are as follows:

1. Paul, a **prophetic figure** through and through, was certainly (as even most of his critics concede) a quite coherent theologian. However, like the prophets of Israel, he was not a systematic one, who would have left us a closed system of faith with no contradictions. He is no ivory-tower scholar who developed an abstract theological set of problems relating to law and faith; in the middle of his restless activity as a missionary (and while earning his living as a tentmaker), he was reflecting on the consequences of his conversion from Pharisaism to belief in Christ, and on all the implications of this faith for the Jewish-Christian and particularly the Gentile-Christian communities.

2. Paul's theological writings are **letters**, indeed most of them are occasional writings governed by the situation: German exegetes in particular say that they show a development from Galatians to Romans, and Anglo-Saxon exegetes in particular at least say that by different approaches from a constant christological centre they attempt to give responses to different situations and questions, responses which are by no means free of tension and in some cases perhaps contain contradictions.[24] In both instances it is possible that Paul corrected himself in the summary letter to the Romans.

3. In his correspondence, which was written in Greek, Paul does not use the Hebrew word 'Torah' (even as a Hebrew loan word) but the Greek **'nomos/law'**, which had been used for the one word Torah from the Greek translation of the Hebrew Bible (the Septuagint) onwards. But this has the disadvantage that we can never know whether in any particular passage in his correspondence Paul is using 'law' in the wider or the narrower sense: in the **wider** sense as Torah/teaching/instruction (= the corpus of the five books of Moses) or in the **narrower** sense as halakhah/law ('halakhah' understood as the religious law of the rabbis, already grounded in the Torah and now increasingly permeating the whole of life, though at that time it was still not codified).

To be sure, despite the immense difficulties of interpreting the Pauline understanding of the law, there are also **agreements** among Pauline exegetes. Most exegetes might agree if one said:
– The fundamental shift in the life of the Pharisaic Jew Paul did not come about through study of the law but through the personal

experience of a vision of the exalted Christ, whom Paul subsequently proclaimed messiah of Israel and the world.[25]
– Rejected in his preaching by Jews, Paul sees it as his prime task to **proclaim also to the Gentiles** the message of the God of Israel, as this God has definitively showed himself in Jesus.[26]

Paul requires of the **Gentiles** belief in the message of Christ, but spares them **being subjected to the Jewish religious law**. For in future this faith, and not the works of the law, is to be decisive for salvation: here the Jews have no advantage.
– This openness of the apostle to 'outsiders' – and this too is a sign of continuity of substance, despite the often questionable continuity of tradition – was very much **in line with Jesus**, but of course very much more so with Paul's tremendous sacrifices and his suffering under persecution, his renunciation of marriage and his humble service.[27] There is no disputing the fact that he took a radically serious view of being a disciple of Christ.

So what is the **most disputed question** among exegetes? It is the question what 'law' means in Paul on any occasion. This by way of anticipation: it would be crazy to discuss here all the problems connected with the law, which have produced an extraordinarily complex and contradictory scholarly literature – all the questions from christology and soteriology to anthropology and ecclesiology. Here I must concentrate exclusively on the significance of the law – in particular also with a view to the dialogue between Jews and Christians today. And here already it should be noted that Paul's own understanding of the law does not stem from an objective theoretical doctrine (say of guilt and atonement, law and gospel, works and faith or sin and grace), nor even necessarily from an autobiographical psychologizing reflection on a quite personal crisis of conscience over the fulfilling of the law, but rather from his experience of Christ and his call to be apostle to the Gentiles.

So this disputed question is: may we say that for Paul **the Jewish law has ongoing validity**? Does the law still apply, or has it been abrogated? To be specific:
– According to Paul, have the Jews who are zealous for the law really perverted the law?
– May the Jewish law really no longer be observed by Jews who follow Christ? So is Jewish Christianity no longer a legitimate possibility alongside Gentile Christianity?
– Is Judaism, then, wrong not only because it rejects Jesus as the messiah but also because and in so far as it still holds to the law?

5. The continuing validity of the Torah

If we read the numerous Pauline texts on the law as far as possible without traditional schemes, whether Christian ('law and gospel') or Jewish ('abolition of the law'), a **first point** is indisputable. Paul takes it for granted that in so far as 'law' means the **Torah**, the law is and remains **God's law**, i.e. the expression of the will of God. Paul explicitly stresses: 'So the law is holy, and the commandment is holy and just and good.'[28] The law is to 'lead to life':[29] it is 'the embodiment of knowledge and truth';[30] it is 'spiritual'.[31] The 'giving of the law' is one of Israel's 'advantages'.[32] Here, for Paul 'law' clearly means the Torah in the sense of the five books of Moses, which human beings have to obey as God's demand.[33]

A **second point** which is often overlooked is that the **Gentiles**, too, are subject to God's demands, though they have no written law. For the Gentiles, too, can perceive the moral demands of the Torah, particularly the Decalogue.[34] The work which the law requires of them is written in their hearts and attested by their consciences.[35] So Gentiles, like Jews, are judged by the one God, who is not partisan,[36] in accordance with their works.[37] For it is possible at any time even for believers to fail; there is no cheap grace – 'it is not the hearers of the law who are righteous before God, but the doers of the law who will be justified (in the final judgment!)'.[38]

A **third point** follows from this. According to Paul, God's holy law, the Torah of Moses, is in no way abolished even after the Christ event, but remains relevant: as the 'Torah of faith'.[39] Indeed Paul expressly says that it is **not 'overthrown'** ('by no means!'), but 'upheld', '**established**' by faith.[40] Could the Jew Paul, who passionately takes the part of God's people, be against God's holy law? Nowhere does Paul distinguish in principle between the Mosaic law, the Torah, and a law which Christians now have to establish and to fulfil. Nowhere does he call on Jews no longer to observe the law. Paul never gave up the Jewishness of which he was proud. And he admonishes both Jewish and Gentile Christians 'to observe the commandments of God'.[41]

However, a **fourth point** has to be considered. For Paul, since the death of Jesus the law has unmistakably displayed a **double aspect**, indeed has had a **double function**: the law itself may not change, but it does have a different effect, depending on a person's attitude to it.[42]

– Negatively, the Torah may stir human desire to sinful transgression: 'If it had not been for the law, I should not have known sin. I should not have known what it is to covet if the law had not said, "You shall not covet".'[43] So it convicts human beings as sinners;[44] it entangles them in sin and so leads to knowledge of sin.[45] To this degree the law leads to judgment and death, and is a **verdict of guilty** on human beings who have incurred guilt and become lost, an **opponent** which leaves them with nothing to say for themselves.

– Positively, at the same time the Torah shows men and women that they need justification by God himself – not through the works of the law (i.e. not by fulfilling the countless moral and ritual commandments on which they constantly come to grief), but through faith which trusts in God alone. Abraham, who had such great faith that he was ready to sacrifice his pagan homeland and even his son, did all this without the precepts of a law; he is the model of faith and the righteousness before God which comes from faith.[46] So for Christians, too, the law has a function – as to some extent a witness to Christ, who brings all those who believe in him to that true righteousness before God which, according to Paul, is also already 'witnessed by the law and the prophets'.[47] To this extent the law leads to life, and is the **witness** and the **ally** of the believer.

From this we can understand that for Paul – and this is the **fifth point** – **Jesus Christ** does not replace the law, but discloses it: he is not the 'end' of the Torah as the way of salvation – as the Greek term *telos*[48] has often been translated – but primarily its **'goal'** and its **'fulfilment'**. Certainly Christ took the curse upon himself on the cross, but precisely in so doing he fulfilled the judgment of the law.[49] So Paul can even speak of a 'law of faith'[50] and a 'law of the spirit of life'[51] – in a completely true sense, and not just playfully and metaphorically.[52] That means that through the new faith in Christ and through the Spirit of Christ the Mosaic Torah becomes a Torah of faith and the Spirit. The Christian who lives by faith can and should 'keep the commandments',[53] like the Jew! So 'living from faith' means 'fulfilling the law' in the power of the Spirit of Christ.

Hence we can similarly understand that Paul – and this is a **sixth point** – does not write polemic against the law in itself, the Mosaic Torah, but against the **works** of the law, against a **righteousness** from the law. His slogan is not justification through faith 'without the law' (as though faith were an arbitrary, voluntary matter without practical consequences), but 'without works of the law'. In Paul, it is not faith and law which are opposed, but faith and works. Here the fact remains that human beings do not attain righteousness before God by what they do. God himself justifies them, and all that is required of them is faith, unconditional trust. For both Jews and Gentiles, 'no human being will be justified in God's sight by works of the law'.[54] Were one to use the law for one's own justification before God, this would be a 'dispensation of death', a 'dispensation of condemnation',[55] since 'the letter kills'.[56]

And so, on the basis of faith in Jesus Christ, one can now – and this is a **seventh point** – understand the meaning of 'for **freedom** Christ has set us free'.[57] This is not simply freedom from the Torah and its ethical demands but freedom from the works of the law. So that is what is meant by the freedom to which 'you are called',[58] which we 'have in Christ Jesus'.[59] To this extent those who believe in Christ are 'no longer under the law but under grace'.[60]

But what is meant by 'works of the law'? And what does this freedom which Paul so solemnly proclaims mean in practice? How are the new Christian communities of Jewish and Gentile origin to behave?

6. Freedom from the halakhah

It has become clear that if we want to have a viable and to some degree coherent interpretation of Paul's understanding of the law, we have to begin from his experience of Christ and his call to be apostle to the Gentiles. For whereas the rabbis decisively interpret the Torah in terms of the **halakhah** (the legal part of the Torah and the tradition), Paul now interprets it in the light of the **revelation of Christ** which he has received.[61] For the Jew Paul, this revelation of Christ is now the new **material criterion** for redefining the function of the Torah: in respect of both Gentiles and Jews. For Paul now – though his Jewish opponents can hardly follow him here – the new experience of the resurrection and of the Spirit (which is bound up with the resurrection), and as a result **belief in Christ** (which is of course more than just fidelity to the covenant, but rather means a radical reorientation and surrender), is as fundamental as the exodus experience already was for the faith of Israel.

What does that mean for the question of the law? After all that we have heard, the answer can only be: when Paul, who, as we heard, had only a single word (*nomos*) at his disposal in Greek for the two key Hebrew words Torah (teaching) and halakhah (law), speaks to us ambiguously about freedom from the 'law', he is **in no way** speaking **against the Torah in principle**. Following Abraham's example, the Torah in fact teaches justification through faith, and according to Paul its ethical commands even apply to the Gentiles. But Paul does speak **against the halakhah** – without yet using this later terminology – where the halakhah does not make general ethical demands, but calls for the doing of the '**works of the law**', namely – as follows from the context

– those works of the Jewish ritual law (circumcision, commandments relating to purity and food, sabbath and feast days) which may not be imposed on the Gentiles.[62]

That means that it is not the Torah in the general sense as God's teaching or instruction which has lost its fundamental significance, but the Torah in the narrower sense: the halakhah, albeit not in the ethical but in the ritual sense. Paul negates this ritual halakhah for the Gentile Christians and fundamentally relativizes it for Jewish Christians: for it is now to be understood in accord with the Spirit which gives life, and not the letter which kills.[63]

So what follows from this for Christian living? It means something different for Gentile Christians and for Jewish Christians:

– Only the ethical commandments of the Torah, which Paul himself of course obeys, are imposed on Christians of Gentile origin (a point which Paul did not distinguish terminologically or develop theoretically), and not the cultic and ritual commandments which are developed so broadly in the halakhah for the whole life of the Jew, the Jewish life-style;

– Christians of Jewish origin can observe the halakhah, but do not necessarily have to, for it is no longer such 'works of the law' which are decisive for salvation, but faith in Jesus Christ. The works of the law themselves are not to be understood in accordance with the letter but in accordance with the Spirit: a life in the Spirit.[64]

What specifically does that mean for the individual ritual commandments of the halakhah? Here are Paul's answers as far as we know them from the letters; he does not give them systematically, but goes into particular situations and questions:

– Circumcision: for Jewish Christians it remains meaningful, but it is no longer made the condition of salvation; for Abraham trusting faith and not circumcision was already fundamental.[65] However, for those Christians who were once Gentiles, physical circumcision is unnecessary; it is replaced by faith, as 'spiritual' circumcision.[66]

– The Jewish festivals, the sabbath in particular: Jewish Christians can continue to celebrate the sabbath. But the Jewish festal calendar is not an obligation for Gentile Christians.[67]

– Observance of the food laws. That is voluntary: Christians of Jewish origin will continue to observe the sabbath in their own surroundings, but these laws may not be imposed on Christians of Gentile origin. And in no case may they lead to a split in the community.[68] In every area of social life, the question of table-fellowship – whether one may eat together or not – is of supreme practical and symbolic significance, even more so for Christians in the case of the common celebration of

The Twofold Meaning of 'Law' in Paul

Torah / teaching
= Nomos = Law

Haggadah / story: remains valid for (e.g. of Abraham)

Jews
Jewish Christians ⎱ now to be understood in the spirit:
Gentile Christians ⎰ Christ = **fulfilment of the Law**

Halakhah / Law
= Nomos = Law

ethical commandments: remain valid for (e.g. Decalogue)

Jews
Jewish Christians ⎱ now under the criterion
Gentile Christians ⎰ of love: Christ = **freedom from the Law**

ritual commandments: (e.g. commandments about food and purity, circumcision)

remain valid for Jews
are relativized for Jewish Christians ⎱ now under the criterion
are not valid for Gentile Christians ⎰ of love: Christ = **freedom from the Law**

the meal in memory of Jesus (eucharist). So Paul, who has become 'to the Jews a Jew and to the Greeks a Greek',[69] observes the food laws when he is with Jewish Christians, but not when he is with Gentile Christians.

However, the most famous **dispute in the early church, in Antioch**, was precisely over this last point: it was between Paul, who (as had been resolved at a meeting of the apostles in Jerusalem) was responsible for the mission to the Gentiles, and Peter, who was responsible for the mission to the Jews.[70]

– **Peter**, who was open to the mission to the Gentiles, had at first practised table-fellowship in Antioch with the Gentiles in the same way as Paul, but gave this up after the arrival of followers of James from Jerusalem, who were faithful to the law and now stipulated kosher food. For the Jewish Christians, if they wanted to remain Jewish Christians, this at first seemed consistent: no table-fellowship and consequently also no eucharistic fellowship between 'clean' Jewish Christians and 'unclean' Gentile Christians. But had they taken sufficiently seriously Jesus' criticism of the law, and the relativization of the law which had come about through his death?

– **Paul** defended the freedom of the Gentile Christians passionately on this specific point (the account which he gives in Galatians is probably unintentionally biased): he 'opposed Peter to his face'![71] From his perspective this was similarly understandable: he had passionately to oppose the break in table-fellowship and eucharistic fellowship which indeed had destroyed the reconciliation of Jews and Gentiles in the one community of Jesus Christ that for him was central. Even if he never denied his Jewishness and never forbade Jewish Christians to live in accordance with the halakhah, but affirmed it for his own sphere, this Jewish life-style was not to become a divisive factor over against the Gentile Christians. While Paul did not expect the Jewish Christians to repudiate the Mosaic Torah, for the sake of the unity of the community made up of Jews and Gentiles, in this case (not generally!) he probably did expect them to renounce the halakhah – the ritual prescriptions of which prohibited such table-fellowship. The halakhah was to be interpreted according to the Spirit, not the letter. For that was what the freedom brought by Christ freed people for.[72] Faith in Christ must also be fundamental for Jewish Christians.

In all this we cannot overlook the fact that **Paul's critical attitude to the law reflects Jesus' critical attitude to the law**. In specific instances Jesus similarly spoke out for the commandment of God and against the application of the halakhah, the 'tradition of men' or the 'tradition of the fathers',[73] and instead of cultic ritual purity (the washing of hands) had called for the ethically-determined purity of the heart.[74] But did this decision by Paul, as is often asserted, really cast the die for the fate of the Jewish Christians in the Diaspora church that was coming into being? Was the premature break into a Jewish and a Gentile Christian church thus pre-programmed? Was this an unavoidable conflict with a tragic outcome? In the spirit of Jesus an understanding would surely in fact have been possible, indeed necessary.

But if in this way Paul and the Gentile-Christian side with good reason called for freedom from the law, i.e. from the halakhah, some Jews and Jewish Christians asked and still ask precisely the opposite question: does not such Pauline freedom lead to arbitrariness, to hedonism and libertinism?

7. Love as the fulfilling of the law

Paul saw the danger, but said clearly that **freedom from the law**, in the sense of **freedom from the ritual halakhah**, did not mean any wild, subjective capriciousness. Freedom from the law may 'not become an occasion for the flesh'.[75] For while the cultic and ritual commandments of the halakhah no longer hold for Gentile Christians who have been freed from the law, the moral requirements of the Torah retain their validity – albeit on the basis of a decisively new basic attitude. At all events, the important thing is 'to prove what is the will of God, what is good and acceptable and perfect'.[76]

Those who believe in Jesus Christ may and should fulfil the will of God in the secular world. They need not give up all the good things of the world. It is just that they must not surrender to them. Believers can give themselves away, surrender themselves, only to God. So they need not in any way forsake the world: only they must not succumb to it. What is called for is not physical detachment but inner personal detachment from the things of this world.

To those who are freed from the law, according to Paul the great saying 'All things are lawful for me' applies.[77] But at the same time, 'I will not be enslaved by anything'.[78] In the world 'nothing is unclean in itself'.[79] But I cannot lose my freedom to anything in the world and allow myself to be ruled by it, as an idol. In that case, still 'all things are lawful for me', but at the same time, 'not all things are helpful'.[80]

And finally, at the same time we must note that what is both permissible and helpful to me can nevertheless be detrimental to my fellow human beings. What then? Even then it is still the case that 'all things are lawful'. But equally, 'not all things build up!' So, 'Let no one seek his own good, but the good of his neighbour.'[81] Hence the freedom of disciples of Christ can also continually become freedom for renunciation, for renunciation above all of domination: 'For though I am free from all men, I have made myself a slave to all.'[82] Here the freedom of the believer is not denied; on the contrary, here it is claimed to the maximum.

In practice this means that true freedom is not heedless: 'Take care that this freedom of yours does not become a stumbling-block to the weak.'[83] Each is to serve the other,[84] but without giving up his or her own freedom: 'Do not become slaves of men.'[85] In the last resort the believer is never tied to the opinions and judgments, the traditions and criteria, of the other: 'For why should my freedom be determined by another man's scruples?'[86] My own conscience, which can distinguish between good and evil, binds me.[87]

This is a paradoxical combination of independence and obligation, power and renunciation, independence and service, domination and servitude. This freedom of the Christian may be an enigma to the non-Christian, but for the Christian, the enigma is resolved by what **lies at the heart of this freedom: love**, which is the firstfruit of the Spirit. In the love which is at work in faith,[88] in which the distinctions between circumcision and uncircumcision are done away with, the master becomes the servant and the servant the master, independence becomes obligation and obligation becomes independence.[89] The question is: could not the matter of table-fellowship have been solved in such a spirit, and the split between the Jewish-Christian and the Gentile-Christian church have been prevented?

Openness for the others, being there for the others, selfless love for the others – for Paul this is the highest realization of freedom: 'For you were called to freedom, brethren; only do not use your freedom as an opportunity for the flesh, but through love be servants of one another. For the whole law is fulfilled in **one** word, "You shall love your neighbour as yourself."'[90] Whatever God himself requires through the law is aimed at love. **Love** is the **fulfilling of the Torah** in human relationships: 'Owe no one anything, except to love one another; for he who loves his neighbour has fulfilled the law. The commandments, "You shall not commit adultery, You shall not kill, You shall not steal, You shall not covet," and any other commandment, are summed up in this sentence, "You shall love your neighbour as yourself." Love does no wrong to a neighbour; therefore love is the fulfilling of the law.'[91] So the 'law of Christ' is none other than the freedom of love: 'Bear one another's burdens, and so fulfil the law of Christ.'[92] Anyone who is bound to God and thus to the neighbour is freed for true freedom.

IV. The Future of the People of God

But the concern is here not just with the individual, but with the people. And this question still remains open. What, in Paul's view, is the status of Israel, his people? We have to consider this question in intellectual strictness and honesty, without false harmonization, by turning to the classical passage on the relationship between young Christianity and the people of Israel, Romans 9-11: this is not an appendix, but an integral part of Pauline theology.

1. The abiding promise

No one in the whole of the New Testament wrestled so intensively and so constructively with the destiny of the people of God as Paul, the Jew who confessed Jesus as the Christ; and neither the law-gospel model, the allegorical-typological model nor the promise-fulfilment model can capture the riches of his thought.

Here is the question. Has Israel lost its special position as the people of God after the death and resurrection of Jesus? Not at all, says Paul in the letter to the Roman community which in fact became his testament: God does not abandon his faithfulness, despite Israel's 'unfaithfulness'.[1] Christians – whom in these very chapters Paul warned against 'boasting' at the expense of the Jews – should never have forgotten that the election of Israel, the people of God, is permanent, indissoluble, irrevocable. God has not changed his promises, though after Christ their validity must be seen in a different light. The Jews are and **remain God's chosen people, indeed his favourites.**[2] For according to Paul, to the Jews – his 'brothers' by common descent[3] – there still belong:

– the 'sonship': the appointment of the people of Israel as God's 'firstborn son' which already took place in Egypt;
– the 'glory': the glory of the presence of God (the 'Shekinah') with his people;
– the 'covenants': the covenant of God with his people, continually threatened and renewed;
– the 'giving of the law': the good orders of life given by God to his people as the sign of his covenant;
– the worship: the true worship of the priestly people;
– the 'promises': the abiding promises of God's grace and salvation;

– the 'patriarchs': the patriarchs of the former time in the community of the one true faith;

– the 'messiah': Jesus the Christ, born of Israelite flesh and blood, who primarily belongs not to the Gentiles, but to the people of Israel.[4]

All this is preserved for the Jews, even if they have rejected Jesus as messiah, a rejection which fills Paul with 'great sorrow' and 'increasing anguish'.[5] No, it was not Paul who detached Christianity from Judaism (others did that after his death and the destruction of the Second Temple). **As a Christian**, Paul, the Jew who gave up his Pharisaism, **in no way gives up his Judaism.** Whatever one says about him, though he is constantly attacked, misunderstood, defamed, he does not feel that he is transgressing the law, as an apostate, a false teacher. He, the Christian Jew and apostle, is simply fulfilling his Judaism – and in so doing thinks that he has the support of the Torah – with a new, freer, more comprehensive spirit: in the light of the God who also continually acts in a new, unexpectedly new, way even before time.

This God has now acted towards his people in Jesus of Nazareth in a decisive new way, as is confirmed for Paul by his prophetic experience of Christ which he therefore proclaims in his message: this God of Jesus Christ is none other than the God of Abraham, Isaac and Jacob. And the old, yet new, message of this one God first of all went out to Israel. The community of Christians is simply inserted into the people of Israel chosen in Abraham. The one and undivided plan for Israel continues, even in the New Testament. There are **not two contradictory divine plans**: the Torah for the Jews and the gospel for the Christians. For as Paul recognized from the revelation of Christ, the Torah points to Christ, and Christ fulfils the Torah.

But for this reason the Christian churches can never be concerned to engage in a '**mission to the Jews**' either. Even Paul does not call for this. Why not? Because the cause of the gospel, the cause of the Jews, must not be presented to the Jews from outside as something alien to them. Or have the Jews so far had a completely false faith, like the Gentiles? Did they not already believe in the one true God even before the church? Did they not receive the message of the one and true God even before the church – and not just through the church? Truly, the Jews were and are the first to be addressed: the young church comes from Judaism.

But have not the majority of the Jews rejected the gospel of Jesus, the Christ? According to Paul this, too, must not be concealed: the majority of the Jews have **rejected the gospel**. In this letter Paul is not speaking to Jews, but to a community of Christians. And given this serious situation, Paul does not hesitate to speak (completely in the style of the prophets) of the 'blinding', 'hardening', 'obduracy', 'deafness', indeed 'rejection' of Israel. This must be understood in terms of a pain for his people which he never overcame. But here it remains the case that 'God's word has not failed' through the failure of the people.[6]

However, for Paul this is not an excuse to stop bearing witness to, and proclaiming the gospel to, the Jews as well. So it is also true for today that the theology of the Jew Paul, who more than anyone else struggled to bring Christ to his Jewish brothers and sisters, cannot be an occasion for watering down or even neglecting the liberating message of Jesus as the messiah of Israel and the world. For individual Christians **to bear witness** to Christ, even to Jews, is rather different from an organized and systematized mission to the Jews by the powerful Christian churches.

However, today we must also allow Judaism to bear witness. The British Jewish journalist Emma Klein has recently argued rightly against the 'misconception widely entertained among Jews and Christians that Judaism is not a missionary religion'. Of course it all depends on what one means by 'mission', which is not to be understood in the primitive sense, say, of distributing tracts, paying annoying house visits or preaching demagogic sermons on television. But mission rightly understood can be practised as the proclamation of a message and vision which people can make their own in full freedom. That already happened in antiquity, when as a result of its monotheism, its ethics, its ritual and its sense of community Judaism proved attractive to countless people: converts to Judaism are known of until well into the Christian era. That was also the case in the early Middle Ages, and could again be so today.[7] Even Christian theologians cannot dispute this. As Christians, we cannot ask for testimonies and then require others to be 'pluralists'.

For as we have heard, the apostle Paul in particular was anything but a modern pluralist, to whom everything was indifferent, anything was right. He speaks of a **'new covenant'** which has been established through the death and resurrection of Jesus Christ,[8] an expression which is not a Christian invention but points back to the prophetic tradition in the Hebrew Bible. The prophet Jeremiah already spoke of God making 'a new covenant with the house of Israel and the house of Judah', which is not like the covenant that he 'made with their fathers', when he 'took them by the hand to bring them out of the land of Egypt'.[9] This talk of a 'new covenant' made possible through Christ must be taken seriously, and yet for Paul that is no reason for simply declaring the old covenant null or out of-date, as a later fatal Christian substitionary theory thought that it could assume. For Paul, the talk of the new covenant may be the foundation of his preaching, but it is no justification for any Christian arrogance about salvation.[10] At the same time Paul believes that the old 'covenant ordinances' still exist. There is only one God and only one plan of salvation.

And yet Paul – like us today – is confronted with the fact that the majority of the people of Israel have rejected Jesus as the messiah. As a result, a division has grown up within Israel itself, since only a 'holy remnant',[11] the Jewish Christians, has recognized Jesus as the messiah of Israel. Paul makes it clear in these terms: 'not all who are descended from Israel belong to Israel'.[12] In other words, God's promises to Abraham and the fathers which precede the law of Moses, along with all the advantages of Israel, are in no way already to be regarded by all individual Israelites as the natural possession of salvation on which they can simply insist. As essentially all through the previous history of Israel, but now with new, extreme urgency, a distinction must be made between an Israel of the flesh and an Israel of the promise, an elect and a non-elect Israel.[13] How are we to understand this? For Paul here, the level of purely human decisions is transcended. Here God's sovereign freedom and inexplicable grace is at work,[14] unfathomable, indeed scandalous, for human beings, as already in the preference of Isaac over Ishmael, Jacob over Esau.

For what does God do in the face of the obduracy of his elect people, in his sovereign freedom and inexplicable grace? God takes for himself the freedom to make an elect people out of a non-elect people, the Gentiles.[15] Paul is not just concerned, negatively, with the rejection of Israel, but quite positively with the election of the Gentiles: the hardening of Israel is balanced by the election of the Gentiles. However, he continues to maintain that while apart for a small 'remnant', God has indeed hardened, deafened, darkened Israel, God has not finally condemned them nor definitively rejected them. He has not dissociated himself from his plan of salvation. He still had a plan for Israel – for the judgment of his righteousness is the judgment of his grace.

In view of this precarious situation for both sides, one thing is quite groundless: arrogance!
– There is no reason for any **Jewish or Jewish-Christian arrogance**. Neither descent nor any works of the law are decisive, not even circumcision: faith in Jesus Christ makes it possible to be admitted to and to belong to the people of God.
– Nor is there any reason for any **Gentile-Christian arrogance** either. The Gentiles do not have the God-given privileges of the Jews; their

sole credentials for being part of the people of God are faith in Jesus Christ. So the Gentile Christians do not have the least occasion for proving arrogant or even hostile to Israel. All Christian boasting, all contempt, all mockery, all arrogance, all vengeance towards the Jews (and perhaps also towards the Jewish Christians), in short, all anti-Judaism, are a perverse self-deception.

Paul uses a metaphor. The tree, Israel, has certainly not been cut down, even if particular branches have been broken off and only a few branches remain to represent the Israel which has become faithful. The Gentile Christians have been 'grafted' on to this tree, so that they now live from the same root as the people of Israel. This is why Paul can say to the Gentile Christians, who have quite gratuitously become members of the people of God: 'But if some of the branches were broken off, and you, a wild olive shoot, were grafted in their place to share the riches of the olive tree, do not boast over the branches. If you do boast, remember it is not you that support the root, but the root that supports you.'[16]

One last question remains: how does Paul envisage the sequel? Or more precisely: what about the deliverance of Israel, the salvation of all?

2. What will happen about Israel?

Since Paul puts so much emphasis on salvation through faith in Jesus Christ, you might expect that he would state quite clearly that non-believers will not be saved. But this is something which Paul, whose preaching among the Gentiles had such great success and whose preaching among the Jews had so little, does not do. In these three chapters of the letter to the Romans, at any rate, there is no mention of the fate of individual Christians or Jews; that is how Paul's statements in the Reformation dispute over 'predestination' were misunderstood. They are about the people.

But there is no mention in these chapters of the exclusion of the people of Israel from salvation either. On the contrary, Paul, speaking prophetically, talks of an eschatological 'mystery' here: in the end '**all Israel will be saved**'.[17] So Paul is convinced that there is a reprieve for the obduracy of Israel, that its blindness is transitory and its transgression is not final – the reprieve is until 'the full number of the Gentiles' is achieved. Just as the partial hardening of Israel by God's free grace is followed by the redemption of the 'full number of the

Gentiles', so from this, again through God's own grace, will follow the redemption of 'all Israel', of Israel as a whole.[18]

But precisely what will happen to 'all Israel'? What is the specific meaning of 'then all Israel will be saved?' Paul is completely silent as to precisely how things will work out. Does this mean that the Jews must first be converted to Christ and the Christian church (which church?) before they attain salvation? Is it a matter of the Jews being ready for conversion, a kind of 'mass conversion' before the appearing of Christ, forced for example by a Christian 'mass mission'? Not at all. Present-day exegesis runs straight across confessional boundaries in agreeing that Paul's decisive statement here is to be interpreted in strictly eschatological and christological terms.[19] In full, it runs: 'And so all Israel wil be saved, as it is written, "The Deliverer will come from Zion, he will banish ungodliness from Jacob"; and this will be my covenant with them when I take away their sins.'[20] What does this mean?

This is Paul's expectation: when the 'full number of the Gentiles' has been achieved, in other words when all the Gentiles have confessed Christ, then there will be a new creation by God in the still unbelieving remnant of Israel – through the Christ who will return from Zion. So here Paul is speaking against the background of his own imminent eschatological expectation, and in view of his own efforts to win as many people as possible for Christ. But he is **not** speaking of any **achievement of converting the Jews**, but of an **action of God through Christ for the Jews**. For this reason, too, a church mission to the Jews is superfluous. So the church must not take the question of the 'conversion' of Israel to the true faith into its own hands; it can confidently leave this to the grace of God and to the Christ, who will appear at the end of time as the 'deliverer from Zion'.[21]

For there is one thing of which Paul is most deeply convinced, and here he agrees with the rabbis: God's ways are unfathomable. Indeed, Paul even thinks – and this statement will later preoccupy Christianity a great deal – that in the end all, Christians and Jews, will be saved: 'God has consigned all men to disobedience, that he may have mercy upon all.'[22] And so Paul concludes his remarks on Jews and Christians with praise of the wisdom of God, in words from the Hebrew Bible: 'O the depth of the riches and wisdom and knowledge of God! How unsearchable are his judgments and how inscrutable his ways! For who has known the mind of the Lord, and who has been his counsellor?'[23] But Paul's last statement on this matter is a confession of the one and only God, which he would never betray but constantly endorsed: 'For from him and through him and to him are all things. To him be glory for ever. Amen.'[24]

3. Consequences for the relationship between Israel and the church

However, now almost two thousand years have passed. And the return of Christ which was expected by Paul and many of his Jewish contemporaries has not taken place. What has followed has been a long history, which has sometimes been cruel for the relationship between Jews and Christians. As we have heard, it has been a history which often enough was a betrayal of the great statements about Israel made by Paul in Romans 9-11. How often the Gentile church, when it could rely on large numbers, has 'boasted' at the expense of the Jews, boasted about its distinctions, as though it had replaced Israel and made it superfluous. The Jew Paul, who in no way wanted to give up his Judaism, had not wanted this.

Only in our days is a change coming about. A new time of co-existence between Israel and the church has begun – after the Holocaust and the foundation of the state of Israel, after Vatican I, the declarations of the World Council of Churches and many other church communities. From all that has been said, two consequences may impress themselves on us.

1. It has become **impossible** for the Christian church, as the new people of God, **to speak or act** in any way **against the old people of God.** For Paul, too, it is the case that a sure sign of being against the one true God is to be against his chosen people. The God of Jesus Christ and the church is none other than the God of Israel. But the people of Israel is and remains a witness to the reality of the living God, and has been so over the past almost two thousand years. It has often been more a witness than Christianity, in a unique way particularly in the Holocaust, where so many Jews preserved the 'hope against all hope'[25] in the God who brings the dead to life. So after all these historical experiences, must the Pauline categories – faith and works, spirit and letter, spirit and flesh – be divided between Jews and Christians in so heedless a way?

2. It has **proved necessary** for the church, as the new people of God, to **enter into understanding dialogue** with the old people of God in every way. Even in the perspective of Paul this dialogue is not closed, but open: today we need not simply stop with Paul, who of course could not foresee the development of 2,000 years. Happily, the shared foundation of Israel and the church has again become visible: it is one

and the same God who leads both. Like Israel, so too the Christian church seeks to be the wandering people of God: constantly setting out anew in the exodus from slavery; constantly once again on the way through the wildernesses of this age; constantly preparing itself anew for the entry into the messianic kingdom, the goal which is constantly postponed.

Only one thing is allowed to the church of Jesus Christ on this joint wandering: instead of just conveniently 'tolerating' Israel in a passive way, or even 'missionizing', it may 'provoke to jealousy'.[26] According to Paul it may make Israel jealous of the 'salvation' which it has experienced,[27] in order to provoke Israel to emulation. But how – after 2,000 years of predominantly disaster for the Jews, inflicted by a church which boasted that it was in exclusive possession of salvation? In all Christian humility and modesty, the answer can only be that in its whole existence the church must be the symbol of the salvation that it has achieved. And is it? Throughout its existence it must bear witness to the messianic fulfilment. But does it? Throughout its existence it must compete with Israel in bearing witness in a world often alienated from God to the manifest God, the fulfilled word, the revealed righteousness, the grace that has been grasped, the rule of God which has dawned. But is the church as it really exists truly a call to believe in the good news and repent, to unite with it and thus with its messiah? It is here – not in theoretical debate but in existential dialogue, not in an uncommitted verbal dispute but in a committed argument over values – that the decision between the church and Israel is made. In short, throughout the life that it lives, the church must bear witness to the reality of redemption.

Happily, today in the sphere of the church there are signs of a new attitude towards the people of Israel. In 'Pastoral Guidelines', in 1973 the French episcopal conference formulated programmatic statements on the 'attitude of Christians to Judaism'. It is worth noting that in clarity these go beyond anything said by Rome, Geneva and the German bishops. Taking up Pauline theology, especially that of Romans, the French bishops state: 'Israel and the church are not two institutions which supplement each other. The permanent contrast between Israel and the church is the sign of God's still unfulfilled plan. The Jewish and the Christian people are thus in a state of mutual self-questioning or, as the apostle Paul says, mutual zeal, over unity (Rom.11.13; cf.Deut.32.21). The words of Jesus himself and the teaching of Paul bear witness to the function of the Jewish people in the fulfilment of the unity of the human race as a unity of Israel and the nation which is ultimately to be brought about. Moreover, in this way the search for unity which Judaism is undertaking today cannot be unconnected with the divine plan of salvation. Nor can it be unconnected with the efforts of Christians to restore their own unity, although very different ways lead to these two plans. Though Jews and Christians fulfil their calling in different ways, history shows us that these ways constantly cross. Are not the messianic times the object of their common concern? So we must hope that they may ultimately take the way of mutual recognition and mutual understanding, that they will set aside their old enmity and turn to the Father with a shining hope which will be a promise for the whole world.'[28]

Indeed, the church must always keep one thing in view: if it does not heed such words, it must not be surprised at **questions put to it from the Jewish side**. Let us listen once again to Shalom Ben-Chorin: 'So we must ask in the light of the Bible whether the message of the Old Testament is fulfilled only in the New Testament or whether it is fulfilled in history – in the history experienced and endured by us and our ancestors. And there, my Christian readers, we must shake our heads and say, "No, there is no kingdom and no peace and no redemption, and it is still in a more distant or nearer future (according to both Jewish **and** Christian faith, no one can determine that), when the *malkuth shadday*, the kingdom of God, will dawn." '[29]

However, Christians, too, are convinced that the **final, manifest redemption of the world, the kingdom of God is still to come**. With Israel, the church, too, asserts a 'not yet', and prays with Israel for the coming of the kingdom which is expected in the future. However, for the church this 'not yet' presupposes a decisive 'but already'. Precisely because the church – unlike Israel, but also and primarily for Israel – believes in the hidden redemption of the world in Jesus the Christ which has already taken place – with Israel and so ultimately also for Israel – it hopes for the manifest and final redemption of the world.

And what is to happen in the meantime? It seems to me that on the basis of such an attitude of common waiting it could also be easier to talk about how we want to, how we should, deal with what separates us. For example with the Sabbath, or Sunday. This is an instance which I want to single out here as a test case for a practical and theoretical approach. To conclude this chapter on the human way and the law, I shall briefly discuss this extremely topical question – as an illustration and a further clarification of the problem of the law.

4. How do we deal with the Sabbath and Sunday today?

The biblical commandment on the Sabbath runs: 'Six days you shall labour and do all your work, but the seventh is a Sabbath to the Lord your God.'[30] The seventh day, dedicated to the creator God, is to be a breathing space for human beings and animals, and particularly for the poor and the weak. The Sabbath is observed nowadays in Jerusalem, very much more strictly than, say, in Tel Aviv: buses and other forms of public transport may not run, cafes and restaurants are shut, and there are no performances in cinemas and theatres.

Can we not understand how a Jewish woman like **Lea Fleischmann**, having first lived for a long time in the hectic atmosphere of modern Germany, of course took some time to get used to the Sabbath in Jerusalem but now sings the 'praise of the Sabbath'? 'The day of reflection, the day of the Lord, the day of the family.' What would it be like if such a day were observed all over the earth: 'Just think: one day in the week on which no automobiles were driven, no planes flew, no telephones rang, no television sets flickered, no machines droned. On one day of the week the air would not be polluted and the rivers would be less contaminated. Silence would prevail, and the soul could take its rest. On one day in the week we would use less energy and spare nature.'[31] A lovely dream, one can certainly say, but it is also worth thinking about and analysing more closely.

The vast majority even of non-Orthodox Jews today are not against but for the Sabbath, one of the oldest institutions of Jewish life, which is also meant to recall the exodus from Egypt. But there is also vigorous dispute in Judaism about what form the Sabbath should take, just as there are now disputes in Christianity over how to keep Sunday. And here, too, economic, political and religious issues are fused into an explosive mixture which can become dangerous in any society.

Beyond doubt the Christian **Sunday**[32] has a **different origin from the Jewish Sabbath**: as the 'first day of the week' in the Easter stories,[33] or the 'day of the Lord (Jesus)',[34] from a very early stage it was the day on which the community met regularly for the 'breaking of the bread'.[35] This 'Lord's Day' (with the 'Lord's Supper') – in Latin *dies dominica* and in the Romance languages *domenica, domingo, dimanche* – was certainly not understood and celebrated as a rest day or 'Christian Sabbath' in the first centuries. 'Sunday' or German 'Sonntag' (Latin *dies solis*) derives from pagan Roman tradition, in which from the first century before Christ the seven-day week and the names of the seven planets for the seven days of the week had become established. It was the Emperor Constantine who in 321 first declared the day of the sun (which was worshipped by many) to be a day without legal proceedings, replacing the day of Saturn (Samstag, Saturday), which was supposed to bring misfortune and therefore was the day on which many people did not work. Later emperors first prohibited servile tasks (*opera servilia*) on that day (also to enable slaves to go to church), and the Germanic kings were the first to ban any hard labour at all (as *opera servilia*). So from the Christian side the day of the Lord as a day on which no work is done is a relatively late phenomenon.

However, since in the course of the first millennium Sunday came to be associated with restrictions on work, the Christian **Sunday does in fact stand in the succession of the Jewish Sabbath,** that age-old weekly holiday which along with circumcision and food laws permanently shaped the image of the 'Jew' even in the ancient world. But this means that the fact that a weekly day of rest and a holiday also became established in the Christian world (and with the spread of Christianity then came to be observed all over the world) is due to the people of Israel and its celebration of the 'seventh day of the week', the 'Sabbath', as a day of rest dedicated to God – a blessing for humankind which can hardly be praised too much.

Christians of Jewish origin for a long time continued to celebrate both days together. A legal and liturgical Christian church order compiled in the fourth century ordains that the Sabbath and Sunday shall be celebrated as rest days: the Sabbath as the day of creation and the Lord's Day as the day of resurrection.[36] In the Eastern churches, from the fourth century onwards Saturday was generally celebrated with a service as the day of creation, and the West was criticized for fasting on this day: we read in the church fathers that the Sabbath and Sunday are like brother and sister.[37] In Christian (originally Jewish-Christian?) Ethiopia even now the Sabbath still has a place alongside Sunday. It follows from all this that in the age of a Jewish-Christian ecumene there would be no theological objections to a week with five working days and two rest days.

Although the **week** does not have an astronomical basis like the month and the year, it would equally stand as a humane ordering of time in our culture. Even political revolutions have been unable to change this. For regardless of whether the week was structured on the Jewish (Saturday), Christian (Sunday) or Muslim (Friday) day of rest, neither the French Revolution with its 'decade' (a ten-day rhythm) nor the Russian Revolution with its equally impracticable five-day week could make any headway against a day of rest from work which had a religious foundation. During the industrial revolution, Sunday, the day free of work, was a battleground for the workers' movement and its trade unions against the total utilitarianism of the industrial age: the **weekly day of rest as a criterion for a humane rhythm to life,** nowadays even defended in the name of a 'biorhythm'.

But the changed economic conditions of the 'post-industrial age' now represent a very much more serious **threat to both the Sabbath and Sunday.** How are Jews and Christians to react to this?

(*a*) We live in a time in which the sacred Jewish day of rest, like that of Christians, is under massive attack from economic and technological utilitarianism. A religious day of rest means even greater loss of profit and competitiveness in the face of machines which are more efficient and expensive machines yet not used to capacity, new methods of continuous production and the constant worldwide pressure of competition. Time is money; it must be calculated and earned: that is the economic understanding of time. Wouldn't it be consistent to sacrifice the Sabbath or Sunday to the technical pressures and economic necessities that there are supposed to be? Wouldn't it be consistent to exchange the Sabbath or Sunday successively for just any working day (with flexi-time holidays for all)? The answer is: as a Christian, in principle one must agree with believing Jews who are energetically resisting any attack on the Sabbath. We should **protect the common rest-day,** whether this is the Sabbath or Sunday.

Of course the Sabbath/Sunday was never 'profitable' in economic terms: it would have been more profitable to give servants and maids a day off each in rotation. But this common holiday was beneficial to human beings in many respects. And modern technological pressures and economic necessities always follow from our own value-judgments and decisions. Besides, we can make a paradoxical observation: the more time we have, gained by time-saving technologies, the less time we have. That is because the more expensive time becomes, the more we want to exploit it to the full. Therefore, despite immeasurable gains in time in all spheres, there is a growing lack of time, a pressure over deadlines about which everyone complains. The result is nervousness, stress, exhaustion. Is this exploitation of time 'round the clock' really profitable?

Human beings with their spiritual needs are now no more than maltreated cattle, even more than cogs in the process of production: before God they find their self-esteem and human value, as the Catholic exegete Josef Blank pointed out shortly before his all too premature death: 'We must note this humane and psychological understanding of time if we are to understand the significance of the day of rest properly.

This cannot be replaced at will by "leisure time for hobbies". The price for that might look something like this: now that the ecological balance is already been out of joint, in this way the human balance in our society would be severely shaken, with unforeseeable consequences. What would be lost here? The answer is quite simple: our time together would be lost. Shared time in our society, shared time in the family; and if we reflect further, we can see that all cultural and even sporting calendars rest on this presupposition of shared time.'[38] Indeed, without synchronized times we would have even more broken families, broken associations, anonymous societies.

(*b*) We live in a time of changed demands, reduced working hours and extended leisure. Is it worth treating the Sabbath (or Sunday) with so to speak Jewish Orthodox, Roman mediaeval or even Puritan Protestant legalism as an unbreakable tabu, a rigorous law, a cultural or religous monument? While the shared day of rest, if it is to be retained, should not just turn into a 'free day' or a lazy day, on the other hand it should not be a totally regulated day. Christians who attempt to go by Jesus' words and the practice of freedom can hardly quarrel with present-day Jews who argue against a finely-spun rabbinic casuistry over the Sabbath in favour of reasonable solutions which benefit human beings. Christians and Jews should not re-legalize the day of freedom from the pressures of work. They should not **let the shared day of rest**, whether this is Sabbath or Sunday, **become a burden.**

For if it is true that human beings are not there for machines, computer systems and production, it is also true, as we have seen, that human beings are not there for the Sabbath either. On the contrary, the Sabbath (and of course also Sunday) is there for human beings. The original social and humanitarian significance is thus once again brought into the centre: the day of rest, not as a burden and pressure, but as help and joy.

(*c*) Is there any solution at all in this dilemma between rigoristic mediaeval Orthodoxy and all too zealous modern adaptation? If there is, then it may lie in preserving the decisive features of the Sabbath (which is important for the religious identity of Judaism) and Sunday (which is not unimportant for the religious identity of Christianity): **standing back from everyday life** to gain a physical and spiritual breathing-space. On the one hand it is important to guard against complete randomness and chronological disorientation and to protect this day of rest, which has a religious foundation and is older than any state and its legislation, so that it survives into a new era of the world.

On the other hand, however, it is important not to overlook the new social conditions, which do call for a revival of the culture of holidays and a transformation of the day of rest and its worship, currently undergoing a crisis in both Judaism and Christianity. This is not to succumb to the modern trend nor to aim to attract more people into the synagogues (or the churches), but to seek the well-being of men and women (and in particular of families and all other communities), who need a **shared** day of rest and celebration, in the secular as well as in the religious sphere. So it is vitally important to stand back from everyday life, no matter whether the emphasis is more on rest from work (as in the Jewish tradition), communal worship (as in the Catholic tradition), or concern with the Word of God (as in the Protestant tradition). Ideally, rest from work, worship and the word of God form a unity.

If we look at the essentials of a day of rest and reflection which has a religious orientation, it is possible to justify the shifting of Sabbath worship to Friday evening or Sunday worship to Saturday evening (the celebration of the vigil = night watch was moved back to the eve of the feast as early as the early Middle Ages); conversely, some Jewish Reform communities have at least temporarily postponed the celebration of the Sabbath to Sunday. In the age of the 'five-day week', what seems to me to be more important than the precise date is this: there is as much need for a less boring, more lively and more spontaneous Sabbath as there is for a more interesting Sunday liturgy that is more positive towards men and women in a postmodern period in which the leisure industry, media and sport have become extraordinarily strong 'competition' for worship.[39]

Be this as it may: human beings as a production conveyor belt – all the year round, twenty-four hours a day, three hundred and sixty five days a year, and so on – cannot be the ideal for the future. Just a free day now and then is not enough for a meaningful life with some quality to it. Work is not the meaning of life. Nor, however, is leisure time, which in addition to leisure stress can also give rise to leisure frustration. Human beings urgently need focal points for communal life; collective interruptions in the hectic pace of modern life; a shared way of rising above pressures; oases of quiet, reflective pauses and room to breathe spiritually: legally protected 'days of rest from work and spiritual elevation' (as Article 140 of the Basic Law of the Federal German Republic puts it). People need a day of freedom for God, who is the ultimate depth, the ultimate meaning, of human life.

C. Jews, Muslims and the Future of the State of Israel

I. The Great Ideal

'Yes, we are strong enough to form a state, and, indeed, a model state. We possess all human and material resources necessary for the purpose.'[1] So wrote Theodor Herzl, the founder-father of the Jewish state, in 1896, in his programmatic work. And indeed, it will be decisive for the future of the state of Israel whether in the face of the notorious difficulties the humane intention which was so important for the founding of the state will be maintained and indeed will perhaps be realized again even better.

1. The state of the Jews – the signal for a paradigm shift

Despite all the clashes in more recent Jewish history, it is impossible to overlook the fact that towards the end of the twentieth century, after the fearful catastrophe of the Holocaust, the **resurgence of the state of Israel is the most important event** in Jewish history **since the destruction of Jerusalem and the Second Temple by the Romans in the year 70 CE.** It has taken almost 1900 years for it again to be possible for there to be a Jewish state in Palestine. I have recounted the history of the rise of this new state very briefly. What does it mean? How is this event to be interpreted in the context of our analysis of the religious situation of the time?

The resurgence of the state of the Jews is the unmistakable signal for an epoch-making paradigm shift in Judaism, in which once again everything is changing. For Judaism, too – after modern assimilation and modern antisemitism with the absolute nadir of the Holocaust – **the postmodern era has begun.** Of course, even now certain constants will remain for believing Jews: it is still a matter of the same **people** with the remembrance of the same **covenant** in connection with the same **land**.[2]

But out of the life-threatening crisis of the Holocaust a transition is now coming about, a shift into a completely **new entire constellation** of convictions, values, attitudes. There is a new macroparadigm.

- The centre of Jewish life is being shifted from Europe back into the 'promised land' of its beginnings.
- The people of Israel is again being given the possibility of organizing itself into a state and of political self-determination.
- The whole of Judaism, even in the Diaspora, is experiencing a new spiritual orientation.

A new spiritual orientation? Indeed, for Christians too there is no mistaking the fact that the resurrection of this people which was believed dead, in the form of their own state, has **finally shattered that anti-Jewish Christian theology and ideology** (which prevailed up until the Second Vatican Council) which saw the Jews as accursed for ever and condemned to dispersion (Ahasver – the 'eternal Jew'). No, the Jewish people has not been annihilated; the biblical promises of land have manifestly not been annulled. On the contrary, even non-Zionists must concede that the state of Israel has rescued a people condemned to final destruction in the Holocaust from its defencelessness, helplessness and despair. The state of Israel has restored its dignity, its self-esteem, its powers of resistance, its readiness to defend itself, its birthright. The old ugly stereotypes and insulting insinuations that the Jews were work-shy, cowardly and greedy have been stunningly refuted by the new state of Israel, which has been particularly successful in the spheres of agriculture and settlement policy (the *kibbutz* and *moshav* movements), sport and self-defence. The word 'Jew' no longer conjures up the ideal of the rabbi reflecting on the Torah but that of the Maccabaean fighter and modern pioneer. There is no doubt about it: a new world age has dawned for the people of the Jews.

But even more, cannot the rebirth of Israel also be regarded with some justification by believing Jews as a trace of the transcendent in this world-age, specifically as a **sign of the fidelity and grace of God**? How difficult it was for a long time for Jews to believe in a living and a just God! How difficult it was for a long time for Jewish parents to teach their own children that to be a Jew is a blessing and not a curse! And how much easier it is now, in the face of the imposing achievements of the state of Israel, to stress the positive side to being a Jew, for example in the spheres of education and health! So has not the belief in God and his promises for people and land, which has been so sorely tried through history, itself been confirmed in a glorious way? That is what many Jews think, above all believing Jews. And Christians – what do they think of the state of Israel?

2. Israel – a religious or a political entity?

First of all, by way of qualification, it should be noted that Jews are primarily responsible for the state of Israel – whether by identification or by criticism. Mindful of their somewhat inglorious attitude to Judaism, Christians should show a basic sympathy to the state of Israel, especially in view of the Holocaust. However, in the context of the Jewish-Christian dialogue the question inescapably arises: what should be the attitudes of Christians, as Christians, to this state and its policies? What should they think of this Israel which is a state of just over 4.5 million inhabitants (as opposed to the 100 million Arabs who surround it), and which has had to live with a constant sense of threat, if no longer from the anti-Judaism of the church, then now from the Arab world (for a long time supported by the Soviet bloc). An Israel which since its foundation has been a bone of contention among the superpowers and which even after four wars still lives a very uncertain existence, as the 1991 Gulf War once again showed to all the world? Is this Israel really a state like any other, whose 'existence' is to be judged not in 'religious' terms, but only in accordance with the 'universal principles of international law', as is still presupposed even by the 1985 Vatican document on Jewish-Christian relations,[3] so that for Christians the state of Israel (and its diplomatic recognition) would be a purely political question?

Not without justification, in Jewish-Christian dialogue the state of Israel is often made a shibboleth, a password and a watchword, a test as to whether one is really taking Jewish-Christian understanding seriously. However, a precise distinction needs to be made here.

First of all, there is no disputing the fact that constitutionally the modern state of Israel is not a religious but a **political entity**. The state of Israel itself does not seek to be a sacral, theocratic, indeed eschatological kingdom but a modern, worldly, secular, tolerant society which constitutionally and legally is organized in the form of a parliamentary multi-party democracy – the only one in the Near East, as is constantly stressed in Israel. The **right of the state of Israel to exist** – founded ultimately on the indisputably more than 3,000-year-old relationship of the Jewish people to this land, even in times of exile – must be recognized. Precisely as a free democratic state – if we leave aside the occupied territories – Israel too deserves **full diplomatic recognition**: above all from the Vatican, which has so often recognized and courted dictatorships. It also deserves unambiguous recognition from the Palestine Liberation Organization (PLO), the only power

which speaks for the great majority of Palestinians. For because the
PLO will not recognize Israel clearly and unequivocally, any peace in
the Near East and any positive political solution for its own people are
ruled out from the start.

A second point must also be noted: Israel is *de facto* **not simply the
state of the Jews**. First of all there are also **non-Jewish Israeli citizens**:
as compared with statistics which have often been tampered with,[4] we
must assume that already before the First World War around 600,000
Arabs were living alongside (at that time) 85,000 Jews in Palestine.[5]
Thus when the state of Israel was founded, right from the beginning it
also included numerous citizens belonging to other peoples (Arabs)
and religions (Muslims, Druze, Christians, even one or two Jewish
Christians). In 1989 – leaving aside the occupied territories – the
proportion of Muslims in the total population was 14% and that of
Christians 2%.

Conversely, it is equally a fact that **not all Jews are citizens of
the state of Israel**. As is well known, Judaism is greater and more
comprehensive than the Jewish state, and by no means always connected
with it. And despite all the affirmation of a secure existence for the
state of Israel, despite all the understanding of the history of Jewish
suffering which stands behind the foundation of the state, and despite
all the recognition also of the unique significance of the state of Israel
for contemporary Judaism, Judaism and Zionism may not simply be
identified. Strictly speaking, the state of Israel is not the state of Judaism
as a religion but the state of the Jews as the Jewish people. Moreover,
the majority of Jews still do not want to live in the state of Israel. There
always have been and always will be non-Zionist Jews. In other words,
while the ethnic-national aspect and the ethical-religious aspect cannot
be completely separated, the one may not be reduced to the other. So
the state of Israel and Judaism are in no way identical, but have an
indissoluble relationship to each other.

The answer to the question must therefore be: the present-day state of
Israel is a **political entity**, but by virtue of its whole tradition it also has
a **religious dimension**. Or, as was already stated ten years ago by the
Council of the Evangelical Church in Germany – in contrast to the
Vatican document of 1985 – the state of Israel, a 'political entity', at
the same time 'stands in the framework of the history of the chosen
people'.[6] We might reflect:
– Its very name 'Israel' (as opposed to say 'Palestine') betrays its origin
with the chosen patriarch Jacob, called Israel.

– The foundation document thus explicitly puts the new state in the biblical tradition of Judaism.

– For this very reason, this state also regards its task as being to guarantee and safeguard the existence of this people in the land of its fathers.

– So the constant in the continuity of the history of the chosen people is the fact that it is not the state but the 'land' that is the content of the promises of the Hebrew Bible, and political Zionism would be unthinkable had not many believers held firm to the promise of this land.

– Israel's official language is a modernized form of that of the Bible: Israel's history-writing and archaeology (in Israel almost a popular sport) follow its traces.

– The legal holiday is the Sabbath, the legal days of rest are the Jewish festivals, like Purim, Passover, Shavuot and Simḥat Torah.

– The Jewish food laws have to be observed in the army, state and public institutions (and in fact are also observed in most restaurants and tourist establishments).

– The dates of the old Hebrew calendar – reckoned from the year of creation – appear on all official documents (the year 5751/52 corresponds to the year 1991).

However, a distinction must be made between the historical and the religious perspectives, and for a long time not all those who affirm the former have also recognized the latter. It is certainly an unmistakable **historical fact** that Judaism lives on as a people: that is indisputably the case for believers and non-believers. But it is by no means a generally shared **conviction of faith** that the particular history of God with this people is continuing, though at the same time this faith is evidently ineradicable. It is also true from the perspective of believing Christians, as we saw, that the **covenant** of God with his people is manifestly not annulled but has endured. God's **people** is again living in the **land** of the original promise. Accordingly, for Jews and Christians the state of the Jews which has come into being again is a real symbol to indicate that **God** is alive and active. For believing Jews, there can be no purely secular world history, any more than there can be for believing Christians. How then? It is the hidden God himself who, for believers, permeates from within the history of the whole world and quite specifically also the history of Israel.

The state of the Jews which has come into being again, as a real symbol of God's activity: is that also still true of the state of Israel half a century after its foundation? Here concerns for the future begin.

3. Religious pluralism or state religion in the Jewish state?

Since the foundation of the state, indeed since the beginning of Zionist immigration, **religion has been a central problem.**

It is **first** a central problem in Israel's relationship to Muslims and Christians. And to this degree the social and legal religious form of the state is a disputed question between Jews and non-Jews to which understanding ecumenical dialogue needs to be devoted. Here it must be acknowledged that the state of Israel guarantees free access to all the holy places of the different religions and the right of worship there, and punishes any violation or desecration with heavy penalties (Law on the Protection of the Holy Places, 1967). But the granting of equal civil rights to the Muslim and Christian inhabitants of the state of the Jews is an urgent question.

Secondly, religion is a central problem for the Jews themselves, in particular in relations between Israelis. Orthodox (and Hasidic) Jews had already immigrated into Palestine in the nineteenth century, i.e. already before the start of the new Zionist immigration at the beginning of the twentieth century, which brought an overwhelming majority of socialist, secular and in part even explicitly anti-religious Jews to Palestine. So in terms of religious policy, from the beginning Orthodoxy (which was largely Hasidic) had a monopoly in legal religion which, coupled with the internal autonomy given to ethnic groups in the Turkish empire, had effects in a great variety of legal spheres. If Zionism wanted to win over the Orthodox, it had to take note of this. Moreover, already at an early stage there was a religious Zionist movement (the Mizrachi) which combined the Zionist work of settlement with prophetic and messianic hopes, and after the First World War gained increasing influence through its own workers' wing and its own *kibbutz* movement. The personal faith of the middle-class Jews who then immigrated in the 1920s and 1930s was in any case mostly Orthodox, and they could not imagine a new Israel without the traditional Jewish values and practices. The religious Jews had their recognized head in the Ashkenasy Chief Rabbi; as long as this was Abraham Isaac Kook, who died in 1935 and characteristically had a very tolerant attitude towards the non-religious, the disputes within Judaism were kept within bounds.

Alongside the modern trend to religious pluralism, which regarded Reform and Conservative Judaism as true alternatives to Orthodoxy on the one hand and secularism on the other, there was also a marked counter-trend towards Orthodoxy which, though numerically small, had a key position in both religion and politics. The Orthodox Jews are blatantly making efforts to develop their institutional power base with all possible means, not only in order to prevent a total secularization of the new Jewish community but also to bring religious practice to secularized Jews through mission. This has led to constant conflicts, especially since a parliamentary system was established with the founding of the state.

Should we not remember here the words of the visionary founder of the state? Theodor Herzl asked in his programmatic work: 'Shall we end by having a theocracy?', and gave a clear 'No!' to this question. 'Shall we end by having a theocracy? No indeed. Faith unites us, knowledge gives us freedom. We shall therefore prevent any theocratic tendencies from coming to the fore on the part of our priesthood. We shall keep our priests within the confines of their temples, in the same way as we shall keep our professional army within the confines of their barracks. Army and priesthood shall receive honours high as their valuable functions deserve. But they must not interfere in the administration of the State, which confers distinction upon them, else they will conjure up difficulties without and within.'[7] Theodor Herzl was to be proved right – on this question too.

For how much the clergy in particular has to say in the new state of Israel, alongside the army which is also becoming increasingly more influential, became evident in the question of the halakhah of the Jewish **religious law**. We have discussed that in detail. To touch on the theme of 'law' is to touch on a problem which is explosive in both its religious and its political aspects. As we saw, the various trends within Judaism divide, indeed fight over it. And as far as Israel is concerned, this means that nowadays in Israel real '**cultural struggles**' are fought, for or against the 'law', which involve not only verbal aggressiveness and political manoeuvring but also acts of violence.[8]

The Orthodox Rabbi David Hartman has given a memorable description of these tensions within Judaism in Israel: 'Jews from everywhere have come home. No longer does one meet one's people in history through praying for the Ingathering of the Exiles. Yet only in the home to which we have returned do we find that we are actually so divided. Here we may even wonder, have we really been a family? The slogan We Are One sounds questionable when Jew meets Jew and each of us wonders if we can understand each other. The most serious question in Israel is, Could the chronic dissension turn into civil war? The polarization between religious and secular is increasing. In the newspapers, the big issues are often not security, but whether the cable car will run on the Sabbath in Haifa or whether a Petah Tikvah cinema will show a film this Friday night. The chief rabbi of the town, locked

in jail for leading a violent illegal demonstration against the opening
of that cinema, claims to be above the law of the state because he is
speaking in the name of God. Four hundred policemen could not spend
the Sabbath with their children because they were trying to prevent
Jews from fighting with one another. Anger, cyncism, and intense
polarization are created over religious issues between brothers who
have come home after praying so long for the Ingathering of the Exiles.'[9]

But why this constant escalation, which involves Israeli society in
constant tensions? The reason is that religious ultra-Orthodoxy in
Israel with increasing emphasis keeps calling for the complete subjection
of both public and private life to the norms of the halakhah; and it has
no small success to show here. In its claim to totality, such Orthodoxy
now recognizes no division between private and public, individual and
society: **all of human life** stands under God's will as Orthodoxy
understands it.

Here we must not forget that already at the founding of the state of
Israel, with its secular-pluralist orientation, the predominant authority
of Orthodoxy, for which the foundations had already been laid before
and during the Zionist immigration, secured from the first Prime
Minister David Ben-Gurion (a socialist!) gained **political concessions
in the religious sphere for the Orthodox religious parties.** The assurances of 19 June 1947 related to sabbath and food laws, and also to
marriage and divorce, which can only be performed by rabbis – and
Orthodox rabbis at that – under the supervision of the Chief Rabbinate.
This has existed since the mandate and is composed of rabbis and party
politicians; thus – to the offence of many – the elected Chief Rabbis
are the supreme religious arbiters in Israel. For in Israel judicial power
is divided, and it is not the state courts but the religious courts which
are responsible for marital law (i.e. in cases of marriage and divorce).
Even the Supreme Court can only assign a specific case to a religious
court for dealing with; it cannot make a decision itself.

In 1947/48 the Orthodox parties were still by no means powerful,
and even after more than forty years they make up no more than 15%
of the electorate. However, given the balance of power in the Israeli
parliament between the Labour Party and the conservative Likud block,
this is enough to tip the scales. So it is because of the influence of these
Orthodox groups that from the beginning there has been **neither civil
marriage nor civil divorce in the state of Israel** – as was formerly also
the case in the authoritarian Catholic states (Italy, Spain, Portugal,
Ireland, Latin America) – on the basis of the Jewish religious laws
imposed on the Israeli state. Moreover, with the foundation of the

state, **halakhic regulations** *de facto* became state law in a whole series of other instances – as is also the case with the *shari'a* in some Islamic countries. Religious pluralism or a single state religion – those are the alternatives here. So a basic question for the state of Israel is:

4. Who is a Jew?

What is under debate here is not, say, just the theoretical definition of Jewish identity, which, as we saw, had to take into account ethnic as well as religous components. What is being debated for the future is the quite practical **question of Israeli citizenship**, which according to the 'Law of Return' passed immediately after the foundation of the state is automatically granted to **all Jews**. Specifically the dispute breaks out over the question, 'What about those who have been converted, not to Orthodox Judaism, but to Conservative and Reform Judaism? Are such converts really, and legally, Jews?' As late as 1987 the then ultra-Orthodox Minister of the Interior decided the question firmly in the negative and laid down the strict conditions for conversion according to the precepts of the halakhah. When the Israeli Supreme Court ruled against this, the minister chose to resign rather than to abandon his religious conviction and obey the legal ordinance.

Since the national conservative Likud government under Menachem Begin (1977), **religious Orthodoxy** – both the party and the equally Orthodox Chief Rabbinate – has considerably stepped up pressure on legislation in the country and imposed far-reaching restrictions: on hotels, on public transport, on the airline El Al, and on many sports organizations. The prohibitions and commands relate above all to eating customs and the observance of the sabbath. As we heard, the vast majority of Israelis want to retain this day of rest, which has been holy from time immemorial, in the face of all modern pressures – but not necessarily in the manner of the Orthodox, who declare the doing of thirty-nine kinds of work on the sabbath tabu, including walking more than two thousand paces. Many Jews also recite the Shema Israel and observe particular Jewish customs, not because they are convinced by the divine commandment but because they want to express their Jewish otherness and authenticity. But the influence of Orthodoxy is growing, and after the Labour Party lost power, even the Socialist leader Shimon Peres (a former Prime Minister and Foreign Minister) though it important to take private instruction in the teachings of Torah and Talmud...

So to what Judaism will the future belong? Perhaps to the Orthodox, to the nationalists, even to the military? **Writers** have recently been issuing warnings. There is certainly no lack of literature of all kinds which depicts the life of Jews in the state of Israel positively, indeed often in romantic colours, and celebrates it. Whereas from the War of Independence to the late 1950s Israeli literature, both prose and poetry, had a marked ideological and social concern, from the 1960s it concentrated more on the identity and the world of the individual. But since the 1980s there has been another alarming literary genre: plays by Israelis which are critiques of society, not meant as destructive criticism but as a warning against wrong directions. There is the fear of a fundamentalist military state. Hence the musical satire *The Last Secular Jews* of 1987, critical of Orthodoxy, which parodied on the stage the Israel of the future as a Jewish theocracy, and therefore promptly ran into difficulties with the censors. Similarly, there was a warning against false patriotism in a play like *The Patriot* in 1986, in which an Israeli tries to emigrate from Israel back to the USA. Or there was the warning against militarism in *Ephraim Returns to the Army* (1986), which depicts the effects of the occupation of the West Bank on the young Israeli soldiers. Finally, already before the Intifada, *The Palestinian Woman* (1985) and *The Jerusalem Syndrome* (1987) took the Israeli-Palestinian conflict as their theme and pulled no punches – both are plays by Joshua Sobol, the Israeli playwright whose works are most frequently staged.

Here too the question is unavoidable: will the future belong to escapism from modernity into the Orthodox Middle Ages – in Judaism and Christianity? Many Jews (and Christians) doubt it, and suffer with the *Tragedy of Zionism*, as it has been described, for example, by the Canadian Jew Bernard Avishai:[10] Avishai lived for a long time in Israel and constantly returns there. I have already gone sufficiently into the controversies within Judaism over the halakhah, the religious law, to be able to say that a basic consensus is possible over the fundamental constants of 'Israel as God's people and land', but that in the face of these basic constants which are fundamental to being a Jew, the question of the practice of the halakhah, which arose later, must be secondary.[11]

So we can ask: what will be the positive solution if in all probability neither complete secularization nor renewed sacralization wins the day? Perhaps a more consistent separation of synagogue and state? Will there possibly one day be a state which is neutral towards religion as a guarantee of religious freedom (including that of Arab, Muslim or Christian citizens) and thus of religious peace? But given the present tensions and the deep resentment on the part of the Sephardic and Eastern Jews (who now make up around two-thirds of the population) of the largely Ashkenasy Israeli establishment (who come from Europe), who knows? Here are tensions which any day could lead to a crucial test.

In particular in present conditions, the old controversy takes on new force. Who is a Jew anyway? First of all, it must be stated as a matter of principle that the state of Israel can define who is a citizen of the state of Israel, but cannot define who is or is not a Jew – Jews also say that. Non-Jews (Muslims and Christians) can also be citizens of Israel and, conversely, non-citizens of Israel can be Jews. So the definition of who is a Jew has to be made, not in the light of contemporary legislation, but **in the light of the great Jewish tradition, though it needs to be reflected on again**. Here, however, once more a twofold perspective has to be distinguished.

- In the **ethnic** sense (belonging to the Jewish people), a Jew is any child of a Jewish mother or – as Reform Judaism now rightly adds – a Jewish father. So in this sense anyone is a Jew who by descent is a member of the Jewish community of fate – whether believer or non-believer, whether a member of a synagogue or not, voluntarily or involuntarily.
- In the **religious** sense (belonging to the Jewish religion) a Jew is anyone who shares the faith in the one God of Abraham, Isaac and Jacob, in the election of the people and the promise of the land: a Jew in this sense is anyone who by faith belongs to the Jewish community of faith – whether in connection with a synagogue or not, whether Orthodox, Conservative or Reform, whether from birth or through conversion.

Our analysis in Part One indicated that the decisive and central element in Jewish faith over three thousand years is the covenant, God's relationship to his people – through all the paradigm shifts and epochs – which has a reference to a particular land. The **modern crisis** of Judaism is that Judaism in the ethnic sense and Judaism in the religious sense no longer *a priori* correspond: formerly, a Jew by origin was also a Jew by faith. And the **postmodern possibility** for Judaism is that being a Jew in both the ethnic sense and the religious sense can be rediscovered by a new future-orientated reflection on the Jewish tradition, on God's covenant and God's ethical commandments, which are not just identical with the halakhic system that was first fully developed in the Jewish Middle Ages and has largely survived into modern times.

But after this description of who is a Jew there is a further fateful question: the question of the limits, not of the people, but of the land.

II. The Tragic Conflict

Here again I have reached an extraordinarily sensitive point in my account. Just as many Roman Catholics immediately search any book on the church for the passage on the pope, and then either stop reading or continue, so in a book on Judaism many Jews first of all look at the chapter on the state of Israel and its **frontiers**. Is the author 'for us' or 'against us'? No matter how positively one may write on the Catholic church or Judaism, if one has a different view from the reader on this one point, one is quite often pigeon-holed or even written off.

And yet I think that at this point too I am obliged to intellectual honesty, to fairness on all sides, and to doing the greatest possible justice. The very history of the origin of the state of Israel which I described at length in Part Two compels me to this approach, and since I have reported time and again and at length the Christian failure towards Jews over the course of the long history of the church up to the Holocaust, so with similar openness and honesty I shall now report on Israeli failure towards the Arabs or Palestinians. I shall do this, not to level out all the failure, or to compare two things which bear no comparison, or to play off Christian failure towards Jews against Jewish failure towards Arabs, but inspired by the passionate wish that there may be that peace between Israelis and Palestinians which is also desired by the majority of Israelis, along with an understanding between Jews, Christians and Muslims. After the Gulf War this is more urgent than ever. And as a study by the Centre for Strategic Studies at Tel Aviv University has recently shown, after the Gulf War now 58% of Israelis (as opposed to 50% last year and only 46% five years ago) are in favour of returning the occupied territories.[1] So direct surveys produce a different picture from that disseminated by the present government. I would like to begin at this point, and follow the desires of this great majority of Israelis.[2]

1. The dispute of two peoples over a land – and no insight?

The recognition remains that for Jews, and especially for Israelis, 'people' and 'land' fundamentally belong together. But since the Jewish resettlement of this land, and even more since the foundation of a Jewish state, it has become abundantly clear that now **two peoples** are confronting each other, the Jewish and the Arab-Palestinian peoples – both of which have an **awareness**, deeply rooted for three thousand years or over the past thousand years, that **this land legitimately belongs to them** and them alone. Here the Jews refer above all to the empire of David and Solomon after the year 1000 BCE, and the Palestinians to the conquest of the land by the Arabs in 636 CE. To this degree, the question which the British historian James Parkes chose as the title of his 'History of the Palestinian People', *Whose Land?*, is a justified one.[3]

There were political possibilities of avoiding a life-and-death struggle between these two peoples.[4] As early as 1947/48, each of the two parties had in hand the founding of its own state, a Jewish state and an Arab state, committed to mutual recognition and political and economic co-operation. At that time it was above all **the Arabs who rejected the foundation of their own state** – and here they unintentionally fell in with the plans of Ben-Gurion – inspired by the deceptive hope that they could again destroy the supposedly weak Jewish state soon after its foundation. An unintended side-effect of the war then was the mass flight (and indeed the expulsion) of many hundreds of thousands of Palestinians from their ancestral territories, born of anxiety and bitter struggles.[5] However, in view of the most recent historical research, can we now say without qualification that the Arabs bear the main responsibility for the first two decades of the conflict? Is it solely their fault that in this space of time there were three wars instead of peace? At all events, there are reasons for the foundation in 1964 of the Palestine Liberation Organization (PLO), an organization which since 1969 has been under the leadership of Yassir Arafat's Al Fatah liberation movement.

One thing is certain: **after the Six Days War** in 1967 the scenario changed decisively. And no one in Israel drew attention so early and so resolutely to the dangerous development which was afoot here than that famous Jewish scholar who forty years earlier had settled in Israel as a convinced Zionist because he had had enough of the lordship of the Goyim over the Jewish people. He fought in the War of Independence, and down to most recent times has spoken out increasingly critically because he longs for another Israel, a peace-loving Israel which is respected by all sides. I mean, of course, the scientist and scholar of Judaism, **Yeshayahu Leibowitz**, Professor at the Hebrew University of Jerusalem, who is already very well known to us. He states soberly: 'The Six Days War was a historical catastrophe for the state of Israel.'[6] Why? Because since then **Israel** has clearly borne **the main responsibility for the absence of peace** in the Near East: 'In fact we are the ones who are not ready to negotiate and share. Israel did not want peace in the past, nor does it want peace today. It is interested only in maintaining its rule over the occupied territories... But in the last resort our stubbornness then led to the Yom Kippur War.'[7]

The renewed turbulent development of the state of Israel in its second phase makes the prospects for the future seem gloomier.[8] In 1974 the PLO was recognized by the Arab powers as the sole legitimate representative of the Palestinian people: it is not a full member of the Arab League, but has observer status at the United Nations; since it was driven out of Lebanon in 1982, its base has been in Tunis. However, also in the view of many Israelis who are critical of the regime, the occupation of Palestinian territories is having increasingly **devastating effects** on Israel's politics, economy, army and international reputation. This has caused not a few Israelis (including some Soviet Jewish immigrants) to emigrate again. And it is attacked by Yeshayahu Leibowitz with almost prophetic remorselessness. If we follow him, what was the price paid for the lasting possession of the Arab territories?
– Establishing and maintaining a **rule of force over the Palestinian people**. In the first two decades of the state of Israel one could 'hope that the state would become the arena in which the decisive Jewish struggles could be dealt with; but since 1967 it has been decided that Israel represents a means of rule by force'.[9]
– A **denial of the right** of the Palestinian people **to exist**. The slogan 'There is no Palestinian people', proclaimed above all by Golda Meir (Foreign Minister 1956-1965, Prime Minister 1969-1974)[10] to the Knesset, prompts the question: 'Are there not enough historians, sociologists and other intellectuals – throughout the world and even in Israel – who dispute the existence of a Jewish people? At any rate we know well enough what the slogan "There is no Palestinian people" means – genocide! Not in the sense of a physical annihilation of the Palestinian people but in the sense of the annihilation of a national and/ or political unity.'[11]
– **Domination by the Israeli secret service**. As early as 1967 it could be foreseen that 'the Secret Service, the Shin Bet (the Israeli security service) and the secret police will become the central institutions of the state of Israel. If the system of Jewish rule by force over another people is to be maintained, then there is no other choice than to make the Shin Bet the centre of political reality.'[12]
– **Misuse of the army**: 'An eighteen-year-old who is conscripted into the army today is not conscripted to defend the state of Israel but is sent into the Arab towns and villages to intimidate the population there. The more sensitive among young people sense that very clearly.'[13]
– **Loss of international respect**: 'Nowadays the world has no respect

Palestine under Changing Rule

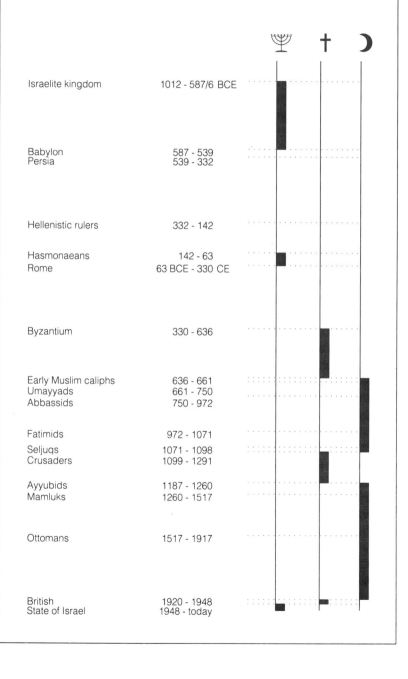

Israelite kingdom	1012 - 587/6 BCE			
Babylon	587 - 539			
Persia	539 - 332			
Hellenistic rulers	332 - 142			
Hasmonaeans	142 - 63			
Rome	63 BCE - 330 CE			
Byzantium	330 - 636			
Early Muslim caliphs	636 - 661			
Umayyads	661 - 750			
Abbassids	750 - 972			
Fatimids	972 - 1071			
Seljuqs	1071 - 1098			
Crusaders	1099 - 1291			
Ayyubids	1187 - 1260			
Mamluks	1260 - 1517			
Ottomans	1517 - 1917			
British	1920 - 1948			
State of Israel	1948 - today			

and esteem, not to mention honest sympathy, for the state of Israel, as was customary in widespread circles after the foundation of the state.'[14] – Loss of internal credibility: 'It is even more decisive that the state of Israel itself is becoming increasingly alien to most Jews – and by no means the worst among them – because in its present condition the state is really no laurel wreath for the Jewish people... The state of Israel is increasingly losing its significance for the existential problems of the Jewish people and of Judaism.'[15]

Voices like that of Leibowitz – an admirer of Maimonides and a great Israeli, even to those who do not share his views – show that specifically within Israel, too, the situation is felt to be intolerable. The much-celebrated economic boom in the occupied territories (gross national product, electrification, foreign trade, standard of living) cannot disguise the fact. And many Israelis also bewail the loss of the original Zionist ideals, to be replaced by unrestrained neo-capitalism and an economy with a strong focus on armaments, which uses the Palestinians above all as a cheap labour force for building, agriculture, and the service industries. I have to confess that this disastrous development in the state of Israel has changed my own political attitude to its official policy – for all the sympathy which remains: I have moved from an almost unqualified endorsement of the policy of the Israeli government of the time to a critical attitude which combines the unconditional recognition of the right of Israel to exist with a serious consideration of the possibility of the Palestinians becoming a nation, with a national right to self-determination. But what does the Israeli population feel about this situation, which is increasingly coming to a head?

2. Hanging on – withdrawing – repressing?

Israeli society is deeply polarized over the decisive question of relations with the Palestinians. We have heard that more than half of present-day Israelis would be ready to give up the occupied territories again. But according to the results of the last Knesset election, around half the Israeli population, represented by Likud and the religious parties, evidently saw nothing reprehensible in the violence of the policy of occupation. On military or religious grounds they stuck to the **three** 'no's: 'No to conversations with the PLO; no to withdrawal to the 1967 frontiers; no to the Palestinian state.' **'Hang on, sit it out, act tactically'** – right down to the most recent negotiations with the American Secretary of State James Baker, that has been the basic attitude, which seeks to combine constant obstruction ('the Arabs are to blame for everything') with the appearance of friendly co-operation ('we do not rule out any possibility'): waiting to see who has the greater stamina.

Small parties or movements to the left of the political spectrum are clearly and openly for peace on this question ('Peace Now', 'Mapam', 'Ratz') and that cannot be had without withdrawal from the occupied territories. Their slogan, 'Land for Peace', was happily also taken up after the Gulf War by the American President George Bush – as it had been earlier by the USSR and the EC.

But why, one asks, is a moderate group, representing between 30% and 40% of the electorate, and drawn above all from the Social Democrat spectrum of the parties, so anxious and depressed about the present situation? Why does it not take some decisive action to change things? **'Don't look too closely'** is the attitude of the undecided in the centre, most of whom have virtually no direct links with the Palestinians. According to the investigations of Stanley Cohen, Professor of Criminology at the Hebrew University,[16] these passive voters are recruited above all from the liberal descendants of European Jews, all of whom represent a 'rational, respectable Zionism with a conscience'. Although there is no way in which they can be unaware of the cruel facts of the Israeli occupation policy towards the Palestinians, they will not accept reality as it is. Why not? Because some information is simply 'filtered out'. Threatening information falls 'into the black holes of consciousness' or is so transformed that it becomes interchangeable. Hence the self-deception and the 'vitally necessary lies', without which the world of their own ideals woud collapse. According to Cohen, the more recent history of Judaism is also a factor. Many Israelis have found it difficult to see themselves as aggressors rather than victims, because they live by the conviction that the Jewish state is in any case morally in the right because of the Holocaust. Acts of injustice by their own country, committed by their own army, are therefore automatically restructured: the army endured intolerable provocation, or these are isolated cases, for example involving Sephardic Jews who immigrated from Arab territories... Cohen's account suggests that to a large extent many Israelis are repressing the real problems.

The underlying problem is: may the Holocaust be used to justify a more than problematical policy? Here, inconvenient Jewish voices, which nevertheless need to be taken very seriously, warn that the **Holocaust trauma of the survivors** must **not** become the **Holocaust syndrome of those born later**, who now project all evil on to the Arabs in general

and the Palestinians in particular. Here are just two voices, which emphasize two important aspects of the use of the Holocaust as an instrument:
– The American Jewish theologian Marc H.Ellis has pointed out that present-day post-Holocaust Judaism in Israel, with its military strength, should not be compared with weak European pre-Holocaust Judaism. Rather, one day, in a fundamentally changed world-political situation, the state of Israel would have to fear a Holocaust if it continues its present policy. The end of the state of Israel would be fearful, but no matter what Jewish Holocaust theologians say about it, it would not be the end of the Jewish people.[17] In fact, the majority of Jews still live outside Israel, and in a significantly large number of countries they have absolutely equal rights, are in no danger and are respected: a minority, like many other minorities, may sometimes be attacked, but at the same time it is sufficiently protected by a highly-developed political culture which is concerned to look after minorities.[18]
– The Israeli politician, scientist and contemporary historian Professor Michael Wolffsohn has made it clear how in different conditions the past which influences the Israeli present holds for both Jews and Arabs. For the Jews, the Holocaust syndrome is by no means limited to Germany. Certainly Germany symbolized the Holocaust, but this in turn was a 'benchmark for the past which is at work in Israel's present'. Here, he argues, we have as it were the 'filter' through which and with which those involved see their environment. Here, on each occasion, the Holocaust syndrome also functions as a 'political argument': 'Thus, for example, the PLO is often identified with National Socialism, as was Nasser, who in 1956 and 1967 was supposed to have wanted a new Holocaust, or even did want it. The past which influences the present is additionally reinforced by the present.'[19]

And what about the Palestinians? Around 850,000 Palestinians had fled or been expelled from their ancestral territories as a result of the 1948 war and were forbidden to return. To them, the land of Israel seems like a 'crusader state' intent on plundering land. As Wolffsohn warns, the Holocaust trauma can also appear among those who have been despised, expelled, persecuted by the Israelis, but this time directed against the Israelis: 'For the Arabs living in and around Palestine, the events of 1947/1948 are certainly also a kind of Holocaust trauma, the long-term effects of which are politically significant. The Beirut massacre of 16/17 September 1982 might also take on this role. In the political psychology of the Palestinian Arabs, Dir Yassin and the mass flight (others say expulsion) of Palestinian Arabs in 1948/49, 1967 and 1982 are certainly on the same level as Auschwitz is for the Jewish Israelis.' Of course we must make historical distinctions here, and Wolffsohn does so. But he is not concerned 'with the comparability of the actual dimension, the distinction between defenceless concentration-camp inmates and civilians, at least some of whom are armed'. He is not concerned 'with the "objectively historical truth" (is there such a thing?) so much as with the truth of history as it is felt collectively and subjectively'.[20] And should not those who have been expelled be able to understand above all those who have also been expelled, those who today above all have to lament the fragmentary remains of their former possessions?

There is no mistaking the fact that the Palestinians, and especially their leader Arafat (incredibly tenacious in surviving all crises, but at the same time not very trustworthy in his promises and alliances), have played a considerable part in causing the absence of peace in the Near East. But the Palestinians are permanently on the defensive, especially in the face of the strategic activity over settlements in the occupied territories. There is certainly a need to reflect on the long-term effects of these settlements, which Michael Wolffsohn describes like this: 'The efforts to "Judaize" the West Bank must paradoxically lead to the "de-Judaizing" of the Jewish state, to watering down its Jewish substance or even dissolving it altogether. Unintentionally, the super-hawks are creating the dream goal of the super-doves: the **bi-national**, i.e. Jewish-Arab, state – instead of a community which is determined purely by Jews. Only one **alternative** would be conceivable: the **abolition of democracy**.'[21] This brings us to the decisive point.

3. A democratic society or a national security state?

In view of this difficult situation, it is to the credit of the Israeli nation in the land of the prophets that nevertheless many of its citizens have the courage to make constructive criticisms. People have virtually stopped talking of Israel as a moral Jewish 'model state'. Critical Israelis sometimes observe, not without irony, that the state of Israel is a Western democracy the majority of whose population is agnostic, with a partly theocratic legislation and a totalitarian policy of occupation.

With greater historical accuracy, on the basis of the analysis in Parts One and Two above it has to be said that the situation in the state of Isarel is so contradictory and prone to conflict because different paradigms coexist in it, **elements of different epoch-making paradigms:**

- The Davidic paradigm of the kingdom (P II) is present through national claims to territory, biblically-based frontiers and Jerusalem as a capital.
- The post-exilic paradigm (P III) is alive through an independent religious judiciary.
- The mediaeval rabbinic paradigm (P IV) lives on through the decisive influence of the Chief Rabbinate on private and family law.
- The paradigm of modernity (P V) makes its mark through modern parliamentarianism, modern administration, the army, the police, science and the trade unions.

However, the great question is: which elements will finally win through? Let us focus once again the question of the future of the state of Israel.
– In the end will both private and public life be subjected to the religious law: a fundamentalist state with the halakhah as a universally valid norm?
– Or will there be a complete secularization of state and society: a pluralistic state and a liberal and social democracy with a Western stamp as a model?
– Or in time will there even be a political and militaristic dictatorship, given the strong Arab opposition in the country itself (one example of this is the 'state of emergency' with a weeks-long curfew for 1.7 million people in the occupied territories during the Gulf War of 1991): a fascist-militaristic system barely restrained by democracy – perhaps even a fundamentalist system – with apartheid between Jews and Arabs?

It is worth noting that according to opinion polls a tendency towards democracy and tolerance ranks higher among non-religious citizens than among religious traditionalists. The **un-democratic developments** in Israel are in fact so numerous today that they can no longer be kept secret out of concern for the state of the Jews. Despite the obfuscating Israeli terminology (only the others are 'murderers') and the official whitewashing (in the end everything is eventually just 'prevention of terrorism'), in America in particular an increasing number of journals (including the otherwise pro-Israeli *New York Times*) are publishing critical articles on the situation in Israel; however, in Israel most recently even the previously liberal *Jerusalem Post* has been bought up by conservative groups: this led to the walk-out of a large part of the editorial staff with the result that this paper, too, has fallen in with the

official line of the present-day conservative religious government. Here are some facts:
– Since 1985 more Jews have been leaving their state than entering it (only the forced Soviet mass immigration has now changed the figures).
– Even those Arabs who since the foundation of the state have formally been citizens of Israel with equal rights (at any rate amounting to more than 700,000) see themselves being increasingly marginalized and isolated by the policy of their government; they have recently been identifying themselves with the Palestinians in revolt.
– Three small reactionary groupings of religious Orthodoxy decide upon the two major parties, the Labour Party and the Likud block (there is no middle-class liberal party between the right-wing party and the Labour Party) and thus on the fate of the state of Israel. One of them (Agudat Israel = Israel Union) is even financed by the Lubavich rabbi in New York: he has never been in Israel, though many Israeli politicians, even some who are in no way Orthodox, make pilgrimages to him. All these groups receive payment for their collaboration in the form of government posts, more money for Torah schools and halakhic concessions.
– As time goes on, radical right-wing Israeli politicians are already finding a growing following among the young, who already seem to be taking Israeli military control over all Palestine for granted; according to surveys many are prepared to sacrifice democracy for the ideological and political unity of the country. For example, the aggressive Zionist New York rabbi Meir Kahane, founder of the Jewish Defense League, who lived in Israel from 1971, was even a Knesset delegate from 1984 and finally had to leave the land of Israel. He was abhorred by many Israelis as a 'Jewish Nazi' because of his racist ideas and his proposals to deport all Arabs from Israel; Kahane's assassination in New York in November 1990 has meanwhile been a warning signal that those who sow violence also reap violence.[22]
– To the dismay of many Israelis, one of the champions of the ideology of deportation was ostentatiously rewarded with a ministerial post during the Gulf War.

At all events, the devastating consequences of the policy of occupation, including the moral consequences, are becoming increasingly clear to many Israelis. And as one who has so openly attacked the silence of Pius XII and the German bishops over the Jewish question, I may not keep silent about what Israelis are doing over the Palestinian question – though that would be much more convenient.

4. A danger for human rights and peace

An increasing number of Israeli Arabs and also 'Jews of Conscience' (as they call themselves in Israel[23]) are demanding extensive investigations of racial discrimination and general **abuses of human rights**, of the cruel practices of the military regime and the armed groups of extremist settlers (who in contrast to other Israelis do not need an arms permit), and also of censorship and above all of the feared state police (Shin Bet). According to credible reports their methods go so far as introducing electrodes into sexual organs.[24] The mere suspicion of the military commander is enough for the internment of Palestinians. So people are asking: does the national end justify the terrorist means? Does terrorism, used for reasons of state, become heroism?

The situation in the occupied territories is oppressive: there are so many Jewish doctors who do not heal Palestinians; lawyers who do not help; judges who do not administer justice; defence forces which murder and torture; the persecuted who now have become the persecutors... Here there really is an Israeli-Palestinian tragedy. And probably no one has described it more impressively than the Israeli writer and radio producer **David Grossmann**, who has been awarded various prizes. He has visited refugee camps, Arab settlements, Israeli judicial hearings and factories employing Palestinians at minimal wages and interviewed the Israeli military, and put all this down in a documentary report written in Hebrew which has become a best-seller in Israel.[25] Here are crimes against humanity which for the most part remain unpunished because of the practice of the Israeli military courts and which are reported on the Israeli media only in official language which trivializes them. And the friends of Israel are particularly depressed by the fact that all this is happening in a state which was set up as a result of the nationalism and racism of the Nazi regime. Here is a new kind of antisemitism: of Semites against Semites (Palestinians). As though international law did not apply to the Palestinian people!

These negative developments in internal policy are matched by an all-encompassing **military aggressiveness** externally. Israel has found sympathy for its two preventive wars, and when the Iraqi despot Saddam fired missiles at Israel during the 1991 Gulf War, sympathies for the Jewish state were still unbroken all over the world. At that time Israel's government was well advised to refrain from its own military intervention (even if only on political and tactical grounds), but to leave the reaction above all to the allied troops (who were eventually sucessful).

But none of this can disguise the numerous **disproportionate military retaliatory strikes**, for example the incessant air attacks on villages in Palestine and southern Lebanon, which were resumed even after the ceasefire in the Gulf: instead of 'an eye for an eye, a tooth for a tooth', as the Hebrew Bible says (by way of limitation), the aim has often been both eyes and all the teeth. And even the Gulf War cannot undo the baneful Israeli invasion and occupation of **Lebanon** in 1982/83 which cost hundreds of lives: even now Israel also has Lebanese territory under its control. Here for the first time in its history the state of Israel quite unambiguously waged an **aggressive war**. The massacre of several hundred Palestinians in the Sabra and Chatila refugee camps by 'Christian militia' under the shadow of the Israeli army was only ended by American intervention. By all this, Israel did itself military, political, economic and moral damage, but at the same time it hastened the downfall of Christian rule in Lebanon instead of preventing it (which was the intention). Syria was the victor!

In Israel itself, however, for the first time tens of thousands of the **Peace Now movement** protested publicly against the war, on the occasion of the invasion of Lebanon. Even the former head of the Israeli military defence force warned the Begin government against the 'Bar-Kokhba syndrome' (transforming catastrophe into a heroic act)[26] and critically challenged 'Israel's fateful decisions', especially since the Likud block had taken over government.[27] And Amnon Rubinstein, the Dean of the Faculty of Law at Tel Aviv University, took the same view in criticizing the fatalistic Israeli apocalypticism that arose in the Six Day War, which sees Israel as the successor to the 'constantly persecuted Jews' instead of as a strong and responsible state which has to pursue a realistic policy.[28]

No 'psychology of the extreme situation' can justify the aggression. And how are we to undestand the fact that **Ariel Sharon**, the greatest warmonger and the one most responsible for the invasion of Lebanon, has subsequently been made Israeli Minister of Housing? Here is a man who – although in 1967 the Israeli government recognized the Muslim quarter of the Old City – quite unscrupulously took up a third home in the middle of Arab Old Jerusalem, with a bodyguard a company strong, and then master-minded the confiscation of the Orthodox Christian St John Hospice in the middle of the Christian quarter of Jerusalem (secretly financed by the government) as a prelude to further similar actions. He is now, where possible, massively pushing forward the Israeli settlements in Arab territories as a continuation of the war by other means. No wonder that Washington officials want to have nothing to do with him!

So far Israel and the United States, especially their armies and secret services, have worked very closely together. But even American Jews and Israelis are now criticizing Israel's **unscrupulous dealings**: spies of their own country in the United States (Israel's protective force!) and at the same time the entanglement of Israel in the Iran Contra affair (which according to President Reagan's memoirs was even devised by Israel); the new giant corruption scandal in the Israeli air force at the expense of the American taxpayers; and finally the close economic and military ties of the state of Israel (and numerous former Israeli officers at every level) with dictators and military juntas from South Africa to Chile and El Salvador, with the Somozas, Duvaliers, Pinochets, Marcos's and Mobutus – particularly over police training, police equipment and the development of nuclear weapons (as is reported with a vast amount of data by Benjamin Beit-Hallahmi, Jewish professor at the University of Haifa[29]).

People have begun to ask questions even in the American government: in such circumstances is Israel still a strategic **asset to the United States**? Despite or precisely because of the Gulf War, there is cause for scepticism here in the medium term. Even if there is still strong support for Israel in Congress (because of the strong influence of the American Jewish organizations) and in the Pentagon (because of the intensive military collaboration), the Gulf War in particular has shown how dangerous Israel's policy against the Palestinians can be from the perspective of world politics. The Iraqi dictator could easily make the unresolved Palestinian question an excuse for his attacks on Israel and encourage the Arab masses everywhere. No, in this still oppressive and externally aggressive form the state of Israel could prove a problematic strategic asset for the USA (after the liquidation of the East-West conflict), whereas not only Saudi Arabia and its oil, but also Egypt and the other Arab allies have become far more important than before and now count on American loyalty and support.

5. The Arab dilemma: Israel either un-Jewish or un-democratic

Abba Eban, Israel's Foreign Minister from 1966 to 1974, was right when he clear-sightedly used the following arguments in favour of conversations with the Palestine Liberation Organization: 'There are no dangers in an Israeli-Palestinian agreement to compare with the volcanic certainties of a *status quo* which is obscuring our vision of peace, weakening our economy, damaging our tourism, distorting our image, undermining our international friendships, dividing our nation, worrying our Jewish Diaspora and undermining our most precious Jewish and democratic values.'[30]

But there is yet another argument which also makes many American Jews anxious: in the meantime the Palestinian 'demographic bomb' in Israel has itself increasingly become a test case for the nation. What will the longer-term future be? A **Jewish national state** or a **Jewish-Arab two-nation state**? There is no doubt that through its policy of occupation after the 1967 war the state of Israel has manoeuvred itself into a difficult situation, accentuated by the settlements in Jerusalem, in 'Samaria and Judaea' (these biblical terms are now used instead of West Jordan, though as we saw, down the centuries Samaria was at the opposite pole to Judaea) and the Gaza Strip (1.7 million Palestinians in all). These settlements first crept in, and have been pushed on vigorously since the Likud government by Prime Minister Begin – the former terrorist leader who first became politically respectable as a result of the Government of National Unity which became necessary in 1967. For whereas formerly official government policy tended simply to deny the Palestinians as political subjects on Israeli territory, today it is impossible either at home or abroad to close one's eyes to the fact that the Arab minority within the present *de facto* state frontiers (including the occupied territories) amounts to almost 40% of the population. Precisely as a result of the temporary closing of the frontiers (the 'green line') before, during and after the Gulf War, the Israeli military have demonstrated to the whole world that the occupied territories of 'Judaea and Samaria' are not in fact part of the state of Israel.

Certainly, the relative strength of Jews and Arabs in Israel cannot be compared with that of white and black, say, in South Africa (not, at least, if one leaves out of account the roughly 100 million Arabs around Israel). But the dilemma of such an expanded 'Greater Israel' is analogous: because of the birth-rate among the Arab population, which is almost double, according to official forecasts by the year 2000 the approximately 4.5 million Jews will be confronted with more than 2 million Arabs. In 'Greater Israel', since 1985 for the first time there have been more Arab children under four years of age (370,000) than Jewish (365,000). Even now there are clear Jewish majorities only in the major cities and in the 'defensive villages', and according to all the forecasts (high and low), because their birthrate is more than twice as high, the Arabs will soon make up almost half the population: in the year 2000 they will amount to between 42% and 46%.[31] A similar development also took place in Lebanon.

The immigration of Jews from the Soviet Union to Israel in particular, pushed by Israel with every possible means and vigorously criticized by the Arabs – 1989: 13,000; 1990: 210,000 (many of them, who are barely religious, and many perhaps who are not even really Jewish, would have preferred to emigrate to the USA) – is deeply ambivalent. On the one hand it aggravates the situation, especially in Arab East Jerusalem, where so far 10% of the immigrants arriving up to May 1990 have settled. On the other hand, in Israel it increases both the unemployment rate (1991: 11%, with the danger of a rise to 18%) and the tremendous burden of state debt, which is the main economic and political problem (in 1989 it was already 30.6 billion dollars); it is estimated that by 1992 the building of 30,000 new homes alone will have cost around 1.2 billion dollars.[32] These are not peasants; more than 6,000 doctors – who will certainly be very much missed in the Soviet Union – have settled in Israel within a year: after Switzerland, Israel has the greatest density of doctors in the population anywhere in the world (12,000 out of 4.5 million). Most recently of all, however, because of the bad conditions in Israel, almost half the Soviet Jews who want to emigrate would prefer to remain in the Soviet Union or go to another country (even Germany). According to a May 1991 report of the Bank of Israel, unless the labour market changes, up to 200,000 Soviet Jews who entered Israel will leave it again over the next few years.

So in these circumstances, what will Israel's future look like? In its practical policy the Jewish state faces the **alternative**:
– Either it acts in a consistently **democratic way**, in which case it runs the risk of becoming **un-Jewish**. For constitutionally the enormous Arab minority would have to be given the same rights as those given to citizens of Jewish descent, which would result in a bi-national Jewish-Arab state. But what Martin Buber above all had formerly advocated, along with left-wing Socialist groups and with Judah Magnes, for many years President of the Hebrew University, is now ruled out by most Israelis: a Zionism which did away with itself?!
– Or the state of Israel remains **Jewish**. But in that case it runs the risk of becoming **undemocratic**. For unless the policy is changed, the land will be exposed to increasing internal tensions: a further radicalization of the Arab minority, coupled with the simultaneous radicalization of small Jewish groups, the settlers, and possibly also the army – the former murdering in desperation, the latter in revenge. Even now the occupied territories are ruled by martial law under a state of emergency. So is this a democracy which might turn into a dictatorship?

After the terrifying reinforcement of right-wing conservative forces in Israel and America and the widespread flight into the past (not least in 'patriotic archaeology'), unfortunately the second possibility looks the more likely for the near future. But could not the tragedy of Greater Lebanon, which already in the 1920s brought too large a Muslim population under the rule of the Christian elite (after Christian Lebanon had survived reasonably well under Muslim rule since the Muslim conquest in the seventeenth century) be a serious warning to Greater Israel?

6. The Intifada and the Palestinian state

What disturbs many serious Israelis is that all Israeli oppressive measures have only strengthened the resolve of the Palestinian people not to come to terms with the occupation of their land in any way. Indeed, in the face of the paralysing immobility, the endless delay and the sit-it-out tactics of official Israel, as in Eastern Europe a decisive turning point has already been reached which the PLO neither brought about nor even foresaw: the **active resistance of the Palestinian people itself**, who have given up their former passivity and taken their cause into their own hands. A new generation of Palestinians (many from the new middle class) has replaced the well-to-do conciliatory notabilities of the West Bank. This is causing extreme irritation to Israeli society and is polarizing it still more, so that – according to the Israeli philosopher Avishai Margalit – some would like to say 'To hell with the Arabs', and others (more to themselves than out loud) 'To hell with the occupied territories.'[33]

Since as long ago as 9 December 1987 the Palestinian population in the occupied territories has been in revolt against the Israeli repression which has now lasted for so many years. This is the '**Intifada**' (literally 'shaking off', 'popular revolt'),[34] which for many in Israel is sinister writing on the wall. In fact this is one of those liberation and emancipation movements which, as the Jews and the state of Israel themselves have shown, usually achieve their goal. But what a change of roles: today the Palestinians are in the role of the stone-slinging **David**, and Israel is in that of the armed but helpless **Goliath**. The Palestinians are provoking the well-organized Israeli army of occupation, armed to the teeth and often brutal, with stones (and sometimes petrol bombs) thrown by small groups mostly consisting of youths and children, and by other heroic actions, and the army (accustomed to open warfare) cannot effectively prevent this kind of thing.

Throughout the world there has rightly been indignation over Saddam Hussein's Scud missile attacks on Israeli cities (fortunately with few victims and little damage to housing). But the Palestinians – out of a mixture of despair, calculation and blindness on Saddam Hussein's side – saw and see this differently. They refer to the **oppressive measures** which have become an everyday affair in Israel's occupied territories: from the closing hours, curfews and bans on demonstrations, through the cutting off of water and electricity and the closing of schools to the destruction of hundreds of homes, mass arrests, the deportation of leading Palestinians, and concentration camps. During the Gulf War the Palestinians lived as if in a giant prison, under a curfew of inhuman proportions. Certainly attempts are made to conceal all this from the world media by systematic news blackouts on the occupied territories, but it has become sufficiently well known.[35] The parallels to South Africa's former apartheid policy spring to mind.

A **further radicalization,** and an escalation of hatred, fury and enmity on both sides, threatens sooner or later: an intensification of the Intifada, which could easily move from stone-throwing though mass killing to the placing of bombs. Former Jewish 'terrorists' now in power are hardly justified in rejecting negotiations with the Palestinian 'terrorists', who, envisaging a Palestinian state, are following the Jewish model in strategy and tactics. Not a few are seriously afraid for the fate of Jerusalem, where many Jews too are infuriated at the constant growth of the ultra-Orthodox communities which are settling in Arab East Israel: with 330,000 members they now already make up a third of the Jewish population of Jerusalem. At all events many people are reckoning with the possibility of increased Arab terrorism and Israeli counter-terrorism and with heightened Jewish-Christian-Muslim tensions in the 'holy city' itself. In this connection, too, here are just a few **indications of the trend:**
– In many countries, even in the United States, voices are increasingly being raised against the *de facto* annexation (which also has a religious basis) of the Arab territories, their infrastructure (control of electricity, water and roads, of markets and the supervision of labour) and their landholdings. Now already more than 50% of the land in the occupied territories has simply been confiscated for allegedly public or military use or for cultivation.
– In these circumstances (within the framework of what are of course the justified interests of Israel's security and certain necessary frontier corrections, especially in the Golan), an increasing number of voices are calling not just for autonomous administration but political self-

determination of the occupied territories and indeed for Palestinian sovereignty over them. 'Judaea and Samaria' are now no longer Israelite states or Roman provinces, but the home of the Palestinians living there.

Since the rebellion of the approximately 1.7 million Palestinians in the occupied territories (140,000 in East Jerusalem) which began at the end of 1987, up to autumn 1990 more than 1,000 Palestinians had been killed by Israeli soldiers and Jewish settlers, who are often even more brutal. Well over 100 of the dead were under sixteen, and well over 300 were between sixteen and twenty-five. And on the Israeli side? Around 50 dead.[36] This is vivid evidence of the disproportionate use of deadly weapons by the occupying troops. The number of Palestinian wounded, who for fear often never go to hospitals, runs into tens of thousands; they have now long ceased to be those who, according to official claims, have been shot in self-defence.

How explosive the situation has become in the meantime was shown less by the fatal indications of sympathy for the 'liberator' Saddam Hussein during the Gulf War from the Palestinians, frustrated, and once again led astray by Arafat, than above all by the **massacre** on the **Temple Mount in Jerusalem** on 8 October 1990. In reaction to the announcement of a procession of a small radical Jewish group (Temple Mount Faithful) to lay the foundation-stone of a Third Temple to replace the Al-Aksa mosque, young Palestinians threw stones at Israeli soldiers (the reason for whose intervention was not explained) on the west balustrade of the Temple Court and (only indirectly) at the Jews praying below at the Wailing Wall. No one on the Jewish side was killed, nor were there any injured to complain of. But the Israeli police retaliated for the stone-throwing with a brutal massacre – leaving around 20 Palestinian dead and around 150 wounded.[37]

Vengeance and retaliation as a **substitute for constructive foreign policy?** Will peace ever be achieved in the Near East in this way? As early as 1955, the then Foreign Minister Moshe Sharret wrote in his diary: 'In the 1930s we reined in impulses to vengeance and educated the public to see vengeance as an absolutely negative impulse. Today, however, for pragmatic considerations we argue for the principle of retaliation... We have loosened the spiritual and moral reins which we had put on this instinct and have taken things so far that ...vengeance is regarded as a moral virtue.'[38] No Israeli government hitherto has ever behaved so uncompromisingly and brusquely in questions relating to the peace process, the settlement policy, and action against the Palestinian revolt as has the right-wing conservative and Orthodox religious coalition government of **Itzhak Shamir** (born 1914 in Poland).

In the government programme he proclaimed 'the eternal right of the Jewish people to the whole land of Israel', including the occupied territories, and announced an extension of the Jewish settlements. But all this has tended to be counter-productive even among the friends of Israel, and in Israel itself has intensified the perplexity and in part the sense of guilt rather than diminishing it. Once again: will peace ever be achieved for Israel and the Near East with hatred, a quest for vengeance and retaliation? It was with good reason that in Part Two of this book, in another connection, I drew attention to the possibility of forgiveness, reconciliation and sharing – necessarily also among the nations.

The Intifada of the Palestinian people itself, which came about so surprisingly, has compelled both Jordan and the PLO to **change their overall strategy**.

– On 31 July 1988 King Hussein II of Jordan announced the legal and administrative separation of the West Bank from Jordan.

– On 15 November 1988 the Palestinian National Council proclaimed in Algiers an independent state of Palestine which would embrace the occupied territories of West Jordan, the Gaza Strip and also Old Jerusalem as a capital (the basis for this was UN Resolution 181 of 1947); at the same time, in the face of radical groups, the majority of the PLO implemented the acceptance of UN Resolutions 242 and 338, which recognize the existence of the state of Israel.

– So all in all: a **Palestinian state alongside the Jewish state, not instead of it**.

Anyone can understand the Israeli anxiety over security, brought on by Jewish history and the Holocaust. But here Israel is more on the offensive than on the defensive. The greatest obstacle to peace in the Near East is posed by the **Israeli settlements** in the occupied territories. Since 1977 it has been this aggressive settlement policy of the Likud government which has most deeply disturbed the Palestinians, and has also split public opinion in Israel and throughout the world. For this is no longer primarily a matter of agricultural pioneering work (only a few, say, of the Soviet Jewish immigrants go even into the new cities in the Negeb desert), but most of all of the planned erection of city-like settlements of middle-class 'commuters' as part of a military strategy: **'defensive villages'**, illegal houses and fortifications protected with barbed wire and searchlights, and strategically planned roads which are meant to cut the Arab cities and villages off from one another and encircle them. And this has happened increasingly down to the present day: although the Israeli government has promised the Soviets, who made possible the emigration of Soviet Jews, and the Americans, who are said to be financing the 'settlements' for Soviet Jews to the tune of 400 million dollars a year, that it would establish no settlements in the occupied territories and East Jerusalem, the settlements went on in secret, with tricks and the supplying of false figures. Indeed, as late as April 1991 they were continued in a provocative way, with caravans and mobile homes as the new wonder weapon, in protest against the peace efforts of the American Secretary of State James Baker. More than 7,500 acres of land vitally necessary for subsistence were officially confiscated from Arab villages on the West Bank in the two months after the Gulf War, and around 1,000 acres were requisitioned by the military with a view to confiscation. According to the latest reports, ex-General and Housing Minister Sharon is now even planning 'the greatest building programme of settlements ever to be launched in the occupied territories', building 14,000 new units in the next two years in order to increase the Jewish population in the occupied territories of 90,000 by more than 50%, thus deciding to whom the land belongs by a *fait accompli*.[39]

What will the **United States** do? The USA already provides almost 4 billion dollars per year towards the annual Israeli military budget of 5.5 billion dollars. Even according to the view of critical Israelis, that means that only an unambiguous and consistent policy on the part of the USA, coupled if need be with action of the kind at least announced by President Bush in spring 1991 for the solution of the Palestinan problem, may prod the Israeli government (this one or a future one) into making overdue political decisions on an intolerable situation which has been accepted for all too long.

Would a committed peace policy cost George Bush victory at the presidential elections in 1992? Hardly, since happily in America, too, the Jewish Diaspora has again become more independent, so that people are talking of a 're-emancipation of the Jewish Diaspora'. The true friends of Israel in the USA and elsewhere should therefore not just look at the ongoing tragedy with feelings of depression and helplessness, or out of opportunism, cowardice or convenience. Many of them are increasingly coming to feel that today the Arabs have a right of self-determination in the face of Israeli military power, just as the Jews did under the British mandate.

Or does the Palestinian people itself have no right to a 'home' in Palestine? From a religious perspective this is a very much more fundamental question.

7. Belief in the nation instead of belief in God?

Informed Jews, too, are increasingly recognizing what tremendous and 'unthinkable' possibilities could arise after the Holocaust: that the Jews, forced on to the defensive – and now probably already in possession of the atom bomb – could be the perpetrators, rather than the victims, of a new genocide. Self-critical Israelis were already thinking about that long before the Gulf crisis. The clinical psychologist **Israel W.Charny** of Tel Aviv University, born in America and living in Israel, had the courage to discuss these problems in two books: *How Can We Commit the Unthinkable?* and *Toward the Understanding and Prevention of Genocide.*[40]

Here, at any rate, in quite a different way from the cases of Iraq and Kuwait, there is not only a political but also a serious religious question which friends of Israel put with the greatest concern: in present circumstances, half a century after the foundation of the state, what remains of Herzl's 'model state', of Ben-Gurion's ideal of an Israel as the 'light among the nations'? Or if we simply apply the quite normal criteria of a democratic state: is Israel in future to be a bastion of nationalism and oppression rather than an island of peace?

However, the issue here is not just that of the credibility of Israeli democracy, but also of the **credibility of Jewish faith**. One might ask oneself whether **belief in the one God** of Abraham, Isaac and Jacob, who in the Decalogue also requires respect for the life and property of the neighbour, may be replaced by **belief in the nation** (drawn from Europe) – for both religious and non-religious Jews? Only between 25% and 30% of Jews describe themselves as 'religious', though many of the 'non-religious' presumably mean by religion the religious Orthodoxy which they have repudiated. Nevertheless the question arises: is Israelism now to take the place of the Jewish monotheism which has lasted for more than three thousand years, an Israelism which in place of the God of Israel now elevates Israel as people and land to a cultic object? Will the idol of nationalism which has brought so much disaster to the peoples of Europe bring salvation to the people of Israel?

At any rate the friends of the state of Israel, who heartily desire not just its existence but its well-being, are asking themselves how this state will continue. The Jewish theologian **Marc H.Ellis** sees it as 'an essential task of Jewish theology to deabsolutize the state of Israel', and calls for 'a theological conversion of the Jewish people toward those whom we often see as the enemy': the only way of ultimately avoiding a military defeat is 'to make peace when you are powerful'.[41]

Once again I quote an evocative comment by **Yeshayahu Leibowitz** to indicate the seriousness of the situation: 'If we continue on the way which we have taken, this will lead to the downfall of the state of Israel within a period of a few years – there is no need of generations for that. Internally Israel will become a state with concentration camps for people like me, as soon as representatives of the right-wing nationalist parties like Kahana, Raful, Druckmann and Sharon come to power. Externally Israel will entangle itself in a life-and-death war with the whole Arab world fom Morocco to Kuwait. That is the perspective for the near future.'[42] As for American support: 'As long as the state of Israel persists in abysmal folly and thinks that American support will last for ever, it will not of course be interested in peace. Therefore Israel will end up like South Vietnam, which also trusted in American help for ever.'[43]

Along with Leibowitz, Christians in particular, who feel especially indebted to the Jews, hope that this will remain a **nightmare** and that the present crisis will be overcome. After all, there is still a great **longing for just solutions** and thus for peace among the great mass of Palestinians – just as there is among the Israelis. Does everything really have to remain as it is in the face of this situation, which at first sight seems hopeless? After all the negative experiences, not least in connection with the Gulf War, in time will not reason reassert itself along with belief in the one true God, and in this way lead through a relaxation of internal tension to a national consensus which is at present lacking, on the following basis:

• Military, yes, but not a militarism which glorifies the army;
• Nation, yes, but not a nationalism which becomes a substitute religion;
• State, yes, but not an idolizing of the state which sacrifices hundreds of human lives to the state.

I hope that what I have had to write here about the tragic conflict between two peoples over one land will soon prove to be unfounded. After the Gulf War most of the Arab nations would also be interested in a peaceful new order in the Near East. But is there a realistic solution to all these problems, even a realistic vision of peace?

III. On the Way to Peace

When indeed will the endless dispute over the Holy Land finally be settled? When will the war be ended, the tragedy over? After the new dramatically heightened world situation as a result of the Gulf War, the Jewish state is evidently in danger of remaining fixated on the past because of its foundation so late in history, instead of being open to the future. It is in danger of persisting

– either in a **mediaeval** paradigm of Orthodoxy, which includes theocratic elements (in no corresponding Western state other than the Vatican are there as many restrictions on the life of individuals based on religion as there are in Jerusalem);

– or in an obsolete **modern** paradigm of the secularists, which is often determined by nationalism, indeed racism, and which threatens to split Israeli society into religious and non-religious Jews.

Here the state of Israel is amazingly like certain Islamic countries which similarly threaten to repress the challenges of **postmodernity**: a postmodernity which despite all the old political, ethnic and religious contrasts, and those which have newly emerged, will have less of a national than an international orientation; which will no longer encourage aggressive antagonism but peace between the nations, and which will no longer strive for fanaticism, but for the peaceful co-existence, indeed the pro-existence of the various religions. What is to be done here? Instead of national mythologies and illusions, the call here is for **realism and pragmatism for the sake of survival**. At this point a political and theological survey of perspectives on the future may be of some help.

1. Extreme positions without a chance

One thing is certain: neither side can simply dictate conditions to the other. So negotiations beween those responsible are unavoidable; thus far an all-or-nothing standpoint has led to nothing but blood and tears. However, there are hardliners on both sides: on the one side aggressive Israeli terrorists, for example the religious and nationalistic 'Gush Emunim' = 'Believers' Block', mostly of European and American origin, who represent the leading edge of Israeli expansionism and have established around a quarter of all the settlements in the occupied territories, and all those who even before the death of the racist Rabbi Kahane shouted 'Death to the Arabs' and propagated 'Arabs out!'. On the other side there are fanatical Palestinian terrorists, especially the secret fundamentalist militant alliance Hamas, which is steadily increasing in number because of the desperate plight of the Palestinians. Both sides should keep in mind the Protestants in Northern Ireland, the Christian Falangists in Lebanon, the Basques in Spain, the Sikhs in India and the Tamils in Sri Lanka to see that only endless suffering can follow from political and religious intransigence on both sides.

The **extreme positions** of the agitators (the 'hawks') on both sides, **without prospect of success**, have become clear:

– Many **Israelis** are supporters of a **Greater Israel**: for geopolitical or religious reasons, with the help of the army, special police and armed Jewish defensive settlements they want to maintain political control over the occupied territories for ever (if need be even by the 'transfer' of population, land permits, deportations and resettlements). Here not only the increasing numbers of the Arab population but also the Arab self-awareness which has grown through the Intifada should have made it clear that after the Gulf War the Palestinians and the Arab states will be less happy with the occupation than ever. After a war which in fact has lasted for forty years, do these Israelis want to expose themselves to a war which will last another forty years or longer?

– Some **Arabs** are supporters of a **Greater Palestine**: for political reasons and with the help of terrorist actions they want to force into being a great state, destroy the state of Israel, and as far as possible drive all Jews 'into the sea'. For some Palestinians the 1968 'Charter' still holds; this aims at an 'elimination of Zionism in Palestine', declares the division of Palestine in 1947 and the foundation of the state of Israel 'completely illegal', and regards as 'null and void' the Balfour Declaration and everything that derives from it. According to this charter, the Jews are not a people with their own nation, but 'citizens of the states to which they belong'. However, have the Palestinians (Arafat included) learned nothing from their mistaken involvement and stunning defeat in the Gulf War?

At the beginning of the 1990s it should have become clear that both uncompromising positions are disastrous illusions which block each other and have constantly led to unimaginable bloodshed. Neither has a future. Instead, beyond question a **realistic view** must be taken by reasonable people on both sides, aimed at arriving at a political (rather than a military) solution. As conversations in Jerusalem during the Gulf crisis convinced me, the reorientation of the PLO, their recognition of the existence of Israel as early as 1988/89 and the acceptance of the two-states ruling has certainly remained the basic conviction of the leaders of the Palestinians, at least in the country itself. But now after the Gulf War, in which the Palestinians, frustrated for decades, and yet again led astray, were enthusiastic supporters of a bloodstained leader simply because he was the only Arab leader who dared to oppose the Americans (and thus the Israelis), a fundamental clarification of the Palestinian position is urgently needed. By their enthusiasm for Saddam Hussein they have all too firmly endorsed and reinforced the Israeli unwillingness for peace. They have all too firmly disillusioned and disappointed those who are ready for peace. A redefinition of the Palestinian position – and possibly individuals should also take the consequences for wrong decisions – is imperative. Do the former PLO resolutions still hold, or is there a willingness at last definitively to recognize Israel's right to exist?

More or less secret conversations between key Israeli politicians and PLO emissaries have already taken place at different times. Immediately before the Gulf Crisis, **Faisal Husseini**, son of Abdul Kader Husseini, the Palestinian commander-in-chief in the 1948 war and today the main leader of the Palestinians on the West Bank, and **Yael Dayan**, son of the famous general and Minister of Defence Moshe Dayan, and today a member of the Central Committee of the Israeli Labour Party, showed in an exemplary way that a basic understanding is not impossible. They stated: 'While we do not agree over a series of problems, we are united in working towards our ultimate goal: a negotiated settlement based on the principle "land for peace" – a settlement which will result in self-determination and security for Israel and for Palestine. Peace calls for painful compromises from both sides.'[1] Indeed: but through a peace agreement there will be no losers, only winners!

However, the decisive question is: **how** are such compromises to be achieved? The UN partition plan of 1947 already envisaged a Jewish and a Palestinian state and in 1967 called for renunciation of violence on both sides (Resolution 242); in 1973 it also called for the recognition of Israel (Resolution 338). Since 1989/1990 – strengthened by the Gulf War – the UN General Assembly, and also the USA, the USSR, the EC and many Arab states, have called for an international or regional peace conference, but this has been rejected above all by the right-wing conservative and religious Orthodox Israeli government, because it will not accept the Palestine Liberation Organization as a negotiating partner and wants unconditionally to hold on to the occupied territories.

The reactionary Likud government is supported in the **United States**

by the powerful pro-Israel lobby (especially AIPAC = the American
Israel Public Affairs Committee),[2] which attempts to suppress all
criticism of Israel as far as possible. It is in a position to offer financial
incentives and to suppress critical enquiries right up to the level of
congressional elections. These lobbyists evidently do not see that
AIPAC has alienated itself from already important trade-union, Black,
feminist and also Christian groups by its completely one-sided policy,
which ignores all Palestinian concerns. Nor does it see the danger of a
new antisemitism in the face of an over-strong, paralysing Jewish
influence on US foreign policy.

Still, leading American Zionists like Nahum Goldmann, Arthur
Hertzberg and others have for these reasons criticized and continue
to criticize AIPAC publicly, thus making themselves spokesmen of
possibly the majority of American Jews, almost half of whom in
any case are not organized into Jewish associations. Moreover since
September 1989, the European Jewish Congress has also adopted a
more complex attitude to the state of Israel, which can be described with
the term 'critical solidarity'. And even major US Jewish organizations –
like the American Jewish Congress and the Union of American Hebrew
Congregations (an organization of 800 communities of the 1.3 million
Reform Jews in the USA) – have recently been calling for a peace
conference. As early as 1985 'a tendency towards the self-ghettoization
of Jewish life' in America was lamented in a report by this organization:
'Combined with this trend is the tendency to develop "one-issue"
organizations and mentalities. And combined with this trend is the
tendency to limit the kind of "Jewish discussion" of problems relating
to Israel or America, or at least not to contribute to the process of
extending them which is necessary in view of the complexities of this
new era.'[3]

And in **Israel** itself? Here, as we saw, society is deeply divided, and
of the major political forces only the Labour Party has spoken out at
least in principle for a peace conference, though at the cost of a
break with the Likud and even then not with the forthrightness and
consistency that is called for. In Israel people are still fond of using the
'rhetoric of weakness', which constantly presents Israel to the world
as an 'underdog' and 'victim'. But that can hardly convince informed
and unprejudiced contemporaries. For this small land has the best-
equipped and best-trained giant army of 540,000 soldiers, with around
3,800 tanks, 682 planes and thousands of pieces of artillery and
missiles. By contrast, the PLO has just over 8,000 men, spread over
various places, no tanks and planes, a few pieces of artillery and no

missiles; just a lot of hand grenades, mortars, bottles and stones.[4] Who is weak, the underdog, the victim, here?

2. Land for peace?

After the Gulf War, an opportunity of a kind unprecedented since the foundation of the state of Israel has arisen for Israelis and Arabs to gather round one table. Aggressive, revolutionary pan-Arabism seems discredited. The obstruction of the Soviet Union to an understanding with Israel has given way to constructive collaboration with the USA. The United States itself also has matters well in hand to compel Israel, which it protected effectively against missile attacks, to turn towards a peace policy, if gratitude (which is rare in world politics) does not lead the state of Israel (and also states like Saudi Arabia and Syria) to come to an agreement. Clearly at the moment the demand has been made in the international community for there at last also to be a **new peaceful order** in the Near East, to be achieved by **effective peace negotiations.**

And indeed, like Europe, so too the Near East does not need to be a powder keg of international tensions. Peace is possible between the 'arch-enemies', the state of Israel and the Arab states, just as it was between the 'arch-enemies' France and Germany. But as between French and Germans, so too between Israelis and Palestinians, rational conversations, specific treaties and precise agreements are needed. In concrete, this means that after preparatory dialogues brokered by the USA among the various interested parties, one or more **regional or international conferences** must be convened under the aegis of either the UN or the USA/USSR/EC, in which not only the Palestinians but as far as possible all the direct or indirect neighbours of Israel – Egypt, Saudi Arabia, Jordan, Syria and Lebanon – would have to be involved.

Israelis and Palestinians would have to realize that the **Gulf War** has now **changed strategic and political thinking in the Near East.** It has changed:
– the relations (hitherto hostile) of the USA to certain Arab states;
– the liaison (hitherto one-sided) of the USA with the state of Israel;
– the policy (now unified) of the UN Security Council opposed to the occupation of Kuwait and also to the occupation of the Palestinian territories.

Moreover:
–the extremists among the Palestinians and Jordanians seem weakened;
– those maintaining a rigid position in Israel are under pressure from

the USA, the EC and the UN to concede territory in order to make peace possible.

What we need in the Near East in 1991 is what we needed in Europe in 1946: reconciliation between former enemies and mutual economic, ecological and political interdependence, so that each side has its own interest in maintaining peace and stability. That means that despite all the difficulties the hour of destiny for the Jewish state has now come closer, and thus the hour of destiny for a goverment which, while constantly calling for direct negotiations with the Arab states, has yet been able skilfully to hinder effective peace negotiations (in particular with the PLO, who are primarily involved here). But it will transpire that this hour of destiny cannot be lived through by obstinate obstruction or one-sided demands to the USA and UN, far less – if there should be no peace agreement – by a new and hopeless trial of arms. The only possible course is a constructive strategy of negotiation, orientated on the future.

Be this as it may, under the healthy pressure of the super-powers and the world public a **political solution** must be worked out by efforts on all sides – rather like the Camp David agreement between Israel and Egypt under a Jimmy Carter II. Beyond question, it would have to include a **return of the occupied territories to their rightful owners** – on the basis of UN Security Council Regulations 242 of 1967 and 465 of 1980 (with a special clause for Jerusalem, which I want to go into separately). (This return would have above all to cover the West Bank and the Gaza Strip, now 23% instead of the 42.9% of Palestine which the UN had promised the Palestinians in 1947).

Is this, then, the 'land for peace' which is now also called for by the current American President George Bush? This standard formula is widely accepted outside Israel, but it is too simple. Here one must show some sympathy with the Israelis. For peace in the real and complete sense involves not just a peace treaty, but very much more. If 'land for peace' is to be understood realistically, it must be given concrete form as follows:

– Land for full **diplomatic relations** with the Arab states, and normalization on the economic-political and spiritual-cultural levels;
– Land for **security**: through arms control, guarantees of security and possibilities of concete implementation and verification;
– Land for **money**: Israel urgently needs financial support towards providing for the Soviet Jews and balancing the enormous state deficit;
– Land for **penetrable frontiers**: free and secure access for Israelis to 'Judaea and Samaria', and conversely free access for Palestinians to

their old homeland before 1948 or 1967; here, as in Germany, the payment of compensation to the Arabs would be possible.

But at the same time the solution would have to be **acceptable to the main parties**. Those involved in the negotiations must themselves be able to decide who belongs to a particular delegation (especially on the Palestinan side), to ensure genuine representation. Peace cannot be brought to the Near East through a *Diktat* in Versailles style; there must be a Brussels-style solution in which, as I have said, there are no losers, but only victors. In view of what has already been said, this will involve:

- The full diplomatic recognition of the state of **Israel** by all neighbouring states and at the same time the guarantee of secure frontiers (with meaningful revisions, say, on the Golan) by the great powers (as in Sinai) or the UN;
- Respect for **Syria**'s legitimate demands for the restoration of territory (on the Golan) and for the legitimate interests of the kingdom of **Jordan,** which because of the Arab-Israeli conflict has already had to bear heavy demographic, economic and financial burdens;
- Realization of the right of the **Palestinian people** to undiminished exercise of their civil rights, their political self-determination and their independence as a state (perhaps limited to begin with, say, in respect of an army: Austria after the Second World War under Four Power Status might be a model). In other words, the **foundation of a sovereign Palestinian state** – perhaps after a transitional stage under an international protectorate (the UN), or with a joint Israeli-Arab administration.

But is a sovereign Palestinian state viable at all? The question is a legitimate one. However, even in the view of Palestinians, the sovereignty of a Palestinian state does not exclude, but rather includes, scientific, technical and economic **co-operation**, perhaps even **association** with Israel on the one hand and Jordan on the other.[5] Indeed, an economic union was already a presupposition of the 1947 UN partition plan.

As a **model** for an association of Israel, Jordan and Palestine today one might cite above all the **Benelux states.** Here the three states of Belgium, the Netherlands and Luxembourg, different in many ways, agreed on a **customs and economic union** (a state treaty was signed in 1960, to last fifty years). In addition to almost complete liberalization of movement of goods, capital and labour, this provides for a harmonization of foreign trade and agricultural policies and a co-ordination of policies on currency and political and economic structure (the political organs are a committee of ministers, a consultative parliamentary council, an economic and a social council, and a court of social justice). So imagine:

– How much could such a **Palestinian state** gain if it were supported by Israeli science, technology and business?

– And how much could the **state of Israel** also gain if instead of its tremendous investment in arms it could invest in its worn-out state infrastructure and its crisis-ridden economy, and at the same time export on a large scale?

– Even more, how much could **Jordan** gain, poor and weakened as it is by the refugee problem and the Gulf crisis, if at the same time it could collaborate with the Palestinian and the Israeli states?

– Moreover, given an association, why should not the Jewish **settlements** remain in the Palestinian territories, and conversely, why should not the Palestinian settlements remain in the Israeli territories?

It would be a tragedy of historic proportions if the present opportunities for peace were not taken by the state of Israel. How often, already in ancient Israel, did prophets like Isaiah and Jeremiah warn against a false policy of strength! Only a constructive solution to the Palestinian problem will allow the realization of the **obligation** which the state of Israel took upon itself in its prophetic **1948 Declaration of Independence**: 'The state of Israel will be open to Jewish immigration and the gathering of Jews in exile. It will devote itself to the development of the land, for the welfare of all its inhabitants. It will be based on freedom, justice and peace in the sense of the visions of the prophets of Israel. It will guarantee equal social and political rights to all its citizens, without distinction of religion, race or sex. It will guarantee freedom of faith and conscience, freedom of language, education and culture; it will take the holy places under its protection, and it will remain true to the basic principles of the United Nations charter.'

However, not only religious mini-parties but in fact also the present Israeli government would interject at this point: does not Israel have a claim to the whole of 'biblical Israel', guaranteed by divine revelation?

3. Biblical arguments for state frontiers?

Just as one can appeal to 'natural' frontiers, so one can also appeal to 'supernaturally' appointed frontiers. One can do politics with theology as well as with geography. The question is this: can one here and now, with reference to the Bible, lay down specific **political frontiers** and make quite specific **territorial demands**? Questions like this are asked not only by the Arabs, but also by many Jews. Is it permissible to take particular texts from the Hebrew Bible and apply them literally in a completely changed situation: to frontiers 'promised by God', guaranteed by God once and for all?

Such **biblical texts** are in fact cited again and again. For example, from the book of Genesis: 'On that day the Lord made a covenant with Abraham, saying, "To your descendants I give this land, from the river of Egypt to the great river, the river Euphrates."'[6] Or from the book of Deuteronomy, where Moses hands on instructions from the Lord to the people of Israel: 'Turn and take your journey, and go to the hill country of the Amorites, and to all their neighbours in the Arabah, in the hill country and in the lowland, and in the Negeb, and by the seacoast, the land of the Canaanites, and Lebanon, as far as the great river, the river Euphrates. Behold, I have set the land before you; go in and take possession of the land which the Lord swore to your fathers, to Abraham, to Isaac and to Jacob, to give them and to their descendants after them.'[7] And later on, the same book even says: 'Every place on which the sole of your foot treads shall be yours; your territory shall be from the wilderness to Lebanon and from the river, the river Euphrates, to the western sea.'[8] One hardly needs to spend much time pointing out that such texts, applied directly to the present situation, contain a good deal of political dynamite.

The question of **normativeness** arises: what counts – historical realities or the ancient biblical texts? The frontiers which have become historic or the frontiers promised in the Bible? Can the political geography (e.g. the Jordan frontier) be over-trumped by a political theology, so that – as in the Psalms – Israel's future messiah king can even be ascribed a kingdom from sea to sea, from the Euphrates to the ends of the earth?[9]

A look at our paradigm analysis can also bring clarification here. As we saw, the Jewish people, too, experienced a revolutionary paradigm shift in its history. It existed both **with a state and without a state,** lived **with both these frontiers and those frontiers,** and – hypothetically speaking – could again live with or without a state, with these or those frontiers. So the question to be asked of a politically loaded religious fundamentalism must be: why quote these particular 'proof texts' from the Bible and not others? Do not historical developments in fact forbid the direct and anachronistic application of just any biblical passage to the present, even to the point of making it the criterion for a particular (military) policy? As if the biblical promises were aimed at an independent modern Jewish **state** rather than a secure **home** for the elect people!

As if the boundaries of this home were not drawn very much more narrowly, even in the Bible![10] As if today one could form a greater Israel with the Jordan at its centre – 'from the river of Egypt to the Euphrates'! As if all the frontiers of Israel had been clear right down the millennia! As if the land west of the Jordan, inhabited by Muslim (and Christian) Arabs, had simply remained historically Jewish land! As if the present-day Arab-Muslim inhabitants, who have been settled here for around 1200 years, did not possess any legitimate rights to a home and could even be deported! As if two-thirds of the Jewish inhabitants of Israel (as Sephardic Jews) did not themselves come from Arab lands! In short, one asks oneself, in the question of frontiers, what is **God's revelation** and what is **nationalistic ideology?**

There are without doubt important differences between the claims of a Saddam Hussein to autonomous Kuwait – already a settlement by Arab Bedouins three centuries ago – and Israel's claim to West Jordan (conquered in a defensive war against Jordan!). But how can one reject as megalomania the claims of a Mesopotamian despot who appeals simultaneously to Nebuchadnezzar's Babylonian empire, the caliphs of Baghdad, and the Qur'an, while at the same time appealing to the 'biblical Israel', in fact to the kingdom of David and Solomon, to justify a 'Greater Israel'? And this 'Greater Israel' is thought of as extending from the Mediterranean to the Jordan (and sometimes even beyond the Jordan). Is it not a dangerous game to conjure up for one's own territorial demands the demons of '**irredentism**', of the 'unredeemed territories', the '*terre irredente*', as the Italian nationalists did in the First and Second World Wars? 'Unredeemed', enslaved, maltreated and betrayed: that is how nowadays above all the Arabs of Palestine feel (and also the Kurds in northern Iraq) – to whom the Jewish side even wants to deny the name 'Palestinian' and the character of a people, simply because they never could and should build a nation and a state. What has happened to the second part of the Balfour Declaration, to the first part of which appeal has constantly been made for the resettlement of Palestine?

Truly, it does make a difference whether the former Israeli Labour Party governments occupied the Arab territories as a buffer against attacks and as a pledge for forthcoming peace negotiations, or now the Likud governments claim these territories as the Holy Land from biblical times and an eternal Jewish possession, no square metre of which may be given up. The well-known Jewish scholar **Jakob J.Petuchowski**, Professor at Hebrew Union College in Cincinnati, Ohio, rightly accuses politicizing Orthodoxy of making a highly **selective use of scripture**: 'When pro-Israeli apologists refer to the importance of the "land" in biblical religion, our first question should be whether these apologists really want to set Judaism back to its biblical phase, i.e. whether they also long for the reintroduction of animal sacrifices, the official toleration of slavery, the death penalty for certain transgressions of the ritual laws and the constitution of a theocratic state. Or do we have here simply an emphasis on the role of the "land" for biblical religion, torn right out of its context – as though in its further Jewish development this religion had not gone through a variety of stages which finally led to an independence of the Jewish religion from the "land"?'[11] These questions focus on the quite essential distinction, worked out all through this book, between the abiding substance of faith and the changing paradigm. For completely secularized Jews, who have replaced their Jewish faith with a nationalist 'Israelism' (like 'Japanism') without religious substance, the question is sharpened still further: can a people which no longer stands by the Bible still have a claim to the 'biblical land'?

Another question arises for Christians: are the Palestinian Arabs now perhaps to **pay for the injustice of Christians**, the injustice which 'Christians' (above all German Christians) formerly inflicted on the Jews? So not least Christians – and many Arabs in Israel and the occupied territories are Christian – have reason not to take a particular side, but to make use of their contacts with both sides to demolish prejudice, hatred and fanaticism: to work towards a religious understanding, a basis for mutual trust, a permanent political solution – in a truly postmodern paradigm. After all, what did Theodor Herzl promise? 'Every man will be as free and undisturbed in his faith or in his disbelief as he is in his nationality. And if it should occur that men of other creeds and different nationalities come to live amongst us, we should accord them honourable protection and equality before the law.'[12]

But now, let us turn to Christians. What should be their future attitude to the state of Israel? Given the view set out in Part Two, that the state of Israel is a political entity with a religious dimension, the following prospects come to mind.

4. For Christians: critical solidarity

How should Christians and Christian churches act in future in practical policies towards the state of Israel? Towards an Israel which is no longer the weak and beleaguered state that it once was, but the strongest military power in the Middle East, with nuclear weapons in the background? For the future there should be:

(a) **No diplomatic and detached ignoring** of the state of Israel. This state remains a geopolitical reality, no matter what one may think about it from a political and a theological perspective. Judaism is not just a religion, but also a people. And no matter what injustice (towards Arabs) may be bound up with the foundation of the state of Israel (as with the foundation of so many states), history, justice, compassion and humanity all call for **diplomatic recognition** of the state of Israel – by the Arabs and also by the Vatican: of course not just 'implicit' recognition but, as is customary elsewhere, official recognition, to form a basis for peaceful collaboration. I have emphasized in various ways how, because of its centuries-old anti-Jewish history and its complete failure over the Holocaust, the Roman Curia has a special debt to repay.

But in addition, **all Christian churches** – not just the Roman Catholic but also the Greek Orthodox, the Armenian and the German Protestant churches – must say more clearly than before that they will **not assert any sovereign rights to land in Palestine on a theological basis**. Of course the holy places should remain in the possession of those to whom they have belonged, often for centuries, and it is to the credit of the state of Israel that it not only guarantees the protection of the holy places by law but in fact also implements this protection effectively. However, precisely for that reason it can be said that private and public rights of possession by Christians or Christian churches to particular places may not be heightened by theological or quasi-state rights of sovereignty, as though Jesus had willed that his successors should become co-heirs of the biblical land. In contrast to Judaism which, as I demonstrated in Part One, is and remains essentially bound to the 'promised land', Christianity is by nature bound to the person of Jesus Christ, but not to a particular land. That also applies to the holy city of Jerusalem, as we shall see. But there is yet another side to the problems of the relationship between Christians and the state of Israel:

(b) There must be **no uncritical identification** with the policies of the state of Israel. No matter how enormous the significance of the Holocaust for Judaism may be, no guilt feelings after it, however great, may lead to a complete identification with any current Israeli state policy (which is often simply party politics and is sometimes more than questionable). I have already pointed out that just as there is no innocent, 'righteous' religion, far less is there any innocent, 'righteous' nation. And particularly in Israel there is all too large a gulf between Herzl's original ideal of the 'model state' and its subsequent realization: ideology and reality are too disparate. The same holds for numerous world states, but in the case of Israel the gulf is particularly striking because of the loftiness of the claim. No matter how much fundamental sympathy they may have for Israel, those who criticize the policy of an Israeli government, whether they be Christians, Muslims or Jews, are not necessarily *a priori* 'enemies of Israel'. Indeed, compared with those who opportunistically pay lip service, they may in fact be **honest friends** of Israel. I certainly am, and remain so! But neither American Jews nor European Christians need to be 'more Israeli than the Israelis'. After all, as we saw, happily there are many courageous Israelis (outside the Peace Now movement e.g. the former Israeli Prime Minister Abba Eban) and leading American Jews (following Nahum Goldmann, until 1968 President of the Zionist World Organization, and now Arthur Hertzberg and the American Jewish Congress) who openly criticize the policy of the present government of Israel towards the Arabs. This is done out of concern for the future well-being of the state of Israel.

(c) What is required, rather, is **critical solidarity of Christians** with the state of Israel. In the Middle East conflict, where manifestly there is right on both sides, over the Palestinian problem and over Jerusalem, the Holy City of Jews, Christians and Muslims, Christians in particular should not *a priori* take one side or the other.[13] After all, both peoples on Palestinian-Jewish soil, Jews and Palestinians, have suffered enormously. After all, both have made mistakes, committed acts of violence and allowed terrorism. But at the same time, among both peoples a broad spectrum of opinions has emerged from the present political stalemate, and there is also good will and a love of peace, which, after so many wars and in view of all the destruction caused by the Gulf War, is also a longing for nothing more than to be able to live without a threat to one's existence. So in the future, Christians should devote themselves even more as steadfast bridge-builders to seeking a **balance between the justified claims of the Jews and those of the Palestinian Arabs**, not heaping all the costs of the conflict on either one side or the other.[14]

So in future, for Christians in particular it will be impossible to ignore the religious dimension of the state of Israel, as still happens in conservative Catholic circles. As though there were no longer any abiding promises of God to his people! Nor can the state of Israel be seen in apocalyptic enthusiasm as a sign of the end-time. As though the prophetic predictions were being fulfilled in this state (down to the planting of trees, irrigation, and the mass influx of pilgrims and tourists)! Religious and political conservatives, like Protestant fundamentalists, tend to propagate this, at the same time having on their cryptic agenda a hope for a conversion of the Jews, which they still expect before the imminent apocalyptic end of the earth with the return of Christ. Fine friends of Israel they are!...

And yet, although even believing Jews refuse to see the secular Jewish state as something like a 'messianic sign' and the 'beginning of our redemption', there is no escaping the need to sketch out a realistic vision of peace. That is important for survival, if future goals are not to be submerged by the sheer weight of present problems.

It is the great religious tradition of Judaism itself which offers the possibility of showing a way of reconciling all the opposites. And referring to the Bible, the Talmud and Maimonides, an Orthodox rabbi like **David Hartman** has described this way as being in concrete terms the **love of the stranger**: 'The experience of diversity in Israel, the presence of the dignified other, be it a Christian, a Muslim, or a Palestinian, brings home to Jewish spiritual consciousness the important empirical fact that no one person or community exhausts all spiritual possibilities. The Bible emphasizes two important notions of love, one related to the love of the neighbour and the other to the love of the stranger. In neighbourly love, we meet one with whom we share common values, familial and communal solidarity. The neighbour who is like oneself gives expression to a love which extends the self and expands one's communal solidarity. In the love of the stranger we meet the other, the different one, the one who cannot be defined exclusively by our own categories. In this context, the Bible frequently recalls our own historical experience of suffering under a totalitarian system, within which we had no dignity because we did not fit into the ruler's framework of values. Ours was an abused life in which differences were not respected, but rather became a source of fear and intolerance. It is this experience of Egypt, says the Bible, that must teach us how to empathize with and not feel threatened by those who are other. "And you shall love the stranger because strangers you were in the land of Egypt." '[15] It would mean a good deal if such notions could become the basis for an understanding between Israelis and Palestinians...

IV. A Real-Utopian Vision of Peace

'Seek peace and pursue it,' says the Psalm.[1] And the vision of terror which is also unfolded in Jewish circles must ultimately be replaced by a **vision of peace**. Since the Intifada and the Gulf War it has become even clearer that so many frustrated Israeli soldiers and so many oppressed Palestinian liberation fighters, indeed so many Jews and Arabs, uninvolved and involved, are longing for peace in this terrible situation. This land no longer needs 'heroes' but good entrepreneurs, technicians, skilled workers of all kinds in order to survive economically in a world which has changed as a result of the dissolution of the military blocks. What is needed is no longer the armaments industry and its weapons but a highly developed peace economy! And who will be able to guarantee the Israelis peace and security for economic development if not the Palestinians – since the highly-qualified Israeli army cannot cope with the Intifada?

1. What could become of Israel

The Lebanon used to be called the '**Switzerland of the Middle East**'. And it is a pity that through the fault of the Christians, then the Palestinians, and finally the other groups, at least for the moment this land has forfeited such a role as a result of the longest civil war in the Middle East, with 150,000 dead. Cultural plurality and economic prosperity plummetted into destruction and anarchy. Could not the state of Israel – if there should be a real peace – play a similar mediating (not dominating) role to that formerly played by Lebanon? In a few years, what today seems so utterly impossible, illusory and utopian could become reality.

Israeli self-awareness and self-esteem has markedly increased over the decades. In the framework of a confederation with a new Palestinian state and Jordan, the state of Israel could transform itself from an armed camp with a highly-equipped warrior people into a peaceful **bridge state** and a **peaceful people** – as did the Swiss confederation (for all its weaknesses). It, too, was once all for military expansion and 'safe frontiers'; it sent mercenaries in all directions, but eventually, through victories and defeats, became an island of peace. An island of peace – even in the midst of Europe during two world wars! An island, however, on which different cultures and peoples had to learn from many crises how to live peacefully and to the common good.

Just imagine for a moment: what would it mean for the whole
Middle East, for Egypt, Syria, Jordan, Iraq and Saudi Arabia, all the
neighbouring states, if so developed a land as Israel were to embark on
peaceful co-operation? Here is a land which gives its inhabitants a high
level of education (a 'people of the book') and has a highly sophisticated
educational system (with seven universities). It is a land with a developed
health system (numerous clinics, the highest number of doctors and the
best medical research in the Middle East) and maintains the social
services at a high level. It is above all a land with an unusual capacity
for economic achievement and technological innovation. So what
would it mean for such a land to be able to resolve on co-operation
with its neighbours, a give-and-take relationship? Think how much
Israel could achieve if it could divert its military energies into peaceful
activity, as Germany succeeded in doing after totally exhausting itself
in bloody wars not only against France but also against the Eastern
states and the Soviet Union?

Israel would be quite prepared for such a mediating role. Today it is
already no longer a homogeneous Western country but one in which
different large groups of population live together, groups which have
preserved their linguistic, historical and cultural identity within the one
state. It is a **multi-cultural land** embracing Jewish communities with
different systems of education, culture and life-styles which have grown
up as a result of the customs of the various countries (not least the Arab
countries) in which the Jewish people settled and to which it adapted
over the centuries of dispersion. It is a state which is striving for unity
but not uniformity, consisting of Ashkenasy, Sephardic and Eastern
Jews, long settled there or new immigrants. It is a society which has
now learned how to unite people of different origins and cultural
traditions, to integrate cultural elements of the West, East and South.
It is a region which already has two school systems and two radio
programmes, one Jewish (where the language is Hebrew) and one Arab-
Druze (where the language is Arabic), and its school system already
makes provision for three different forms of religious instruction: for
Jews, Christians and Muslims.

Indeed, what would it mean if this state, having become peaceful like
the Swiss Confederation four hundred years ago, became a mediating
bridge country in the Middle East – not least because of its **universalist
ethical and religious heritage**, in which Christianity and Islam share?
All men and women could profit from that. Is that unrealistic? Israel's
coat of arms contains the menorah, which also appears on the cover of
this book, the seven-branched candlestick as a symbol of Jewish identity
and history, but flanked by two olive branches: they are meant to

express the desire of the Jewish people for peace. And at a time when the **European** states, when Germany and France, Germany and Poland – and even the USA and USSR – have sought and found peace and collaboration, could it not be possible for Israelis and Palestinians, indeed for Jews and Arabs also to usher in a peaceful future in the crisis-torn **Middle East**? After so many decades of feuding and no peace in their own camp, the time is pressing.

But the most difficult question of all arises here: how is a solution to be found for the city of Jerusalem, which is holy to both sides, indeed holy to Jews, Muslims and Christians, and is anything but a matter of indifference even to secular Jews?[2]

2. And Jerusalem?

There can be no solution of the Palestine question without a settlement of the Jerusalem question: without a realistic solution for Yerushalayim, the city which according to popular etymology contains within its name the word 'shalom', 'peace', but which has constantly been a city not of peace, but of war.

Jerusalem, on the hills of Judaea (about 2,500 feet above sea level, and little more than twenty miles from the Jordan) is a modern major city with 400,000 inhabitants, and at the same time has been lived in without a break for longer than almost any city on earth. Indeed Jerusalem is a world city, not an industrial city. It is a city with 2,500 houses of prayer, synagogues, churches and mosques (none of which pay any taxes) and with 1,000 historical monuments (which cost a great deal of money). All this explains why so culturally rich a city as Jerusalem is financially a poor city, but it does not explain why the Arab population is so blatantly disadvantaged in comparison with the new Jewish quarter near to the 'Wailing Wall', the monumental government and museum quarter, and the Israeli satellite cities circling the old city. At any rate, the Israelis are being made to think by the increase in the Arab population under Israeli administration from 70,000 to 150,000. But, the bitter retort goes from the Arab side, this is not to be attributed to a fantastic birth rate or immigration, but to the illegal incorporation of more than 20% of the whole territory of the West Bank into the city area of Jerusalem, which as we know is all treated by the state of Israel as an integral part of Israel (not as occupied territory).

Yet despite everything, the real problems of Jerusalem do not lie primarily in the social sphere but in that of religious politics. To whom does the city belong? Historically this question is hard to answer. For down to its architecture, as the most recent excavations show, Jerusalem does not reflect so much the history of the Jewish people as the history of the **different ruling powers** over the centuries: Canaanite, Jewish, neo-Babylonian, Persian, Seleucid-Hellenistic, Jewish-Maccabaean, Roman, Christian-Byzantine, Caliphate-Islamic, mediaeval Christian, Turkish-Islamic, British and now again Jewish rule. Excavations by the Israel Exploration Society on the south slope of the Temple Mount have uncovered many layers of settlement: from the time of king Solomon in the tenth century BCE through Christian remains from the Byzantine period to the caliph's palace in the eight century CE; in the area of the city of David even pre-Davidic, Canaanite-Jebusite remains have been found . . .

'Unfortunately the bloody dispute over the Holy Land does not obey the dictates of political reason,' observes the knowledgeable journalist Peter Scholl-Latour, 'but is overlaid with the power of primaeval myths.'[3] Indeed, the destiny of the city of Jerusalem in world history is that it is simultaneously **holy to all three Abrahamic religions**. And it is so because of Abraham: 'There is a real "religious geography" in which Jerusalem is more the focal point than the centre...', says Jacques Madaule, Professor at the Sorbonne. He adds: 'The city is a kind of common horizon for the three religions which derive from Abraham.'[4] But in addition each religion also has specific 'holy' ties to Jerusalem. For the Jews the fundamental figure is **David**, the king who made this city the centre of a great empire. For Christians it is **Jesus** of Nazareth, whose death and resurrection are commemorated here. For Muslims it is the prophet **Muhammad**, whose ascent into heaven – which is particularly important for the mystical literature of Islam – is believed to have taken place here. The largely visible architectural symbols of Jerusalem, from the Dome of the Rock to the great city wall of the Old City which is still standing, are ultimately Muslim in origin – not Jewish or Christian.

There should be no dispute among the various religions that the Holy City should remain 'holy' to all three religions. It was the Muslims who called Jerusalem 'The Holy', 'al-Quds'. But the decisive question is, **'To which of the three religions should the Holy City belong?'** For since each of the three religions has possessed it for a longer or shorter time, and since each religion can demonstrate the special significance of this city for itself in particular, basically each of the three religions takes more or less for granted, or at least thinks it appropriate, that the Holy City should belong to it and it in particular.

Jerusalem

The holy city of three world religions.
Place of Abraham's meeting with Melchizedek
and the binding of Abraham's son.
The city of David (since c. 1000 BCE)
and Solomon's Temple.

Yerushalayim – the city of Israel.	Hierosolyma – the city of Christians.	Al-Quds – the city of Muslims.
Temple Mount: place of the gracious presence of God.	Golgotha and the Church of the Resurrection: place of the passion, death and resurrection of Jesus Christ.	Sacred Rock: place of the transporting of the prophet Muhammad to heaven (632: miraj).
From 70/135: place of mourning and lament over the destruction of the Temple and the city.	From 30 the home of the earliest community.	From 638 an Islamic possession: building the Dome of the Rock 691 and Aksa Mosque – third most important place of pilgrimage after Mecca and Medina.
11th/12th centuries: Jewish persecutions as a result of the Crusades.	Crusades: 1099: massacre of Jews, Eastern Christians and Muslims.	Christian persecutions: 1099: destruction of Church of the Resurrection.
19th century: intensified Jewish return. Institution of a Jewish Chief Rabbinate.	19th century: establishment of Anglican and Prussian-Protestant churches (1841) and a Latin Patriarchate (1847).	19th century: development of the city on the basis of Turkish reforms and the strengthening of Egypt.
1917: Balfour Declaration: 'national home' in Palestine promised.	1920: British mandate.	1918: Collapse of the Osman empire and end of Muslim political rule.
1948: Founding of the state of Israel: partition of the city. 1967: Israeli conquest of the Old City and East Jerusalem.	1964: Meeting of Pope Paul VI and Athenagoras the Ecumenical Patriarch of Constantinople	After 1948: Five Jewish-Arab wars: division and loss of the city.
City of promise: goal of Jewish longing. End of all dispersion and the place of messianic consummation.	City of promise: the 'earthly Jerusalem'. Prototype of the 'heavenly Jerusalem'. Place of Christ's return.	City of promise: place of the final judgment and the opening of the gate to paradise.

Today Jerusalem is **in fact under Jewish rule**: it is under the rule of the state of Israel, which captured West Jerusalem in the 1948 War of Independence and at that time drove out between 30,000 and 60,000 Arab inhabitants (however, the old Jewish quarter in the Arab part was also destroyed). In the Six Day War in 1967 Israel also occupied East Jerusalem and annexed it out of hand. In 1980, under the Likud government, by a 'basic law' of the Knesset Jerusalem was unilaterally declared Israel's 'indivisible capital'.

But what is the **legal situation**? No one even in Israel can overlook the fact that in international law **Israel has no sovereign rights over Jerusalem**. Consequently all the foreign embassies have refused to move from Tel Aviv to Jerusalem. The state of Israel, whose international credentials rest on the 1947 UN partition resolution (with Jerusalem as an international zone) was called on to withdraw its troops from the occupied territories after the Six Day War in 1967 by Resolution 242 of the Security Council – in exchange for Arab assurances of recognition and respect for a secure Israel. Security Council Resolution 465 of 1 March 1980 stated, with the endorsement of the USA: 'All measures taken by Israel to alter the physical character, the demographic composition, the institutional structure or the status' of the territories occupied since 1967, 'including Jerusalem or any part of it, have no legal validity'.

Israel's government and the Knesset certainly did not think that they had to pay any attention to UN resolutions and world opinion, any more than did Saddam Hussein. They passed the 'Basic Law' mentioned above, which solemnly proclaimed all Jerusalem the capital of Israel. But this self-decreed 'legality' has no international 'legitimacy' (the support of all parties involved and the world community). Even the USA refused to endorse this resolution and continued to keep its embassy in Tel Aviv. Indeed, in 1990 President Bush confirmed the position of the USA over the illegality of the *de facto* annexation of east Jerusalem – and in so doing incurred the public wrath of Prime Minister Shamir – by explicitly calling for the participation of Arabs from East Jerusalem in the international peace conference. When a further UN resolution on the Middle East condemned Israel for the deportation of Palestinians, Shamir declared to the international community, with an arrogance which also pained many Jews, that this UN Resolution would gather dust in the archives like all the resolutions against Israel before it. Now, after the Gulf War, we shall see how far the United States of America, with the backing of the United Nations, will exert the necessary pressure on its protégé in the Middle East so that a solution can finally be found.

Whereas even the Palestinians can have no illusions over West Jerusalem remaining Jewish, the status of Arab East Jerusalem still continues to be the centre of controversy. In the cold light of everyday reality, the **Jerusalem 'united'** by Israel is an **illusion**. The situation is quite the contrary. For a long time Jerusalem had been a peaceful island in the storm, but since the Intifada, from early afternoon on, the Old City of Jerusalem has been a largely dead city with closed shops. This a city which since 1967 has been more divided than ever: the Jews (and the Americans) no longer dare to go into Arab Jerusalem, and the Arabs no longer dare to go into Jewish Jerusalem. Since the massacre on the Temple Mount, each group has had a paralysing anxiety about the other and this has given rise to some Palestinian and Israeli revenge killings; violent acts have become so common that hardly any Israeli cab driver will venture into the Arab part of Jerusalem or even the surrounding area. More than stones could fly, and an assassination or a blood bath could again become a reality at any time.

The standpoints are harsh and unreconciled. For the Israeli government, Jerusalem is not a part of the occupied territories but the sovereign capital of Israel. But the **Palestinians also claim Jerusalem as their capital** – for so many centuries it has been an Arab city. And they cannot conceive that for example Nablus or Hebron, Ramallah or Jericho, could become the capital of Palestine. How can such a difficult question be resolved?

3. Two flags over the 'city of peace'?

Quite a number of Israelis are working in Jerusalem towards understanding. That has been done and is still being done for Jerusalem above all by **Teddy Kollek** (born in Vienna in 1915, and a Zionist from his youth up). Anwar el-Sadat once described him as 'the best mayor in the world'. No one has been more concerned than Kollek, since 1965 regularly re-elected as mayor of Jerusalem, to bring peace, harmony, civilization and beauty to this city in the face of all the anxiety, hatred and violence. But as a result of the most recent bloody developments, even his indefatigable activity to enable if not exactly friendship, at least the possibility of mutual esteem, between Jews and Arabs in this city seems to be flagging. Mutual mistrust is the greatest obstacle to any understanding. However, as I was able to ascertain personally, Teddy Kollek will not give up, and he too is calling for peace talks to end the violence and bloodshed: 'For the goal of co-existence to be attainable once more, we must kindle a light at the end of the tunnel for the Arabs. We must show them that we want to negotiate seriously, that it is not our goal to lord it over more than one and a half million Arabs.'[5]

More than anyone else, Teddy Kollek knows that Jerusalem is not just a piece of land but a **religious symbol**. As the Jews did once, so now the Palestinians, too, are seeking a political identity; they are claiming recognition and want their own flag. But need religious and national symbols necessarily be exclusive? Why should not peaceful co-existence be possible in a new time? Here Christians, for whom the time of the Crusades is happily past, could set a good example. The cross on many towers and buildings shows what important places and buildings have been in Christian possession, mostly for centuries. And yet there is an essential difference between the Christian claim to possession and that of Jews and Muslims. Why?

– The **Jews** lay claim to Jerusalem as a capital on the basis of biblical promises and their former possession of it, extending over many centuries.

– The **Muslims** similarly lay claim to Jerusalem as a capital on the basis of religious ties and subsequent possession, extending over many centuries.

– But in religious terms **Christians** cannot and should not make any claims to sovereignty in Jerusalem, the place of Jesus' ministry – not even through internationalization.[6]

I must point out once again that Christians have a **personal** bond with the Holy Land through the person of Jesus, and not a **territorial** bond through the land of Palestine. The third promise in the **Sermon on the Mount**, that the 'meek' or 'non-violent' will 'inherit (or possess) the land',[7] does not refer to an earthly territory but to a heavenly kingdom. And this kingdom will not be given to the powerful, who want to impose their power, but to the non-violent (Hebrew *anawim*), who acknowledge their helplessness to God. In our present historical context, that third promise of the Sermon on the Mount is to be taken with the seventh commandment, according to which the 'peacemakers' are to be called the 'sons (or daughters) of God'.[8] It follows from this that on the basis of their own message Christians should be active as peacemakers who voluntarily, unequivocally and publicly renounce any claims to sovereignty in Jerusalem and instead co-operate in balancing the apparently irreconcilable territorial claims of Jews and Muslims, with their religious basis, in a fair solution which is acceptable to both sides.

As it is essential for such a fair solution to be found for the sake of peace, it seems to me worth putting forward some suggestions which might seem very bold. As a **first element** in an overall political and religious solution for Jerusalem: why should not **two flags fly over Jerusalem**, the flag of Israel with the Star of David and the flag of Palestine with or without the Crescent? Since both sides so tenaciously lay claim to Jerusalem, and on the other hand a continuous partition would make no economic, political and social sense to either side, why should not this symbolic city be the **capital for both the state of Israel and the Palestinian state**, an 'indivisible capital', which unites and does not divide?[9]

Realistic **Palestinians**, too, are now ready for reasonable negotiations with this goal in view. Leading Palestinians have described it like this: 'A Palestinian and Israeli vision for the Jerusalem of the future can become possible only if and when official Israel realizes that the exercising of Palestinian sovereignty over the Arab state does not conflict with the exercising of Israeli sovereignty over the Israeli state.

Today there is a need to prepare the ground for the investigation of practical options for the future of the city. No one can afford to wait, since there is manifestly an urgent need for an open and pertinent discussion, aimed at shaping a just and better future. And there is also a need to think about the nature of the administration of the city and the civic institutions of the two neighbouring capitals.

Similarly, there is a need to address the question of Jerusalem as an open city: without the walls which separate the different quarters, yet not "united" under Israeli authority and control.

Because of the central and strategic position of the city, there is the additional need to discuss the geographical, demographic and economic implications for Palestinian and Israeli society of any future arrangements.

Free access to the city is another necessity which must be considered, along with the sacred right to worship and pilgrimage. Every effort must be made to ensure the preservation of the aesthetic and historical character of the city – to the satisfaction of the three religious communities.

As for the main issue of sovereignty, it is important to take different standpoints and scenarios into account: for example, "two independent sovereignties", "shared sovereignty" or "collective sovereignty", which could operate under very different flags, whether Palestinian, Israeli, UN, Red Cross or others.'[10]

Is there perhaps a historical model for such an arrangement? Yes, for **two flags** – the Italian flag and the Vatican flag – also fly **over Rome**, which is equally a highly symbolic city. Rome is the capital of Italy and

– as the 'extra-territorial' residence of the Pope – the capital of the
Vatican state, a sovereign international body ('Statto e Città del
Vaticano'), to which a diplomatic corps is also accredited, different
from that accredited to the Quirinal. In Rome, too, over the decades, the
religious (Vatican) side had been closed to any political understanding:
'*Non possumus*. We cannot.' So said the popes, until they saw that
with this strategy of refusal they were isolating, blocking and boycotting
themselves. So why should it not be possible in Jerusalem, too, for there
to be **two political authorities and yet only one city administration**?

A **second element** in the future status of Jerusalem could be provided
by a complete differentiation between capital and seat of goverment,
with the stipulation that these must in no way coincide. Very often, for
the sake of the unity of a country, the capital is by no means the
strongest city, either economically or politically: hence we have not
Zurich, but Bern; not Amsterdam, but The Hague; not Sydney, but
Canberra; not Rio, but Brasilia; not New York, but Washington. In
the USA, Washington was chosen as capital because it lay on the
boundary between the northern and the southern states. However (and
this should be a warning!), Washington became the real capital of two
parts which were very different, both politically and culturally, only
after a terrible civil war. As the District of Columbia, it is not answerable
to any of the states, but directly to Congress. Why should capital
and seat of government necessarily coincide? This question has been
discussed in particular in connection with the reunification of Germany.
And after all, the France of the *Ancien Régime* was ruled from Versailles.

So if Jerusalem were to become the capital for both states, why
should it not be possible to have the Israeli seat of government in Tel
Aviv and that of the Arabs in Ramallah, a new foundation by the
caliphs which for a long time was the capital of Muslim Palestine? Or
if, as is to be expected, the Israeli government is in no way willing to
withdraw from the western New City of Jerusalem, why could not the
Old City of Jerusalem, the only part which is symbolic, be the neutral
capital of Israel **and** Palestine? In other words, the **Israeli centre
of government** could remain in Jewish New Jerusalem, while the
Palestinian centre of government could be brought into being in Arab
new Jerusalem. In this way neither centre of government would be on
the neutral territory common to both, but each would be on its own
territory. Specific conditions could be negotiated. Where there is an
ethical will – namely to create peace – there is usually also a political
way!

But how can the question of the old **Temple Court**, the **Haram es-**

Sherif ('noble, holy place', where there can be no fighting) in the centre of Israel be incorporated into a peaceful solution? For as in countless other instances, unless the religious dimension is taken seriously, here in particular a political solution will prove quite impossible. And in the long term neither a religious nor a political solution call just for speeches and treaties; they also require actions and symbols which speak to people over and above the sheerly rational level, to their emotions and their passions. Some constructive pressure in this direction – the **third element** in an overall political and religious solution for Jerusalem – must be ventured here: over the Temple or perhaps another sanctuary.

4. Rebuilding of the Temple?

Not only millions of Jews but also hundreds of millions of Muslims and Christians have a strong, even **emotional tie to Jerusalem,** because this city has a special significance for the origin of their faith. With good reason, for centuries there have been Jewish, Muslim and Christian (both Armenian and Greek) quarters in the Old City of Jerusalem.

However, for **Christians** the Temple Mount is of secondary significance: certainly, it was here that the confrontation between Jesus and the Temple establishment took place (and according to the Gospels the pinnacle of the Temple was the scene of Jesus' temptation to power). However, the real 'holy' places of Christianity are outside the Temple precinct: the circular Church of the Holy Sepulchre or Church of the Resurrection (Greek Anastasis), with the small Chapel of the Sepulchre in the centre and right next to it and – already incorporated into the Constantinian basilica – the equally small Golgotha chapel, according to tradition built on the rock on which Jesus was crucified.

For the majority of **Jews,** the west wall of the Temple left after 70 CE, a mighty protective wall built by Herod and known as the 'Wailing Wall', has greater significance than the Temple Court proper. Both religious and non-religious Jews can gather here for personal and private (or also for public and national) rituals. Most of them have no vision of a restoration of the Temple – with all the sacrificial slaughtering of animals, large and small. Moreover, after the conquest of east Jerusalem in the Six Day War, General Moshe Dayan was well advised to forbid the raising of the Israeli flag and the setting up of any indication of Israeli supremacy on the Temple Mount, and to hand the keys back to the Muslim authorities. And it is to the credit of three hundred rabbis of very different trends, from the most Orthodox to the most liberal, that they then stated in a letter that they had no intention of going up on to the Temple Mount.

But as among all religions and nations, so too among the Jews there are also fanatics, in this case explicit **Temple Mount activists** who have envisaged a rebuilding of the destroyed Temple and a resumption of Temple worship by an appropriate body of priests. They are relearning the old biblical laws for the Temple, building models and holding exhibitions. Indeed, a numerically insignificant but particularly radical group, under the leadership of Gershom Salomon of Jerusalem, the nationalist religious 'Faithful of the Temple Mount', whom we have already come across, want to go up to the Temple Mount again in order to lay the foundation stone for the Third Temple there, after prior purification. So far, however, this has been forbidden them by Israel's Supreme Court. Another group in favour of rebuilding the Temple is already publishing a magazine which has on the cover an aerial view of Jerusalem with the rebuilt Temple. Indeed, there are fanatical Israelis who even planned to blow up the Muslim Dome of the Rock on the Temple Court. Can one rule out the possibility of that in the future, unless there is eventually a peaceful solution. One shudders to think of the consequences...

Of course the question arises: is not the **Temple an essential part of Judaism**? Should not, indeed must not, the Temple be rebuilt for Jews? In the light of the foregoing paradigm analyses in Part One, the answer can be summarized briefly: Temple and priesthood – the two essentially belong together – play no role in the settlement paradigm (P I). In the paradigm of the kingdom (P II) the Temple plays only a subordinate role, since King David still managed without a Temple and it was King Solomon who built it – as many people think, against Yahweh's will. This means that according to the accounts in the Hebrew Bible, Israel became a people before it possessed a land; and it possessed the land long before it built a temple in Jerusalem. Moreover, for centuries Yahweh could also be worshipped appropriately without a temple or without any concentration on the Temple. The Temple really plays a dominant role only in the few centuries after the Babylonian exile, in the Jewish theocracy paradigm (P III). This was that Second Temple which went up in flames in 70 CE, in the Jewish-Roman war. Later, as we saw, the Temple was replaced by the synagogues, the priesthood by the rabbis and hierocracy by cathedocracy (P IV).

It follows from all this that for the greater part of its history Israel has lived without a temple. Unlike people and land, the Temple is not part of the essence of Judaism, but only part of a particular historical constellation. This observation opens the way to a further consideration.

5. The Dome of the Rock – a sign of unity for the Abrahamic ecumene?

For **Muslims,** the 'Haram esh-Sharif' is the third holiest place in the world after Mecca and Medina, and they guard it as the apple of their eye. For according to a tradition (albeit late and not Qur'anic), from here the prophet Muhammad ascended into heaven, and even now one can still see his footprints. So the Muslims have also made the Temple Mount 'their' sanctuary: in the middle of the Court stands the 'Dome' over the giant, irregular bare rock which has been here from time immemorial, and then on the edge of the Temple Court a mosque which almost has the form of a basilica and bears the name 'al-Aksa', 'the distant'. Remarkably enough, the 'distant' Jerusalem, so-called from the perspective of Arabia, is not mentioned in the Qur'an, either under its own name or any other. But according to universal Islamic Qur'an exegesis the beginning of surah 17, 'The nocturnal journey', refers to Jerusalem: 'Glory to Him who by night took His servant (i.e.Muhammad) journeying from the sacred place of prayer (in Mecca) to the **distant place of prayer,** whose precincts we have blessed, in order to show him Our revelations.'[11] And Jerusalem has been identified with this 'distant place of prayer'.

What then? Given the complexity of the situation, which extends from a lack of interest in religious veneration to an aggressive lust for conquest, can something 'holy', something healing and reconciling, go forth from this holy place – not just for Muslims, but also for Jews and Christians? Perhaps the suggestion of a Muslim can help us here – that of **Anwar el-Sadat,** to whom Israel owes peace with Egypt. Anwar el-Sadat, who for the sake of this peace, to the surprise even of Christians resolved on a journey to Jerusalem, had to pay for it later with his life. He was assassinated. He knew what he was saying when he made the suggestion that the three Abrahamic religions need a religious symbol, a common sanctuary, as a great sign that all three worship the one God of Abraham, in other words as a great sign that they have something fundamental in common which could overcome all divisions and all enmity. Peace, founded on common faith and symbolized in a common holy place – that was his great idea. And according to Sadat this holy place was to be built in Sinai.

But is there today the slightest prospect that such a sanctuary could ever be realized, far less built in the foreseeable future? Nevertheless, the suggestion is well worth thinking about, precisely because it is related to a very deep concern for peace between the religions, which is the presupposition for peace among the nations. So I venture to make a suggestion here. To some people today it might seem quite crazy, but perhaps it is worth thinking about in connection with a future solution to the problem of Jerusalem – this is the **third** element. For anyone who comes to Jerusalem, whether as a Jew, Christian or Muslim, is confronted with the inescapable fact that there **already is a sanctuary for the one God of Abraham**. Indeed it is precisely this unique sanctuary in the ancient Temple Court in Jerusalem, the 'Dome of the Rock' (Arabic *Kubbet es-Sakhra*), often wrongly called the Omar Mosque, although it is not a mosque at all and was only subsequently attributed to Omar, who had not himself captured Jerusalem. The Dome of the Rock is an architectural masterpiece, built, as I have said, on the site of the original Holy of Holies in the year 72 after the Hijra, in 691-2 of our era, under the Omayyad Abd al-Malik; it has been restored time and again, most recently between 1956 and 1964 under the guidance of Egyptian and Jordanian architects. The Dome of the Rock is regarded as the oldest, most beautiful and most perfect achievement of Islamic architecture; amazingly, it has not been imitated anywhere else in the Islamic world. It is a unique monument in many respects.[12]

Here it is important to know that no worship takes place in the Dome of the Rock with its gilded cupola, visible from afar. For it would be impossible even to carry out the strict order of prayer which is customary for Muslims in this circular building, since in the midst of the Dome, as I have already indicated, is the giant naked rock of Mount Moriah on which according to tradition Abraham was preserved by divine grace from having to sacrifice his son Isaac. It is here, too, according to Muslim traditions, that the first human being was created, and here too that the judgment of the world will take place. So for **Muslims** this is an eminent place for remembering the one God of Abraham. It is a place of silent prayer – no more; for as we know, Islam has neither temple nor sacrifice, neither priest nor sacraments. By Muslim worship of God this holy place, which was desecrated by the Romans and neglected by the Byzantine Christians, has been hallowed anew. But could Muslim, Christians and Jews pray together at all **here**? Indeed, could they **pray together** at all anywhere?

6. Praying together?

First of all let us consider quite generally and as a matter of principle the question of Jews, Christians and Muslims praying together. As is well known, **Christians and Jews** have few difficulties if they want to pray psalms or other prayers from the Hebrew Bible or the Jewish tradition together. Those Christians who have already taken part in a Jewish service know that they can join in most of the prayers, even if, for example, they understand the term 'Torah' differently – as also do some Jews: more in the sense of a 'spiritual law'. Conversely, some Jews might find no insuperable difficulties in, for example, joining in saying the Our Father in a Christian service, since its essential elements after all go back to the Hebrew Bible.

Similarly, for Christians and Jews there might be no theological difficulties in saying some of the fine prayers from the Qur'an **with Muslims**. After all, the Qur'an states that the same God spoke to Abraham, the prophets, Jesus and Muhammad. And those Christians who have joined in the impressive common prayer of Muslims know that it can make good sense for them to prostrate themselves to the one God of Abraham, even if they do not acknowledge the prophet Muhammad in the same way. Conversely, given time, there may be an increasing readiness, particularly in Diaspora Islam, in some circumstances also to pray Jewish or Christian prayers to the one all-merciful God. All this means that within the three prophetic religions it might in principle be possible also to address one and the same God through a common prayer.

But what about Jerusalem? Let us presuppose for a moment that peace among the religions and nations came about in the Near East: could the **Dome of the Rock also be a place of prayer for Christians**? For centuries Christians have tended to avoid the Temple Court, but in the time of the Crusades they made the Dome of the Rock a Christian church (*Templum Domini*), which was entrusted to the Templars. In more recent times, great hosts of Christians have also constantly visited this Dome, and no Muslim should prevent them from praying in the silence in this place to the one God of Abraham, if they want to do so. Nor need the Qur'anic inscriptions within this Dome, an admonition not to give up faith in the oneness of God, be any obstacle: strikingly, the ascension of Muhammad is not mentioned anywhere. In any case, the octagonal substructure with the Byzantine pillars on which rests the elegant and light golden cupola, decked inside with a marvellous mosaic with Byzantine and Persian motifs, strongly reminds Christians of Roman-Byzantine buildings like the Lateran baptistery, the San Vitale baptistery in Ravenna, the Church of the Nativity in Bethlehem and the original Church of the Sepulchre in Jerusalem. Indeed, the Dome of the Rock may have been conceived as a Muslim counterpart to the last-mentioned of these. And the theme of paradise, judgment and resurrection with which the rock has been associated even from Jewish times, and which is symbolized particularly on the mosaic by fruit trees and jewels, is a theme which is common to Jews, Christians and Muslims.[13] So Christians and Jews would not need to feel strange in this 'Dome'. I myself prayed there during the Gulf crisis (shortly after the massacre on the Temple Mount).

But what about the Jews? Many Orthodox do not go on the Temple Mount, for fear of treading on the site of the Holy of Holies, which can no longer be located with certainty. That is the place which only the high priest could enter on the Day of Atonement. But – in a new situation of peace! – any Jew who did not feel prevented by the halakhah could similarly come on to the Temple Mount and make this Dome of the Rock a place of prayer. Why not? Have not Jews prayed for centuries at this place to the God of Abraham, Isaac and Jacob? And even if no Third Temple were to be built on the site of the Holy of Holies of the First and Second Temples, could not this place again be hallowed by Jewish prayers? So should Jews be prevented from praying here today simply by the fact that the architecture is not theirs and the building was not erected by Jews? Have not synagogues, too, always had changing architecture and changing founders? So is it completely absurd to believe that after a religious and political settlement between Israelis and Palestinians, in this holy place Jews and Arabs, Muslims, Christians and Jews, could pray to the one God of Abraham, the God of the living and not the dead – in silence, or in future perhaps even aloud together on certain occasions?

What was possible in Assisi between the representatives of very different world religions must surely also be possible in Jerusalem among Jews, Christians and Muslims, who are so closely related spiritually, namely common prayer. And here I am thinking of not just one prayer after another, as in Assisi, but prayer together, perhaps like this:

Hidden, eternal, unfathomable, all-merciful God,
beside you there is no other God.
You are great and worthy of all praise;
your power and grace sustain the universe.

God of faithfulness without falsity, just and truthful,

you chose Abraham, your devout servant,
to be the father of many nations,
and you have spoken through the prophets.
Hallowed and praised be your name throughout the world.
May your will be done wherever people live.

Living and gracious God, hear our prayer:
our guilt has become great.
Forgive us children of Abraham our wars,
our enmities, our misdeeds towards one another.
Rescue us from all distress and give us peace.

Guardian of our destiny,
bless the leaders and rulers of the nations,
that they may not covet power and glory,
but act responsibly
for the welfare and peace of humankind.
Guide our religious communities and those set over them,
that they may not only proclaim the message of peace
but also show it in their lives.
And to all of us, and to those who do not belong among us,
give your grace, mercy and all good things,
and lead us, God of the living,
on the right way to your eternal glory.

In this way the Dome of the Rock – at present a sign of the times, representing tragic religious tensions – could become a sign of unity for the Abrahamic ecumene, a **Dome of Reconcilation** for the three religions which stem from Abraham. In the first four centuries of Muslim rule these religions lived side by side in relative peace and equality (the Jews were readmitted there, the Christian churches were not attacked, and there were countless pilgrimages – of Christians and above all Jews). Just as in the Middle Ages Jerusalem was regarded as the centre of the earth, and some maps of the world were centred on Jerusalem, so this place of prayer, with its gleaming golden cupola, would become a central symbol for the whole world, indicating that the three religions, while certainly differing on decisive points, can gather together in faith and prayer to the one God – all as a sign of an understanding which would, moreover, also result in practical collaboration.[14]

However, many people could not say such a prayer, because for them – after the abysmal experience of the Holocaust – all **talk of God** has become questionable. Theology has to take this terrible experience with unconditional seriousness as a question to God. Hence our question: after Auschwitz, is there still a future for talk of God?

D. The Holocaust and the Future for Talk of God

In Judaism itself, theological discussion of the Holocaust has begun after **a remarkable time-lag** – not until two decades later – and has therefore been all the more vigorous.[1] There has been much puzzling in America over the reasons for this.

I. The Holocaust in Jewish Theology

What are the reasons for this delayed discussion of the Holocaust?
– In addition to all the involvement was it also a **guilt complex among American Jews**, who together with their great organizations had largely kept silent and remained inactive over the fate of their European brothers and sisters after 1940?
– Was it the opening-up brought about by the **Eichmann trial** or the shattering literary work of **Elie Wiesel**, especially his book *Night*, on the 'Holo-caust' (whole offering) (he introduced this problematic religious term for the annihilation of the Jews)?
– Was it the **civil rights movement** and the stress on the 'ethnicity' of the Blacks, and then also of the Indios, Poles and finally the Jews, who had become unexpectedly well-to-do and culturally influential as a religious minority after the Second World War, and had developed a new, almost euphoric, self-awareness?
– Or was it the disillusionment which set in during the crisis of the **Six Day War** in 1967 in the face of the ongoing passivity of the American government and the silence of Christian organizations? Was it in reaction to this disillusionment that there was now vigorous support for the state of Israel, formerly by no means universally accepted, but now under deadly threat?
– Or was it, finally, the wave of the **'death of God' theology** (the death of God in modern culture as a cultural fact), lapping high in the same decade, which brought out, particularly through Rabbi Richard

Rubenstein's *After Auschwitz*,[2] the irreligion also latent in many Jews and made belief in a God who rules the world seem empty in the livid light of threatening atheism.

1. Holocaust fixation?

Who would deny that all this together contributed to the concentration on the Holocaust experience in the late 1960s? It became evident – and I need not spell this out at length here[3] – that those **age-old answers in the form of a theodicy**, which attempted to vindicate the righteous and good God in the face of the evil of this world, completely **collapsed** in the face of **this** suffering. All the talk of God's allowing evil for the sake of human freedom; of punishment for the sins of the Jewish people and reward in or after this life; of suffering out of love and for the salvation of others; of redemption by the messiah and the coming of the kingdom of God... all these well-meant theses seemed to fail completely to explain the monstrosity of the Holocaust event.[4]

People honestly asked how God could really have acted in such a cruel way in history, with Adolf Hitler and his SS butchers as the divine instruments. Could a good and righteous God ever have allowed all this without intervening? Inconceivable! However, such a naive notion of an Almighty who intervened directly, who imposed the Holocaust as a punishment for failing to observe the Jewish law, was never put forward by enlightened Jewish or by Christian theologians. Nevertheless, the questions remain.

Since then, Jewish (and Christian) theologians have been driven by one particular question: must the **Holocaust experience** also be 'central' for future talk of God or not?[5]

For many **Jewish theologians**, if they go into the question theologically at all, the Holocaust is no less and also no more than a further example of the monstrous **evil of human beings** which is attested in the Bible from beginning to end. What happened in the Holocaust is just one of the many historical catastrophes which are familiar to Jewish thought. So even a theologian like **Jacob Neusner** refuses to draw particular consequences from the Holocaust. Neusner expressly asks: 'What consequences, then, are to be drawn from the Holocaust? I argue that none are to be drawn, none for Jewish theology and none for the life of Jews with one another, which were not there before 1933. Jewish theologians do no good service to believers when they claim that "Auschwitz" denotes a turning point... In reality, Jewish piety has always been able to react to catastrophes.'[6] And Neusner refers to the Orthodox Jewish theologian **Michael Wyschogrod**, who says of the Holocaust: 'The God of Israel is a redeeming God; that is the only message which we are justified in preaching, no matter how false it may seem in the eyes of unbelief. Should the Holocaust cease to be a marginal phenomenon of the faith of Israel and penetrate the Holy of Holies, and become a dominant voice to which Israel hearkens, then the voice that it heard could only be a demonic voice. No salvation can be gained from the Holocaust, no tottering Judaism can revive through it, no new foundation for the ongoing existence of the Jewish people can be found in it. If there is hope after the Holocaust, there is hope because for believers the voice of the prophets speaks louder than Hitler, and because the divine promise extends beyond the crematoria and reduces the voice of Auschwitz to silence.'[7]

With that the Christian theologian can only agree. After all that I have described in this book, it has to be emphasized **against any fixation on the Holocaust**:
– The essence and identity of Judaism are not to be defined from a historical situation but from the Jewish religion.
– The long history of Jewish suffering may not be reduced to the Holocaust, its presuppositions and consequences; the most recent history of the Jewish people must not be cut off from its former history.
– Holocaust must not become a secular substitute religion; holocausto-logy must not become a substitute theology, the Shoah Day must not become a substitute liturgy, and the Yad Vashem memorial in Jerusalem must not be made a secular substitute Temple.[8]

But once one has taken a clear stand in this way against the Holocaust as a substitute religion and against a secular functionalization of the Holocaust, conversely, the question arises: does a theological reduction of the Holocaust to the level of the other catastrophes of Jewish history really do justice to this event? Does not such a view play down the Holocaust all too much, historically as well as theologically?

2. The Holocaust – a new Sinai?

For other Jewish thinkers, like **Emil Fackenheim**, the Holocaust is a **qualitatively unique event**, in the light of which present-day Judaism has to see its God, humanity and itself anew. Here belief in God is not abandoned (in contrast to the view of Richard Rubenstein) in favour of 'the Holy Nothingness', but affirmed in a new form.[9]

At a very early stage, Fackenheim begged his Jewish brothers and sisters to hold fast to belief in God so as not to help Hitler and his butchers to gain a victory after the event, the victory of nihilism and cynicism over the dignity of Jewish people, which was what the Nazis wanted. To secular and religious Jews he says passionately: 'Jews are forbidden to hand Hitler posthumous victories. They are commanded to survive as Jewish, 'lest the Jewish people perish. They are commanded to remember the victims of Auschwitz lest their memory perish. They are forbidden to despair of man and his world, and to escape into cynicism or otherworldliness, lest they cooperate in delivering the world over to the forces of Auschwitz – Finally, they are forbidden to despair of the God of Israel, lest Judaism perish. A secularist Jew cannot make himself believe by a mere act of will, nor can he be commanded to do so... And a religious Jew who has stayed with his God may be forced into new, possibly revolutionary relationships with Him. One possibility, however, is wholly unthinkable. A Jew may not respond to Hitler's attempt to destroy Judaism by himself cooperating in its destruction. In ancient times, the unthinkable Jewish sin was idolatry. Today, it is to respond to Hitler by doing his work.'[10]

In other words, Fackenheim refuses to replace theology by holocaust-ology, as is happening among some Jewish (and also some Christian) theologians. He has recognized the danger that in principle or in practice no longer God himself but the Holocaust will be made the centre of theology, indeed of religion. In fact a fixation on the Holocaust (which justifies any policy) and thus on Germany (even for all the Jews who in America, Israel and elsewhere are in no way 'survivors of the Holocaust') leads to an evacuation of Judaism – often in favour of an Israelism which becomes a pseudo-religion. Therefore in his newest, most comprehensive account of Jewish faith under the title *What is Judaism?*, Fackenheim quite resolutely puts God and God's covenant with the Jewish people at the centre of his theology.[11]

In historical terms I have set out in detail how neither moral levelling out and historical relativization nor mystifying over-heightening and unhistorical absolutizing will do justice to this truly singular cata-strophe. While the Holocaust does not mark the end of Judaism, it does mark the end of a whole Jewish paradigm, that of assimilation. The Holocaust is and remains for Judaism a **break in continuity of epoch-making extent**. It remains an event far surpassing all previous history of suffering, an event of an unspeakable suffering of the people of the Jews which cannot be 'understood' theoretically. It has a fundamental significance for our era, but one which is by no means exclusive for the future. Truly, one does the mass murderers too much credit if one stylizes 'Auschwitz' as virtually a new revelation event, if one elevates it to what Richard Rubenstein has termed a '**new Jewish Sinai**'. As if what was 'revealed' here were not so much God's decree as human disintegration. No, this is no revelation of values and criteria, but a complete perversion and obsfucation of them. So a counter-thesis would seem in place.

3. The Holocaust as the anti-Sinai of modernity

Auschwitz is not a place of revelation but **the** modern anti-Sinai. It is not a new beginning, but radically the end of that past era which produced it: European modernity. I have referred several times to the many factors which led to National Socialism: there can be no question of a monocausal explanation any more than there can be of a metaphysical historical construction. But it was not a theologian but a historian, **Fritz Stern**, the American Jew of German descent who addressed the German Bundestag in 1985 and in his book on the 'drama of German history'[12] pointed out that the creeping and ultimately total secularization, this tacit acknowledgment of the 'death of God' (Friedrich Nietzsche) in the nineteenth century, the culminating 'de-mystification of the world' (Max Weber) and **secular belief in the nation**, have proved to have fatal consequences both for modern Jews and modern Germans:
– This secularistic substitute faith alienated **Jews** from their own traditional identity: it left them morally helpless and defenceless when Hitler also robbed them of their Germanhood, i.e. their nationality.
– At a very early stage the silent secularization left in its wake among **Germans** a feeling of emptiness and boredom which could not be overcome by the identification of the divine with the nation (people, state) and the existing order (university, art). Especially after the devaluation of this surrogate faith in 1918 there was a call for more: so all too easily many people now believed in Hitler's mystifying, obfuscating talk of miracles, providence, myth, mystery, authority; they believed as it were in a new Pentecost with the outpouring of the Holy Spirit in the year of salvation 1933. A 'thousand-year kingdom' – that age-old figure of a utopian-chiliastic millenarianism[13] – was imminent. The few who resisted had other moral and religious criteria.

Thomas Mann in particular – the representative of the German spirit in a time of demonry in Germany – himself emphasized to German emigrants in America, against all interpretations which played down this event, that 1933 had been an enthusiastic revolution striking sparks, a German popular movement with a tremendous spiritual investment of faith and enthusiasm, but a revolution of a unique kind, without the idea, against the idea, against all that is higher, better, respectable; against freedom, truth, right; in short a 'revolution of nihilism... mixed with sinister credulity in the inhumane, the pre-rational and chthonic, in earth, people, blood, past and death'.[14] No one should excuse such an assessment in terms of the history of ideas: on the contrary, here before everyone's eyes was **the reversal of an idealistic modernity to become its nihilistic opposite.**

Modern men and women in particular cannot overlook the fact that the prophecy of the 'madman' **Friedrich Nietzsche**[15] has been fulfilled in Auschwitz, as also in the Gulag and in all the countless camps and compulsory ghettos of this world. Those who deny the supreme value and thus declare that God is dead, those who cut the earth loose from its sun, and want to drink the sea dry, are on their way to that void of Western civilization, that nihilism, which along with the supreme value also devalues all other values.[16] This European **nihilism** finally made its dramatic breakthrough and showed its empty grimace in the Nazism of Hitler, who, cursing his people before his cowardly suicide, attempted to drag them down in defeat – to an extent which Nietzsche himself, with his typical mixture of banality and evil, had probably never anticipated.[17]

But this oppressive and repressive world which was coming into being had been anticipated by a Prague Jew named **Franz Kafka**. He himself did not have to experience the SS terror, but his beloved sister Ottla perished in a concentration camp. In his work, Kafka created a world which with good reason has become proverbial in all languages – 'the **Kafkaesque world**'. What this term describes is the late phase of the labyrinthine modern world, the world of our century with its anonymous powers and insuperable structures, with its monstrous world wars and its practices of exploitation, a world which with concentration camps and Gulags is ultimately capable of surpassing even Kafka's visions of terror.

Let us make no mistake about it: with all this, the **paradigm of modernity** which had so grandiose a beginning has **come to an end.** It is utterly different from the end of all former paradigms: overshadowed in its crisis not only, like all transitional periods, by human nervousness, uncertainty and anger, but by an unprecedented remoteness of God, indeed a '**darkness of God**'. As we heard, Martin Buber, Kafka's Jewish conversation partner, made this the key concept of the time between the world wars: 'the darkening of the light of heaven, the darkness of God, is the character of the world hour in which we live'.[18]

Indeed, belief in modernity and in substitute gods like reason, progress, culture, nation, race, class – and humanity – has been **shattered** once and for all. Is God a human projection? With the assertion of the 'death of God' (originally a cry of freedom), Ludwig Feuerbach's theory of projection has turned back on itself. What human beings projected was none other than their own death, the 'death of man'. In the abysses of the Holocaust, what was broken was the **modern belief of human beings in human greatness**, which had also been widespread among European and American Jews: 'We believed in the goodness of man and trusted that education and culture would direct it rightly, while psychotherapy healed its rifts,' writes Eugene Borowitz: 'We counted on politics to bring in the Messiah, with an assist from social science. We followed the commandments of self-realization and looked forward to perfecting humankind. Sitting in our homes, walking on the way, lying down, rising up, we spoke of human progress and put our faith in new projects. For us, humanity sat on God's throne.'[19] In other words, the **'dialectic of modernity'** rules everywhere – a dialectic which was acutely analysed by the agnostic German Jews Theodor W. Adorno and Max Horkheimer in the 1930s and 1940s, but which had already clearly been perceived by the early Christian critics of liberal Culture Protestantism and the bourgeoisie, by Barth, Brunner, Gogarten, Bultmann and Tillich; by Jaspers and Wittgenstein; and also by Thomas Mann, Hermann Hesse and many writers and artists after the First World War. So once again: what is our situation today, half a century **after** Auschwitz?

4. The consequences: the overcoming of nihilism

Of course I have no intention here of discrediting modernity generally, with all its many positive achievements in philosophy, science, technology, industry and democracy. What reasonable person would want to go back from modernity into the Middle Ages or even into the time of the Reformation? But the Holocaust has shown one thing: wherever that modernity, which had begun so effectively and so hopefully, set itself loose in total secularization from all ethical and religious ties, it could turn into barbarism, whether with the French Revolution ('the Terror'), the Russian Revolution ('the Gulag') or even with the National Socialist 'seizure of power' (the concentration camps). Without religion, civilization is often only a thin veneer, but that does not mean that the crimes which have been committed in the name of religion (crusades, witch-hunts, inquisition, earlier persecutions of the Jews) can be trivialized or even disputed. And in this sense one can follow the New York rabbi Irving Greenberg in calling the Holocaust an '**orienteering event**', above all for modern culture (and then also for the Jewish and Christian religion).[20]

To put it pointedly: **humanity without divinity can become bestiality**. For all its backward-looking romantic mythological ideology, Nazism was externally a movement claiming to be modern, with an enthusiasm for technology – with highly modern organization, bureaucracy, propaganda and above all armaments and army. Specifically, Nazism demonstrated that:

- Without ethical ties, modern science can turn into the lie of propaganda.
- Without ethical ties, modern democracy can end in mass domination by the seduction and terror of a single 'Leader' and his party.
- Without ethical ties, technology can end in the technically perfect murder of millions.
- Without ethical ties, industry can slide into the almost complete industrial mass annihilation of a whole people.

So the Holocaust is a warning to **all** modern nations. Why? Because rationality, technology and industrialization, the whole complicated organization of industrial mass-murder invested here by the 'engineers' Himmler and Heydrich – although without doubt a German invention and a perversion of German thoroughness – was completely in line with a secularistic **European modernity** which had become godless. The way from Robespierre's guillotine through Lenin's mass shootings to Hitler's gas ovens – the technical perfecting of murder – was not inconsistent. Had not the great European nations at that time **all** worshipped the god nation (race, class), to which in some circumstances they sacrificed everything: freedom, law, art, religion – and millions of human lives? And were they not all 'rewarded' by this god: with militarism, imperialism and racism, and at the individual level with moral indifference, apathy and that lack of basic humanity towards the Nazi victims which was so extraordinarily prevalent even among German women (only recently has this aspect come to be discussed by feminists)?

Indeed, after two world wars, after Gulag, Holocaust and atom bombs, a paradigm shift, a change of entire constellation, is overdue, indeed is happily already well under way. A modernization of modernity is not enough: there is a need for the transcending 'sublation' of modernity into postmodernity. Rabbi **Irving Greenberg** is right: 'The cultural shift which is needed is a complex, differentiated process... The frontier of reason – established everywhere from psychoanalysis to the sociology of knowledge – must be redefined. This process can break the tyranny of modern categories and allow a new dialectical relationship to the claims of reason and science. It is not simply a matter of going back to tradition. It is more a question of a move to postmodernity.'[21] And it seems to me that now – for both Jews and Christians – this primarily includes a postmodern understanding of God which has been purified by the experiences of modernity.

For here we have to note an almost paradoxical phenomenon: in the abysses of unspeakable terror, for many people **the armour of religionlessness** was also broken. Reflecting on Auschwitz has also allowed many secular Jews to concede their concealed, repressed religious feelings and the untenability of their negative attitude. That is also a symptom of postmodernity: for all the doubts and constraints, a number of Jews have begun to feel their way towards the mystery of the God hidden in this world – through textual studies, liturgy, mysticism or social activities. As Eugene B.Borowitz has commented: 'In recovering our Jewish identity in depth, we find ourselves on new terms with what our tradition called God. The almost unbelievable, dialectical outcome of our attention to the Holocaust has been that a sizeable minority in the Jewish comunity is now involved in exploring the dimensions of their personal relationship to God. Theirs is a fragmentary faith but in this empty era even a partial belief is a lot to have gained.'[22] At this point I want to shed a little more light on this 'relationship to God', this 'faith'.

II. Understanding God after Auschwitz

The Holocaust, this event of unique human brutality, raises the question of God with unprecedented profundity. And in order that here, too, we do not get swamped by the infinity of questions, I propose to continue the line taken in this book so far and engage in discussion above all with Jewish conversation partners.[1] So I shall embark on the problems by discussing a piece of 'speculative theology'[2] which **Hans Jonas**, the Jewish philosopher of religion from the New School of Social Research in New York, has boldly put forward. In 1984, Jonas gave a lecture at the University of Tübingen on the 'concept of God after Auschwitz'. It was gripping because of his own personal situation (he was driven out of Germany by the Nazis and his mother died in Auschwitz). If I go on to add a few critical remarks, I do so not with the attitude of someone who thinks he knows better, but in solidarity with the difficulty, indeed the ultimate insolubility, of this question.

1. God helpless in the face of suffering?

After Auschwitz, can one still speak of God as the omnipotent, good and comprehensible 'Lord of history'? No, for Jonas, after Auschwitz this particular age-old conventional idea of God, with its traditional predicates and nomenclature, has become impossible. After Auschwitz, it has now finally become clear[3] that one cannot reconcile the omnipotence, goodness and comprehensibilty of God. Either God is omnipotent and utterly good – in which case it is incomprehensible why he did not prevent something as cruel as Auschwitz. Or God is omnipotent and comprehensible, in which case Auschwitz is the refutation of his goodness. Or God is good and comprehensible, in which case Auschwitz is the proof of his impotence. For Jonas, after Auschwitz it is no longer possible to have all three attributes – omnipotence, absolute goodness, comprehensibility – together at the same time. What is the alternative?

– Against the biblical conception of divine majesty Jonas sets the **suffering God**: 'That **from the moment of creation on**, and certainly from the creation of human beings on, the relationship of God to the world involves suffering on the part of God.'[4]

– Against the God who remains identical in his perfect being through eternity, Jonas sets the **God who is coming to be**, not 'an indifferent and dead eternity... but one which grows with the harvest of time as it accumulates'.[5]

– Against a remote, exalted God who is shut in on himself Jonas sets the **caring God** who is 'entangled in what he cares for': 'an endangered God, a God with his own risk'.[6]

– Against God's omnipotence Jonas sets **God's impotence**, that of a God who in Auschwitz and elsewhere kept silence and did not intervene, 'not because he did not want to, but because he could not'.[7] In other words, Jonas maintains God's goodness and his comprehensibility – even after Auschwitz. The omnipotence of God must be sacrificed.

All these ideas are not simply Jonas' invention. On the contrary, Jonas is here deliberately taking his stand in a tradition which, as we heard in Part One, has been revived in the twentieth century by the great Jewish scholar Gershom Scholem: **the tradition of Jewish mysticism, the Kabbala**.[8] And indeed in the Kabbala, in the sixteenth century, in Isaak Luria – the 'lion' ('Ari') – whom we have already met (and who was later disowned by the pseudo-messiah Sabbatai Zwi),[9] there is cosmological speculation about how creation could come about at all. Luria's answer is that since God is everything, it is only through a voluntary 'withdrawal', taking himself back, limiting himself, that God could create. In the Kabbala this is the doctrine of *zimzum*, and similar notions of God's 'self-renunciation', 'de-selfing' and 'condescension' are expressed in Hasidic conceptions.

The term *zimzum* is older than the Kabbala. Originally it means the 'concentration' or 'contraction' of God's holy presence on the Holy of Holies in the Temple or on Mount Sinai. However, Luria not only expanded this term so that it took on cosmogonic dimensions, but also reinterpreted its content. It came to denote a **self-limitation of God right at the beginning of time** – in order to make it possible for him to give the world an autonomous existence, space and time at all. According to Scholem, 'the existence of the universe' has been 'made possible by a process of concentration in God'.[10] God has 'opened up an area in his being from which he has retreated, a kind of mystical primal space, into which he could emerge in creation and revelation'.[11] So here creation is understood as an act no longer of divine self-unfolding, but of divine self-limitation! Here, according to Jonas, is a God who to some degree negates himself by the existence of creation and who, 'having given himself wholly into the world that was coming to be' has 'nothing more to give'.[12] It is now for human beings to give to him.

Jonas's lecture on the concept of God after Auschwitz stood out for its great earnestness and was presented with 'fear and trembling' – beyond any flat negation critical of religion or any full-throated orthodox affirmation of God. And yet is it a completely satisfactory answer – for Jews or for Christians? One thing must be seen clearly: here we no longer have an inter-religious controversy between Jews and Christians, since on the one hand many Jews differ from the Kabbalists on this matter, and on the other, individual Christian theologians, too, attempt among other things to get behind the mysteries of God with the help of this kabbalistic 'secret doctrine' and to decipher the **how** of creation and the **why** of human suffering.[13]

But the question of suffering is a deep abyss, above all the question of unmerited suffering, of suffering that people have not brought upon themselves: the private individual suffering, say, of innocent children which so tormented Dostoievski and Camus, and even more the suffering in world history, the senseless natural catastrophes, the great earthquakes with tens of thousands of dead and the inhuman tragedies of humankind, above all the Holocaust. For a long time I attempted to go my own way over this question,[14] but in view of all my experiences, in view of the tremendous amount of suffering and unimaginable evil, instead of embarking on cosmogonic speculations deriving from Gnosticism (Basilides; the book of the Great Logos!) in the style of Luria or Jakob Böhme, in the last resort I prefer to keep to the great classical tradition.[15] As also over the question of creation.

2. Creation of the world – self-limitation on God's part?

Should we really assume as the presupposition for creation such a **self-limitation** or **self-enfolding** of the infinite God from himself and in himself? This seems to me to be an extremely anthropomorphic conception (Scholem, too, calls it 'coarse', 'solid'[16]), even if self-limitation is explained as an expression of God's omnipotence. For God to have to draw himself together, contract into himself in order to give being and essence to another alongside himself, to allow space, to give time,[17] seems to me to rob God of his infinity, eternity and perfection. Moses Maimonides already wrote polemic against the idea that God has something like a mysterious, radiant body. Were not Jewish Kabbalists and Christian theologians drawn too much into anthropomorphism when by means of the concept of a *zimzum* God they wanted to know not only **that** God creates, but **how** he creates? Is there not a danger that God will become a 'lesser God', even a 'shrunken God'?

Moreover, with good reason, present-day Jewish theology keeps its distance from the Kabbala and strictly rejects the idea of a God who is limited where evil is concerned. Thus for example perhaps the most knowledgeable Jewish systematic theologian of the present day, **Louis Jacobs**,[18] who is also a distinguished expert on the Kabbala, unmistakably conveys his scepticism about the Kabbala: 'Unless one believes, as the Kabbalists did, that the doctrine is a direct divine revelation concerning the mystery of God's being, one sees the Kabbala as a gigantic speculative scheme in which Jews meditated on ideas – neo-Platonic and Gnostic – which had come down from the past.'[19] In particular, Louis Jacobs keeps his distance from the doctrine of the '*zimzum*' in the framework of Luria's unprecedentedly complicated doctrine of creation, in which ten divine potencies (properties, powers, manifestations) are poured from the unfathomability of God into creation – something which the Christian advocates of *zimzum* are unwilling to recognize: 'The Lurianic ideas will be accepted as revealed truth by very few modern Jews.'[20] No, constantly and with extreme acuteness, this Jewish theologian maintains the unity of God and sharply rejects any trinitarian interpretation of the Jewish tradition.[21] That is particularly true of the idea of a limitation of God in the face of the evil in the world: 'It invites the suspicion that such a limited God has no reality but is an invention of the acute human imagination. For these reasons, and in spite of its brilliant advocates, the doctrine of the finite God has succeeded in winning few adherents. The stark adherents for man are belief in God as traditionally conceived, that is the God who is omnipotent, or out and out atheism.'[22]

The leading theologian of American Orthodoxy, **Joseph B. Soloveitchik**, rejects recent Kabbalistic interpretation of the *zimzum* even more sharply, since this 'does not at all affect questions of cosmogony in the halakhah': 'The (kabbalistic) mystic regards the existence of the world as a kind of "affront" – God forbid – against God's honour; the cosmos as it now is limits the infinity of the creator.'[23] To this Soloveitchik objects: 'The creation of the world does not add any blemish to the idea of the Godhead; it does not limit infinity. On the contrary, it is the will of God that his Shekinah, his divine presence, draws itself together and limits itself in the sphere of empirical reality.'[24] That means that what I have constantly presented in terms of Christian theology also applies to traditional Jewish theology: God is to be understood as the infinite in all finitude, the transcendent in the concrete, the divine in the empirical reality of the world.[25]

In view of this, as a Christian theologian, too, one does better not to embark on speculative Jewish or Christian experiments but to keep to the classic confession of *Deus semper maior*, the God who is always greater, who as the maximum is also the minimum and thus transcends both minimum and maximum, as Nicolas of Cusa pointed out in his early *magnum opus De docta ignorantia* ('On Learned Ignorance'): 'From the standpoint of negative theology, in God there is nothing but infinity.'[26]

Therefore in classical Christian tradition, too, **creation 'from nothing'** does not mean from some quasi-black nothing before or alongside God, an independent void which God must open up in order to engage in any creative activity at all. Creation 'from nothing' is a sober expression that the world as a whole – including space and time, as Augustine already stresses – owes itself to the first cause, God alone, and to no other cause. Contrary to the assumptions of Jewish and Christian theologians whose thought is anthropomorphic, the finite cannot *a priori* limit the infinite. Why not? Because God is wholly other: infinitely pure spirit, whom nothing limits. And because things, human beings, the world, **do not exist alongside** or **under** God, but *a priori* in God, the infinite. It is not **alongside**, but **in** his divine being and essence that the Creator grants being and essence, accords space, gives time.

So God need not draw himself together and as it were hold his breath, in order to breathe out on creation. At 'creation' God does not hold himself back, but rather gives himself. For he is not active in the world in the manner of the finite and the relative. He is active as the **infinite in the finite** and the absolute **in the** relative: not 'the being' alongside or above being, but dynamic **Being itself** (Thomas Aquinas), in whom all being participates. Thus the world can be understood as *participatio* (Plato) or better as *explicatio Dei* (Nicolas of Cusa): as an **unfolding** of that **God** who is himself the many without multiplicity and who is the opposite in identity – without the world losing itself in God or, conversely, God dissolving himself in the world. This is not pantheism, but very much pan-en-theism. The Infinite is not active towards the world from above or outside. It is active in the process of the development of the world from within, as the most dynamically real reality, and simultaneously makes possible, pervades and completes this process. That is how God is to be understood according to Nicolas of Cusa's late work ('The Not-Other'): as the 'centre of the centre, goal of the goal, designation of the designation, being of being and non-being of non-being'.[27] In other words, God does not work **above** world history, but **in** world history, **in** and **with** human beings and things – as their primal origin, primal ground and primal goal. God is the all-embracing, all-pervasive infinite **ground of meaning** of the world and world history, the reality which is both immanent and transcendent, the first reality of all and the ultimate reality of all, though this can only be accepted in that reasonable trust which we call faith.

Of course this confession of the incomprehensible God, of the *Deus semper maior*, the God who is always more, does not make any easier a 'theodicy', a 'justification of God', a defence of God in the face of the infinite misery of the world which is laid at his door, the uncannily dark dimensions of world history and quite specifically the Holocaust. And we have learned not least from the biblical Job that we human beings have the right to ask and enquire, indeed to beseech and accuse. However, in the face of so many misunderstandings and ambiguities in current discussions about God and suffering between and among Jews and Christians, first of all I want to indicate clearly some basic convergences in this question before I comment on the differences.[28]

3. God neither uninvolved nor compassionate but involved in suffering

Indeed one cannot put too much emphasis on the **convergences** between Christians and Jews in the postmodern **understanding of God** after Auschwitz, Hiroshima and the Gulag Archipelago.

- Jews and Christians largely agree on **negative delimitation**: on the joint Jewish-Christian criticism of a God apart from the world, who does not get involved, is unhistorical, impassible, cruel and **lacking in compassion.**
- But Jews and Christians also largely agree on **positive affirmation**: on shared Jewish-Christian faith in a **God** who is present in a hidden way, is truly involved in history, is merciful and indeed **compassionate.**

This conception already runs through the Hebrew Bible and is also basically taken for granted by the New Testament.[29] And how, after Auschwitz in particular, would it be possible to have an understanding of God which extracted God from the events of the world, left him unaffected, as it were purely with the status of an observer?

However, caution is needed here: at the same time the **Old Testament prohibition against images** must not simply be abandoned in relation to God himself. Christians are advised to be cautious precisely by the great Jewish tradition of having no images of God (not to mention Greek philosophy). In what way? Precisely because this tradition warns Christians against demoting, cheapening the transcendence of God in the face of changing human experiences, against moderating it in favour of an excessive anthropomorphism.

No, for the sake of the divinity of God, there should be no **neglect of transcendence**.

Certainly **criticism** is in place in connection with an undialectical understanding of the **omnipotence of God**, who as the 'ab-solute' power, 'detached' from everything, directs everything, makes everything or could make everything.

But: criticism is equally clearly indicated when to explain the meaninglessness of suffering the conceptuality is conjured up of a dialectic of the power and powerlessness of God, of strength and weakness, even a conceptuality which simply replaces God's power with powerlessness, God's wisdom with folly, indeed God's holiness with God's guilt. Here I no longer recognize the God of the Bible.

Certainly one may **object to a theocratic creator God** who controls everything, an authoritarian high God, even a despot.

But: criticism is no less appropriate of a powerless and defenceless, impotent God who has abandoned any providence and decree in world history. That, too, is indisputably no longer the biblical God.

Certainly **doubt is in place about** the notion of an **impassible God**, of Platonic immobility and uninvolvement.

But: equally clearly, doubts must be expressed about a wholly anthropomorphic, foolish God, who suffers and even dies in human fashion, a God who can no longer give, indeed on whom human beings must now for their part have compassion and mercy. This would no longer be a compassionate God but a **God to feel sorry for**. This God, too, is not the God of the Bible.

It is my conviction that the riddle of human suffering cannot be solved with such bold phantasmagoria, nor do they help in coping with a monstrous reality like Auschwitz. Muslims, more concerned for God's transcendence than some Christians and Jews, rightly give their ironic and critical commentaries on such a 'run-down', 'pitiful' picture of God. Here the christology of which Christian theologians often make excessive use for their image of God is particularly open to criticism, and undifferentiated thinking needs differentiation. Hence the question:

4. A crucified God?

After the Second World War, Christians, referring to a remark by
Dietrich Bonhoeffer, often sought to tackle the problem of suffering by
assuming a 'suffering God'. God is 'weak and powerless in the world,
and that is precisely the way, the only way, in which he is with us and
helps us... only the suffering God can help'.[30] In respect of the Holocaust,
some theologians have even concluded from this that the 'inexpressible
suffering of the six million is also the voice of the suffering God'.[31] Yet
other theologians have thought that they could deal with the problems
of suffering in a highly speculative way by means of a history of
suffering within the Trinity which is played out dialectically between
God and God, indeed God **against** God.

However, taught by the great Judaeo-Christian tradition and with
awareness of Hegel's problematical thought-model, we do well to be
reserved towards speculations more inspired by Hegel than by the
Bible, about a suffering God, a 'crucified God',[32] even a 'death of
God'.[33] They were always impossible for Jews and Muslims, and even
today they are also difficult for many Christians. As if christological
speculations and conceptual manipulations of the concept of God
could really put the immense and especially the innocent, meaningless
suffering of this human life, this human history, and finally also of the
Holocaust on a 'higher plane' and deal with it that way! Jewish
theology, at any rate, tries to make a theological response to the
challenge of the Holocaust without such devices of christological
reflection. And for Christian theologians too – for all God's 'humanity',
or more precisely loving-kindness, towards human beings (*philanthro-
pia*[34]) which is manifest in Christ Jesus – there must be no levelling-
down of transcendence, no sell-out of the Godness of God, even in the
face of so much incomprehensible suffering and grief.

A look at scripture may sober up such speculative boldness. According
to the **Old Testament**, people keep crying to God in trust that God will
hear their cries and weeping, but their crying, suffering and dying does
not simply become the crying, suffering and dying of God. Granted, in
anthropomorphic fashion the Hebrew Bible sometimes attributes the
whole range of human feelings and patterns of behaviour to God:
anger, complaint and pain at the conduct of his people, and also, time
and again, patience and the cessation of his anger. But nowhere is the
distinction between God and human beings done away with, nor is the
pain and suffering of human beings simply declared to be the suffering
and pain of God and thus transfigured. Nowhere does God's Godliness

become ungodliness, his faithfulness unfaithfulness, his reliability unreliability, his divine mercy human pitifulness. For the Old Testament, though human beings fail, God does not fail; when human beings die, God does not die with them. For 'I am God and not man, the holy one in your midst', states Hosea 11 against any anthropomorphic presentation of God, although there the talk of God's compassion on his people is more anthropomorphic than elsewhere.

Also according to the **New Testament**, Jesus, the Son of God, cries out to God his Father because he believes that he has been abandoned by God in the depths of his suffering. But nowhere does God cry to God, nowhere is God himself weak, helpless, suffering, crucified, or even dead. If one identifies human suffering so much with God that it is also God's suffering, if the cry of human beings becomes the cry of God, then does not human sin also become God's own sin (the crimes of the SS butchers)?

No, a Christian theologian thinking biblically cannot avoid the sobering observation that the message which, according to Paul, is the **word of the cross**, is weakness and folly only for non-believers; for believers it is the **power** of God and **the wisdom** of God.[35] This is a paradox, but not a contradiction, and it is important for Jewish-Christian dialogue: in the cross of Jesus Christ – according to the whole of the New Testament, here very much in line with the Hebrew Bible and contrary to all Gnostic-Kabbalistic speculations – it is **not** simply God who has been crucified: **the God, ho** *theos, Deus pater omnipotens* (far less, of course, God's Holy Spirit). How else could the crucified Jesus, forsaken by God, have cried out to God, 'My God, my God'?[36] No, according to the New Testament, here we have no 'speculative Good Friday',[37] no *'salto mortale'* by God himself. And despite the seductive voice in Elie Wiesel's famous Auschwitz story of the young boy on the gallows,[38] it is not 'God' hanging there on the cross, but God's anointed, his 'Christ', the 'Son of Man'.

In other words, the cross is not the symbol of the 'suffering', 'screaming' God, indeed 'the symbol of God suffering the distress of death', but the symbol of **humanity** suffering the distress of death. God himself (*ho theos*), the Father, did not die on the cross, but God's **'Messiah'** and **'Christ'**, God's **'Image, 'Word'** and **'Son'**. At a very early stage the church rightly condemned an unbiblical patripassianism, the view that God the Father himself suffered! And if Jewish theologians rightly protest against a sadistic and cruel picture of God, according to which a bloodthirsty God calls for the sacrifice of his Son, I hope that Christian theology will no less emphatically protest against a masochistic, tolerant understanding of God according to which a weak

God had to torture himself to resurrection by suffering and death, if he was not to suffer eternally.

Indeed, when confronted with speculation about God 'at a low' I ask myself: does it really make any difference to the situation of human suffering if God, too, is directly drawn into it? As I once heard Karl Rahner ask, 'Do things go better for human beings when they are going badly even for God?'[39] Is that not an unbiblical anthropomorphism? Precisely in the light of the New Testament, it must be said as a matter of principle that a helpless, foolish, weak, crucified God has not become 'visible' in the folly and helplessness of the cross. And had God really himself died on the cross, we would be confronted with the unanswerable question, 'Who raised this dead God to new life?' Only in Hegel's system of dialectic, dictated by logical necessity, is the dead God himself brought to life again through a dialectical upswing – a purely speculative solution. But in the light of the New Testament? In the perspective of this book, any notion of a self-redemption of God is foolish.

So as theologians, too, let us make no mistake about it: seen in itself the cross is a sheer fiasco, into which nothing is to be secretly introduced. It is an unprecedented abandonment of the one sent by God, by both human beings **and** by God. To this extent we must agree with the philosopher Hans Blumenberg when he seeks to read out of Jesus' cry of lament over his godforsakenness the 'failure of God' in his work, God's 'self-sublation'. If we concentrate solely on the death of Jesus on the cross, we can hardly contradict Blumenberg. But Johann Sebastian Bach's *St Matthew Passion*, which Blumenberg uses in his interpretation, ends, like the Gospels themselves, with the certainty of resurrection and redemption, and the 'covenant of peace' between humankind and God.[40] Only in the light of the resurrection of Jesus to life is God's hidden presence accepted in faith after the event, in his manifest absence. This cannot be understood speculatively in the sense of a self-resurrection of God. For again, according to the whole of the New Testament, what is proclaimed is not the raising of God to new life, but only that of Jesus, the **Son**. But who is the subject of this raising? Obviously God himself (*ho theos*), who is a God of the living and not of the dead: the **Father**. As Paul says clearly, not of God, but of Christ, the Son of God, 'he was crucified in weakness, but lives by the power of God (= the Father)'.[41]

Indeed, only in this way, by the acceptance of this Son into God's eternal life, does God show himself to be near in solidarity with believers as he is with this unique Son (and thus with all his sons and daughters), even in extreme suffering, in forsakenness and dying: as the one who is also bound up with our grief and our suffering (merited or unmerited); as the one who is also affected by our suffering and by all injustice, **sharing the suffering** in a hidden way and yet precisely in so doing, right to the end the infinitely **good** and **powerful** God.

That is the most I may say on the basis of scripture about the question of God and suffering. On the basis of this conviction of faith, is talk about God after Auschwitz also possible? For does not the question of theodicy, the question of the vindication, the defence, of God, arise here in a quite different, radical, way?

5. An answer to the question of theodicy

Having been constantly preoccupied for decades with all the attempts at theodicy – in modern times from Gottfried Wilhelm Leibniz to Hans Jonas – I can confidently say quite bluntly that there seems to me to be **no theoretical answer** whatsoever to the **theodicy problem**. On the basis of a an attitude of faith only one thing can be said:

- **If** God exists, then God was also in Auschwitz! Even in this death factory, believers of different religions and confessions maintained that, despite everything, God lives.
- But at the same time the believer also has to concede that there is no answer to the question, '**How** could God have been in Auschwitz without preventing Auschwitz?'

Despite all pious apologetic, one has to concede soberly that any theologians who seek to get behind the mystery, the mystery of God himself, will at best discover their own theologoumenon, their own little theological discovery there. Neither the Hebrew Bible nor the New Testament tells us **how** the good, gracious and powerful God – in the end of the day none of these attributes can finally be abandoned if we are still to talk of **God** – has been able to allow such immeasurable suffering in his world in things both small (but what is 'small' here?) and great (indeed excessively great), how he could 'watch' while Auschwitz was made possible and 'look on' while the gas streamed out and the crematorium ovens were burning.

Or should I simply console myself over all the suffering of the Holocaust with the classical theological formula that God does not will suffering; however, he does not not will it either: rather, he simply 'allows it' (*permittit*). But does that solve all the riddles? No, it did not solve them yesterday any more than it does today. But, it might be asked, in that case cannot we simply eliminate this primal human problem? On the basis of what new insights, on the basis of what experiences of our own? We do not need the Holocaust to confront us with this problem. Sometimes simply failure at work, an illness, the loss, betrayal or death of a single person, is enough to cast us into despair. That is precisely what happened to the American rabbi Harold S.Kushner. Because he lost a child through a tragic illness, he wrote a book which went on to become a best seller, *When Bad Things Happen to Good People*.[42] His suggested solution was that the notion of God's **omnipotence** should be abandoned. Others feel no less troubled by the thought of 'When Good Things Happen to Bad People', and because of that would want to deny God's **goodness** and **justice**. But neither of these courses offers a way out of the dilemma. For a God robbed of all omnipotence ceases to be God, and the idea that God is cruel and arbitrary rather than gracious and just is even more intolerable.

For better or for worse, we have to put up with the fact that the problem is not solved by either such over-hasty negations or such highly speculative affirmations. What a presumption of the human spirit it is, whether it comes in the guise of theological scepticism, philosophical metaphysics, idealistic philosophy of history or trinitarian speculation! Perhaps we can learn from this to understand the arguments of Epicurus, Bayle, Feuerbach or Nietzsche against such theodicy less as blasphemy of God than as mockery of human beings and especially of the arrogance of theologians. At this extreme point, on this difficult question, a **theology of silence** would seem to be better: 'If I were to know him, I would be him', goes an old Jewish saying. And some Jewish theologians who prefer to dispense with any ultimate vindication of God in the face of all suffering simply quote the terse word of scripture which follows the report of the death of the two sons of Aaron, killed by divine fire: 'And Aaron held his peace.'[43]

None of the great minds of humanity – whether Augustine or Thomas or Calvin, Leibniz or Hegel – has solved the basic problem: Immanuel Kant wrote *On the Failure of all Philosophical Attempts at a Theodicy* in 1791, when in Paris people were thinking of doing away with God and replacing him with the goddess Reason. But to put the question the other way round: is **atheism**, then, the solution? An atheism which would see its Faustian pledge in Auschwitz? Is Auschwitz the rock of atheism? Or perhaps Auschwitz might rather be the consequence and the end of atheism? Is that a better explanation of the godlessness of the world? Of its grandeur and its misery? Does unbelief explain the world as it is now? Can unbelief bring consolation in unmerited, incomprehensible, meaningless suffering? As if all **unbelieving** reason did not have its limits in such suffering! No, here the anti-theologian is no better off than the theologian.

Above all the Jewish writer **Elie Wiesel**, whose autobiographical Auschwitz book I have already mentioned, has showed through all his extensive plays and prose works that one cannot deal adequately with Auschwitz either by theological speculation or by an anti-theology. To the question whether we could speak about God after Auschwitz, he replied pointedly: 'I do not believe that we can speak **about** God; we can only – as Kafka put it – speak **to** God. It all depends on who is speaking. What I am attempting is to speak **to** God. Even if I speak **against** him, I am speaking **to** him. And even if I am angry at God, I am attempting to show him my anger. But that in itself contains a confession of God, not a negation of God.' Can there still be any theology at all after Auschwitz? Wiesel replied: 'I personally do not believe so. There cannot be any theology **after** Auschwitz and certainly not any theology **about** Auschwitz. For we are lost whatever we do; whatever we say is inappropriate. One can never understand the event **with** God, and one cannot understand the event **without God**. Theology, the Logos of God? Who am I to explain God? Some people attempt it. I believe that they fail. Nevertheless... It is their right to make the attempt. After Auschwitz everything is an attempt.'[44] So what is left, if it is still right to make a theological attempt?

6. Meaningless suffering cannot be understood theoretically, but must be endured in trust

There is no avoiding the sobering acknowledgment that if neither a theological nor an anti-theological 'theory' explains suffering, then another basic attitude is called for. It is my insight, which has grown over the decades and to which so far I have not found a convincing alternative, that suffering, excessive, innocent suffering, **meaningless suffering** – both individual and collective – **cannot be understood theoretically, but can only be lived through**. For Christians and Jews there is only a **practical answer** to the problem of theodicy. What is that? In this question both Jews and Christians may point to different, yet interconnected, traditions:

In extreme suffering both **Jews** and Christians have in view the figure of **Job**, who indicates two things: in the last resort God is and remains incomprehensible to human beings, and yet human beings are given the possibility of showing an unshakeable, **unconditional trust** in this incomprehensible God, rather than resignation or despair. In the light of Job they can trust that God also respects the human **protest** against suffering and finally manifests himself as the creator of human beings who redeems them from suffering.

For Christians – and why not also for Jews? – in extreme suffering (over and above the figure of Job, who in the last resort is fictitious), there shines out the truly historical figure of the suffering and dying 'servant of God',[45] the **man of grief from Nazareth**. His betrayal, his being handed over, flogged and scorned, his slow dying on the cross, has anticipated what Susan Shapiro has described as the fearful threefold experience of the victims of the Holocaust:[46] namely, that all-pervasive experience of being abandoned by all human beings, even robbed of one's humanity, indeed of being abandoned by God himself.

In his book on the Holocaust Martin Gilbert tells the story of the sixteen-year-old Zvi Michalowski. On 27 September 1941 the young man should have been executed with more than 3,000 Lithuanian Jews. He had fallen into the pit a fraction of a second before the volley of shots which killed those standing with him. That night he crept out of the mass grave and escaped to the nearest village. A peasant who opened the door to him saw the naked figure, covered with blood, and said, 'Jew, go back to the grave where you belong!' In despair Zvi Michalowski finally beseeched an elderly widow: 'I am your Lord, Jesus Christ. I came down from the cross. Look at me – the blood, the pain, the suffering of the innocent. Let me in.' The widow, Zvi remembered, threw herself at his feet and hid him for three days. Then the young man made his way to the nearby forest. There he survived the war as a partisan.[47]

Did Jesus' death have a meaning? One should not seek by means of all kinds of anthropomorphic theories to overplay and exalt this dying, forsaken by God and human beings. Why not? Because only after the event, as a result of belief in the resurrection of Jesus to new life through and in God, does a '**meaning**' enter into this **meaningless, godforsaken dying**. Only on the basis of this faith is the crucified Jesus, exalted to God's eternal life, also the invitation in hope **to trust** in a meaning even in senseless suffering, and in this life to practise **endurance** and **persistence** to the end. So there is no expectation of a happy ending on earth, as in the story which frames the book of Job, who in the end even has his three daughters restored to him. Rather, there is the quite radical offer of the possibility of affirming a meaning even in meaningless suffering (if need be, endured to the bitter end): a hidden meaning, which human beings cannot uncover by themselves, but which can be given in the light of this one person, forsaken by God and man, and yet justified. For scripture, suffering and hope belong indissolubly together.[48] This is hope in a God who despite everything will prove and establish himself not as an arbitrary God, capricious and impassible, but as a God of redeeming love.

So without suffering being trivialized, reinterpreted or glorified, or even just accepted stoically, impassively, without feeling, it can be recognized in the light of Jesus, the suffering servant of God, and confessed with almost desperate hope, in protest and prayer:

– that even when suffering is apparently meaningless, God is nevertheless hiddenly present;

– that while God does not preserve us **from** all suffering, he does preserve us **in** all suffering;

– that wherever possible we should show solidarity in suffering and attempt to share in bearing it;

– indeed, that in this way we are not only enduring suffering but, where possible, fighting against it, less in individual matters than in the structures and relationships which are caused by suffering.

We must all decide for ourselves whether this is an answer which can be lived out; which does not lead us to forget suffering, but to come to terms with it. I have been moved and encouraged by the fact that even in Auschwitz, countless **Jews** and also some **Christians** believed in the God who despite all the terrors was nevertheless hiddenly present, in the God who not only suffered with them but also had mercy on them. They trusted and – this is often overlooked – **prayed even in the hell of Auschwitz**. Since then, many shattering testimonies have been collected which show that in the concentration camps not only was the Talmud recited secretly, were the festivals observed, but that there were also prayers in trust to God even in the face of death.[49] Thus Rabbi **Zvi Hirsch Meisel** reports how on Rosh Hashanah, the Jewish New Year's Day, at risk of his life, he blew the shophar ('ram's horn') one last time at the request of 1,400 young men condemned to death. When he left their block, a young man cried out: 'The Rebbe has strengthened our spirits by telling us that "even if a sharp sword rest on a man's throat, he should not despair of God's mercy". I say to you, we can hope that things will get better, but we must be prepared for them to get worse. For God's sake, let us not forget to cry out *shema yisrael* with devotion at the last moment.'[50] And so countless Jews (and some Christians) in the concentration camps trusted that it made sense to accept their own suffering, to call on the hidden God and where possible to support others. And because people prayed even **in** Auschwitz, while prayer **after** Auschwitz has not got any easier, at all events it can never become meaningless.

7. A third way

And did people in Auschwitz – whether Jews or Christians – cry in their prayers to a weak, foolish, imprisoned, helpless, dead God! That is unimaginable! If they prayed at all, they will have cried out to a living, involved God, even if he was absent and hidden, a God in whose power they trusted – through all the violence and evil of human beings: to the sun which is completely covered by dark clouds. As a Jew wrote on the walls of the Warsaw ghetto:

> *I believe in the sun even when it does not shine.*
> *I believe in love, even when I cannot feel it.*
> *I believe in God, even when I do not see him.*

No, it is not the impotent God but the compassionate God of love, strength, goodness and mercy who made the victims strong enough to withstand the cruelty. So to confess the merciful God in the death camps did not mean to bear witness to God as himself **as prisoner, as victim, as** dead. It meant to confess God himself as a living God **for** the prisoners, **for** the victims, **for** the dead. At all events he is a God who clearly stands on the side of the victims and not on the side of the executioners. According to our common Jewish and Christian faith there is a God to whom the future will belong, who in justice creates rights for those who have no rights and so will show his power to the impotent – a God of the living and not of the dead.

To sum up: by this answer I have not solved the concrete question why God 'did not intervene', 'did not prevent it', because I cannot. But I have attempted to relativize it. It seems to me that in view of the tremendous negativity, theologically a **middle way** is offered for us, Christians and Jews. On the one hand there is the godlessness of those who think to find in Auschwitz their strongest argument against God, and yet who nevertheless fail to explain anything. And on the other hand there is **the type of faith in God** of those who speculatively incorporate Auschwitz into trinitarian theology and elevate it into a dialectic of suffering within God, yet do not explain the ultimate cause of suffering either. This middle, modest way is **the way of unshakeable (not irrational, but completely reasonable) trust in God – despite everything**: of faith in a God who remains the light despite and in abysmal darkness. Because there is Auschwitz, say the godless, the idea of God is intolerable. And those who believe in God, whether Jews or Christians, may answer, 'Only because there is God is the thought of Auschwitz tolerable to me at all.'

That is also the view of the Orthodox American theologian **Michael Wyschogrod**, from the perspective of Jewish theology: 'Jewish faith is therefore from the beginning faith that God can do what is incomprehensible to human beings. In our time that includes the belief that despite Auschwitz, God can fulfil his promise to redeem Israel and the world. Can I understand how that is possible? No. Far less can I understand how God can ever make it up to those who perished in the Holocaust. But with Abraham I believe that he will do this. Is this faith offensive? Does it take the suffering of those who were murdered too lightly? In one way, yes, quite definitely, from a human perspective. However, God can and will do this. He is not bound to what is possible for human beings. He has promised to redeem us, and he will do it.'[51]

It seems to me that there must be more talk about this between Jews and Christians in the future. After all, this is precisely what the apostle Paul means by those statements which sound like a hymn but which nevertheless come from his own experience of suffering. Today he could write them even above Auschwitz, Hiroshima and the Gulag Archipelago: 'If God is for us, who is against us...? For I am sure that neither death, nor life, nor angels, nor principalities, nor things present, nor things to come, nor powers, nor height, nor depth, nor anything else in all creation, will be able to separate us from the love of God in Christ Jesus our Lord.'[52]

But only at the end will what the agnostic Jewish philosopher Max Horkheimer hoped so much from 'the wholly other', 'that the murderer may not triumph over the innocent victim', be made manifest.[53] And our Jewish brothers and sisters, too, will be able to join in what is written on the last page of the New Testament, taking up the prophets, about the eschaton as a testimony of hope: 'And God himself will be with them; he will wipe away all tears from their eyes, and death shall be no more, neither shall there be mourning nor crying nor pain any more, for the former things have passed away.'[54]

Epilogue: No New World Order without a New World Ethic

We live in exciting times. Within a few hectic years the world scene has changed with tremendous turbulence: the collapse of the Soviet system, the reunification of Germany, the democratization of the former Eastern-bloc states, the Gulf War... Despite the enormous economic difficulties of the former 'Warsaw Pact' countries and indeed East Germany, on the whole there has perhaps been a turn for the better; despite the devastating consequences of the Gulf War for the whole environment and whole peoples (the Kurds), consequences which will take a long time to deal with, on the whole there are still perhaps prospects of peace not only in the Gulf but also in Palestine. Israel's most dangerous opponent has been conquered – without the intervention of Israel.

All these developments also show how difficult political developments are to diagnose and to prognosticate. Here is a test question. What did you think of a military intervention – before, then during, and finally after the Gulf War? In some detailed assessments everyone was wrong – including the governments, the generals and the secret services. Not only has the USSR frittered away billions for information which it would have done better to glean without prejudice from careful reading of the serious press, but for three decades the CIA, now with 20,000 employees, has given one American president after another false briefings about the extent and growth of the Soviet economy (and also the strength of the Iraqi army) because it was trapped in its own prejudices. After the end of the Cold War there is also an urgent need for the disarming of the often useless and uncontrolled armies of the secret services. However, even more urgent is the abandonment of absurd projects like SDI, Star Wars, for which – leaving aside the basic technological preconditions – there is neither the money (20.9 billion dollars in seven years with a new demand for 120 billion) nor the relevant enemy ('the evil empire'); or the French nuclear experiments on Muroroa Atoll, which are continuing despite all the protests; and new German plans for arms purchases. On the other hand, are not at long last the humanitarian use of American troops (e.g. 8,000 US soldiers for the Kurds and 12,000 for Bangladesh) or German aid for reconstruction in the Eastern European countries (85 billion DM for the Soviet Union and neighbouring countries – along with 20 billion for sharing the burden of the Gulf War) a hopeful sign of a new thinking which also needs to be extended to the immense North-South problems?

Without going too much into detailed political assessments here, I think that the urgency of the three postulates 'world ethic, religious peace, religious dialogue', which I developed in *Global Responsibility* (1990, English translation 1991) and which are the quite matter-of-fact basic convictions of this book, has become even more evident. So here are a few brief remarks – not in the spirit of any superior theological knowledge, but as a sober analysis of the political situation after the Gulf War – which are of long-term importance for Judaism, Christianity and Islam. Having spent many hundreds of pages saying what it seems to me necessary to say about Judaism itself, here I shall be discussing current political problems which affect all three religions.

The third chance for a postmodern world order

As one can see more clearly in retrospect, the modern order, which has beyond doubt shown enormous successes in science and technology, industrialization and democratization, had already entered into a radical crisis in the First World War. In a fourteen-point programme, the then American President Woodrow Wilson, Nobel Peace Prize Winner in 1919, had set down what the new world order after 1918 should be. But the opportunity was missed. 'Versailles' became the symbol of the continuation of the old struggle for hegemony and the intent of the European powers on revenge. Unfortunately the 'League of Nations' suggested by Wilson and founded in 1920 emerged stillborn. Europe and the world paid dearly for that: with Fascism and National Socialism, with Communism and Japanese militarism, and in their wake with the Second World War, the Holocaust, the Gulag Archipelago and Hiroshima. Instead of a world order there was unprecedented world chaos.

After 1945 there was another chance of a new world order, and the United Nations which was now founded was meant to help towards this. But this new attempt, too, was a mixed affair. The old Europe, given generous economic support by the United States under President Truman, had certainly come together in a very transitory, but nevertheless functioning European Community. But it was above all the Stalinist

Soviet Union which in Eastern Europe and elsewhere got in the way of a better order and dug its own grave through totalitarianism within and hegemony without. Instead of a world order there was a division of the world. To an unbridled capitalism with negative consequences, above all in Latin America and Africa, there was now added a socialism which brought unprecedented human slavery and the exploitation of nature from the Elbe to Vladivostock – until it could go on no longer.

Now – after the collapse of Marxist socialism in 1989 and the dissolving of the blocs, we have been given a **third opportunity for a 'postmodern' world order**. From a political perspective this presupposes democratic constitutions, and from an economic perspective a market economy with both a social and an ecological orientation. This is affirmed at least in principle in Washington, Brussels and now also in Moscow, though it is still some way from being realized. But such a world order will not come into being without a new understanding between the nations, of the kind that is taking shape in the European community, which has thus become an attractive model from Eastern Europe to Black Africa, South America and the Pacific.

Of course it is impossible to find a simultaneous solution to all the numerous problems of the world – in which so often the various religions are involved: one has only to think of all the regional **trouble-spots**, in the Balkans (Serbia, Slovenia and Croatia), in Central America (Guatemala and El Salvador), in South America (Colombia and Peru) and southern Asia (Afghanistan, Kashmir, the Punjab, Tibet, Sri Lanka), in the Far East (Burma, the Philippines, Cambodia) and in most African countries (especially Liberia and the Sudan). Certainly, in some countries – for example in South Africa, Angola, Ethiopia, Haiti, El Salvador and Nepal – there is now a more resolute concern than elsewhere for democracy, internal peace and social reforms. That is important. But the final removal of some of the notorious trouble-spots which impinge on the whole world beyond an individual nation is an element in a new world order. And top of the agenda in the international community after the Gulf War is the **Palestine question**, which for more than four decades has poisoned international relations, and which from the beginning was also linked with the Gulf War.

Land for peace!

Just as the division of Germany, which had led to a disastrous division of Europe, was overcome, so now the Palestinian question must be solved in order to bring about a peaceful order in the Middle East. That is a central concern of this book. For:

– What a liberation and a joy it would be for **Judaism** everywhere if Israel, the state of the Jews, finally gained universal recognition and could live in security and peace, devoting itself to civil reconstruction in the whole region instead of military defence!

– What a liberation and a new opportunity for the future it would also be for the **Arab world** if after the foundation of a Palestinian state the Arab states could at last concentrate wholly on social reforms and the building up of economically and politically strong democracies (instead of strong armies), without highly emotional and far-fetched political rhetoric.

– And finally, what would it mean for the whole **world community** if instead of concentrating on the Middle East it could concentrate on other important trouble-spots, especially in the countries of the South.

All in all, there is a tremendous opportunity for the state of Israel. With the UN, the USSR and the EC, the US government is now affirming the principle 'land for peace' as a settlement of the Palestinian question. But the present government of Israel under Shamir is still inexorably rejecting this, with every kind of objection and legalistic hair-splitting. Indeed, it is attempting systematically to exclude the UN from taking part in the peace talks and refusing to accept the Security Council resolutions as criteria binding on all states. I have already indicated that in the meantime, neither the geopolitical nor the biblical reasons for the insolent new 'conquest' are convincing. However, some Israelis think that Jordan (which is in fact itself part of the Davidic kingdom) is after all the 'Palestinian state' and are again arguing for the emigration or exiling of the remaining 1.7 million Palestinians to Jordan. But such a solution, in the style of totalitarian systems, would not be tolerated either by the majority of the Israeli people or by the USA, the EC or the USSR. Sensible spiritual leaders of Judaism, like the former Chief Rabbi of Great Britain, Lord Jakobovits, are now raising their voices and warning that Israel cannot 'for ever rule over one and a half million Arabs'. In more than thirty years these would be 'in the majority'. So the Palestinians have concerns which cannot be 'denied for ever' (*The Tablet*, 15 June 1991). Therefore the only alternative is: either to hand back the occupied territories or wage a further war which will come sooner or later. Those Arab states which have not been offered back any territory, as Egypt has, are still in a state of war with Israel and are now rearming.

But will such a solution come about without external political pressure? Such pressure would help no one more than the Israelis themselves, as the majority of people in the country see quite clearly. But now that President Bush has missed the favourable moment for a Middle Eastern trip immediately after the Gulf War, America's irresolution so far has simply been exploited by the hotheads on the one hand and the blockheads on the other. Since the secret diplomacy of Secretary of State Baker, carried on all too gingerly with kid gloves (despite the support of the Soviet Foreign Minister) got hopelessly bogged down in procedural questions after four Near Eastern trips and was made to look ridiculous by the provocative new Israeli settlements in the occupied territories (the offical count is 105,000 settlers on the West Bank and 4,500 on the Gaza strip, 10% more than at the beginning of January 1991), **another strategy** is now being considered in Washington. 58% of Americans (as opposed to 30% earlier) are now refusing to give Israel's strength and security top priority if Israel rejects the American proposals for a solution to the Arab-Israeli conflict (*Time* magazine, 3 June 1991). How is any progress to be made here if only friendly personal letters are sent, and Israel's government is secretly given a *de facto* veto against the Palestinians?

No solution is possible without dramatic action from the superpowers, which for the moment would put a strain on American-Israeli relations, though it would give support to the majority in Israel who are concerned for peace. Some American observers also share the view that a necessary scenario would be:

– The convening of a **peace conference** by the two superpowers (with observer status for the EC and the UN), which would be attended by Israel and the Arab nations involved.

– A **clear indication** of the purposes and goals, and also – without further negotiations – of the rules and procedures (relating to timing, the plenary conference and sub-conferences);

– **Consequences for non-attendance**: withdrawal of military, financial and economic support by the superpowers (and the EC).

– Just as President Truman after 1945 and President Carter in 1979 became quite personally involved (through trips to Cairo and Jerusalem, and the Camp David conference), so too the present **American President George Bush** should not hesitate to put his office and the whole prestige of the United States – to which Israel owes so much – on the line.

– At the same time, **public opinion** in the states concerned must be activated positively, so that the immense advantages of a peaceful solution can be clearly recognized, along with the concessions which are unfortunately needed as well. Instead of exclusive secret diplomacy there should be an appeal to the people.

In **Israel** this could result in a new majority and the formation of a new government. At any rate, many people see enormous advantages which could arise from a peace conference of the kind proposed by President Bush and Secretary of State Baker. Thus the former Israeli Foreign Minister and USA ambassador Abba Eban writes: 'The advantages would include: negotiations with the Arab states, dialogue with the majority representatives among the Palestinians, close co-operation with the United States in a peace process, a new status in the European community and diplomatic relations with the Soviet Union. The whole result would be an economic boom which would help Israel to solve the problems which have now arisen as a result of the providential arrival of immigrants from the Soviet Union and Ethiopia' (*International Herald Tribune*, 14 June 1991). In contrast to Shamir, Eban has no objections to the symbolic presence of UN observers.

It remains to be hoped that with the elections which are again looming in the United States, neither the powerful Israel lobby nor the gigantic arms industry can sabotage the peace efforts, a failure over which will lead sooner or later to a new Middle East crisis which will endanger the whole world. Or is the world to wait until not only Israel, but also one of the seventeen Arab states between Morocco and Pakistan which see Israel as their enemy, gets hold of the atom bomb? How would occupied territories and security zones help then? The present rearmament on all sides bodes no good.

What can be learned from the Gulf War

Some lessons can be learned from the Gulf War for a new world order in the Middle East:

1. A mass murderer and megalomaniac dictator cannot be allowed decisive power over a region which is vital to the life of the whole world. Stalin (in Finland) and Hitler (throughout Europe) have demonstrated that **peace at any price is not worth while**. Resistance must be offered to a man who wreaks bloody terror within his country and wages a ten-year war against his neighbour Iran, with around a million dead. Anyone who fights with hostage-taking, poison gas and oil pollution, and who threatens another state, Israel, with total annihilation by 'non-conventional' weapons, is not a negotiating partner. He must be stopped.

2. But a **war** was **not inevitable from the start**: (*a*) American

diplomacy (including the CIA) had a stunning failure in the lead-up to the crisis; in her conversation with Saddam Hussein immediately before the invasion of Kuwait the US ambassador had not threatened US intervention, but rather had indicated that the whole affair was solely a matter for the Arabs. (*b*) An earlier solution to the Palestinian question was long overdue; instead of this, there had been opposition to linkage between the Gulf crisis and the Palestinian crisis, which we know to have been the main reason for the disputes between the Arabs and Israel/America. (*c*) Economic sanctions could have been given longer to work and could have been combined with demands for the resignation of the Iraqi head of state; instead of this, a whole people was fearfully punished and the dictator and his whole clique were left in power.

3. However, an absolute pacifism, for which peace is a supreme good to which everything must be sacrificed, is irresponsible. **Legitimate self-defence** in accordance with article 51 of the UN charter is not ruled out even by the Sermon on the Mount; the demand for the renunciation of violence must not be interpreted in a literalistic and fundamentalist way. Pacifism is not enough to preserve peace. What is called for is not an idle peace, but peace as a work of justice, and in some circumstances this means defending those who are attacked and disarming the attackers. What is in place here is not a dispositional ethic unconcerned for the consequences, but an **ethic of disposition and responsibility** which as far as possible takes the consequences into account. Some 'peace fighters' must be told that mere moral disposition without reason can have catastrophic effects.

4. Conversely, of course, it is also the case that merely **efficient politics without morality have a tendency to lead to criminal actions.** Here the Gulf War in particular has shown that pointing to Saddam Hussein in no way answers the question who is to blame for this war. No, a **searching of consciences**, particularly after the war, must go further afield. Here we have more than just black and white, villains and innocent, good and bad, God and Satan. The demonization of the opponent often serves as an excuse for oneself. Everyone wooed Iraq and equipped it with money, technology and advisors – regardless of the power blocs: China, the Soviet Union, and then above all the West. With the benevolent toleration and complicity of the United States, in particular France, England, Italy and – through the irresponsible tolerance of activity of criminal firms – unfortunately also Germany were involved. Up to 80% of the weapons provided for the region came from the five permanent members of the Security Council.

5. **Wars**, particularly in the twentieth century, are **neither 'holy' nor**

'just' nor 'clean'. The time of the 'Wars of Yahweh' and the 'Crusades'
is happily now long past, and that of the militant 'jihad' (which does
not mean 'holy war' but primarily moral 'effort' for God's cause)
should similarly at last be a thing of the past. Those Islamic guardians
of the grail who met in Lahore, Pakistan, from 15-17 February 1991
and took their stand behind Saddam Hussein and his 'jihad' against
the 'unbelievers' and 'hypocrites' (Iraq's neighbours to the south of the
Gulf) did not do the cause of God any service, any more than did the
American president, who in Crusader fashion resorted to the name of
God in connection with the war and the victory celebrations, shed tears
for his own 'boys', called on the Kurds and Shi'ites to rebel, and
immediately afterwards cold-bloodedly left them in the lurch (to the
advantage of Saddam Hussein). Instead of removing the main culprit,
this latest war, waged and won with high technology, has resulted in
incalculable loss of human life, the destruction of the whole infrastructure of a country, millions of fleeing refugees, and ecological disaster
on a vast scale – all consequences which are making even some of those
who were in favour of the war now ask whether, in view of all the
military, financial, ecological, social and moral consequences, it was
really worth while. Pompous military parades to celebrate victory over
a second-rate opponent would have had a less hollow feel if at least the
first dawning of the 'new world order' in the Middle East were visible.

6. **Wars do not solve the internal problems of states** either: those
who put on a strong front externally can be weak internally. And in
particular, excessive technological armaments can be an important
reason why in time a superpower finds itself on the verge of economic
collapse (the USSR) or can no longer cope with a tremendous budget
deficit and astronomical foreign debt (USA). As is well known, the war
now being celebrated in the USA had to be financed by Saudi Arabia,
Germany and Japan. The rebuilding of a worn-out infrastructure (roads
and bridges) and the development of a stagnating industry is also being
neglected in the USA, where the decayed public school system results
in defective elementary education at primary and secondary levels.
'Smart bombs' do not take the place of investment, and 'patriot' missiles
are not good weapons against the Japanese automobile and computer
industy; 'intelligent weapon systems' do not create an intelligent
society. The euphoria of victory (which I experienced in California)
does not solve any of the problems of peace: 378 American dead in the
Gulf War, but around 23,000 murder victims in the USA itself (in the
year 1990 alone). No, victory in the Gulf War cannot bring forgetfulness
of organized and unorganized crime, the increasing mass poverty, the
stagnation for twenty years of the family income of 80% of the

population, the growing illiteracy, the lack of basic health care (37 million Americans have no health insurance), the Black ghettos and drug addiction. The programme for a new order in foreign policy does not replace a domestic political agenda and resolute action for a new order at home. It is here – in domestic policy – that the harder front of our times runs. When in the USA two-thirds of the research and development budget of around 70 billion dollars is still devoted to military purposes (in Japan the proportion is only 5%), one cannot be surprised that the decline in the automobile and steel industry is also being followed by a decline in newer areas of industry. In the long run a military superpower (the USA) can hardly compete with industrial superpowers (Japan, the EC). But now, after the victory celebrations, the vast majority of Americans want the economic and social problems of America to be tackled with similar energy and comparable means. Here there will be much to think about.

Postulate 1: No world survival without a world ethic

If in this way we learn lessons from the Gulf War, we may first of all note that a new, **better world order is possible** – on certain conditions: not only in Europe, but also in the Near East and other crisis-spots of the world. By a better world order I do not mean a foretaste of paradise, an ideal state without economic rivalry, social tensions or ethnic and national conflicts; there never was a whole world, nor will there ever be in this age. By a better world order I mean a state of relative economic stability, and peace and security of the kind that the European states have achieved after centuries of economic and political rivalry and military conflicts. But how will it be introduced? **On what basis?**

A new, better world order will **not** be introduced on the basis
– of diplomatic offensives alone. All too often, these are aimed only at the governments and not at the peoples, and all too often they seem incapable of guaranteeing the peace and stability of a region;
– of humanitarian aid (food, medicines) alone. This cannot replace political action (against expulsions or wars);
– of primarily military intervention. This usually tends to have negative rather than positive consequences;
– of 'international law' alone, as long as this rests on unlimited state sovereignty and has the rights of states more in view than those of peoples and individuals (human rights).
The Gulf War in particular has shown that **international law** in its

hitherto minimal form is not enough, but needs ethical motivation, support and expansion. If a ruler ruling by force attempts to murder or drive out a whole people (the Kurds), one cannot simply refer to the UN charter, the sacrosanct principles of state sovereignty, territorial integrity and the prohibition against intervention in the domestic affairs of a nation. In that case, it is the international law of the UN that needs to be changed in accordance with ethical perspectives, in such a way that the Declaration of Human Rights does not just remain 'recommendations' by the nations, but becomes universally binding law, so that in cases of blatant crimes against humanity (genocide) the principle of non-intervention in the internal affairs of a state is abrogated in favour of legal safeguards and appropriate intervention by the international community. At any rate the moral conscience of the world public, alarmed by the very detailed reporting of the media, has quite rightly forced a change in the supercooled pragmatic policy of the American president. This demonstrates, in the face of all the cynics, that when the world's conscience is aroused, an appeal to morality, a call for human dignity and human rights can still change things even now. So protest is meaningful – protest wherever morality is sacrificed to 'reasons of state' or 'Realpolitik'. Morality must also motivate the further development of international law which is so urgently needed, in opposition to all international or even national rule by force.

So in the end a new world order will ultimately be **brought about** only **on the basis of**:
– more shared visions, ideals, values, aims and criteria;
– a heightened global responsibility on the part of the nations and their leaders;
– a new binding ethic which unites the whole of humankind, including the states and those who hold power in them, one which embraces cultures and religions. That is what is mean by the first thesis of my *Global Responsibility*: **no new world order without a new world ethic.**

Law cannot combat the double standards and double talk in world politics; only ethics can. A world politics without a world ethic will end in world chaos. But the **new world ethic is indivisible.** Specifically, that means:
– You cannot declare that the violation of Kuwait is a moral challenge and discuss the distress of the Kurds and the Shi'ites purely in terms of power politics; you cannot treat the Kuwaitis as victims and ignore the Palestinians; you cannot fight for freedom and democracy in Kuwait

and then tolerate once again the restoration of the mediaeval feudalistic regime of an Emir and its vengeful justice.

– You cannot punish a whole people with the destruction of its technological infrastructure and then want to use the butcher of Baghdad – in fear, above all, of the Shi'ites in Southern Iraq – as a 'stabilizing factor' for the whole region, instead of putting him on trial like the major Nazis and guaranteeing the status of an autonomus province in a federal Iraq for the Kurds in the north and the Shi'ites in the south.

– You cannot argue for a new peaceful order and at the same time ask the American Congress to provide billions of dollars of credits so that the poorer countries can buy weapons in America again (allegedly for security and as a deterrent).

– You cannot present disarmament plans (involving atomic, ballistic and chemical weapons) for the Middle East and at the same time provide weapons (conventional weapons) to the tune of billions to both Saudis and Israelis (Israel and the states of the Middle East squander around 25% of their GNP on weapons).

– You cannot guarantee the Jewish people a homeland, livng rights and existence as a state and refuse this to the Palestinian people.

– You cannot rapidly implement the UN decisions on the Gulf with 550,000 American soldiers, but keep UN resolutions on the question of Palestine in the air and be deterred by the talk of a government which is manifestly unwilling for peace.

– You cannot liberate 250,000 Soviet and 14,000 Ethiopian Jews and then oppress the Palestinians and rob them of their land even more.

Let us not deceive ourselves: a policy which leaves ethics out of account is not a good policy – at least in the long term. An immoral 'Realpolitik' is not a realistic policy. And even if world history is not always judgment on the world, as Hegel assumed, the peoples often pay dearly after decades or centuries for the sins which they have committed – whether in the time of colonialism or imperialism, or in the time of National Socialism or Communism.

Postulate 2: No world peace without religious peace

After the Gulf War, new opportunities for peace have opened up in the Middle East.

1. The war in the Gulf was not **a war of religions**. It was not a war between Christianity and Islam; Christians and Muslims were involved on both sides. Nor is there ancestral enmity between Jews and Muslims,

who lived together relatively peacefully until the twentieth century. No, the justified indignation over Saddam Hussein must in no way lead to sweeping condemnations of Islam as an aggressive and warlike religion with a contempt for humanity.

2. But beyond doubt the **religious dimension also** played a part in this conflict between the peoples: religion can reinforce, but it can also have a mitigating effect. Religion can foment and prolong wars, but it can also prevent and shorten them. And although the last war was not a war of religion, it was a war which on both sides was legitimated by the religions, and in part was inspired and emotionally charged by them.

3. In this war it has again become obvious how easily religion can be **misused** even by the irreligious. A war criminal like Saddam Hussein had a very subtle understanding of how to make himself popular among the Islamic masses: by taking up the Israel question; by active resistance to America and the West; by demanding the 'liberation' of the Islamic holy places (Mecca, Medina and Jerusalem!) from the Saudis or the Jews and social equilibrium between the rich and poor Arab states. All these were demands with social and religious undertones, presented by someone who – despite all the propaganda – as we know, has no religious convictions.

4. But peaceful revolutions in Poland, the ex-German Democratic Republic, Czechoslovakia, South Africa and the Philippines have shown that religion can also have an influence **in making peace**. Hence the urgent question: is it an illusion to believe that the Gulf War could have been prevented, had the Palestinian question, which for decades has poisoned the relationship between the Western world and the Arab world, finally been taken seriously? If the ecumenical dialogue between Christians, Jews and Muslims had been pressed further in the interests of preserving world peace, but also resolving the question of Palestine? What would it mean for hundreds of millions of people if the representatives of the great religions ceased to foment wars, and instead began on a broad basis to encourage reconciliation and peace between the nations?

5. However, to achieve a new world order and world peace there is at the same time a need for a **great coalition of believers and non-believers.**

– So there can be no **retrogressive 're-evangelization'** of Europe or the world, which in fact – as e.g. in Eastern Europe – amounts to a mediaeval 're-Catholicizing' (with a concentration on sexual morality, marriage legislation and the restoration of the power of the church).

– However, there also cannot be **any further 'secularization'**, as in

Western Europe, in the direction of a godless secularism which in fact deprives people of any meaningful horizon in life, any moral criteria and any spiritual home.

6. What is needed, rather, is a **spiritual renewal** of Europe and the world. The religions could make a special contribution to this if each began to contribute from its own tradition, despite all dogmatic differences, to a **common ethic for humanity**. This ethic does not need to be 'invented', but is already deeply rooted in the religious traditions: in the Ten Commandments of the Hebrew Bible and in the key texts of the New Testament and the Qur'an – with parallels also in the great revealed writings of the other religions (of Indian and Chinese origin). No, we do not primarily need stricter laws and speedier punishment of criminals, although this too is sometimes necessary (say in the case of those who export weapons illegally). Rather, we need more reflection on the moral actions and ideals that we have achieved. For *Quid leges sine moribus*? What is the use of any law without morals? What is the use even of a supra-national legal system if the moral will of human beings is not there to observe it? What is the use of a diplomacy whose only value is national utility? Truth, fairness and generosity cannot be prescribed by law. What we need is unprejudiced self-examination, more ethical commitment on the part of all those who bear responsibility in business and science, in government, politics and diplomacy. It is not just a matter of questions involving technology and organization; very profound ethical questions are also at stake.

7. At the moment the cards have been reshuffled. And as might be expected, it is more difficult to win the peace than the war. Powerful aggressive emotions have come to the surface – almost as at the time of the Second World War. But sobriety has already set in on all sides – even among the victors. Only 13% of Americans now believe that the war against Iraq was completely successful; 32% think that it was largely successful; 46% that it was only partially successful; and 7% that it was unsuccessful (*Time Magazine* of 3 June 1991). Humankind, like individuals, seems only to learn from experiences, which are usually bitter. Are we not now mature enough, as after the Second World War, to achieve a new peaceful order in the Middle East of the kind that has been achieved in Europe? And generally, a non-violent world culture as opposed to the senseless arms race and arms trade which endanger peace? As we have experienced, peace can be achieved. The religions and their representatives, who so far have been so passive, must be active here, and make the task of the politicians easier.

Postulate 3: No religious peace without religious dialogue

Having discussed the problem area of Judaism – the state of Israel and the Palestinian question – at length in this book, I shall now briefly refer to the problem areas in Christianity and Islam, as a foretaste of the next two volumes of this research project.

(a) Re-evangelization = Re-Catholicization?

The presupposition for any dialogue between the religions is **self-criticism** on the part of the religions involved, **Christianity** included. This self-criticism is hardly to be found at present on the part of official Roman Catholicism. Nowadays in Christianity there is a good deal of complaint about fanatical Islamic (and in part Jewish) fundamentalism, and too little recollection that the word 'fundamentalism' derives from that Protestantism which seeks certainty for itself and against others by keeping firmly to the letter of the Bible. But there is also a variant of fundamentalism in Catholicism, in so far as the present church government is seeking to identify the Catholic faith with the very last church traditions and by means of a 're-evangelizing' = 're-Catholicizing' to force Catholics back into a mediaeval paradigm of church and society – thereby neglecting and marginalizing Protestants, Orthodox and Jews.

I already warned in *Global Responsibility* against the dangers of an anti-modern (and also anti-Reformation and anti-Orthodox) 're-Catholicizing' in Poland, in a country which has hitherto been the unacknowledged papal model for a 're-evangelizing' of other countries. For in the meantime the Catholic Church there – according to opinion polls – has become the most powerful (though not the most popular) institution, more powerful than the government, president, parliament, army or Solidarity. 74% of Poles now think that the political role of the church is too great. But with this power – especially exercised through delegates who are anxious about being re-elected – the church has begun energetically to restore the mediaeval *status quo*, so that complaints can be heard not only from Orthodox and Protestant Christians and Jews, but also from open-minded Catholics (for example, the former Prime Minister Tadeusz Mazowiecki):
– By-passing parliament, religious instruction was introduced in Polish schools, which is to be given by a clergy which has had no kind of pedagogical training for it.

– Although 59% of Poles are in support of at least a limited legalization of the termination of pregnancy, one of the most rigorous anti-abortion laws in the world (with two years in prison for women and doctors who practise abortions) has been introduced even in cases of rape, genetic damage to the embryo, and the sickness of the mother (the only exception is when her life is in danger).

– State subventions for contraceptive pills have been abolished (despite the horrific number of abortions each year), so that many women will no longer be able to buy pills, now that they are three times as expensive as they were.

– New laws are also expected against divorce, pornography and much else.

– The rank of general has been introduced for the senior military chaplain, and the church hierarchy are now usually present at important public ceremonies.

– Many bishops are calling for the abolition of the article in the constitution which separates church and state.

– Psychological terror is often being used against dissenters at a local level (for example, those calling for a referendum on the abortion law), and the influence of the church on elections and politicians is growing steadily.

'Church, church over all'? That is what people are writing on the wall. What people? Those who fear a clerical state that will be ruled in accordance with the dictates of the Polish messiah pope. But because after the shift to democracy the church has all too rapidly changed from being a political, powerless haven of freedom to an authoritarian fortress of power, its credibility has been rapidly declining (from 83% in 1990 to 58% in April 1991). A general polarization of Polish society threatens. This process was encouraged by the papal visit in June 1991, in which Karol Wojtyla travelled through his country in the style of a clenched-fist crusading pope and (to the scandal of all Democrats) challenged the right of parliament to pass a liberal abortion law. To the scandal of the Jews, he compared the abortion of embryos with Auschwitz and finally – having in effect affirmed a total pacifism in the Gulf War – praised national political heroism with tens of thousands of soldiers and now affirmed 'the legitimate right to defence'. By contrast, the pope did not devote a single word to the question of an authentic parliamentary democracy.

What particularly stirred the pope was a national survey on the eve of his visit: he doubtless knew about it, though the Polish media maintained almost complete silence on it, and far too little attention was paid to it in the Western press. It showed abundantly clearly what new fronts have formed in post-Communist Poland. To the question whether the Catholic Church has the right to compel people to submit to its teaching, 81% of all Poles replied 'certainly not' or 'probably not' over contraception. 71% gave the same answer over abortion, 61% over pre-marital or extra-marital relationships, and 63% over divorce. And over abortion, even 62% of Poles living in country areas replied 'probably not' or 'certainly not'. This figure rose to 81% in cities with more than 500,000 inhabitants, like Lodz, Warsaw and even Krakow. Such figures show that on these disputed questions the church hierarchy in Poland in no way has the majority of the population behind it. Certainly it should not simply give way to the spirit of the time and tacitly tolerate permissiveness. But it would be well advised to rethink its rigorous and sweeping teaching, particularly in matters of sexual morality. Otherwise it risks forfeiting the credibility which it urgently needs for the real spiritual renewal of this land. Those who are alienated from ordinary men and women on these questions can hardly expect to be followed on other vitally important issues.

Now in his most recent social encyclical *Centesimus Annus* (May 1991), the pope has also attempted to enlighten **the whole world** on present-day social distress. At the same time he is using the practices of the Inquisition to muzzle the representatives of Latin-American liberation theology. He is noting with satisfaction the downfall of the Marxist systems of the East, and is rightly criticizing the excesses of capitalism and all forms of exclusion and exploitation, especially in the Third World. But cheap criticism of the 'materialistic and consumerist' West, which does not cost anything, and the regaining of ground in Eastern Europe by exploiting the situation, is not real spiritual renewal.

As for the Third World, the church's *magisterium* is making itself an accomplice in the mass misery, the hunger and the death of millions upon millions of children throughout the world in continuing its worldwide campaign **against birth control** (and more recently also against condoms in the fight against AIDS). Like many of his prede-cessors since the days of Luther, Galileo and Darwin, does not this pope, too – blinded by the doctrine of infallibility in matters of faith and morality – realize that here he is trapped in error? In this way he is becoming one of those chiefly responsible for the uncontrollable population explosion and thus also the wretchedness of children in Latin America, Africa and other countries of the South. Incapable of self-criticism, he fails to understand that it is a contradiction in terms to fight against abortion and contraception at the same time, when contraception could be the most effective way of bringing down abortion rates, which are in any case too high. At 600,000 per year, Poland has the highest abortion rate in Europe, because abortion has become the main method of birth control. This is for want of contraceptives of any kind, all of which are repudiated by the pope and the hierarchy.

But the pope will not understand that it does little help to call for human rights (freedom of thought, speech, teaching and religion) now, all of which his anti-democratic predecessor Leo XIII, whom he so reveres, condemned a century ago, when for millions of people, particularly in the Third World, a worthwhile human life is *a priori* impossible. It is impossible because the number of people in the pre-industrial, poor, Third World, who already make up two-thirds of humankind, is increasing at such a hectic pace that there is no way in which the human investment needed can keep up any longer. About the time of Christ's birth, around 200 million people were living on our earth; at the time of the discovery of America 500 million; in the middle of the eighteenth century 700 million. With the Industrial Revolution, as early as 1830 the figure topped the billion mark; it doubled in 1925 to two billion and again doubled as early as 1975 to four billion. According to the figures in the annual UN demographic report published in May 1991, there are now 5.4 billion people on this planet. By the end of our century this will already be 6.4 billion, and in the year 2025 already 8.5 billion. Since Paul VI's unfortunate 1968 encyclical *Humanae Vitae* against contraception, the population has risen from 3.5 billion to 5.4 billion. John Paul II has learned nothing from this. In his encyclical *Centesimus Annus* he simply keeps silent on this fundamental human problem.

Though countless people do not have basic food, water and energy, let alone homes, jobs and health-care organizations, and the environment is increasingly being destroyed by the great cities and slums which are mushrooming, certainly there is no case for compulsory birth control measures. But family planning must be striven for by all legitimate political means and relevant social measures (a change in the role of women); here there can be no more effective support than that of the religions. For in the countries of the so-called Third World the religions often reach people's heads and hearts more than great political campaigns. Without the support of the religious authorities, the peoples of these lands will not change the moral behaviour which the religions have instilled in them over the centuries.

(*b*) Re-Islamicization

However, **self-criticism** is called for not only from Judaism and Christianity but also from **Islam**. Remarkably, traditionalist Islam, orientated on its Middle Ages, faces similar questions to those faced by Roman Catholicism, which is also orientated on its Middle Ages. **Birth control** is only one instance. For example, in traditionalist Pakistan the population has risen from 90 million to 140-150 million, with tremendous political, social, economic and ecological consequences. Bangladesh, visited in May 1991 by a devastating flood, is a prime example of the catastrophes which can befall a land with a birth rate which has doubled in twenty-five years: gross over-population, boundless poverty, a catastrophic lack of space and therefore no dykes or too steep dykes, the sinking of the land below sea level, no protection against flooding, almost 200,000 dead...

But even apart from the population explosion, many Islamic states have enormous problems. Particularly among the Arab states is there not an ongoing, intolerable **social gap between rich and poor** which conflicts with the Qur'anic demand for justice: between the super-rich oil-producing countries (Saudi Arabia, Kuwait, the Emirates) and poor lands like Egypt and Jordan? Was this not the subsequent, dubious, justification for the invasion by oil-rich, prosperous Iraq of its smaller but super-rich neighbour, since Saddam Hussein's debts had become excessively large as a result of a high level of armaments and a senseless war against Iran? Could not an ethically motivated social policy among the Arab states long since have broken down such social contrasts, thus preventing many tensions from the start? Has backwardness, poverty, misery and a lack of democracy also perhaps something to do with religion – in both Islamic and Catholic countries? Surely the Qur'an and the Bible are not slow in calling for social justice in both the individual and the social spheres?

Given the partly devastating results of Western secularization, though, one can understand why many Muslims who are very much in favour of a **modernization** of their country, strictly reject a **secularization** which they identify with hostility to religion and with godlessness, indeed seeing it as the main enemy of Islam and humankind generally. But the decisive question is: can one have the modern world – modern science, technology and industry – without conceding a guaranteed amount of intellectual freedom: freedom of thought, speech, religion, freedom of the press and of assembly? The Islamic states – so completely different from the states of East and South-East Asia, which are shaped more by a Confucian ethic – will long lag behind modern developments unless they grant these 'bourgeois freedoms', unless they realize tolerance, respect for human dignity and human rights, and construct democracies worthy of the name.

So is not democratization (the introduction of at least a constitutional monarchy, for example in 'liberated' Kuwait, which is again being ruled in authoritarian fashion) and better implementation of human rights in many Islamic states more urgent than ever after this war? Will these states ever link up with the hectic postmodern development without independent thought and free social exchanges? It is a welcome sign of change that now, after the Gulf War, even in Saudi Arabia several hundred university professors and theologians have sent a petition to King Fahd in which they are calling for better protection of human rights, an end to corruption, just distribution of wealth in the country, and better democratic representation (with the aid of a completely independent council of people of integrity and competence).

So the questions to be put to antimodern (rather than postmodern) 're-Islamicization' are quite similar to those to be put to equally antimodern (rather than postmodern) 're-evangelization':
– Internally: the process of re-Islamicization is meant to renew the 'Islamic order' ('*Nizam ul-Islam*') and Islamic society (the 'Umma') throughout the Islamic world. Does that mean that just as church law is being imposed in Poland, so now Islamic sacral law (the *shari'ah*) will again be imposed on all Islamic states? Does that mean that an authoritarian, Islamic state ('**Dar ul-Islam**') is to be established, similar to the clerical Catholic state, which at best affords limited freedom of religion and human rights and grants the other religions only an inferior status?
– Externally: the process of re-Islamicization is also to advance beyond the Islamic world, and as the '**Islamic mission**' (Da'wah = invitation, challenge) it has an explicitly expansionist character. Does this mean that as in the former Christian colonialist mission, the starting point is the conviction of possessing the only truth – excluding all the others? Does this not mean the erection of new dividing walls once again, when a religion in fact regards itself as the one religion which brings salvation and seeks to assert itself with money and political power – an enterprise which is in any case doomed to failure?

(c) Research into the foundations

In the two subsequent volumes of this trilogy, on Christianity and Islam, I hope to develop all these questions similarly along three major lines: I shall be analysing, first, the paradigms of the Christian and Islamic **past** which still have an influence today; then, the challenges of the **present** to Christianity and Islam; and finally, possibilities for the **future** – in all this comparing the problems of all three Abrahamic religions closely. This makes the basic question for the three prophetic religions that much more acute. What would an international policy look like which was guided by a responsibility for the future? What special responsibility do the representatives of the religions have for overcoming these problems?

The presupposition for any dialogue between the religions is **research into the foundations**, religious and theological. The Gulf War in particular has again popularized that literature which *a priori* attacks Islam – that ancient great religion which is the foundation of Arab culture – brands it a religion of violence, and makes Christians anxious, as though Islam were in process of converting the whole human race 'by fire and sword'. This will drive Muslims even more into fundamentalism. It should not least be the task of theological faculties in Western countries, in conjunction with departments of religious studies, to see that every young theologian is familiarized with the basic conceptions of the other great religions, so that both the divergences and the convergences between them become part of the general content of education. In the face of the international, multi-cultural and multi-religious world situation, this is the only course to take in the church and in society. No responsible religious instruction can fail to give a good deal of space to dialogue with and information about other religions. No Christian community is still credible which does not also show hospitality to non-Christian believers (in particular to Jews and Muslims).

(d) The contribution of religions to changing the world situation

If they did this, the religions would be better capable of identifying their priorities and at the same time making a basic contribution to changing the world situation:
– In **furthering world peace**. Why not at last put a stop to the arms business? Why yet more gigantic rearming in the USA, with its enormous level of debt? Why more weapons sales to Saudi Arabia and the Gulf

states amounting to billions of dollars after the victory over Iraq? Why yet more free weapons (planes, missiles) to Israel, now the strongest military power in the Middle East? Why not make the Middle East a zone which is not only free of nuclear, biological and chemical weapons but also has a freeze on all new armaments? However, a solution to the Palestinian question would be the presupposition of all this. The representatives of the religions cannot remove the strategic and security problems, but if they only spoke with one voice they could help to find that spirit of understanding, trust and peace which is the presupposition of any arms control policy.

– In the **fight against poverty**. The representatives of the religions could and should argue resolutely that the needs of the peoples should be taken more seriously than the will of their rulers; with the end of East-West confrontation and the end of military aid from both sides in Africa (e.g. in Angola and Ethiopia) or Indochina (Cambodia), the prospects are very much better. Furthermore, the religious leaders should support the plans of the World Bank and the International Monetary Fund that the military expenditure of the lands concerned should be taken into account in the giving of credits. In future, developing countries which spend more on their armies than on health and education should go away empty-handed. According to information supplied by the United Nations, in Black Africa and Southern Asia, where the need is greatest and the cry for help is understandably loudest, some governments are spending two to three times as much on weapons as on education and health. Public expenditure needs to be examined, and money needs to be spent more effectively to combat poverty. According to the UN development programme, just a simple freeze on military expenditure in the Third World (instead of the annual increase of 7.5%) would release 15 billion dollars of investment for the most urgent human needs and development: the Third World has a growth rate in military expenditure between two and three times higher than that in the West (from 24 billion dollars in 1960 to 173 billion dollars in 1987). By the elimination of costly and inefficient government programmes and a fight against corruption and the flight of capital, a further 35 billion could be saved.

– In the **overcoming of ethnic tensions**: deeply rooted in the history of the peoples, they break out anew in the progress of democratization and the attaining of more freedom. They cannot always be overcome by the founding of new states and the setting of new boundaries, but they can be overcome by the granting of political, economic and cultural autonomy in respect of language, schools and media, and above all a secure basis for living. Who would be better suited to take action

against ethnic prejudices and resentments, and to work for mutual understanding, than the religions of Abrahamic origin, which believe in a God before whom **all** human beings are equal?
– In **freedom of religion within their own territory**. The religion of the majority must also be concerned for the freedom of other religions. A religion which does not respect the freedom of other religions does not deserve any respect itself. The religions and their representatives have to take a stand against the ideologies and ideologues of hatred and enmity. Wherever power is put above right and reason, the religions have to make their claim. Missions nowadays can no longer be carried on in colonialist, imperialistic fashion, but must give free testimony to the faith which inspires them, whether this be Jewish, Christian or Islamic.

Presuppositions for peace in the Middle East

There will be no peace in the Middle East, no solution to the Gulf question, no solution to the Palestinian question, unless the Abrahamic ecumene can be made an effective force in world politics. How else are the pious fanatics to be kept at bay in all camps? To put this positively:

- On the basis of the **Hebrew Bible** and the **New Testament, Jews** and **Christians** should work together for the dignity of the Arab and Islamic peoples, who do not want to be the last colonies on this earth.
- On the basis of the **Qur'an** and the **New Testament, Muslims** and **Christians** should work together for the right to life of the Jewish people, which has suffered more than any other people in the last two thousand years and came close to being exterminated.
- On the basis of the **Hebrew Bible** and the **Qur'an, Jews and Muslims** should work together for the threatened freedom of Christian communities in some lands of the Near East and Middle East.
- So there is a need for a common commitment from all three religions to peace, justice and freedom, to human dignity, to human rights and the preservation of creation – of course also in collaboration with peoples from **Indian, Chinese** or **Japanese** traditions.

Here the religions in particular should reflect on their own programme, in which the word 'peace' – in the Hebrew Bible **shalom**, in the Qur'an **salam** and in the New Testament **eirene** – plays so large a role:
– 'Seek peace and pursue it', we have already heard from the Psalms (Ps.34.15). 'And they shall beat their swords into ploughshares' is the

prophet Isaiah's vision of peace: 'Nation shall not lift up sword against nation, and they shall learn war no more' (Isa 2.4).
– 'Blessed are the peacemakers, for they shall be called the sons of God', we hear in the Sermon on the Mount. And the apostle Paul says, 'Recompense no one evil with evil' (Rom.12.17).
– And the Qur'an, for all its summons to arm against the unbelieving enemies, commands: 'And if they (the enemies) incline to peace, make peace with them and put your trust in God' (surah 8.61). Also, 'If they (the unbelievers) keep away from you and cease their hostility and offer you peace, God bids you not to harm them' (surah 4.90).

This is my wish for the future: that there should no longer be a single synagogue, church or mosque that does not make a contribution towards religious understanding. In all synagogues, churches and mosques there should not only be prayers but also an active concern and work for peace. For that we all need a vision; we need imagination, courage and indefatigable, creative commitment.

Abbreviations and Lexicons

LEXICONS

Bibellexikon, ed. H.Haag, Zurich 1968

Contemporary Jewish Thought. Original Essays on Critical Concepts, Movements and Beliefs, ed. A.A.Cohen and P.Mendes-Flohr, New York 1987

Dictionnaire des Religions, ed. P.Poupard, Paris ²1985

Die Religion in Geschichte und Gegenwart. Handwörterbuch für Theologie und Religionswissenschaft, ed. K.Galling (6 vols.), Tübingen ³1957ff.

Encyclopaedia Judaica, ed. C.Roth and G.Wigoder (17 vols.), Jerusalem nd

Enzyklopaedie des Islam. Geographisches, ethnographisches und biographisches Wörterbuch der muhammedanischen Völker, ed. M.T.Houtsma et al. (5 vols.), Leiden 1913-1938

Jüdisches Lexikon. Ein enzyklopädisches Handbuch des jüdischen Wissens in vier Bänden, founded by G.Herlitz and B.Kirschner, Vols. I-IV.2, Frankfurt ²1987

Lexikon der jüdisch-christlichen Begegnung, ed. J.J.Petuchowski and C.Thoma, Freiburg 1989

Lexikon der Religionen, ed. H.Waldenfels, Freiburg 1987

Lexikon für Theologie und Kirche, ed. J.Höfer and K.Rahner (9 vols.), Freiburg 1957ff.

Reallexikon für Antike und Christentum. Sachwörterbuch zur Auseinandersetzung des Christentums mit der Antiken Welt, ed. T.Klausner (14 vols.), Stuttgart 1950ff.

The Encyclopaedia of Islam, new edition by H.A.R.Gibb et al. (6 vols.), Leiden 1960-1990

The Encyclopaedia of Religion, ed. M.Eliade (16 vols.), New York 1987 (the articles on Judaism are also collected in *Judaism: A People and its History*, ed. Robert M.Seltzer, New York and London 1989

Theologische Realenzyklopädie, ed. G.Krause and G.Müller (17 vols.), Berlin 1977ff.

Theological Dictionary of the New Testament, ed. G.Kittel (1933ff.) (10 volumes), Grand Rapids 1964ff.

Wörterbuch des Christentums, ed. V.Drehsen, H.Häring, K.-J.Kuschel and H.Siemers, Gütersloh 1988

ABBREVIATIONS

Biblical commentaries

AB	The Anchor Bible, New York
ATD	Das Alte Testament Deutsch, Göttingen
BK	Biblischer Kommentar Altes Testament, Neukirchen
CNEB	Cambridge Bible Commentary on the New English Bible, Cambridge
EKK	Evangelisch-Katholischer Kommentar zum Neuen Testament, Neukirchen
HAT	Handbuch zum Alten Testament, Tübingen
HNT	Handbuch zum Neuen Testament, Tübingen
HTK	Herders Theologischer Kommentar zum Neuen Testament, Freiburg
IB	The Interpreter's Bible, Nashville and New York
KAT	Kommentar zum Alten Testament, Leipzig and Gütersloh
KEK	Kritisch-Exegetischer Kommentar über das Neue Testament, Göttingen
NBC	Nelson's Bible Commentary, Edinburgh
NCB	New Clarendon Bible, Oxford
NCeB	New Century Bible, London
NTD	Das Neue Testament Deutsch, Göttingen
ÖTK	Ökumenischer Taschenbuchkommentar zum Neuen Testament, Gütersloh
OTL	Old Testament Library, London and Philadelphia
WBC	Word Biblical Commentary, Waco, Texas

Works by the author

Church	*The Church* (1967), London and New York 1968
CR	*Christianity and Chinese Religions* (with **Julia Ching**) (1988), New York 1989
CWR	*Christianity and the World Religions. Paths of Dialogue with Islam, Hinduism and Buddhism* (with **J.van Ess, H.von Stietencron** and **H.Bechert**) (1984), London and New York 1985
DGE	*Does God Exist? An Answer for Today* (1978), London and New York 1980, reissued 1991
EL	*Eternal Life?* (^{2}1982), London and New York 1984, reissued 1991
GR	*Global Responsibility. In Search of a New World Ethic* (1990), London and New York 1991
OBC	*On Being a Christian* (1974), London and New York 1976, reissued 1991
TTM	*Theology for the Third Millennium* (1987), New York 1988 and London 1991

Notes

PART ONE:
THE PAST THAT IS STILL PRESENT

A. Origins

A. I. Abraham, the Tribal Ancestor of Three World Religions

1. After initial excavations by C.Warren (1868), E.Stellin and C.Watzinger (1907-1909) and J.Garstang (1930-1936), the investigations were continued between 1952 and 1956 by an Anglo-American expedition under **K.M.Kenyon.** She is also the editor of the research report, *Excavations at Jericho*, Vols. I and II, London 1960-65.

2. Cf. **D.Diringer**, *Writing*, New York 1962; **J.Friedrich**, *Geschichte der Schrift. Unter besonderer Berücksichtigung ihre geistigen Entwicklung*, Heidelberg 1966; **M.Cohen**, *La grande invention de l'Ecriture et son invention*, Vols.I-III, Paris 1958; **I.J.Gelb**, *A Study of Writing. The Foundations of Grammatology*, Chicago 1952; **C.H.Gordon**, *Forgotten Scripts*, New York ²1982.

3. The Indus valley appears within the horizon of the Hebrew Bible first with Alexander the Great in I Maccabees (1.4), which has only been preserved in Greek. China does not come within its horizon at all.

4. Rome is mentioned for the first time in the Bible only at a late stage (I Macc.1.10).

5. Cf. Ex.1.

6. Cf. Gen.1-11.

7. Cf. Gen.12-50.

8. For the **history of Israel**, as well as the earlier overall accounts by J.Wellhausen, A.Schlatter, E.Schürer, R.Kittel. W.O.E.Oesterley/T.H.Robinson, cf. among more recent works: **W.F.Albright**, *From the Stone Age to Christianity. Monotheism and the Historical Process*, Baltimore 1940, ²1946; id. *The Biblical Period from Abraham to Ezra*, New York 1963; **M.Noth**, *History of Israel* (1950), London and Philadelphia ²1959; **M.A.Beek**, *A Short* (US edition *Concise*) *History of Israel from Abraham to the Bar Kochba Period*, London 1963 and New York 1964; **J.Bright**, *A History of Israel*, Philadelphia 1959 and London 1960, ³1981; **M.Metzger**, *Grundriss der Geschichte Israels*, Neukirchen 1963, ⁶1983; **B.Netanyahu** et al. (eds.), *The World History of the Jewish People. First Series: Ancient Time*, Vols.I-VIII, Tel Aviv and London 1964-77; **E.L.Ehrlich**, *A Concise History of Israel from the Earliest Times to the Destruction of the Temple in AD 70*, London 1962

and New York 1965; **R.de Vaux**, *The Early History of Israel* (1971-3), London and New York 1978; **A.H.J.Gunneweg**, *Geschichte Israels bis Bar Kochba*, Stuttgart 1972, ⁴1982; **S.Herrmann**, *A History of Israel in Old Testament Times*, London and Philadelphia ²1981; **H.H.Ben-Sasson** (ed.), *History of the Jewish People*, Cambridge 1976; **G.Fohrer**, *Geschichte Israels. Von den Anfängen bis zur Gegenwart*, Heidelberg ³1982; **J.H.Hayes and J.M.Miller** (eds.), *Israelite and Judaean History*, London and Philadelphia 1977; **H.Donner**, *Geschichte des Volkes Israel und seiner Nachbarn* (2 vols.), Göttingen 1984; **M.Grant**, *A History of Ancient Israel*, London 1984; **M.Claus**, *Geschichte Israels. Von der Frühzeit bis zur Zerstörung Jerusalems (587 v.Chr.)*, Munich 1986; **J.H.Hayes and J.M.Miller**, *A History of Ancient Israel and Judah*, Philadelphia and London 1986. **I.M.Zeitlin**, *Ancient Judaism. Biblical Criticism from Max Weber to the Present*, Cambridge 1984, surveys the famous study by **Max Weber**, *Ancient Judaism* (1920), Glencoe 1952 on the basis of more recent research.

The emphasis is placed on the history of (post-exilic) Judaism in **H.Graetz**, *Geschichte der Juden von den ältesten Zeiten bis zur Gegenwart* (11 vols.), Leipzig 1853-1875, ⁵1902-9; **S.Dubnow**, *Weltgeschichte des jüdischen Volkes* (10 vols.), Berlin 1925-1929; **S.W.Baron**, *A Social and Religious History of the Jews* (3 vols.), New York 1937, ²1952-1969; **J.Maier**, *Geschichte der jüdischen Religion. Von der Zeit Alexander des Grossen bis zur Aufklärung mit einem Ausblick auf das 19./20.Jahrhundert*, Berlin 1972; id., *Das Judentum. Von der biblische Zeit bis zur Moderne*, Munich ²1973; **A.Bein**, *Die Judenfrage. Biographie eines Weltproblems* (2 vols.), Stuttgart 1980; **P.Sigal**, *The Emergence of Contemporary Judaism* (3 vols.), Pittsburgh 1977-1984; id., *Judentum*, Stuttgart 1986; **P.Johnson**, *A History of the Jews*, London and New York 1987.

For the history of **Jewish literature** cf. **M.Waxman**, *A History of Jewish Literature*, new edition (5 vols.), New York 1960 (this begins with the completion of the biblical canon in 400 BCE and ends in 1960 CE); **I.Zinberg**, *A History of Jewish Literature* (12 vols.), Cleveland and New York 1972-1978 (this begins with the Spanish-Arab period and ends with the Haskala at its height).

9. Gen.17.1-5, 7-8, 11; this is translated, and provided with a very full commentary, by **C.Westermann**, *Genesis 12-36*, Minneapolis and London 1985, 253ff.

10. Cf. Gen.17.15-21.

11. For **Abraham** (or Ibrahim) cf. the articles in *Bibellexikon* (A.van den Born); *Dictionnaire des Religions* (H.Cazelles, E.Cothenet, K.Hruby, G.Harpigny); *Die Religion in Geschichte und Gegenwart* (A.Weiser); *Encyclopaedia Judaica* (I.M.Ta-Shma, D.Kadosh, S.D.Goitein, J.Dan, H.Rosenau); *Jüdisches Lexikon* (A.Spanier, A.Kristianpoller, A.Sandler); *Lexikon der jüdisch-christlichen Begegnung* (J.J.Petuchowski, C.Thoma); *Lexikon der Religionen* (F.L.Hossfeld/B.Schumacher, G.Risse); *Lexikon für Theologie und Kirche* (V.Hamp, J.Schmid); *Lexikon religiöser Grundbegriffe* (P.Navè Levinson, G.Evers, S.Balic); *Reallexikon für Antike und Christentum* (T.Klauser); *The Encyclopaedia of Islam* (R.Paret); *The Encyclopaedia of Religion* (J.van Seters); *Theologische Realenzyklopädie* (R.Martin-Achard, K.Berger, R.P.Schmitz, J.Hjärpe); *Theological Dictionary of the New Testa-*

ment (J.Jeremias); *Wörterbuch des Christentums* (J.Ebach); cf. further Donner, *Geschichte* (n.8), I, 72-84.

Important works specifically on the dialogue on Abraham: W.Gross, *Glaubensgehorsam als Wagnis der Freiheit. Wir sind Abraham*, Mainz 1980; R.Martin-Achard, *Actualité d'Abraham*, Neuchâtel 1969; Y.Moubarac, *Abraham dans le Coran. L'histoire d'Abraham dans le Coran et la naissance de l'Islam*, Paris 1958; W.Zuidema (ed.), *Isaak wird wieder geopfert. Die 'Bindung Isaaks' als Symbol des Leidens Israels. Versuche einer Deutung*, Neukirchen 1987.

The study by F.E.Peters, *Children of Abraham. Judaism – Christianity – Islam*, Princeton 1982, is particularly helpful in this connection. The author makes an illuminating and informative comparison of the structures of the three Abrahamic religions with reference to seven themes: the understanding of scripture, the understanding of the different 'axial periods' (the experience of the exile in Judaism, the appearance of Jesus in Christianity, the emergence of Muhammad in Islam), the community and the hierarchy, the law, the relationship between scripture and tradition, liturgy, asceticism and mysticism, and theology. I have gone into many of these themes in the present book. We shall have to return to others when, in the course of this trilogy on Judaism, Christianity and Islam, we turn explicitly to the question of the trialogue.

12. For the **book of Genesis**, in addition to the classic works by H.Gunkel, J.Skinner and O.Procksch, see the following more recent commentaries: B.Jacob, Berlin 1934; W.Zimmerli, 1943 (ZBK: only Gen.1-11); H.Junker, Würzburg 1949; J.Chaine, Paris 1951; G. von Rad (ATD 1953), OTL London and Philadelphia ²1972; R.de Vaux, Paris 1956; G.Aalders, Kampen 1933-1936; F.Michaeli, Neuchâtel 1960; U.Cassuto (2 vols.), Jerusalem 1961; J.de Fraine, Roermond 1963; J.Morgenstern, New York 1965; A.van Selms (2 vols.), Nijkerk 1967, ³1979; W.G.Plaut, in *The Torah*, New York 1974; E.A.Speiser, 1981 (AB); C.Westermann (BK 1981), Minneapolis and London 1984-7 (3 vols.). There is a good survey of the exegesis of Genesis in C.Westermann, *Genesis 1-11*, Darmstadt ³1985; id., *Genesis 12-50*, Darmstadt ²1987.

13. H.Gunkel and H.Gressmann were the first to recognize that many of the biblical narratives are **sagas**; their insight was later developed comprehensively by A.Alt, M.Noth, and many other German Old Testament scholars, often with negative historical results. Against this some American scholars, especially those associated with W.F.Albright, called for closer attention to the results of archaeology. Summary works include: W.F.Albright, *The Archaeology of Palestine*, Harmondsworth, England and Cambridge, Mass. 1971; A.Parrot, *Studies in Biblical Archaeology* (7 vols.), London 1955ff.; G.E.Wright, *Biblical Archaeology*, Philadelphia and London 1957; J.B.Pritchard, *Archaeology and the Old Testament*, Princeton 1958; K.M.Kenyon, *Archaeology in the Holy Land*, London ⁴1979 (which contains a good survey of Kenyon's excavations in Jericho, putting them in context); V.Fritz, *Einführung in die biblische Archäologie*, Darmstadt 1985.

14. Cf. recently G.W.Coats, *Genesis, with an Introduction to Narrative Literature*, Grand Rapids 1983; id. (ed.), *Saga, Legend, Tale, Novella, Fable: Narrative Forms in Old Testament Literature*, Sheffield 1985.

15. Cf. H.Haag, *Das Land der Bibel. Gestalt – Geschichte – Erforschung*, Stuttgart 1989, 50-63.

16. Cf. Gen.11.

17. For Abraham's origin from Ur see Gen.11.28,31; 15.7; from Haran, Gen.11.31; 24.4, 10; 27.43.

18. Gen.12.6-9.

19. Gen.23.4.

20. Cf. Gen.23.19f.

21. Gen.14.13.

22. For the 'Hebrews'/'Apiru', cf., as an endorsement of G.E.Mendenhall's view, **M.Weippert**, *The Settlement of the Israelite Tribes in Palestine*, London 1971, 63-101; O.Loretz, *Habiru – Hebräer. Eine sozio-linguistische Studie über die Herkunft des Gentiliziums c ibri vom Appellativum habiru*, Berlin 1984.

23. For the genealogy cf. **Westermann**, *Genesis 1-11* (n.12), 558-66.

24. Cf. Gen.25.1,6.

25. Gen.21.2f.

26. Gen.16.5.

27. Cf. Gen.25.12-18, and on this **E.A.Knauf**, *Ismael. Untersuchungen zur Geschichte Palästinas und Nordarabiens im 1.Jahrtausend vor Christus*, Wiesbaden 1985: ' "Ismael" was a proto-Bedouin confederation which embraced the whole of northern Arabia from the Nefud to the margins of the Fertile Crescent' (113). Cf. also **Donner**, *Geschichte* 1 (n.8), 58.

28. Cf. Gen.25.1-4.

29. Cf. **de Vaux**, *Early History* I (n.8), 274-81, 454-62.

30. Cf. **Westermann**, *Genesis 12-36* (n.12), 265f., excursus on circumcision.

31. Cf. Lev.12.3.

32. Cf. Gen.15.6.

33. Cf. Gen.22.1-12.

34. Cf. **H.Küng**, GR, ch.C III.

35. Cf. Gen.26.24.

36. Cf. Isa.41.8.

37. Cf. Sir.44.19-23.

38. The text can be found in **J.H.Charlesworth** (ed.), *The Old Testament Pseudepigrapha*, Vol.I, *Apocalyptic Literature and Testaments*, New York and London 1983, 681-705, translated with an introduction by R.Rubinkiewicz.

39. For the text see ibid., 871-902, translated with an introduction by E.P.Sanders.

40. Cf. Gen.12.12f.

41. Cf. Gen.21.14.

42. Cf. Gen.25.6.

43. Sir.44.19.

44. Cf. Gen.26.5.

45. Cf. Talmud, tractate Yoma: bYom 28b.

46. Thus in the legendary midrashic work on the book of Genesis, Bereshit Rabba 14.6. Here we have the parable of Abraham as the main beam of a building: 'It is like a man who wants to build a dining hall. He has a big strong beam. Where does he put this beam? Does he not put it along the middle of the dining hall? It is there to support the beams which are before and after. So why did the Holy One, blessed be He, create Abraham in the midst of the generations? So that he might support the earlier and the later generations.'

47. Isa.41.8; Jer.33.26.

48. Ps.47.10.
49. Gen.12.1-3.
50. Cf. Mark 12.26; Luke 19.9.
51. Cf. Luke 16.19-31.
52. Cf. James 2.23.
53. Cf. Matt.3.7-10; Luke 3.7-9.
54. Cf. Matt.3.9.
55. Cf. Matt.8.11f.
56. Cf. Rom.4.9-12; 9.6-8; Gal.3.6-29.
57. Cf. Rom.2.29.
58. Cf. Rom.4.1-25.
59. Cf. Gal.4.21-30.
60. Cf.surah 2.125; 3.97; 22.26-31. However, there is no historical evidence that Abraham would have travelled so far south: cf. **W.Montgomery Watt and A.T.Welch**, *Der Islam, I, Mohammed und die Frühzeit – Islamisches Recht-Religiöses Leben*, Stuttgart 1980, 122-4. In particular the works of **A.Geiger**, *Was hat Mohammed aus dem Judenthume aufgenommen*, Leipzig ²1902, and **C.Snouck Hurgronje**, *Het Mekkaansche Feest*, Leiden 1880, resulted in a great debate on Muhammad's development with reference to his relationship to Abraham and Ishmael. Cf. **R.Paret**, *Encyclopedia of Islam*, III, 980f.
61. Cf. surah 4.125.
62. Cf. surah 3.67.
63. Cf. surah 6.74-81; 21.55-67.
64. Cf. surah 2.124; 37.102-6.
65. **P.Antes** concludes his scrupulously documented article on 'Abraham in Judentum, Christentum und Islam', in id., *Christen und Juden. Ein notwendiger Dialog*, Hanover 1988, 11-15: 15, with this question.
66. Jesus Christ is spoken of particularly clearly as a descendant of Abraham in Matt.1.1-17, and also in Luke 3.23f.
67. Cf. Rev.3.13.
68. Cf. Gal.5.6.
69. Cf. John 8.39.
70. Cf. James 1.22-25.
71. Cf. **H.Strack and P.Billerbeck**, *Kommentar zum Neuen Testament aus Talmud und Midrasch* III, Munich 1926, 186-201. Many passages are collected here.
72. Cf. **Petuchowski**, *Lexikon* (n.11), col.4.
73. **D.Flusser**, 'Christianity', in A.A.Cohen and P.Mendes-Flohr (eds.), *Contemporary Jewish Religious Thought. Original Essays on Critical Concepts, Movements and Beliefs*, Jerualem 1972, reissued New York 1988, 62. Like the Lexicons, this key theological work will be cited in abbreviated form.
74. **K.Rudolph**, 'Juden – Christen – Muslime. Zum Verhältnis der drei monotheistischen Religionen in religionswissenschaftlicher Sicht', *Judaica* 44, 1988, 214-32: 223.
75. For the 'trialogue' between Jews, Christians and Muslims cf. **I.Maybaum**, *Happiness outside the State: Judaism, Christianity, Islam – Three Ways to God*, Stocksfield 1980: **F.E.Peters**, *Children of Abraham: Judaism/Christianity/Islam*, Princeton 1982; **M.Stöhr** (ed.), *Abrahams Kinder: Juden – Christen – Moslems*, Frankfurt 1983; **W.Strolz**, *Heilswege der Weltreligionen*, I, *Christliche Begegnung mit Judentum und Islam*, Freiburg 1984; **J.Falaturi**

et al. (eds.), *Drei Wege zu dem einen Gott. Glaubenserfahrung in den monotheistischen Religionen*, Freiburg 1976.
76. **Vatican II**, Declaration on the Relationship of the Church to the Non-Christian Religions, *Nostra Aetate*, 4.
77. Ibid., 3.

A.II Problems over Beginnings

1. Cf. **M.Noth**, *The World of the Old Testament* (1957), Philadelphia and London 1966.
2. For Israel's involvement in the religious world of its time, cf. **J.B.Pritchard**, *Ancient Near Eastern Texts relating to the Old Testament*, Princeton 1950, ³1969; **W.Beyerlin** (ed.), *Near Eastern Religious Texts relating to the Old Testament*, London and Philadelphia 1978.
3. Cf. Ex.5-15.
4. Cf. Ex.7-11.
5. Cf. Ex.12.
6. Text in **Pritchard**, *Near Eastern Texts* (n.2), 378; text and illustration in **G.E.Wright**, *Biblical Archaeology*, Philadelphia 1957, 71. According to **G.W.Ahlström**, *Who Were the Israelites?*, Winona Lake 1986, 'Israel' on the stele is only a territorial name for the central hill-country of Palestine (only at a later stage did it then become the name of a people, subsequently a religious and liturgical name, and finally an ideologically restricted concept). **E.Otto** points out that on the stele 'Israel' is given 'the determinative "people"' (*Theologische Revue* 85, 1989, 8).
7. Cf. Ex.2.1-10.
8. Text in **Beyerlin**, *Near Eastern Religious Texts* (n.2), 98f.
9. For Thomas Mann, cf. my contribution in **W.Jens** and **H.Küng**, *Anwälte der Menschlichkeit. Thomas Mann – Hermann Hesse – Heinrich Böll*, Munich 1989; for Sigmund Freud, cf. **H.Küng**, *Freud und die Zukunft der Religion*, Munich 1987.
10. Cf. **H.J.Kraus**, *Geschichte der historisch-kritischen Erforschung des Alten Testaments von der Reformation bis zur Gegenwart*, Neukirchen 1956.
11. Even **O.Eissfeldt's** monumental *The Old Testament – An Introduction* (²1956), Oxford 1965 (totalling more than 1100 pages in the German), can give only a limited impression of this. **V.Fritz, J.W.Rogerson, B.J.Diebner** and **O.Merk**, in 'Bibelwissenschaft', *Theologische Realenzykopädie* VI, Berlin and New York 1980, 316-409, show how complex and literally unchartable biblical scholarship has become in our day. **N.K.Gottwald**, The Hebrew Bible. A Socio-literary Introduction, Philadelphia 1985, does the same thing for the Hebrew Bible.
12. The varied use of two Hebrew words for God – 'Yahweh' and 'El' (plural 'Elohim') – in the **Pentateuch** was noted at an early stage; only at the time of the French Enlightenment was it discovered that the Yahweh passages on the one hand and the Elohim passages on the other each form a connected whole. The famous French doctor **J.Astruc**, physician to Louis XV, who went over from Protestantism to Catholicism, was the first to make a systematic investigation and thus became the founder of critical research into the Pentateuch (1753). **G.Eichhorn** later worked out the characteristics and

content of the two sources more accurately (1799). After further long arguments, in the nineteenth century **H.Hupfeld** then succeeded in distinguishing four anonymous sources in the Pentateuch (1853): J (Jahwist) and E (Elohist), along with P (Priestly Writing, especially for cultic and priestly ordinances) and D (Deuteronomy). **J.Wellhausen** gave classic form to the documentary theory in his work *Die Composition des Hexateuch und der historischen Bücher des alten Testaments*, Berlin 1865; ⁴1963. The dating of the book of Deuteronomy by **W.M.L.de Wette** (as early as 1805) to the period of King Josiah (II Kings 22) in the seventh century BCE formed the basis for the dating of the manifestly older sources J and E (after Julius Wellhausen, P was usually dated to the Babylonian exile in the sixth century). This analysis been accepted down to the present day, though source criticism was later modified in many ways and supplemented with tradition criticism. **H.Gunkel** in his commentaries on Genesis and other books of the Bible, and **H.Gressmann** in his work *Mose und seine Zeit. Ein Kommentar zu den Mose-Sagen*, Göttingen 1913, concentrated on traditions which had already existed before being fixed in writing and attempted to define their 'Sitz im Leben' in the social conditions of Israel.

13. The original German title of **W. Keller**, *The Bible as History*, London and New York 1956.

14. **Gottwald**, *Hebrew Bible* (n.11), 608.

15. Ex.20.2-4; cf. Deut.5.6-8.

16. **Y.Kaufmann**, *The Religion of Israel. From Its Beginnings to the Babylonian Exile* (abridged version translated from the Hebrew by M.Greenberg), Chicago 1960, 60.

17. Ibid., 121.

18. Some standard works on the historical criticism of the Old Testament: **A.Alt**, *Kleine Schriften zur Geschichte des Volkes Israel* (2 vols.), Munich 1953 (partial ET in *Essays on Old Testament Religion*, Oxford 1966, especially 'The Settlement of the Israelites in Palestine' [1925], 133-69; 'The God of the Fathers' [1929], 1-77; 'The Formation of the Israelite State in Palestine' [1930], 171-237; and 'The Origins of Israelite Law' [1934], 79-132); **Noth**, *The World of the Old Testament* (n.1); id. *A History of Pentateuchal Traditions* (1948), Englewood Cliffs NJ, 1972; id., *Gesammelte Studien zum Alten Testament* (2 vols), Munich 1957-1969 (ET of the first volume, *The Laws in the Pentateuch*, Edinburgh 1966, reissued London 1984; the study which gives the title to this book is particularly important); **G.von Rad**: in addition to his studies of Deuteronomy, the works of Chronicler and the Hexateuch, and his Genesis commentary, see above all his *Old Testament Theology* (2 vols.), Edinburgh 1962, 1965, reissued London 1975; **O.Eissfeldt**: in addition to his Introduction to the Old Testament and his *Hexateuchsynopse* (1922), cf. above all *Die ältesten Traditionen Israels. Ein kritischer Bericht über C.A.Simpson's* The Early Traditions of Israel, Berlin 1950, and his brief synthesis *Die Genesis der Genesis*, Tübingen 1958.

19. There is a comprehensive survey of methodologies in contemporary biblical criticsm in **Gottwald**, *Hebrew Bible* (n.11), 6-34, 612-65.

20. Cf. **M.Smith**, *Palestinian Parties and Politics that Shaped the Old Testament*, New York 1971; second, corrected edition London 1987, esp. 15-56.

21. **O.Keel** (ed.), *Monotheismus im alten Israel und seiner Umwelt*, Fribourg

1980 (and the editor's own 'Gedanken zur Beschäftigung mit dem Mono-theismus', 11-30: 21).

22. Cf. **B.Lang** (ed.), *Der einzige Gott. Die Geburt des biblischen Mono-theismus*, Munich 1981, esp.47-83; cf. similarly **A.de Pury**, *Exclusivism and Integration in the Faith of Ancient Israel. Is Monotheism Comparable with a 'Convival' Religion?*, printed in manuscript form for the 'Abrahamic Sym-posium' organized by the Geneva Cultures Dialogue Institute in Cordoba, 12-15 February 1987.

23. Isa.2.8,18; 10.10; 19.3.

24. Jer.2.11; 5.7.

25. Jer.2.5; 10.8; 14.22.

26. Isa.45.21.

27. According to Deut.6.4.

28. Cf. **H.Haag**, *Abschied vom Teufel*, Zurich 1969; id., *Teufelsglaube. Mit Beiträgen von K.Elliger, B.Lang and M.Limbeck*, Tübingen 1974, Part II, 'Dämonen und Satan im Alten Testament', 141-269.

29. Cf. Isa.63.7-64,11.

30. Cf. Gen.1.27.

31. For this very complex set of problems see the judicious analyis by **E.S.Gerstenberger**, *Jahwe – ein patriarchaler Gott? Traditionelles Gottesbild und feministische Theologie*, Stuttgart 1988.

32. Cf. **K.Jaspers**, *Die grossen Philosophen*, I, Munich 1957, 68.

33. Cf. **H.Renckens**, 'Adam', in *Bibellexikon*.

34. Cf. Gen.1.26-28.

35. Cf. Gen.14.18-20.

36. Cf. Ps.110.4.

37. Cf. Heb.5.1-7, 28.

38. Gen.9.9-11.

39. Gen.9.6.

40. Cf. **A.Lichtenstein**, *The Seven Laws of Noah*, New York 1981.

41. Cf. **J.J.Petuchowski**, 'Noachidische Gebote', *Lexikon der jüdisch-christ-lichen Begegnung*; cf. **D.Novak**, *The Image of the Non-Jew in Judaism. An Historical and Constructive Study of the Noahide Laws*, New York 1983.

B. The Centre

B.I The Central Structural Elements

1. Ex.6.6f.

2. Cf. Ex.1-15.

3. For the book of **Exodus**, in addition to the earlier commentaries by H.Holzinger, B.Baentsch and G.Beer/K.Galling, cf. those by **J.C.Rylaarsdam**, 1952 (IB); **M.Noth** (ATD 1958), London and Philadelphia 1972 (OTL); **G.te Stroete**, Roermond 1966; **U.Cassuto**, Jerusalem 1967; **J.P.Hyatt**, 1971 (NCeB); **R.E.Clements**, 1972 (CNEB); **B.S.Childs**, 1974 (OTL); **W.H.Schmidt**, 1974 (BK); **F.C.Fensham**, Nijkerk ²1977; **W.G.Plaut**, in *The Torah*, New York 1981.

4. Cf. Ex.6.14-20.

5. Cf. Gen.35.22-26.

6. There is a survey of the most recent literature on the name Yahweh and Ex.3.14 in **W.H.Schmidt**, *Exodus-Kommentar*, 1988 (BK), 169-71.

7. Ex.3.14. For discussion of this classic passage cf. ibid., 171-9.

8. Hos.13.4.

9. For the key concepts like people, covenant and land which are developed here and subsequently, cf.the relevant sections in the standard theologies of the Old Testament: **W.Eichrodt**, *Theology of the Old Testament* (1933-9), London and Philadelphia 1961, 1967 (2 vols.); **L.Köhler**, *Old Testament Theology* (1936), London and Philadelphia 1957; **O.Procksch**, *Theologie des Alten Testaments*, Gütersloh 1949; **E.Jacob**, *Theology of the Old Testament*, London and New York 1958; **T.C.Vriezen**, *An Outline of Old Testament Theology*, Oxford and Newton, MA 1958, ²1970; **G.von Rad**, *Old Testament Theology* (2 vols.), Edinburgh 1962, 1965, reissued London 1975; **G.Fohrer**, *Theologische Grundstrukturen des Alten Testaments*, Berlin 1972; **W.Zimmerli**, *Old Testament Theology in Outline* (1972), Richmond, Va. 1978; **J.L.McKenzie**, *A Theology of the Old Testament*, New York 1974; **C.Westermann**, *Elements of Old Testament Theology* (1978), Atlanta, Ga. 1986.

10. Ex.19.5f.

11. Cf. Ex.19.10-20,21.

12. Cf. Ex.24.

13. Cf. **H.Gese**, 'Bemerkungen zur Sinaitradition' (1967), in id., *Vom Sinai zum Zion*, Munich 1974, 31-48. Cf. also **H.Donner**, *Geschichte des Volkes Israel und seiner Nachbarn in Grundzügen*, I, Göttingen 1984, 97-115. There is a survey of the discussion (above all in German works) in **W.H.Schmidt**, *Exodus, Sinai und Mose. Erwägungen zu Exodus 1-19 und 24*, Darmstadt 1983.

14. Cf. **L.Perlitt**, *Bundestheologie im Alten Testament*, Neukirchen 1969: 'The Deuteronomic covenant theology was not stimulated initially by any law book but by the "chief commandment".' Israel itself 'developed hardly any other theological concept in such breadth. *Berit* could formulate the sharpest ethical demand, compel an unconditional religious decision and offer insight into one's own guilt; *berit* could similarly rouse hope and invoke Yahweh's fidelity' (284). Of course such a covenant theology should not be fixed to a so-called 'covenant formulary'. Cf. **D.J.McCarthy**, *Treaty and Covenant*, Rome 1963.

15. Cf. Gen.15.

16. Cf. Gen.17.19, 21; 24.7; 26.1-5.

17. Gen.28.3f.

18. Cf. Deut.26.16-19.

19. Cf. Ex.20-23.

20. Cf. **A.Alt**, 'The Origins of Israelite Law (1934)', in *Essays in Old Testament Religion*, Oxford 1966, 79-132.

21. Cf. **M.Noth**, 'The Laws in the Pentateuch', in id., *The Laws in the Pentateuch*, Edinburgh 1966, reissued London 1984, 1-107.

22. **Von Rad**, *Old Testament Theology* I (n.9), 191.

23. **N.K.Gottwald**, *The Hebrew Bible. A Socio-Literary Introduction*, Philadelphia 1985, 209.

24. **G.Fohrer**, *History of Israelite Religion*, Nashville and London 1977, 85.

25. Josh.1.1-4.

26. Cf. **F.Stummer** and **H.Haag**, 'Palästina', in *Bibellexikon*.

27. Cf. already those to the 'patriarchs', Gen.12.1-3,7; 13.14-17; 15.7, 18-21; 28.13-15.
28. Cf. **M.Sharon** (ed.), *The Holy Land in History and Thought*, Leiden 1988.
29. Cf. Josh.1.4.
30. Cf. Gen.9.9-16.
31. Cf. Gen.17.20.
32. Cf. Gen.25.12-18.

B.II The Central Leading Figure

1. Cf. Ex.2.15-22; Ex.18.
2. Cf. Ex.3-4.
3. Cf. Ex.1.11-14; 4.29.
4. Cf. **J.Wach**, *Sociology of Religion*, Chicago [5]1950, who distinguishes the following types of religious authority: founder of a religion, reformer, prophet, seer, magician, diviner, saint, priest, *religiosus*.
5. There is a recent survey in **H.Donner**, *Geschichte des Volkes Israel und seiner Nachbarn in Grundzügen*, I, Göttingen 1984, 107-15. Earlier exegetical works on exegesis and the history of religion: **P.Volz**, *Mose. Ein Beitrag zur Untersuchung über die Ursprünge der israelitischen Religion*, Tübingen 1907; **H.Gressmann**, *Mose und seine Zeit. Ein Kommentar zu den Mose-Sagen*, Göttingen 1913; **E.Sellin**, *Mose und seine Bedeutung für die israelitisch-jüdische Religionsgeschichte*, Leipzig 1922.
6. Cf. **M.Noth**, *A History of Pentateuchal Traditions* (1948), Englewood Cliffs, NJ 1972, 172-91.
7. For **Moses** see the articles in *Bibellexikon* (**H.Cazelles**), *Encyclopaedia Judaica* (**I.Abrahams, M.Greenberg, D.Winston, I.Jacobs, A.Rothkoff, D.Kadosh, H.Z.Hirschberg, B.Bayer**), *Enzyklopaedie des Islam* (**B.Heller**), *Jüdisches Lexikon* (**A.Kristianpoller, N.M.Soloweitschik**), *Lexikon der jüdisch-christlichen Begegnung* (**J.J.Petuchowski and C.Thoma**), *Lexikon der Religionen* (**F.-L.Hossfeld and C.Frevel**), *Lexikon für Theologie und Kirche* (**J.Schmid**), *Die Religion in Geschichte und Gegenwart* (**E.Osswald**), *Theological Dictionary of the New Testament* (**J.Jeremias**), *Wörterbuch des Christentums* (**R.Liwak**).
Important monographs on the dialogue about Moses: **M.Buber**, *Moses* (1944), in *Werke*, Munich 1964, II, 9-230; **H.Cazelles et al.**, *Moise. L'Homme de l'Alliance*, Paris 1955; **L.Ginzberg**, *The Legends of the Jews*, I-II, Philadelphia 1909-10; **A.Néher**, *Moïse et la vocation juive*, Paris 1956; **H.Schmid**, *Die Gestalt des Mose. Probleme alttestamentlicher Forschung unter Berücksichtigung der Pentateuchkrise*, Darmstadt 1986.
8. Cf. Ex.4.16; 34.29-35.
9. Cf. Ex.3-4.
10. **F.Heiler**, *Prayer*, Oxford 1932, 142f.
11. Num.12.8.
12. Deut.18.15.
13. There is an edition of the text in **P.Riessler**, *Altjüdisches Schrifttum ausserhalb der Bibel*, Freiburg 1928, [5]1984, 138-55.
14. For the text see ibid., 485-95.

15. Cf. already II Kings 14.6.
16. Cf. Mark 7.9f.
17. Cf. Luke 16.29-31.
18. Cf. Matt.2.
19. Cf. John 6.25-34.
20. Cf. Luke 24.25-27.
21. Cf. surah 20.10-98.
22. Cf. surah 7.104-158; 20.10-98; 26.10-68; 28.4-43.
23. Cf. **R.Smend**, *Die Mitte des Alten Testaments*, Zurich 1970; Rudolf Smend's two articles which, though brief, have excellent historical documentation, ranging from W.M.L.de Wette (1813) and Wilhelm Vatke (1835), the founders of a modern biblical theology, through Julius Wellhausen (1880) to Martin Buber (1932), Walther Eichrodt (1933-39) and Gerhard von Rad (1957-60) have helped me to make my own standpoint more precise in the light of history (my only criticism is the constant neglect of the promise of the land which goes with the election of the people).
24. Already for **J.Wellhausen**, *Israelitische und jüdische Geschichte*, Berlin 1894, ⁹1958, the statement 'Yahweh the God of Israel, Israel the people of Yahweh' had been the brief embodiment of Israelite religion. 'Yahweh the God of Israel, Israel the people of Yahweh: that is the beginning and the abiding principle of the political and religious history which follows... The foundation on which the common awareness of Israel rests at all times was the belief: Yahweh the God of Israel and Israel the people of Yahweh' (23, 28).
25. The substance of the bipolar description also occurs in numerous other authors, for example in **G.Fohrer**, who speaks of the kingship of God and the community of God to express the living relationship between God and people. For further discussion of the centre of the Old Testament, cf. **H.Graf Reventlow**, *Problems of Old Testament Theology in the Twentieth Century*, London and Philadelphia 1985, ch.IV, 'The "Centre" of the Old Testament'.
26. **T.S.Kuhn**, *The Structure of Scientific Revolutions*, Chicago 1962, 175.
27. Cf. **H.Küng**, TTM, B II-IV C 1, similarly GR, Part C.

C. History

C.1 The Tribal Paradigm of the Period before the State

1. **T.S.Kuhn**, *The Structure of Scientific Revolutions*, Chicago 1962, 175.
2. Cf. **H.Küng**, TTM, ch. C 1.4, 'Does Paradigm Shift mean Progress?'.
3. **R.de Vaux**, *The Early History of Israel*, I, London and New York 1978, 475; for the settlement cf. II, 523-680.
4. There is a good survey of the most recent discussion in **M.L.Chaney**, 'Ancient Palestinian Peasant Movements and the Formation of Premonarchic Israel', in *Palestine in Transition. The Emergence of Ancient Israel*, ed. D.N.Freedman and D.Graf, Sheffield 1983, 39-90. Cf. also **R.B.Coote and K.W.Whitelam**, *The Emergence of Early Israel in Historical Perspective*, Sheffield 1987. I owe valuable information to personal conversations with the Old Testament scholar **Don C.Benjamin** during my guest semester at Rice University, Houston, Texas, in autumn 1987.

5. In addition to Albright's and Wright's works (cf. ch.A I) cf. also the first edition of **J.Bright**'s *History of Israel*, Philadelphia 1959 and London 1960, and **H.H.Rowley**, *From Joseph to Joshua. Biblical Tradition in the Light of Archaeology*, London 1950.

6. Cf. **A.Alt**, 'The Settlement of the Israelites in Palestine' (1925), in *Essays on Old Testament Religion*, Oxford 1966, 133-69; **id.**, 'Erwägungen über die Landnahme der Israeliten in Palästina' (1939), in *Kleine Schriften zur Geschichte des Volkes Israel*, I, Munich 1953, 126-75; **M.Noth**, *History of Israel*, London and Philadelphia ²1959; **M.Weippert**, *The Settlement of the Israelite Tribes in Palestine*, London 1971. For criticism cf. **C.H.J.de Geus**, *The Tribes of Israel. An Investigation into Some of the Presuppositions of Martin Noth's Amphictyony Hypothesis*, Assen 1976. There is some confirmation from archaeology in **Y.Aharoni**, *The Archaeology of the Land of Israel. From the Prehistoric Beginnings to the End of the First Temple Period*, Philadelphia and London 1982.

7. Cf. **G.E.Mendenhall**, 'The Hebrew Conquest of Palestine', *The Biblical Archaeologist* 25, 1962, 66-87; **id.**, *The Tenth Generation. The Origins of the Biblical Tradition*, Baltimore 1973; **id.**, 'Ancient Israel's Hyphenated History', in Freedman and Graf (eds.), *Palestine in Transition* (n.4), 91-103.

8. Cf. **N.K.Gottwald**, *The Tribes of Yahweh: A Sociology of the Religion of Liberated Israel 1250-1050*, Maryknoll and London 1979.

9. In addition to **M.L.Chaney**, who goes into the arguments of M.Weippert in particular, cf. above all **N.K.Gottwald**, *The Hebrew Bible*, Philadelphia 1985, 272-6.

10. Cf. **I.Finkelstein**, *The Archaeology of the Israelite Settlement*, Jerusalem 1988, 306-14, 352-6. Cf. also the criticism of the conquest model, ibid., 295-302.

11. **I. Finkelstein**: 'The origins of the Israelite settlers must ultimately be sought at the end of the Middle Bronze period, when the network of villages in the hill country broke apart and groups of people dropped out of this sedentary rural framework. These groups then underwent a lengthy pastoralist stage. They were particularly active in marginal areas, including the hill country, and their existence is attested in documents from the Late Bronze period. A change in political and economic circumstances led to their resedentarization throughout the Iron I period' (ibid., 353).

12. Ibid. Cf. the objections by **A.J.Hauser** to Mendenhall's theory, and further contributions to the discussion in *Journal for the Study of the Old Testament* 7, 1978.

13. **G. Fohrer**, *History of Israelite Religion*, Nashville and London 1977, 64.

14. The recent *History of Ancient Israel and Judah* by **J.M.Miller and J.H.Hayes**, Philadelphia and London 1986, completely gives up any attempt to reconstruct the history of the early Israelites, and **J.A.Soggin** also thinks (though without taking account of the most recent American discussion) that a reliable history of Israel can only begin with the foundation of the state by David: *A History of Israel. From the Beginnings to the Bar Kochba Revolt, AD 135*, London and Philadelphia 1984.

15. **M.Claus**, *Geschichte Israels*, still takes no account of the intensive discussion of the last two decades, in contrast to **J.Bright** in his third edition and in German exegesis **H.Donner**, *Geschichte des Volkes Israel und seiner Nachbarn in Grundzügen*, I, Göttingen 1984.

16. **Donner**, *Geschichte Israels* (n.15), 127.
17. Cf. **Gottwald**, *The Hebrew Bible* (n.9), 143f.
18. Cf. Judg.5.
19. Judg.5.7.
20. Judg.5.3.
21. **J.Wellhausen**, *Israelitische und jüdische Geschichte*, Berlin 1894, ⁹1958, 23, cf. 28.
22. **M.Buber**, *The Kingship of God* (1932), London 1967.
23. Buber does not seem to me to have refuted the objections made to this by **G.von Rad** in 'Basileus', *Theological Dictionary of the New Testament*, cf. *Kingship of God* (n.22).
24. Cf. **L.Perlitt**, *Bundestheologie im Alten Testament*, Neukirchen 1969.
25. Cf. **W.Eichrodt**, *Theology of the Old Testament* (1933-1939), London and Philadelphia 1961, 1967 (2 vols.).
26. Cf. **H.Haag**, *Das Land der Bibel. Gestalt – Geschichte – Erforschung*, Stuttgart 1989, 63-72.
27. Cf. Judg.5.11-13.
28. Cf. **Gottwald**, *The Hebrew Bible* (n.9), 285.

C.II The Paradigm of the Kingdom: The Period of the Monarchy

1. Judg.8.22f.
2. However, this is one-sidedly described as a continuous development – completely neglecting the external threat from the Philistines which stands in the foreground for the Old Testament texts – by **R.B.Coote and K.W.Whitlam**, *The Emergence of Early Israel in Historical Perspective*, Sheffield 1987, 139-66. The study by **F.S.Frick**, *The Formation of the State in Ancient Israel. A Survey of Models and Theories*, Sheffield 1985, seems more balanced; he is able to connect models and data from archaeology, comparative ethnology and anthropology with the biblical texts. Cf. further the contributions by **H.Donner, A.D.H.Mayes, B.Oded** and **J.A.Soggin** in *Israelite and Judaean History*, ed. J.H.Hayes and J.M.Miller, London and Philadelphia 1977; **B.Halpern**, *The Constitution of the Monarchy in Israel*, Chico 1981; **A.D.H.Mayes**, *The Story of Israel between Settlement and Exile. A Redactional Study of the Deuteronomistic History*, London 1983.
3. Cf. Deut. 17.14-20. On this cf. **M.Noth**, *The Deuteronomistic History*, Sheffield ²1991, and *The Chronicler's History*, Sheffield 1987 (the two volumes are a translation of *Überlieferungsgeschichtliche Studien* I, ²1957); **M.Weinfeld**, *Deuteronomy and the Deuteronomic School*, Oxford 1972; **R.D.Nelson**, *The Double Redaction of the Deuteronomistic History*, Sheffield 1981.
4. Cf. Judg.8.22f.; 9.8-15. For this cf. **A.D.H.Mayes**, 'The Period of the Judges and the Rise of the Monarchy', in *Israelite and Judaean History* (n.2), 285-331.
5. Cf.I Sam.8; 10.17-27; 11.12-14.
6. Both are brought together in a single composition in I Sam.8-12.
7. Cf. **G.Fohrer**, *Geschichte Israels. Von den Anfängen bis zur Gegenwart*, Heidelberg ³1982, 86f.; **D.M.Gunn**, *The Fate of King Saul. An Interpretation of a Biblical Story*, Sheffield 1980.
8. Cf. I Sam.31.4.

9. For David and his abiding significance cf. the articles in *Bibellexikon* (A.van den Born), *Die Religion in Geschichte und Gegenwart* (R.Bach), *Encyclopaedia Judaica* (B.Oded, I.M.Ta-Shma, L.I.Rabinowitz, G.Sholem, D.Flusser, H.Z.Hirschberg, A.Goldberg, B.Narkiss, B.Bayer); *Jüdisches Lexikon* (H.Fuchs, A.Sandler); *Lexikon für Theologie und Kirche* (M.Rehm), *Reallexikon für Antike und Christentum* (J.Daniélou), *The Encyclopaedia of Religion* (J.van Seters), *Theologische Realenzyklopädie* (L.A.Sinclair, C.Thoma), *Wörterbuch des Christentums* (U.Rüterswörden).

In the Jewish-Christian-Muslim 'trialogue', David has so far been given far less attention than, say, Abraham and Moses. Here the heading 'David' is often missing.

10. Cf. **G.von Rad**, 'The Beginnings of Historical Writing in Ancient Israel' (1944), in *The Problem of the Hexateuch*, Edinburgh 1966, reissued London 1984, 166-204, esp. 189f.

11. The series of **stories about David** begins with I Sam.16 and ends with I Kings 2.12; there are already marked idealizing tendencies in the two books of Chronicles. Basic exegetical articles are: **A.Alt**, 'Die Staatenbildung der Israeliten in Palästina' (1930) and 'Das Grossreich Davids' (1950), in *Kleine Schriften zur Geschichte des Volkes Israel* II, Munich 1953, 1-75, and the relevant chapters in the histories of Israel used here (cf. chapter A I), especially **Fohrer**, 91-104; **Donner**, I, 169-215; **J.A. Soggin**, *A History of Israel. From the Beginnings to the Bar Kochba Revolt, AD 135*, London and Philadelphia 1984, 41-68. Cf. further **D.M.Gunn**, *The Story of King David. Genre and Interpretation*, Sheffield 1978. Also the commentaries on the books of Samuel including, more recently, **H.W.Herzberg** (ATD 1956), 1964 (OTL); **H.J.Stoebe**, I, 1973 (KAT); **P.K.McCarter**, 1980/1984 AB. There is further literature on the kingdom of David and Solomon in **N.K.Gottwald**, *The Hebrew Bible. A Socio-literary Introduction*, Philadelphia 1985, 635-40.

12. Cf. II Sam.1.19-27.

13. Cf. II Sam.5.5.

14. Cf. II Sam.5.6-9.

15. Cf. II Sam.5.7.

16. Read the narrative II Sam.6, which is surrounded with sagas.

17. **Soggin**, *History* (n.11), 55.

18. Cf. **G.Fohrer**, *History of Israelite Religion*, Nashville and London 1977, 102-22.

19. Cf. II Sam.3.10; 17.11; 24.15.

20. Cf. II Sam.24.9; I Chron.22.2.

21. Josh.1.4; cf. also I Kings 5.1,4; II Chron.9.26.

22. Cf. II Sam.7.16.

23. Cf. I Chron.10-29.

24. Cf. Neh.3.16.

25. Cf. Acts 2.29.

26. **C.Thoma**, *Theologische Realenzyklopädie* VIII, 384.

27. Cf. ibid., 384-7.

28. Cf. Pss.1; 19; 119.

29. Cf. Ruth 4.17,20-22; I Sam.22.3-4.

30. Cf. Mark 2.23-28.

31. Cf. Matt.2.1-12: also **F.Hahn**, *Christologische Hoheitstitel. Ihre Geschi-*

chte im frühen Christentum, Göttingen 1961, ³1966, 242-79; C.Burger, *Jesus als Davidssohn. Eine traditionsgeschichtliche Untersuchung*, Göttingen 1970.

32. Cf. Luke 2.4-11.

33. Cf. Matt.1.1-17.

34. Cf. Luke 3.23-38.

35. Cf. Mark 10.47f.

36. Cf. Ps.2.

37. Cf. Acts 13.33.

38. Cf. surah 5.78.

39. Cf. surah 2.251.

40. Surah 17.55: on the corresponding surah 4.163, in his commentary **Rudi Paret** remarks: 'The word *zabur* is to be explained as an amalgamation of the Hebrew *mizmor* (Ethiopian *mazmur*), "psalm", and the Arabic *zabur*, "scripture" (which has probably come in from southern Arabic).'

41. Cf. I Kings 1-2.

42. For **Solomon** cf. the fundamental studies by **A.Alt**, 'Israels Gaue unter Salomo' (1913), 'Die Weisheit Salomos' (1951), in *Kleine Schriften* (n.11), 76-99, and the relevant chapters in the histories of Israel used here (cf. ch.A.I), especially **Fohrer**, 104-19; **Donner**, I, 215-32; **Soggin**, 69-85. In addition, of course, also the commentaries on I Kings: the most recent include **M.Noth** (only chs.1-16; his work was cut short when he was on the preliminaries to the exegesis of the Elijah narratives), 1968 (BK); **J.Gray**, 1964 (OTL); **E.Würthwein**, 1977 (ATD).

43. Cf. I Kings 1.

44. Cf. I Kings 5.12.

45. Cf. I Kings 3.4-15.

46. **Fohrer**, *History of Israelite Religion* (n.18), 128.

47. Cf. I Kings 5.9-14.

48. Cf. I Kings 5.15-9.25.

49. Cf. I Kings 9.26-10.29.

50. Cf. I Kings 11.

51. Cf. I Kings 3.16-28.

52. Cf. especially the commentary by **E.Würthwein**.

53. There is a comprehensive article on the First Temple – history, structure and ritual – by **Y.M.Grintz** and **Y.Yadin**, 'Tempel', *Encyclopaedia Judaica*. Cf. also **S.Krauss, J.P.Kohn, A.Kristianpoller**, 'Tempel', in *Jüdisches Lexikon*.

54. Cf. I Kings 8.12f.

55. Cf. I Kings 12.

56. Cf. **H.H.Rowley**, *Prophecy and Religion in Ancient China and Israel*, London 1956.

57. Cf. **H.Küng**, CR II.2.

58. Rowley himself has to concede this at the end of his book (125f.).

59. Cf. Ex.15.20f.

60. Cf. Judg.4f.

61. Cf. II Kings 22.14-20.

62. Cf. Isa.8.3.

63. For **prophecy**, in addition to the theologies of the Old Testament (cf. ch.A. I), cf. the articles in *Bibellexikon* (**P. van Imschoot/H.Haag, J.Kürzinger**)*; Dictionnaire de Religions* (**J.Jomier, L.Monboulou, E.Cothenet**)*; Die Religion in Geschichte und Gegenwart* (**G.Mensching, R.Meyer, J.Fichtner, A.Jepsen,**

P.Vielhauer, E.Fascher), *Encyclopaedia Judaica* (S.M.Paul, L.I.Rabinowitz, R.Lerner, W.S.Wurzburger), *Enzyklopaedie des Islam* (J.Horovitz); *Jüdisches Lexikon* (M.Wiener); *Lexikon der Religionen* (F.-L.Hossfeld/E.Reuter, A.Schimmel); *Lexikon für Theologie und Kirche* (G.Lanczkowski, H.Gross, J.Schmid, K.Rahner); *Lexikon religiöser Grundbegriffe* (D.Vetter, R.Glei, S.Balic); *The Encyclopedia of Religion* (G.T.Sheppard/ W.E.Herbrechtsmeier, R.R.Wilson), *Theologisches Handwörterbuch zum Alten Testament* (J.Jeremias); *Theological Dictionary of the New Testament* (H.Krämer); *Wörterbuch des Christentums* (R.Liwak).

Important recent publications about the dialogue on the prophets include: M.Buber, *Prophetic Faith*, New York 1977; K.Koch, *The Prophets*, London and Philadelphia 1982, 1983 (2 vols.); A.Néher, *L'essence du prophétisme*, Paris 1955; C.Westermann, 'Propheten', in *Biblisch-historisches Wörterbuch*, Göttingen 1960, 1496-1512; Fohrer, *History of Israelite Religion* (n.18), 223-91; id., *Theologische Grundstrukturen des Alten Testaments*, Berlin 1972, 71-86; R.R.Wilson, *Prophecy and Society in Ancient Israel*, Philadelphia 1980; J.Blenkinsopp, *A History of Prophecy in Israel*, Philadelphia 1983; D.L.Petersen (ed.), *Prophecy in Israel. Search for an Identity*, Philadelphia 1987; J.F.A.Sawyer, *Prophecy and the Prophets of the Old Testament*, Oxford 1987; H.W.Wolff, *Studien zur Prophetie. Probleme und Erträge*, Munich 1987; J.Barton, *Oracles of God. Perceptions of Ancient Prophecy in Israel after the Exile*, London 1986.

64. Cf. Isa.6.

65. Cf. Jer.1.4-10.

66. Cf. Ezek.1.1-3.15.

67. Cf. H.von Stietencron, in H.Küng, CWR, ch. B.I 1.

68. Cf. J.Ching, in H.Küng, CR, ch.II.1.

69. On this cf. the literature referred to in ch.A II above, by B.Lang, M.Smith and A.de Pury.

70. Cf. I Kings 19.10,14.

71. Isa.2.4; cf. Micah 4.1-3.

72. Cf. Hos.9.7; Jer.29.26; II Kings 9.11.

73. Cf. C.Thoma, 'Prophet', in *Lexikon der jüdisch-christlichen Begegnung*.

74. Talmud, tractate Berakhot: jBer 1.4 (3b).

75. Cf. F.Rahman, *Prophecy in Islam. Philosophy and Orthodoxy*, London 1958.

76. Cf. II Kings 17.1-6.

77. Cf. II Kings 17.14-34.

78. There is an account of the reform in II Kings 22-23.

79. Cf. Donner, *Geschichte* II, 368f.; Soggin, *History*, 232f.

80. The classic study of the Deuteronomistic history work is by M.Noth, *The Chronicler's History*, Sheffield 1987, a translation of the second part of *Überlieferungsgeschichtliche Studien* I, ²1957 (see n.3 above). There is a comprehensive survey of research in H.D.Preuss, *Deuteronomium*, Darmstadt 1982.

81. Nor, however, is it probable that there was a 'pious deception' in the discovery of the book, though this is constantly asserted. Cf. recently H.Spieckermann, *Judah unter Assur*, Göttingen 1982, 156ff.

82. Deut. 12.5.

83. Cf. II Kings 24.14.

84. Cf. II Kings 25.4-7.
85. Cf. Jer.52.11.

C.III The Paradigm of Theocracy: Post-Exilic Judaism

1. Cf. Lev.26.
2. Cf.Ps.137.
3. Cf. Ezek.1.1 for the **Babylonian exile**. Among more recent publications, in addition to the histories of Israel cited in ch.I A (**Ben-Sasson, Donner, Fohrer** and **Gottwald** are particularly important) cf. **W.Eichrodt**, *Krisis der Gemeinschaft in Israel*, Basel 1953; **E.Janssen**, *Juda in der Exilszeit. Ein Beitrag zur Frage der Entstehung des Judentums*, Göttingen 1956; **C.F.Whitley**, *The Exilic Age*, London 1957; **P.R.Ackroyd**, *Exile and Restoration. A Study of Hebrew Thought of the Sixth Century BC*, London and Philadelphia 1968; id., *Israel under Babylon and Persia*, Oxford 1970; **R.W.Klein**, *Israel in Exile. A Theological Interpretation*, Philadelphia 1979; **J.D.Newsome, Jr**, *By the Waters of Babylon. An Introduction to the History and Theology of the Exile*, Edinburgh 1979; **J.A.Soggin**, *A History of Israel. From the Beginnings to the Bar Kochba Revolt, AD 135*, London and Philadelphia 1984.
4. Cf. Ps.137.
5. Cf. Ezek.37.1-14.
6. Cf. **G.Fohrer**, *History of Israelite Religion*, Nashville and London 1977, 324.
7. There is a debate over the influence of the 'Deuteronomist(s)' on other biblical books. Cf. the literature by **M.Noth** and **H.D.Preuss** cited in the previous chapter.
8. For the **history of Judah in the Persian empire**, in addition to the histories of Israel see among the more recent publications: **K.Galling**, *Die Krise der Aufklärung in Israel*, Mainz 1952; id., *Studien zur Geschichte Israels im persischen Zeitalter*, Tübingen 1964; **C.C.Torrey**, *The Chronicler's History of Israel. Chronicles-Ezra-Nehemiah Restored to Its Original Form*, New Haven 1954; **O.Plöger**, *Theocracy and Eschatology*, Oxford 1968; **S.Mowinckel**, *Studien zu dem Buche Ezra-Nehemia*, I-III, Oslo 1964-5; **H.C.M.Vogt**, *Studien zur nachexilischen Gemeinde in Esra-Nehemia*, Werl 1966; **J.D.Purvis**, *The Samaritan Pentateuch and the Origin of the Samaritan Sect*, Cambridge 1968; **R.S.Foster**, *The Restoration of Israel. A Study in Exile and Return*, London 1970; **K.-M.Beyse**, *Serubbabel und die Königserwartungen der Propheten Haggai und Sacharja. Eine historische und traditionsgeschichtliche Untersuchung*, Stuttgart 1972; **R.J.Coggins**, *Samaritans and Jews. The Origins of Samaritanism Reconsidered*, Atlanta 1975; **M.Avi-Yonah** and **Z.Baras** (eds.), *Society and Religion in the Second Temple Period* (The World History of the Jewish People. First Series: Ancient Time, Vol.VIII), Jerusalem and London 1977; **S.Safrai**, *Das jüdische Volk im Zeitalter des Zweiten Tempels*, Neukirchen 1978; **W.D.Davies and L.Finkelstein** (eds.), *The Cambridge History of Judaism*, I, *Introduction. The Persian Period*, Cambridge 1984.
9. Cf. Isa.41.2.
10. Cf. Isa.44.28.
11. Cf. Isa.45.1.

12. The original Aramaic version is in Ezra 6.3-5.

13. Cf. Ezra 1.1-4.

14. According to **Donner**, *Geschichte*, II, 409-12, the permission to return may have been added later by the author of the Chronistic history work (from the fourth/third century).

15. Thus **H.Haag**, *Das Land der Bibel. Gestalt – Geschichte – Erforschung*, Stuttgart 1989, 93f.

16. The homecoming of those who returned, some of them well-to-do – 42,360 and more than 7,300 slaves, according to Ezra 2 (including those who had remained in the land?), did not take place until the 520s. Thus **Donner**, *Geschichte*, II, 409-12.

17. Cf. Hag.1.2-4.

18. Cf. Zech.4.9.

19. Cf. Hag.2.23.

20. Cf. Zech.4.1-6, 10,14.

21. There is a comprehensive article on the Second Temple, its history, structure and ritual, by **B.Porten, Y.M.Grintz, M.Avi-Yonah** and **S.Safrai**, 'Tempel', in *Encyclopaedia Judaica*. Cf. also **S.Krauss, J.P.Kohn, A.Kristian-poller**, 'Tempel', in *Jüdisches Lexikon*.

22. Cf. Ezra 6.15-18.

23. Cf. Mal.3.1.

24. Cf. Neh.5.14.

25. **A.van Hoonacker**, *Néhémie et Esdras. Nouvelle hypothèse sur la chronologie de l'époque de la restauration*, Louvain 1890.

26. Cf. Ezra 7.12, 21.

27. Cf. Neh.8.10.

28. There is a survey in **U.Kellermann**, 'Erwägungen zum Esra-Gesetz', *Zeitschrift für die alttestamentliche Wissenschaft* 80, 1968, 373-85.

29. Cf. Lev.17-26.

30. **Fohrer**, *History of Israelite Religion* (n.6), 314.

31. Ibid.

32. Ibid., 315.

33. Cf. Ezra 7-10.

34. Cf. Neh.1-7; 10-13.

35. **Fohrer**, *History of Israelite Religion* (n.6), 374.

36. Cf. II Macc.6.2.

37. **Soggin**, *History*, 278.

38. Cf. **Donner**, *Geschichte* II, 43-9, 'Das dunkle Jahrhundert'.

39. Cf. I and II Chronicles, Ezra, Nehemiah.

40. The complex redaction-critical and literary-critical process has been described at a high level by **N.K.Gottwald**, *The Hebrew Bible. A Socio-Literary Introduction*, Philadelphia 1985, ch. 11 (Law and Prophets) and 12 (Writings).

41. **I.Elbogen**, *Der jüdische Gottesdienst in seiner geschichtlichen Entwicklung*, Frankfurt 1913, ³1931.

42. **J.Heinemann**, *Prayer in the Talmud. Forms and Patterns*, Berlin 1977, 15.

43. **J.Neusner**, *The Way of Torah. An Introduction to Judaism*, Belmont ³1979, 53.

44. **J.H.Charlesworth**, 'A Prolegomenon to a New Study of the Jewish

Background of the Hymns and Prayers in the New Testament', *Journal of Jewish Studies* XXXIII, 1982, 272.

45. Cf. Isa.56-66.

46. Cf. Zech.9-14.

47. Ps.74.9.

48. Cf. Talmud tractate Yoma, bYom. 9b. **R.Then**, '*Gibt es denn keinen mehr unter den Propheten?' Zum Fortgang der alttestamentlichen Prophetie in frühjüdischer Zeit*, Frankfurt 1990, demonstrates an ongoing interest in the prophets and projections back on to David and others rather than the existence of real prophets in early Judaism.

49. Cf. John 6.14; 7.40,52; Acts 3.22; 7.37.

50. Cf. I Cor.12.28.

51. Cf. I Cor.14.1-3.

52. Cf. I Cor.14.

53. Cf. Rom.12.6.

54. Cf. Eph.4.11f.

55. Cf. **A.Schimmel**, 'Prophet', in *Lexikon der Religionen*.

56. Cf. Jer.18.18.

57. Cf. **M.Hengel**, *Judaism and Hellenism. Studies in their Encounter with Special Reference to Palestine to the Middle of the Second Century BCE*, London and Philadelphia 1974 (2 vols.), I, 127.

58. There is a good survey of the recent state of scholarship in **K.-J.Kuschel**, *Geboren vor aller Zeit? Der Streit um Christi Ursprung*, Munich 1990 (ET in preparation, *Born Before All Time?*, London and New York 1992).

59. For the **history of Judah in the Hellenistic period**, in addition to the histories of Israel (ch.A. I), see among more recent publications **W.O.E.Oesterley**, *The Jews and Judaism during the Greek Period: The Background of Christianity*, London 1941; **V.Tcherikover**, *Hellenistic Civilization and the Jews*, Philadelphia 1959; **S.Zeitlin**, *The Rise and Fall of the Judaean State. A Political, Social and Religious History of the Second Commonwealth* (2 vols.), Philadelphia 1962-1967; **D.S.Russell**, *The Jews from Alexander to Herod*, Oxford 1967; **M.Hengel**, *Judaism and Hellenism* (n.57); id., *Jews, Greeks and Barbarians. Aspects of Hellenization of Judaism in Pre-Christian Times*, London and Philadelphia 1980; **H.Temporini and W.Haase** (eds.), *Aufstieg und Niedergang der römischen Welt. Geschichte und Kultur Roms im Spiegel der neueren Forschung*, Part II, Vol.21.1-2: *Religion (Hellenistisches Judentum im römischer Zeit: Philon und Josephus)*, Berlin 1983-1984.

60. The Tübingen scholar **Martin Hengel** refers explicitly to this possibility of a 'world religion' (= Diaspora religion) which is not only in fact spread all over the world externally, but is genuinely universal by virtue of its intrinsic character: 'In the Hellenistic period, say from the second half of the second century BC, Judaism was well on the way towards becoming a *world religion* as a result of the rapid extension of the Diaspora and a partially very active mission – the success of the Maccabean period had also raised its self-awareness in this respect. The anxious and zealous fixation on the letter of the Torah which we meet in Pharisaism was, of course, in manifest opposition to this. Even in Greek-speaking Judaism there was only a slightly greater freedom towards the law here; the allegorical interpretation did not do away with the literal sense, and the concrete commands and prohibitions remained unqualifiedly in force even in Philo' (*Judaism and Hellenism* I [n.57], 313).

61. **Donner**, *Geschichte*, II, 439.

62. Cf. Dan.11.31; 12.11.

63. For the Maccabaean period, in addition to the histories of Israel (ch.A.1), among more recent publications cf. **W.W.Buehler**, *The Pre-Herodian Civil War and Social Debate. Jewish Society in the Period 76-40 BC and the Social Factors Contributing to the Rise of the Pharisees and the Sadducees*, Basel 1974; **W.R.Farmer**, *Maccabees, Zealots and Josephus. An Inquiry into Jewish Nationalism in the Greco-Roman Period*, New York 1956; **O.Plöger**, *Aus der Spätzeit des Alten Testaments. Studien*, Göttingen 1971.

64. Cf. **Flavius Josephus**, *Antiquities* 13,380f.; id., *Jewish War*, I, 97f.

65. Thus, tendentiously, **M.Stern**, 'The Period of the Second Temple', in Ben-Sasson, *History of the Jewish People*, 14f.; this is realistically opposed by **Zeitlin**, *Rise and Fall* (n.59), Vol.I.

66. **Gottwald**, *The Hebrew Bible* (n.40), 448.

67. For the **history of Judah under the Romans**, in addition to the histories of Israel (ch.A.1), among more recent publications cf. **E.Schürer**, *Geschichte des jüdischen Volkes im Zeitalter Jesu Christi* (3 vols), Leipzig [4]1901-1909; new edition ed. M.Goodman, F.Millar, G.Vermes, *The History of the Jewish People in the Age of Jesus Christ (175 BC – AD 135)*, Vols. I-III.2, Edinburgh 1973ff.; **J.Jeremias**, *Jerusalem in the Time of Jesus* (1923, [2]1958), London and Philadelphia 1969; **M.Hengel**, *The Zealots. Investigations into the Jewish Freedom Movement in the Period from Herod I to 70 AD* ([2]1976), Edinburgh 1989; **P.Prigent**, *La fin de Jérusalem*, Neuchâtel 1969; **H.Kreissig**, *Die sozialen Zusammenhänge des jüdischen Krieges. Klassen und Klassenkampf im Palästina des 1.Jahrhunderts vor unsere Zeit*, Berlin 1970; **D.M.Rhoads**, *Israel in Revolution 6-74 CE. A Political History based on the Writings of Josephus*, Philadelphia 1976.

68. **G.Fohrer**, *Geschichte Israels*, Heidelberg 1979, 296f.

69. For **Herod**, in addition to the histories of Israel (ch.A.1), cf. above all Schürer's work, which sums up briefly and pertinently the information to be found in Josephus. In contrast to the descriptions of Herod by Heinrich Grätz (1906-1908), who condemns him from the perspective of Talmudic orthodoxy; of Hugo Willrich (1929), who defends him against the Jews as a victim of politics; and Joseph Klausner (1949-1951), who defends the Hasmonaeans one-sidedly against the 'alien usurper Herod', **Abraham Schalit**, following Walter Otto (1913), attempts to do justice to Herod in a comprehensive critical approach. His work, written in Hebrew, was substantially enlarged and extended for the German edition (now almost 900pp.), *König Herodes. Der Mann und sein Werk*, Berlin 1969. There are more recent biographies by **S.Sandmel**, *Herod. Profile of a Tyrant*, Philadelphia 1967; **M.Grant**, *Herod the Great*, London 1971.

70. **Jeremias**, *Jerusalem* (n.67), gives a comprehensive account of economic, socal and religious conditions in Jerusalem.

71. For **apocalyptic** cf. **O.Plöger**, *Theocracy and Eschatology* (1959), Oxford 1968; **C.Rowland**, *The Open Heaven. A Study of Apocalyptic in Judaism and Early Christianity*, London and New York 1982; **D.Hellholm** (ed.), *Apocalypticism in the Mediterranean World and the Near East: Proceedings of the International Colloquium on Apocalypticism (Uppsala, August 12-17, 1979)*, Tübingen 1983; **G.W.E.Nickelsburg and M.E.Stone**, *Faith and Piety in Early Judaism. Texts and Documents*, Philadelphia 1983; **J.J.Collins**, *The*

Apocalyptic Imagination. An Introduction to the Jewish Matrix of Christianity, New York 1984; **M.Goodman**, *The Ruling Class of Judaea. The Origins of the Jewish Revolt against Rome, AD 66-70*, Cambridge 1987; **P.D.Hanson**, *Old Testament Apocalyptic*, Nashville 1987.

72. **E.Zenger**, 'Jesus von Nazareth und die messianische Hoffnung des alttestamentlichen Israel', in W.Kasper (ed.), *Christologische Schwerpunkte*, Düsseldorf 1980, 37-78: 70.

73. Cf. Dan.12.3.

74. There is an illuminating text from the pre-Christian period, which combines the figure of the 'son of David' with that of the Messiah, in Psalm 17 of the pseudepigraphical Psalms of Solomon (17.21-46). But the figure depicted here is an earthly liberator who is to crush the godless rulers and purify Jerusalem from the Gentile nations. This notion has only a very few features in common with Jesus as the Christian Son of David. For the development of the ideas of Son of Man and Messiah in the pre-Christian and New Testament period according to the latest state of scholarly research cf. **Kuschel**, *Geboren vor aller Zeit* (n.58), 262-310.

75. For the pre-history of the Jewish rebellion cf. above all **Hengel**, *The Zealots* (n.67).

76. **Rhoads**, *Israel in Revolution* (n.67), offers a precise analysis of the causes of the war.

77. Only around 150 years ago (in 1838) did the American scholars E.Smith and E.Robinson succeed in identifying with the fort of Masada the ruins lying west of the Dead Sea and called 'es-Seddeh' by the Arabs. In subsequent years international expeditions, the most comprehensive of which was led in 1963-5 by Yigael Yadin, reconstructed the plan and function of the mighty fortress not least through the indications given by Josephus. Cf. **Y.Yadin**, *Masada. Herod's Fortress and the Zealots' Last Stand*, London and New York 1966.

78. **Prigent**, *Fin de Jérusalem* (n.67),deals with both Jewish-Roman wars.

79. Cf. **Y.Yadin**, *Bar Kokhba – The Rediscovery of the Legendary Hero of the Last Jewish Revolt against Imperial Rome*, London and New York 1971.

C.IV The Mediaeval Paradigm: The Rabbis and the Synagogue

1. Cf. **F.Hahn**, *Christologische Hoheitstitel. Ihre Geschichte im frühen Christentum*, Göttingen 1963, [2]1966, 75f.

2. Cf. **F.Hüttenmeister** and **G.Reeg**, *Die antiken Synagogen in Israel* (2 vols), Wiesbaden 1977.

3. Sayings of the Fathers 1.2.

4. **J.Neusner**, 'Varieties of Judaism in the Formative Age', in A.Green (ed.), *Jewish Spirituality. From the Bible through the Middle Ages*, New York and London 1987, 171-97: 172, 171.

5. Cf. **I.Elbogen**, *Der jüdische Gottesdienst in seiner geschichtlichen Entwicklung*, Frankfurt [3]1931.

6. Cf. especially **S.Safrai**, in H.H.Ben-Sasson (ed.), *A History of the Jewish People*, Cambridge 1976, 373-82.

7. **Neusner**, 'Varieties' (n.4), 172.

8. For Judaism in **the period of Mishnah and Talmud** cf. **J.Maier**, *Das Judentum. Von der biblischen Zeit bis zur Moderne*, Munich [2]1973, 287-379;

Safrai (n.6), 305-82; **G.Alon**, *Jews, Judaism and the Classical World. Studies in Jewish History in the Times of the Second Temple and Talmud*, Jerusalem 1977; **H.Temporini and W.Haase** (eds.), *Aufstieg und Niedergang der römischen Welt. Geschichte und Kultur Roms im Spiegel der neueren Forschung*, Part II, Vol.21.1-2: *Religion (Judentum: Allgemeines, Palästinisches Judentum)*, Berlin 1979; **G.Stemberger**, *Geschichte der jüdischen Literatur. Eine Einführung*, Munich 1977; *id., Das klassische Judentum. Kultur und Geschichte der rabbinischen Zeit (70 n.Chr. bis 1040 n.Chr)*, Munich 1979; *id., Epochen der jüdischen Literatur*, Munich 1982. The book edited by the rabbi **J.Winter** and the Christian Judaist **A.Wünsche**, *Die jüdische Literatur seit Abschluss des Kanons. Eine prosaische und poetische Anthologie mit biographischen und litterargeschichtlichen Einleitungen* (2 vols.), Trier 1894 reprinted 1964, is still useful as a reference work; **G.Karpeles**, *Geschichte des jüdischen Literatur* (2 vols.), Berlin 1886 reprinted 1963, is a popular compilation. Cf. now the two excellent multi-volume works on Jewish literature: **M.Waxman**, *A History of Jewish Literature* (5 vols.), new edition New York 1960; **I.Zinberg**, *A History of Jewish Literature* (12 vols.), Cleveland and New York 1972-1978. However, all research into the Mishnah and Talmud has been put on a new footing by **Jacob Neusner**, the leading scholar of Talmudic and rabbinic literature. His *A History of the Jews in Babylonia* (5 vols.), Leiden 1965-1970, and *A History of the Mishnaic Law of Purities* (22 vols.), Leiden 1974-7, are basic works. He attempted a systematic account of the Mishnah in *Judaism, The Evidence of the Mishnah*, Chicago 1981. See also among his other works: *The Formation of the Babylonian Talmud. Studies in the Achievements of Late Nineteenth and Twentieth Century Historical and Literary-Critical Research*, Leiden 1970; *Torah. From Scroll to Symbol in Formative Judaism*, Philadelphia 1985; *Ancient Judaism and Modern Category-Formation. 'Judaism', 'Midrash, 'Messianism' and Canon in the Past Quarter-Century*, Lanham 1986; *The Religious Study of Judaism* (2 vols.), Lanham 1986; *The Wonder-working Lawyers of Talmudic Babylonia; The Theory and Practice of Judaism in its Formative Age*, Lanham 1987; *Why no Gospels in Talmudic Judaism?*, Atlanta 1988; *Wrong Ways and Right Ways in the Study of Formative Judaism. Critical Method and Literature, History, and the History of Religion*, Atlanta 1988; *Medium and Message in Judaism*, First series, Atlanta 1989.

9. Cf. 'Talmud' in *Jüdisches Lexikon* (**B.Kirschner**) and *Encyclopaedia Judaica* (**E.E.Urbach**).

10. **G.Stemberger**, *Der Talmud. Einführung – Texte – Erläuterungen*, Munich 1982, ²1987, 37. **R.Mayer**, *Der Talmud*, Munich ³1980, also offers a good selection of important texts.

11. Cf. the articles in *Jüdisches Lexikon* (**J.Krengel**) and *Encyclopaedia Judaica* (**E.Berkovits, B.Bayer**).

12. So the Gemara is the exposition of the Mishnah in the Talmud: Mishnah + Gemara = Talmud. In addition to the Gemara there is also the Tosephta, a collection which largely coincides with it. There are further traditions in the Midrashim (Bible commentaries) and Targums (periphrastic renderings of the Bible into the Aramaic vernacular).

13. **Stemberger**, *Talmud* (n.10), 46. So given the very complex development it is important to keep in mind the following phases of the rabbinic movement and doctrinal tradition:

First-second centuries, the **Tannaites** (from Aramaic *tanna'im* = 'repeater', 'tradent', 'teacher'): masters of oral tradition. Their work is the Mishnah = halakhah = the binding law or religious law.

Third-fifth centuries, the **Amoraim** (from Hebrew *amar* = say): the commentators on Tannaitic doctrine: they produced the Gemara (= teaching, expansion of the Mishnah), which together with the Mishnah forms the Talmud (Palestinian and Babylonian).

Sixth-seventh centuries, the **Saborim** (from Hebrew *sabar* = think): those (only in Babylonia) who arranged the **Babylonian** Talmud and edited it comprehensively; it contains far more haggadic material than the Palestinian Talmud. **Seventh-eleventh centuries, the Geonim** or **Gaons** (from Hebrew *gaon* = exalted): the leaders of the Talmudic academies, who taught the Talmud and based their religious decisions on it.

14. The tractates of the **Babylonian Talmud** are quoted in abbreviated form, prefaced by b; tractates from the Jerusalem/Palestinian Talmud are prefaced by j. There is an English translation edited by I.Epstein, *The Babylonian Talmud* (35 volumes), London 1948-52; an American edition is beginning to appear, edited by **J.Neusner**, *The Talmud of Babylonia. An American Translation*, Chico, California 1984ff. (36 volumes are planned).

In addition to the classical introduction by **H.L.Strack**, *Einleitung in den Talmud* (1887; from ⁵1921 retitled *Einleitung in Talmud und Midrasch*, reprinted 1962, ET of seventh completely revised edition by **H.L.Strack and G.Stemberger**, *Introduction to the Talmud and Midrash* [1982], Edinburgh 1991), cf. also **B.M.Bokser**, 'An Annotated Bibliographical Guide to the Study of the Palestinian Talmud', in Temporini and Haase, *Aufstieg* (n.8), Vol.19.2, 1239-56; **D.Goodblatt**, 'The Babylonian Talmud', ibid., 257-336; **G.Stemberger**, *Der Talmud*; id., *Midrasch. Vom Umgang der Rabbinen mit der Bibel. Einführung – Texte – Erläuterungen*, Munich 1989. The great systematic work on the theology of the Talmud (the rabbinic view of God, humankind, the world, the law and the people of Israel) is **E.E.Urbach**, *The Sages. Their Concepts and Belief* (in Hebrew, Jerusalem 1969; English edition, Jerusalem 1975), new edition, Cambridge, Mass. and London 1987. But cf. **J.Neusner**, *From Literature to Theology in Formative Judaism. Three Preliminary Studies*, Atlanta 1989. **A.Cohen**, *Everyman's Talmud* (1932), reissued New York 1975, is a constantly reprinted popular systematic compilation of texts.

Cf. also the articles in *Dictionnaire des Religions* (**K.Hruby**), *Die Religion in Geschichte und Gegenwart* (**R.L.Dietrich**), *Encyclopaedia Judaica* (**B.Bayer**, **E.Berkovits**), *Jüdisches Lexikon* (**B.Kirschner, J.Krengel**), *Lexikon der jüdisch-christlichen Begegnung* (**J.J.Petuchowski**), *Lexikon für Theologie und Kirche* (**K.Schubert**), *The Encyclopedia of Religion* (**R.Goldenberg**).

15. According to the Council of Trent *pari pietatis affectu*, 'with equally pious affect', **H.Denziger**, *Enchiridion Symbolorum*, Freiburg ³¹1960, no.783.

16. For the **history of the Jews in the Middle Ages** cf. Ben Sasson, *History of the Jewish People*, 383-723; **I.Elbogen**, *Geschichte der Juden in Deutschland*, Berlin 1935; **Maier**, *Judentum* (n.8), 381-601; **I.Husik**, *A History of Mediaeval Jewish Philosophy*, New York 1916; **I.R.Marcus**, *The Jew in the Medieval World. A Source Book. 315-1971*, Westport, Conn. ²1975; **Y.H.Yerushalmi** et al., *Bibliographical Essays in Medieval Jewish Studies*, New York 1976; **L.Sievers**, *Juden in Deutschland. Die Geschichte einer 2000-jährigen Tragödie*, Hamburg 1977 (also the modern period); **H.Greive**, *Die*

Juden. Grundzüge ihre Geschichte im mittelalterlichen und neuzeitlichen Europa, Darmstadt 1980; I. Twersky, *Studies in Jewish Law and Philosophy*, New York 1982; H.and M.Simon, *Geschichte der jüdischen Philosophie*, Munich 1984; A.Green, *Jewish Spirituality* (n.4).

17. There is a survey of the latest state of research into **Philo** in **W.Haase** (ed.), *Aufstieg und Niedergang der römischen Welt. Geschichte und Kultur Roms im Spiegel der neueren Forschung*, Part II, 21.1 *(Hellenistisches Judentum in römischer Zeit: Philon und Josephus)*, Berlin 1984. Cf. here especially **E.Hilgert**, 'Bibliographie Philonienne 1935-1981', and the survey of research by **P.Borgen**, 'Philo of Alexandria. Critical and Synthetical Survey of Research since World War II'. Cf. also in addition to the basic works by É.Bréhier, I.Heinemann, W.Völker and H.A.Wolfson, from a Jewish standpoint the more recent synthetic accounts by **D.Winston**, 'Philo and the Contemplative Life', in Green, *Jewish Spirituality* (n.4), 198-231, and **Y.Amir**, 'Philo Judaeus', in *Enyclopaedia Judaica*. However, these works hardly go into the question why Philo remained an episode. It was only in the ninth century that the **Karaites** took up Philo again, in their polemic against anthropomorphic conceptions of God, with the result that even their opponent the **Gaon Saadia** had to go into these philosophical and theological problems.

18. Cf. **R.Goldenberg**, 'Talmud', *Encyclopedia of Religion* XIV, 256-60; id., 'Law and Spirit in Talmudic Religion', in Green, *Jewish Spirituality* (n.4), 232-52.

19. Cf. **S.W.Baron**, *A Social and Religious History of the Jews* (new edition in 18 volumes), New York 1952-1983, I, 167-71.

20. Already in the fifth century, for five brief decades there was a Jewish-Arab kingdom of Himiar in Arabia; cf. **S.Safrai**, in Ben-Sasson, *History* (n.6), 358f.

21. **R.Goldenberger**, 'Talmud', 259.

22. **Council of Florence**, *Decretum pro Jacobitis*, in **H.Denzinger**, *Enchiridion Symbolorum*, Freiburg [31]1960, no.714.

23. This has been worked out very emphatically by **A.F.Segal**, *Rebecca's Children. Judaism and Christianity in the Roman World*, Cambridge, Mass. 1986, esp.163-81.

24. For **antisemitism** (usually understood in the broader sense of anti-Judaism), see the articles in: *Dictionnaire des Religions* (**P.Pierrard**), *Die Religion in Geschichte und Gegenwart* (**W.Holsten**), *Encyclopaedia Judaica* (**B.Eliav**), *Jüdisches Lexikon* (**F.Goldmann, S.Kaznelson, B.Kirschner, J.Kreppel, W.Levinger, J.Meisl, A.Tänzer, A.Zweig**), *Lexikon der jüdisch-christlichen Begegnung* (**C.Thoma**), *Lexikon der Religionen* (**K.-H.Minz**), *Lexikon für Theologie und Kirche* (**K.Thieme**); *Reallexikon für Antike und Christentum* (**J.Leipoldt**), *The Encyclopedia of Religion* (**A.Davies**), *Theologische Realenzyklopädie* (**G.B. and T.C.de Kruijf, W.P.Eckert, N.R.M.de Lange, G.Müller, C.Thoma, E.Weinzierl**), *Wörterbuch des Christentums (***P.Maser***)*.

Important publications about the inter-religious dialogue on antisemitism are: **L.Goppelt**, *Christentum und Judentum im ersten und zweiten Jahrhundert. Ein Aufriss der Urgeschichte der Kirche*, Gütersloh 1954; **L.Poliakov**, *Histoire de l'antisémitisme* (4 vols), Paris 1955-77; **J.Isaac**, *Génèse de l'antisémitisme. Essai historique*, Paris 1956; **H.Andics**, *Der ewige Jude. Ursachen und Geschichte des Antisemitismus*, Vienna 1965; **E.H.Flannery**, *The Anguish of the Jews. Twenty-three Centuries of Antisemitism*, New York 1965; **M.Stern** (ed.), *Greek and Latin Authors on Jews and Judaism* (2 vols), Jerusalem 1974-1980; C.Klein, *Theologie und Anti-Judaismus. Eine Studie zur deutschen theologischen Literatur der Gegenwart*, Munich 1975; H.Jansen, *Christelijke Theologie na Auschwitz*, I, *Theologische en kerkelijke wortels van het antisemitisme*, The Hague 1981; K.H.Rengstorf and S.von Kortzfleisch (eds.), *Kirche und Synagoge. Handbuch zur Geschichte von Christen und Juden. Darstellung und Quellen* (2 vols.), Stuttgart 1968-1970, Munich 1988. In Vol.1 cf. especially B.Blumenkranz, 'Die Entwicklung im Westen zwischen 200 und 1200', 84-135; B.Kötting, 'Die Entwicklung im Westen der orientalischen Kirchen', 175-209; H.Greive, *Geschichte des modernen Antisemitismus in Deutschland*, Darmstadt 1983; D.Berger (ed.), *History and Hate; The Dimensions of Anti-Semitism*, Philadelphia 1986; E.Endres, *Die gelbe Farbe. Die Entwicklung der Judenfeindschaft aus dem Christentum*, Munich 1989.

25. Cf. J.N.Sevenster, *The Roots of Pagan Anti-Semitism in the Ancient World*, Leiden 1975, esp. 89-144.

26. Flavius Josephus, *Contra Apionem* I, 26-31.

27. Sevenster, *Roots of Pagan Anti-Semitism* (n.25), 118.

28. Quoted ibid., 90.

29. This had been preceded by the ban on the tax for the patriarchs (399) and the abolition of the privileges of the patriarch (415); possibly the extinction of the family of patriarchs was the immediate occasion for this. Cf. G.Stemberger, *Juden und Christen im Heiligen Land. Palästina unter Konstantin und Theodosius*, Munich 1987, 208-13.

30. Maier, *Judentum* (n.8), 582.

31. Ibid., 283: 'The Pharisaic-rabbinic components of the middle way not only proved to be the guideline which would determine the future in the catastrophe of 66-70 CE, but down to the Enlightenment in the eighteenth century remained the stepping stone from which to break new ground, depending on the particular situation. Moreover they were a point to which to return after disappointments', cf. 435.

32. P.Johnson has written an illuminating chapter in his *A History of the Jews*, London and New York 1987, under the title 'Cathedocracy' – the 'unique formula for self-government' in Judaism – , 169-232, cf. 149-68, on the significance of the scholars, their academies and great families, their many-sidedness and their economic success, and also of the different trends between nationalism and mysticism (Kabbala) and their most significant representatives: along with Nahmanides, of course above all Maimonides.

33. Cf. N.R.M.de Lange, 'Antisemitismus IV', in *Theologische Realenzyklopädie* 3, 128-37.

34. Ibid., 128.

35. J.W.Parkes, 'Jews and Christians in the Constantine Empire', in C.W.Dugmore and C.Duggan (eds.), *Studies in Church History* I, London 1964, 69-79: 71.

36. On this cf. H.Schreckenberg, *Die christlichen Adversus-Judaeos Texte und ihr literarisches und historisches Umfeld (1-11 Jahrhunderten)*, Frankfurt 1982; A.L.Williams, *Adversus Judaeos. A Bird's-Eye View of Christian Apologiae until the Renaissance*, Cambridge 1935; S.G.Wilson (ed.), *Anti-Judaism in Early Christianity*, II, *Separation and Polemic*, Waterloo 1986.

37. Melito of Sardis, *On Pascha*, in S.G.Hall (ed.), *Melito of Sardis. On Pascha and Fragments*, Oxford 1979, 94, 96 (lines 693-5, 715-16).

38. Stemberger, *Juden und Christen*, 46.

39. Cf. **Chrysostom**'s eight anti-Jewish sermons, *Patrologia Graeca* 48, 843-942 – an arsenal for anti-Jewish campaigns.

40. **N.A.Stillman**, *The Jews of Arab Lands. A History and Source Book*, Philadelphia 1979; **S.D.Goitein**, *Jews and Arabs. Their Contacts through the Ages*, New York 1955; B.Lewis, *The Jews of Islam*, Princeton 1984; **A.Cohen**, *Jewish Life under Islam. Jerusalem in the Sixteenth Century*, Cambridge, Mass 1984; **B.Ye'or**, *The Dhimmi. Jews and Christians under Islam*, London 1985.

41. Cf. **Ben-Sasson**, *History of the Jews*, 403.

42. For the political environment and internal organization of Judaism from the Arab conquest to the expulsion from Spain (638-1492), cf. **Maier**, *Judentum*, 383-434.

43. As a halakhist, philosopher and doctor, **Maimonides** (the abbreviated form of his name is Rambam) is portrayed by **A.Sandler, J.Guttmann, M.W.Rapaport** and **I.Lewin**, 'Maimonides', in *Jüdisches Lexikon*, and by **L.I.Rabinowitz, J.I.Dienstag, A.Hyman** and **S.Muntner** in *Encyclopaedia Judaica*. Cf. also **S.W.Baron**, 'Moses Maimonides', in S.Noveck (ed.), *Grosse Gestalten des Judentums*, I, Zurich 1962, 103-30.

44. On Mishnah Sanhedrin 11.1. Cf.**Elbogen**, *Der jüdische Gottesdienst* (n.5), 88. **S.Ben-Chorin**, *Jüdischer Glaube. Strukturen einer Theologie des Judentums anhand des Maimonidischen Credo. Tübinger Vorlesungen*, Tübingen 1975, attempts an explanation of Maimonides' confession of faith for our time.

45. Research into the social and religious history of Judaism was decisively stimulated by: for earlier Israelite history, **M.Weber**, *Ancient Judaism* (1920), Glencoe 1962; for modern Jewish history, **W.Sombart**, *Die Juden und das Wirtschaftsleben*, Leipzig 1911. **S.W.Baron** was stimulated by Weber and Sombart to write his often-quoted monoumental work, *A Social and Religious History of the Jews*.

46. See 638 n.8 above.

47. Cf. **Ben Sasson**, *History of the Jewish People*, 385f.

48. This danger is basically present in any history of antisemitism. One might take as an example **Hellmut Andics**, *Der Ewige Jude*, the individual chapters of which, written in the spirit of dialectical materialism, bear the following titles: 'The Designated', 'The Elect', 'The Outcast', 'The Despised', 'The Defenceless', 'The Liberated', 'The Feared', 'The Riven', 'The Slain', 'The Damned', 'The Inexorable'.

49. **Baron**, *Social and Religious History of the Jews*, II, 31.

50. **B.Blumenkranz**, *Juifs et chrétiens dans le monde occidental 430-1096*, Paris 1960.

51. **P.Riesenberg**, 'Jews in the Structure of Western Institutions', *Judaism* 28, 1979, 402-15.

52. Cf. **S.M.Blumenfeld**, 'Raschi', in Noveck (ed.), *Grosse Gestalten*(n.43), 131-50.

53. Cf. **Johnson**, *History* (n.32), 233-310 (Part IV: 'Ghetto').

54. **Riesenberg**, 'Jews' (n.51), 415.

55. Cf. **D.Biale**, *Power and Powerlessness in Jewish History*, New York 1986.

56. Cf. **W.P.Eckert**, 'Hoch- und Spätmittelalter', in Rengstorf and Kortzfleisch, *Kirche und Synagoge*(n.14) I, 210-72.

57. Cf. **A.H.and H.E.Cutler**, *The Jew as Ally of the Muslim. Medieval roots of Anti-Semitism*, Notre Dame 1986.

58. The 'hardened' and therefore 'unredeemed' Jews, 'slaves of sin', are to be treated legally and socially as 'slaves', as the property of Christian rulers, which for the Jews meant that they were under direct taxation and jurisdiction.

59. Cf. **R.Chazan**, *European Jewry and the First Crusade*, Berkeley 1987; id., *Daggers of Faith. Thirteenth-Century Christian Missionizing and Jewish Response*, Berkeley 1989. In the first riots of 1096, the Christians were generally on the side of the Jews, so that the Jews could flee to their Christian neighbours. Cf. also the volume of essays edited by Chazan, *Church, State, and Jew in the Middle Ages*, West Orange, NJ 1980.

60. **J.Cohen**, *The Friars and the Jews. The Evolution of Medieval Anti-Judaism*, Ithaca 1982.

61. For the whole historical context cf. **H.J.Schoeps**, *Jüdisch-christliches Religionsgespräch in 19 Jahrhunderten. Geschichte einer theologischen Auseinandersetzung*, Berlin 1937; **E.I.J.Rosenthal**, 'Jüdische Antwort', in Rengstorf and Kortzfleisch, *Kirche und Synagoge* (n.24) I, 307-62.

62. Cf. **H.Maccoby** (ed.), *Judaism on Trial. Jewish-Christian Disputations in the Middle Ages*, London 1982.

63. Cf. **Johnson**, *History* (n.32), 222.

64. **J.Maier**, *Jesus von Nazareth in der talmudischen Überlieferung*, Darmstadt 1978, 263f.

65. Cf. **J.J.Petuchowski**, 'Polemik' and 'Disputationen', in *Lexikon der jüdisch-christlichen Begegnung*.

66. I have already analysed these anti-semitic judgments in the chapter 'The Church and the Jews' in my book *The Church* (1967). **E.Eliav** offers a good survey of current prejudices with illuminating pictorial material in 'Anti-Semitism', *Encyclopaedia Judaica*.

67. **J.Maier** provides a convincing refutation of this charge from the Christian side with a broad account of Jewish commercial life in the Middle Ages, *Das Judentum* (n.8), 577-601.

68. Cf. Ex.22.24; Lev.25.35-37; Deut.23.20f.

69. For the passion plays see **S.Schaller** et al., *Passionsspiele heute? Notwendigkeit und Möglichkeiten*, Meitingen 1973; **R.Pesch**, ' "Sein Blut komme über uns und unsere Kinder."Ein Nachwort', in *Das Oberammergauer Passionspiel 1990. Textbuch*, ed. by the Oberammergau community, 1990, 111-15.

70. In addition to the relevant sections in the histories of Judaism (esp. **S.W.Baron, H.H.Ben-Sasson, P.Johnson**), cf. **Z.Ankori**, *Karaites in Byzantium. The Formative Years, 970-1100*, New York 1959; **P.Birnbaum** (ed.), *Karaite Studies*, New York 1971 (which contains two articles in on Gaon Saadia's Anti-Karaite works); **J.Mann**, *The Collected Articles*, Vol.III, *Karaitic and Genizah Studies*, Gedera 1971; **L.Nemoy** (ed.), *Karaite Anthology. Excerpts from the Early Literature*, New Haven 1952; **J.J.Petuchowski**, *The Theology of Haham David Nieto. An 18th Century Defense of Jewish Tradition*, New York ²1970; id., 'Karäer', in *Lexikon der jüdisch-christlichen Begegnungen*. There is a well-documented summary of the history and doctrine of the Karaites in **J.E.Heller and L.Nemoy**, 'Karaites', *Encyclopaedia Judaica* 10, cols. 761-82.

71. **Heller and Nemoy**, 'Karaites' (n.70), 765.

72. Cf. **Saadja Fajjumi**, *Emunot we-Deot oder Glaubenslehre und Philoso-phie*, ed. J.Fürst, Leipzig 1845. The most recent English translation from the Arabic and Hebrew is that of **S.Rosenblatt**, *Saadia Gaon. The Book of Beliefs and Opinions*, New Haven 1989. Cf. **T.Weiss-Rosmarin**, 'Der Gaon Saadia', in Noveck, *Grosse Gestalten* (n.43), 63-80.

C.V The Modern Paradigm: Assimilation

1. For the **Kabbala**, cf. above all **G.Scholem**, *Major Trends in Jewish Mysticism*, London 1955; id., *Judaica* (3 vols.), Frankfurt 1963-1970; **I.Twer-sky and B.Septimus** (eds.), *Jewish Thought in the Seventeenth Century*, Cambridge, Mass. 1987; **A.Steinsaltz**, *La rose aux Treize Pétales*, Paris 1989.
2. Cf. **M.Idel**, 'Mysticism', in *Contemporary Jewish Religious Thought*; id., *Kabbalah. New Perspectives*, New Haven 1988.
3. Cf. Ezek.1.15-28. The texts are in **P.Schäfer** (ed.), *Synopse zur Hekhalot-Literatur*, Tübingen 1981. For the interpretation cf. **G.Scholem**, *Jewish Gnosti-cism, Merkabah Mysticism, and Talmudic Tradition*, New York 1960, and **J.Dan**, 'The Religious Experience of the "Merkavah"', in A.Green (ed.), *Jewish Spirituality. From the Bible to the Middle Ages*, New York and London 1987, 289-307.
4. Significant Kabbalists of this time are: Abraham ben Isaac from Narbonne, his son-in-law Abraham ben David, his son Isaac the Blind, and the Kabbalists of Gerona with the famous Moses ben Nachman (Nachmanides) at their head.
5. Cf. **L.Fine** (ed.), *Safed Spirituality. Rules of Mystical Piety. The Beginning of Wisdom*, New York 1984.
6. For historical **Hasidism** cf. above all **G.Scholem**, *Major Trends in Jewish Mysticism*, London 1955; id, *The Messianic Idea in Judaism and Other Essays on Jewish Spirituality*, New York 1971; **S.Dubnow**, *Geschichte des Chassidismus* (2 vols), Berlin 1931; **H.M.Rabinowicz**, *The World of Hasidism*, London 1970; **K.E.Grözinger**, 'Chasidismus, osteuropäischer', in *Theolog-ische Realenzykopädie*.
7. Cf. **L.N.Newman**, 'Der Baalschemtow', in S.Noveck (ed.), *Grosse Gestal-ten des Judentums* I, Zurich 1972, 177-204.
8. Cf. **M.Buber**, 'Writings on Hasidim', *Werke*, Vol.III, Munich 1963; id., *The Origin and Meaning of Hasidism*, edited and translated by M.Friedman, New York 1960.
9. Cf. **G.Scholem**, 'Martin Bubers Deutung des Chasidismus', in the collec-tion of his studies, *Judaica*, I, 165-206.
10. **J.Reuchlin**, *De rudimentis hebraicis libri* III, Pforzheim 1506, facsimile reprint Hildesheim 1974. For what follows cf. **W.Maurer**, 'Reuchlin und das Judentum', *Theologische Literaturzeitung* 77, 1952, cols. 535-44; **W.P.Eckert**, 'Humanismus und christliche Kabbala', in K.H.Rengstorf and S. von Kortzflei-sch (eds.), *Kirche und Synagoge. Handbuch der Geschichte von Christen und Juden. Darstelluing mit Quellen*, I, Stuttgart 1968, Munich 1988, 272-306.
11. **J.Reuchlin**, *De verbo mirifico* (1494); *De arte cabalistica* (1517), facsimile reprint in one volume, Stuttgart 1964.
12. A by-product of the whole controversy was the *Epistolae obscurorum virorum* ('Letters of Obscure Men'), published anonymously, which was addressed to the spokesmen of the Cologne Dominicans against Reuchlin;

with its remorseless criticism of conditions in the church; this helped to prepare for the Reformation. For research into the Kabbala from Reuchlin to the present cf. **G.Scholem**, *Judaica* III, 247-63.

13. **Maurer**, 'Reuchlin', col.542; cf. also **I.Elbogen**, *Geschichte der Juden in Deutschland*, Berlin 1935, 104f.

14. **For Luther's attitude to Judaism** cf. **R.Lewin**, *Luthers Stellung zu den Juden. Ein Beitrag zur Geschichte der Juden in Deutschland während des Reformationszeitalters*, Berlin 1911; **E.Mills**, *Martin Luther and the Jews. A Refutation to his Book 'The Jews and Their Lies'*, Vienna 1968; **J.Brosseder**, *Luthers Stellung zu den Juden im Spiegel seiner Interpreten. Interpretation und Rezeption von Luthers Schriften und Äusserungen zum Judentum im 19. und 20.Jahrhundert vor allem in deutschsprächigen Raum*, Munich 1972 (here 22f., list of Luther's writings on the Jews); **G.Müller**, 'Antisemitismus (VI, 16. und 17. Jahrhundert)', *Theologische Realenzyklopädie*; **W.Maurer**, 'Die Zeit der Reformation', in Rengstorf and Kortzfleisch, *Kirche und Synagoge* (n.14), I, 363-452; **C.B.Sucher**, *Luthers Stellung zu den Juden. Eine Interpretation aus germanistischer Sicht*, Nieuwekoop 1977; **H.A.Oberman**, *Wurzeln des Antisemitismus. Christenangst und Judenplage im Zeitalter von Humanismus und Reformation*, Berlin 1981; **W.Bienert**, *Martin Luther und die Juden. Ein Quellenbuch mit zeitgenössischen Illustrationen, mit Einführungen und Erläuterungen*, Frankfurt 1982; **H.Kremers** (ed.), *Die Juden und Martin Luther – Martin Luther und die Juden. Geschichte, Wirkungsgeschichte, Herausforderung*, Neukirchen 1985.

15. Cf. **M.Luther**, 'That Jesus Christ was born a Jew' (1523), in *Luther's Works* (henceforth abbreviated *L W*), 45, 195-230.

16. Ibid., 201.

17. Ibid., 229.

18. The Reformed historian **H.A.Oberman**, *Die Reformation. Von Wittenberg bis Genf*, Göttingen 1986, esp.162-207, rightly keeps stressing the apocalyptic horizon and the firm belief in the devil in Luther's theology.

19. **M.Luther**, 'Against the Sabbatarians' (1538), in *L W* 47, 57-98.

20. **Id.**, 'On the Jews and their Lies', (1543), in *L W* 47, 121-306: in addition there are two more anti-Jewish works 'On The Tetragrammaton and the Genealogy of Christ' ('Vom Schem Hamphoras und vom Geschlecht Christi', 1543), *Weimarer Ausgabe* 53, 573-618 (there is no ET in *L W*), and 'The Last Words of David' (1523), *L W* 15, 265-351.

21. **Id.**, 'On the Jews and their Lies' (n.20), 272

22. **Maurer**, in Rengstorf and Kortzfleisch, *Kirche und Synagoge* (n.14), I, 447.

23. **Sucher**, *Luthers Stellung zu den Juden* (n.14), preface.

24. The standard German history of the papacy by **F.X.Seppelt**, revised by **G.Schwaiger**, *Geschichte der Päpste*, V, Munich [2]1959, 70-90, 119-75, maintains a complete silence on the countless anti-Jewish activities of the 'great popes of the Catholic Reformation' (Paul VI, Pius V and Gregory XIII), apart from barely seven lines on the Rome ghetto. **L.von Pastor**, *Geschichte der Päpste seit dem Ausgang des Mittelalters*, IX, Freiburg [11]1958, at least gives a brief account, though it is vague and mitigating, e.g. on Gregory XIII, 223-6.

25. The text of the bull *Antiqua Judaeorum improbitas*, issued on 10 June 1581, is given, along with other documents, by **W.P.Eckert**, 'Katholizismus

zwischen 1580 und 1848 (Stellung der Juden im Kirchenstaat)', in Rengstorf and Kortzfleisch, *Kirche und Synagoge* (n.14), II, 222-43, 275f.

26. Cf. **W.Philipp**, 'Spätbarock und frühe Aufklärung. Das Zeitalter des Philosemitismus', in ibid., 23-86.

27. Cf. **M.Schmid**, 'Judentum und Christentum im Pietismus des 17./18. Jahrhunderts', in ibid., 87-128.

28. For Judaism in the **modern world** and especially in **Germany**, in addition to the major works on the history of Judaism which we have already encountered – above all **Ben-Sasson** and **Maier** – cf. **W.Kampmann**, *Deutsche und Juden. Studien zur Geschichte des deutschen Judentums*, Heidelberg 1963; **H.Greive**, *Die Juden. Grundzüge ihrer Geschichte in mittelalterlichen und neuzeitlichen Europa*, Darmstadt 1980; **P.R.Mendes-Flohr** and **J.Reinharz** (ed.), *The Jew in the Modern World. A Documentary History*, New York 1980; **J.Bab**, *Leben und Tod des deutschen Judentums*, Berlin 1988; **F.Stern**, *Dreams and Delusions. The Drama of German History*, New York 1987; **A.J.and H.Edelheit**, *The Jewish World in Modern Times. A Selected, Annotated Bibliography*, Boulder, Co 1988; **N.T.Gidal**, *Die Juden in Deutschland von der Römerzeit bis zur Weimarer Republik*, Gütersloh 1988; **M.-R.Hayoun**, *Le judaïsme moderne*, Paris 1989; **H.M.Kirn**, *Das Bild vom Juden im Deutschland des frühen 16.Jahrhunderts, dargestellt an den Schriften des Johann Pfefferkorns*, Tübingen 1989; **F.Battenberg**, *Das europäische Zeitalter der Juden. Zur Entwicklung einer Minderheit in der nichtjüdischen Umwelt Europas* (2 vols), Darmstadt 1990, esp. II, *Von 1650 bis 1945*.

29. There is a pioneering account (inspired by Max Weber) of the most significant German national economists of the first half of the century by **W.Sombart**, *Die Juden und das Wirtschaftsleben*, Berlin 1911, in which 'the objective aptitude of the Jews to capitalism' is investigated (198-224), against the background of the 'significance of Jewish religion for economic life' (255-95). The decisive contribution of Jewish court finance to the modern state (e.g. to the Habsburgs, from first to last, from Amschel Oppenheim to Baron Louis de Rothschild) is shown by the investigations of **H.Schnee**, *Die Hoffinanz und der moderne Staat. Geschichte und System der Hoffaktoren an deutschen Fürstenhöfen im Zeitalter des Absolutismus* (5 vols), Berlin 1953-1965.

30. According to serious Jewish historians, too – **S.E.Morison, S.W.Baron, J.L.Blau** – there is no evidence that Christopher Columbus was of Jewish descent, but indubitably Jews or Marranos, including the ship's doctor, took part on the first expedition to America.

31. Cf. **M.U.Schappes** (ed.), *A Documentary History of the Jews in the United States 1654-1785*, New York [3]1971. He quotes Peter Stuyvesant's letter to the Dutch West India Company, from which it emerges that, contrary to their expectations, the twenty-three Jewish refugees from Brazil, now controlled by the Portuguese and the Inquisition, were unwelcome in New Amsterdam (1f.).

32. For the **history of Jews in America** cf. **J.L.Blau**, *Modern Varieties of Judaism*, London 1966; id., *Judaism in America. From Curiosity to Third Faith*, Chicago 1976; **J.L.Blau** and **S.W.Baron** (ed.), *The Jews of the United States 1790-1840. A Documentary History* (3 vols), New York 1963; **N.Glazer**, *American Judaism*, Chicago 1952, [2]1972; **M.Rischin**, *An Inventory of American Jewish History*, Cambridge, Mass. 1954; **D.Rudavsky**, *Modern*

Jewish Religious Movements. A History of Emancipation and Adjustment, New York 1967, ²1979.

33. Cf. the fair theological assessment by **J.Moltmann**, ' "What would a God be who only intervened from outside?" In Memory of Giordano Bruno', in *History and the Triune God*, London and New York 1991, 156-64.

34. Cf. **P.de Mendelssohn**, 'Sass Baruch Spinoza jemals vor Rembrandts Staffelei? Mutmassungen über die Verbindung zwischen den bankrotten Maler und dem verdammten Ketzer von Amsterdam', *Frankfurter Allgemeine Zeitung*, 26 February 1977.

35. Cf. **Chronicon Spinozanum** (5 vols.), The Hague 1921-1927; **N.Altwicker** (ed.), *Texte zur Geschichte des Spinozismus*, Darmstadt 1971 (with bibliography 1924-1968). There is also a good summary account by **Altwicker** – based on the fundamental interpretations by H.A.Wolfson, K.Jasper, K.Löwith, W.Cramer and M.Gueroult, 'Baruch Spinoza', in *Die Grossen der Weltgeschichte*, VI, ed.K.Fassmann, Zurich 1975, 32-47.

36. Cf. **Y.Yovel**, *Spinoza and Other Heretics. The Marrano of Reason*, Princeton 1989.

37. Ibid., 200.

38. Cf. **B.de Spinoza**, *Tractatus theologico-politicus*, 'Hamburg' (in fact 'Amsterdam') 1670; there is an English edition, *A Theologico-Political Treatise*, London 1883, reissued New York 1951, translated by R.H.M.Elwes.

39. Cf. **R.Simon**, *Histoire critique du Vieux Testament*, Paris 1678, with a new preface, Amsterdam 1685. There followed a critical history of the New Testament (1689), of the translations of the New Testament (1690) and of the most important commentators on the New Testament (1693) – all appeared in Amsterdam.

40. Cf. **B.de Spinoza**, *Ethica ordine geometrico demonstrata*, no place of publication, 1677; ET *Ethics*, London 1882, reissued New York 1951.

41. That Einstein's Spinozism was responsible for his repudiation of quantum mechanics was shown in **H.Küng**, DGE, ch.G II.2, ' "Does God Play Dice?", Albert Einstein'.

42. This is developed from Spinoza through Fichte and Hegel to Pierre Teilhard de Chardin and Alfred North Whitehead in **ibid.**, Part B, 'The New Understanding of God', especially 'Interim Results II: Theses on the reality and historicity of God'.

43. Cf. **J.Toland**, *Reasons for Naturalizing the Jews in Great Britain and Ireland, on the same foot with all other Nations. Containing also, a Defence of the Jews against all vulgar Prejudices in all Countries*, London 1714.

44. Cf. **A.Hertzberg**, *The French Enlightenment and the Jews*, New York 1968; **K.H.Rengstorf**, 'Der Kampf um die Emanzipation', in Rengstorf and Kortzfleisch, *Kirche und Synagoge* (n.14), II, 129-76.

45. **Montesquieu**, *De l'esprit des lois*, published anonymously in 1748; it went through twenty editions in two years. New edition by G.Truc (2 vols.), Paris 1949, livre XXV, ch.13.

46. **Voltaire**, *Dialogues et anecdotes philosophiques*, ed. R.Naves, Paris 1939, 143f. There are similar contemptuous remarks in Voltaire's *Dictionnaire Philosophique*, Basle 1764, s.v. 'Juifs'.

47. Cf.**W.Jens** and **H.Küng**, *Dichtung und Religion*, Munich 1985, 81-119.

48. Cf. **G.E.Lessing**, *Nathan the Wise*, Act 4 scene 7.

49. There are illuminating documents on Moses Mendelssohn in **H.Knob-**

loch, *Herr Moses in Berlin. Auf den Spuren eines Menschenfreundes*, Berlin 1979, ³1981.

50. Cf. **M.Mendelssohn**, 'Jerusalem oder über religiöse Macht und Judentum' (1783), in *Gesammelte Schriften, Jubiläumsausgabe*, Vol.8, Stuttgart 1983, 99-204.

51. Cf. **J.Maier**, who in his great work *Das Judentum. Von der biblischen Zeit bis zur Moderne*, Munich² 1973, also gives a good survey of the course of the Enlightenment in Judaism. Also the articles in *Jüdisches Lexikon* (**J.Meisl**) and *Encyclopaedia Judaica* (**A.Shochat** and **Y.Slutsky**).

52. **G.W.F.Hegel**, *Early Theological Writings*, translated by T.M.Knox and edited by Richard Kroner, Chicago 1948. Cf. **H.Küng**, *The Incarnation of God. An Introduction to Hegel's Theological Thought as Prolegomena to A Future Christology* (1970), Edinburgh 1987, III.2., 'Alien God and Alienated Man'; VII.4, 'Christ in Religion'.

53. Cf. **F.D.E.Schleiermacher**, *On Religion. Speeches to its Cultured Despisers*, London 1893 reissued New York 1958.

54. Cf. the impressive list of baptized Jews in **F.Goldmann**, 'Taufjudentum', in *Jüdisches Lexikon*. Cf. **S.Hensel**, *Die Familie Mendelssohn, 1729-1847. Nach Briefen und Tagebüchern* (3 vols.), Berlin 1879. Also the fine illustrated volume by **E.Klessmann**, *Die Mendelssohns. Bilder aus einer deutschen Familie*, Zurich 1990.

55. Cf. **M.Wyschogrod**, 'Verbunden für alle Zeit: die jüdische und die deutsche Geschichte', in *Deutsches Allgemeines Sonntagsblatt*, 2 October 1988.

56. Cf. **K.H.Rengstorf**, 'Der Kampf um die Emanzipation'; **R.Lill**, 'Der Heilige Stuhl und die Juden', both in Rengstorf and Kortzfleisch, *Kirche und Synagoge* (n.14), II, 222-79, 358-69.

57. For the extremely turbulent history of the Jews in Poland and Russia – full of Jewish successes and anti-Jewish measures on the part of the church – cf. **J.Meisl**, *Geschichte der Juden in Polen und Russland*, I-II, Berlin 1921-1925, esp. Vol.I, *Von den ältesten Zeiten bis zu den Kosakenaufständen in der Mitte des 17. Jahrhunderts*.

58. **Maier**, *Judentum*, 670f.

59. The Israeli historian **S.Volkov**, *Jüdisches Leben und Antisemitismus im 19. und 20. Jahrhundert. Zehn Essays*, Munich 1990, 110-45, gives an excellent analysis of this development.

60. In addition to **Leopold Zunz** (history of liturgy) and **Moritz Steinschneider** (bibliography of the sources), above all **Abraham Geiger** (the founder of the scientific theology of Judaism and the *Zeitschrift für jüdische Theologie*), **Zacharias Frankel** (the Mishnah and Talmud scholar) and **Heinrich Graetz** (author of the standard work *Geschichte des Judentums*), all of whom will concern us later. Although the Science of Judaism is concentrated in Germany, it also has representatives elsewhere: **Salomo Munk** in France and **Samuel David Luzzatto** in Italy. Here I should mention an impressive, though little mentioned example of this immense scholarly activity, a work on the dividing line between Judaism and Islam: **M.Steinschneider**, *Die arabische Literatur der Juden. Ein Beitrag zur Literaturgeschichte der Araber, grosstenteils aus handschriftlichen Quellen*, Frankfurt 1902. Steinschneider had already had published *Die hebräischen Übersetzungen des Mittelalters und die Juden als Dolmetscher*, Berlin 1893.

61. English text in **Glazer**, *American Judaism* (n.32), 42.

62. Cf. **S.L.Gilman**, *Jewish Self-Hatred, Anti-Semitism and the Hidden Language of the Jews*, Baltimore 1986.

63. There is more on **Schechter** in Part Three below.

64. Cf. the figures given in **Glazer**, *American Judaism* (n.32), 84f.

PART TWO:
THE CHALLENGES OF THE PRESENT

A. From the Holocaust to the State of Israel

A.1 A Past That Will Not Go Away

1. For the scientific assessment of the number of victims cf. **A.Suzmann** and **D.Diamond**, 'Der Mord an sechs Millionen Juden. Die Wahrheit ist unteilbar', in *Aus Politik und Zeitgeschichte*, supplement to *Das Parlament*, Bonn, B30, 1978, 4-21; **G.Wellers**, 'Die Zahl der Opfer der "Endlosung" und der Korherr-Bericht', ibid., 22-39. In ten years of research a team from the Munich Institute for Contemporary History examined these figures; they concluded that the certain minimum number was 5,290,000, but that the actual number of Jews murdered probably even exceeds the 6 million already mentioned by Eichmann. Cf. **W.Benz** (ed.), *Dimensionen des Völkermords. Die Zahl der jüdischen Opfer der Nationalsozialismus*, Oldenburg 1991. So the number of Jews murdered was: in Poland at least 2,700,000, in the Soviet Union 2,100,000, in Hungary 330,000, in Romania 211,000, and in the then German Reich 160,000. The work of exterminating the Jews did not just fall to a small number of murderers; this genocide was assisted in various ways by the army and the civil service.

2. Cf. **A. and M.Mitscherlich**, *Die Unfähigkeit zu trauern. Grundlagen kollektiven Verhaltens*, Munich 1977; **J.Müller-Hohagen**, *Verleugnet, verdrängt, verschwiegen. Die seelischen Auswirkungen der Nazizeit*, Munich 1988.

3. It is to the credit of the city of Nuremberg, at that time the city of the Reich Party Conferences and the race laws, that to commemorate 'Reichskristallnacht' in 1988, in collaboration with the cities of Fürth, Erlangen and Schwabach it arranged more than 400 different events in an attempt to work out the problems of the repression of guilt. Cf. the first-hand reports and analyses in **J.Wollenberg** (ed.), *'Niemand war dabei und keiner hat's gewusst.' Die deutsche Öffentlichkeit und die Judenverfolgung 1933-1945*, Munich 1989.

4. The monumental facsimile documentation (with English translations) edited by **J.Mendelsohn**, *The Holocaust. Selected Documents*, New York 1982 (18 vols.), is essential for understanding the **National Socialist persecution of the Jews** from a **historical** perspective. Vol. XI, for example, includes the notorious Wannsee protocol on the implementation of the 'final solution' to the Jewish question. On the basis of 220 key documents, **P.Longerich** attempts to depict the totality of the National Socialist murder of the Jews and to describe the mechanism of Europe-wide extermination: *Die Ermordung der europäischen Juden. Eine umfassende Dokumentation des Holocaust 1941-1945*, Munich 1989.

Important monographs include: **R.Hilberg**, *The Destruction of European Jews*, 1961; **H.Arendt**, *Eichmann in Jerusalem. Ein Bericht von der Banalität des Bösen*, Munich 1964; **U.D.Adam**, *Judenpolitik im Dritten Reich*, Düsseldorf 1972; **S.Adler-Rudel**, *Jüdische Selbsthilfe unter dem Naziregime 1933-1939. Im Spiegel der Berichte der Reichsvertretung der Juden in Deutschland*, Tübingen 1974; **L.S.Dawidowicz**, *The War against the Jews 1933-1945*, New York 1975; **Y.Bauer**, *A History of the Holocaust*, London 1978; **G.Hausner**, *Die Vernichtung der Juden: Das grösste Verbrechen der Geschichte*, Munich 1979; **Y.Bauer** and **N.Rotenstreich** (eds.), *The Holocaust as Historical Experience. Essays and a Discussion*, New York 1981; **H.U.Thamer**, *Verführung und Gewalt, Deutschland 1933-1945*, Berlin 1986. What documents by themselves cannot convey can be communicated by the recollections of the few survivors, as in the shattering account by **Ruth Elias**, who gave birth to a child in Auschwitz and lost it as a result of the camp doctor, Dr Mengele: **R.Elias**, *Die Hoffnung erhielt mich am Leben. Mein Weg von Theresienstadt und Auschwitz nach Israel*, Munich 1988. There is a survey of the various explanatory models of the origin and nature of National Socialism in **I.Kershaw**, *The Nazi Dictatorship. Problems and Perspectives of Interpretation*, London 1985. The comprehensive *Encyclopaedia of the Holocaust*, Tel Aviv and New York 1990, involved the collaboration of more than 100 scholars. An international congress on the Holocaust, 'Remembering for the Future', held in Oxford between 1 and 13 July and in London on 15 July 1988, centred above all on two themes, 'Jews and Christians during and after the Holocaust', and 'The Effect of the Holocaust on the Contemporary World'. The proceedings were published in three volumes, totalling in all 3,002 large-format pages: **Y.Bauer** et al., *Remembering for the Future. Working Papers and Addenda*, Oxford 1989.

5. The standard academic work on the struggle (and finally the downfall) of **the opposition to Hitler** in the 1930s and 1940s is **P.Hoffmann**, *The History of the German Resistance 1933-1945* (1969), London 1970.

6. The original German title of **F.Fischer**, *Germany's Aims in the First World* (1961), London 1967: 'As Germany willed and coveted the Austro-Serbian war and, in her confidence in her military military superiority, deliberately faced the risk of a conflict with Russia and France, her leaders must bear a substantial share of the historical responsibility for the outbreak of general war in 1914' (104). Cf. the recent studies by **R.J.W.Evans** and **H.Pogge von Strandmann** (eds.), *The Coming of the First World War*, Oxford 1988: 'All the available evidence suggests that it was mainly Germany which pushed for war and that without the German drive to extend her hegemony a major war would not have started in Europe in 1914' (Pogge, 121). **I.Geiss**, *Der lange Weg in die Katastrophe. Die Vorgeschichte des Ersten Weltkriegs 1815-1914*, Munich 1990, attempts a global historical synthesis. For the ideological support by church and theologies, **K.Hammer**, *Deutsche Kriegstheologie 1870-1914*, Munich 1974, is illuminating.

7. For the 'historians' dispute', cf. *'Historiker-Streit.' Die Dokumentation der Kontroverse um die Einzigartigkeit der nationalsozialistischen Judenvernichtung*, published by Piper Verlag, Munich 1987 (= *Piper-Dokumentation*).

8. **J.Habermas**, in *Piper-Dokumentation*, 62.

9. **E.Nolte**, in *Piper-Dokumentation*, 14.

10. Ibid.

11. Ibid., 15.

12. Cf. **S.Haffner**, *Anmerkungen zu Hitler*, Munich 1978.

13. Ibid., 124.

14. **H.Senfft**, *Kein Abschied von Hitler. Ein Blick hinter die Fassaden des 'Historikerstreits'*, Hamburg 1990, gives a retrospective survey which is both illuminating and critical (especially in connection with the revisionist historical policy of the *Frankfurter Allgemeine Zeitung*).

15. Cf. the crucial documents on the preparation and organization of the 'final solution', with a commentary, in **Longerich**, *Die Ermordung* (n.4), 65-102, which includes important documents on the question of knowledge and apathy, 427-52.

16. Cf. the summary of the cruelty of the 'Final Solution', in **Thamer**, *Verführung und Gewalt* (n.4), 696-710. The thesis of the English historian **D.Irving**, *Hitler's War*, London 1977, that the mass murder was committed behind Hitler's back by Himmler, on the latter's own initiative, is now regarded as refuted.

17. **E.Jäckel**, in *Piper-Dokumentation* (n.7), 118.

18. This came about – in the face of the obstructive measures of the Israeli government and the threats of the Turkish government – at an international conference in Tel Aviv, in which prominent experts on genocide research such as H.Fein, L.Kuper and R.G.Hovannisian took part under the leadership of **Israel W.Charny**, who also edited the proceedings of the congress, *Toward the Understanding and Prevention of Genocide. Proceedings of the International Conference on the Holocaust and Genocide*, Tel Aviv 1982 and Boulder, Colorado 1984. **Alfred Grosser**, in *Le crime et la memoire*, Paris 1989, has made a careful and detailed comparison with other mass murders: the Terror at the time of the French Revolution, the genocide of the Armenians by the Osman Turks, the Gulag Archipelago, the massacre of the Kurds, and the killings in Vietnam and Cambodia. Although he is himself of Jewish origin, he was abused by German Jews at a commemoration of the Nazi victims in 1990, in Berlin, because of his historical incorruptibility and humane tolerance.

19. **A.Solzhenitsyn**, *The Gulag Archipelago* (3 vols.), London and New York 1974-8. At the conference on genocide mentioned in the previous note, **L.H.Leaters** spoke of 15 million murdered Soviet peasants (60-6).

20. The 'defenders of the West' and the 'people of the eternal yesterday' in Germany should be told that Hitler and his followers were solely responsible for allowing Stalin's sphere of rule to extend as far as Berlin and Weimar. However, there should be no doubt that, for all the essential ideological differences between them, **both** National Socialism and Communism were equally 'totalitarian' systems which involved the whole person and which seduced the masses into self-sacrifice and slavery. **Hannah Arendt**, *The Origins of Totalitarianism*, New York 1951, pointed this out at an early stage, analysing National Socialism and Stalinism as kindred types of rule in the context of antisemitism and imperialism. Thus that left-wing conceptual politics dictated by political interests which attempted to ban the word 'totalitarianism' (as being anti-Communist) and at the same time to inflate the Italian word 'Fascismo' (to include both National Socialism and often also Communism) bent the question and confused the issue. The Bonn historian **K.D.Bracher** rightly observes: 'The outlawing of the term totalitarianism blurred what is common to both right-wing and left-wing systems of oppressive

dictatorship, and made the use of the word suspect as being anti-communistic; at the same time the current theories about Fascism underestimated the central significance of the National Socialist ideology and racial policy' (113).

21. There remains a fundamental difference between Nazism and Bolshevism, and any historical comparison would be irresponsible which sought to gloss over the uniqueness of the Holocaust and say that it was not as bad as all that. The Bielefeld historian J.Kocka puts it like this: 'There remains a qualitative difference between the bureaucratized, dispassionate, perfected system of mass murder in Hitler's industrialized, comparatively highly organized Reich, and the brutal mix of the excesses of civil wars, mass liquidations, slave labour and starvation in Stalin's retrograde empire' (134). Without doubt some historians would do better to compare Hitler's Germany with contemporary France or England rather than with the regimes of Pol Pot in Cambodia and Idi Amin in Uganda. Indeed, they would do better to make the great cultural tradition of Germany itself the criterion – that tradition, so often cited elsewhere, of German idealism, German philosophy, literature, art, music and indeed even theology. This would show the singularity of that barbarian aberration.

22. E.Jäckel, J.Kocka, C.Meier, H. and W.Mommsen; cf. their contributions to the *Piper-Dokumentation*. The criticism of Nolte's thesis by the Tübingen historian D.Langewiesche, 'Der "Historikerstreit" und die "Historisierung" des Nationalsozialismus', in K.Oesterle and S.Schiele (eds.), *Historikerstreit und politische Bildung*, Stuttgart 1989, 20-41, is equally trenchant.

23. Cf. S.Volkov, *Jüdisches Leben und Antisemitismus im 19. und 20. Jahrhundert. Zehn Essays*, Munich 1990. This front was already reflected in the Wilhelmine empire, in the discussion between the Central Association of German Citizens, which argued for assimilation, and the Zionist Association for Germany. For the same period, from the German side, cf. D.Bering, *Der Name als Stigma. Antisemitismus im deutschen Alltag 1812-1933*, Stuttgart 1987; W.Jochmann, *Gesellschaftskrise und Judenfeindschaft in Deutschland 1870-1945*, Hamburg 1988.

24. In Germany, too, recent investigations are showing how there were phases of fruitful collaboration between Jewish and non-Jewish Germans in German-Jewish history before the catastrophic rift in the development caused by National Socialism. And the Salomon Ludwig Steinheim Institute for German-Jewish History at the University of Duisburg, founded by Julius H.Schoeps (cf. Vol.1 of *Menorah. Jahrbuch für deutsche Geschichte 1990*, Munich 1990) is attempting to sound out points of contact and connecting links within the German-Jewish partnership and to indicate the lines of continuity which were interrupted by National Socialism.

25. Volkov, *Jüdisches Leben* (n.23), 9, 65f.

26. J.A. Gobineau, *L'essai sur l'inégalité des races humaines*, Paris 1853-55.

27. Cf. M.Zimmermann, *Wilhelm Marr. The Patriarch of Anti-Semitism*, New York 1986.

28. Cf. I.Elbogen, *Geschichte der Juden in Deutschland*, Berlin 1935, 313.

29. Volkov, *Jüdisches Leben* (n.23), 35f., 54-75.

30. T.Mann, 'Deutschland und die Deutschen' (1945), in *Reden und Aufsätze*, Vol.III, Frankfurt 1960, 1143, 1136. Cf. P.Reichel, 'Hoffen auf den starken Mann. "Ich fühle euch, und ihr fühlt mich!" – Erfolg und Verfall des

Führer-Mythos', *Die Zeit*, 12 May 1989. Cf. also **J.C.Fest**, *Hitler*, London and New York 1974: 'Interlude: The Great Dread' (87-106) is important. Anxiety about the Communist revolution, hatred of the West, of the Enlightenment, of rationality, of democracy, of Judaism; Nazism as 'an odd mixture of mediaevalism and modernity... Hitler's fling at hegemony, carefully planned, cold-blooded and realistic as it was, and dependent on the most modern weaponry, was justified in the name of a quaint and vanished Germanism. The world was to be conquered for the sake of thatched roofs and an upright peasantry, for folk dances, celebrations of the winter solstice and swastikas' (103f.).

31. The impressive volume of essays, *Juden im deutschen Kulturbereich*, ed. S.**Kaznelson**, Berlin 1935 (considerably expanded second edition 1959), which runs to more than 1000 pages, gives an impressive picture of the cultural achievements of German Jews, from literature and art through the various sciences to social life and sport (there is also a well-informed article by I.Meisl on the Science of Judaism). However, in her investigation of the social causes of Jewish success in science (ibid., 146-65), S.**Volkov** makes it clear that most of the extraordinary Jewish scientists were settled in marginal academic areas which often proved to be particularly creative, and in subordinate academic positions, which in contrast to the established chairs made specialization possible: 'extraordinary achievements... paradoxically and in the end fatefully came about not *despite* but also *because of* prejudice' (162). That Jews had a key role in all the significant intellectual movements of German culture is demonstrated in 'homage to the German Jews of our century' by the impressive volume edited by **H.J.Schultz**, *Es ist ein Weinen in der Welt*, Stuttgart 1990. There are discussions of S.Freud, G.Mahler, W.Rathenau, E.Lasker-Schüler, R.Luxemburg, G.Landauer, M.Reinhardt, A.Schoenberg, M.Buber, L.Meitner, A.Einstein, F.Kafka, E.Bloch, W.Benjamin, M.Horkheimer, A.Freud, E.Fromm, A.Seghers, M.Sperber, H.Arendt. The role of Jewish women philosophers is often overlooked: they all made an acute analysis of the militaristic and totalitarian tendencies of their time. **R.Wimmer** has produced a summary monograph on them, *Vier jüdische Philosophinnen. Rosa Luxemburg, Simone Weil, Edith Stein, Hannah Arendt*, Tübingen 1990.

32. For the role of **industry** in National Socialism, which is a particularly disputed by experts, in addition to earlier investigations from what used to be East (W.Bleyer, D.Eichholtz and the Brown Book of 1965) and West Germany (W.A.Boelcke, M.Broszat, W.Fischer, L.P.Lochner, D.Petzina, R.Wagenführ) and the USA (B.H.Klein, A.Schweitzer) and the controversies between D.Stegman and H.A.Turner (over big business and Hitler's rise) and between D.Abraham and U.Nocken (over the downfall of the Weimar Republic), among more recent monographs cf. above all **E.Czichon**, *Wer verhalf Hitler zur Macht? Zum Anteil der deutschen Industrie an der Zerstörung der Weimarer Republik*, Cologne ⁴1976; **R.Neebe**, *Grossindustrie, Staat und NSDAP 1930-1933. Paul Silverberg und der Reichsverband der Deutschen Industrie in der Krise der Weimarer Republik*, Göttingen 1981; **H.-E.Volkmann**, *Wirtschaft im Dritten Reich. Eine Bibliographie*, Vol.1, *1933-1939*, Munich 1980; II, *1939-1954*, Koblenz 1984. For the role of important individual firms, e.g. I.G.Farben, cf. **J.Borkin**, *The Crime and Punishment of I.G.Farben*, New York 1978; *US Group Control Council – Finance Division*, Investigations into I.G.Farben AG, September 1945; **P.Hayes**, *Industry and*

Ideology, IG Farben in the Nazi Era, Cambridge 1987. For Daimler-Benz AG cf. **H.Pohl, S.Habeth** and **B.Brüninghaus**, *Die Daimler Benz AG in den Jahren 1933-1945. Eine Dokumentation*, Stuttgart 1986. For criticism of this see *Das Daimler-Benz-Buch. Ein Rüstungskonzern im 'Tausendjährigen Reich'. Schriften der Hamburger Stiftung für Sozialgeschichte des 20. Jahrhunderts*, Nördlingen 1987; **K.Roth** and **M.Schmid**, *Die Daimler-Benz AG 1916-1918. Schlüsseldokumente zur Konzerngeschichte*, Schriften der Hamburger Stiftung für Sozialgeschichte V, Nördlingen 1987.

33. There is now a comprehensive overall account of the role of the judiciary: **L.Gruchman**, *Justiz im Dritten Reich 1933-1940. Anpassung und Unterwerfung in der Ära Gürtner*, Munich 1988. **I.Staff** (ed.), *Justiz im Dritten Reich. Eine Dokumentation*, Frankfurt 1964, expanded second edition 1978, gives a very helpful survey. **J.Friedrich**, *Freispruch für die Nazi-Justiz. Die Urteile gegen NS-Richter seit 1948. Eine Dokumentation*, Reinbek 1983, documents how German post-war justice glossed over, approved, indeed rewarded offences of murder, killing and genocide. Cf. the polemical work by **H.Senfft**, *Richter und andere Bürger, 150 Jahre politische Justiz und neudeutsche Herrschaftspublizistik*. Nördlingen 1988; Senfft calculates among other things that the lawyers of the 'Third Reich' atoned after 1945 for the 30,000 death sentences that they had handed out with only 27 years and 2 months imprisonment. Cf. further **I.Müller**, *Furchtbare Juristen. Die unbewältigte Vergangenheit unserer Justiz*, Munich 1987; **B.Diestelkamp** and **M.Stolleis** (eds.), *Justizialtag im Dritten Reich*, Frankfurt 1988; **R.Dreier** and **W.Sellert** (eds.), *Recht und Justiz im 'Dritten Reich'*, Frankfurt 1989.

34. For the role of the **medical profession**, and in particular the darkest chapter of Nazi medicine, 'racial hygiene' and euthanasia, which claimed hundreds of thousands of mentally ill and physically handicapped victims, cf. **E.Klee**, *'Euthanasie' im NS-Staat. Die 'Vernichtung lebensunwerten Lebens'*, Frankfurt 1983; **id.** (ed.), *Dokumente zur 'Euthanasie'*, Frankfurt 1983: **id.**, *Was sie taten – Was sie wurden. Ärzte, Juristen und andere Beteiligte am Kranken- oder Judenmord*, Frankfurt 1986; **P.Weingart** et al., *Rasse, Blut und Gene. Geschichte der Eugenik und Rassenhygiene in Deutschland*, Frankfurt 1988; **R.N.Proctor**, *Racial Hygiene. Medicine under the Nazis*, Cambridge, Mass. 1988; **R.J.Lifton**, *The Nazi Doctors. Medical Killing and the Psychology of Genocide*, New York 1986.

35. Too little research has so far been done into the role of **journalism**; cf. **O.Köhler**, 'Schreibmaschinen-Täter. Journalisten im dritten Reich und danach: eine vergessene Vergangenheit, eine unwillkommene Debatte', *Die Zeit*, 15 January 1988.

36. For the role of the **army** cf. **E.Klee, W.Dressen** and **V.Riess**, *'Schöne Zeiten'. Judenmord aus der Sicht der Täter und Gaffer*, Frankfurt 1988; **A.J.Mayer**, *Why Did the Heavens Not Darken? The 'Final Solution' in History*, New York 1988; **E.Klee** and **W.Dressen** (eds.), *'Gott mit uns'. Der deutsche Vernichtungskrieg im Osten 1939-1945*, Frankfurt 1989. It emerges from these publications how much not only the SS but also the Wehrmacht was engaged in the anti-Soviet, antisemitic crusade and war of annihilation.

37. Happily, printed series of lectures on the role of the **universities** appeared as early as the mid-1960s from three German universities – Tübingen, Berlin and Munich: cf. **A.Flitner** (ed.), *Deutsches Geistesleben und Nationalsozialismus*, Tübingen 1965; *Nationalsozialismus und die deutsche Universität*.

Veröffentlichung der Freien Universität Berlin, Berlin 1966; **H.Kuhn** et al., *Die Deutsche Universität im Dritten Reich*, Munich 1966. More recently too, this problem, which is clearly still a tricky one, has been tackled in different ways both for the German academic world as a whole during the Third Reich and in the case of individual universities, disciplines and scholars. The latest study is of Göttingen, cf. **H.Becker** et al. (eds.), *Die Universität Göttingen unter dem Nationalsozialismus. Das verdrängte Kapitel ihrer 250-jährigen Geschichte*, Munich 1987.

38. The most recent discussion has shown what the so-called French 'Postmodernists', along with some German admirers of Heidegger, have failed to perceive: **Martin Heidegger**'s entanglement in National Socialism was more serious and more lasting than was assumed for a long time. The most recent debate was sparked off by the book *Heidegger et le Nazisme*, Lagrasse 1987, by **V.Farías**, a Chilean living in Berlin. While detailed statements are open to attack, the book as a whole is very worth-while. The language above all has been improved for the German edition, *Heidegger und der Nationalsozialismus*, with a foreword by Jürgen Habermas, Frankfurt 1989. **H.Ott**, *Martin Heidegger. Unterwegs zu seiner Biographie*, Frankfurt 1989, is historically accurate. There are various views on the Heidegger affair in **B.Martin** (ed.), *Martin Heidegger und das 'Drittes Reich'. Ein Kompendium*, Darmstadt 1989, which contains the most important documents from the years 1933 (especially Heidegger's rectoral address) and 1945 (his de-Nazification).

39. Cf. **C.Schmitt**, *Staat, Bewegung, Volk. Die Dreigliederung der politischen Einheit*, Hamburg 1933. On this see **Senfft**, *Richter* (n.33), 159-61 (here also on Schmitt's opportunism and antisemitism); **K.Sontheimer**, 'Der Macht näher als dem Recht. Zum Tode Carl Schmitts', *Die Zeit*, 19 April 1985; **B.Rüthers**, *Carl Schmitt im Dritten Reich. Wissenschaft als Zeitgeist-Verstärkung?*, Munich 1989.

40. **W.Laqueur**, *The Terrible Secret*, London 1980, 201. Here too there is a comprehensive survey of the then state of information among the neturals, the Allies, the Jews in German occupied Europe, and world Jewry.

41. Cf. **C.E.Bärsch**, *Erlösung und Vernichtung. Dr.phil.Joseph Goebbels. Zur Psyche und Ideologie eines jungen Nationalsozialisten 1923-127*, Munich 1987. Goebbels, who was brought up a Catholic (though not by Jesuits!) and always remained one (he stayed in the church right to the end), was certain as early as 1929 that Christ could not have been a Jew: 'The Jew is the lie made flesh. In Christ for the first time in history he nailed the eternal truth to the cross. That was repeated dozens of times in subsequent centuries and still keeps repeating itself. The idea of the victim first took visible form in Christ. The victim is part of the essence of socialism. Giving oneself for others. The Jew has no understanding of this' (ibid., 126). **R.G.Reuth** wrote his biography, *Goebbels*, Munich 1990, on the basis of the whole Goebbels archive made available exclusively to Piper Verlag; it again makes clear Goebbels' pioneering role in the policy on the Jews.

42. I stated this openly as early as 1965 – in one of a number of publications which summed up the achievements of the Second Vatican Council – and in return received a first official censure from the President of the German episcopal conference, Cardinal **Julius Döpfner**. The Cardinal did not reply when I sent him the chapter on 'The Church and the Jews' which I had already completed for my book *The Church* (1967).

43. Cf. Fest, *Hitler*, (n.30).
44. Cf. E.Jäckel, *Hitler's World View* (1969), Cambridge, Mass. 1981.
45. Ibid.
46. H.-U.Thamer, *Verführung und Gewalt. Deutschland 1933-1945*, Berlin 1986.
47. Jäckel, *Hitler's World View* (n.44), 89.
48. Thamer, *Verführung und Gewalt* (n.46), 88.
49. Quoted in Jäckel, *Hitler's World View* (n.44), 55.
50. Cf. A.Hitler, *Mein Kampf*, London 1969, 5.
51. Cf. F.Heer, *Der Glaube des Adolf Hitler. Anatomie einer politischer Religiösität*, Munich 1968.
52. Cf. W.Daim, *Der Mann, der Hitler die Ideen gab. Die sektierischen Grundlagen des Nationalsozialismus*, Vienna 1957, [2]1985.
53. Heer, *Der Glaube des Adolf Hitler* (n.51), 272.
54. Only the former Archbishop of Vienna, Cardinal **Franz König**, the successor to that Cardinal **Theodor Innitzer** who wrote a covering letter to the declaration of the capitulation of the Austrian episcopate on 18 March 1938 with a handwritten 'Heil Hitler', according to the Catholic Press Agency made an unequivocal confession of guilt in connection with the most recent events, at a gathering of Catholic Action in St Pölten on 26 September 1987: 'In retrospect, as Christians we too must without doubt also say a *nostra culpa* for the failure and above all the errors of the church authorities of the time.'
55. H.Krätzel, 'Vergiftete Brunnen. Antwort auf Proteste von Gläubigen', *Publik-Forum*, 11 March 1988.

A.II The Repression of Guilt

1. *Die Zeit* gave this report of the 'Heroic Act of a District President' in its issue of 4 November 1988.
2. L.van Dick (ed.), *Lehreropposition im NS-Staat. Biographische Berichte über den 'aufrechten Gang'*, new edition, Frankfurt 1990, shows that it was not necessary to conform completely, even in the schools.
3. The following figures, too, are contained in the report which appeared in *Die Zeit* on 4 November 1988 under the title 'Man wollte an die Vermögen heran'. For 'Reichskristallnacht', cf. R.Thalmann and E.Feinermann, *La nuit de Cristal*, Paris 1972; H-J.Döscher, *'Reichskristallnacht'. Die Novemberpogrome 1938*, Frankfurt 1988; id. (ed.), *'Reichskristallnacht'. Die Novemberpogrome 1938 im Spiegel auserwählter Quellen*, Bonn 1988; W.H.Pehle (ed.), *Der Judenpogrom 1938. Von der 'Reichskristallnacht' zum Völkermord*, Frankfurt 1988.
4. For the **relationship of the churches to National Socialism** cf. especially *Akten deutscher Bischöfe über die Lage der Kirche 1933-1945* (6 vols.), ed. B.Stasiewski and L.Volk, Mainz 1968-85. There is a clear account with the most important documents in G.Denzler and V.Fabricius, *Die Kirchen im Dritten Reich. Christen und Nazis Hand in Hand?, I. Darstellung, II. Dokumente*, Frankfurt 1984 (= Denzler-Fabricius); cf. also the important collection of documents by R.Rendtorff and H.H.Henrix (eds.), *Die Kirchen und das Judentum. Dokumente von 1945 bis 1985*, Paderborn 1988 (= Rendtorff-Henrix). In English cf. H.Croner (ed.), *More Stepping Stones to*

Jewish-Christian Relations. An Unabridged Collection of Christian Documents 1975-1983, New York 1985. **E.Röhm and J.Tierfelder,** *Juden, Christen, Deutsche, 1933-1945, I: 1933-1935,* Stuttgart 1990, is an overall account of the history of Jews and Christians with a wealth of illustrations: four volumes are planned. Cf. also the following monographs: **G.C.Zahn,** *German Catholics and Hitler's Wars,* New York 1965; **G.Lewy,** *The Catholic Church and Nazi Germany,* New York 1964; **L.Siegele-Wenschkewitz,** *Nationalsozialismus und Kirchen. Religionspolitik von Partei und Staat bis 1935,* Düsseldorf 1974; **ead.,** *Neutestamentliche Wissenschaft vor der Judenfrage. Gerhard Kittels theologische Arbeit im Wandel deutscher Geschichte,* Munich 1980; **K.Scholder,** *The Churches and the Third Reich,* I, *Preliminary History and the Time of Illusions 1981-1934* (1977), London and Philadelphia 1987; II, *The Year of Disillusionment 1934. Barmen and Rome* (1985), London and Philadelphia 1988; **G.Denzler,** *Widerstand oder Anpassung? Katholische Kirche und Drittes Reich,* Munich 1984; **J.Fischel and S.Pinsker** (eds.), *The Churches' Response to the Holocaust,* Holocaust Studies Annual Vol.II, Greenwood 1986; **O.D.Kulka** and **P.E.Mendes-Flor** (eds.), *Judaism and Christianity under the Impact of National Socialism,* Jerusalem 1987; **R.P.Ericksen,** *Theologen unter Hitler. Das Bündnis zwischen evangelischer Dogmatik und Nationalsozialismus,* Munich 1988 (on G.Kittel, P.Althaus and E.Hirsch); **M.Greschat and J.C.Kaiser** (eds.), *Der Holocaust und die Protestanten. Analysen einer Verstrickung,* Frankfurt 1988; **E.Klee,** *'Die SA Jesu Christi'. Die Kirchen im Banne Hitlers,* Frankfurt 1989; **K.Repgen** and **K.Gotto** (eds.), *Die Katholiken und das Dritte Reich,* third enlarged edition, Mainz 1990.

5. Cf. the 'pronouncement' by the whole episcopate of 28 March 1933, in *Akten deutscher Bischöfe* I (n.4), 30-2; Denzler-Fabricius, 42-4.

6. **H.-U.Thamer,** *Verführung und Gewalt. Deutschland 1933-1945,* Berlin 1986, 435.

7. Quoted from Denzler-Fabricius, 255.

8. Cf. the address by **R.Moeller,** the president of the Kirchentag, at the First German Evangelical Kirchentag in Dresden, 1 September 1919, in Denzler-Fabricius, 13f.

9. Cf. **Greschat and Kaiser,** *Der Holocaust* (n.4), especially the contribution by H.U.Thamer.

10. Quoted from Denzler-Fabricius, 37f.

11. Quoted from Denzler-Fabricius, 76.

12. Article 1, ibid., 83.

13. Article 4, ibid.

14. Cf the text in Denzler-Fabricius, 77-83.

15. Cf the text in Denzler-Fabricius, 84-7.

16. Cf. **K.Barth,** *Theological Existence Today,* 24-25 June 1933, London 1933.

17. Thus the synod declares: 'We repudiate the false teaching that there are areas of our life in which we belong not to Jesus Christ but to other lords' (no.2).

18. Cf. **H.U.Stephan** (ed.), *Das eine Wort für alle. Barmen 1934-1984. Eine Dokumentation,* Neukirchen 1986.

19. Cf. **M.Greschat** (ed.), *Zwischen Widerspruch und Widerstand. Texte zur Denkschrift der Bekennenden Kirche an Hitler (1936),* Munich 1987.

20. Cf. **C.-R.Müller,** *Dietrich Bonhoeffers Kampf gegen die nationalsozialis-*

tische Verfolgung und Vernichtung der Juden. Bonhoeffers Haltung zur Judenfrage im Vergleich mit Stellungnahmen aus der evangelischen Kirche und Kreisen des deutschen Widerstandes, Munich 1990.

21. Text in Rendtorff-Henrix, 528. Cf. **M.Greschat** (ed.), *Im Zeichen der Schuld. 40 Jahre Stuttgarter Schuldbekenntnis. Eine Dokumentation,* Neukirchen 1985.

22. Quoted from Denzler-Fabricius, 256.

23. This is pointed out by **F.Hermle**, *Evangelische Kirche und Judentum – Stationen nach 1945,* Göttingen 1990. The General Secretary of the ecumenical Refugee Commission, **Adolf Freudenberg**, was a key figure in working out the Jewish question theologically in the face of all the resistance in the church government. The text of the 'Statement on the Jewish Question' made by the Evangelical Church of Germany in April 1950 is in Rendtorff-Henrix, 548f.

24. For this see the comprehensive collection of documents by the historian **C.Vollnhals**, *Entnazifizierung und Selbstreinigung im Urteil der evangelischen Kirche. Dokumente und Reflexionen 1945-1949,* Munich 1989; id., *Evangelische Kirche und Entnazifizierung 1945-1949. Die Last der nationalsozialistischen Vergangenheit,* Munich 1989.

25. Pacelli's personality, politics and position in church history, which are discussed in all the relevant studies of the history of the time, are analysed particularly perceptively in relation to Germany, National Socialism and Hitler by **Friedrich Heer**, *Der Glaube des Adolf Hitler. Anatomie einer politischen Religiosität,* Munich 1968, chs.26-31.

26. Cf. the text in Denzler-Fabricius, 61-74.

27. Cf. *Konkordate seit 1800,* collected and edited by **L.Schöppe**, *Dokumente,* Vol.35, Frankfurt 1964, 29-35, esp.33.

28. Cf. **K.Adam**, 'Deutsches Volkstum und katholisches Christentum', *Theologische Quartalschrift* 114, 1933, 40-63: 41, 58-61.

29. Id., 'Jesus, der Christus und wir Deutsche', *Wissenschaft und Weisheit. Vierteljahresschrift für systematische franziskane Philosophie und Theologie in der Gegenwart* 10, 1943, 73-103: 'I personally find it an uplifting thought that the best, the noblest dispositions and forces at the disposal of the human race generally, were alive in the genes, the genetic make-up, which Mary passed on to her divine Son, thanks to a mysterious guidance of God who watched over the development of her family. This view is based on the truth of faith that Mary was conceived without original sin – "without original sin", i.e. without the consequences of original sin, in other words in perfect purity and beauty, i.e. with the noblest disposition and powers. It is this dogma of the immaculate conception of Mary which in the Catholic view makes all those malicious questions and complaints so completely senseless, as if we had to recognize Jesus as a 'descendant of the Jews' despite all his finer qualities. For it testifies to us that Jesus' mother Mary had no physical or moral connection with those ugly dispositions and forces which we condemn in full-blooded Jews. Through the miracle of the grace of God she is beyond these Jewish hereditary traits, a figure who transcends Judaism' (90f.).

30. Cf.**C.Falconi**, *Il silenzio di Pio XII,* Milan 1965.

31. Cf. the text in Denzler-Fabricius, 104-50.

32. For the encyclical there are drafts by three Jesuits (J.La Farge, USA; G.Gundlach, Germany; P.Desbuqouis, France), all of which betray considerable anti-Jewish prejudices. It was then the Polish Jesuit General **Vladimir**

Ledochowski who delayed the publication of the enyclical, probably because he saw Hitler as an ally against Bolshevism; cf. **J.H.Nota**, 'Edith Stein und der Entwurf für eine Enzyklika gegen Rassismus and Antisemitismus', *Freiburger Rundbrief* 26, 1974, 35-41. As early as 1933, in a sealed letter to Pius XI, Edith Stein had personally asked urgently for an encyclical on the Jewish question – without success.

33. Cf. **Falconi**, *Silenzio* (n.30), Part III. **V.Dedijer**, *Jasenovac – das jugoslawische Auschwitz und der Vatikan*, ed. G.Niemietz, Freiburg 1988, is biassed (the figures are disputed).

34. That at this time aid measures were argued over at a diplomatic level even in Jewish circles is shown by the case of the acting president of the Hungarian Zionist movement, **Rezsö Rudolf Kasztner**: despite reliable information about what had been going on in the German extermination camps since 1944, the Hungarian Jews were not warned, but only a few thousand Jews were evacuated on the basis of secret negotiations with the German leadership ('blood for goods'), sometimes with Eichmann personally. So in 1953 Kasztner was accused in Israel of collaboration with the Germans and condemned in 1955; however, he was rehabilitated in 1958, having been shot the year earlier on a public street. Cf. **R.L.Braham**, 'What Did They Know and When?', in *The Holocaust as Historical Experience. Essays and a Discussion*, ed. Y.Bauer and N.Rotenstreich, New York 1981, 109-31; **Y.Marton**, 'Kasztner, Rezsö Rudolf', in *Encyclopaedia Judaica*.

35. Quoted from **P.Longerich** (ed.), *Die Ermordung der europäischer Juden. Eine umfassende Dokumentation des Holocaust 1941-1945*, Munich 1989, 445.

36. E.von Weizsäcker, telegram to the Foreign Office, 17/28 October 1943; quoted from **Longerich**, *Ermordung* (n.35), 445f.

37. Cf. the memoirs of Gasperi's daughter and secretary **Maria Romana Catti-de Gasperi**, *De Gasperi, uomo solo*, Milan 1964, 317-39, esp. 335 (a papal audience was refused even on the occasion of the prime minister's thirtieth wedding anniversary and the taking of 'perpetual' religious vows by his second daughter Lucia).

38. **J.F.Morley**, *Vatican Diplomacy and the Jews during the Holocaust 1939-1949*, New York 1980.

39. Ibid., 209.

40. Cf. **P.I.Murphy**, '*La Popessa*', New York 1983, esp.59-170, 192-215.

41. The chapter 'Das vatikanische Labyrinth', in **N.Goldmann**, *Le paradoxe juïf. Conversations avec Léon Abramovicz*, Paris 1976, is illuminating on the attitude of Pius XII and the Curia. (Unfortunately, at least in the German edition, the names of Fr Robert Leiber and the Jesuit General J.B.Janssens are given wrongly; Sr Pasqualina becomes Sr Angelina, and the Gregorian Papal University becomes the University of Georgia.)

42. **J.Kaiser**, 'Die Bühne als publizistische Anstalt?', *Süddeutsche Zeitung*, 25 April 1988.

43. Cf. also the apostolic letter by **Pope John Paul II** on the fiftieth anniversary of the beginning of the Second World War, 27 August 1989.

44. **A.Momigliano**, 'Independent People', in *The New York Review of Books*, 8 October 1987.

45. Cf. Pope **Paul VI**'s new formulation of the Good Friday intercessions

for the Jews in the *Missale Romanum* of 26 March 1970, in Rendtorff-Henrix, 56-60.

46. Cf. the text of the Council Declaration *Nostra aetate* no.4. For the whole declaration see **K.-J.Kuschel**, 'Ökumenischer Konsens über das Judentum?', in *Christlich-jüdisches Forum. Mitteilungsblatt der christlich-jüdischen Arbeitsgemeinschaft in der Schweiz* 53, ed. E.L.Ehrlich, Basel 1981, 17-33.

47. For the activity of the **German bishops** generally cf. above all the publications of the Commission for Contemporary History at the Catholic Academy in Bavaria, the two series of which – sources and researches – already amount to more than 80 volumes. The six volumes of the 'Acts of the German Bishops on the Situation of the Church, 1933-1945'(n.4 above) are particularly important for our theme.

48. As far as I know, the word comes from the Catholic historian **K.Repgen**, of Bonn, who with R.Mosey edited the Acts of the German Bishops. Cf. also **Repgen and Gotto,** *Katholiken* (n.4).

49. Cf. **Scholder,** *The Churches* (n.4), I, 237-53. According to K.D.Bracher (in an opinion on the concordat process in the 1950s), Scholder convincingly demonstrated against K.Repgen, R.Morsey and L.Volk, the journalistic exponents of the Catholic Commission for Contemporary History, that there is a direct connection between the beginning of the negotiations between the Vatican and Germany over a 'Reich concordat' and the assent of the Catholic Centre Party to the Enabling Law for Hitler on 3 March 1933. In addition to the volumes mentioned, cf. **K.Scholder,** 'Altes und Neues zur Vorgeschichte des Reichskonkordats. Erwiderung auf Konrad Repgen', in *Die Kirchen zwischen Republik und Gewaltherrschaft*, Berlin 1988, 171-203, the volume of Scholder's collected articles posthumously edited by K.O.von Aretin and G.Besier.

50. **Scholder,** 'Altes und Neues' (n.49), 194.

51. **Id.,** *The Churches* (n.4), I, 253.

52. On this see **Lewy,** *Catholic Church* (n.4), 267-83.

53. Cf. **H.Hürten,** *Verfolgung, Widerstand und Zeugnis. Kirche im National-sozialismus. Fragen eines Historikers*, Mainz 1987.

54. Quoted in **J.Köhler,** *Haben die deutschen Bischöfe während der national-sozialistischen Herrschaft Widerstand geleistet? Der deutsche Katholizismus zwischen Widerspruch und nationaler Loyalität*, unpublished manuscript, 22. I am grateful to Professor **Joachim Köhler**, church historian in the Catholic Theological Faculty of the University of Tübingen, for valuable additions and corrections to this whole chapter.

55. Cf. **S.Rahner** et al., *'Treu deutsch sind wir – wir sind auch treu katholisch.' Kardinal von Galen und das Dritte Reich*, Münster 1987.

56. The text of Preysing's memorandum of 17 October is in *Akten deutscher Bischöfe* (n.4), Vol.IV, 356-61; Denzler-Fabricius, 161-6.

57. Cf. **D.R.Bauer and A.P.Kustermann** (eds.), *Gelegen oder ungelegen – Zeugnis für die Wahrheit. Zur Vertreibung des Rottenburger Bischofs J.B.Sproll im Sommer 1937*, Rottenburg 1989; here **J.Köhler** points out how active Sproll already was in the peace movement in the 1920s (cf. 17-55).

58. There is no answer to this, even in the most recent biography by **E.Endres,** *Edith Stein. Christliche Philosophin und jüdische Märtyrin*, Munich 1987.

59. **Denzler,** *Widerstand oder Anpassung?* (n.4), reports how the president of the episcopal conference, Cardinal Adolf Bertram, was still sending the most

friendly congratulations to the 'Führer' on his last birthday on 20 April 1945 (!), After Hitler's cowardly suicide ten days later Bertram was thinking in terms of a requiem (though this did not come about). Denzler also mentions the Nazi leanings of the bishops of Freiburg (Conrad Gröber was a patron of the SS, along with all his cathedral chapter) and Osnabrück (Wilhelm Berning was a Prussian state councillor), Nazi Benedictine abbots, collaborators, brown-shirted professors of theology and clergy, and finally the servile papal nuncio Orsenigo in Berlin, who in his heart of hearts (like a majority of the Roman Curia after the concordat with Mussolini in 1929) had become a Fascist.

60. Cf. the text in Rendtorff-Henrix, 260-80.

61. The General Synod of the Dioceses in the Federal Republic of Germany, resolution, 'Unsere Hoffnung. Ein Bekenntnis zum Glauben in dieser Zeit', of 22 November 1975, in Rendtorff-Henrix, 245.

62. Cf. the account in *Herder-Korrespondenz* 45, 1991, 7f., with the title 'Stagnation'.

63. That a Jew could also do this is shown by the example of the Polish Jewish doctor, teacher, educator and educational reformer **Janusz Korczak**, who in 1942 went from the Warsaw ghetto with 200 of 'his' children from the Jewish orphanage to Treblinka, having previously refused all offers of escape. Cf. **B.J.Lifton**, *The King of Children. A Biography of Janusz Korczak*, New York 1988.

64. Cf. **A.Smolar**, 'Unschuld und Tabu' (the original Polish version is in *Aneks* nos.41-42, London 1986), in *Babylon. Beiträge zur jüdische Gegenwart* 2, 1987.2, 40-71: 66. This Polish author is concerned to give an account of the complex relationship between Poles and Jews which is fair to all sides. I am grateful to **Helga Hirsch** of Warsaw for drawing my attention to this article.

65. **W.Bartoszewski**, *Uns eint vergossenes Blut. Juden und Polen in der Zeit der 'Endlosung'*, Frankfurt 1987. Cf. **W.Bartoszewski and Z.Lewin** (eds.), *Righteous among Nations. How Poles helped the Jews 1939-1945*, London 1969. In contrast to the Polish literature with its marked apologetic colouring, **Y.Gutman and S.Krakowski**, *Unequal Victims. Poles and Jews during World War Two*, New York 1986, point out that the situation of the Polish population under the Nazi regime was in no way comparable with the fate of the Jews. Certainly the Poles too suffered considerably under expulsion, forced labour and National Socialist persecution, but the Jews were 'from the beginning the object of a special degree of persecution and terror': persecution, plundering, ghettoizing and finally systematic total annihilation. With a few exceptions, there was no help from the Polish side, not only because of the generally difficult situation under the Nazi occupiers but also because of the 'subjective Polish attitude, the attitude of the different levels of the Polish population and the position of the different political forces and the church' (thus the Foreword), which soon after the war again led to anti-Jewish campaigns and pogroms. Cf. also the commentary by **S.Krakowski** on Z.Zielinski, in O.D.Kulka and P.R.Mendes-Flohr, *Judaism and Christianity* (n.4), 395-9. Cf. also the volume of essays edited by **B.Vago** and **G.L.Mosse**, *Jews and Non-Jews in Eastern Europe 1918-1945*, New York 1974; **G.Rhode** (ed.), *Juden in Ostmitteleuropa. Von der Emanzipation bis zum Ersten Weltkrieg*, Marburg 1989.

66. Text quoted in **Smolar**, 'Unschuld und Tabu' (n.64), 56.

67. **J.H.Schoeps**, 'Unbequeme Erinnerungen. Polen und Juden in der Zeit

der "Endlosung"', *Die Zeit*, 9 October 1987. For the German problems cf. id., *Leiden zu Deutschland. Vom anti-semitischen Wahn und der Last der Erinnerung*, Munich 1990. Cf. the work by the American theologian of Polish origin, **R.Modras**, 'The Catholic Church in Poland and Antisemitism, 1933-1939', in Y.Bauer et al. (eds.), *Remembering for the Future. Working Papers and Addenda*, I, Oxford 1989, 183-196.

68. **M.Nierzabitowska** and **T.Tomaszewski**, *Die letzten Juden in Polen*, Schaffhausen 1987.

69. Cf. here the book by the Princeton Orientalist **B.Lewis**, *Treibt sie ins Meer. Die Geschichte des Antisemitismus*, Berlin 1987, 28.

70. **M.Checinski**, 'The Kielce Pogrom. Some Unanswered Questions', in *Soviet Jewish Affairs* 5.1, 1975, 57-72, investigates the more immediate circumstances and finally arrives at the following verdict: 'The pogrom was a pretext for strenghtening repressive measures in Poland, and served to gain support in liberal Western circles for the Soviets and their protégés who posed as the defenders of the persecuted remnant of Polish Jewry from the "antisemitic inclinations of the Polish people"... The fact that the elimination of the Jews from Poland would be welcomed by the chauvinistic and antisemitic Poles probably also played a role in the calculations of the Soviets who hoped to gain the support of these circles. – The Polish anti-Communist underground, the émigré circles and the Catholic hierarchy saw in the pogrom a sign of weakness on the part of the Warsaw Government, and no doubt welcomed the Jewish exodus from Poland' (71).

71. For what follows see the extensive report by **T.Mechtenberg**, 'Zum jüdisch-polnischen Verhältnis', *Orientierung* 52, 1988, 117-19, 124-7, 140-2.

72. **J.Blonski**, 'Diedni Polacy... (Die armen Polen schauen auf das Getto', *Tygodnik Powszechny*, 11 January 1987, quoted in ibid., 140f.

73. *Tygodnik Powszechny*, 12 February 1987, ibid., 141.

74. In Auschwitz the Jewish 'nationality' is assigned just as much 'exhibition space' as the other nationalities (the Italian pavilion does not in fact contain any specific material). See the museum guide by **K.Smolen**, *Auschwitz 1940-1945. Ein Gang durch das Museum*, Katowice 1981; **id.** (with others), *Ausgewählte Probleme aus der Geschichte des Kl.Auschwitz*, Auschwitz ³1988. In the historical museum of the city of Warsaw the uprising in the Warsaw ghetto is presented as a Polish but hardly as a Jewish revolt; in a single month in 1943 56,000 Jews were killed or deported from there; cf. **D.Dambrowska**, 'Warsaw', *Encyclopaedia Judaica*. For the Jewish resistance generally cf. **F.Kroh**, *David kämpft. Vom jüdischen Widerstand gegen Hitler*, Reinbek 1988.

75. Quoted from *Herder-Korrespondenz* 45, 1991, 97.

76. Cf. **A.A.Häsler**, *Das Boot ist voll. Die Schweiz und die Flüchtlinge 1933-1945*, Zurich 1967, ²1968.

77. Between 1933 and 1945 the following well-known personalities, among others, found temporary or permanent refuge in Switzerland: Fritz Adler, Albert Bassermann, Maria Becker, Ernst Bloch, Bert Brecht, Alfred Döblin, Käthe Dorsch, Walter Fabian, Therese Giehse, Stefan Hermlin, Paul Hindemith, Alfred Kerr, E.L.Kirchner, Arthur Koestler, Oskar Kokoschka, Emil Ludwig, Thomas Mann, Hans Mayer, Robert Musil, Max Ophüls, Rudolf Pannwitz, Wolfgang Pauli, Hermann Rauschning, Erich Maria Remarque,

Wilhelm Röpke, Hermann Scherchen, Ignazio Silone, Margarete Susman, Kurt Tucholski, Bruno Walter, Jakob Wassermann, Carl Zuckmayer. This is from information supplied by the Swiss Police Department in **A.A.Häsler**, ibid., 339.

78. Cf. ibid., 338.

79. Cf. **Evangelischer Pressedienst**. *EPD*, November 1988.

80. Cf. **F.Gsteiger**, ' "Tödlicher Schweigen am Genfer See." ' Warum das Internationale Rote Kreuz im Oktober 1942 die Welt nicht über den Holocaust aufklärte', *Die Zeit*, 23 September 1988. Also **H.Lichtenstein**, *Angepasst und treu ergeben. Das Rote Kreuz im 'Dritten Reich'*, Cologne 1988; **J.-C.Favez**, *Das Internationale Rote Kreuz und das Dritte Reich. War das Holocaust aufzuhalten?*, Munich 1989.

81. Cf. **S.Klarsfeld**, *Vichy-Auschwitz. Die Zusammenarbeit der deutschen und französichen Behörden bei der 'Endlösung der Judenfrage' in Frankreich*, Nördlingen 1989.

82. Cf. **A.Grosser**, *Le crime et la mémoire*, Paris 1989, 149-207x.

83. Cf. **D.S.Wyman**, *The Abandonment of the Jews. America and the Holocaust, 1941-1945*, New York 1984; further connections are discussed by **M.Gilberî**, *Auschwitz and the Allies*, **London 1981**.

84. Cf. **R.Modras**, 'Father Coughlin and the Jews. A Broadcast Remembered', *America*, 11 March 1989.

85. **Wyman**, *The Abandonment of the Jews* (n.83), 431.

86. Cf. **Y.Bauer**, *American Jewry and the Holocaust. The American Jewish Joint Distribution Committee 1939-1945*, Detroit 1981.

87. Cf. **C.Genizi**, *American Apathy. The Plight of Christian Refugees from Nazism*, Ramat-Gan, Israel 1983.

88. **M.Wolffsohn**, *Ewige Schuld? 40 Jahre deutsch-jüdisch-israelische Beziehungen*, Munich 1988, 51f. In his most recent book, *Keine Angst vor Deutschland!*, Erlangen 1990, **Wolffsohn** defends himself against quite inappropriate attacks above all from his German Jewish fellow-believers.

89. **M.Buber**, 'Das echte Gespräch und die Möglichkeiten des Friedens', in *Friedenspreis des Deutschen Buchhandels. Reden und Würdigungen 1951-1960*, published by the Börsenverein des Deutschen Buchhandels e.V., Frankfurt 1961, 67-74: 67f.

90. Cf. *Time* magazine, 11 February 1991.

91. Cf. **Wolffsohn**, *Keine Angst vor Deutschland!* (n.88), 184. The book also contains illuminating chapters which show the degree to which the past was nevertheless assimilated in post-war Germany. Cf. also **M.Brumlik** et al. (eds.), *Jüdisches Leben in Deutschland seit 1945*, Frankfurt 1986; **J.Wetzel**, *Jüdisches Leben in München 1945-1951. Durchgangstation oder Wiederaufbau?*, Munich 1987; **R.Ostow**, *Jüdisches Leben in der DDR*, Frankfurt 1988.

A.III The Return to Israel

1. Ps.137.1.

2. For the prehistory and history of Zionism cf. **N.M.Gelber, H.H.Schachtel** and **R.Weltsch**, 'Zionismus (II.Geschichte)', in *Jüdisches Lexikon*; **J.Katz, S.Ettinger** and **A.Hertzberg**, 'Zionism (Forerunners, Hibbat Zion, Ideological Evolution)', in *Encyclopaedia Judaica*. Then the monographs by **J.** and

D.Kimche, *The Secret Roads – The 'Illegal' Migration of a People 1938-1948*, London 1954; C.Sykes, *Crossroads to Israel*, London 1965; Y.Bauer, *From Diplomacy to Resistance. A History of Jewish Palestine 1939-1945*, Philadelphia 1970; W.Laqueur, *A History of Zionism*, London 1972; N.Goldmann, *Le paradoxe juif. Conversation avec Léon Abramowicz*, Paris 1976; H.M.Sachar, *A History of Israel*, I. *From the Rise of Zionism to Our Time*, New York 1976; II. *From the Aftermath of the Yom Kippur War*, New York 1987; G.Luft, *Heimkehr ins Unbekannte. Eine Darstellung der Einwanderung von Juden aus Deutschland nach Palästina vom Aufstieg Hitlers zur Macht bis zum Aufbruch des Zweiten Weltkriegs, 1933-1939*, Wuppertal 1977; M.Stöhr (ed.), *Zionismus. Beiträge zur Diskussion*, Munich 1980; A.L.Avneri, *The Claim of Dispossession. Jewish Land-Settlement and the Arabs 1878-1948*, New York 1982; M.Krupp, *Zionismus und Staat Israel. Ein geschichtlicher Abriss*, Gütersloh 1983; J.H.Schoeps (ed.), *Zionismus. Texte zu seiner Entwicklung*, Wiesbaden ²1983; J.Peters, *From Time Immemorial. The Origins of the Arab-Jewish Conflict Over Palestine*, New York 1984; Y.Eloni, *Zionismus in Deutschland. Von den Anfängen bis 1914*, Gerlingen 1987.

3. The different '*aliyahs*' or waves of immigration have been worked out in particular by **Laqueur**, *History* (n.2), and **Sachar**, *History* (n.2).

4. Cf. **N.M.Gelber**, 'Pinsker, Jehuda Löb (Leon)', in *Jüdisches Lexicon*; **I.Klausner**, 'Pinsker, Leon', in *Encyclopaedia Judaica*.

5. Cf. **L.Pinsker**, *Auto-Emancipation. A Call to his People by a Russian Jew* (1882), London 1947.

6. Ibid., 9.

7. Ibid., 34.

8. Cf. **A.Friedemann**, 'Herzl, Theodor', in *Jüdisches Lexikon*; **A.Bein**, 'Herzl, Theodor', in Encyclopaedia Judaica.

9. Cf. **T.Herzl**, *The Jewish State* (1896), London 1946. The book appeared in eighty different editions and eighteen languages.

10. Ibid., 15.

11. Ibid., 8.

12. The great extent to which the ideals of the German youth movement were realized in the Israeli kibbutz movement is shown by the vivid documentation on the founding of the Hasorea kibbutz by young German Jews in 1934: **W.B.Godenschweger and F.Vilmar**, *Die rettende Kraft der Utopie. Deutsche Juden gründen den Kibbuz Hasorea*, Frankfurt 1990.

13. Cf. **N.M.Gelber**, 'Weizmann, Chajim', in *Jüdisches Lexikon*; **A.Eban**, 'Weizmann, Chaim', in *Encyclopaedia Judaica*. *Cf* also **C.Weizmann**, *Trial and Error*, New York 1950, and the enormous documentary source material, *The Letters and Papers of Chaim Weizmann*, ed. B.Litvinoff, Series A (Letters, 23 vols.); Series B (Papers, 2 vols.), Oxford, New Brunswick and Jerusalem 1968-1983.

14. The original text of the declaration runs: 'His Majesty's government view with favour the establishment in Palestine of a national home for the Jewish people, and will use their best endeavours to facilitate the achievement of this object...' (quoted from a facsimile in *Encyclopaedia Judaica* IV, col.131).

15. Ibid.

16. Cf. **S.Flapan**, *The Birth of Israel*, London and New York 1987.

17. Cf. **Weltsch**, 'Zionismus' (n.2).

18. Cf. **Hertzberg**, 'Zionism' (n.2).

19. Cf. **Y.Slutsky**, 'Ben-Gurion, David', in *Encyclopaedia Judaica*; also **D.Ben-Gurion**, *Israel. Die Geschichte eines Staates*, Frankfurt 1973. For the state of Israel cf. especially **A.Eban**, *My Country. The Story of Modern Israel*, 1972; **D.M.Zohar**, *Political Parties in Israel. The Evolution of Israeli Democracy*, New York 1974; **M.Wolffsohn**, *Politik in Israel. Entwicklung und Struktur des politischen Systems*, Opladen 1983; id., *Israel. Grundwissen-Länderkunde. Politik-Gesellschaft-Wirtschaft*, Opladen ²1987; **T.Segev**, *1949. The first Israelis*, New York 1986. The article 'Israel' in *Encyclopaedia Judaica* is an account of the state of Israel – history, constitution, population, immigration, government, law, army, economy, religion, education, science and culture, running to 940 columns. Cf. also the great works on the history of the Jewish people or on Judaism by **H.H.Ben-Sasson** (especially the contribution by **S.Ettinger**), **P.Johnson** and **J.Maier** often cited in Part One above.

20. For V.Jabotinsky see the relevant article by **J.B.Schechtman** in *Encyclopaedia Judaica*.

21. However, the official Israeli propaganda of the Likud governments, which try to ignore the existence of a Palestinian people, sees the policy of terror and intimidation only on the other side. Cf. the pamphlet *Facts about Israel*, Jerusalem 1985, produced by the 'Department of Information of the Foreign Ministry' and disseminated as a travel guide. Similarly **M.Comay**, *Zionism, Israel and the Palestinian Arabs*, Jerusalem 1983.

22. **E.W.Said**, the Palestinian American Professor of English at Columbia University and a member of the Palestinian National Council, reflects on the sorry Palestinian experiences in *The Question of Palestine*, New York 1980.

23. Cf. the comprehensive account by **H.Baumgarten**, *Befreiung in den Staat. Geschichte der palästinensischen Nationalbewegung*, Frankfurt 1991.

24. Cf. **M.Begin**, *The Revolt. Story of the Irgun*, Tel Aviv 1964.

25. Cf. **N.Goldmann**, *Memories*, London 1970; there is an enlarged two-volume German version: *Mein Leben als deutscher Jude*, Munich 1980; *Mein Leben. USA – Europe – Israel*, Munich 1981.

26. **Flapan**, *Birth of Israel* (n.16), 8.

27. Ibid., 8.

28. Ibid.

29. Ibid., 10.

30. For the first four wars and the peace efforts relating to them cf. **S.D.Bailey**, *Four Arab-Israeli Wars and the Peace Process*, London 1990.

31. **Flapan**, *Birth of Israel* (n.16), 5.

B. The Dispute between Jews and Christians

B.I. Jesus in Jewish-Christian Dialogue Today

1. Cf. **The German Bishops**, *Declaration on the Relationship of the Church to Judaism*, 28 April 1980 (a more accurate title would have been: The German Catholic Bishops...*Catholic Church*), German text in *Die Kirchen und das Judentum. Dokumente von 1945 bis 1985*, ed. R.Rendtorff and H.H.Henrix, Paderborn and Munich 1988, 260-80.

2. Ibid., 261.

3. Cf. **Küng**, OBC, Part Two B: The Distinction.

4. Cf. **A.von Harnack**, *What is Christianity?* (1900), London 1901 reissued New York 1957.

5. **L.Baeck**, 'Harnack's Vorlesungen über das Wesen des Christentums', *Monatsschrift für Geschichte und Wissenschaft des Judentums* 45, 1901, 97-102: 118.

6. Cf. **G.Lindeskog**, *Die Jesusfrage im neuzeitlichen Judentum. Ein Beitrag zur Geschichte der Leben-Jesu-Forschung*, Uppsala 1938, esp. 94-126, a work which gives the broad outlines of the situation.

7. Cf. **J.Salvador**, *Jésus-Christ et sa doctrine. Histoire de la naissance de l'église, de son organisation et de ses progrès pendant le premier siècle* (2 vols.), Paris 1838.

8. Cf. **S.Hirsch**, *Die Religionsphilosophie der Juden oder das Prinzip der jüdischen Religionsanschauung und sein Verhältnis zum Heidentum, Christentum und zur absoluten Philosophie*, Leipzig 1842.

9. Cf. **A.Geiger**, *Das Judentum und seine Geschichte* (3 vols.), Breslau 1864-1871.

10. Cf. **H.Graetz**, *Geschichte der Juden. Von den ältesten Zeiten bis zur Gegenwart* (11 vols.), Leipzig 1853-1875, ²1902-1909.

11. Cf. **J.Klausner**, *Jesus of Nazareth. His Life, Times, and Teaching* (original Hebrew 1922), London 1925.

12. Ibid., 374.

13. Cf. **C.G.Montefiore**, *The Synoptic Gospels* London 1909, ²1927.

14. Quoted from **S.Ben-Chorin**, *Bruder Jesus. Der Nazarener in jüdischer Sicht*, Munich 1967, 11.

15. **P.Lapide**, *Ist das nicht Josephs Sohn? Jesus im heutigen Judentum*, Stuttgart and Munich 1976, 42.

16. **H.Küng and P.Lapide**, *Jesus im Widerstreit. Ein jüdisch-christlicher Dialog*, Stuttgart 1976, 19.

17. **M.Buber**, *Two Types of Faith*, London 1951, 12.

18. **Ben-Chorin**, *Bruder Jesus* (n.14), 12.

19. Ibid.

20. **German Bishops** (n.1), 275.

21. Mark 10.18.

22. **German Bishops** (n.1), 275.

23. **Küng** and **Lapide**, *Jesus im Widerstreit* (n.16), 21.

24. Ibid.

25. Ibid.

26. More detailed information about the relevant scriptural passages for these and the following sections, which does not all need to be repeated in this brief summary, can be found in my OBC.

27. Cf. **W.Vogler**, *Jüdische Jesusinterpretationen in christlicher Sicht*, Weimar 1988.

28. Cf. **S.Sandmel**, *A Jewish Understanding of the New Testament*, Cincinnati 1956.

29. Cf. **A.Schweitzer**, *The Quest of the Historical Jesus* (1906), London ³1950.

30. Cf. **R.Bultmann**, *Jesus and the Word* (1926), New York 1934, reissued London 1958.

31. **Sandmel**, *Jewish Understanding* (n.28), 33.

32. Cf. the careful summary by **Vogler**, *Jüdische Jesusinterpretationen* (n.27), 84-8, whose conclusions agree with mine in OBC I-IV. There is a good survey of more recent research into Jesus in **W.G.Kümmel**, *Dreissig Jahre Jesus-Forschung (1950-1980)*, Königstein 1985.

33. Cf. **H.Küng**, OBC, C II 2, 'Miracles?'

34. Cf. ibid., C IV 1, 'The Decision'.

35. **J.H.Charlesworth**, 'From Barren Mazes to Gentle Rappings. The Emergence of Jesus Research', *The Princeton Seminary Bulletin* 7, 1986.3, 221-30:225. After philological research into the Bible had been shaped above all by German scholarship, biblical archaeology was carried on principally by American, English and French scholars: the school of W.F.Albright, the Ecole Biblique founded by Lagrange and the British School of Archaeology might be mentioned as examples. As a result, a good deal of the information in the Gospels (primarily including statements in the Gospel of John which were assumed to be improbable) has been confirmed in a surprising way. This relates not least to the place of Jesus' condemnation (Greek *lithostroton*, Aramaic *gabbatha*) and the place of his crucifixion (Golgotha), which according to most recent excavations must have lain outside the Western city wall in the area of the present-day Church of the Sepulchre. Cf. the survey of archaeological resarch by **J.H.Charlesworth**, *Jesus within Judaism. New Light from Exciting Archaeological Discoveries*, New York 1988, 103-30.

36. Cf. **F.F. Bruce**, *The Hard Sayings of Jesus*, Illinois 1983.

37. Cf. **E.P.Sanders**, *Jesus and Judaism*, **London and Philadelphia 1985.**

38. Cf. **G.Cornfeld** (ed.), *The Historical Jesus. A Scholarly View of the Man and his World*, New York 1982.

39. Cf. **D.Flusser**, *Jesus in Selbstzeugnissen und Bilddokumenten*, Reinbek 1968; **id.**, *Last Days of Jesus in Jerusalem – A Current Study of the Easter Week*, Tel Aviv 1980; **id.**, *Entdeckungen im Neuen Testament*, I, *Jesusworte und ihre Überlieferung*, ed. M.Majer, Neukirchen 1987; **id.**, *Judaism and the Origins of Christianity*, Jerusalem 1988; **id.**, *Das Christentum – eine jüdische Religion*, Munich 1990.

40. Cf. **G.Vermes**, *The Gospel of Jesus the Jew. The Riddell Memorial Lectures*, Newcastle 1981.

41. A book which is representative of this trend but which has yet to be discussed thoroughly is **E.P.Sanders**, *Jesus and Judaism* (n.37). This book has rightly been found liberating by many Anglo-Saxon exegetes trapped in traditional Protestant schemes, but now it manifestly exaggerates in the other direction. I must leave detailed criticism to the exegetes, but cannot suppress some hesitations on matters of principle.

Sanders thinks that 'what he (Jesus) claimed for himself was **tantamount** to claiming kingship', though he has to confess that 'the only direct statement...is the symbolic gesture of entering Jerusalem on an ass' and 'some, quite reasonably, have worries about the authenticity of that story' (32). Here we can also see the one-sidedness of Sanders' hermeneutical principle that we must start primarily from 'facts', from Jesus' actions and not from his words. Here Jesus' proclamation (in complete contrast to that of other prophets) is *a priori* assigned second place. According to Sanders, the Sermon on the Mount is in any case to be attributed 'to Matthew or a pre-Matthaean author or editor' (323). So the Sermon on the Mount does not count for the self-understanding and proclamation of Jesus.

And what about the controversy over the halakhah, which Jesus could not avoid with his proclamation? Sanders asserts that 'opposition to Sabbath, food and purity do not belong to the bedrock of the tradition', although he has to concede that the controversies 'are prominent in the Gospels' (325). He alleges that these controversies, too, are essentially to be attributed to the later community. What for Sanders is most certain about the proclamation of Jesus is all that it 'had in common with Jewish restoration eschatology: the expectation that Israel would be restored' (323).

In this way Sanders, 'a liberal, modern, secularized Protestant, brought up in a church dominated by low christology and a social gospel' (334), shows two things: on the one hand how to make Jesus innocuous by classing him as an apocalyptist, and on the other how to foist the controversy with the Judaism of his time on to the earliest community (and then of course Paul). It is not surprising that in this way he sees Jesus as being more in 'agreement' with Pharisaism than opposed to it (337).

The American rabbi **H.Falk**, *Jesus the Pharisee. A New Look at the Jewishness of Jesus*, New York 1985, sees Jesus very much as following the line of the school of Hillel against the school of Shammai.

42. Thus in the most recent German book on Jesus, **J.Gnilka**, *Jesus von Nazaret. Botschaft und Geschichte*, Freiburg 1990, there is no reference to Sanders, though this could also be because of the language barrier.

43. Cf. **J.Maier**, 'Gewundene Wege der Rezeption. Zur neueren jüdischen Jesusforschung', *Herder-Korrespondenz* 30, 1976, 313-19: 'Alongside the horizon of expectation of the Christian circles in question, which largely begin from the assumption that Jewish descent in principle already guarantees a deeper insight and replaces knowledge of Judaism, political and psychological considerations also play a role. The shades of the past evidently hamper a normal estimation and reaction, and with the demonstration of success at the same time impose both a dissatisfaction over content and suppressed murmuring' (318).

44. It is not my concern here to endorse in principle the classical (German) line of interpretation running from Albert Schweitzer through Bultmann, Käsemann, Fuchs, Bornkamm, Kümmel, to Eduard Schweizer, which controlled my account of Jesus in OBC. I am concerned with an issue which I see to be represented by both the German and the Anglo-Saxon exegetes whom I mention. Thus an expert in early Judaism, **J.H.Charlesworth**, regards the argument put forward by Sanders that Jesus stood within the general framework of a Jewish eschatology of restoration as 'exaggerated and fraught with numerous problems'. Charlesworth also firmly dismisses the assumption of a single type of normative Judaism ('covenantal nomism', cf. the review in *Journal of the American Academy of Religion* 55, 1987, 622-4). Charlesworth is right in saying that 'Jesus was clearly upset by the Jerusalem-based rigid norms for purity and isolation. Jesus' actions in the Temple may well fit within this overarching concern: the Temple was polluted by corrupt sacerdotal aristocratic priests. It needed to be purified' (Charlesworth reminds Sanders of the most recent Israeli excavations in Jerusalem, which unearthed stone vessels, pointing to the strict regulations for purification within the framework of the Temple).

45. Cf. **D.Flusser**, *Das Christentum – eine jüdische Religion*, Munich 1990.

46. The Catholic religious **B.J.Lee**, in *The Galilean Jewishness of Jesus.*

Retrieving the Jewish Origins of Christianity, I, New York 1988, claims to have traced the Galilean origins of Jesus' Judaism on a historical basis – a legitimate and worthwhile undertaking. But he clearly expresses his heuristic interest at the end of the first volume as follows: 'As a Christian I must think through my own Jewish identity.' That is certainly at first 'a loss', but then for him as 'a good Jewish Christian' it is 'a gain' (140). Do not some Jews also feel such Jewish identity to be too much of an intrusion? But the author continues: 'So here we are, Americans of the twentieth century... who are once again interpreting the significance of Jesus of Nazareth. Although we always remain bound to the event that we are interpreting, our free construction is an essential ingredient' (ibid). No wonder that, with his 'free construction', Lee is a wholehearted follower of E.P.Sanders (cf. 141-4).

47. Klausner, *Jesus of Nazareth* (n.11), 369.

48. Cf. **K.Barth**, *Church Dogmatics* I.1 (1932), Edinburgh ²1975, §8-12; cf. I.2, §13-15, 'The Incarnation of the Word'. Of course this does not mean that there is no valuable material for Jewish-Christian dialogue in Barth's developed christology (IV.1-4: The Doctrine of Reconciliation).

49. How the difficult problem of the pre-existence of Christ could also be discussed today in Jewish-Christian dialogue is shown by **K.-J.Kuschel**, *Geboren vor aller Zeit? Der Streit um Christi Ursprung*, Munich 1990 (ET in preparation, *Born Before All Time?*, London and New York 1992), above all in the epilogue.

50. **J.Moltmann**, *The Way of Jesus Christ. Christology in Messianic Dimensions*, London and New York 1990, 3.

51. Ibid.

52. Ibid., 28-37.

53. Ibid., 53.

54. Ibid. Cf. **id.**, *The Trinity and the Kingdom of God. The Doctrine of God*, London and New York 1981.

55. **Id.**, *The Way of Jesus Christ* (n.50), 72.

56. **F.-W.Marquardt**, *Das christliche Bekenntnis zu Jesus, dem Juden. Eine Christologie*, Vol.I, Munich 1990. Nor is this aspect really a theme in Vol.2, which appeared in 1991. What is worthwhile about Marquardt's christology is that he resolutely attempts to do christology in the context of the people of Israel. He rightly defends himself against the charge that such an approach detracts 'from the Christian confession'. He answers this with the testimony 'how much gratitude one owes to the God of **Israel** that one can still confess oneself a Christian and may seek reasons for that' (Vol.II, 445).

57. Cf. **P.M.van Buren**, *A Theology of the Jewish-Christian Reality* (3 vols.), New York 1980-88. The individual volumes bear the titles: I. *Discerning the Way*; II. *A Christian Theology of the People Israel*; III. *Christ in Context*. The Catholic theologian **L.Volken**, *Jesus der Jude und das Jüdische im Christentum*, Düsseldorf 1983, attempts an approach to the 'Christ of Chalcedon' from 'Jesus the Jew'.

58. For the following sections on a christology in the light of the Jewish context cf. **H.Küng**, OBC, Part C; **E.B.Borowitz**, *Contemporary Christologies. A Jewish Response*, New York 1980, does not comment on the christology of *On Being a Christian* (1974). For the Jewish-Christian dialogue in the light of its historical origins cf. **L.Boadt** et al. (eds.), *Biblical Studies. Meeting Ground of Jews and Christians*, New York 1980; **H.Flothkötter and B.Nacke** (eds.),

Das Judentum – eine Wurzel des Christlichen. Neue Perspektiven des Miteinanders, Würzburg 1990.

B.II Who Was Jesus?

1. Cf. **D.Flusser**, 'Christianity', in *Contemporary Jewish Religious Thought*. Recent literature on the historical Jesus and New Testament christology: **G.Bornkamm**, *Jesus of Nazareth* (1956), London and New York 1960; **O.Cullmann**, *The Christology of the New Testament* (1957), London and New York [2]1963; **N.Perrin**, *Rediscovering the Teaching of Jesus*, London and New York 1967; **E.Schweizer**, *Jesus* (1968), Nashville and London 1971; **H.Braun**, *Jesus. Der Mann aus Nazareth und seine Zeit*, Stuttgart 1969; **C.H.Dodd**, *The Founder of Christianity*, London and New York 1970; **J.Gnilka**, *Jesus nach frühen Zeugnissen des Glaubens*, Munich 1970; id., 'Zur Christologie des NT', in **W.Kasper** (ed.), *Christologische Schwerpunkte*, Düsseldorf 1980, 79-91; **F.Hahn**, *Christologische Hoheitstitel. Ihre Geschichte im frühen Christentum*, Göttingen 1974; **C.F.D.Moule**, *The Origin of Christology*, Cambridge 1977; **J.D.G.Dunn**, *Christology in the Making. A New Testament Enquiry into the Origins of the Doctrine of the Incarnation*, London and Philadelphia 1980; **C. and W.Feneberg**, *Das Leben Jesu im Evangelium*, Freiburg 1980; **J.Riches**, *Jesus and the Transformation of Judaism*, London 1980; **G.O'Collins**, *Interpreting Jesus*, London 1983; **P.Pokorny**, *Die Enstehung der Christologie. Voraussetzungen einer Theologie des Neuen Testaments*, Berlin 1984; **E.P.Sanders**, *Jesus and Judaism*, London and Philadelphia 1985; **L.Swidler**, *Yeshua: A Model for Moderns*, Kansas City 1988. There are surveys of research in **H.J.Leroy**, *Jesus. Überlieferung und Deutung*, Darmstadt 1978, 1-48; **W.G.Kümmel**, *Dreissig Jahre Jesusforschung (1950-1980)*, Königstein 1985; **F.Mussner**, 'Rückfrage nach Jesus. Bericht über neue Wege und Methoden', in *Theologische Berichte XIII (Methoden der Evangelienexegese)*, ed. J.Pfammatter and F.Furger, Zurich 1985, 165-82.

2. **J.Klausner**, *Jesus of Nazareth: His Life, Times, and Teaching* (original Hebrew 1922), London 1925, 222.

3. Cf. **R.Eisler**, *Jesous basileus ou basileusas. Die messianische Unabhängigkeitsbewegung vom Auftreten Johannes des Täufers bis zum Untergang Jakobs des Gerechten nach der neuerschlossenen Eroberung von Jerusalem des Flavius Josephus und den christlichen Quellen* (two vols.), Heidelberg 1929-30. For the trial of Jesus, along these lines cf. **P.Winter**, *On the Trial of Jesus*, Berlin 1961, [2]1974; **W.Fricke**, *The Court-Martial of Jesus. A Christian Defends the Jews against the Charge of Deicide*, New York 1990.

4. Cf. **J.Carmichael**, *The Death of Jesus*, New York and London 1962, [2]1982.

5. **S.G.F.Brandon**, *Jesus and the Zealots*, Manchester 1967; id., *The Trial of Jesus of Nazareth*, London 1968.

6. Cf. **P.Lapide**, *Der Rabbi von Nazareth. Wandlungen des jüdischen Jesusbildes*, Trier 1974, 'messianic revolutionary' (38). In his view, Jesus' failure led to a 'clear shift in the direction of militancy' (34) with the aim of 'taking possession of the Temple' (39). After dialogue lectures with me at the University of Tübingen in the summer semester of 1989 on the theme 'Christians and Jews Today. An Invitation to Dialogue', Lapide toned down

these statements. Cf. id., *Jesus – ein gekreuzigter Pharisäer?*, Gütersloh 1990. Here Jesus is a 'threefold rebel of non-violence' (120, cf. 109-21).

7. Cf. Luke 22.35-38.

8. Cf. Luke 22.51.

9. Matt.26.52.

10. Cf. Mark 11.15-19 par. Cf. **G.Theissen**, 'Die Tempelweissagung Jesu. Prophetie im Spannungsfeld von Stadt und Land', in id., *Studien zur Soziologie des Urchristentums*, Tübingen 1979, [3]1989, 142-59.

11. **E.P.Sanders** rightly stresses this one complex (the Temple) at Jesus' condemnation – cf. Mark 13.1f.; 14.58f.; Matt.27.39f.; John 2.18-22 (cf. pp.61-76). But it is evident throughout all the Gospels, Paul and Acts that a second complex led to the life-and-death conflict (cf. already Mark 3.6, etc.): that of the Law. Cf. also the testimony from the accusation against Stephen (Acts 6.13f.): 'This man never ceases to speak words against this holy place and the law; for we have heard him say that this Jesus of Nazareth will destroy this place, and will change the customs which Moses delivered to us.'

12. Mark 12.17.

13. Cf. **W.Vogler**, *Jüdische Jesusinterpretationen in christlicher Sicht*, Weimar 1988, 48.

14. **H.-J.Schoeps**, 'Jesus', in id., *Gottheit und Menschheit. Die grossen Religionsstifter und ihre Lehren*, Darmstadt 1954, 56.

15. Cf. **A.Schweitzer**, *The Quest of the Historical Jesus* (1906), London [3]1950.

16. For the **Pharisees**, in addition to the various lexicon articles, works on the New Testament enivronment and commentaries on the Synoptic Gospels and the letters of Paul, from the abundant Jewish literature cf. also **I.Abrahams**, *Studies in Pharisaism and the Gospels*, Cambridge 1917; **I.Finkelstein**, *The Pharisees. The Sociological Background of their Faith* (2 vols.), Philadelphia 1946; **J.Neusner**, *The Rabbinic Traditions about the Pharisees before 70* (3 vols.), Leiden 1971; **F.Mussner**, *Tractate on the Jews* (1979), Philadelphia 1984; id., *Die Kraft der Wurzel. Judentum -Jesus – Kirche*, Freiburg 1987; **F.Dexinger, C.Thoma and R.Mayer**, 'Die Pharisäer', *Bibel und Kirche 35*, 1980, 113-29, are representative of what Mussner has called 'the Christian process of relearning about the Pharisees'.

17. The **German Bishops**, 'Declaration on the Relationship of the Church to Judaism', of 28 April 1980; German text in *Die Kirchen und das Judentum. Dokumente von 1945-1985*, ed. R.Rendtorff and H.H.Henrix, Paderborn 1988 (= Rendtorff-Henrix), 276.

18. Ex.19.6.

19. Cf. **C.Thoma**, 'Der Pharisäismus', in J.Maier and J.Schreiner (eds.), *Literatur und Religion des Frühjudentums*, Würzburg 1973, 254-72; id., 'Spiritualität der Pharisäer', *Bibel und Kirche 35*, 1980, 117-22; **J.Gnilka**, *Das Evangelium nach Markus* I, Zurich 1978, 107-9.

20. Cf. e.g. most recently the Canadian sociologist **I.M.Zeitlin**, *Jesus and the Judaism of his Time*, Oxford 1988, esp. 73-84, where Matthew is preferred to the more radical Mark, who in turn is said not to give the standpoint of Jesus but that of later Gentile-Christian communities.

21. Cf. Matt.5.17.

22. **P.Lapide**, *The Sermon on the Mount* (1982), Maryknoll 1986.

23. **Mussner**, *Tractate* (n.16), 98 n.102.

24. **Mussner** refers to jEx 84; jBer IX.7; jPeah VIII.8; jHag II.7; jSot III.4.

25. Talmud, tractate bSota (as translated and interpreted by Mussner).

26. Matt.23.4.

27. Cf. Luke 18.9-14.

28. Luke 18.13.

29. **Thoma**, 'Spiritualität der Pharisäer' (n.19), 118.

30. There is a wealth of interesting detail on all these controversial questions in the learned, often multi-volume, commentaries on the Synoptic Gospels by distinguished exegetes published in recent years. I have made use of the commentaries on Mark by **J.Gnilka, W.H.Kelber, R.Pesch and W.Schmithals**; on Matthew by **J.Gnilka** and **U.Luz**; on Luke by **F.Bovon, J.A.Fitzmyer, G.Schneider** and **H.Schürmann**.

However, as a systematic theologian one is often perplexed by the general uncertainty over detail and the delight in constructing hypotheses. The warnings issued by the Bern exegete **U.Luz**, 'Markusforschung in der Sackgasse?', *Theologische Literaturzeitung* 105, 1980, 641-55, drawn from a comparison of three recent commentaries on Mark, need to be taken very seriously:

1. 'There should be limits to the game of constructing hypotheses... Reflecting that a combination of three hypotheses, each of which has a fifty per cent probability, ends up as a third-degree hypothesis with a probability of just over ten per cent, one will be very careful, and say more often and more clearly how little we really know.'

2. 'The scepticism which has grown up about the viability of traditio-historical reconstruction... There is urgent need for an attempt at a traditio-historical methodology which takes us a step beyond the unfortunately and inevitably subjective criteria about what is a unity and what is in tension, what is contradictory and what is coherent, and at least makes it possible to communicate traditio-historical hypotheses.'

3. 'In the traditio-historical jungle of present-day research... two postulates are important': 'the postulate of simplicity' and 'the postulate of traditio-historical continuity'. 'In my view it is *a priori* more probable for a historical event to continue to be retold than for it to be invented. In my view, it is more probable that there were stories about Jesus from the beginning than that someone invented them seventy years later' (653f.).

31. Cf. the survey in **Vogler**, *Jüdische Jesusinterpretationen* (n.13), 107-12.

32. **H.-J.Schoeps**, 'Jesus und das jüdische Gesetz', in his *Studien zur unbekannten Religions- und Geistesgeschichte*, Göttingen 1963, 41-61: 46f.

33. Matt.5.18f.

34. Mark 2.7.

35. Matt.12.41; Luke 11.32.

36. Matt.12.42; Luke 11.31.

37. **P.Lapide**, *Jesus – ein gekreuzigter Pharisäer*, Gütersloh 1990, thinks that the following answer can be given to the question 'whether a liberal Pharisee other than Jesus was ever crucified': 'Under the regime of Pontius Pilate alone, thousands of Pharisees, liberal, less liberal and even Zealot, were crucified by the Romans' (25). In answer to that I can only repeat the remark that I already made in our dialogue lectures: that here there is a confusion and an extrapolation. There are figures that can be verified: about a hundred years

before Christ, 800 rebellious Pharisees were crucified by the Jewish king and high priest Alexander Jannaeus, whereupon another 8,000 fled (Josephus, *Jewish War* I, 96-103; *Antiquities* XIII, 380-3 – the earliest example of the penalty of crucifixion being used by a Jewish prince on his own people). Later, 6,000 Pharisees who after a rash intrigue in the first years of the reign of Herod I, still before the birth of Christ, refused to give an oath of loyalty to the emperor and his king, were punished not with the death penalty but with a fine; Herod had only a few troublemakers and conspirators from his own family executed (*Antiquities* 17, 41-45). Finally, under the legate Publius Quinctilius Varus, between six and four years before Christ 2,000 Jewish rebels were crucified (*Jewish War* II, 75). However, there is no mention of Pharisees here. We know of Pontius Pilate that in Caesarea he spared the Jews who were protesting over the Roman standards in Jerusalem and only ordered executions in exceptional cases – the Galileans of Luke 13.1 who were murdered at the altar.

38. Cf. Mark 14.43.

39. Cf. John 18.12.

40. Cf. **A.Strobel**, *Die Stunde der Wahrheit. Untersuchungen zum Strafverfahren gegen Jesus*, Tübingen 1980.

41. Cf. **J.Blinzler**, *Der Prozess Jesu. Das jüdische und das römische Gerichtsverfahren gegen Jesus Christus auf Grund der ältesten Zeugnisse dargestellt und beurteilt*, third considerably revised edition, Regensburg 1960.

42. **Strobel**, *Stunde der Wahrheit* (n.40), 129.

43. Cf. **Y.Yadin** (ed.), *Megillat Hamikdasch* (3 vols.), Jerusalem 1977.

44. Cf. **O.Betz**, *Jesus, der Messias Israels. Aufsätze zur biblischen Theologie*, ed. M.Hengel, I, Tübingen 1987, 59-74.

45. For the different questions about procedure cf. **K.Kertelge** (ed.), *Der Prozess gegen Jesus. Historische Rückfrage und theologische Deutung*, Freiburg 1988 (especially the articles by J.Gnilka and K.Müller)

46. **Strobel**, *Stunde der Wahrheit* (n.40), 116f.; cf. also **J.Gnilka**, *Jesus von Nazareth. Botschaft und Geschichte*, Freiburg 1990, 291-318.

47. **Vatican II**, Declaration on the Relationship of the Church to the Non-Christian Religions, *Nostra Aetate*, 4.

B.III Belief in Jesus as the Messiah

1. For the problems connected with the **resurrection**, in addition to the books on Jesus and the christologies mentioned in the previous chapter, see the contributions by **H.Merklein**, 'Die Auferweckung Jesu und die Anfänge der Christologie', *Zeitschrift für die neutestamentliche Wissenschaft* 72, 1981, 1-26, and **H.W.Bartsch**, 'Inhalt und Funktion des urchristlichen Osterglaubens', with a bibliography on the theme 'The Resurrection of Jesus Christ', 1862-1959 (a selection) and 1960-1973 by **H.Rumpelts**, and 1975-1980 by **T.Pola**, in *Aufstieg und Niedergang der römischen Welt*, ed. W.Haase, 25.1, Berlin 1982, 794-890. **P.Hoffmann**, 'Auferweckung Jesu', in *Neues Bibel-Lexikon*, Zurich 1989, 202-15, gives a brief analysis of the biblical evidence. Cf. also the volume of essays edited by **P.Hoffmann**, *Zur neutestamentlichen Überlieferung von der Auferstehung Jesu*, Darmstadt 1988.

2. Cf. Rom.4.24; 8.11; II Cor.4.14; Gal.1.1; Acts 13.33.

3. Cf. Rom.10.9; I Cor 6.14; 15.15; Acts 2.32; 13.34.

4. Thus the simple, brief confession of I Cor.15.5-8. This possibly derives from the earliest Jerusalem community and in any case was 'taken over' by Paul in the period between 35 and 45 and 'delivered' to the Corinthians (cf. Gal.1.16; I Thess.4.14): that the risen Christ 'was seen' (Greek passive *ophthe*), 'made visible' (by God), 'showed himself', 'appeared', 'manifested himself' (many witnesses are said still to be alive).

5. **A.A.Cohen**, 'Resurrection of the Dead', in *Contemporary Jewish Religious Thought*, 807-13: 807.

6. There is a detailed analysis of these 'Easter experiences' and the 'Easter message' in **H.Küng**, OBC C. V: 'The New Life'.

7. Cf. **Flavius Philostratos**, *The Life of Apollonius of Tyana* VIII, 31.

8. Cf. **P.Lapide**, *Auferstehung. Ein jüdisches Glaubenserlebnis*, Stuttgart 1977.

9. **A.L. and A.R.Eckhardt**, *Long Night's Journey into Day. A Revised Retrospective on the Holocaust*, Detroit 1982 and Oxford 1985, 139.

10. Phil.2.8f.

11. **H.Küng**, OBC C.V, 1: (here 'Legends? Origin of Faith').

12. For the ideas of the Messiah in Judaism cf. **J.Neusner** et al. (ed.), *Judaisms and Their Messiahs at the Turn of the Christian Era*, Cambridge 1987.

13. **A.A.Cohen**, *The Myth of the Judeo-Christian Tradition and Other Dissenting Essays*, New York 1971, is right when in view of the hostility extending over many hundreds of years, he speaks of the 'Jewish-Christian tradition' as a myth. It is hopeful that with reference to the last, more positive, decades he is in favour of a 'Judeo-Christian humanism' (189-223). However, for me this again has its basis precisely in those things which were originally common to Jews and Christians.

14. Cf. Acts 15.1; Gal.5.2f.

15. Cf. Matt.24.20.

16. Cf. Col.2.16.

17. Cf. Gal.2.12f.; Acts 21.20-26.

18. Cf. Matt.5.23; Acts 2.46; 3.1.

19. Cf. **J.H.Charlesworth**, 'A Prolegomenon to a New Study of the Jewish Background of the Hymns and Prayers in the New Testament', *Journal of Jewish Studies* 23, 1982, nos.1-2, 262-85.

B.IV The History of an Alienation

1. Cf. **H.Koester**, *Introduction to the New Testament*, Berlin and Philadelphia 1982 (2 vols), II, 87.

2. **R.Bultmann**, *Theology of the New Testament* I, New York and London 1952, 53.

3. For the history of research cf. **H.R.Balz**, *Methodische Probleme der neutestamentliche Christologie*, Neukirchen 1967.

4. Cf. **M.Hengel**, *Judaism and Hellenism. Studies in their Encounter with Special Reference to Palestine up to the Middle of the Second Century BC*, London and Philadelphia 1974.

5. For the history of earliest Christianity cf. **H.Conzelmann**, *History of Primitive Christianity*, London 1973; **H.Koester and J.M.Robinson**, *Trajector-*

ies through Early Christianity, Philadelphia 1971; **P.Vielhauer**, *Geschichte der urchristlichen Literatur*, Berlin 1975; **H.M.Schenke and K.M.Fischer**, *Einleitung in die Schriften des NT* (2 vols.), Gütersloh 1978-1979; **G.Dautzenberg, H.Merklein and K.Müller** (eds.), *Zur Geschichte des Urchristentum*, Freiburg 1979; **H.Goldstein** (ed.), *Gottesverächter und Menschenfeinde? Juden zwischen Jesus und frühchristlicher Kirche*, Düsseldorf 1979; **M.Hengel**, *Acts and the History of Earliest Christianity*, London and Philadelphia 1979; **Koester**, *Introduction to the New Testament* (n.1); **H.Kraft**, *Die Entstehung des Christentums*, Darmstadt 1981; **W.Schneemelcher**, *Das Urchristentum*, Stuttgart 1981; **W.Grundmann**, *Die frühe Christenheit und ihre Schriften*, Stuttgart 1983; **N.A.Beck**, *Mature Christianity. The Recognition and Repudiation of Anti-Jewish Polemic of the New Testament*, London 1985; **K.M.Fischer**, *Das Urchristentum*, Berlin 1985; **H.Jansen**, *Christelijke Theologie na Auschwitz*, Part 2: *Nieuwtestamentische wortels van het semitisme*, 1, The Hague 1985; **A.F.Segal**, *Rebecca's Children. Judaism and Christianity in the Roman World*, Cambridge, Mass. 1986; **J.Becker** et al., *Die Anfänge des Christentums. Alte Welt und neue Hoffnung*, Stuttgart 1987; **J.Neusner**, *Judentum in frühchristlicher Zeit*, Stuttgart 1988; **L.Schenke**, *Die Urgemeinde. Geschichtliche und theologische Entwicklung*, Stuttgart 1990; **D.Stegmann**, *Jüdische Wurzeln des Christentums. Grundstrukturen des alttestamentlichen und nachtestamentlichen Glaubens bis zur Zeit Jesu*, Essen 1990.

6. Cf. Acts 6.1.

7. Cf. **M.Hengel**, 'Christology and New Testament Christology. A Problem in the History of Earliest Christianity', and 'Between Jesus and Paul. The "Hellenists", the "Seven" and Stephen (Acts 6.1-15; 7.54-8.3)', both in *id.*, *Between Jesus and Paul*, London and Philadelphia 1983, 30-47, 1-29.

8. Cf. Acts 6.11-14.

9. Cf. Acts 6.12.

10. Cf. Acts 7.54-60.

11. Cf. Acts 8.1.

12. Acts 11.19f.

13. **Hengel**, *Acts and the History of Earliest Christianity* (n.5), 74.

14. **K.Löning**, in **Becker** et al., *Anfänge des Christentums* (n.5), 83.

15. Acts 11.19.

16. Acts 11.20.

17. Cf. **R.E.Brown** and **J.P.Meier**, *Antioch and Rome. New Testament Cradles of Catholic Christianity*, New York 1983.

18. **Hengel**, 'Between Jesus and Paul' (n.7), 25.

19. Ibid., 25f.

20. **R.Ruether**, *Faith and Fratricide: The Theological Roots of Anti-Semitism*, New York 1974, 62: subsequently, in her quite justified concern to destroy Christian antisemitism root and branch, this Christian theologian sees the development too one-sidedly from the standpoint of the synagogue.

21. The sayings collected together by Matthew in ch.23 beginning 'Woe to you' are particularly bad.

22. Cf. Matt.12.39; 16.4.

23. Whereas the word 'hypocrites' is used just once in the earliest Gospel (Mark 7.6), in the later Gospel of Matthew it is used 13 times, principally of the 'scribes and Pharisees'. For the whole complex of questions cf. **H.J.Becker**,

Auf der Kathedra des Mose. Rabbinisch-theologisches Denken und antirabbinische Polemik in Mt 23,1-12, Berlin 1990.

24. This is particularly evident in the Gospel of John.

25. Matt.27.25. For the history of the influence of this saying cf. **R.Kampling**, *Das Blut Christi und die Juden. Matt.27.25 bei den lateinsprachigen christlichen Autoren bis zu Leo dem Grossen*, Münster 1984.

26. Cf. Acts 7.2-53.

27. Cf.Acts 7.59.

28. Acts 8.3.

29. Phil.3.5f.

30. Gal.1.13f.

31. Ibid.

32. I Cor.17-31; Gal.3.1-14.

33. Cf. **H.Küng**, OBC, C.V 1 'Origin of Faith'.

34. Cf. I Cor 9.1; 15.8-10; Gal.1.15f.; Phil.3.4-11. On this cf. **J.Blank**, *Paulus und Jesus. Eine theologische Grundlegung*, Munich 1968, ch.4, 'Die Berufung des Paulus als offenbarungshafter Grund seines Christusverhältnisses, seines Apostolats und seiner Theologie'.

35. II Cor.11.23-26.

36. Cf. John 14.6.

37. John 6.35; cf. John 6.22-59.

38. John 5.18.

39. John 10.33.

40. For this whole issue, incorporating the latest research, cf. **K.-J.Kuschel**, *Geboren vor aller Zeit? Der Streit um Christi Ursprung*, Munich 1990 (ET in preparation, *Born Before All Time?*, London and New York 1992).

41. From the Cairo Genizah text published by S.Schechter, quoted from **Reuven Kimelman**, '*Birkat Ha-Minim* and the Lack of Evidence for an Anti-Christian Jewish Prayer in Late Antiquity', in *Jewish and Christian Self-Definition*, ed. E.P.Sanders with A.I.Baumgarten and Alan Mendelson, 226.

42. **P.Schäfer**, *Studien zur Geschichte und Theologie des rabbinischen Judentums*, Leiden 1978, 48.

43. **I.Elbogen**, *Der jüdische Gottesdienst in seiner geschichtlichen Entwicklung*, Frankfurt ³1931, 36.

44. For the whole question cf. **K.Wengst**, *Bedrängte Gemeinde und verherrlichter Christus. Der historische Ort des Johannes-Evangeliums als Schüssel zu seiner Interpretation*, Neukirchen 1981; **R.Brown**, *The Community of the Beloved Disciple. The Life, Loves and Hates of an Individual Church in New Testament Times*, New York 1979.

45. John 9.22.

46. John 12.42.

47. John 19.38.

48. However, there is already 'supersessionism' and the demonization of other religions in the Hebrew Bible – in dealings with the Canaanites, Edomites and Amalekites. This is pointed out by the Jewish scholar **J.D.Revenson**, 'Is There a Counterpart in the Hebrew Bible to New Testament Antisemitism?', *Journal of Ecumenical Studies* 22, 1985, 242-60.

B.V A First Christian Paradigm Shift: From Jewish Christianity to Gentile Christianity

1. For **research into Paul** cf. the early important articles by **R.Bultmann, K.Holl, H.Lietzmann, A.Oepke, R.Reitzenstein, A.Schlatter and A.Schweitzer** collected by **K.H.Rengstorf**, *Das Paulusbild in neueren deutschen Forschung*, Darmstadt 1964. For orientation on the state of scholarship, which in fact is almost impossible to take in, cf. the **account of research** by **B.Rigaux**, *St Paul et ses lettres. État de la question*, Paris 1962; **H.Hübner**, 'Paulusforschung seit 1945. Ein kritischer Literaturbericht', in *Aufstieg und Niedergang der römischen Welt. Geschichte und Kultur Roms im Spiegel der neueren Forschung*, ed. W.Haas and H.Temporini, II, 25.4, Berlin 1987, 2649-840 (which also contains detailed contributions on the latest state of interpretation of the individual letters of Paul); **O.Merk**, 'Paulus-Forschung 1936-1985', *Theologische Rundschau* 53, 1988, 1-81. For an introduction to the person and work of the apostle Paul, in addition to the Introductions to the New Testament cf. especially **M.Dibelius** (ed. W.G.Kümmel), *Paul*, London 1953; **P.Seidensticker**, *Paulus, der verfolgte Apostel Jesu Christi*, Stuttgart 1965; **G.Bornkamm**, *Paul* (1969), London and New York 1971; **O.Kuss**, *Paulus. Die Rolle des Apostels in der theologischen Entwicklung der Urkirche*, Regensburg 1971; **K.Stendahl**, *Paul among Jews and Gentiles*, Philadelphia 1976 and London 1977; **F.F.Bruce**, *Paul. Apostle of the Free Spirit*, Exeter 1977; **E.P.Sanders**, *Paul and Palestinian Judaism*. London and Philadelphia 1977; id., *Paul, the Law and the Jewish People*, Philadelphia 1983 and London 1985; id., *Paul*, Oxford 1991; **J.C.Beker**, *Paul the Apostle. The Triumph of God in Life and Thought*, Philadelphia and Edinburgh 1980; **K.H.Schelkle**, *Paulus. Leben – Briefe – Theologie*, Darmstadt 1981; **G.Lüdemann**, *Paul. The Apostle to the Gentiles. Studies in Chronology* (1980), Philadelphia and London 1984; id., *Opposition to Paul in Jewish Christianity* (1983), Minneapolis 1989; **W.A.Meeks**, *The First Urban Christians. The Social World of the Apostle Paul*, New Haven 1983; **H.Räisänen**, *Paul and the Law*, Tübingen 1983; **G.Theissen**, *Psychological Aspects of Pauline Theology* (1983), Philadelphia and Edinburgh 1987; **F.Watson**, *Paul, Judaism and the Gentiles. A Sociological Approach*, Cambridge 1986; **J.Becker**, *Paulus. Der Apostel der Völker*, Tübingen 1989.

2. For **Paul from the Jewish side** and in **Jewish-Christian dialogue** cf. the following more recent literature: **S.Sandmel**, *The Genius of Paul. A Study in History*, New York 1958; **H.-J.Schoeps**, *Paul. The Theology of the Apostle Paul in the Light of Jewish Religious History* (1959), London 1961; **S.Ben-Chorin**, *Paulus. Der Völkerapostel in jüdischer Sicht*, Munich 1970; **M.Barth** et al., *Paulus – Apostat oder Apostel? Jüdische und christliche Antworten*, Regensburg 1979; **F.Mussner**, *Tractate on the Jews* (1979), Philadelphia 1984; **P.Lapide** and **P.Stuhlmacher**, *Paulus – Rabbi und Apostel. Ein jüdisch-christlicher Dialog*, Stuttgart 1981; **P.von der Osten-Sacken**, *Grundzüge einer Theologie im christlich-jüdischen Gespräch*, Munich 1982; id., *Evangelium und Tora. Aufsätze zu Paulus*, Munich 1987; **F.-W.Marquardt**, *Die Gegenwart des Auferstandenen bei seinem Volk Israel. Ein dogmatisches Experiment*, Munich 1983; **E.Biser** et al., *Paulus – Wegbereiter des Christentums. Zur Aktualität des Völkerapostels in ökumenischer Sicht*, Munich 1984; **L.Swidler**,

L.J.Eron, G.Sloyan and L.Dean, *Bursting the Bonds? A Jewish-Christian Dialogue on Jesus and Paul*, New York 1990. A.F.Segal, *Paul the Convert. The Apostolate and Apostasy of Saul the Pharisee*, New Haven 1990, makes a new methodological approach from the Jewish side.

3. **Lapide and Stuhlmacher**, *Paulus – Rabbi und Apostel* (n.2), 58f.

4. Cf. **H.Maccoby**, *The Mythmaker. Paul and the Invention of Christianity*, Cambridge and New York 1986.

5. Cf. **Segal**, *Paul the Convert* (n.2).

6. Ibid., xi.

7. Ibid., xiii.

8. Cf. the study by **W.Thüsing**, *Per Christum in Deum. Studien zum Verhältnis von Christozentrik und Theozentrik in den paulinischen Hauptbriefen*, Münster 1965.

9. I Cor.15.28.

10. As is generally recognized in exegesis, the legitimation of the Gentile Christian communities which have broken away from the law is the sociological background to Paul's criticism of the law. **Watson**, *Paul, Judaism and the Gentiles* (n.1), attempts to go beyond this and demonstrate that Paul has a basically sectarian attitude. I do not find this very convincing (cf. e.g. the collection for the Jerusalem community). **G.Lüdemann**, *Opposition to Paul in Jewish Christianity* (n.1), points out how strong the opposition to Paul was in the Jewish-Christian communities before and after 70.

11. **P.Lapide**, 'Missionar ohne Beispiel. Paulus – Rabbi, Ketzer und Apostel', *Süddeutsche Zeitung*, 6-8 June 1987.

12. At least 20 passages can be quoted from the authentic letters of Paul where Paul clearly bases himself on the Jesus tradition in the Gospels.

13. Cf. I Cor.1.18.

14. Cf. the letter to the Galatians.

15. Cf. both the letters to the Corinthians.

16. Cf. I Cor.3.11.

17. Phil.2.21: 'They all look after their own interests, not those of Jesus Christ'; cf. I Cor.7.32-34, 'the affairs of the Lord'.

18. **E.Käsemann**, 'Wo sich die Wege trennen', *Deutsches Allgemeines Sonntagsblatt*, 13 April 1990.

19. II Sam.7.14.

20. **J.Neusner** has demonstrated for the periods 70-300 and 300-600 CE that the concept of Israel changed not only in Christianity but also in Judaism, along with corresponding changes in these religions themselves – with reference to the development in Paul and early Christianity: *Judaism and Its Social Metaphors. Israel in the History of Jewish Thought*, Cambridge 1989.

21. For this development cf. **L.H.Schiffman**, *Who was a Jew? Rabbinic and Halakhic Perspectives on the Jewish Christian Schism*, Hoboken, NJ 1985.

22. **A.F.Segal**, *Rebecca's Children. Judaism and Christianity in the Roman World*, Cambridge, Mass. 1986, 179.

B.VI Christian Self-Criticism in the Light of Judaism

1. Cf. **D.Flusser**, 'Christianity', in *Contemporary Jewish Religious Thought*, 63.

2. 'Guidelines on Religious Relations with the Jews (*Nostra aetate* 4)', in *Vatican Council II. The Conciliar and Post-Conciliar Documents*, ed. A.Flannery, Leominster 1981, 742-9.

3. Cf. the 'Declaration on the Encounter between Lutheran Christians and Jews', approved at the Conference of the Lutheran European Commission on Church and Judaism, Driebergen, Netherlands, 8 May 1990.

4. Ibid., I.2.

5. Ibid., III.2.

6. C.Thoma, *Christliche Theologie des Judentums*, Aschaffenburg 1978, 43.

7. Ibid.

8. From the Jewish side cf. **S.E.Rosenberg**, *The Christian Problem. A Jewish View*, New York 1986.

9. Cf. **H. Küng**, OBC, especially C; **id.**, DGE, G.III; **id.**, CWR, A.IV.3, B.IV.2; C.I.2; **id.**, CR ch.II.2.

10. Cf. **K.-J.Kuschel**'s comprehensive study of pre-existence christology, *Geboren vor aller Zeit? Der Streit um Christi Ursprung*, Munich 1990 (English translation in preparation, *Born Before All Time?*, London and New York 1992).

11. **Thoma**, *Christliche Theologie* (n.6), 43.

12. Cf. e.g. Deut 32.6, 18; Jer.3.4; Isa.64.8; Mal.2.10.

13. Cf. e.g. Ex.4.22f.; Hos.11.1; Jer.31.9.

14. Cf. e.g. Deut.14.1.

15. Cf. e.g. Hos.1.10.

16. Cf. e.g. II Sam.7.14; Ps.2.7; 89.7f.

17. Ps.2.7.

18. Cf. Mark 12.36; Matt.22.44; Luke 20.42; Acts 2.34; Heb.1.3. Moreover, reference is also often made to the case of the Galilean ecstatic and miracle worker **Chanina ben Dosa**, who is a contemporary parallel to Jesus. Rabbis (even the great Rabban Johanan ben Zakkai) called him a special son of God, since he had a specially intimate relationship with God (whom like Jesus he addressed as 'Abba').

19. Cf. **K.Kohler**, *Jewish Theology, Systematically and Historically Considered*, New York 1918, reissued 1968, 198f., who develops the idea at length.

20. Ibid. The quotations have come from the 1910 German edition, 148f.

21. Isa. 57.15.

22. Deut.4.7.

23. **C.Thoma**, *Theologische Beziehungen zwischen Christentum und Judentum*, Darmstadt²1989, 112. The American theologian **J.T.Pawlikowski**, *Christ in the Light of Jewish-Christian Dialogue*, New York 1982, demonstrates the degree to which incarnational christology in particular has increasingly divided Jews and Christians.

24. Cf. Gal.4.4; Rom.8.3.

25. Cf. John 1.

26. Cf. **Kuschel**, *Geboren vor aller Zeit?* (n.10), 393.

27. Ibid., 390. The quotation in Kuschel comes from **B.v.Iersel**, 'Son of God in the New Testament', *Concilium* 153, 1982, 45.

28. Cf. **Flusser**, 'Christianity' (n.1), 64.

29. John 17.3.

30. John 20.17.

31. This is how **Kuschel** convincingly sums up the state of recent Catholic and Protestant exegesis, *Geboren vor aller Zeit?* (n.10), 502. The quotation in Kuschel comes from **H.Strathmann**, *Das Evangelium nach Johannes*, Göttingen 1951, 170.

32. **Kuschel**, *Geboren vor aller Zeit?* (n.10), 502.

33. For the problems connected with the virgin birth cf. **H.Küng**, OBC, C VI.3.

34. Deut.6.4.

35. Cf. the comprehensive survey of the Jewish commentaries in **L.Jacobs**, *Principles of the Jewish Faith. An Analytical Study*, London 1964, 95-117.

36. John 1.14.

37. Col.2.9.

38. John 3.16.

39. **P.Lapide**, *Warum kommt er nicht? Jüdische Evangelienauslegung*, Gütersloh 1988, 59.

40. Ibid.

41. **H.Küng**, OBC (1974!), 424.

42. Cf. ibid., C VI.2: Interpretations of Death.

43. **W.Vogler**, 'Jesu Tod – Gottes Tat? Bemerkungen zur frühchristlichen Interpretation des Todes Jesu', *Theologische Literaturzeitung* 113, 1988, cols. 481-92: 488.

44. **G.Friedrich**, *Die Verkündigung des Todes Jesu im Neuen Testament*, Neukirchen 1982, 30f.

45. **Vogler**, 'Jesu Tod' (n.43), col.289.

B.VII Jewish Self-Criticism in the Light of the Sermon on the Mount?

1. Cf. **A.Unterman**, 'Forgiveness (In Talmud and Jewish Thought)', in *Encyclopaedia Judaica*.

2. Sir.28.6f.

3. Cf. **G.Willmann**, *Kriegsgräber in Europa. Ein Gedenkbuch*, Munich 1980, 317. In the First World War there were 9,737,000 victims to mourn.

4. Matt.6.12; cf. Luke 11.4.

5. Cf. Matt.18.21-35.

6. Matt.18.22; cf. Luke 17.4.

7. Cf. Luke 23.34.

8. Matt.7.1 par.

9. Cf. Ps.130.1,3f.

10. Matt.18.33.

11. **A.H.Friedlander**, *A Thread of Gold. Journeys towards Reconciliation*, London 1990, 135.

12. Ibid., 5.

13. Another example of impressive work towards reconciliation in the United States is **Dr Edith Eva Eger** of La Jolla, California, whom I met in California. She survived Auschwitz at the age of sixteen and uses her terrible experiences at that time positively, in psychotherapy, to help people to survive in difficult situations.

14. *Cf. Das Parlament*, Bonn, 3 September 1977.

15. Cf. Matt.18.32-35.

16. Cf. Luke 19.18.
17. Cf. Mark 2.17 par.
18. Cf. *Das Parlament*, Bonn, 3 September 1977.
19. This and the following texts were printed in *Die Zeit*, 6 January 1989.

C. The Overcoming of Modernity

C.I Ways out of the Identity Crisis

1. For the **more recent history of the Jews in America** cf. **N.Glazer**, *American Judaism*, Chicago 1952, ²1972; **M.Rischin**, *An Inventory of American Jewish History*, Cambridge, Mass. 1954; **J.L.Blau**, *Modern Varieties of Judaism*, New York 1966; **id.**, *Judaism in America. From Curiosity to Third Faith*, Chicago 1976; **A.W.Miller**, *God of Daniel S.In Search of the American Jew*, London 1969; **G.S.Rosenthal**, *Four Paths to One God. Today's Jew and His Religion*, New York 1973; **C.S.Liebman**, *Aspects of the Religious Behaviour of American Jews*, New York 1974; **W.W.Brickman**, *The Jewish Community in America. An Annotated and Classified Bibliographical Guide*, New York 1977; **M.L.Raphael**, *Profiles in American Judaism. The Reform, Conservative, Orthodox, and Reconstructionist Traditions in Historical Perspective*, San Francisco 1984.
2. Cf. **W.Herberg**, *Protestant – Catholic – Jew. An Essay in American Religious Sociology*, New York 1956.
3. Cf. **id.**, *Judaism and Modern Man. An Interpretation of Jewish Religion*, New York 1951.
4. Cf. **C.E.Silberman**, *A Certain People. American Jews and Their Lives Today*, New York 1985. Part One is about 'An American Success Story' and Part Two 'A Jewish Success Story'; in the last part, 'Notes on the Future', the author sees the main danger for Judaism in the exclusive concentration of many leading Jews (especially Jewish politicians) on exclusively Jewish concerns, especially support for the state of Israel.
5. **A.J.Feldman**, *The American Jew. A Study of Backgrounds*, New York 1937, reissued 1979, 49.
6. Cf. *Encyclopaedia Judaica, Year Book 1986/87*, 389-91.
7. For **A.J.Heschel** cf. **F.A.Rothschild**, 'Heschel, Abraham Joshua', in *Encyclopaedia Judaica*; **id.** (ed.), *Between God and Man. An Interpretation of Judaism from the Writings of Abraham J.Heschel*, New York 1959.
8. Cf. **A.J.Heschel**, *Die Prophetie*, Krakow 1936.
9. Cf. **id.**, *Maimonides. Eine Biographie*, Berlin 1935.
10. Cf. **id.**, *Man is Not Alone: A Philosophy of Religion*, New York 1951.
11. Cf. **id.**, *God in Search of Man: A Philosophy of Judaism*, New York 1955, 168f.
12. Ibid.
13. Ibid., 31.
14. Ibid., 164.
15. Ibid., 259.
16. Ibid., 260f.
17. Ibid., 415.

18. Ibid., 416.
19. Ibid., 169.
20. Cf. the attempt at a critical/self-critical dialogue with modern criticism of religion in **H.Küng**, DGE, C, 'The Challenge of Atheism'.
21. **Heschel**, *God in Search of Man* (n.11), 274.
22. Ibid., 341.
23. Ibid., 348.
24. Ibid., 351.
25. Ibid.

C.II Basic Religious Options for the Future?

1. For **Orthodox Judaism in America**, cf. **I.Epstein**, *The Faith of Judaism. An Interpretation for our Time*, London 1954; **I.Herzog**, *Judaism: Law and Ethics*, articles selected by C.Herzog, London 1974; **C.S.Liebman**, 'Orthodoxy in American Jewish Life', in *Aspects of the Religious Behaviour of American Jews*, New York 1974, 111-87; **W.B.Helmreich**, *The World of the Yeshiva. An Intimate Portrait of Orthodox Jewry,*, New York 1982; **R.P.Bulka** (ed.), *Dimensions of Orthodox Judaism*, New York 1983. For the **training of rabbis** in Orthodox Judaism cf. **Z.Charlop**, 'The Making of American Rabbis: Orthodox Rabbis', in *Encyclopaedia Judaica, Yearbook 1983-85*, 84-90; **M.H.Danzger**, *Returning to Tradition. The Contemporary Revival of Orthodox Judaism, New Haven* 1989.

2. Along with his friend and later opponent Abraham Geiger, **Samson Raphael Hirsch**, born in Hamburg, studied in Bonn and for eleven years was rabbi of the principality of Oldenburg, five years later rabbi of Moravia and finally (from 1851) rabbi of the Orthodox 'Israelite Society of Religion' in Frankfurt; between 1864 and 1870 he was editor of the journal *Jeschurun*, a 'Monthly Journal for the Furtherance of the Jewish Spirit and Jewish Life in Home, Community and School'. Particularly through his numerous publications (Torah exegesis, a new translation of the Bible, etc.), in his commitment to a uniform renewed Judaism, Hirsch **became head of German neo-Orthodoxy**. Cf. the articles by **M.Joseph** (*Jüdisches Lexicon*) and **S.Katz** (*Encyclopaedia Judaica*).

3. Cf. **Liebman**, *Orthodoxy* (n.1), 117-20.

4. For these three categories and especially for modern Orthodoxy cf. **E.Rackman**, 'Modern Orthodoxy', in *Encyclopaedia Judaica, Yearbook 1986-87*, 118-22.

5. **Joseph D.Soloveitchik** comes from a famous family of Lithuanian rabbis. Born in Poland and trained as a Talmudic scholar in Brest-Litovsk, at the age of twenty-two he arrived at Berlin University, was very impressed by Neo-Kantianism and Hegel, and gained a doctorate in philosophy with a dissertation on the epistemology and metaphysics of Hermann Cohen, the most significant Jewish representative of neo-Kantianism. In 1931 he married Tonya Lewit, who had a doctorate from the University of Jena and was a loyal assistant to him until her death in 1967. In 1932 they both emigrated to the USA and Soloveitchik became rabbi of the Orthodox community in Boston and founder of both the first Jewish day school in New England and a Talmudic school. In 1941 he succeeded his father as Professor of Talmud at the Yeshiva University.

Here he became the spiritual mentor of the majority of orthodox Rabbis trained in America, and also the influential chairman of the Halakhah Commission of the Orthodox Rabbinical Council of America. He refused the post of Ashkenasy Chief Rabbi of Israel in 1959. Soloveitchik was influential above all through his lectures in English, Hebrew and Yiddish. He published relatively little. He gives a good introduction to his thought in *Halakhic Man*, New York 1983, and in his discussion *The Halakhic Mind. An Essay on Jewish Tradition and Modern Thought*, similarly written as early as 1944, but only published in New York in 1986. Cf. the article by **A.Rothkoff** in *Encyclopaedia Judaica*. For enlightened Orthodoxy cf.also **Z.Kurzweil**, *The Modern Impulse of Traditional Judaism*, Hoboken 1985, which includes a chapter on J.D.Soloveitchik, A.I.H.Kook and E.Berkovits.

6. **Soloveitchik**, *The Halakhic Man* (n.5), 19.
7. Ibid., 29.
8. Ibid., 36.
9. Ibid. 37f.
10. Ibid., 40.
11. **Id.**, *The Halakhic Mind* (n.5), 85.
12. Ibid., 88.
13. Ibid., 90.
14. Ibid., 101.
15. Ibid., 102.
16. For what follows see **Rackman**, 'Modern Orthodoxy' (n.4). Rackman's own orthodox views appear under the title *One Man's Judaism*, Tel Aviv nd.
17. After more than thirty bus stations were burned down by the Orthodox in 1985/6 for 'immoral' advertising and many others were disfigured, in 1986 a Yeshiva in Tel Aviv was broken into and prayer books and objects of religious art were desecrated – obviously as a warning. For the conversion of secular Jews to Orthodox Judaism in the state of Israel cf. the investigation by **J.Aviad**, *Return to Judaism. Religious Renewal in Israel*, Chicago 1983.
18. **Abraham Geiger**, born in Frankfurt, was active as a rabbi in Wiesbaden, Frankfurt, Breslau and Berlin. Although antipathetic to frantic Reformism he was nevertheless regarded with considerably hostility and was only appointed lecturer at the Berlin College for the Science of Judaism two years before his death (1872-1874). Through his many-sided academic work on Bible and Mishnah, and on exegetical, historical, philosophical and poetic literature of the Middle Ages and modern times, through his influence on the important rabbinic assemblies of the 1840s and his journals *Wissenschaftliche Zeitschrift für jüdische Theologie* (6 vols, 1835-1847) and *Jüdische Zeitschrift für Wissenschaft und Leben* (11 vols, 1862-75), he became the spiritual **leader of Reform Judaism**. His work *Urschrift und Übersetzungen der Bibel in ihrer Abhängigkeit von der inneren Entwicklung des Judentums*, Breslau 1857, ²1928 is characteristic of his evolutionary view of Judaism, which he sees culminating in prophecy. His posthumous writings were edited by his son Ludwig in five volumes, 1875-1878. Cf. the articles by **M.Joseph** (*Jüdisches Lexikon*) and **J.S.Levinger** (*Encyclopaedia Judaica*).
19. After his retirement **Hermann Cohen**, born in Coswig (Anhalt), from 1876-1912 professor in Marburg, went to the Berlin College for the Science of Judaism where he taught the philosophy of religion until his death in 1918; his wife died in Theresienstadt concentration camp shortly after being sent

there. Important works are: *Die Religion der Vernunft aus den Quellen des Judentums*, Frankfurt 1919, second revised edition 1929; *Jüdische Schriften* (3 vols.), Berlin 1924.

20. For **Reform Judaism in America** cf. D.Philipson, *The Reform Movement in Judaism*, 1907 reissued New York 1967; G.W.Plaut, *The Rise of Reform Judaism. A Source Book of its European Origins*, New York 1963; id., *The Growth of Reform Judaism. American and European Sources until 1948*, New York 1965; A.J.Feldman, *The American Reform Rabbi. A Profile of a Profession*, New York 1965; J.L.Blau (ed.), *Reform Judaism. A Historical Perspective. Essays from the Yearbook of the Central Conference of American Rabbis*, New York 1973; E.B.Borowitz, *Reform Judaism Today* (3 vols.), New York 1977-78; id., *Liberal Judaism*, New York 1984. For the **training of rabbis** in Reform Judaism cf. A.Gottschalk, 'The Making of American Rabbis: Reform Rabbis', in *Encyclopaedia Judaica, Yearbook 1983-85*, 96-100; **M.A.Meyer**, *Response to Modernity. A History of the Reform Movement in Judaism*, New York 1988.

21. Text in the *Yearbook of the Central Conference of American Rabbis* XLVII, 1937, 97f., quoted in **N.Glazer**, *American Judaism*, Chicago 1952, ²1972, 103f. The texts of both the 'Pittsburgh Platform' (1885) and the 'Columbus Platform' (1937) are in **Plaut**, *The Growth of Reform Judaism*, 33f., 96-9.

22. **Louis Jacobs** received his training first in the rabbinic schools of Manchester and London and then also at London University. After that he was active as a rabbi at synagogues in Manchester and in the 1950s in the West End of London. After his work as tutor at Jews' College (1959-62) he was to become its director. However, a veto from the English Chief Rabbi Israel Brody prevented this, and also the appointment of Jacobs as minister of the modern New West End Synagogue. Rabbi Jacobs has written several books. *We Have Reason to Believe. Some Aspects of Jewish Theology Examined in the Light of Modern Thought*, London 1957, was the first to cause offence. Then appeared *Jewish Values*, London 1960, and finally *Principles of the Jewish Faith. An Analytical Study*, London 1964, an exposition of the creed of Maimonides. Cf.the unsigned article in *Encyclopaedia Judaica*.

23. Cf. I.Epstein, *The Faith of Judaism. An Interpretation for Our Times*, London 1954.

24. Jacobs, *Principles of the Jewish Faith* (n.22), viii.

25. Ibid., x.

26. Id., *A Jewish Theology*, London 1973.

27. Cf. **K.Kohler**, *Jewish Theology: Systematically and Historically Considered*, New York 1918, reissued 1968. The work has three main parts: God – Man – Israel and the Kingdom of God.

28. Jacobs, *A Jewish Theology* (n.26), 204.

29. Ibid., 205.

30. For **Conservative Judaism** in America cf. R.Gordis, *Judaism for the Modern Age*, New York 1955; id., *Understanding Conservative Judaism*, New York 1978; **M.Waxman** (ed.), *Tradition and Change. The Development of Conservative Judaism*, New York 1958; **M.Davis**, *The Emergence of Conservative Judaism. The Historical School in Nineteenth-Century America*, Philadelphia 1963; **S.Siegel** (ed.), *Conservative Judaism and Jewish Law*, New York 1977; **H.Rosenblum**, *Conservative Judaism. A Contemporary History*,

New York 1983. For the **training of rabbis** in Conservative Judaism cf. **R.Hammer**, 'The Making of American Rabbis: Conservative Rabbis', in *Encyclopaedia Judaica Yearbook 1983-85*, 91-5.

31. **Zacharias Frankel** was first of all Chief Rabbi in Dresden, and then from 1854 until his death director of the newly-founded Jewish theological seminary and founder of the most significant journal on Judaistics (which survived until 1939!), the *Monatsschrift für Geschichte und Wissenschaft des Judentums*. Frankel was the spiritual **leader of the Conservative mediating party**, the historical-positive ('Breslau') school, in the great controversies within Judaism at the time, and such was criticized both by Abraham Geiger, the leading representative of the 'Science of Judaism', and Samson Raphael Hirsch, the head of neo-Orthodoxy (in Frankfurt). Frankel was active in three directions: he was active politically through his legal opinions and writings on the emancipation of the Jews (the 'Jewish oath'), historically through his research into the rabbinic writings (introduction to the Mishnah and Jerusalem Talmud, preliminary studies on the Septuagint, studies on hermeneutics, on judicial evidence and on the marriage law), and finally academically and pedagogically through his pupils and his considerable influence on the training of rabbis. Cf. the articles by **S.Gans** (*Jüdisches Lexikon*) and **J.E.Heller** (*Encyclopaedia Judaica*).

32. From 1902 until his death in 1915, **Solomon Schechter** (born 1847 in Rumania) was president of the Jewish Theological Seminary of America in New York. After a thorough rabbinic training and studies in Vienna and at the Berlin College for the Science of Judaism, Schechter went to England as tutor of his fellow-student Claude G.Montefiore. In 1892 he became a lecturer in rabbinic literature in Cambridge. He achieved fame by bringing (along with C.Taylor) more than 100,000 fragments from the Geniza of Al Fustat in Cairo to Cambridge (the Taylor-Schechter Collection). In America, through the selection of an outstanding faculty (L.Ginzberg, I.Friedlaender, I.Davidson, A.Marx and M.M.Kaplan) and through the organization of the Synagogue of America he became the **chief architect of Conservative Judaism in America** and an influential promoter of Zionism. Important works are: *Some Aspects of Rabbinic Theology, London 1909; id., Seminary Addresses and Other Papers, Cincinnati 1915, new edition Westmead 1960; id., Studies in Judaism. A Selection*, New York 1958 (a selection of still relevant essays from Schechter's three-volume *Studies in Judaism* of 1896-1924). Cf. the articles by **I.Elbogen** (*Jüdisches Lexikon*) and **M.Ben-Horin** (*Encyclopaedia Judaica*).

33. Cf. **J.Neusner**, 'Conservative Judaism in a Divided Community', *Conservative Judaism* 20, 1965-66, no.4, 1-19; also **L.Ginzberg**, *Students, Scholars and Saints*, 1928, new edition New York 1960 (this also contains articles on the most important representatives of the Conservative school tradition: in addition to Zacharias Frankel and Solomon Schechter also Israel Salanter, Isaac Hirsch Weiss and David Hoffman); **H.Parzen**, *Architects of Conservative Judaism*, New York 1964.

34. **Mordecai Menahem Kaplan**, of Lithuanian descent, emigrated to the USA at the age of nine. Between 1909 and 1963 he taught homiletics and the philosophy of religion at Jewish Theological Seminary or at its Teachers Institute. As head of the Teachers Institute he became the **founder of the Reconstructionist movement**. Cf. the article by **J.J.Cohen** in *Encyclopaedia Judaica*.

35. **M.M.Kaplan**, *Judaism as a Civilization. Towards a Reconstruction of American Jewish Life*, New York 1935, x.

36. Ibid.

37. Ibid., 178.

38. Ibid., 179.

39. Ibid., 305f.

40. Cf. ibid., 311-31; cf. **id.**, *Judaism without Supernaturalism. The Only Alternative to Orthodoxy and Secularism*, *New York 1958;* **id.**, *Judaism in Transition*, New York 1936.

41. For the **Reconstructionist movement in America**, in addition to the works of M.M.Kaplan cf. **H.L.Goldberg**, *Introduction to Reconstructionism*, New York 1957; **C.S.Liebman**, *Reconstructionism in American Jewish Life* (n.x), 189-285. For the **training of rabbis** in the Reconstructionist movement cf. **R.T.Alpert**, 'The Making of American Rabbis: Reconstructionist Rabbis', *Encyclopaedia Judaica, Yearbook 1983-85*, 101-5.

42. **Kaplan**, *Judaism as a Civilization* (n.35), x.

43. Cf. **Jacobs**, *A Jewish Theology* (n.26), 223f.

44. Ibid., 350, 381. Cf. **id.**, *The Greater Judaism in the Making. A Study of the Modern Evolution of Judaism*, New York 1960.

45. **Glazer**, *American Judaism* (n.21), 133.

46. Ibid., 133f.

47. **Y.Leibowitz** (with M.Shashar), *Al olam umlo'oh*, Jerusalem 1987; German *Gespräche über Gott und die Welt*, Frankfurt 1990, 86.

48. Ibid.

49. Ibid., 83.

50. Ibid., 84.

PART THREE:
POSSIBILITIES FOR THE FUTURE

A. Judaism in Postmodernity

A.I The Origin of Postmodernity

1. Cf. **H.Küng**, *Global Responsibility*, London and New York 1991, esp. 2-24, 65-70, 135-8.

2. For Buber's biography cf. **S.H.Bergman**, 'Buber, Martin', in *Encyclopaedia Judaica*, cols. 1429-32. Buber's philosophical and theological works are published in **M.Buber**, *Werke* (3 vols.), Munich 1962-1964. However, Buber's works on Judaism, Zionism and the state of Israel are also important. They are collected in **id.**, *Der Jude und sein Judentum. Gesammelte Aufsätze und Reden*, Cologne 1963.

3. The Buber-Rosenzweig translation of the Bible appeared in the following four volumes: *Die Fünf Bücher der Weisung, Bücher der Geschichte, Bücher der Kündung, Schriftwerke*, revised edition Cologne 1954-1962.

4. All these discussions are in **Buber**, *Werke*, Vol.II.

5. **Id.**, 'The History of the Dialogical Principle', in *Between Man and Man*, New York 1965, 209–24.

6. Ibid., 304.

7. Cf. ibid., 291-305.
8. Cf. ibid., 299.
9. **Id.**, *I and Thou*, Edinburgh ²1958, 18.
10. Ibid., 99.
11. Ibid., 91.
12. Cf. **id.**, 'Biblical Humanism', in *Biblical Humanism. Eighteen Studies*, ed. Nahum N.Glatzer, London 1968, 221-20.
13. Ibid., 211.
14. Ibid.
15. Ibid.
16. Ibid., 212.
17. Ibid.
18. Ibid., 213.
19. **Id.**, 'Das Problem des Menschen', in *Werke* I, 307-407: 403f.
20. **Id.**, *Eclipse of God: Studies in the Relation between Religion and Philosophy*, London 1953, 17f.
21. Quoted in **Bergman**, 'Buber' (n.2), col.1430.
22. **Y.Leibowitz** (with Michael Shashar), *Gespräche über Gott und die Welt*, Frankfurt 1990, 55f.
23. Ibid.

A.II Judaism in Postmodernity

1. I would refer to the very different studies by **S.Volkov**, quoted above.
2. **B.Halpern**, 'The Jewish Consensus', *Jewish Frontier*, September 1962, quoted in **J.Neusner**, *The Way of Torah. An Introduction to Judaism*, Belmont, Ca. ³1979, 129f.
3. Cf. **Neusner**, *The Way of Torah* (n.2), 130.
4. Ibid.
5. Cf. ibid., 131.
6. Ibid., 131f.
7. For what follows see **D.Marmour**, *Beyond Survival. Reflections on the Future of Judaism*, London 1982, 205.

B. Conflicts in Life and the Future of the Law

B.I The Ambivalence of the Law

1. All the works on the different trends in Judaism quoted in the last chapter of Part Two contain detailed chapters on the law and its interpretation.
2. **G.Horowitz**, *The Spirit of the Jewish Law. A Brief Account of Biblical and Rabbinical Judisprudence. With a Special Note on Jewish Law and the State of Israel*, New York 1953, gives a compact survey (around 800pp!) of the most important principles of the Jewish law as it has developed from the beginnings in the Bible through the Talmud to the works of the later great masters. Cf. further the more recent monographs by **D.W.Halivini**, *Midrash, Mishnah and Gemara. The Jewish Predilection for Justified Law*, Cambridge,

Mass. 1986 (seeks to replace Alt's distinction between apodeictic and casuistic laws with that between categorical and vindicatory/justificatory laws); E.N.Dorff and A.Rosett, *A Living Tree. The Roots and Growth of Jewish Law*, Albany 1988. P.H.Weisbard and D.Schonberg, *Jewish Law. Bibliography of Sources and Scholarship in English*, Littleton, Co 1989, gives a comprehensive English-language bibliography.

3. D.Hartman, *A Living Covenant. The Innovative Spirit in Traditional Judaism*, New York 1985.

4. Ibid., 5.

5. Ibid., 5f.

6. Ibid., 28f.

7. Ibid., 98.

8. Cf. **H.Zoller**, 'Jude sein in Israel is kein Zuckerschlecken', *Der Spiegel*, 1, 1987.

9. Cf. **M.Waxman** (ed.), *Tradition and Change. The Development of Conservative Judaism*, New York 1958, 349-407; S.Siegel (ed.), *Conservative Judaism and Jewish Law*, New York 1977.

10. Cf. **A.H.Neulander**, 'The Use of Electricity on the Sabbath', in Waxman (ed.)., *Tradition and Change* (n.9), 401-7.

11. **Zoller**, 'Jude sein in Israel' (n.8).

12. Cf. **H.Denzinger**, *Enchiridion symbolorum, definitionum et declarationum de rebus fidei et morum* (1854), Freiburg ^{31}1960. There is a German selection in **J.Neuner** and **H.Roos**, *Der Glaube der Kirche in den Urkunden der Lehrerverkündigung* (1938), Regensburg ^{5}1958. For a critique of the selection cf. **H.Küng**, 'Veröffentlichungen zum Konzil. Ein Überblick', *Theologische Quartalschrift* 143, 1963, 56-82.

13. Cf. **H.Küng**, *Infallible?*, London and New York 1972; id., *Fehlbar. Eine Bilanz*, Zurich 1973.

14. Cf. **id.**, *Truthfulness: The Future of the Church*, London and New York 1968, B.VIII: Manipulation of the Truth.

15. Cf. **Denzinger** (n.12), no.714.

16. Cf. the Constitution *Lumen Gentium* of the **Second Vatican Council** (1965), no.16.

17. Cf. Ex.16.29; Jer.17.22.

18. Cf. **Z.Kaplan**, 'Eruv', in *Encyclopaedia Judaica*; W.Lewy and S.Krauss, 'Eruv', in *Jüdisches Lexikon*.

19. Cf. **B.Z.Schereschewsky**, 'Mamzer', in *Encyclopaedia Judaica*; M.Cohn, 'Mamser' in *Jüdisches Lexikon*.

20. Cf. Deut.23.2; Zech.9.6.

21. Cf. **D.Novak**, *Halakhah in a Theological Dimension*, Chico, Ca. 1985, 27f.

22. Quoted ibid., 28.

23. Cf. **L.Jacobs**, *A Tree of Life. Diversity, Flexibility, and Creativity in Jewish Law*, Oxford 1984, Appendix B, 257-75. Cf. also **id.**, *Theology in the Responsa*, London 1975; id., *The Talmudic Argument. A Study in Talmudic Reasoning and Methodology*, London 1984.

24. **Id.**, *A Tree of Life* (n.23), 236.

B.II For God's Sake?

1. Cf. **Y.Leibowitz**, *The Faith of Maimonides*, New York 1987.
2. **Y.Leibowitz**, 'Commandments', in *Contemporary Jewish Religious Thought*, 70.
3. Ibid., 71.
4. Ibid.
5. Ibid.
6. Ibid.
7. Ibid., 75.
8. **Id.** (with Michael Shashar), *Gespräche über Gott und die Welt*, Frankfurt 1990, 105f.
9. Cf. ibid., 107, 110-16.
10. Ibid., 107.
11. Cf. **G.Frankel**, 'Israel's 2000-Year-Old Divorce Laws Turn Ties That Bend into Chains', *International Herald Tribune*, 14 March 1989.
12. Cf. Gen.1.27.
13. Cf. **J.Plaskow**, *Standing Again at Sinai. Judaism from a Feminist Perspective*, San Francisco 1990.
14. Cf. **E.Schüssler Fiorenza**, *In Memory of Her. A Feminist Theological Reconstruction of Christian Origins*, New York and London 1983.
15. **Plaskow**, *Standing Again at Sinai* (n.13), 3.
16. Ibid., 75.
17. Ex.19.15.
18. Cf. **Plaskow**, *Standing Again at Sinai* (n.13), 25.
19. Ibid., 25, 27.
20. Ibid., 71f.
21. Ibid., 89f.
22. Ibid., 71.
23. Cf. **E.B.Borowitz**, *Choices in Modern Jewish Thought. A Partisan Guide*, New York 1983; **id.**, *Liberal Judaism*, New York 1984.
24. Ibid., 243f.
25. Cf. **id.**, 'Freedom', in *Contemporary Jewish Religious Thought*, 261-7.
26. Ibid., 266.
27. **Id.**, *Choices in Modern Jewish Thought* (n.23), 281.
28. Ibid.
29. **Id.**, 'Freedom' (n.25), 266.
30. Ibid., 268.
31. **S.Novak**, *Halakha in a Theological Dimension*, Chico, Ca. 1985, esp. 116-31 has recently demonstrated how the halakhah must be understood in the logic of the covenant.
32. **Franz Rosenzweig**, the son of cultivated parents who sat loosely to Judaism, studied philosophy, history and classical philology, among other subjects, at various universities. At first he resolved on conversion to Christianity, but in 1913 he declared that from now on he understood himself as a Jew and wanted to rediscover Judaism for himself and others. After several studies on Christianity and Judaism and his two works on German Idealism, in 1921 his main work *The Star of Redemption* appeared. This was an attempt at a 'new thought', a demand for a philosophical theology of Judaism and

Christianity. After the First World War, with the help of Jewish intellectuals (including M.Buber, E.Strauss and E.Fromm) he organized the 'Free Jewish House of Learning'. After 1922, when he was in fact paralysed, speechless and confined to his house, he composed numerous translations from Hebrew into German of liturgical songs, hymns and poems, and from 1924, in collaboration with Martin Buber, also the Bible. Cf. the article by **S.S.Schwarzschild** in *Encyclopaedia Judaica*. For the translation of the Bible cf. **F.Rosenzweig**, 'Sprachdenken. Arbeitspapiere zur Verdeutschung der Schrift', in **id.**, *Gesammelte Schriften* IV.2, Dordrecht 1984.

33. Cf. **F.Rosenzweig**, *The Star of Redemption* (1921), New York 1930, reissued Boston 1971.

34. **Rosenzweig** responded **to Buber**'s *Reden über das Judentum*, Frankfurt 1923, with the article 'Die Bauleute. Über das Gesetz. An Martin Buber' (1923), in *Kleinere Schriften*, Berlin 1937, 106-21.

35. Buber evidently did not want to respond to Rosenzweig's article 'Die Bauleute', but there is a conversation on the law in the correspondence. Cf. **F.Rosenzweig**, 'Briefe und Tagebücher', in **id.**, *Gesammelte Schriften*, I, Dordrecht 1979. The details of this are brought out by **G.Bonola**, 'Franz Rosenzweig und Martin Buber. Die Auseinandersetzung über das Gesetz', in W.Schmied-Kowarzik (ed.), *Der Philosoph Franz Rosenzweig (1886-1929). Internationaler Kongress, Kassel 1986*, Vol.I, Freiburg 1988, 225-28.

36. Gal.4.4f.

B.III For the Sake of Human Beings

1. Cf. Part Two, B.II.

2. Matt.5.19.

3. The Jewish-Christian Matthew, who writes very good Greek, evidently attached his Gospel far more decidedly to the law than the Gospel of Mark (Gentile-Christian and also written in Greek). However, precisely by doing this he wrote very polemically against the rabbinic Judaism which was reforming after the catastrophe of the year 70. Certainly no new Moses appears in the Gospel of Matthew to command obedience, but there is a revealer of the Father who issues an invitation to take up the easy burden of his teaching (Matt.11.25-30). In principle he sets love above the Jewish ceremonial law. This disciple, too, 'was a follower of Jesus in his understanding of the law and not a Pharisee': 'Although for him the ritual law and the commandment of circumcision were valid, the weight did not lie here. In my view the distinction between the *barytera tou nomou* (the most important things in the law), i.e. the commandment to love, the Decalogue, the moral law (Matt.23.23) and the more peripheral ceremonial laws, including the commandments about purity, the sabbath and circumcision, explain why it could be possible for later followers of Matthew to dispense with these for the Gentiles.'U.**Luz**, *Das Evangelium nach Matthäus*, I, Zurich 1985, 68.

4. Matt.5.20.

5. Mark 12.34.

6. For Matt.5.21-48, in addition to the commentary by U.Luz, cf. also that by **J.Gnilka**, *Das Matthäusevangelium*, Vol.I, Freiburg 1986.

7. Love of neighbour is already mentioned in Lev.19.18, among all kinds of religious and moral precepts.
8. Mekilta de Rabbi Ishmael, tractate Shabbat I, 26,43.
9. Mark 2.27.
10. J.Gnilka, *Das Evangelium nach Markus*, Zurich 1978, 123.
11. Mark 3.4.
12. Matt.12.12.
13. Cf. Luke 10.25-27.
14. Mark 12.34.
15. Cf. Deut. 10.18f.
16. Phil.3.6.
17. S.Ben-Chorin, *Paulus. Der Völkerapostel in jüdischer Sicht*, Munich 1980, 11. Contrary to Ben-Chorin's view, Luther himself also experienced this suffering under the law (of the church) and with him so did some Catholic monks, priests and laity.
18. Ibid., 57. In contrast to the Jew Ben-Chorin, the non-Jew E.P.Sanders, *Paul*, Oxford 1991, shows little sensitivity to this problem, which is fundamental to the Pauline understanding of the law; he describes the problems discussed in Rom.7 as those of a 'neurotic' (98).
19. Cf. H.Hübner, *Das Gesetz bei Paulus. Ein Beitrag zum Werden der paulinischen Theologie*, Göttingen 1978, ³1982, 115f.: 'Freedom from the perverted law', etc.
20. For the letter to the Romans: there is a comprehensive survey of the literature in J.D.G.Dunn, 'Paul's Epistle to the Romans. An Analysis of Structure and Argument', in *Aufstieg und Niedergang der Römischen Welt*, ed. H.Temporini and W.Haase, II, 25.4, Berlin 1987, 2842-90. More recent commentaries: E.Käsemann (HNT, 1973), Grand Rapids and London ²1982; C.E.B.Cranfield, 1975/79 (International Critical Commentary); H.Schlier, 1977 (HTK); U.Wilckens (3 vols.), 1978-82 (EKK); J.D.G.Dunn (2 vols.), 1988 (WBC); W.Schmithals, Gütersloh 1988; P.Stuhlmacher, 1989 (NTD). More recent works: G.Bornkamm, 'Der Römerbrief als Testament des Paulus', in id., *Glaube und Geschichte* II (Gesammelte Aufsätze 4), Munich 1971, 120-39: W.G.Kümmel, *Römer 7 und das Bild des Menschen im NT. Zwei Studien*, Munich 1974; U.Wilckens, 'Über Abfassungszweck und Aufbau des Römerbriefs', in id., *Rechtfertigung als Freiheit*, Neukirchen 1974, 110-70; W.Schmithals, *Der Römerbrief als historisches Problem*, Gütersloh 1975; H.Moxnes, *Theology in Conflict. Studies in Paul's Understanding of God in Romans*, Leiden 1980; F.Mussner, 'Heil für Alle. Der Grundgedanke des Römerbriefs', *Kairos* 23, 1981, 207-14.
21. For the letter to the Galatians: there is a comprehensive survey of the literature in K.H.Schelkle, *Paulus. Leben – Briefe – Theologie*, Darmstadt 1981, 80f. More recent commentaries: H.Schlier (1949), 5th edition of the revision, 1971 (KEK); F.Mussner, 1977 (HTK); D.Lührmann, Zurich 1978; H.D.Betz, Philadelphia 1979 (Hermeneia); U.Borse, Regensburg 1984; J.Becker, 1985 (NTD); W.Egger, Würzburg 1985.
More recent works: J.Eckert, *Die urchristliche Verkündigung im Streit zwischen Paulus und seinen Gegnern nach dem Galaterbrief*, Regensburg 1971; G.Howard, *Crisis in Galatia. A Study in Early Christian Theology*, Cambridge 1979; H.Feld, 'Christus Diener der Sünde. Zum Ausgang des Streits zwischen Petrus und Paulus', *TQ* 153, 1983, 119-31; A.Suhl, 'Der

Galaterbrief – Situation und Argumentation', in *Aufstieg und Niedergang der Römischen Welt*, II 25.4, 3067-134; **J.D.G.Dunn**, *Jesus, Paul and the Law. Studies in Mark and Galatians*, London 1990.

22. **H.Hübner**, review of E.P.Sanders, in *Studien zum Neuen Testament und seiner Umwelt* 11, 1986, 241.

23. There is hardly a book on Paul which does not contain a section on Paul and the law, and which does not tackle the contrast between the polemical Galatians and the later more balanced Romans (cf. the literature on Pauline scholarship in Part Two, B. V, and **G.Klein**, 'Gesetz: Neues Testament', in *TRE*). Paul's theology is not of course a single edifice. But alleged or real discrepancies and contradictions in the different letters of Paul, all of which were written from different situations to different recipients at different times, cannot disguise the intrinsic unity of his theology (and possibly his theological development). Unfortunately **H.Räisänen**, *Paul and the Law*, Tübingen 1983, ²1987, argues to the contrary. Even in the preface to the second edition Räisänen expresses the view that for Paul the main and intractable problem was that 'a **divine** institution has been **abolished** through what God has done in Christ' (xxiv, cf. the first edition, 264f.). But precisely this is not the case, as we shall see. On the other hand even Räisänen must concede that Paul himself felt that his teaching ' "really fulfils" or "upholds" the law' (254). A fair interpretation will attempt to understand any author on the basis of his central convictions instead of imputing to him contradictions which the interpreter has in part created himself. Cf. also **H.Hübner**'s criticism of Räisänen, *Theologische Literaturzeitung* 110, 1985, cols. 894-6.

24. Thus **E.P.Sanders**, *Paul and Palestinian Judaism. A Comparison of Patterns of Religion*, London 1977; id., *Paul, the Law and the Jewish People*, Philadelphia 1983 and London 1987; id., *Paul*, Oxford 1991.

25. In his publications, **E.P.Sanders** has rightly and clearly emphasized the Christ-experience as the existential starting point for the theology of the apostle Paul (in contrast to a theological systematic account which begins with human fallenness). However, this experience of Christ may not become a 'meteor-from-heaven' interpretation of the conversion of Paul, an objection rightly made by **J.C.Beker**, 'The New Testament View of Judaism', in J.H.Charlesworth (ed.), *Jews and Christians. Exploring the Past, Present and Future*, New York 1990, 72. Cf. id., *Paul the Apostle. The Triumph of God in Life and Thought*, Philadelphia and Edinburgh 1980, esp. ch.11. We need to remember that: 1. like any pious person, of course Saul, the blameless Pharisee and zealot for the law, would be able to have his own often ambivalent experiences of the law. 2. Saul the persecutor of Christians might have known why he persecuted Christians: to the zealot for the law, the criticism of the law stemming from the Jewish Christians (probably above all the Hellenistic Jewish Christians) and reflecting Jesus' criticism of the law must have been a scandal. So there is a continuity of substance between Jesus, the earliest community and Paul, even if there is no direct continuity of tradition.

26. Cf. Gal.1.15f. and in most detail from the Jewish side **A.F.Segal**, *Paul the Convert. The Apostolate and Apostasy of Paul the Pharisee*, New Haven 1990, chs. 1-3 and appendix.

27. Cf. **A.J.M.Wedderburn** (ed.), *Paul and Jesus. Collected Essays*, Sheffield 1989, especially also the contributions by C.Wolff. **K.-J.Kuschel**, *Geboren vor aller Zeit? Der Streit um Christi Ursprung*, Munich 1990, 340-96 (ET in

preparation, *Born Before All Time?*, London and New York 1992), shows that there is no pre-existence christology in Paul.

28. Rom.7.12; Sanders, *Paul*, 1991, 92-5, differs.

29. Rom.7.10; cf. 10.5; Gal.3.12.

30. Rom.2.20.

31. Rom.7.14.

32. Rom.9.4.

33. E.P.Sanders has rightly rejected the frequent Christian charge against Judaism 'that **Judaism necessarily tends** towards petty legalism, self-serving and self-deceiving casuistry, and a mixture of arrogance and lack of confidence in God' (*Paul and Palestinian Judaism*, n.24, 427). Cf.similarly F.Mussner, *Die Kraft der Wurzel. Judentum – Jesus – Kirche*, Freiburg 1987, 13-26. However, Sanders should take equally seriously the fact that 'some individual Jews misunderstood, misapplied and abused their religion' (ibid.). That means that there were sufficient grounds in the life of Jews at the time as they lived it for the criticism of their piety by Jesus and the apostle Paul. To this degree the passages critical of piety in the Gospels and the letters of Paul may not be eliminated hermeneutically or conjured away by interpretation. Who would want to judge, say, late mediaeval Christianity simply by its theological texts (which speak against a righteousness by works) while neglecting the criticism made by Luther and the Reformation?

34. Cf. Rom.2.1-3.20; 13.8-10; Gal.5.14.

35. Cf. Rom.2.14f.

36. Cf. Rom.2.11.

37. Rom.2.6; I Cor.3.12-15.

38. Rom.2.13; cf. the commentary by P.Stuhlmacher, 1989: Excursus V: 'Das Endgericht nach den Werken', 44-6.

39. Rom.3.27. G.Friedrich, 'Das Gesetz des Glaubens', *Theologische Zeitschrift* 10, 1954, 401-17, was the first to interpret 'law' (*nomos*) in Rom.3.27 as the Mosaic Torah. Similarly for Rom.8.2, E.Lohse, '*Ho nomos tou pneumatos tes zoes*. Exegetische Anmerkungen zu Röm 8,2' (1973), in id., *Die Vielfalt des Neuen Testaments*, Göttingen 1982, 128-36. He is followed by P.von der Osten-Sacken, *Römer 8 als Beispiel paulinischer Soteriologie*, Göttingen 1975; C.E.B.Cranfield, *The Epistle to the Romans* I, Edinburgh 1975, 375f.; F.Hahn, 'Das Gesetzesverständnis im Römer- und Galaterbrief', *Zeitschrift für die neutestamentliche Wissenschaft* 67, 1976, 29-63, esp.47-51; H.Hübner, *Das Gesetz bei Paulus* (n.19); U.Wilckens, *Der Brief an die Römer*, II, 122f.

40. Cf. Rom.3.31.

41. I Cor.7.19.

42. Whereas among more recent authors H.Räisänen and E.P.Sanders simply set the negative and positive understandings of the law side by side, as though they expressed above all the unresolved conflict in the person and theology of the apostle Paul, P.von der Osten-Sacken, *Der Heiligkeit der Tora. Studien zum Gesetz bei Paulus*, Munich 1989, esp.9-59, rightly argues for a dialectical view of the Pauline understanding of the law, which sees *nomos* coherently as the Mosaic Torah. I go on to summarize this view briefly here. Cf. already at an earlier date id., *Grundzüge einer Theologie in christlich-jüdischem Gespräch*, Munich 1982; id., *Evangelium und Torah. Aufsätze zu Paulus*, Munich 1987. An overall intention to interpret Paul more in connection

with Judaism than in opposition to it can also be found in **L.Gaston,** *Paul and the Torah,* Vancouver 1987.

43. Rom.7.7; cf. 7.8-13.
44. Cf. Gal.3.22-24.
45. Cf. Rom.3.20; 4.15; 5.20.
46. Cf. Rom.4.
47. Rom.3.21; cf. 1.17.
48. Rom.10.4.
49. Cf. Gal.3.13.
50. Rom.3.27.
51. Rom.8.2.
52. Thus, against H.Räisänen and E.P.Sanders, **P.von der Osten-Sacken** and others, e.g. **R.Bring,** *Christus und das Gesetz. Die Bedeutung des Gesetzes des Alten Testaments nach Paulus und sein Glauben an Christus,* Leiden 1969; **M.Barth,** 'Das Volk Gottes. Juden und Christen in der Botschaft des Paulus', in **M.Barth** et al., *Paulus – Apostat oder Apostel? Jüdische und christliche Antworten,* Regensburg 1977, 45-134; **C.E.B.Cranfield,** *The Epistle to the Romans,* Vol.II, 515-20. Recently this interpetation has been confirmed by the monograph by **R.Bardenas,** *Christ the End of the Law. Romans 10.4 in Pauline Perspective,* Sheffield 1985 (which works through the whole history of interpretation and all the biblical and extra-biblical word-field of *telos*), esp.38ff., 150: 'its fulfilled *telos*'.
53. I Cor.7.19.
54. Rom.3.20; cf. Gal.3.10.
55. II Cor.3.7,9.
56. II Cor.3.6.
57. Gal.5.1.
58. Gal.5.13.
59. Gal.2.4.
60. Rom.6.14; cf. 7.5f.
61. Cf. von der Osten-Sacken, *Heiligkeit der Torah* (n.42), 48.
62. Following several Christian exegetes like M.Barth, J.G.Gager and J.D.G.Dunn, the Jewish scholar **A.F.Segal** in particular has stressed that here according to the context Paul is speaking of the particular ritual ('ceremonial') commands of the Torah (halakhah): 'Although "works of the law" is a direct translation of the Hebrew *ma'asei hatora,* Paul is not referring to Torah but to the **observance** of Jewish ceremonial practices. "Works of the law" means the ceremonial Torah, those special ordinances that separate Jews from Gentiles' (*Paul the Convert,* n.26, 124). In all these passages Paul would not be theologizing, as many New Testament scholars have thought, but 'talking about the proper role of Jewish observances in the Christian community' (food laws, feast days, purity and circumcision).
63. Cf. II Cor.3.6.
64. Against L.Gaston, J.G.Gager and K.Stendahl, **A.F.Segal** rightly remarks that Paul not only wants to open up the way to salvation for Gentiles through belief without the Jewish ritual commandments but in addition is challenging the view that Jews can attain salvation through observing the law. According to Segal, 'the idea of two separate paths – salvation for Gentiles in Christianity and for the Jews in Torah – does not gain much support from Paul's writings' (cf. 130). But does Segal sufficiently reflect on the third completely Pauline

option: that of the Jewish Christians, who also according to Paul can combine
their belief in Jesus Christ with observance of the Law – if they fulfil it in the
spirit of Jesus Christ, in the spirit of freedom and love?
  65. Cf. I. Cor.7.19; Gal.6.15; Rom.4.
  66. Cf. Rom.2.29; in Pauline tradition Col.2.11.
  67. Cf. Gal.4.10f: similarly Col.2.16f.
  68. Cf. Rom.14.1-6; Gal.2.
  69. Cf. I Kings 9.19-23; Gal.3.28.
  70. Cf Gal.2; Acts 15.1-34. The best analysis is given by Eckert, *Urchristliche
Verkündigung* (n.20). For the wider context cf. **W.A.Meeks and R.L.Wilken**,
*Jews and Christians in Antioch in the First Four Centuries of the Common
Era*, Missoula, Montana 1978.
  71. Cf. Gal.2.11.
  72. Cf. Gal.5.1.
  73. Cf. Mark 7.8; 7.4.
  74. Cf. Mark 7.1-23.
  75. Gal.5.13.
  76. Rom.12.2; cf. Phil.1.10.
  77. I Cor.6.12.
  78. Ibid.
  79. Rom.14.14; cf. Titus 1.15, 'To the pure, everything is pure.'
  80. I Cor.6.12.
  81. I Cor.10.23f.
  82. I Cor.9.19.
  83. I Cor.8.9.
  84. Cf. I Cor.9.19; Gal.5.13.
  85. I Cor.7.23.
  86. I Cor.10.29.
  87. Cf. I Cor.8.7-12; 10.25-30.
  88. Cf. Gal.5.6.
  89. The Jewish historian of religion **H.-J.Schoeps** has made it clear that the
understanding of the law in Paul could also be accepted within Judaism in this
sense, cf. *Paul. The Theology of the Apostle in the Light of Jewish Religious
History*, London 1961, esp. 280ff. Schoeps also recognizes the apostle's
criticism of the law as a 'problem within Judaism': 'If the law seems not to be
capable of fulfilment here and now as a whole, does that not perhaps indicate
that the will of God is not completely exhausted in the law? Can fulfilment of
the law of Moses be made to agree without contradiction with pursuit of the
divine will?' (280). In this sense, according to Schoeps, Paul raised 'a decisive
question' for which 'the tradition is in his debt' (281). Indeed, for Schoeps
there is 'a mission of the Rabbi Saul within Judaism which has not yet been
carried out today' (285).
  90. Gal.5.13f.
  91. Rom.13.8-10.
  92. Gal. 6.2.

B.IV The Future of the People of God

1. Rom.3.3.
2. Cf. Ex.4.22.
3. Cf. Rom.9.3.
4. Cf. Rom.9.4f. F.Mussner has convincingly summed up the 'great heritage of Israel's faith' from a present-day perspective: *Tractate on the Jews*, Philadelphia 1984, 52-108. He stresses the following elements: monotheism, the idea of creation, humanity, the 'image of God', fundamental attitudes before God, the covenant, the messianic idea, the discovery of the future, the yearning for a just world, atonement and representation, conscience and the Decalogue, remembrance, the sabbath, the raising of the dead.
5. Cf. Rom.9.2.
6. Rom.9.6.
7. Cf. E.Klein, 'Making the Jewish Voice Heard', *The Times*, 9 April 1991.
8. I Cor.11.25; cf. II Cor.3.6 ('servants of the new covenant'); Gal.4.21-31 (two sons).
9. Jer.31.31f.
10. There is a good survey of the various covenant theologies (one covenant or several?) in the article by J.T.Pawlikowski, 'Judentum und Christentum', *Theologische Realenzykopädie* 17, 390-403. On the basis of the authentic letters of Paul there is no avoiding talk of **a saving plan** of God which encompasses Israel and the church, but at the same time without falling into the fatal mistake of the traditional substitutionary model of **two covenants**, an old covenant and a new covenant.
11. Cf. Rom.11.2-10.
12. Rom. 9.6.
13. Cf. Rom.9.8-13.
14. Cf. Rom.9.14-29.
15. Cf. Rom.9.22-26.
16. Rom.11.17f.
17. Rom.11.26.
18. Cf. Rom.11.25f.
19. Cf. M.Löhrer, 'Gottes Gnadenhandeln als Erwählung des Menschen', in *Mysterium Salutis. Grundriss heilsgeschichtlicher Dogmatik*, ed. J.Feiner and M.Löhrer, IV.2, Zurich 1973, 818-25. Similarly the commentaries on Romans by Käsemann, 313f.; Schlier, 340; Wilckens, II, 263-8; Stuhlmacher, 154-7.
20. Rom.11.26f.
21. Cf.also the controversy over F.Mussner's thesis of the 'special way of Israel' in redemption with reference e.g. to the study by M.Theobald, *Überfliessende Gnade*, 1982, in F.Mussner, *Die Kraft der Wurzel*, 48-54. Cf. Mussner, *Tractate on the Jews* (n.4), 53-5. Theobald has developed the results of his study with reference to Israel and reflected on it hermeneutically in his article 'Kirche und Israel nach Römer 9-11', *Kairos* 29, 1987, 1-22.
22. Rom.11.32.
23. Rom.11.33-35.
24. Rom.11.36.

25. Cf. Rom.4.20.

26. Cf. Rom.11.11,14: '*parazeloun*'.

27. Rom.11.11.

28. **French Conference of Bishops**, 'The Attitude of Christians to Judaism. Pastoral Guidelines', 16 April 1973, German text in R.Rendtorff and H.H.Henrix (eds.), *Die Kirchen und das Judentum. Dokumente von 1945 bis 1985*, Paderborn 1988, 149-56: 155f.

29. **S.Ben-Chorin**, *Paulus. Der Völkerapostel in jüdischer Sicht*, Munich 1980, 142.

30. Ex.20.9f. For the **sabbath** generally cf 'Sabbath', in *Encyclopaedia Judaica*: in the Bible (**M.Greenberg**), in the apocrypha and rabbinic literature, Jewish philosophy and legislation (**L.Jacobs**), in the Kabbala (**E.Gottlieb**) and in art (**A.Kanof**).

31. Cf. **L.Fleischmann**, 'Lob des Schabbat. Ein Tag für die Natur', *Die Zeit*, 6 April 1990: the sabbath as 'the day of reflection, the day of the Lord, the day of the family'. For the 'battle for the sabbath in Israel' cf. **T.Segev**, *The First Israelis*, New York 1986, ch.8.

32. Cf. **W.Rordorf**, *Sunday. The History of the Day of Rest and Worship in the Earliest Centuries of the Christian Church* (1962), London and Philadelphia 1968: Rordorf's work is rightly divided into Part One, The Day of Rest (the sabbath problem and Sunday as a day of rest); Part Two, The Day of Worship (origin, oldest forms and names for Sunday). Cf. also the lexicon articles on Sunday or Sunday rest in *Lexikon für Theologie und Kirche* (**L.Koep, A.Stiegler**), *Die Religion in Geschichte und Gegenwart* (**E.Hertzsch, H.W.Surkau**). Interestingly, while there are long articles in the *Encyclopedia of Religion* on 'Sun' and 'Sun Dance', there is not one on 'Sunday'.

33. Matt.28.1; Mark 16.2.

34. Acts 1.10.

35. Cf. I Cor.16.2; Acts 20.7.

36. Cf. *Apostolic Constitutions* VIII, 33, in *Didascalia et Constitutiones Apostolorum*, ed.F.X.Funk, Vol.I, Paderborn 1905, 539.

37. Cf. **W.Rordorf**, *Sabbat und Sonntag in der Alten Kirche*, Zurich 1972. This volume contains all the important texts of the Greek and Latin fathers on the Sabbath and Sunday, with a German translation.

38. **J.Blank**, 'Den Sonntag verkaufen?', in *Zur Debatte*, November/ December 1989, 9.

39. The 'Joint Statement of the German Episcopal Conference and the Council of the Evangelical Church in Germany', made on the First Sunday in Advent, 1984, is typical of the mediaeval and unworldly attitude of the present Catholic church government and of ecumenical stagnation. It attempts to prevent as far as possible not only the eucharistic fellowship already long practised by many Christians but also ecumenical services on Sunday. One gets the impression that it is better to have even fewer churchgoers.

C. Jews, Muslims and the Future of the State of Israel

C.I The Great Ideal

1. T.Herzl, *The Jewish State* (1896), London 1946, 27.
2. Cf. H.R.Greenstein, *Judaism – An Eternal Covenant*, Philadelphia 1983, who investigates the covenant and its elements in Reform, Conservative, Orthodox and 'Reconstructionist' Judaism.
3. Cf. the **Commission for Religious Relations with Judaism**, 'Guidelines for a Correct Presentation of Jews and Judaism in the Preaching and the Catechesis of the Catholic Church', 24 June 1985, Art.25, German text in R.Rendtorff and H.H.Henrix (eds.), *Die Kirchen und das Judentum. Dokumente von 1945 bis 1985*, Paderborn 1988, 102. Given the well-known position of the Vatican, it is not surprising that many Roman Catholic documents either do not mention the state of Israel at all, or if they do, it is only briefly and then from a purely political perspective. It is again the statement by the **French Conference of Bishops**, 'The Attitude of Christians to Judaism. Pastoral Guidelines', 16 April 1973, ch. V, which goes furthest: it not only stresses the right of the state of Israel to exist ('the conscience of the world cannot forbid the Jewish people... the right and the means to a political existence among the peoples'), but also takes account of its religious self-understanding ('Christians... must take note of the interpretation which the Jews themselves give of their gathering around Jerusalem') (German text in ibid., 154).
4. E.g. J.Peters, *From Time Immemorial. The Origins of the Arab-Jewish Conflict over Palestine*, New York 1984, esp chs.7-8.
5. The figures come from **Yehoshua Porath**, an Israeli historiographer of the Palestinian Arabs.
6. **Council of the Evangelical Church of Germany**, study on 'Christians and Jews', May 1975, Art.III.3, German text in Rendtorff and Henrix (eds.), *Die Kirchen und das Judentum* (n.3), 573.
7. **Herzl**, *The Jewish State* (n.1), 71.
8. For the **halakhah** cf. **G.Horowitz**, *The Spirit of Jewish Law. A Brief Account of Biblical and Rabbinical Jurisprudence with a Special Note on Jewish Law and the State of Israel*, New York 1963. For **law** in Israel cf. **A.Bin-Nun**, *Einführung in das Recht des Staates Israel*, Darmstadt 1983.
9. **D.Hartman**, *Conflicting Visions*, New York 1990, 258f.
10. Cf. **B.Avishai**, *The Tragedy of Zionism. Revolution and Democracy in the Land of Israel*, New York 1985.
11. The American rabbi **M.N.Kertzer**, *What is a Jew?* (1953), New York [4]1978, replies to all the practical questions relating to being a Jew.

C.II The Tragic Conflict

1. Cf. *International Herald Tribune*, 30 April 1991.
2. Until the last, I hoped that the negotiations of Secretary of State James

Baker would produce some concrete results and that I would be able to delete some paragraphs in this chapter 'The Tragic Conflict' as now being without foundation. But this kind of secret shuttle diplomacy has again come to grief – as it did earlier under Secretary of State George Schultz. Arab resistance could have been overcome had the Israeli government declared itself ready to exchange land for peace. So attention must be drawn all the more clearly to the disastrous effects of present Isaraeli policy (cf. also the Epilogue).

3. Cf. **J.Parkes**, *Whose Land? A History of Palestine*, Harmondsworth ²1970.

4. There is a good survey of the conflicts in the Near East since the First World War in **F.Schreiber and M.Wolffsohn**, *Nahost. Geschichte und Struktur des Konflikts*, Opladen 1987.

5. Cf. the careful and differentiated analysis by **B.Morris**, *The Birth of the Palestine Refugee Problem, 1948-1949*, Cambridge 1987. It concludes: 'The Palestinian refugee problem was born of war, not by design, Jewish or Arab. It was largely a by-product of Arab and Jewish fears and of the protracted, bitter fighting that characterised the first Israel-Arab war; in smaller part, it was the deliberate creation of Jewish and Arab military commanders and politicians' (286). But at the same time the conclusions of the investigations by **S.Flapan** in *The Birth of Israel*, reported in Part Two above (A. III), must be noted.

6. **Y.Leibowitz** (with M.Shashar), *Al olam umlo'oh*, Jerusalem 1987; German: *Gespräche über Gott und die Welt*, Frankfurt 1990, 11.

7. Ibid., 10f.

8. This is also confirmed by the historian **H.S.Sachar**, *A History of Israel*, II, *From the Aftermath of the Yom Kippur War*, New York 1987.

9. **Leibowitz**, *Gespräche mit Gott* (n.6), 15.

10. Cf. **G.Meir**, *My Life*, London 1975.

11. **Leibowitz**, *Gespräche mit Gott* (n.6), 16.

12. Ibid., 11f.

13. Ibid., 11.

14. Ibid., 13.

15. Ibid.

16. For the different attitudes among the population and for Cohen's view cf. the instructive report by **P.Rosenkranz**, 'Zum Teufel mit den Arabern – oder mit den besetzten Gebieten', in *Vaterland* (Lucerne), 21 April 1990, from which the following quotations are taken.

17. Cf. **M.H.Ellis**, *Toward a Jewish Theology of Liberation. The Uprising and the Future*, Maryknoll and London 1988, Maryknoll ²1989, 133f.

18. Cf. **P.Levy**, *Die jüdische Mitte – politische Aspekte*, lecture in Zurich, 1 March 1990 (manuscript).

19. **M.Wolffsohn**, *Israel. Grundwissen – Länderkunde. Politik – Gesellschaft – Wirtschaft*, Opladen, ²1987, 28.

20. Ibid., 29f.

21. Ibid., 24.

22. On the occasion of Kahane's murder **R.I.Friedman**, author of the book *The False Prophet: Rabbi Meir Kahane, From FBI Informant to Knesset Member*, wrote: 'Kahaneism – the hatred of Arabs, liberal Jews and Western culture – has had anything but a limited impact in Israel. Indeed, some of Mr Kahane's ideas have taken root and have become respectable... No cult is likely

to develop around Mr Kahane now... But the rabbi will leave behind a legacy of hatred and violence that will trouble Israelis and American Jews for some time.' Id., 'Kahane's Message of Hatred and Violence Will Fade', *International Herald Tribune*, 8 November 1990.

23. Particular mention should be made here of the Israeli Committee for Human Rights under Professor **Israel Shahak** of Jerusalem.

24. Cf. the report on the occupied Arab territories by Amnesty International, London 1990; also the report by Middle East Watch, in *International Herald Tribune*, 1 August 1990. By contrast the pernickity interrogation of those flying to Tel Aviv airport, of a kind that one did not use to experience even in the Communist states, is harmless – and useless.

25. Cf. **D.Grossmann**, *The Yellow Wind*, New York 1988.

26. Cf. **Y.Harkabi**, *The Bar Kokhba Syndrome. Risk and Realism in International Politics*, Chappaqua, NY 1983.

27. Id., *Israel's Fateful Decisions*, London 1988.

28. Cf. **A.Rubinstein**, *The Zionist Dream Revisited. From Herzl to Gush Emunim and Back*, New York 1984.

29. Cf. **B.Beit-Hallahmi**, *The Israel Connection. Who Israel Arms and Why*, New York 1987.

30. **A.Eban**, 'Talking to the PLO Doesn't Mean Approval', *International Herald Tribune*, 25 July 1989.

31. Information from Israel's Central Bureau of Statistics, *New York Times*, 19 October 1987.

32. Figures from *Aktuell '91. Das Lexikon der Gegenwart*, Dortmund 1990, 475.

33. Reported by **Rosenkranz**, 'Zum Teufel mit den Araben' (n.16).

34. Cf. **A.Flores**, *Intifada. Aufstand der Palästinenser*, Berlin 1988, ^{2}1989.

35. For important information on the latest situation I am indebted to **Felicia Langer**, a Jewish patriot who since 1967 as an advocate has constantly been defending Palestinians before Israeli courts. However, when she felt threatened and could no longer be of any use, she closed her office in Jerusalem and retreated to Tübingen to continue her work of explanation. In 1990 she was given the Alternative Nobel Prize for her works for human rights. She wrote *An Age of Stone*, London 1988, on her experiences from 1979 to 1988. The German-born Israeli journalist **U.Avnery**, *My Friend, the Enemy*, London 1986, gives an account of the dialogue between Israelis concerned for peace and PLO representatives.

36. Cf. *International Herald Tribune*, 24 October 1990.

37. One can hardly be surprised at the numerous and rarely reported excesses of violence against Palestinians if a few days after the event one personally seen the bloodstains and bullet holes from wild shooting on the Temple Court, and even inside the mosque on the Temple Mount, and a few months earlier – immediately before the murder of seven Palestinians in Tel Aviv by an allegedly mentally-disturbed Israeli – has heard from the commander of a tank unit that all Palestinians are 'monkeys', not human beings (Begin spoke of the PLO as 'two-legged animals'). Nor is it at all amazing that following the one-sided massacre on the Temple Mount in Jerusalem there was hardly a word of apology from Israeli Prime Minister Shamir; instead, there was repeatedly coarse rejection of a committee of enquiry into Jerusalem which had been resolved on unanimously by the UN Security Council, and a snubbing of the

United States, Israel's closest ally. Will not such a manifest lack of feeling towards the suffering and grief of others and a policy which is deaf to all claims to reason, which does not impress Israel's enemies and perplexes Israel's friends, do even more damage to the state of Israel?

38. **M.Sharett**, *Diaries*, 31 March 1955, 840, quoted in S.Flapan, *The Birth of Israel*, New York 1987.

39. Cf. *International Herald Tribune*, 6/7 April 1991.

40. Cf. **I.W.Charny**, *How Can We Commit the Unthinkable? Genocide: The Human Cancer*, Boulder, Co 1982; **id.** (ed.), *Toward the Understanding and Prevention of Genocide. Proceedings of the International Conference on the Holocaust and Genocide, Tel Aviv 1982*, Boulder, Co 1984.

41. **Ellis**, *Toward a Jewish Theology of Liberation* (n.17), 132, 134, and preface to the second edition.

42. **Leibowitz**, *Gespräche mit Gott* (n.6), 21f.

43. Ibid., 22.

C.III On the Way to Peace

1. **F.Husseini** and **Y.Dayan**, 'The Mideast Moderates Must Make a Stand', *International Herald Tribune*, 23/24 June 1990.

2. Cf. **E.Tivnan**, *The Lobby. Jewish Political Power and American Foreign Policy*, New York 1987: 'The lobby is powerful enough to engender fear among dissenters in the uppermost levels of American government and the American Jewish community' (12). The conclusion of this extremely informative book is: 'In American domestic political terms, AIPAC had become a symbol of the final arrival of the Jews as Americans. They had quickly suceeded in business, banking, and the arts, and now politics. US representatives and senators feared and cultivated "Jewish muscle"; few ambitious American politicians could even dream of higher office without the prospect of Jewish money. And thus AIPAC's policies affected the politics of America, and the policy of the US government. AIPAC's role was not only impressive, it was phenomenal' (242).

3. Quoted ibid., 251f.

4. The former Israeli Foreign Minister **Abba Eban** refers to these figures from the Research Centre for Strategic Studies in Tel Aviv and to the improbability of a renewed military attack by the other Arab powers on behalf of the PLO, and therefore sees Israel as strong enough for dialogue: 'The friends of Israel should be careful not to build up a false myth of Israeli weakness. Israel must now struggle towards accepting UN Resolution 242 and the principle of "territory in exchange for peace". And Israel is strong enough to take this step.' **A.Eban**, 'Stark genug zum Dialog. Israel sollte das Umdenken der PLO begrüssen', *Die Zeit*, 20 January 1989.

5. This also does not exclude a 'greater regional and inter-regional co-operation', as say by Jordan in the framework of the Arab Cooperation Council (ACC: Jordan, Egypt, Iraq and North Yemen). Cf. **Crown Prince Hassan**, 'From Jordan. A New Bid to Free the Dove', *International Herald Tribune*, 28/29 April 1990.

6. Gen.14.18.

7. Deut.1.7f.

8. Deut.11.24.
9. Cf. Ps.72.8.
10. Cf. Num.34.3-15; Ezek. 47.15-20.
11. J.J.Petuchowski, 'Drei Stadien im christlich-jüdischen Gespräch', *Orientierung* 49, 1985, 66.
12. T.Herzl, *The Jewish State* (1896), London 1946, 71.
13. Cf. the discussion between **H.Bookbinder**, the long-time representative of the American Jewish Committee in Washington, and **J.G.Abourezk**, the founder of the American-Arab Anti-Discrimination Committee: *Through Different Eyes. Two Leading Americans – a Jew and an Arab – Debate US Policy in the Middle East*, Bethesda, Maryland 1987.
14. The view of a Christian Palestinian, **N.S.Ateek**, *Justice, and only Justice. A Palestinian Theology of Liberation*, New York 1989, is very constructive. The book ends with the following words: 'The challenge to Palestinian Christians, and indeed to all Palestinians and to all people in this conflict in Israel-Palestine, is: do not destroy yourself with hate; maintain your inner freedom; insist on justice, work for it, and it shall be yours' (187). It was only after completing this manuscript that I became aware of another book on the Israeli-Palestinian conflict from a Christian theological perspective, **R.Radford Ruether** and **H.J.Ruether**, *The Wrath of Jonah. The Rise of Religious Nationalism in the Israeli-Palestinian Conflict*, San Francisco 1989.
15. **D.Hartman**, *Conflicting Visions*, New York 1990, 265.

C.IV A Real-Utopian Vision of Peace

1. Cf. Ps.34.15.
2. **Hans Mayer** of Tübingen, the German Jewish literary critic of Marxist provenance, felt himself challenged by a visiting semester in Jerusalem to begin on his autobiography: *Ein Deutscher auf Widerruf. Erinnerungen* (2 vols.), Frankfurt 1982/84.
3. **P.Scholl-Latour**, in id. (ed.), *Knaurs Weltspiegel '90. Die kompakte Information zum Zeitgeschehen*, Munich 1989, 30.
4. **J.Madaule**, *L'Universo dello Spirito. Gerusalemme. La città santa di tre religioni*, Milan 1981, 105 (with splendid photographs by the Japanese Y.Zenyoji); cf. **T.Kollek** and **M.Pearlman**, *Jerusalem. Sacred City of Mankind. A History of Forty Centuries*, London 1968; **A.Elon**, Jerusalem. City of Mirrors', Boston 1989.
5. **T.Kollek**, 'Wir haben die Araber vernachlässigt', *Die Zeit*, 2 November 1990.
6. Professor **Clemens Thoma** of Lucerne has drawn my attention to this aspect of the question.
7. Cf. Matt.5.5.
8. Cf. Matt.5.9.
9. In connection with the peace plan put forward by US Secretary of State James Baker, this solution was suggested on different occasions not only in Arab Jerusalem, but also in Europe and in the USA. Very much along these lines, **M.C.Hudson**, Professor of International Law and a member of the Centre of Contemporary Arabic Studies at Georgetown University, Washington DC,

and editor of a book announced under the title *The Palestinians: New Directions*, comments: 'Given the new flexibility being shown by the Palestine Liberation Organization and leading Palestinians in the occupied territories, as well as the creative thinking within Israeli public opinion, it should not be beyond the wit of the negotiators to find a formula whereby Jerusalem remains a unified municipality and the capital of both the Israeli and the Palestinian states', cf. **M.C.Hudson**, 'Jerusalem: Bush Returns the Spotlight to an Unsettled Issue', *International Herald Tribune*, 3 April 1990.

10. **M.Abul Hadi** and **B.Sabella** (Palestine Academic Society), *Jerusalem: Out of the Dark Tunnel*, 4f. Manuscript of 26 October 1990.

11. Based on the translation by **R.Paret**, *Der Koran*, surah 17.1, Stuttgart 1979, 196. English translations, e.g. **K.Cragg**, *Readings in the Qu'ran*, London 1988, 205, tend to translate, 'from the sacred mosque to the distant mosque'. In his commentary volume (Stuttgart 1971, ³1980), **Paret** makes it clear on his translation of the Qur'an on p.296 that 'the distant place of prayer (*al-masgid al-aqsa*)' means Jerusalem (or a place within Jerusalem). According to Muslim tradition the creation of mankind took place here, and the judgment will also take place here. There is no holier mountain in Islam than this mountain of Jerusalem.

12. Cf. **M.Rosen-Ayalon**, *The Early Islamic Monuments of Al-Haram Al-Sharif. An Iconographic Study*, Jerusalem 1989. The most recent attempt at an interpretation of the Dome of the Rock (*qubbat al-sakhra*) as 'tent' (Arabic *qubba*) over the throne of God on the rock has been put forward by **J.G.van Ess**, 'Abd al-Malik and the Dome of the Rock. An Analysis of Some Texts', in J.Raby (ed.), *'Abd al-Malik's Jerusalem*, Oxford (forthcoming: there is a copious bibliography at the end of the article).

13. Ibid., esp. 46-72.

14. The field of education is particularly important for the praxis of shared Jewish and Christian life. Cf. the special issue of *Journal of Ecumenical Studies*, 1984, 21.3, *Jews and Judaism in Christian Education*, edited by Professor **Leonard Swidler** (Temple University, Philadelphia). This journal regularly contains articles, reports and reviews on Jewish-Christian-Muslim dialogue. In addition to the literature on dialogue already mentioned, cf. also the following helpful books: **R.Pfisterer**, *Von A bis Z. Quellen zu Fragen um Juden und Christen*, Neukirchen 1971, new and enlarged edition 1985; **J.J.Petuchowski** (ed.), *Where Jews and Christians Meet*, New York 1988; **D.Novak**, *Jewish-Christian Dialogue. A Jewish Justification*, New York 1989; **M.Saperstein**, *Moments of Crisis in Jewish-Christian Relations*, London and Philadelphia 1989.

D. The Holocaust and the Future of Talk of God

D.I The Holocaust in Jewish Theology

1. For the **history** of the Holocaust cf. the literature in Part Two, A.I. For a **theological evaluation** cf. among many others **F.H.Littell**, *The Crucifixion of the Jews*, New York 1975 (it is to the credit of Professor Littell that he was one of the first Christian theologians to recognize the problems of the Holocaust

and to get them discussed widely by his extensive writing on the issue); I.J.Rosenbaum, *The Holocaust and Halakha*, New York 1976; J.T.Pawlikowski, *The Challenge of the Holocaust for Christian Theology*, New York 1978; A.J.Peck (ed.), *Jews and Christians after the Holocaust*, Philadelphia 1982; J.Kohn, *Haschoah. Christlich-jüdische Verständigung nach Auschwitz*, Munich 1986; G.B.Ginzel (ed.), *Auschwitz als Herausforderung für Juden und Christen*, Heidelberg 1980.

2. Cf. R.L.Rubenstein, *After Auschwitz. Radical Theology and Contemporary Judaism*, Indianapolis 1966. In a 1988 article Rubenstein concedes a change in his views: 'When I wrote *After Auschwitz* I stressed both the punitive and exclusivist aspects of the doctrine of covenant and election. Over the years I have come to appreciate the other side of the picture: humanity's profound need for something like the covenant or its functional equivalent'; id., 'Covenant and Holocaust', in Y.Bauer et al. (eds.), *Remembering the Future. Working Papers and Addenda*, Vol.I, Oxford 1989, 662-71: 666.

3. For the theodicy problem cf. H.Küng, OBC, ch.VI.2; id., DGE, ch.G.III.2.

4. To provide a definition of this monstrosity and to prevent any language which plays down the fact of the Holocaust, in an impressive plea the Jewish theologian A.A.Cohen has suggested the terms 'tremendum' and 'caesura': *The Tremendum. A Theological Interpretation of the Holocaust*, New York 1981.

5. For a survey of the discussion cf. M.Brocke and H.Jochum (eds.), *Wolkensäule und Feuerschein. Jüdische Theologie des Holocaust*, Munich 1982 (here in particular the contributions by I.Maybaum, I.Greenberg and M.Wyschograd); E.B.Borowitz, *Choices in Modern Jewish Thought. A Partisan Guide*, New York 1983, ch.9, and the issue of the international theological journal *Concilium* 175, 1984, *The Holocaust as Interruption*, ed. E.Schüssler Fiorenza and D.Tracy.

6. J.Neusner, 'Holocaust – Mythos und Identität', in Brocke and Jochum (eds.), *Wolkensäule und Feuerschein* (n.5), 195-212: 211.

7. M.Wyschogrod, quoted in ibid., 207f.

8. Cf. the indication of the dangers in M.Wolffsohn, *Ewige Schuld? 40 Jahre deutsch-jüdisch-Israeli Beziehungen*, Munich 1988, 65-71: 81.

9. Cf. E.L.Fackenheim, *To Mend the World. Foundations of Future Jewish Thought*, New York 1982. However, Fackenheim opposes not only R.Rubenstein but also E.Berkovitz (*With God in Hell*, New York 1979), for whom faith after the Holocaust, although deeply shaken, has not changed as a result (309). Cf. id., 'Holocaust', in *Contemporary Jewish Religious Thought*, 399-408.

10. E.L.Fackenheim, *God's Presence in History. Jewish Affirmations and Philosophical Reflections*, New York 1970, 84 (Fackenheim quotes this passage from an earlier article of his under the title 'Jewish Faith and the Holocaust', *Commentary*, 1967).

11. Cf. id., *What is Judaism? An Interpretation for the Present Age*, New York 1987.

12. Cf. F.Stern, *Dreams and Delusions. The Drama of German History*, New York 1987.

13. Cf. Rev.20.1-6.

14. T.Mann, 'Meine Zeit', in *Gesammelte Werke*, XI, Frankfurt 1960, 35.

15. Cf. F.Nietzsche, *The Gay Science*, III, 125.

16. For the problem of nihilism in Nietzsche cf. **H.Küng**, DGE, D.I.3, 'What is Nihilism?'; D.II 'Conquest of Nihilism'.

17. In his books *Die Revolution des Nihilismus. Kulisse und Wirklichkeit im Dritten Reich* (1938); *Gespräche mit Hitler* (1940), H.Rauschning, the Danzig National Socialist and President of the Danzig Senate, drew attention to Hitler's nihilism at a very early stage. However, he resigned in a conflict with the Gauleiter in 1934 and in 1936 emigrated to Switzerland; cf. **T.Schieder**, *Hermann Rauschnings 'Gespräche mit Hitler' als Geschichtsquelle*, Opladen 1972.

18. **M.Buber**, *Werke*, Vol.I, Munich 1962, 520.

19. **Borowitz**, *Choices in Modern Jewish Thought* (n.5), 215.

20. Cf. **I.Greenberg**, 'Religious Values After the Holocaust: A Jewish View', in Peck (ed.), *Jews and Christians after the Holocaust* (n.1), 63-86.

21. Ibid., 73.

22. **Borowitz**, *Choices in Modern Jewish Thought* (n.5), 216f.

D.II The Understanding of God after Auschwitz

1. In addition to the following works, cf. the literature in Part Two, A.I and Part Three, D.I.

2. **H.Jonas**, *der Gottesbegriff nach Auschwitz. Eine jüdische Stimme*, Tübingen 1984, paperback edition Frankfurt 1987, 7.

3. Cf. ibid., 37-42.

4. Ibid., 25f.

5. Ibid., 30f.

6. Ibid, 32f.

7. Ibid., 41.

8. Cf. **G.Scholem**, *Die jüdische Mystik in ihren Haupströmungen*, Zurich 1957.

9. Cf. Part One, C IV 1.

10. **Scholem**, *Die jüdische Mystik* (n.8), 286.

11. Ibid.

12. **H.Jonas**, *Der Gottesbegriff nach Auschwitz* (n.2), 47.

13. Cf. **J.Moltmann**, *The Trinity and the Kingdom of God*, London and New York 1981, esp. IV.2,2 'God's Self-Limitation'; id., *God in Creation. An Ecological Doctrine of Creation*, London and New York 1985, esp. IV 3: 'Creation out of Nothing'; E.Jüngel, 'Gottes ursprüngliches Anfangen als schöpferische Selbstbegrenzung. Ein Beitrag zum Gespräch mit Hans Jonas über den "Gottesbegriff nach Auschwitz"', in *Gottes Zukunft – Zukunft der Welt. Festschrift für Jürgen Moltmann zum 60.Geburtstag*, ed. H.Deuser et al., Munich 1986, 165-75.

14. Cf. **H.Küng**, *The Incarnation of God. An Introduction to Hegel's Theological Thought as Prolegomena to a Future Christology* (1970), Edinburgh 1987, esp. ch.VIII, 'Prolegomena to a Future Christology', and Excursuses I-V.

15. Cf. **id.**, OBC, DGE, CWR III. 2.

16. **Scholem**, *Die jüdische Mystik* (n.8), 286.

17. Cf. **Jüngel**, 'Gottes ursprüngliches Anfangen' (n.17).

18. **L.Jacobs**, *A Jewish Theology*, London 1973.

19. Ibid., 31.

20. Ibid., 34.

21. Cf. ibid., 25-7.

22. Ibid., 77. In his earlier work, *Principles of the Jewish Faith. An Analytical Study*, London 1964, Jacobs pointed out that not only all Catholic and Islamic thinkers but also many influential Protestant and Jewish (and especially all mediaeval Jewish) theologians reject the idea of a 'finite God': 'The basic objection to the idea is that a finite God would not be God at all, just as a slightly flat circle would not be a circle at all' (148). I have explained in DGE, B, 'The New Understanding of God', what can be said critically and constructively about a God in the becoming, as presented in Hegel, Whitehead or Teilhard de Chardin.

23. J.B.Soloveitchik, *Halakhic Man*, New York 1983, 49.

24. Ibid., 52.

25. Cf. ibid., 48.

26. Nicolas of Cusa, *De docta ignorantia* (1440), Book I, 26.

27. Id., *Directio speculantis seu de non aliud* (1462).

28. I find confirmation of my own criticism of the notion of the 'suffering God' in J.B.Metz, 'Theologie der Theodizee?' in W.Oelmuller (ed.), *Theodizee – Gott vor Gericht?*, Munich 1990, 103-18: 'Let me explain my reservations. How is it that talk of the suffering God is not ultimately just a sublime duplication of human suffering and human impotence? How is it that talk of suffering in God or of suffering between God and God does not lead to a perpetuation of suffering... I do not believe that christology necessitates or even legitimates talk of the suffering God or of suffering in God' (117).

29. It is in this that I also see basic agreement with my Tübingen colleagues and friends **Jürgen Moltmann** and **Eberard Jüngel**, both of whom have been concerned, with admirable intensity, solely to deepen the understanding of God in the face of the tremendous negativity of suffering and death.

30. **D.Bonhoeffer**, *Letters and Papers From Prison. The Enlarged Edition*, ed. E.Bethge, London and New York 1971, 361.

31. Cf. **D.Tracy**, 'Religious Values after the Holocaust. A Catholic View', in A.J.Peck (ed.), *Jews and Christians after the Holocaust*, Philadelphia 1982, 87-107: 106.

32. Cf. **J.Moltmann**, *The Crucified God. The Cross of Christ as Ground and Criticism of Christian Theology*, London and New York 1974, esp.ch.VI, 'The "Crucified God"'. Cf. **H.Küng**, 'Die Religionen als Frage an die Theologie des Kreuzes. Zur Kreuzestheologie J.Moltmanns', *Evangelische Theologie* 33, 1973, 401-23. However, the criticism of **A.R.Eckardt**, 'J.Moltmann, the Jewish People, and the Holocaust', *Journal of the American Academy of Religion* 44, 1976, 675-91, seems to me to be exaggerated. We are at one in criticizing the triumphalism of Christian theology towards the Jews; but that does not mean that one may brand any attempt at a distinctive Christian profile as itself already open or concealed triumphalism, which is what Eckardt does in the case of Moltmann.

33. Cf. **E.Jüngel**, *God as the Mystery of the World. On the Foundation of the Theology of the Crucified One in the Dispute between Theism and Atheism* (1977), Grand Rapids and Edinburgh 1983, especially §13, 'God's Unity with Perishability as the Basis for Thinking God; §22 'The Crucified Jesus Christ

as "Vestige of the Trinity'"; id., *Tod*, Stuttgart 1971, esp. B.V, 'Der Tod Jesu Christi – Der Tod als Passion Gottes'.

34. Titus 3.4.

35. Cf. I Cor.1.18-31.

36. Mark 15.34.

37. By a philosophical understanding of the Absolute in the unity of the infinite and the finite, Hegel seeks not only to restore the 'historical' (of that time) but the truly 'speculative' (historical-eternal) 'Good Friday... in the whole truth and severity of its godlessness' (*Erste Druckschriften*, ed. Lasson-Hoffmeister, I, 346). For the interpretation of the text cf. **Küng**, *The Incarnation of God* (n.14), ch.IV, 'The Death of God'.

38. E.Wiesel, *Night* (1961), Harmondsworth 1981, esp. 76f.

39. **K.Rahner** has also publicly expressed this idea, and among others has criticized J.Moltmann, in *Karl Rahner in Dialogue. Conversations and Interviews 1965-1982*, ed. P.Imhof and H.Biallowons, New York 1986, 126f. **Moltmann**'s most recent reaction to this can be found in 'The Question of Compassion and God's Impassibility', in *History and the Triune God*, London and New York 1991, 122-4. Moltmann answers Rahner's charge that his own view of the suffering is a kind of Gnosticism, patripassianism and Schellingian speculation by making psychologizing insinuations (celibacy, Jesuit training, an old man) against a man who can no longer defend himself against them. As far as the issue is concerned, of course there are no objections to supposing that God is capable of love and suffering, in the sense of com-passion (this is also affirmed by Rahner). But the difficulties begin in christology where Moltmann speaks directly of a 'crucified God' and in practice does away with the difference between God himself, the Father, and the Son. I would define my own standpoint as follows: neither the *Deus impassibilis et immutabilis* (Rahner's presupposition) nor the *Deus crucifixus, mortuus et sepultus* (Moltmann's consequence), but rather the *Deus compassibilis et compatiens* as he is manifested in Christ Jesus *crucifixus, mortuus, sepultus et resurrectus*.

40. Cf. **H.Blumenberg**, *Matthäuspassion*, Frankfurt 1988; also **E.Bieser**, 'Theologische Trauerarbeit. Zu Hans Blumenbergs *Matthäuspassion*', *Theologische Revue* 85, 1989, 441-52.

41. II Cor.13.4.

42. **H.S.Kushner**, *When Bad Things Happen to Good People*, New York 1981.

43. Cf. Lev.10.3. A systematic theology of the silence of God – as the hidden side of God in contrast to that which is 'visible' in the Word – is developed from the Jewish side by **A.Néher**, *L'exil de la parole. Du silence biblique au silence d'Auschwitz*, Paris 1970; cf. id., 'Silence', in *Contemporary Jewish Religious Thought*, 873-85. From the Christian side cf. the issue of the international theological journal *Concilium* 169, 1983, *Job and the Silence of God*, edited by **C.Duquoc** and **C.Floristán**.

44. **E.Wiesel**, 'Eine Quelle für die Hoffnung finden. Gespräch mit R.Boschert', *Süddeutsche Zeitung*, 28/29 October 1989. Cf. similarly the basic biography of the person and work of Elie Wiesel, **R.McAfee Brown**, *Elie Wiesel. Messenger to all Humanity*, Notre Dame 1983, esp. ch.5, 'The Silence of God'.

45. Cf. Isa.52.13-53.12.

46. Cf. **S.Shapiro**, 'Hearing the Testimony of Radical Negation', *Concilium* 175, 1984, 3-10.

47. Cf. **M.Gilbert**, *The Holocaust*, London and New York 1986, 200f.
48. This has again been brought out only recently in a biblical theological study by **J.C.Beker** of Princeton, *Suffering and Hope. The Biblical Vision and the Human Predicament*, Philadelphia 1987.
49. Cf. **I.J.Rosenbaum**, *The Holocaust and Halakhah*, New York 1976.
50. Ibid., 111.
51. Thus **M.Wyschogrod**, in response to I.Greenberg, 'Gott – ein Gott der Erlösung', in **M.Brocke** and **H.Jochum** (eds.), *Wolkensäule und Feuerschein. Jüdische Theologie des Holocaust*, Munich 1982, 178-94: 185.
52. Rom.8.31, 38f.
53. **M.Horkheimer**, *Die Sehnsucht nach dem ganz Anderen. Ein Interview mit Kommentar von H.Gumnior*, Hamburg 1970, 61f.
54. Rev.21.3f.

Indexes

Detailed discussion of persons or subjects is indicated in **bold**; mentions of authors in the notes are in *italic*.

INDEX OF NAMES

Gregory the Great, Pope, 155
Gregory VII, Pope, 150, 164
Gregory XIII, Pope, 185, 665
Greive, H., 659, 661, 666
Greschat, M., 677, 678
Gressmann, H., 634, 643, 646
Grintz, Y. M., 651, 654
Gröber, C., Archbishop, 265, 681
Grözinger, K. E., 664
Gross, H., 652
Gross, W., 639
Grosser, A., 274, 671, 683
Grossmann, D., 540, 720
Grotius, H., 186, 190
Gruchman, L., 674
Grundmann, W., 695
Gsteiger, F., 683
Gueroult, M., 667
Gumnior, H., 728
Gundlach, G., 678
Gunkel, H., 639, 648
Gunn, D. M., 649, 650
Gunneweg, A. H. J., 638
Gutman, Y., 681
Guttmann, J., 662

H

ha-Am, A., 287
Haag, H., xix, 639, 644, 645, 649, 651, 654
Haase, W., 655, 658, 660, 697, 711
Habermas, J., 220, 222, 670, 675
Habeth, S., 674
Hadi, M. A., 723
Hadrian, Emperor, 148, 149
Häsler, A. A., 273, 682, 683
Haffner, S., 223, 671
Hagar, 9, 11, 12, 47
Haggai, 101, 110
Hahn, F., 650, 657, 690, 713
al-Hakim, Sultan, 163
Halivini, D. W., 707

Hall, S. G., 661
Hallevi, J., 173
Halpern, B., 456, 649, 707
Hammer, K., 670
Hammer, R., 705
Hamp, V., 638
Hanson, P. D., 657
Harkabi, Y., 720
Harlan, V., 189
Harnack, A. von, 307, 686
Harpigny, G., 638
Hartman, D., xx, 465–7, 525, 565, 708, 718, 722
Hassan, bin Talal, Crown Prince, 721
Hauff, W., 189
Hauser, A. J., 648
Hausner, G., 670
Havel, V., 388
Hayes, J. H., 638, 648, 649
Hayes, P., 673
Hayoun, M.-R., 666
Hebbel, F., 120
Hecataeus of Abdera, 148
Heer, F., 237, 676, 678
Hegel, G. F. W., 36, 194, 201, 419, 667, 668, 702, 726, 727
Heidegger, M., 232, 449, 450, 452, 675
Heiler, F., 50, 646
Heine, H., 202, 212, 405
Heinemann, G., 249
Heinemann, I., 660
Heinemann, J., 109, 654, 660
Heisenberg, W., 194
Heller, B., 646
Heller, J. E., 173, 663, 705
Hellholm, D., 656
Helmreich, W. B., 702
Hengel, M., 350, 353, 378, 449, 452, 600, 602, 604, 621, 655–7, 693–5
Henrikx, H. H., 676, 678, 680, 681, 685, 691, 717, 718
Hensel, S., 668

Herberg, W., 401, 701
Herbrechtsmeier, W. E., 652
Herder, J. G., 197
Hermle, F., 678
Hermlin, S., 682
Herod Antipas, 314
Herod the Great, 119, 120, 353, 576, 656, 693
Herrmann, S., 638
Hertzberg, A., 555, 564, 667, 683, 684
Hertzberg, H. W., 650
Hertzsch, E., 717
Herzl, T., **285–8**, 291, 292, 296, 309, 519, 525, 550, 562, 563, 684, 718, 721
Herzog, C., 702
Herzog, I., 702
Heschel, A. J., 405–12, 418, 436, 452, 701, 702
Hess, M., 283
Hesse, H., 590
Heydrich, R., 225, 233, 235, 591
Hezekiah, King, 80, 92
Hilberg, R., 235, 670
Hilgert, E., 660
Hillel, 129
Himmler, H., 182, 224, 225, 233, 256, 591, 671
Hindemith, P., 682
Hippolytus, 152
Hirsch, E., 672
Hirsch, H., 681
Hirsch, S. R., 308, 309, 414, 415, 420, 423, 428, 430, 436, 686, 702, 705
Hirsch Meisels, Z., 607
Hirsch Weiss, I., 705
Hirschberg, H. Z., 646, 650
Hitler, Adolf, 182, **221–6, 232–9**, 242, 244–6, 248, 249, **252–6**, 258, 261, 262, 267, 273, 283, 286, 293, 294, 298, 400, 451, 585–9, 591, 616, 670–3, 676, 678–81

INDEX OF SUBJECTS